Lecture Notes in Computer Science 16161

Founding Editors

Gerhard Goos
Juris Hartmanis

Editorial Board Members

The series Lecture Notes in Computer Science (LNCS), including its subseries Lecture Notes in Artificial Intelligence (LNAI) and Lecture Notes in Bioinformatics (LNBI), has established itself as a medium for the publication of new developments in computer science and information technology research, teaching, and education.

LNCS enjoys close cooperation with the computer science R & D community, the series counts many renowned academics among its volume editors and paper authors, and collaborates with prestigious societies. Its mission is to serve this international community by providing an invaluable service, mainly focused on the publication of conference and workshop proceedings and postproceedings. LNCS commenced publication in 1973.

Zhouchen Lin · Liang Wang · Yugang Jiang ·
Xuesong Wang · Shengcai Liao · Shiguang Shan ·
Risheng Liu · Jing Dong · Xin Yu
Editors

Image and Graphics

13th International Conference, ICIG 2025
Xuzhou, China, October 31 – November 2, 2025
Proceedings, Part I

 Springer

Editors
Zhouchen Lin
Peking University
Beijing, China

Liang Wang
Institute of Automation, CAS
Beijing, China

Yugang Jiang
Fudan University
Shanghai, China

Xuesong Wang
China University of Mining and Technology
Xuzhou, China

Shengcai Liao
United Arab Emirates University
Abu Dhabi, United Arab Emirates

Shiguang Shan
Institute of Computing Technology, CAS
Beijing, China

Risheng Liu
Dalian University of Technology
Dalian, China

Jing Dong
Institute of Automation, CAS
Beijing, China

Xin Yu
The University of Queensland
Brisbane, QLD, Australia

ISSN 0302-9743　　　　　　　　　　ISSN 1611-3349　(electronic)
Lecture Notes in Computer Science
ISBN 978-981-95-3397-8　　　　　　ISBN 978-981-95-3398-5　(eBook)
https://doi.org/10.1007/978-981-95-3398-5

This Springer imprint is published by the registered company Springer Nature Singapore Pte Ltd.
The registered company address is: 152 Beach Road, #21-01/04 Gateway East, Singapore 189721, Singapore

If disposing of this product, please recycle the paper.

Preface

These are the proceedings of the 13th International Conference on Image and Graphics (ICIG 2025), which was held in Xuzhou, China, on October 31 – November 2, 2025. The conference was hosted by the China Society of Image and Graphics (CSIG), organized by the China University of Mining and Technology, co-organized by Nanjing University of Science & Technology.

ICIG is a biennial conference that focuses on innovative technologies of image, video, and graphics processing and fosters innovation, entrepreneurship, and networking. It features world-class plenary speakers, exhibits, and high-quality peer-reviewed oral and poster presentations.

CSIG has hosted the ICIG conference series since 2000. Details about past conferences are as follows:

Conference	Place	Date	Submissions	Accepted
1st (ICIG 2000)	Tianjin, China	August 16–18	220	156
2nd (ICIG 2002)	Hefei, China	August 15–18	280	166
3rd (ICIG 2004)	Hong Kong, China	December 17–19	460	140
4th (ICIG 2007)	Chengdu, China	August 22–24	525	184
5th (ICIG 2009)	Xi'an, China	September 20–23	362	179
6th (ICIG 2011)	Hefei, China	August 12–15	329	183
7th (ICIG 2013)	Qingdao, China	July 26–28	346	181
8th (ICIG 2015)	Tianjin, China	August 13–16	345	170
9th (ICIG 2017)	Shanghai, China	September 13–15	370	172
10th (ICIG 2019)	Beijing, China	August 23–25	384	183
11th (ICIG 2021)	Haikou, China	December 26–28	421	198
12th (ICIG 2023)	Nanjing, China	September 22–24	409	166

For ICIG 2025, 420 submissions were received and 137 papers were accepted, corresponding to an acceptance rate of 32.62%. Each paper received three double-blind reviews, on average. To facilitate the search for a required paper in these proceedings, the accepted papers have been arranged into different sections according to their topic.

We sincerely thank all the contributors, who came from all over the world to present their advanced work at this event. We would also like to thank all the reviewers, who carefully reviewed all submissions and made their valuable comments for improving the accepted papers. The proceedings could not have been produced without the invaluable efforts of the members of the Organizing Committee, and a number of active members of CSIG.

October 2025

Zhouchen Lin
Liang Wang
Yugang Jiang
Xuesong Wang
Shengcai Liao
Shiguang Shan
Risheng Liu
Jing Dong
Xin Yu

Organization

General Chairs

Yaonan Wang   Hunan University, China
Hongwei Zhao   China University of Mining and Technology, China
Kyoung Mu Lee   Seoul National University, South Korea
Oliver Deussen   University of Konstanz, Germany

Technical Program Chairs

Zhouchen Lin   Peking University, China
Liang Wang   Institute of Automation, CAS, China
Yugang Jiang   Fudan University, China
Xuesong Wang   China University of Mining and Technology, China
Shengcai Liao   United Arab Emirates University, UAE

Organizing Committee Chairs

Huimin Ma   University of Science and Technology Beijing, China
Yuxin Peng   Peking University, China
Bingkun Bao   Nanjing University of Posts and Telecommunications, China
Jun Wang   China University of Mining and Technology, China

Publicity Chairs

Yuanlong Yu   Fuzhou University, China
Jinchang Ren   Robert Gordon University, UK
Wei Jia   Hefei University of Technology, China
Feifei Zhang   Tianjin University of Technology, China
Phoebe Chen   La Trobe University, Australia

Award Chairs

Changsheng Xu	Institute of Automation, CAS, China
Jian Yang	Nanjing University of Science and Technology, China
Jingkuan Song	Tongji University, China
Han Yu	Nanyang Technological University, Singapore

Publication Chairs

Shiguang Shan	Institute of Computing Technology, CAS, China
Risheng Liu	Dalian University of Technology, China
Jing Dong	Institute of Automation, CAS, China
Xin Yu	University of Queensland, Australia

Workshop Chairs

Yao Zhao	Beijing Jiaotong University
Xi Li	Zhejiang University, China
Kun Tan	East China Normal University, China
Guosheng Lin	Nanyang Technological University, Singapore

Tutorial Chairs

Weiwei Xu	Zhejiang University, China
Weishi Zheng	Sun Yat-sen University, China
Zechao Li	Nanjing University of Science and Technology, China
Yong Zhou	China University of Mining and Technology, China

Exhibits Chairs

Cheng Deng	Xi'an University of Electronic Science and Technology, China
Min Xia	Western University, Canada
Shengsheng Qian	Institute of Automation, CAS, China
Yisen Wang	Peking University, China

Sponsorship Chairs

Xucheng Yin	University of Science and Technology Beijing, China
Jin Tang	Anhui University, China
Junchi Yan	Shanghai Jiao Tong University, China
Shan An	Tianjin University, China

Finance Chairs

Xi Peng	Sichuan University, China
Kai Qin	China University of Mining and Technology, China
Zhi Jin	Sun Yat-sen University, China
Yi Jin	Beijing Jiaotong University, China

Website Chairs

Anan Liu	Tianjin University, China
Rushi Lan	Guilin University of Electronic Technology, China
Chenping Hou	National University of Defense Technology, China
Haoyu Wang	China University of Mining and Technology, China

Program Committee

Chenyan Bai	Ping Hu
Jie Cao	Huaibo Huang
Changsheng Chen	Junjun Jiang
Tao Chen	Taisong Jin
Runmin Cong	Rushi Lan
Qiongjie Cui	Chenglong Li
Junxian Duan	Hui Li
Bin Fan	Jia Li
Wei Feng	Tianrui Li
Changxin Gao	Jian Liang
Junyu Gao	Baodi Liu
Chen Gong	Dong Liu

Meng Liu	Xin Yu
Qi Liu	Zhenhua Yu
Chunlei Peng	Hui Yuan
Jie Qin	Donglin Zhang
Dongwei Ren	Hua Zhang
Nong Sang	Jinglin Zhang
Linlin Shen	Bin Zhao
Cong Wang	Liang Zhao
Gaoang Wang	Bineng Zhong
Yuheng Wang	Quan Zhou
Jinjian Wu	Yu Zhou
Chunyan Xu	Anna Zhu
Jufeng Yang	Linchao Zhu
Shiqi Yu	Liang Zou

Additional Reviewers

Chenyan Bai	Huanzhang Dou
Zhengyao Bai	Hong Fan
Yanqi Bao	Junkai Fan
Yi Chang	Yuchun Fang
Bo Chen	Lunke Fei
Cheng Chen	Chen Feng
Gongping Chen	Zhanxiang Feng
Hao Chen	Congrui Fu
Hui Chen	Sichao Fu
Jinyong Chen	Zhaojin Fu
Lu Chen	Zhenqi Fu
Qinghui Chen	Guangwei Gao
Ruoyu Chen	Shaobing Gao
Shuhuang Chen	Shengxiang Gao
Xiaolin Chen	Zhenghao Gao
Zheng Chen	Mingrong Gong
Zhenyuan Chen	Kuangpu Guo
Ming-Ming Cheng	Xiaoying Guo
Chaoran Cui	Conghao Han
Hui Cui	Hong Han
Jinrong Cui	Pengfei Han
Yimian Dai	Changhao He
Haoyou Deng	Xiangteng He
Jiajun Deng	Wang Heng
Hui Ding	Yuqing Hou
Jin Ding	Zhi-Qiang Hou
Neng Dong	Junlin Hu

Dexing Zhong
Guoqiang Zhong
Daoxiang Zhou
Kangneng Zhou
Qian Zhou
Tao Zhou
Tao Zhou
Yong Zhou

Zhen Zhou
Zhou Zhou
Guoqing Zhu
Hancan Zhu
Lei Zhu
Xukun Zhu
Peixian Zhuang
Yuan Zong

Contents – Part I

Biological and Medical Image Processing

Color and Multispectral Processing

Compression, Transmission, Retrieval

Computational Imaging

Computer Graphics and Visualization

Contents – Part II

Contents – Part III

Multimedia Security

Multi-view and Stereoscopic Processing

Surveillance and Remote Sensing

Virtual Reality

Artificial Intelligence

SRG-Net: Semantic Relation-Guided Network for Commonsense Video Captioning

Zeyu Xi, Yijie Li, Haoying Sun, Haoran Zhang, and Lifang Wu[✉]

School of Information Science and Technology, Beijing University of Technology,
Beijing 100124, China
`lfwu@bjut.edu.cn`

Abstract. Commonsense video captioning requires the model not only to describe visible content but also to infer multiple types of commonsense captions, including "Intention", "Effect", and "Attribute". Existing methods generally fall into two categories: one extracts commonsense directly from videos but struggles to bridge the semantic gap between visual content and implicit commonsense under limited knowledge; the other leverages language model-extended textual knowledge, which alleviates this gap but overlooks the semantic relationships among different types of commonsense information, limiting reasoning capability. To address these challenges, we propose a Semantic Relation-Guided Network (SRG-Net) for commonsense video captioning. Specifically, a Commonsense Semantic Relation Modeling (CSRM) module is designed to capture interrelations among different types of extended commonsense knowledge and enhance their representations. Furthermore, a Hierarchical Fusion Decoding (HFD) strategy is adopted. Multimodal video features are first fused, followed by the integration of enhanced commonsense representations, enabling the generation of accurate and fluent commonsense captions. Extensive experiments on the large-scale Video-to-Commonsense dataset demonstrate that SRG-Net achieves superior performance compared to existing methods across multiple metrics.

Keywords: Commonsense video captioning · Commonsense semantic relation modeling · Hierarchical fusion decoding

1 Introduction

Commonsense video captioning [6] is a challenging task in the field of video understanding, as it requires the model not only to generate textual descriptions of video content, but also to perform commonsense reasoning related to the depicted event. As shown in Fig. 1(a), this task involves three types of commonsense descriptions: "Intention" (the motivation behind an event or action), "Effect" (the potential result from the event or action), and "Attribute" (the description of the event or agent in the video). Recently, some methods [6,26]

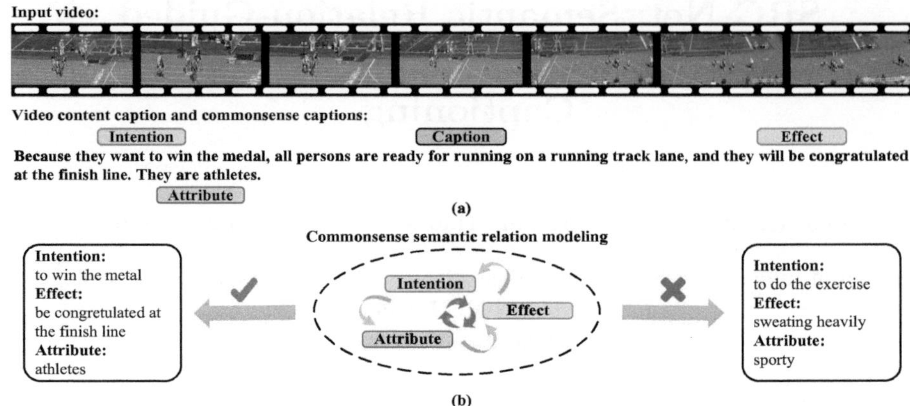

Fig. 1. (a) The example of the video commonsense captioning task. (b) Considering semantic relations enables more accurate commonsense caption generation.

have attempted to directly extract commonsense information from videos. These methods typically decode the extracted multimodal features into textual descriptions of visible video content, and then combine them with the original multimodal features to generate three types of commonsense descriptions. Although such methods have achieved initial success, they still struggle to bridge the semantic gap between visible visual content and implicit commonsense under limited knowledge conditions. To address this issue, Yuan et al. [27] utilize the strong imaginative and generative capabilities of language model to extend three types of textual commonsense knowledge based on the visual description, thereby enhancing commonsense reasoning. However, this method relies solely on the corresponding extended commonsense knowledge when generating each type of description, neglecting the latent semantic relations among the three types, which limits its reasoning performance.

In fact, there exist latent semantic relations among the three types of commonsense knowledge. As shown in Fig. 1(b), in a running scenario, if the model is unaware that the person in the video is an athlete, it may infer that the likely outcome is "sweating heavily". Similarly, if the final result is not to rush towards the finish line and celebrate, then the inferred intention may be to do the exercise rather than win a medal. These examples demonstrate that the three types of commonsense can complement and inform each other. Therefore, enabling the model to capture the latent semantic relationships among different types of commonsense can lead to more accurate, comprehensive, and human-like reasoning in commonsense caption generation.

In this paper, we introduce a semantic relation-guided network (SRG-Net) for commonsense video captioning. To capture the latent semantic relationships among the three types of commonsense knowledge generated by the language model, we propose a Commonsense Semantic Relation Modeling (CSRM) module based on the cross-attention mechanism, which enhances the semantic representation of commonsense knowledge. Additionally, a Hierarchical Fusion Decoding (HFD) strategy is adopted to progressively integrate multimodal features with the enhanced commonsense representations. Experimental results demonstrate the effectiveness of the proposed SRG-Net and the high quality of the generated commonsense descriptions.

In summary, our contributions are summarized as follows: (1) We introduce SRG-Net, a novel semantic relation-guided network for commonsense video captioning, which integrates a Commonsense Semantic Relation Modeling (CSRM) module and a Hierarchical Fusion Decoding (HFD) strategy to enable accurate commonsense mining and reasoning. (2) The proposed CSRM module enhances the semantic representation of extended commonsense knowledge by capturing the latent semantic relations among different types of textual commonsense knowledge. In addition, an HFD strategy is designed to ensure more accurate and coherent generation of commonsense captions. (3) Extensive experiments on the large-scale Video-to-Commonsense dataset [6] demonstrate the superior performance of the proposed SRG-Net compared to existing methods.

2   Related Works

2.1   Video Captioning

Video captioning is an important task in the field of video understanding, which requires the model to describe the video content with fluent natural language sentences. Early template-based methods [10,11] insert extracted semantic attributes into predefined sentence templates to form the complete captions, with the limitation of diversity and flexibility. Recent studies [13,17,18,22,23,25] reformulate the task as the sequence learning problem using encoder-decoder frameworks. Some efforts [2,4] also incorporate detection tools to capture fine-grained visual information and enhance video features. In this work, we utilize multiple pretrained encoders, including I3D [3], ResNet152 [8], and SoundNet [1], to extract dynamic visual, static image, and audio features, respectively. These features are then decoded using a Transformer-based [19] decoder to generate both video content captions and commonsense reasoning descriptions.

2.2   Commonsense Video Captioning

Commonsense video captioning aims to generate not only the video caption but also three types of commonsense descriptions: "Intention", "Effect", and "Attribute". Fang et al. [6] first introduce the task by enhancing the MSR-VTT dataset [24] with the commonsense knowledge base (ATOMIC) [15]. Yu et al. [26] propose a unified framework to generate all three types of commonsense descriptions simultaneously. However, these methods attempt to extract commonsense directly from visual features, overlooking the complex semantic gap between visual content and commonsense, resulting in low performance. Shao et al. [16] exploit inferential commonsense knowledge to assist the training of video captioning model with a novel paradigm for sentence-level semantic alignment. To

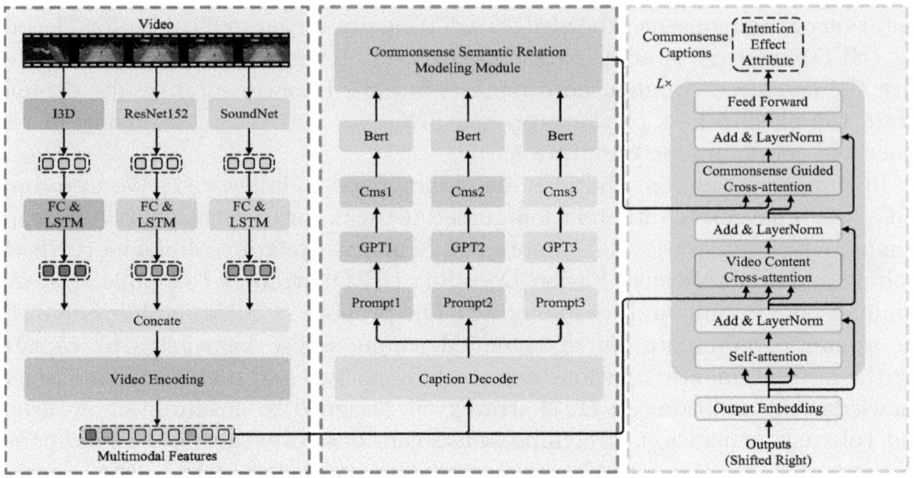

Fig. 2. The architecture of the proposed SRG-Net.

bridge the gap between visual content and commonsense, Yuan et al. [27] employ a language model to extend commonsense knowledge based on the caption of the video, guiding the generation of commonsense descriptions. Nevertheless, this method ignores the semantic relations among the three types of commonsense, limiting the reasoning performance. In this paper, we design a commonsense semantic relation modeling (CSRM) module to compensate for this deficiency. Moreover, we propose a hierarchical fusion decoding (HFD) strategy to further improve the accuracy and coherence of commonsense descriptions.

3 Method

As shown in Fig. 2, SRG-Net mainly consists of three main parts: 1) multimodal feature extraction, 2) knowledge extension and semantic relation modeling, and 3) hierarchical fusion decoder. In the following subsections, we will describe each part of the proposed SRG-Net in detail.

3.1 Multimodal Feature Extraction

To obtain the comprehensive video representation, we utilize multiple encoders, including I3D, ResNet152, and SoundNet, to extract dynamic visual f_{3D}, static image f_{2D}, and audio f_{1D} features, respectively. To reduce the gap between modalities, these features are mapped into a unified vector space, followed by the LSTM to model temporal dependencies. Finally, the features are concatenated.

$$F_V = [\text{LSTM}_1 (W_{3D} f_{3D}), \text{LSTM}_2 (W_{2D} f_{2D}), \text{LSTM}_3 (W_{1D} f_{1D})], \qquad (1)$$

where $W_{3D} \in \mathbb{R}^{1024 \times 512}$, $W_{2D} \in \mathbb{R}^{2048 \times 512}$ and $W_{1D} \in \mathbb{R}^{1024 \times 512}$ denote the learnable mapping layers. [·] is the concatenate function in Python.

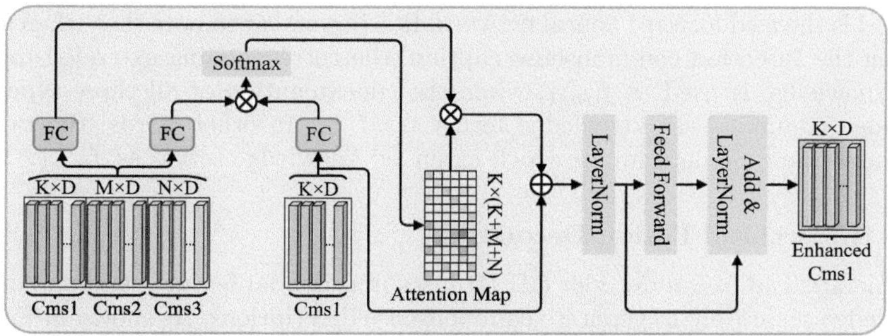

Fig. 3. The architecture of the proposed CRSM module.

To further enhance the multimodal features, an attention-based video encoder is employed to fuse them more effectively. The core component of the encoder, self-attention, is formulated as follows:

$$\widetilde{F_V} = \rho \left(\frac{(W_{Q1}F_V) \cdot (W_{K1}F_V)^{\top}}{\sqrt{d_k}} \right) \cdot (W_{V1}F_V), \tag{2}$$

where W_{Q1}, W_{K1} and W_{V1} denote the learnable mapping layers. $\rho(\cdot)$ is the Softmax function. And d_k is the feature dimension.

3.2 Knowledge Extension and Semantic Relation Modeling

The text decoder generates a video description C from the multimodal features. Based on this, commonsense knowledge is expanded using a pretrained GPT-2 model from [27] with predefined prompts. For "Intention", the prompt is set as "and the aim is"; For "Effect", the prompt is "and the result is"; For "Attribute", we set the prompt as "and the event or person is". The textual feature f_{cms} of the extended commonsense knowledge K_{cms} is then extracted using the pretrained BERT [5]. To enhance the semantic representation of the knowledge, as shown in Fig. 3, we propose a Commonsense Relation Semantic Modeling (CRSM) module based on cross-attention. This module captures latent semantic relations among different types of commonsense knowledge, and the process is detailed as follows:

$$M_{cms} = [f_{cms1}, f_{cms2}, f_{cms3}], \tag{3}$$

$$F_{cms1} = \rho \left(\frac{(W_{Q2}f_{cms1}) \cdot (W_{K2}M_{cms})^{\top}}{\sqrt{D}} \right) \cdot (W_{V2}M_{cms}) + f_{cms1}, \tag{4}$$

$$\widetilde{F_{cms1}} = \ell \left(\ell \left(F_{cms1} \right) + \text{FFN} \left(\ell \left(F_{cms1} \right) \right) \right), \tag{5}$$

where D denotes the dimension of the textual features. $\ell(\cdot)$ denotes the Layer Normalization. W_{Q2}, W_{K2} and W_{V2} are learnable projection matrices. And

FFN $(\cdot)$ is the feed forward neural network. It is important to note that when generating the Intention commonsense caption, the corresponding extended Intention knowledge is used as f_{cms1}, while the concatenation of all three types of extended commonsense knowledge forms as M_{cms}. In other words, the target commonsense type determines which extended knowledge serves as f_{cms1}.

3.3   Hierarchical Fusion Decoder

The hierarchical fusion decoder (HFD) fuses multimodal features and enhanced knowledge separately to generate commonsense descriptions. As shown in Fig. 2, HFD utilizes the video content cross-attention $\mathcal{M}_{vc}(\cdot)$ to integrate the multimodal features with the decoding state d^{t-1} at the decoding time t:

$$e_{vc}^{t} = \ell\left(d^{t-1} + \mathcal{M}_{vc}\left(d^{t-1}, \widetilde{F_V}, \widetilde{F_V}\right)\right). \tag{6}$$

At this stage, the decoder has already captured the main video content. To further infer commonsense descriptions, HFD subsequently employs commonsense-guided cross-attention $\mathcal{M}_{vg}(\cdot)$ to integrate the enhanced commonsense knowledge feature $\widetilde{F_{cms}}$:

$$e_{vg}^{t} = \text{FFN}\left(\ell\left(\mathcal{M}_{vg}\left(e_{vc}^{t}, \widetilde{F_{cms}}, \widetilde{F_{cms}}\right) + e_{vc}^{t}\right)\right). \tag{7}$$

We stack N decoder layers to obtain the final output. The decoder combines probabilities and the word dictionary to decode the corresponding words. Output probabilities are obtained by MLP layer and softmax function:

$$O = \delta\left(\text{MLP}\left(e_{vg}^{t}\right)\right). \tag{8}$$

Following the standard training pattern for caption generation, we utilize cross-entropy loss to optimize the SRG-Net:

$$\mathcal{L}_{\Phi} = -\sum_{t=1}^{M} \log\left(\text{P}\left(y_t^* | y_{0:t-1}^*, \widetilde{F_V}, \widetilde{F_{cms}}; \Theta\right)\right), \tag{9}$$

where $\{y_0^*, y_1^*, ..., y_M^*\}$ is the set of ground-truth tokenized tokens. M denotes the number of tokens. And Θ denotes the optimized parameters.

4   Experiments

4.1   Implementation Details

During the training, the learning rate is set to 3e-5. SRG-Net is trained for 1000 epochs on the Video-to-Commonsense dataset [6] and the batch size is set to 128. We employ Adam [9] as the optimizer and the warm-up is 5000. Beam search with a beam size of 2 is utilized for inference. We employ a single-layer video encoder to extract multimodal video features and a single-layer CSRM module to capture the semantic relations among the three types of commonsense knowledge. Both the caption decoder and the commonsense caption decoder share the same structure, each consisting of 6 Transformer blocks with 8 attention heads.

Table 1. Quantitative comparison results on completion task. Numbers in bold denote the best performance.

Setting	Model	CIDEr	Rouge-L	BLEU-1	BLEU-2	BLEU-3	BLEU-4
Intention	S2VT [21]	51.8	44.3	48.4	39.9	34.3	26.4
	Att-Enc-Dec [7]	52.1	48.0	51.1	42.6	35.5	28.2
	Dense captioner [28]	60.3	53.1	59.3	47.0	37.3	31.5
	CMS transformer [6]	62.0	54.6	60.8	48.4	39.1	34.1
	CAVAN [16]	58.7	59.4	-	-	-	38.6
	Hybridnet [26]	92.6	60.1	69.4	60.5	55.4	53.1
	TKG-Net [27]	100.6	62.0	70.4	62.1	**57.3**	55.7
	Ours	**101.0**	**62.3**	**71.5**	**62.8**	**57.3**	**56.1**
Effect	S2VT [21]	28.3	22.1	24.9	18.6	16.2	14.3
	Att-Enc-Dec [7]	29.5	23.9	26.5	19.4	18.8	15.1
	Dense captioner [28]	36.9	29.9	33.7	24.8	21.0	20.2
	CMS transformer [6]	37.3	30.6	34.8	25.9	22.5	20.4
	Hybridnet [26]	66.2	41.5	49.0	42.9	40.3	38.8
	TKG-Net [27]	77.7	45.3	53.2	48.1	45.5	43.6
	Ours	**78.4**	**45.7**	**53.8**	**48.6**	**46.2**	**44.7**
Attribute	S2VT [21]	-	-	35.9	-	-	-
	Att-Enc-Dec [7]	-	-	38.3	-	-	-
	Dense captioner [28]	-	-	46.0	-	-	-
	CMS transformer [6]	-	-	47.3	-	-	-
	Hybridnet [26]	-	-	58.7	-	-	-
	TKG-Net [27]	-	-	59.1	-	-	-
	Ours	-	-	**59.6**	-	-	-

4.2   Dataset and Metrics

We conduct experiments on the large-scale Video-to-Commonsense (V2C) dataset. It is split into a training set of 6819 videos with 85100 captions, and a testing set of 2903 videos with 36518 captions. The dataset includes three types of commonsense annotations: "Intention", "Effect", and "Attribute". It supports two downstream tasks: the Completion task and the Generation task. In the Completion task, the model is required to infer and generate the three types of commonsense descriptions based on the given video content and ground-truth caption. In the Generation task, the model needs to generate both the video description and the three commonsense texts from the input video content. Following [27], we report the comparative results for metrics CIDEr [20], Rouge-L [12] and BLEU [14].

Table 2. Quantitative comparison results on generation task. Numbers in bold denote the best performance.

Setting	Model	CIDEr	Rouge-L	BLEU-1	BLEU-2	BLEU-3	BLEU-4
Intention+C	S2VT [21]	35.4	58.6	71.3	53.9	41.3	31.2
	Att-Enc-Dec [7]	33.2	59.6	75.4	59.4	45.1	33.5
	Dense captioner [28]	37.0	60.9	76.1	60.2	46.7	35.9
	CMS transformer [6]	37.8	61.9	76.2	61.2	48.1	37.3
	Hybridnet [26]	40.4	62.9	77.5	62.9	50.4	40.2
	TKG-Net [27]	45.0	64.4	78.7	65.3	52.9	42.1
	Ours	**47.1**	**65.5**	**79.8**	**66.5**	**54.5**	**44.0**
Effect+C	S2VT [21]	29.9	55.3	69.8	54.1	39.9	29.1
	Att-Enc-Dec [7]	26.1	53.5	70.2	51.8	38.6	28.7
	Dense captioner [28]	30.6	56.0	72.1	54.5	42.3	33.2
	CMS transformer [6]	32.1	57.4	72.5	56.1	44.3	35.2
	Hybridnet [26]	34.2	58.3	73.2	57.4	46.3	37.2
	TKG-Net [27]	36.5	59.1	75.4	59.6	47.6	38.4
	Ours	**37.8**	**61.2**	**77.3**	**61.0**	**48.1**	**39.5**
Attribute+C	S2VT [21]	38.5	59.1	69.1	53.6	42.0	32.3
	Att-Enc-Dec [7]	34.0	58.0	67.0	51.7	40.7	31.4
	Dense captioner [28]	36.8	57.7	68.4	52.1	39.8	30.0
	CMS transformer [6]	40.2	59.0	70.2	54.8	42.7	32.6
	Hybridnet [26]	41.6	60.4	71.3	57.0	45.6	35.7
	TKG-Net [27]	43.7	61.4	72.5	57.8	46.4	36.4
	Ours	**45.7**	**63.3**	**74.1**	**58.5**	**48.0**	**38.7**

4.3 Performance Comparison

Table 1 and 2 present the performance comparisons on the completion and generation tasks, respectively. The compared methods include S2VT [21], Att-Enc-Dec [7], Dense Captioner [28], CMS Transformer [6], CAVAN [16], Hybrid-Net [26], and TKG-Net [27].

Comparison on Completion Task. SRG-Net outperforms all compared models across all metrics. On the "Intention" part, SRG-Net improves the CIDEr from 100.6 to 101.0 and increases BLEU-4 from 55.7 to 56.1 with the baseline TKG-Net. It outperforms HybridNet by 8.4% on CIDEr and by 3.0% on BLEU-4. On the "Effect" part, SRG-Net consistently improves over the baseline across all metrics. On the "Attribute" part, since the commonsense caption describes events or entities using only a single word, only the BLEU-1 score is reported. SRG-Net achieves the highest BLEU-1 score of 59.6. As shown in Fig. 4, supported by the external language model's strong imagination and generation capabilities, SRG-Net can generate commonsense captions closely related to the video. Thanks to the CSEM module's ability to model semantic relationships among the commonsense knowledge, the generated commonsense captions effectively link "playing games" and "entertainment", making it closer to the ground-truth captions.

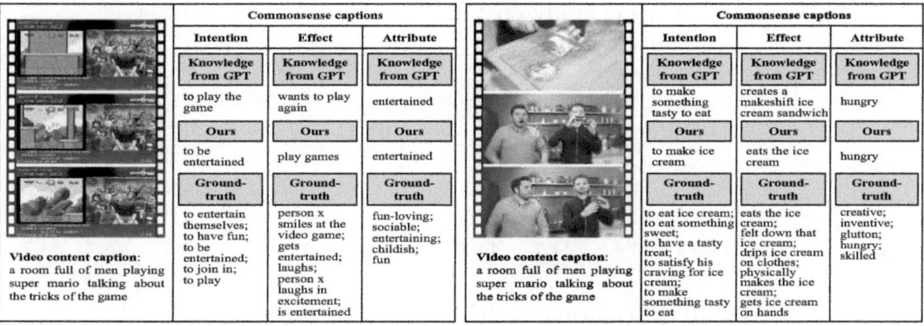

Fig. 4. Qualitative visual results on completion task.

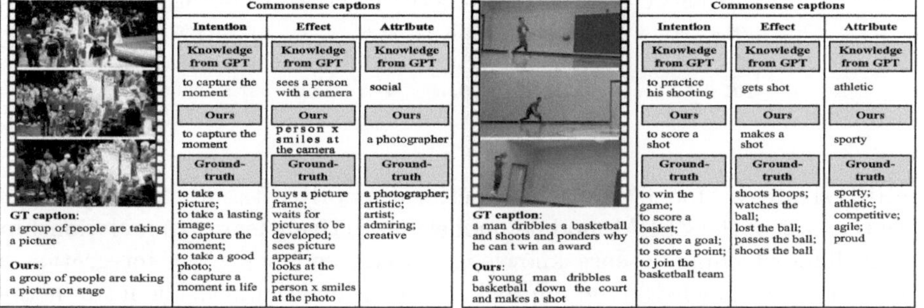

Fig. 5. Qualitative visual results on generation task.

Comparison on Generation Task. SRG-Net achieves the best performance in this task. For "Intention", SRG-Net surpasses the baseline by 2.1% on CIDEr and 1.9% on BLEU-4. For "Effect" part, SRG-Net improves the baseline by 1.3% on CIDEr and 1.1% on BLEU-4. For "Attribute" part, our method also achieves the best scores on all evaluation metrics. These results demonstrate that our method maintains strong robustness in long-text generation tasks. As shown in Fig. 5, the generated video descriptions are closely aligned with ground truth. Moreover, in the example on the right side of the figure, the "Intention" knowledge provided by GPT-2 is "practice shooting". Supplemented by Effect knowledge, SRG-Net gives an intention description that better matches the ground truth. This further confirms that our method not only excels at the completion task but also achieves state-of-the-art performance on the more challenging generation task.

4.4   Ablation Study

Contribution of Each Component. As shown in Table 3, we conduct ablation studies to evaluate the individual contributions of the CSRM module and

Table 3. Ablation study on Video-to-Commonsense dataset.

Model	CSRM	HFD	Completion task					Generation task					
			Intention		Effect		Attribute	Intention+C		Effect+C		Attribute+C	
			CIDEr	BLEU-4	CIDEr	BLEU-4	BLEU-1	CIDEr	BLEU-4	CIDEr	BLEU-4	CIDEr	BLEU-4
①			100.6	55.7	77.7	43.6	59.1	45.0	42.1	36.5	38.4	43.7	36.4
②	✓		100.8	55.9	78.0	44.3	59.5	46.5	43.1	37.5	39.0	45.0	38.2
③		✓	100.7	55.8	77.9	44.1	59.3	46.0	42.8	37.0	38.7	44.7	37.7
④	✓	✓	**101.0**	**56.1**	**78.4**	**44.7**	**59.6**	**47.1**	**44.0**	**37.8**	**39.5**	**45.7**	**38.7**

Table 4. Ablation study on the structure of HFD.

Model	V‖C	C2V	V2C	Completion task					Generation task					
				Intention		Effect		Attribute	Intention		Effect		Attribute	
				CIDEr	BLEU-4	CIDEr	BLEU-4	BLEU-1	CIDEr	BLEU-4	CIDEr	BLEU-4	CIDEr	BLEU-4
(a)	✓			100.8	55.9	78.0	44.3	59.5	46.5	43.1	37.5	39.0	45.0	38.2
(b)		✓		99.5	54.6	77.1	41.9	58.4	43.7	41.2	35.3	37.1	43.0	35.8
(c)			✓	**101.0**	**56.1**	**78.4**	**44.7**	**59.6**	**47.1**	**44.0**	**37.8**	**39.5**	**45.7**	**38.7**

the HFD strategy. Model ① (baseline) performs poorly without any components. With the help of the CSRM module, model ② effectively learns the relationships among different commonsense knowledge pieces, enhancing the integration of complementary knowledge and improving generation accuracy. The introduction of HFD enables the model ③ to first thoroughly understand the video content and then decode the commonsense text in a more structured and coherent manner through the commonsense knowledge. Comparing model ② and model ③, CSRM contributes more significantly, underscoring the importance of semantic relation modeling. With both CSRM and HFD, model ④ achieves the best overall performance. These results validate the effectiveness of each component and highlight the importance of knowledge relation modeling and sequential reasoning for high-quality commonsense captioning (Table 4).

The Structure of HFD. We further investigate the impact of different HFD architectures on performance. As shown in Table 3, three variants are compared: (a) concatenating multimodal features with enhanced commonsense knowledge feature (V‖C); (b) fusing commonsense knowledge feature first, followed by multimodal features (C2V); and (c) fusing multimodal features first, followed by commonsense knowledge feature (V2C). The performance comparison result shows that architecture (b) achieves the worst results. This is because commonsense reasoning must be grounded on a thorough understanding of the video content. Multimodal features provide the factual basis of "what is happening" in the video, while commonsense knowledge offers high-level inference and supplementation. In addition, since multimodal and commonsense features have different semantic properties, directly concatenating them can cause information confusion, thereby limiting the quality of commonsense text generation. These findings further validate the effectiveness and rationality of our HFD design.

5   Conclusion, Limitation and Future Work

In this paper, we explore the latent semantic relationships among different types of commonsense knowledge and demonstrate their benefits for the commonsense reasoning task. Based on this insight, we propose a Semantic Relation-Guided Network (SRG-Net) for commonsense video captioning. SRG-Net effectively captures semantic relations within commonsense knowledge to enhance knowledge representation and improves generation by decoding video content and commonsense in sequence. Despite achieving state-of-the-art performance, SRG-Net has some limitations. First, it mainly focuses on commonsense generation, with limited optimization of the video caption decoder. Second, it depends heavily on the quality of the pretrained language model. Future work will address these issues to further boost performance.

Acknowledgments. This project was supported in part by the Beijing Natural Science Foundation under grant L233008; in part by the Natural Science Foundation of China under Grant 62236010.

References

1. Aytar, Y., Vondrick, C., Torralba, A.: Soundnet: learning sound representations from unlabeled video. In: Advances in Neural Information Processing Systems, vol. 29 (2016)
2. Ayyubi, H.A., Liu, T., Nagrani, A., et al.: Video summarization: towards entity-aware captions. arXiv preprint arXiv:2312.02188 (2023)
3. Carreira, J., Zisserman, A.: Quo vadis, action recognition? A new model and the kinetics dataset. In: Proceedings of the IEEE Conference on Computer Vision and Pattern Recognition, pp. 6299–6308 (2017)
4. Chen, S., Jiang, Y.G.: Motion guided region message passing for video captioning. In: Proceedings of the IEEE Conference on Computer Vision and Pattern Recognition (ICCV), pp. 1543–1552 (2021)
5. Devlin, J., Chang, M.W., et al.: Bert: pre-training of deep bidirectional transformers for language understanding. In: Proceedings of the 2019 Conference of the North American Chapter of the Association for Computational Linguistics: Human Language Technologies, Volume 1 (Long and Short Papers), pp. 4171–4186 (2019)
6. Fang, Z., Gokhale, T., et al.: Video2commonsense: generating commonsense descriptions to enrich video captioning. arXiv preprint arXiv:2003.05162 (2020)
7. Gao, L., Guo, Z., Zhang, H., et al.: Video captioning with attention-based LSTM and semantic consistency. IEEE Trans. Multimedia **19**(9), 2045–2055 (2017)
8. He, K., Zhang, X., Ren, S., et al.: Deep residual learning for image recognition. In: Proceedings of the IEEE Conference on Computer Vision and Pattern Recognition, pp. 770–778 (2016)
9. Kingma, D.P., Ba, J.: Adam: a method for stochastic optimization. arXiv preprint arXiv:1412.6980 (2014)
10. Kojima, A., Tamura, T., Fukunaga, K.: Natural language description of human activities from video images based on concept hierarchy of actions. Int. J. Comput. Vision **50**, 171–184 (2002)

11. Krishnamoorthy, N., Malkarnenkar, G., Mooney, R., et al.: Generating natural-language video descriptions using text-mined knowledge. In: Proceedings of the AAAI Conference on Artificial Intelligence, vol. 27, pp. 541–547 (2013)

12. Lin, C.Y.: Rouge: a package for automatic evaluation of summaries. In: Text Summarization Branches Out, pp. 74–81 (2004)

13. Lin, K., Li, L., Lin, C.C., et al.: Swinbert: end-to-end transformers with sparse attention for video captioning. In: Proceedings of the IEEE/CVF Conference on Computer Vision and Pattern Recognition, pp. 17949–17958 (2022)

14. Papineni, K., Roukos, S., Ward, T., et al.: Bleu: a method for automatic evaluation of machine translation. In: Proceedings of the 40th Annual Meeting of the Association for Computational Linguistics (ACL), pp. 311–318 (2002)

15. Sap, M., Le Bras, R., Allaway, E., et al.: Atomic: an atlas of machine commonsense for if-then reasoning. In: Proceedings of the AAAI Conference on Artificial Intelligence, vol. 33, pp. 3027–3035 (2019)

16. Shao, H., Fang, Z., Yang, Y.: Cavan: commonsense knowledge anchored video captioning. In: 2022 26th International Conference on Pattern Recognition (ICPR), pp. 4095–4102. IEEE (2022)

17. Shen, Y., Gu, X., Xu, K., et al.: Accurate and fast compressed video captioning. In: Proceedings of the IEEE/CVF International Conference on Computer Vision, pp. 15558–15567 (2023)

18. Tang, M., Wang, Z., et al.: Clip4caption: clip for video caption. In: Proceedings of the 29th ACM International Conference on Multimedia, pp. 4858–4862 (2021)

19. Vaswani, A., Shazeer, N., Parmar, N., et al.: Attention is all you need. In: Advances in Neural Information Processing Systems, vol. 30 (2017)

20. Vedantam, R., Lawrence Zitnick, C., Parikh, D.: Cider: consensus-based image description evaluation. In: Proceedings of the IEEE Conference on Computer Vision and Pattern Recognition (CVPR), pp. 4566–4575 (2015)

21. Venugopalan, S., Rohrbach, M., et al.: Sequence to sequence-video to text. In: Proceedings of the IEEE International Conference on Computer Vision, pp. 4534–4542 (2015)

22. Xi, Z., Shi, G., Li, X., et al.: A simple yet effective knowledge guided method for entity-aware video captioning on a basketball benchmark. Neurocomputing **619**, 129177 (2025)

23. Xi, Z., Shi, G., Sun, H., et al.: Eika: explicit & implicit knowledge-augmented network for entity-aware sports video captioning. Expert Syst. Appl. **274**, 126906 (2025)

24. Xu, J., Mei, T., Yao, T., et al.: MSR-VTT: a large video description dataset for bridging video and language. In: Proceedings of the IEEE Conference on Computer Vision and Pattern Recognition, pp. 5288–5296 (2016)

25. Ye, H., Li, G., Qi, Y., et al.: Hierarchical modular network for video captioning. In: Proceedings of the IEEE/CVF Conference on Computer Vision and Pattern Recognition, pp. 17939–17948 (2022)

26. Yu, W., Liang, J., Ji, L., et al.: Hybrid reasoning network for video-based commonsense captioning. In: Proceedings of the 29th ACM International Conference on Multimedia, pp. 5213–5221 (2021)

27. Yuan, M., Jia, G., Bao, B.K.: GPT-based knowledge guiding network for commonsense video captioning. IEEE Trans. Multimedia **26**, 5147–5158 (2023)

28. Zhou, L., Zhou, Y., Corso, J.J., et al.: End-to-end dense video captioning with masked transformer. In: Proceedings of the IEEE Conference on Computer Vision and Pattern Recognition, pp. 8739–8748 (2018)

EAANet: Edge-Aware Attention Network for Real-Time Road Scene Understanding

Chuyu Bai[1], Jianlin Yu[1], Xiaochun Lei[1,2(✉)], and Zetao Jiang[1,2]

[1] School of Computer Science and Information Security, Guilin University of
Electronic Technology, Guilin 541010, Guangxi, China
[2] Guangxi Key Laboratory of Image and Graphic Intelligent Processing, Guilin
University of Electronic Technology, Guilin 541004, Guangxi, China
`lxc8125@guet.edu.cn`

Abstract. To address the accuracy-speed trade-off in semantic segmentation for resource-constrained driver assistance systems, this study proposes EAANet (Edge-Aware Attention Network). Building upon a Lightweight Progressive Scalable Network (LPSNet) as the baseline, we first embed Squeeze-and-Excitation (SE) channel attention into feature fusion layers to establish channel-wise adaptive feature selection. The Atrous Spatial Pyramid Pooling (ASPP) module is then enhanced through four parallel branches for improved multi-scale feature extraction. Further optimizations include reconstructing the decoder with depthwise separable convolutions and compressing the model size via parameter pruning. Experiments on the Cityscapes dataset demonstrate that EAANet achieves 76.7% mIoU, surpassing LPSNet by 3.2% points while reducing parameters to 1.2M. When deployed on NVIDIA Jetson Xavier NX edge devices, it attains real-time inference at 33.5 frames per second, with specific accuracy improvements of 9.0% for vehicles and 14.7% for traffic signs. The proposed model significantly enhances critical object recognition while maintaining real-time performance, offering a cost-effective semantic segmentation solution for vehicular edge computing platforms.

Keywords: Semantic segmentation · driver assistance · Lightweight Neural Networks · attention mechanism

1 Introduction

With the rapid development of intelligent networked vehicle technology, the environmental sensing capabilities of autonomous driving systems face the dual challenges of high accuracy and real-time performance. As a core technology, although traditional semantic segmentation methods excel in accuracy, their substantial computational demands make them difficult to meet the real-time requirements of in-vehicle platforms.

In recent years, lightweight semantic segmentation networks have gradually balanced performance through architectural optimization. However, significant

Z. Lin et al. (Eds.): ICIG 2025, LNCS 16161, pp. 15–26, 2026.
https://doi.org/10.1007/978-981-95-3398-5_2

limitations persist: when facing complex scenes, their ability to segment details of safety-critical targets like pedestrians and vehicles is often insufficient, and they struggle to adapt to practical challenges such as varying lighting conditions, occlusions, and multi-scale targets. Existing research primarily focuses on architecture lightweighting, which is prone to losing small target features, and dynamic computation, which can introduce extra latency in embedded devices due to dynamic routing mechanisms. Although the combination of multi-scale feature fusion and attention mechanisms has become a trend, the naive stacking of modules often leads to insufficient interaction, and fixed parameter configurations struggle to adapt to diverse scene changes.

There are three major bottlenecks in current approaches: (1) lightweight designs often sacrifice spatial details, leading to blurred key target boundaries; (2) multi-scale modules frequently suffer from parameter redundancy; and (3) a significant discrepancy exists between the theoretical acceleration of dynamic computation and actual hardware performance. To address these issues, this paper proposes the EAANet framework, which significantly improves network performance through three core innovations: integrating the channel attention mechanism, optimizing the multi-scale perception module, and streamlining the computational process. Experiments demonstrate that the improved model enhances segmentation accuracy by 3.2% while maintaining real-time performance, particularly for safety-critical targets, thereby providing an efficient and reliable perception solution for autonomous driving systems.

2   Related Work

2.1   Semantic Segmentation Evolution

Modern semantic segmentation evolved from FCN's end-to-end framework [1], with subsequent advances addressing accuracy-speed trade-offs. The DeepLab series [2] improved boundary precision via atrous convolution and ASPP, yet incurred high computation (100G FLOPs [3]). Encoder-decoder architectures (U-Net [4]/SegNet [5]) enhanced feature fusion but struggled with multi-scale adaptation. Recent lightweight designs prioritize edge deployment: ENet [6] reduced computation 20× through asymmetric structures but sacrificed small-target accuracy; BiSeNet [8] achieved 62FPS via dual-path processing, while ESPNetV2 [10] compressed models through spatial pyramids. SCTNet's [21] CNN-Transformer hybrid reached 80.5% mIoU but maintained high resource demands. A persistent challenge remains balancing detail preservation and computational efficiency, particularly for sub-2M parameter models.

2.2   Attention and Multi-scale Fusion

Attention mechanisms revolutionized feature enhancement, with SENet's [13] channel attention and DANet's [14] dual attention improving dynamic calibration. Lightweight variants like BiSeNetV2 [16] integrated refined attention yet suffered insufficient multi-scale interaction. Parallel developments in multi-scale processing saw ASPP [18] expand receptive fields via dilated convolutions, while PSPNet's [19] pyramid pooling enhanced global context. LPSNet [20] emerged as a balanced solution, achieving 72.3% mIoU through progressive fusion, though its fixed dilation rates limited scale adaptation.

2.3   LPSNet Limitations

As our baseline, LPSNet's scalable architecture enables flexible capacity adjustment through: 1) Multi-path feature interaction, 2) Lightweight backbone, 3) Progressive fusion. However, three critical limitations persist in autonomous driving scenarios: 1) Blurred small-target boundaries due to aggressive downsampling, 2) Fixed-scale ASPP configurations inadequate for dynamic urban environments, 3) Redundant computations in cross-path interactions. Our EAANet addresses these through SE-enhanced attention and optimized multi-scale processing.

3   Method

EAANet extends the LPSNet encoder-decoder framework with three strategic enhancements, as depicted in Fig. 1. The encoder incorporates Squeeze-and-Excitation (SE) attention during multi-path interactions to amplify critical features, while a redesigned Atrous Spatial Pyramid Pooling (ASPP) module handles multi-scale context. The decoder undergoes structural optimizations to eliminate redundancy. The complete pipeline is expressed as:

$$F_{\text{out}} = D(A(\varepsilon_{\text{SE}}(X))) \tag{1}$$

where ε_{SE} denotes the SE-augmented encoder, A the lightweight ASPP, and D the optimized decoder.

3.1   Channel Attention Integration

As shown in Fig. 2, SE modules are inserted after each convolutional path to dynamically recalibrate channel-wise feature responses. This process first compresses spatial information through global average pooling, then applies two fully-connected layers with reduction ratio $r = 16$ to generate attention weights:

$$W_{\text{SE}} = \sigma(W_2\delta(W_1 \cdot \text{GAP}(F))) \tag{2}$$

where σ denotes sigmoid activation. The SE-enhanced features are subsequently fused across paths, adding only 0.2M parameters while improving pedestrian IoU by 9.5%.

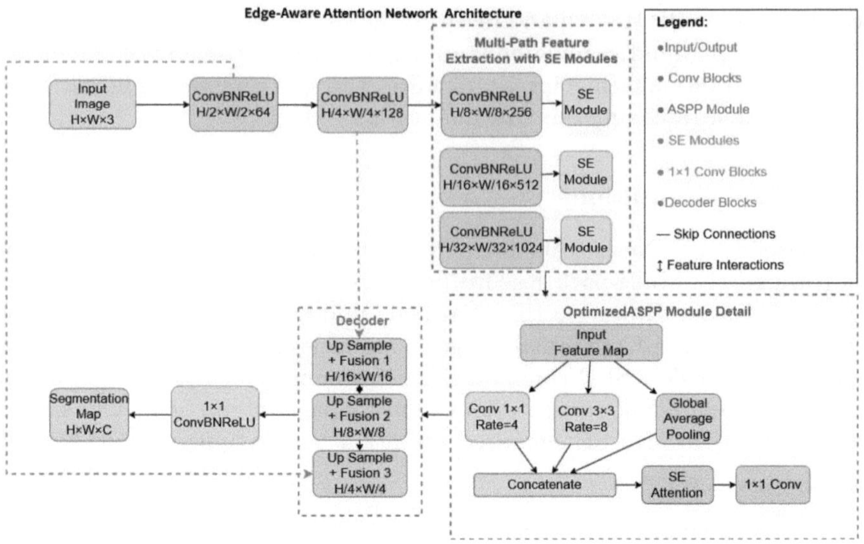

Fig. 1. EAANet architectural improvements: (1) SE blocks in multi-path fusion, (2) Four-branch ASPP with adaptive pooling, (3) Pruned decoder with gradual upsampling.

3.2   Multi-scale Feature Extraction

The improved ASPP module (Fig. 3) employs four parallel branches to capture diverse receptive fields: two cascaded 1×1-3×3 convolutional chains, a standalone 1×1 convolution, and an adaptive pooling branch. Branch outputs are concatenated and weighted by a shared SE module before final fusion:

$$F_{\mathrm{ASPP}} = \delta(W_{\mathrm{SE}} * \mathrm{Concat}(F_1, F_2, F_3, F_4)) \tag{3}$$

Standard ASPP implementations typically involve multiple parallel dilated convolutions (e.g., 3×3 with various dilation rates) and an image pooling branch, often followed by 1×1 convolutions. While effective for multi-scale context aggregation, these dilated convolutions can be computationally intensive, especially with larger dilation rates and higher channel counts. In contrast, our improved ASPP strategically replaces the majority of these expensive dilated convolutions with more efficient structures. Specifically, the use of two cascaded 1×1-3×3 convolutional chains in the primary branches allows for capturing receptive fields similar to larger convolutions but with significantly fewer FLOPs due to factorization. The straightforward 1×1 convolution and the adaptive pooling branch further contribute to computational efficiency. This streamlined design, particularly when processing 1/16 resolution features, leads to a reduction of FLOPs by 43% compared to conventional standard ASPP implementations, optimizing the balance between multi-scale representation capability and computational cost.

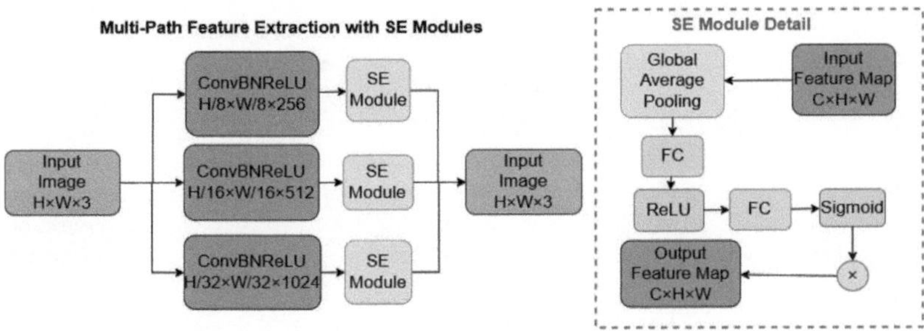

Fig. 2. SE module integration workflow: (a) Feature compression, (b) Excitation weight generation, (c) Channel-wise multiplication.

3.3   Structural Optimization

Three key optimizations address computational bottlenecks in LPSNet. First, adaptive feature aggregation minimizes redundant cross-path computations through learnable weighted fusion $F^l = \sum w_i^l T_i(F_i)$. Second, a gradual upsampling decoder progressively refines features using $F_{\text{dec}}^l = U(\text{Conv}(\text{Concat}[F_{\text{dec}}^{l+1}, F_{\text{skip}}^l]))$, reducing interpolation artifacts. Third, channel pruning based on feature importance analysis [24] removes 35% of shallow layer channels. As detailed in Table 1, these changes, particularly when applied to create the lightweight EAANet variant, maintain accuracy while reducing parameters from EAANet's 1.2M to 0.8M.

4   Experiments

4.1   Experimental Setup and Assessment Methods

This study evaluates the performance of EAANet on the Cityscapes dataset, a standard dataset widely used for semantic segmentation of autonomous driving scenarios, containing street view images from 50 different cities. The dataset consists of 2,975 training images, 500 validation images, and 1,525 test images, each with a resolution of 2048 × 1024 and labeled with 19 categories covering key elements in the autonomous driving scenario such as roads, sidewalks, buildings, vehicles, and pedestrians. In terms of evaluation metrics, this study adopts mIoU as the main measure, which reflects the overall segmentation accuracy. In addition, this study pays special attention to the individual category IoUs of safety-critical categories such as pedestrians, vehicles, and road boundaries. To comprehensively evaluate the model performance, this study simultaneously measures the inference time and frame rate as well as the computational complexity metrics, including floating-point operations and parameter counts, on different hardware platforms. In terms of implementation details, this study uses an input resolution of 768 × 384 for training and 1024 × 512 for testing. The training batch size is set to 16, and the SGD optimizer is used with an initial learning rate of 0.01, momentum of 0.9, and weight decay of 5e-4. The learning

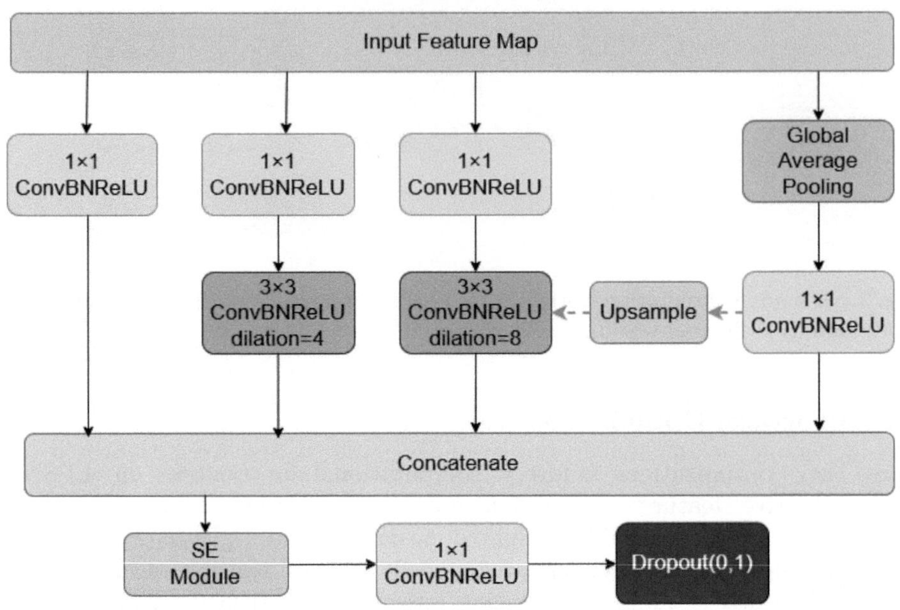

Fig. 3. Lightweight ASPP structure: B1-B3 handle local-dilated-global contexts, B4 provides global priors.

rate is based on a polynomial decay strategy with a decay factor of 0.9, and the total number of training rounds is 200. To enhance the model generalization ability, data augmentation techniques such as random scaling (0.5–2.0), random cropping, random horizontal flipping and color jittering are applied in this study. The experiments are trained on NVIDIA RTX 3090 GPUs and the inference performance is tested on NVIDIA Jetson Xavier NX embedded platform and Intel Core i7-10700K CPU general-purpose computing platform, respectively.

4.2   Comparative Experiments and Analysis

To evaluate the effectiveness of the proposed EAANet and its variants, we first present a detailed performance comparison with the baseline LPSNet on the Cityscapes validation set, as shown in Table 2. Subsequently, a comprehensive comparison against other state-of-the-art lightweight semantic segmentation methods is also provided.

As shown in Table 2, the EAANet ($r = 16$) configuration achieves a top mIoU of 76.7%, which is a significant 3.2% point improvement over the baseline LPSNet (73.5%). While this configuration has a slightly higher parameter count (1.2M vs 0.9M) and GFLOPs (6.8 vs 6.2) compared to LPSNet, its superior precision demonstrates the value of the refined design. Furthermore, EAANet exhibits flexible efficiency-accuracy trade-offs through configuration

Table 1. EAANet Hierarchical Model Comparison

Component	LPSNet	EAANet
Initial Parameters		
ConvBlock 1	Fixed step decay	64 channels
ConvBlock 2	Fixed step decay	128 channels
Multi-source Components		
Path 1	Shared decay	256 channels
Path 2	Shared decay	512 channels
Path 3	Shared decay	1024 channels
ASPP Structure		
Branch 1	–	DualCBR
Branch 2	–	DualCBR
Branch 3	–	1×1 Conv(BN+ReLU)
Branch 4	–	AdaptCBR
Feature Fusion		
Basic fusion	Concatenation	SE attention
Multi-scale	Single-level	MS-Fusion
Attention		
SE Module	–	Adaptive (min=1)
Classifier	channels$_{-1}$ × paths	channels$_{-1}$

Note: CBR: Conv-BatchNorm-ReLU. DualCBR: $1 \times 1 + 3 \times 3$ convolutions. MS-Fusion: Multi-scale fusion. SE: Squeeze-and-Excitation. Subscript -1 denotes final layer dimensions

Table 2. Performance Comparison Between EAANet and LPSNet

Method	Input Size	mIoU (%)	FPS	Params (M)	GFLOPs
LPSNet	768×384	73.5	28.3	0.9	6.2
EAANet($r = 16$)	768×384	76.7	25.8	1.2	6.8
EAANet($r = 8$)	768×384	75.2	33.5	0.8	4.7

Testing platform: Jetson Xavier NX

adjustments. For instance, by setting the SE module's compression ratio 'r' to 8, the lightweight EAANet variant significantly boosts inference speed to 33.5 FPS on the Jetson Xavier NX platform, with reduced parameters (0.8M) and GFLOPs (4.7G). Although its mIoU is slightly lower at 75.2%, it still distinctly outperforms the baseline LPSNet. This demonstrates EAANet's adaptability to resource-constrained scenarios, allowing for optimal balance between performance and computational demands by tuning key hyperparameters. Figure 4 illustrates EAANet's substantial IoU enhancements across critical traffic safety categories. Traffic light recognition improves from 0.57 to 0.67 IoU (17.5% relative improvement), traffic sign detection from 0.68 to 0.78 (14.7% IoU boost), and pedestrian recognition from 0.74 to 0.81 (9.5% increased IoU). Bicycle and

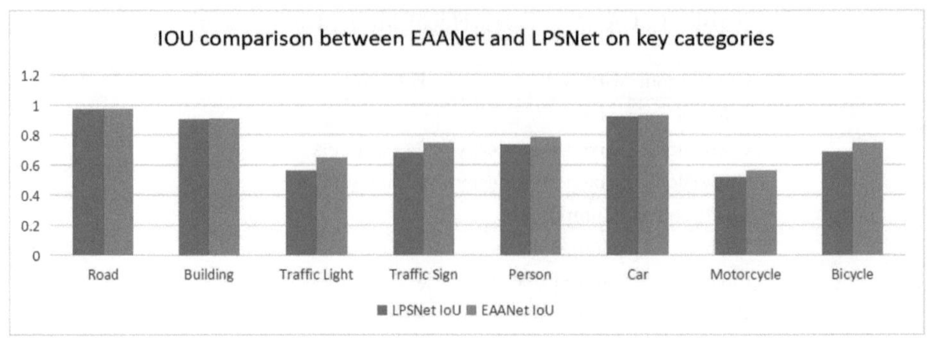

Fig. 4. Category-wise IoU improvements: (a) Traffic lights, (b) Traffic signs, (c) Pedestrians. Red dashed line indicates baseline LPSNet performance, blue bars represent EAANet results. Critical safety categories show 9.5%–17.5% IoU gains. (Color figure online)

Table 3. Performance Comparison with Lightweight Segmentation Methods

Method	Backbone	Input Size	mIoU (%)	FPS	Params (M)	GFLOPs
BiSeNetV2	–	768 × 384	73.4	22.5	3.4	12.3
FastSCNN	–	1024 × 512	70.2	35.6	1.1	3.8
ESPNetV2	–	1024 × 512	67.9	31.2	1.7	4.5
MNV3+DLbV3	MNV3	768 × 384	75.1	18.3	5.3	15.2
PP-LiteSeg	–	768 × 384	74.9	28.7	2.8	8.6
EAANet (r = 16)	–	768 × 384	76.7	25.8	1.2	6.8
EAANet (r = 8)	–	768 × 384	75.2	33.5	0.8	4.7

Testing platform: Jetson Xavier NX.

MNV3+DLV3 = MobileNetV3 + DeepLabV3 combination.

Symbol "–" denotes no backbone usage

motorcycle identification also show respective 13.0% and 11.5% gains, reaching 0.78 and 0.58 IoU scores. Concurrently, the model maintains high performance in fundamental categories, with 0.98 IoU for road segmentation, 0.91 for buildings, and 0.93 for vehicle detection. These advancements significantly strengthen autonomous systems' environmental perception capabilities, particularly in critical operational dimensions such as traffic signal interpretation, regulatory signage compliance, and vulnerable road user detection, which are essential for safe navigation in dense urban environments.

Table 3 demonstrates that our EAANet achieves a superior accuracy-speed equilibrium compared to state-of-the-art lightweight semantic segmentation approaches. When evaluated against methods with comparable segmentation accuracy, such as MobileNetV3-DeepLabV3 and PP-LiteSeg, the proposed network demonstrates 55.8% fewer parameters and 24.6% faster inference speed while maintaining equivalent precision. Conversely, relative to speed-optimized frameworks including FastSCNN and ESPNetV2, EAANet delivers 6.5–8.8% point improvements in mean Intersection-over-Union metrics without compromising real-time performance. These empirical results validate the efficacy of our architectural enhancements in optimizing lightweight segmentation networks, thus establishing an effective solution for deploying high-precision semantic understanding systems on resource-constrained embedded platforms.

4.3   Conclusion

This paper introduces EAANet, a novel architecture designed to achieve an optimal balance between accuracy and speed for semantic segmentation in autonomous driving. By integrating a Squeeze-and-Excitation (SE) attention mechanism and an improved lightweight Atrous Spatial Pyramid Pooling (ASPP) module, EAANet demonstrates superior performance. Experiments on the Cityscapes dataset show that the network achieves 76.7% mIoU, a 3.2% point improvement over the baseline LPSNet, with notable enhancements in the segmentation accuracy of safety-critical targets like pedestrians and vehicles. Furthermore, through optimized network structure and computational flow, EAANet achieves real-time inference at 33.5 FPS on the NVIDIA Jetson Xavier NX platform, effectively meeting the low-latency requirements for in-vehicle systems. Our comprehensive analysis of different EAANet configurations demonstrates the effectiveness of its core components. The integrated SE module significantly enhances key feature representation through dynamic channel weighting. Additionally, the improved ASPP module effectively processes multi-scale features, contributing to a reduction in computational complexity (e.g., a 43% reduction in FLOPs compared to standard ASPP when processing 1/16 resolution features) and an improvement in small target detection rates by 12.6%.

However, it is important to note that a detailed, component-wise ablation study quantifying the individual contribution of each proposed module was not conducted due to current research constraints. This systematic analysis will be a crucial area for future work.

Despite these advancements, EAANet's robustness in complex scenarios, such as extreme lighting conditions, rain, and snow, requires further improvement. Specifically, segmentation accuracy in nighttime environments decreases by approximately 8.3% compared to daytime performance. Furthermore, inherent resolution loss from downsampling limits the recognition rate of distant pedestrians to less than 65%. As a single-frame processing model, EAANet also faces challenges in optimizing dynamic scene segmentation consistency without leveraging temporal information. Lastly, for long-tailed data distributions, the model's segmentation accuracy for less-sampled categories, such as motorcycles and bicycles, remains below 70%, underscoring the persistent challenge of class imbalance.

Future work will focus on several key areas. Firstly, we aim to design a spatio-temporal fusion architecture that integrates optical flow estimation and video sequence analysis to enhance dynamic scene adaptation. Secondly, we plan to explore uncertainty quantification methods to provide a credibility assessment of segmentation results, crucial for robust decision-making systems. Thirdly, we intend to construct a multi-task joint learning framework with a shared feature extraction network to synchronize and optimize the tasks of semantic segmentation and depth estimation. Additionally, further enhancements to model deployment efficiency and generalization ability will involve operator-level optimization and self-supervised pre-training techniques tailored for embedded hardware.

Acknowledgements. This work was supported by the National Natural Science Foundation of China (NSFC) under Grants 62473105 and 62172118, the Guangxi Natural Science Foundation Key Project (2021GXNSFDA196002), the Guangxi Key Laboratory of Image and Graphic Intelligent Processing Research Project (GIIP2305), and the Undergraduate Innovation Training Program (202310595026).

References

1. Long, J., Shelhamer, E., Darrell, T.: Fully convolutional networks for semantic segmentation. In: Proceedings of IEEE Conference on Computer Vision and Pattern Recognition (CVPR), Los Alamitos, pp. 3431–3440. IEEE (2015). https://doi.org/10.1109/CVPR.2015.7298965
2. Chen, L.C., Papandreou, G., Kokkinos, I., Murphy, K., Yuille, A.L.: Deeplab: semantic image segmentation with deep convolutional nets, atrous convolution, and fully connected CRFs. IEEE Trans. Pattern Anal. Mach. Intell. **40**(4), 834–848 (2017). https://doi.org/10.1109/TPAMI.2017.2699184
3. Ronneberger, O., Fischer, P., Brox, T.: U-Net: convolutional networks for biomedical image segmentation. In: Navab, N., Hornegger, J., Wells, W.M., Frangi, A.F. (eds.) MICCAI 2015. LNCS, vol. 9351, pp. 234–241. Springer, Cham (2015). https://doi.org/10.1007/978-3-319-24574-4_28
4. Badrinarayanan, V., Kendall, A., Cipolla, R.: SegNet: a deep convolutional encoder-decoder architecture for image segmentation. IEEE Trans. Pattern Anal. Mach. Intell. **39**(12), 2481–2495 (2017). https://doi.org/10.1109/TPAMI.2016.2644615
5. Siam, M., Gamal, M., Abdel-Razek, M., Yogamani, S., Jagersand, M., Zhang, H.: A comparative study of real-time semantic segmentation for autonomous driving. In: Proceedings of IEEE Conference on Computer Vision and Pattern Recognition Workshops (CVPRW), Los Alamitos, pp. 587–597. IEEE (2018). https://doi.org/10.1109/CVPRW.2018.00086
6. Paszke, A., Chaurasia, A., Kim, S., Culurciello, E.: ENet: a deep neural network architecture for real-time semantic segmentation. arXiv preprint arXiv:1606.02147 (2016)
7. Zhao, H., Qi, X., Shen, X., Shi, J., Jia, J.: ICNet for real-time semantic segmentation on high-resolution images. In: Ferrari, V., Hebert, M., Sminchisescu, C., Weiss, Y. (eds.) ECCV 2018. LNCS, vol. 11207, pp. 418–434. Springer, Cham (2018). https://doi.org/10.1007/978-3-030-01219-9_25
8. Yu, C., Wang, J., Peng, C., Gao, C., Yu, G., Sang, N.: BiSeNet: bilateral segmentation network for real-time semantic segmentation. In: Ferrari, V., Hebert, M., Sminchisescu, C., Weiss, Y. (eds.) ECCV 2018. LNCS, vol. 11217, pp. 334–349. Springer, Cham (2018). https://doi.org/10.1007/978-3-030-01261-8_20

9. Laradji, I.H., Rostamzadeh, N., Pinheiro, P.O., Vazquez, D., Schmidt, M.: Where are the blobs: counting by localization with point supervision. In: Ferrari, V., Hebert, M., Sminchisescu, C., Weiss, Y. (eds.) ECCV 2018. LNCS, vol. 11206, pp. 560–576. Springer, Cham (2018). https://doi.org/10.1007/978-3-030-01216-8_34

10. Mehta, S., Rastegari, M., Shapiro, L., Hajishirzi, H.: ESPNetV2: a light-weight, power efficient, and general purpose convolutional neural network. In: Proceedings of IEEE/CVF Conference on Computer Vision and Pattern Recognition (CVPR), Los Alamitos, pp. 9190–9200. IEEE (2019). https://doi.org/10.1109/CVPR.2019.00941

11. Wang, X., Girshick, R., Gupta, A., He, K.: Non-local neural networks. In: Proceedings of IEEE Conference on Computer Vision and Pattern Recognition (CVPR), Los Alamitos, pp. 7794–7803. IEEE (2018). https://doi.org/10.1109/CVPR.2018.00813

12. Hu, J., Shen, L., Sun, G.: Squeeze-and-excitation networks. In: Proceedings of IEEE Conference on Computer Vision and Pattern Recognition (CVPR), Los Alamitos, pp. 7132–7141. IEEE (2018). https://doi.org/10.1109/CVPR.2018.00745

13. Fu, J., Liu, J., Tian, H., et al.: Dual attention network for scene segmentation. In: Proceedings of IEEE/CVF Conference on Computer Vision and Pattern Recognition (CVPR), Los Alamitos, pp. 3146–3154. IEEE (2019). https://doi.org/10.1109/CVPR.2019.00326

14. Huang, Z., Wang, X., Huang, L., et al.: CCNet: criss-cross attention for semantic segmentation. In: Proceedings of IEEE/CVF International Conference on Computer Vision (ICCV), Los Alamitos, pp. 603–612. IEEE (2019). https://doi.org/10.1109/ICCV.2019.00069

15. Yu, C., Gao, C., Wang, J., Yu, G., Shen, C., Sang, N.: BiSeNet V2: bilateral network with guided aggregation for real-time semantic segmentation. Int. J. Comput. Vision **129**(11), 3051–3068 (2021). https://doi.org/10.1007/s11263-021-01515-2

16. Poudel, R.P., Liwicki, S., Cipolla, R.: Fast-SCNN: fast semantic segmentation network. arXiv preprint arXiv:1902.04502 (2019)

17. Chen, L.-C., Zhu, Y., Papandreou, G., Schroff, F., Adam, H.: Encoder-decoder with atrous separable convolution for semantic image segmentation. In: Ferrari, V., Hebert, M., Sminchisescu, C., Weiss, Y. (eds.) ECCV 2018. LNCS, vol. 11211, pp. 833–851. Springer, Cham (2018). https://doi.org/10.1007/978-3-030-01234-2_49

18. Zhao, H., Shi, J., Qi, X., Wang, X., Jia, J.: Pyramid scene parsing network. In: Proceedings of IEEE Conference on Computer Vision and Pattern Recognition (CVPR), Los Alamitos, pp. 2881–2890. IEEE (2017). https://doi.org/10.1109/CVPR.2017.660

19. Oršić, M., Kreso, I., Bevandić, P., Šegvić, S.: In defense of pre-trained ImageNet architectures for real-time semantic segmentation of road-driving scenes. In: Proceedings of IEEE/CVF Conference on Computer Vision and Pattern Recognition (CVPR), Los Alamitos, pp. 12607–12616. IEEE (2019). https://doi.org/10.1109/CVPR.2019.01290

20. Wei, Y., Liu, S., Wang, F., Pan, J.: LPSNet: lightweight and progressive semantic segmentation network for real-time urban driving scene parsing. IEEE Trans. Intell. Transp. Syst. **22**(7), 4450–4461 (2020). https://doi.org/10.1109/TITS.2020.2996147

21. Xu, F., Li, L., Gao, F., Liang, Y., Li, Z.: SCTNet: capturing lost semantic information in deep supervision for semantic segmentation. In: Proceedings of IEEE/CVF International Conference on Computer Vision (ICCV), Los Alamitos, pp. 2351–2360. IEEE (2023). https://doi.org/10.1109/ICCV51070.2023.00221

22. Fan, M., Lai, S., Huang, J., et al.: Rethinking BiSeNet for real-time semantic segmentation. In: Proceedings of IEEE/CVF Conference on Computer Vision and Pattern Recognition (CVPR), Los Alamitos, pp. 9716–9725. IEEE (2021). https://doi.org/10.1109/CVPR46437.2021.00959
23. Cordts, M., et al.: The cityscapes dataset for semantic urban scene understanding. In: Proceedings of IEEE Conference on Computer Vision and Pattern Recognition (CVPR), Los Alamitos, pp. 3213–3223. IEEE (2016). https://doi.org/10.1109/CVPR.2016.350
24. Zhang, Y., Zhou, D., Chen, S., Gao, S., Ma, Y.: Channel pruning for accelerating very deep neural networks. In: Proceedings of IEEE International Conference on Computer Vision (ICCV), Los Alamitos, pp. 1389–1397. IEEE (2020). https://doi.org/10.1109/ICCV.2017.155
25. Wang, J., et al.: Deep high-resolution representation learning for visual recognition. IEEE Trans. Pattern Anal. Mach. Intell. **43**(10), 3349–3364 (2021). https://doi.org/10.1109/TPAMI.2020.2983686
26. Liu, Y., Chen, K., Liu, C., Qin, Z., Luo, Z., Wang, J.: Structured knowledge distillation for semantic segmentation. In: Proceedings of IEEE/CVF Conference on Computer Vision and Pattern Recognition (CVPR), Los Alamitos, pp. 2604–2613. IEEE (2019). https://doi.org/10.1109/CVPR.2019.00271

Learning A Decomposition-Driven Two Stages Unfolding Artifact Removal Network for Compressed Images

Lijun Zhao[1]($\boxtimes$)(iD), Jie Zhao[1], Jinjing Zhang[2](iD), Hao Ren[1], Yong Zeng[1], and Anhong Wang[1]

[1] Taiyuan University of Science and Technology, Taiyuan 030024, China
leejun@tyust.edu.cn
[2] North University of China, Jiancaoping District, Taiyuan 030051, China
zjj_ginger@nuc.edu.cn

Abstract. In recent years, compression artifact removal technique has garnered significant attention in the field of image compression. However, existing artifact removal methods always adopt black-box networks for image enhancement. Although some explicable networks have better capability on reducing compression artifacts, they attach no importance to the role of image decomposition on network architecture design. To this end, we build a decomposition-driven two stages artifact removal framework for compressed images, which is composed of L1-norm and Low-Rank Constrained Structure Enhancement (LRC-SE) sub-optimization model and L1-norm Constrained Structure-Texture Enhancement (LC-STE) sub-optimization model. These two models can be unfolded into two explicable networks, named LRC-SE network and LC-STE network. The LRC-SE network is proposed to enhance the structure map, which is used as the initialization in the LC-STE network. Additionally, we design a low-rank latent representation block to decompose high-dimension features for effective feature extraction and redundancy reduction. Extensive experimental results demonstrate that the proposed method achieves superior performances for compression artifact removal in terms of PSNR, PSNR-B, and SSIM.

Keywords: Image compression · Artifact removal · Image decomposition · Interpretable neural network

1 Introduction

Lossy compression techniques are often widely used for image and video data, aiming to save network bandwidth and minimize storage space. For example, the main encoding steps of JPEG lossy compression include: dividing the input image into non-overlapping 8×8 blocks, performing Discrete Cosine Transform (DCT) on each 8×8 block to obtain DCT coefficients, DCT coefficients quantization and Huffman lossless coding. However, coarse quantization operations always result

© The Author(s), under exclusive license to Springer Nature Singapore Pte Ltd. 2026
Z. Lin et al. (Eds.): ICIG 2025, LNCS 16161, pp. 27–38, 2026.
https://doi.org/10.1007/978-981-95-3398-5_3

in the loss of high-frequency details in the image. At the same time, quantization operation is irreversible, ultimately leading to obvious visual artifacts. These artifacts not only affect user's visual experience, but also hinder subsequent low-level and high-level image processing tasks. Therefore, more and more researchers focus on how to reduce artifacts caused by lossy image compression.

In recent years, deep learning methods based on Convolutional Neural Networks (CNN) can directly learn different end-to-end nonlinear mappings from JPEG-degraded images to the clean ones. For instance, *Dong et al.* proposed a four-layer shallow network named ARCNN [1] to learn mapping function. Inspired by deep residual learning, *Zhang et al.* proposed a very deep network called DnCNN [2] for general image restoration. *Liu et al.* proposed a multi-scale U-Net in wavelet domain named MWCNN [3]. However, deep learning based methods lack theoretical basis and interpretability. To address the above problems, Deep Unfolding Network (DUN) receives increasing attention on removing compression artifacts. For example, *Fu et al.* [4] established a JEPG-artifacts removal DUN based on sparse convolutional dictionary learning. *Zhang et al.* proposed a low-rank compressed sensing network named LR-CSNet [5] for natural image compressed sensing by learning low-rank matrix factorization through network learning, and transformed it into a DUN architecture. Although these methods take into account various priors to optimize the unfolding network [6–10], these networks have not well combined diverse regularizers together. To this end, we propose a decomposition-driven two stages artifact removal framework for compression artifact removal. The main contributions of our method are summarized as follows:

1) We propose a two-stage decomposition based optimization model and expand it into a Decomposition-driven Two-stage Unfolding Artifact-removal Network (DTUANet) as the post-processing for image compression. The proposed model uses implicit low-rank prior and structure-texture priors for artifact removal in a cascaded manner.
2) Due to the cascaded manner of the proposed method, DTUANet has two essential parts: L1-norm and Low-Rank Constrained Structure Enhancement (LRC-SE) sub-optimization model, L1-norm Constrained Structure-Texture Enhancement (LC-STE) sub-optimization model.
3) In LRC-SE, the low-rank term is incorporated into the sub-optimization problem, which is solved to obtain a smoothed image. To effectively extract key features and reduce redundancy, we introduce a Low-Rank Latent Representation Block (LRLRB) to replace the low-rank optimization, which decomposes high-dimensional features into two low-rank matrices.
4) In LC-STE, the output of LRC-SE is used as the input, and the structure and texture features are optimized in an alternating and progressively-enhancing manner, allowing the structure and texture features to complement each other.

The rest of this paper is organized as follows. In Sect. 2, we will introduce the proposed method in detail. In Sect. 3, we will provide experimental results. Finally, we will draw conclusions in Sect. 4.

2   The Proposed Method

Unlike the traditional CNN-based methods, we formulate compressed images artifact removal problems as a decomposition-driven two stages optimization problem, which is composed of L1-norm and Low-Rank Constrained Structure Enhancement (LRC-STE) sub-optimization model and L1-norm Constrained Structure-Texture Enhancement (LC-STE) sub-optimization model. The LRC-STE sub-optimization model can be written as:

$$\arg \min_{X_S} \|Y_S - X_S\|_2^2 + \lambda_1 f_1(X_S) + \mu R(X_S), \tag{1}$$

in which Y_S is the smoothed image of the compressed image obtained by $L0$ gradient minimization, and X_S is the desired smoothed image. $R(X_S)$ is the nuclear norm on X_S. λ_1 and μ are the trade-off hyper-parameters. We restrict the low-rank components and the $L2$ norm of the signal instead of directly using the nuclear norm to avoid expensive SVD, so we let $R(X_S) = \frac{1}{2}\|X_S - I_S\|_2^2$. The LRC-SE sub-optimization model can be written as:

$$\arg \min_{X} \|Y - S - T\|_2^2 + \lambda f(S) + \eta g(T), \tag{2}$$

where $f(S)$ and $g(T)$ represent two regularizers associated with structure and texture priors, while η and λ are two trade-off parameters. Here, the artifact removal problem can be transformed into joint optimization problem of simultaneously predicting the structure map S and texture map T. These two sub-optimization models can be unfolded into two explicable networks, named LRC-SE network and LC-STE network, as shown in the Fig. 1. The LRC-SE network is obtained by unfolding the solution of Eq. (1), which is designed to predict the smoothed image, as shown in Fig. 2. Within the LRC-SE network, the high-dimensional features are decomposed into the product of two sub-matrices via an LRLRB to replace the original low-rank decomposition. Then the formula to be solved is expanded as the Proximal Gradient Descent Module (PGDM). After fixing LRC-SE network, the output of LRC-SE is used to initialize the structure map of LC-STE, and texture map is obtained by pixel-wise subtraction between the input image and the structure map. By unfolding the solution of Eq. (2), we can get the LC-STE network, as shown in Fig. 5.

2.1   LRC-SE Sub-optimization Model

To get the solution of Eq. (1), the auxiliary variable Z_S is introduced into Eq. (1), which can be written as:

$$\arg \min_{X_S} \|Y_S - Z_S\|_2^2 + \lambda_1 f_1(X_S) + \frac{\mu}{2}\|Z_S - I_S\|_2^2, s.t. X_S = Z_S. \tag{3}$$

Among them, Z_S is the approximation of smoothed compressed image obtained by the $L0$ gradient minimization on X_S. X_S is the desired smoothed image. I_S

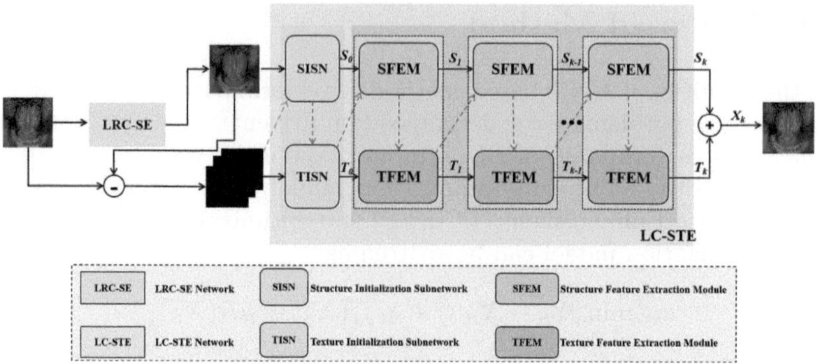

Fig. 1. The diagram of the proposed DTUANet.

is the low-rank component. Subsequently, we convert the constrained optimization problem of (3) into the unconstrained optimization problem, which can be written as:

$$\mathcal{L}(Z_S, X_S) = \frac{1}{2}\|Y_S - Z_S\|_2^2 + \lambda_1 f_1(X_S) + \frac{\mu}{2}\|Z_S - I_S\|_2^2 + \frac{\beta}{2}\|X_S - Z_S\|_2^2, \quad (4)$$

where μ and β are two penalty hyper-parameters. In general, the above optimization problem of Eq. (4) can be handled by solving the two sub-problems alternately. Note that the low-rank component I_S generated by LRLRB is independent of Z_S and X_S.

Update Z_S: In the k-th iteration, the Z_S can be updated as:

$$Z_S^{(k)} = \arg\min_{Z_S} \frac{1}{2}\|Y_S - Z_S\|_2^2 + \frac{\mu}{2}\|Z_S - I_S\|_2^2 + \frac{\beta}{2}\|X_S^{k-1} - Z_S\|_2^2. \quad (5)$$

Since both Z_S and I_S are the approximation of X_S, and the first term contains the original information of the input, we perform a Taylor expansion on the first term to adequately retain the original information, that is, replacing $\frac{1}{2}\|Y_S - Z_S\|_2^2$ with $\frac{l_1}{4}\|Z_S - Z_S^{k-1} + \frac{1}{l_1}(Z_S^{k-1} - Y_S)\| + C1$, which is a linear function that satisfies Lipschitz continuity. Finally, the update of Z_S^k can be written as:

$$Z_S^k = \frac{1}{s}(2\beta X_S^{k-1} + l_1 Z_S^{k-1} + 2\mu I^k - Z_S^{k-1} + Y_S), s = l_1 + 2\mu + 2\beta. \quad (6)$$

Update X_S: In the k-th iteration, the auxiliary variable X_S can be updated as:

$$X_S^{(k)} = \arg\min_{X_S} \frac{\beta}{2}\|X_S - Z_S^k\|_2^2 + \lambda_1 f_1(X_S). \quad (7)$$

Similarly, we perform Taylor expansion of $f_1(X_S)$ at X_S^{k-1} and convert it to the form $\nabla G(x)$ with the $L2$ norm constraint. The update of X_S^k can be written as:

$$x_S^k = \frac{\lambda l_2}{\lambda l_2 + \beta} x_S^{k-1} + \frac{\beta}{\lambda l_2 + \beta} z_S^k - \frac{\lambda}{\lambda l_2 + \beta} \nabla f_1(x_S^{k-1}). \quad (8)$$

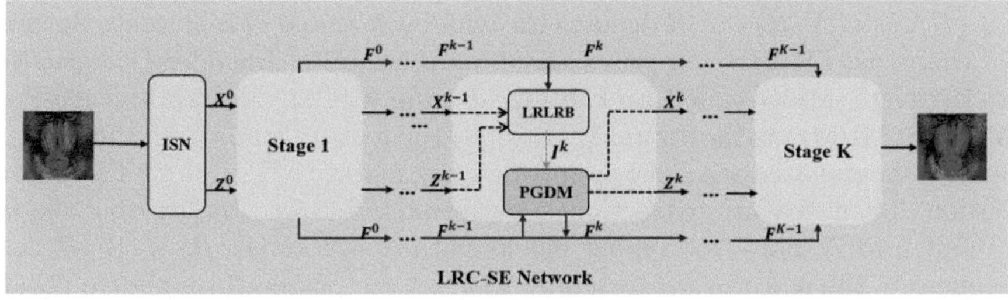

Fig. 2. The diagram of LRC-SE network.

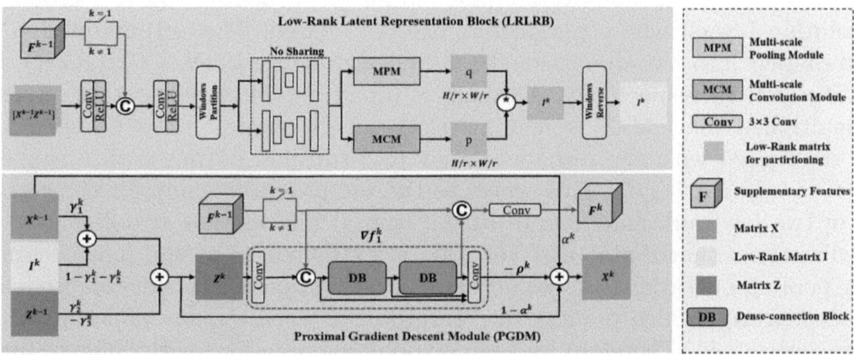

Fig. 3. The structures of LRLRB and PGDM from LRC-SE network at the k-th stage.

Here, the unknown function $\bigtriangledown G(x)$ is replaced by the convolutional layer in LRC-SE. In the specific end-to-end training, we set the penalty coefficients in front of the above variables as a series of learnable variables. After simplification, the iteration formula can be written as:

$$Z_S^k = \gamma_1^k X_S^{k-1} + \gamma_2^k Z_S^{k-1} + (1 - \gamma_1^k - \gamma_2^k)I^k - \gamma_3^k Z_S^{k-1} + \gamma_3^k Y_S,$$

$$\gamma_1^k = \frac{2\beta}{l_1 + 2\mu + 2\beta}, \gamma_2^k = \frac{l_1}{l_1 + 2\mu + 2\beta}, \gamma_3^k = \frac{1}{l_1 + 2\mu + 2\beta}, \tag{9}$$

$$X_S^k = \alpha^k X_S^{k-1} + (1 - \alpha^k)Z_S^{k-1} - \rho^k \bigtriangledown f_1(X_S^{k-1}), \alpha^k = \frac{\lambda l_2}{\lambda l_2 + \beta}, \rho^k = \frac{\lambda}{\lambda l_2 + \beta}. \tag{10}$$

The above Z_S, X_S, and I_S are combined in an explicit manner. Note that, for the update of X_S, $\bigtriangledown G(x)$ is unknown, so we use dense connection blocks to replace it. At the same time, the supplementary features F_{k-1} are all-zero tensor in the first stage, while it are obtained by updating X_S in the subsequent stages. The structure of the PGDM is given in Fig. 3.

LRLRB is responsible to generate a low-rank matrix at each stage, which encapsulates most of the important features from feature map. The low-rank matrix can be conceptualized as the product of two sub-matrices, $I = p \times q$, where

$p \times q \in (H/R) \times (W/R) \times C$, R denotes the window size and C represents the number of channels. LRLRB comprises three main modules: Encoder-Decoder Network (ED-Net), Multi-scale Convolution Module (MCM) and Multi-scale Pooling Module (MPM), as shown in Fig. 4. First, the feature maps from the previous stage are concatenated with the supplementary features F_{k-1} along the channel dimension. Then, feature extraction is performed, followed by dividing the feature maps into N non-overlapping blocks with a size of $(H/R) \times (W/R) \times C$. Subsequently, the features processed by ED-Net are passed through two parallel modules of the MPM and MCM to obtain two sub-matrices, which are multiplied in an element-wise manner to obtain the final low-rank tensor.

In ED-Net, these non-overlapping blocks are processed by two groups of convolution layers, whose parameters are not shared. The outputs of ED-Net are reshaped into two-dimensional tensors of dimensions $N \times C \times (R \times R)$ and $N \times (R \times R) \times C$ respectively. Through a broadcast mechanism, these tensors are multiplied to yield N weight matrices with a shape of $C \times C$, which are then multiplied with the reshaped input to form final output with a shape of $N \times C \times (H/R \times W/R)$. This serves as the pre-processing step for the generation of two low-rank matrices. In MPM, spatial information at different scales and directions (horizontal and vertical) is extracted from the input features using pooling operations. As we all know, pooling operations can compress and extract features, which reduces the resolution of feature maps while increasing the receptive field. Therefore, we employ pooling operations with different directions and strides, including global average pooling in the horizontal and vertical directions with three strides of two, four, and eight. These features obtained from multi-scale pooling and convolution operations are concatenated to form a comprehensive feature representation that is rich in contextual and structural information. The MCM is divided into three branches to extract features from the input feature map. In this module, $1 \times (H/R)$ and $(H/R) \times 1$ convolutional kernels are used to enhance directional features extraction, thereby refining and enriching the feature representation. Additionally, one convolution is employed to reduce the number of channels in the input features from C to 1. This reduces computational complexity, while integrating features across channels, simplifying the feature map and emphasizing the most important features. The features from these three branches are then added using a broadcast mechanism to create a weight map, which is multiplied by the input feature map to produce the final output. Finally, the outputs of the MPM and the MCM are multiplied to obtain the final low-rank feature map.

2.2   LC-STE Sub-optimization Model

The optimization problem of Eq. (2) can be transformed into two sub-problems. These sub-problems can be solved by the proximal gradient descent algorithm. The solutions to these sub-problems are iteratively refined in sequence. The optimization equations for these two sub-problems can be written as:

$$s^{(k)} = S^{(k-1)} - \eta_S(S^{(k-1)} - (Y - T^{(k-1)})), \tag{11}$$

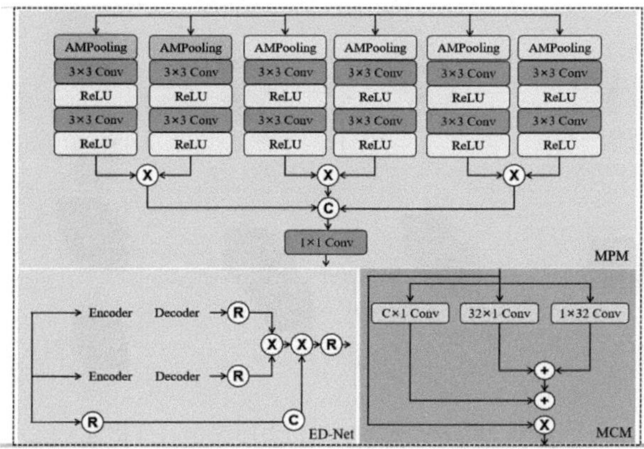

Fig. 4. The structures of ED-Net, MPM and MCM.

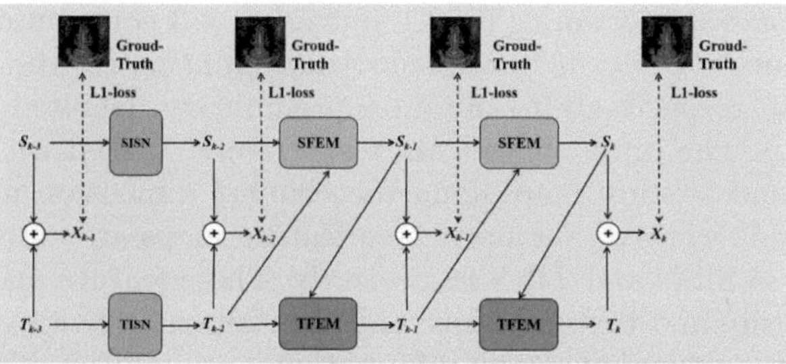

Fig. 5. The diagram of LC-STE network.

$$S^{(k+1)} = prox_{\eta S,\lambda_1}(s^{(k)}) = \arg\min_S \frac{1}{2}\|S - s^{(k)}\|_2^2 + \eta_s\lambda_1 f_1(S), \qquad (12)$$

$$t^{(k)} = T^{(k-1)} - \eta_T(T^{(k-1)} - (Y - S^{(k)})), \qquad (13)$$

$$T^{(k+1)} = prox_{\eta T,\lambda_2}(t^{(k)}) = \arg\min_T \frac{1}{2}\|T - t^{(k)}\|_2^2 + \eta_t\lambda_2 f_2(T), \qquad (14)$$

where k represents the iteration index, η_s and η_t are the learnable step parameters for updating S and T respectively. $prox_{\eta S,\lambda_1}(*)$ and $prox_{\eta T,\lambda_2}(*)$ are the proximal operators about the implicit prior $f_1(S)$ and $f_2(T)$ respectively, whose structure is shown in Fig. 8. According to Eq. (12) and Eq. (14), the iteratively-updated structure map S^k and texture map T^k can be obtained by Eq. (11) and Eq. (13). Finally, the last updated S^k and T^k are added in an element-wise manner to obtain the enhanced image. Equation (12) and Eq. (14) can be unfolded into the Structure Feature Extraction Module (SFEM) and Texture Feature Extraction Module (TFEM). Since the optimization of these two formulas involves two proximal operators $prox_{\eta T,\lambda_2}(*)$ and $prox_{\eta T,\lambda_2}(*)$ of $L1$-norm regularization, it cannot be derived explicitly, so the CNN is used to update S^k and T^k.

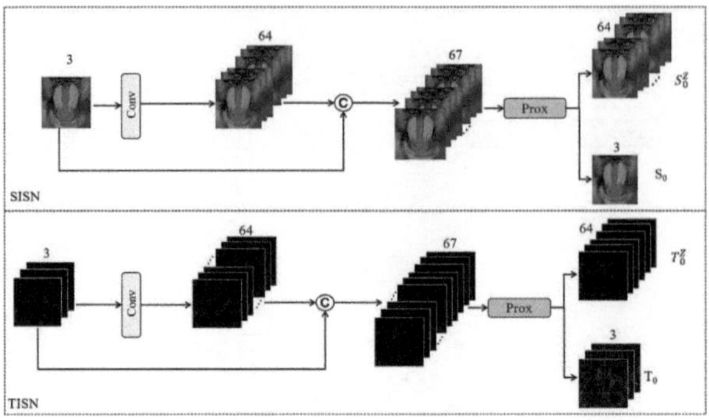

Fig. 6. The structures of SISN and TISN.

As shown in Fig. 6, the Structure Initialization Sub-Network (SISN) and Texture Initialization Sub-Network (TISN) first use 3×3 convolution kernels with all weights of one to perform image smoothing filtering on the structure map and texture map respectively to obtain a preliminary denoised structure map and texture map. The input images are respectively stacked with the obtained structure map and texture map along the channel dimension and sent to the initialization module. Next, the first three feature maps are extracted from the output features of SISN and TISN respectively. These feature maps serve as the initialized structure and texture maps, and the remaining feature maps are sent to the next stage as supplementary information.

The SFEM is primarily designed to update the structural features of the image, as shown in Fig. 1. This module takes the initialized structure and texture feature maps as the input, and processes them using the gradient descent algorithm, resulting in three-channel feature maps. For the proximal mapping approximation in Eq. (12), the three-channel feature maps obtained from the gradient descent algorithm are concatenated with the remaining feature maps from the previous stage along the channel dimension, followed by processing through five residual blocks with a constant number of channels, as shown in Fig. 8. The output feature maps with 67 channels retain the first three channels as the updated S, while the remaining 64 channels are used as supplementary information for the next stage, as shown in Fig. 7. The TFEM is mainly responsible for updating the texture features of the image, as shown in Fig. 1. This module takes the initialized texture image and the structure image updated by SFEM as inputs and processes them by the gradient descent algorithm to produce three-channel feature maps. TFEM and SFEM have same network structure, as shown in Fig. 8 and Fig. 7.

2.3 Loss Function

The Loss of LRC-SE Network. The enhanced images produced by LRC-SE and the original uncompressed image $L0$ gradient minimization are used as

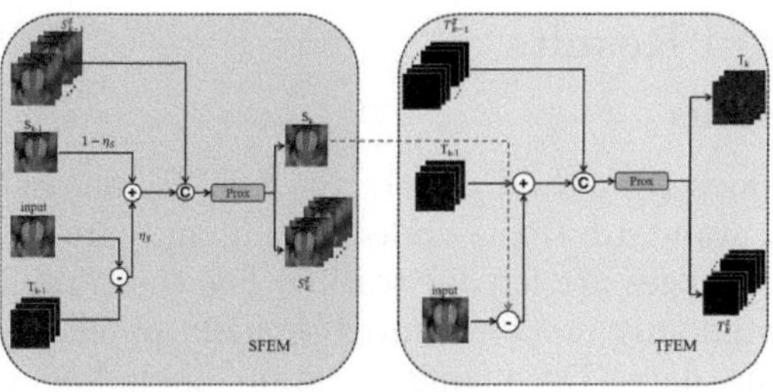

Fig. 7. The diagram of SFEM and TFEM.

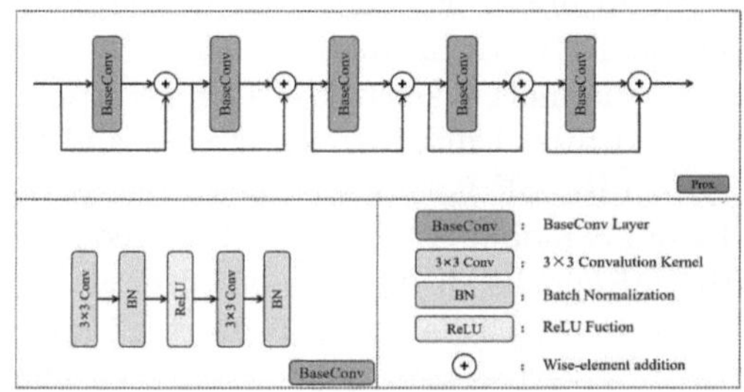

Fig. 8. The diagram of proximal operator (Prox).

the inputs of the loss function for LRC-SE network. The reconstruction loss constrained by the L1 norm is employed to supervise the learning of LRC-SE. The total loss function can be written as:

$$\mathscr{L}_S(X_S, Y_S) = \frac{1}{N}||Y_S - X_S^{(0)}||_1 + \frac{1}{N*K}\sum_{i=1}^{K}||Y_S - X_S^{(i)}||_1, \qquad (15)$$

where $X_S^{(0)}$ is the initialized smoothed image. $X_S^{(i)}$ is the enhanced smoothed image at the i-th stage. N is the total pixel number of the image Y_S, and K is the total number of stages in LRC-SE.

The Loss of LC-STE Network. The image enhanced by LC-STE and the original undistorted image X_{GT} are the inputs of the loss function for the LC-STE network. The reconstruction loss with an L1 norm constraint is used to supervise the learning of LC-STE network. The overall loss function can be written as:

$$\mathscr{L}_{clean}(X, X_{GT}) = \frac{1}{N}||X_{GT} - X^{(0)}||_1 + \frac{1}{N*K}\sum_{i=1}^{K}||X_{GT} - X^{(i)}||_1, \qquad (16)$$

Here, N is the size of image X_{GT}, and K is the total stage number. $X0$ is the initialized enhanced image, and $X^{(i)}$ is the enhanced image in the i-th stage.

3 Experimental Results

3.1 Training Details

To evaluate the proposed method, firstly the DIV2K dataset with 900 images is compressed using standard JPEG codec. 800 images are used for training the DTUANet, and 100 images are left for testing. For the training dataset, each of the 800 images is randomly cropped into 128×128 patches, and these patches serve as the training data. Data augmentation, including random horizontal flipping and 90-degree rotations, are applied. The pre-training details for the LRC-SE model are as follows. The model is trained for a total of 100 epochs using an optimizer, with an initial learning rate of 1e-4, which is reduced by a factor of 5 every 25 epochs. All convolutional kernels in the network have a size of 3×3, and the number of channels is set to 64. The iterative optimization phase of the LRC-SE pre-trained model involves ten stages, and the batch-size is set to eight. The pre-trained LRC-SE network is then used as the first stage of the DTUANet, and the LC-STE model is trained as the second stage. The LC-STE model is trained with 100 epochs, using an optimizer with an initial learning rate of 1e-3, which is reduced by a factor of 5 every 25 epochs. The network's convolutional filters with a kernel size of 3×3 have 64 channels, and it also includes ten iterative stages. The batch-size for training is set to 16. Our method is implemented using the PyTorch deep learning framework, and all experiments are conducted using an NVIDIA RTX A6000 GPU. Five widely-used benchmark datasets are employed: LIVE1, Classic5, BSD68, Set14, and Set5. We evaluate the proposed method by using three common image quality metrics: Peak Signal-to-Noise Ratio (PSNR), Structural Similarity Index (SSIM), and Peak Signal-to-Noise Ratio in the presence of Blocking artifacts (PSNR-B) for compressed images.

Table 1. The average PSNR/PSNR-B/SSIM comparison of different methods.

Methods(QF = 10)	LIVE1	Classic5	BSD68	Set14
JPEG	28.361/0.7935/28.350	28.260/0.7807/28.202	28.775/0.7996/28.711	30.329/0.8399/30.212
FDnCNN [2]	28.594/0.8029/28.580	29.504/0.7984/29.456	28.498/0.7892/28.437	29.079/0.8102/29.011
FFDNet [11]	28.651/0.8053/28.636	29.563/0.8008/29.515	28.549/0.7916/28.487	29.155/0.8129/29.085
FBCNN [12]	29.540/0.8249/28.850	30.490/0.8196/29.681	29.430/0.8108/28.640	30.220/0.8336/29.490
DGUNet [13]	29.724/0.8301/29.7040	30.712/0.8245/30.647	29.489/0.8136/29.411	30.401/0.8379/30.310
DGUNet+ [13]	29.817/0.8324/29.796	30.849/0.8279/30.781	29.520/0.8151/29.442	30.534/0.8406/30.440
CARNet [4]	29.710/0.8316/29.803	30.815/0.8275/30.747	29.587/0.8155/29.507	30.514/0.8400/30.421
RCDNet [14]	29.993/0.8364/29.971	31.052/0.8330/30.976	28.775/0.7996/28.711	29.721/0.8191/29.638
DTUANet(ours)	**30.188/0.8405/30.165**	**31.227/0.8377/31.150**	**29.880/0.8223/29.795**	**30.931/0.8480/30.831**

3.2 Comparison with Inexplicable Compress Artifact Removal Methods

We compare our network with three non-interpretable methods: FDNCNN, FFDNet and FBCNN. Meanwhile, we compare our network with four inter-

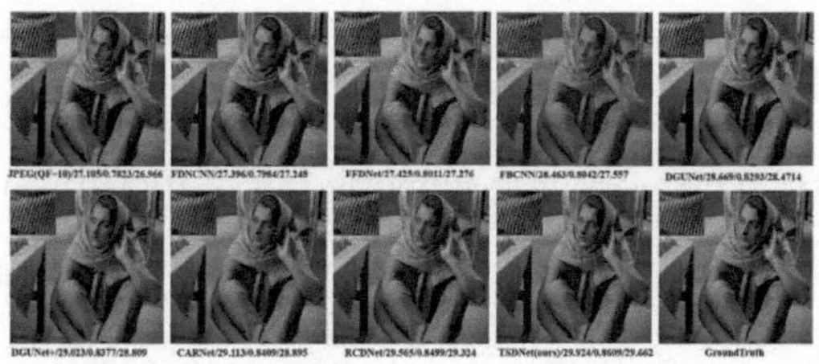

Fig. 9. Visual comparison of different artifact removal methods.

pretable methods: GDUNet, GDUNet+, CARNet and RCDNet. Both FDNCNN and FFDNet are trained on the DIV2K dataset, which are identical to our approach. For these four interpretable methods, we use the authors' provided code and trained them on the same dataset as our method on the RTX A6000. Notably, since CARNet is based on TensorFlow, we re-implement it in PyTorch by following the original paper's guidelines and training strategies. GDUNet+ is an enhanced version of GDUNet. Table 1 shows that, on average, our method achieves 0.46 dB, 0.38 dB, 0.48 dB, and 0.19 dB higher PSNR than GDUNet, GDUNet+, CARNet, and RCDNet, respectively. Figure 9 provides visual comparisons, revealing that although these four interpretable networks effectively remove compression artifacts, they still result in blurring of textures and details. In contrast, our method not only removes compression artifacts but also preserves the clarity of textures and details. As shown in Table 1, our method consistently outperforms the others in terms of average PSNR, SSIM, and PSNR-B across all five test datasets, strongly demonstrating the advantage of interpretable networks over non-interpretable networks. Figure 9 shows visual comparisons on the LIVE1 and Classic5 datasets. FDNCNN and FFDNet fail to effectively remove compression artifacts. Although FBCNN reduces some artifacts, it leads to blurring of edges and details. In contrast, our method not only removes artifacts but also preserves details and contours.

4   Conclusion

This paper introduces an end-to-end artifact removal network for compressed images. Unlike standard state-of-the-art artifact removal methods, DTUANet employs a two-stage unfolding model that leverages prior knowledge of image structure and texture to enhance artifact removal. First, we propose an LRC-SE sub-optimization model, which produces smoothed image to serve as the refined input for the subsequent artifact removal module. Second, we introduce an LC-STE sub-optimization model, which further decomposes the output from LRC-SE into structural and textural components. Through iterative optimization, this model enhances image structure and texture details, thereby achieving superior artifact removal. Additionally, the proposed LRLRB can efficiently generate low-rank features with reduced redundancy while preserving essential structural information. However, our two-stage optimization approach increases model complexity and training time, so our future work will focus on developing lightweight network architectures to address these issues.

Acknowledgements. This work was supported by National Natural Science Foundation of China (62202323), Shanxi Scholarship Council of China (2024-130), Shanxi Province Science Foundation for Youth (202203021222047), The Shanxi Province Third Batch of Outstanding Doctoral Research Initial Funding in 2022 (98001836), The First Batch of Doctoral Research Initial Funding in 2023 (110136051).

References

1. Dong, C., Loy, C.C., He, K., Tang, X.: Learning a deep convolutional network for image super-resolution, pp. 184–199 (2014)
2. Zhang, K., Zuo, W., Chen, Y., Meng, D., Zhang, L.: Beyond a gaussian denoiser: residual learning of deep CNN for image denoising. IEEE Trans. Image Process. **26**(7), 3142–3155 (2017)
3. Liu, P., Zhang, H., Zhang, K., Lin, L., Zuo, W.: Multi-level wavelet-CNN for image restoration, pp. 773–782 (2018)
4. Fu, X., Wang, M., Cao, X., Ding, X., Zha, Z.-J.: A model-driven deep unfolding method for JPEG artifacts removal. IEEE Trans. Neural Netw. Learn. Syst. **33**(11), 6802–6816 (2021)
5. Zhang, T., Li, L., Igel, C., Oehmcke, S., Gieseke, F., Peng, Z.: LR-CSNet: low-rank deep unfolding network for image compressive sensing, pp. 1951–1957 (2022)
6. Zhao, L., Zhang, Y., Wang, X., Zhang, J., Bai, H., Wang, A.: A survey on image compressive sensing: from classical theory to the latest explicable deep learning. Pattern Recognit. 112022 (2025)
7. Zhang, J., Zhao, L., Zhang, J., Wang, A., Bai, H.: Joint deep-unfolding optimization learning for depth map arbitrary-scale super-resolution. IEEE Trans. Multimedia (2025)
8. Wang, X., Zhao, L., Zhang, J., Wang, A., Bai, H.: A wavelet-domain consistency-constrained compressive sensing framework based on memory-boosted guidance filtering. IEEE Trans. Instrum. Meas. **73**, 1–16 (2024)
9. Zhao, L., Zhang, J., Zhang, J., Bai, H., Wang, A.: Joint discontinuity-aware depth map super-resolution via dual-tasks driven unfolding network. IEEE Trans. Instrum. Meas. **73**, 1–14 (2024)
10. Zhao, L., Chen, B., Zhang, J., Wang, A., Bai, H.: RIRO: from Retinex-inspired reconstruction optimization model to deep low-light image enhancement unfolding network. IEEE Trans. Comput. Imaging **10**, 969–983 (2024)
11. Zhang, K., Zuo, W., Zhang, L.: FFDNet: toward a fast and flexible solution for CNN-based image denoising. IEEE Trans. Image Process. **27**(9), 4608–4622 (2018)
12. Jiang, J., Zhang, K., Timofte, R.: Towards flexible blind JPEG artifacts removal, pp. 4997–5006 (2021)
13. Mou, C., Wang, Q., Zhang, J.: Deep generalized unfolding networks for image restoration. In: Proceedings of the IEEE/CVF Conference on Computer Vision and Pattern Recognition, pp. 17399–17410 (2022)
14. Wang, H., et al.: RCDNet: an interpretable rain convolutional dictionary network for single image deraining. IEEE Trans. Neural Netw. Learn. Syst. **35**(6), 8668–8682 (2023)

Martingale-Based Skin Lesion Segmentation from Dermoscopic Images

Yao Lu, Yan Zhao[✉], Shigang Wang, and Jian Wei

Jilin University, Changchun, China
luyao22@mails.jlu.edu.cn, {zhao_y,weijian}@jlu.edu.cn,
wangshigang@vip.sina.com

Abstract. Accurate skin lesion segmentation is of great significance for improving the quantitative analysis of skin cancer from dermoscopic images. However, lesion segmentation remains a challenging problem due to the large differences in color, location, size, shape, and boundary contrast of lesions. In order to solve these difficulties, we construct a novel lesion segmentation algorithm based on martingale, which combines local and global information of the images. In order to combine the global information of the images in the segmentation process, we build a newly defined random power martingale (RPM) based on the statistical and structural features of the images. The unbiased nature of the martingale process optimizes the subtle boundaries and structural changes in the dermoscopic images. We compare our method with different outstanding algorithms and analyze them using some commonly used evaluation indexes in the International Skin Imaging Collaboration 2016 (ISIC-16) skin lesion dataset. Visualization results and quantitative evaluation show that our method can achieve superior performance.

Keywords: Skin Lesion Segmentation · Martingale · Another Expectation Maximization

1 Introduction

Dermoscopy is a widely used clinical diagnostic tool for distinguishing between benign and malignant skin abnormalities [1]. Segmenting lesions from dermoscopic images is a key step in skin cancer diagnosis and treatment planning. The use of a dermatoscope enables clinicians to display the detailed color spectrum and characteristics of skin lesions for better diagnosis. However, even with the use of a dermatoscope, the diagnosis and delineation of lesion areas can be poor as they may require expert visual inspection and interpretation.

Although a lot of research has been devoted to the automatic segmentation and diagnosis of skin lesions, there are still many challenges and difficulties. The main reasons for this difficulty include three aspects: Firstly, the low contrast between the lesion area and the surrounding normal tissue, which makes it difficult to accurately distinguish the boundary. Secondly, artifacts such as hair

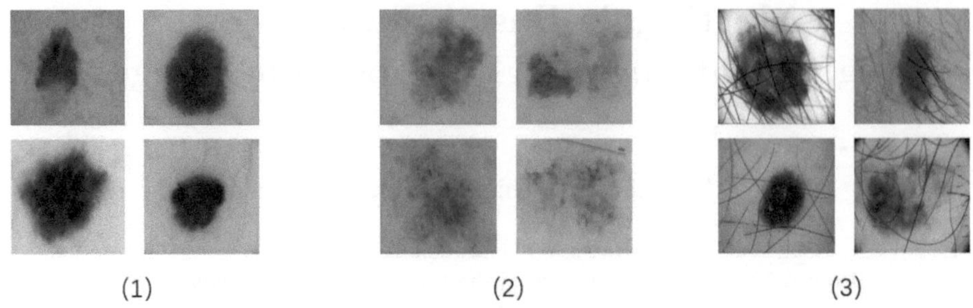

(1)   (2)   (3)

Fig. 1. Typical skin lesions in ISIC-16 dataset.

and bubbles will obscure the lesion area, seriously interfering with the accurate judgment of the size and location of the lesion. Thirdly, as shown in Fig. 1, skin lesions are highly heterogeneous in color, shape, size and spatial position, which increases the complexity of segmentation and diagnosis. In order to achieve accurate diagnosis of skin lesions in clinical practice, it is particularly important to accurately extract the structural features of the lesion area boundary.

Scientists have proposed a variety of segmentation algorithms to deal with the problem of accurate segmentation of skin lesion images.

The first is the threshold method. These methods compare the visual feature values of a single or group of pixels in a dermoscopic image with a threshold value. Examples of threshold segmentation methods include adaptive threshold segmentation [2], histogram threshold segmentation [3] and clustering threshold segmentation [4]. But when light conditions can be uneven, the boundary of skin lesions is usually blurred and color gradient, and the fixed threshold method is difficult to deal with these irregular boundaries.

Compared with the threshold method, the edge and contour-based method can improve the treatment of discontinuities and lesion boundaries. The automatic method uses watershed algorithm [5], active contour [6], and canny edge detector [7]. However, edge detection and contour detection methods do not consider the color, texture, shape and other information of skin lesions. Some other traditional methods include Markov random fields [8], graph-cut [9], and wavelet transform [10].

Recently, many authors have built entirely new Convolutional Neural Network (CNN) segmentation networks by leveraging different deep learning-based segmentation architectures such as U-Net [11]. Transformer models [12] have also been used for automatic segmentation. However, deep learning models also struggle to explain their decision-making processes.

In this paper, we design an automatic skin lesion segmentation algorithm based on martingale theory, which can accurately and efficiently process dermoscopic images even in the presence of reflections, oil bubbles, hair, or other defects. And as far as we know, it is the first time to apply martingale theory in the field of image processing. At the same time, our algorithm does not require any training and can still maintain excellent segmentation accuracy in the face of different textures. Our algorithm combines local edge texture information with global structure statistics through RPM process, which is based on a newly defined discrepancy function that incorporates the global information of the image. To demonstrate the effectiveness of the algorithm, we validate our algorithm and compare with other segmentation methods on skin leison segmentation dataset. The experimental results indicate that our algorithm achieves higher accuracy compared to other segmentation algorithms.

The rest of this paper is organized as follows. The martingale theory and related theorems is discussed in Sect. 2, while the proposed segmentation of skin lesions is detailed in Sect. 3. Section 4 gives a description of the dataset used for the experiments and a quantitative comparison of our method with other well-known segmentation algorithms. Finally, Sect. 5 summarizes the overall algorithm.

2   Martingale Theory and Related Theorems

The application of martingale theory has gained significant attention from researchers in modern probability theory [13], which has been widely used in the fields. However, to the best of our knowledge, it has not yet been applied in image processing. This paper is the first time to apply martingale process to image processing.

Definition 1. *If a random sequence $\{X_n, \forall n \geq 0\}$ satisfies:*

(1) $E[X_n] < \infty$;
(2) $E[X_{n+1}|X_0, ..., X_n] = X_n$

where $E[...]$ represents the expectation of a random variable. Then $\{X_n\}$ is a discrete martingale sequence.

Definition 2. *If $\{X_n, \forall n \geq 0\}$ and $\{Y_n, \forall n \geq 0\}$ are two random sequences, they satisfy:*

(1) $E[X_n] < \infty$;
(2) $\{X_n\}$ is a function of $\{Y_0, \cdots, Y_n\}$;
(3) $E[X_{n+1}|Y_0, ..., Y_n] = X_n$

Then $\{X_n\}$ is a martingale with respect to $\{Y_n\}$.

The martingale convergence theorem is an important theorem in martingale theory, which describes the limiting behavior of martingale under certain conditions.

3   Method

Our algorithm firstly converts the image into a one-dimensional sequence through Hilbert-Peano Scanning and constructs Hidden Markov Chain (HMC). During the segmentation process, random power martingale process is constructed based on the global statistical information and structural information of the image to improve the segmentation ability of the overall algorithm. We judge the algorithm convergence by the property of martingale convergence. The complete algorithm is outlined in Algorithm 1.

Algorithm 1. Skin lesion segmentation algorithm based on martingale

---

Require: $\theta^q = \left(PI^q\left(\omega_i\right), A^q\left(\omega_i, \omega_j\right), \mu_{\omega_i}^q, \left(\sigma_{\omega_i}^q\right)^2 \right)$;

Ensure: The final result of segmentation;

1: **for** $q = 0$ **do**
2:      Calculating $\alpha_n^q\left(\omega_i\right), \beta_n^q\left(\omega_i\right), \gamma_n^q\left(\omega_i, \omega_j\right)$ and $\varepsilon_n^q\left(\omega_i\right)$;
3:      Estimating parameter θ^{q+1} by using Eq. (7), (8), (9) and (10);
4:      Calculating the emission probability by Eq. (5);
5:      Obtaining the global difference information by Eq. (12);
6:      Constructing RPM by Eq. (11);
7:      Determining the final iteration;
8:      $q = q + 1$;
9: **end for**
10: Geting the final segmentation result.

3.1   Hilbert-Peano Scanning

Figure 2 shows the process of Hilbert-Peano Scanning.

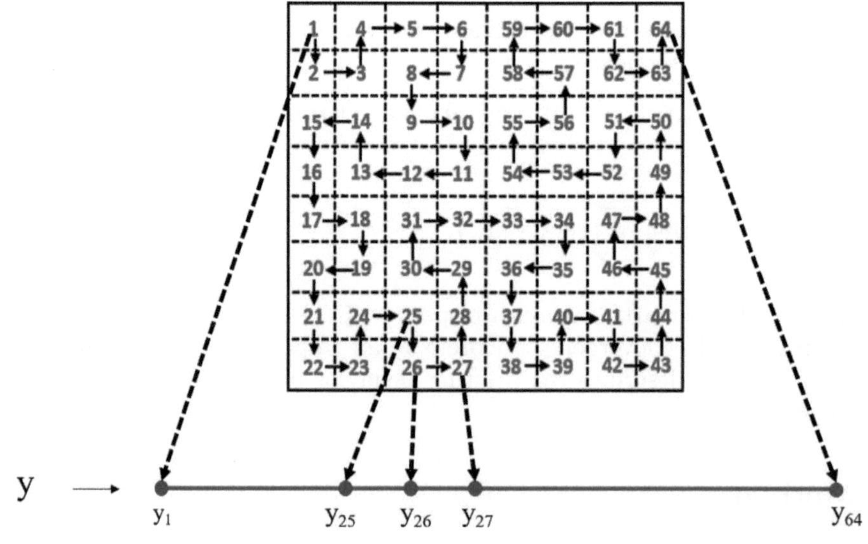

Fig. 2. Illustration of Hilbert-Peano Scanning.

Hilbert-Peano Scanning is defined by the matrix. We define the initial matrix $H_2 = \begin{bmatrix} 1 & 2 \\ 4 & 3 \end{bmatrix}$, and recursively construct the matrix $H_{2^{k+1}}$ with the size of $2^n \times 2^n$ from H_2. When k is odd, the matrix is represented as follows:

$$H_{2^{k+1}} = \begin{bmatrix} H_{2^k}, & \left(4^k+1\right) E_{2^k} - \overline{H}_{2^k} \\ 4^k E_{2^k} + H_{2^k}^T, & \left(3 \cdot 4^k+1\right) E_{2^k} - \overline{H}_{2^k}^T \end{bmatrix} \tag{1}$$

when k is even, the matrix can be represented as follows:

$$H_{2^{k+1}} = \begin{bmatrix} H_{2^k}, & 4^k E_{2^k} \\ \left(4^k+1\right) E_{2^k} - \widehat{H_{2^k}}, & \left(3 \cdot 4^k+1\right) E_{2^k} - \left(\overline{H}_{2^k}\right)^T \end{bmatrix} \tag{2}$$

where matrix E is an equal-order matrix with all elements being 1; $\overline{H_{2^k}} = J \times H_{2^k}$, where matrix J represents the permutation matrix (1 in its anti-diagonal, 0 elsewhere); $\widehat{H_{2^k}} = H_{2^k} \times J$; H^T stands for transpose matrix of H.

3.2   Segmentation Algorithm Based on Martingale

Firstly, we construct the HMC based on the converted one-dimensional sequence. Let $H = \{X, Y\}$ is an HMC. $X = \{X_1, ..., X_N\}$ is a hidden process and each X_n takes its values from set of classes $\Omega = (\omega_1, ..., \omega_K)$. $Y = (Y_1, ..., Y_N)$ is an observed process and each Y_n takes its values from $\mathbb{R}$. The realizations of X and Y are respectively noted by $x_1 = \{x_1, ..., x_N\}$ and $y_1 = \{y_1, ..., y_N\}$.

The prior initial parameter $\theta^0 = \left(PI^0\left(\omega_i\right), A^0\left(\omega_i, \omega_j\right), \mu_{\omega_i}^0, \left(\sigma_{\omega_i}^0\right)^2\right)$ includes: the initial law $PI^0\left(\omega_i\right) = p\left(x_1 = \omega_i\right)$, the transition probability matrix $A^0\left(\omega_i, \omega_j\right) = p\left(x_{n+1} = \omega_j | x_n = \omega_i\right)$ between the class ω_i and the class ω_j, the mean $\mu_{\omega_i}^0$, and the variance $\left(\sigma_{\omega_i}^0\right)^2$ of pixels in the class ω_i.

Then, $\alpha_n\left(\omega_i\right) = p\left(y_1, y_2, ..., y_n, x_n = \omega_i\right)$ is defined as the forward probability. When $n = 1$, it is expressed as $\alpha_1\left(\omega_i\right) = \frac{PI(\omega_i)f_{\omega_i}(y_1)}{\sum_{\omega_j \in \Omega} PI(\omega_i)f_{\omega_j}(y_1)}$. And when $n > 1$, the forward probability can be expressed as:

$$\alpha_n\left(\omega_i\right) = \frac{f_{\omega_i}\left(y_n\right)\sum_{\omega_j \in \Omega} \alpha_{n-1}\left(\omega_j\right) A\left(\omega_i, \omega_j\right)}{\sum_{k \in \Omega} f_k\left(y_n\right)\sum_{\omega_j \in \Omega}\alpha_{n-1}\left(\omega_j\right) A\left(\omega_i, \omega_j\right)} \tag{3}$$

$\beta_n\left(\omega_i\right) = p\left(y_{n+1}, y_{n+2}, ..., y_N | x_n = \omega_i\right)$ is defined as the backward probability. When $n = N$, it is expressed as $\beta_N\left(\omega_i\right) = 1$, and when $n < N$, the backward probability is expressed as:

$$\beta_n\left(\omega_i\right) = \frac{\sum_{\omega_j \in \Omega} A\left(\omega_i, \omega_j\right) f_{\omega_j}\left(y_{n+1}\right)\beta_{n+1}\left(\omega_j\right)}{\sum_{k \in \Omega} f_k\left(y_{n+1}\right)\sum_{\omega_j \in \Omega}\alpha_n\left(\omega_j\right) A\left(\omega_i, \omega_j\right)} \tag{4}$$

where $f_{\omega_i}\left(y_n\right)$ is the emission probability, which follows the Gaussian distribution:

$$f_{\omega_i}\left(y_n\right) = \frac{1}{\sqrt{2\pi\left(\sigma_{\omega_i}\right)^2}}\exp\left[-\frac{\left(y_n - \mu_{\omega_i}\right)^2}{2\left(\sigma_{\omega_i}\right)^2}\right] \tag{5}$$

where μ_{ω_i} and $\left(\sigma_{\omega_i}\right)^2$ are the mean and variance of pixels in class ω_i.

From the Eq. (3), (4) and (5), the joint posteriori probability $\gamma_n\left(\omega_i, \omega_j\right)$ can be expressed as:

$$\gamma_n\left(\omega_i, \omega_j\right) = \frac{\alpha_n\left(\omega_i\right) A\left(\omega_i, \omega_j\right) f_{\omega_j}\left(y_n\right) \beta_{n+1}\left(\omega_j\right)}{\sum_{k \in \Omega} f_k\left(y_n\right) \sum_{l \in \Omega} \alpha_n(l) A\left(l, k\right)} \tag{6}$$

Then, from the Eq. (3) and (4), we can define the posteriori marginal probability $\varepsilon_n\left(\omega_i\right) = \alpha_n\left(\omega_i\right) \cdot \beta_n\left(\omega_i\right)$.

The result of the new parameter iteration is represented by θ^{q+1}, which is obtained by updating the parameters θ^q of the previous generation. Each component of θ^{q+1} is expressed as follows:

$$PI^{q+1}\left(\omega_i\right) = \varepsilon_n^q\left(\omega_i\right) \tag{7}$$

$$A^{q+1}\left(\omega_i, \omega_j\right) = \frac{\sum_{n=1}^{N} \gamma^q\left(\omega_i, \omega_j\right)}{\sum_{n=1}^{N} \varepsilon_n^q\left(\omega_i\right)} \tag{8}$$

$$\mu_{\omega_i}^{q+1} = \frac{\sum_{n=1}^{N} y_n \cdot \varepsilon_n^q\left(\omega_i\right)}{\sum_{n=1}^{N} \varepsilon_n^q\left(\omega_i\right)} \tag{9}$$

$$\left(\sigma_{\omega_i}^{q+1}\right)^2 = \frac{\sum_{n=1}^{N}\left(y_n - \mu_{\omega_i}^q\right)^2 \cdot \varepsilon_n^q\left(\omega_i\right)}{\sum_{n=1}^{N} \varepsilon_n^q\left(\omega_i\right)} \tag{10}$$

where $\gamma^q\left(\omega_i, \omega_j\right)$ and $\varepsilon_n^q\left(\omega_i\right)$ are the joint posteriori probability and marginal posteriori probability in the qth iteration respectively. The emission probability is updated with the new mean and variance. We maximize the posterior probability $X = argmax_{\omega_i \in \Omega}\left[\alpha_n\left(\omega_i\right) \beta_n\left(\omega_i\right)\right]$.

However, when segmentation is based solely on this local information, it can be easily influenced by factors such as uneven intensity or noise, which can influence the stability and accuracy of the segmentation results. To address this problem, we introduce the global structure and statistical information of the image into the segmentation process and build RPM based on this.

The structure of RPM is defined as follows:

$$M_{q+1} = \prod_{q=1}^{N-1}\left[\xi p_{q,q+1}\left(x, y\right)^{\xi-1}\right] \tag{11}$$

where $\xi \in (0.9, 1)$ [14].

Then, the conditional expectation of M_{q+1} with respect to the $p_{q,q+1}\left(x, y\right)$, is given by:

$$E\left[M_{q+1} | p_{1,2}, p_{2,3}, \cdots, p_{q,q+1}\right] = M_q \int_0^1 \xi p_{q,q+1}\left(x, y\right)^{\xi-1} dp_{q,q+1} = M_q$$

where $q \in [1, N-1]$. This property proves that M_{q+1} is a martingale [15].

In RPM, we define a new discrepancy function $p_{q,q+1}(x,y)$ to obtain the differences between the results of adjacent iterations, which can be expressed as:

$$p_{q,q+1}(x,y) = (1 - SSIM(x,y)) \cdot Moment(x,y) \qquad (12)$$

The discrepancy function is composed of the SSIM function and moment function [16]. The SSIM function represents the structural differences between the two adjacent results and can be expressed as follows:

$$SSIM(x,y) = \frac{(2\mu_x\mu_y + C_1)(2\sigma_{xy} + C_2)}{(\mu_x^2 + \mu_y^2 + C_1)(\sigma_x^2 + \sigma_y^2 + C_2)} \qquad (13)$$

where μ_x, σ_x, μ_y and σ_y represent the mean and standard deviation of result x and result y, respectively. The function $Moment(x,y)$ is measured by calculating the statistical differences between two iterative results.

In the segmentation process, we construct RPM based on the global information differences in the image. We employ the martingale convergence theorem within the algorithm to assess overall convergence. During each iteration, we calculate the change $|M_q - M_{q-1}|$ in the martingale, as well as the expectation $E[M_q]$ and variance $\sigma_q^2 = E\left[(M_q - E[M_q])^2\right]$ of the martingale process. When the change $|M_q - M_{q-1}|$ approaches zero, the expectation $E[M_q]$ stabilizes to a constant, and the variance $\sigma_q^2 = E\left[(M_q - E[M_q])^2\right]$ approaches zero, we can effectively determine that the segmentation process has converged or ended based on these three conditions.

4   Experimental Results

4.1   Dataset

For the experiment, we select the ISIC-16 skin lesion segmentation dataset [17], which is widely selected in skin lesion segmentation. ISIC-16 uses images with resolutions of 556×679 to $2,848 \times 4828$ pixels to distinguish between moles and melanomas and includes 1279 images to segment. In our experiments, we adjust these images to 256×256 pixels.

4.2   Evaluation Metrics

We utilize the the widely adopted metrics Accuracy, Dice and Jaccard to assess the performance of different algorithms. They are used to evaluate the accuracy of algorithm segmentation and the similarity with the standard segmentation results. Accuracy represents the ratio of correctly classified pixels to the total number of pixels in the image. Dice measures the overlap between the pixels of two images, such as the predicted segmentation and the standard result. The Jaccard coefficient indicates the similarity between images by measuring the overlap between the pixels of the two images.

They are expressed as followed:

$$Accuracy = \frac{TP + TN}{TP + TN + FP + FN} \qquad (14)$$

$$Dice = \frac{2TP}{2TP + FP + FN} \qquad (15)$$

$$Jaccard = \frac{TP}{TP + FP + FN} \qquad (16)$$

where TP is the number of truly positive pixels, FP is the number of false positives, TN is the number of truly negative pixels, and FN is the number of false negative pixels. Note that all the metrics defined above take values between 0 and 1, with larger values indicating a better match between the segmentation and the ground truth for most of the above defined metrics.

4.3 Quantitative Analysis

In order to evaluate the performance of our proposed algorithm, we compare our method with other segmentation algorithms, including MCET [18], CGFCM [19], DRLSE [20], FBM [21], KLDFCM [22] and RSLC [23]. In order to ensure that the comparative experiment is fair and accurate, all of the methods listed above can be used for skin lesion segmentation in the same dermoscopic images.

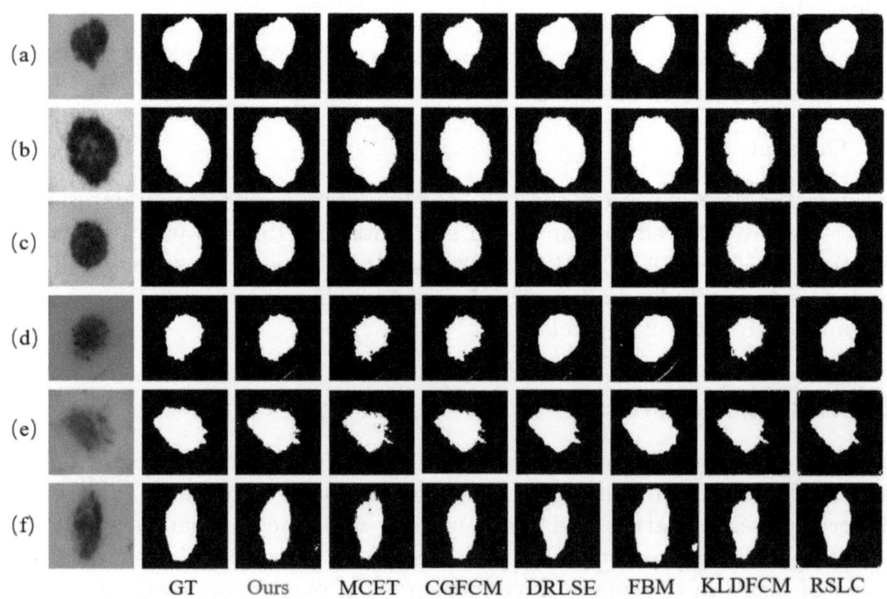

Fig. 3. The performance comparison of different segmentation algorithms.

In terms of visualization results, the segmentation results of our algorithm are shown in Fig. 3. All experimental images are from ISIC-16, the first column is the segmentation image, the second column is the ground turth, the third column is the segmentation results of our algorithm, and the rest are the results of other methods. And it can be clearly seen that the selected images have both strong contrast lesion images and blurred edge images. From the visualization analysis, we can clearly see that MCET, CGFCM and RSLC have fuzzy or inaccurate edges. For example, in image (d), (e) and (f), MCET and CGFCM have obvious jagged, irregular and fuzzy boundaries at the edges. Our method can fit the real contour more accurately, obtain smoother edges and is more in line with GT.

Table 1. Image segmentation results measured by Accuracy in Fig. 3

Methods	Image(a)	Image(b)	Image(c)	Image(d)	Image(e)	Image(f)
Ours	**0.9939**	**0.9796**	**0.9836**	**0.9887**	**0.9703**	**0.9801**
MCET [18]	0.9685	0.9643	0.9615	0.9757	0.9366	0.9429
CGFCM [19]	0.9829	0.9177	0.9732	0.9861	0.9531	0.9602
DRLSE [20]	0.9844	0.9608	0.9760	0.9650	0.9580	0.9367
FBM [21]	0.9286	0.9603	0.9696	0.9651	0.9592	0.9515
KLDFCM [22]	0.9749	0.9737	0.9777	0.9743	0.9478	0.9477
RSLC [23]	0.9715	0.9674	0.9664	0.9766	0.9420	0.9474

In image (d) and (f), FBM produces extra white spots and artifacts that exceed the actual lesion area, causing over-segmentation and increasing false positives. Image (d), image (e) and image (f) are lesion images with low contrast and complex texture, which are more challenging. It can be clearly seen that compared with other methods, our method can better maintain the integrity and shape consistency of the lesion area. The performance of DRLSE and RSLC in such images is significantly reduced and more susceptible to noise interference.

Table 2. Image segmentation results measured by Dice in Fig. 3

Methods	Image(a)	Image(b)	Image(c)	Image(d)	Image(e)	Image(f)
Ours	**0.9847**	**0.9733**	**0.9627**	**0.9690**	**0.9360**	**0.9575**
MCET [18]	0.9106	0.9517	0.9076	0.9267	0.8495	0.8666
CGFCM [19]	0.9447	0.9575	0.9258	0.9593	0.8797	0.8984
DRLSE [20]	0.9810	0.9690	0.9352	0.9008	0.8994	0.8438
FBM [21]	0.8507	0.9503	0.9235	0.9002	0.9181	0.9090
KLDFCM [22]	0.9342	0.9646	0.9475	0.9220	0.8766	0.8106
RSLC [23]	0.9266	0.9566	0.9211	0.9318	0.8659	0.8024

Table 3. Image segmentation results measured by Jaccard in Fig. 3

Methods	Image(a)	Image(b)	Image(c)	Image(d)	Image(e)	Image(f)
Ours	**0.9699**	**0.9481**	**0.9281**	**0.9398**	**0.8797**	**0.9184**
MCET [18]	0.8450	0.9078	0.8308	0.8633	0.8384	0.8645
CGFCM [19]	0.8953	0.9185	0.8169	0.9217	0.8553	0.8155
DRLSE [20]	0.9627	0.9398	0.8783	0.8196	0.8172	0.8298
FBM [21]	0.8402	0.9053	0.8580	0.8215	0.8486	0.8332
KLDFCM [22]	0.8765	0.9317	0.9003	0.8553	0.8304	0.8642
RSLC [23]	0.8632	0.9169	0.8537	0.8724	0.8235	0.8680

Accuracy, Dice and Jaccard are used to measure the segmentation results obtained by all algorithms. As can be seen from Tables 1, 2 and 3, our method achieves the highest accuracy on each image, up to 0.9939, while maintaining boundary integrity and minimizing background interference. All other methods suffer from over-segmentation and artifacts. In terms of Dice, our method achieves the largest value and shows the best region overlap accuracy. MECT and RSLC perform poorly on image(e) and image(f), indicating that they are less robust to low-contrast images. DRLSE and KLDFCM perform second best, which is still a certain gap compared with our results. In terms of Jaccard, the average Jaccard of our method reached 0.9310, which is significantly better than other methods. Other methods have more misclassifications, which leads to significantly lower Jaccard. Low Jaccard indicates that the segmented area is significantly different from the true standard.

5   Conclusion

In this paper, we propose a novel skin lesion segmentation algorithm based onmartingale theory. Our approach firstly incorporates martingale theory into the HMC framework and effectively utilizes the global and local information of the image during the segmentation process. Martingale theory is widely utilized in various fields due to the unbiased characteristics. Additionally, we have developed a discrepancy function to compare results between adjacent iterations, allowing us to evaluate segmentation quality after each iteration and adjust segmentation parameters. Experimental results across various skin lesion demonstrate that our proposed algorithm consistently achieves more accurate segmentation results.

Acknowledgments. This research is supported by the Jilin Provincial Science and Technology Development Plan Project under Grant 20250102208JC.

Disclosure of Interests. The authors have no competing interests to declare that are relevant to the content of this article.

References

1. Ashwini, A., Sahila, T., Radhakrishnan, A., Vanitha, M., Loretta, G. I.: Automatic skin tumor detection in dermoscopic samples using online patch fuzzy region based segmentation. Biomed. Signal Process. Control **100**, 107096 (2025)
2. Thanh, D.N.H., Hien, N.N., Surya Prasath, V.B., Erkan, U., Khamparia, A.: Adaptive thresholding skin lesion segmentation with gabor filters and principal component analysis. In: Solanki, V.K., Hoang, M.K., Lu, Z.J., Pattnaik, P.K. (eds.) Intelligent Computing in Engineering. AISC, vol. 1125, pp. 811–820. Springer, Singapore (2020). https://doi.org/10.1007/978-981-15-2780-7_87
3. Garcia-Arroyo, J.L., Garcia-Zapirain, B.: Segmentation of skin lesions in dermoscopy images using fuzzy classification of pixels and histogram thresholding. Comput. Methods Programs Biomed. **168**, 11–19 (2019)
4. Pereira, P.M.M., et al.: Dermoscopic skin lesion image segmentation based on local binary pattern clustering: comparative study. Biomed. Signal Process. Control **59**, 101924 (2020)
5. Gopal, A., Alagarsamy, P.C., Kalivaradhan, U.M., Gandhimaruthian, L.: An automatic region based optimal segmentation and detection of features on dermoscopy images using V-shaped waterfall and water ridges. Traitement du Signal **40**(2) (2023)
6. Fawzy, S., Moustafa, H.E.-D., Ata, M.M., AbdelHay, E.H.: High performed skin lesion segmentation based on modified active contour. In: 2022 International Telecommunications Conference (ITC-Egypt), pp. 1–5. IEEE (2022)
7. Kavitha, J.C., Subitha, D., Nagarajan, D.: Self-adaptive canny edge detection with reinforcement learning and dominant texture color patterns for melanoma segmentation and classification in dermoscopic images. Eng. Res. Exp. **6**(4), 045254 (2024)
8. Salih, O., Viriri, S.: Skin lesion segmentation using enhanced unified Markov random field. In: Groza, A., Prasath, R. (eds.) MIKE 2018. LNCS (LNAI), vol. 11308, pp. 331–340. Springer, Cham (2018). https://doi.org/10.1007/978-3-030-05918-7_30
9. Jaisakthi, S.M., Mirunalini, P., Aravindan, C.: Automated skin lesion segmentation of dermoscopic images using GrabCut and k-means algorithms. IET Comput. Vision **12**(8), 1088–1095 (2018)
10. Hu, K., et al.: A skin lesion segmentation method based on saliency and adaptive thresholding in wavelet domain. In: Lu, H. (ed.) ISAIR 2018. SCI, vol. 810, pp. 445–453. Springer, Cham (2020). https://doi.org/10.1007/978-3-030-04946-1_43
11. Gu, R., Wang, L., Zhang, L.: DE-Net: a deep edge network with boundary information for automatic skin lesion segmentation. Neurocomputing **468**, 71–84 (2022)
12. Dong, Y., Wang, L., Li, Y.: TC-Net: dual coding network of transformer and CNN for skin lesion segmentation. PLoS ONE **17**(11), e0277578 (2022)
13. Doob, J.L.: What is a martingale? Am. Math. Mon. **78**(5), 451–463 (1971)
14. Vovk, V., et al.: Testing exchangeability on-line. In: Proceedings of the 20th International Conference on Machine Learning (ICML 2003), pp. 768–775 (2003)
15. Lu, G., et al.: A novel framework of change-point detection for machine monitoring. Mech. Syst. Signal Process. **83**, 533–548 (2017)
16. Hu, M.-K.: Visual pattern recognition by moment invariants. IRE Trans. Inf. Theory **8**(2), 179–187 (1962)
17. Gutman, D., et al.: Skin lesion analysis toward melanoma detection: a challenge at the international symposium on biomedical imaging (ISBI) 2016, hosted by the international skin imaging collaboration (ISIC). arXiv preprint arXiv:1605.01397 (2016)

18. Rodríguez-Esparza, E., et al.: An efficient Harris hawks-inspired image segmentation method. Expert Syst. Appl. **155**, 113428 (2020)
19. Oskouei, A.G., et al.: CGFFCM: cluster-weight and group-local feature-weight learning in fuzzy C-means clustering algorithm for color image segmentation. Appl. Soft Comput. **113**, 108005 (2021)
20. Wali, S., et al.: Level-set evolution for medical image segmentation with alternating direction method of multipliers. Signal Process. **211**, 109105 (2023)
21. Brudfors, M., Balbastre, Y., Flandin, G., Nachev, P., Ashburner, J.: Flexible Bayesian modelling for nonlinear image registration. In: Martel, A.L., et al. (eds.) MICCAI 2020. LNCS, vol. 12263, pp. 253–263. Springer, Cham (2020). https://doi.org/10.1007/978-3-030-59716-0_25
22. Wang, C., et al.: Kullback–Leibler divergence-based fuzzy C-means clustering incorporating morphological reconstruction and wavelet frames for image segmentation. IEEE Trans. Cybern. **52**(8), 7612–7623 (2021)
23. Shang, R., et al.: SAR image segmentation using region smoothing and label correction. Remote Sens. **12**(5), 803 (2020)

Research on Adaptive Multi-layer Multi-pass Welding Technology for Medium-Thick Plates

Ruiyun Zhong, Xiaoteng Wang$^{(\boxtimes)}$, and Xili Dai

China Railway Construction Heavy Industry Corporation Limited, No. 88, East Seven Road Changsha Economic and Technological Development Zone, Changsha 410100, Hunan, China
Wangxiaoteng.zg@crcc.cn

Abstract. The rapid development of industries such as heavy machinery, shipbuilding, and energy equipment has led to a sustained increase in the demand for medium-thick plate welding. However, conventional welding methods still heavily rely on manual operations or robotic teaching, resulting in low efficiency and poor consistency in weld quality. These limitations make it difficult to meet the high precision and productivity requirements of modern intelligent manufacturing. To address these challenges, this study proposes an intelligent multi-layer, multi-pass welding system for medium-thick plates, integrating deep learning and adaptive control. First, a deep convolutional neural network (CNN) based on the ResNet101 architecture was developed to automatically classify weld groove types, achieving a classification accuracy of 99.62%. Second, groove feature points were extracted with sub-millimeter precision using a Gaussian Mixture Model (GMM) clustering algorithm, enabling accurate analysis of geometric parameters. Finally, a multi-layer, multi-pass welding process system was designed with three key optimizations: adaptive adjustment of welding sequence and torch pose, dynamic compensation for wire stick-out, and compensation for thermal deformation and scanning errors. Experimental results demonstrate the system's feasibility and effectiveness in industrial applications, significantly improving the level of welding automation. Manual intervention time was reduced by over 91.3%, and welding efficiency increased by 30%. This work offers a practical and engineering-ready solution and establishes a technical paradigm for the intelligent transformation of welding processes under the framework of smart manufacturing.

Keywords: adaptive welding · medium-thick plate · deep learning · robotics · intelligent welding

1 Introduction

Medium-thick plates are widely used in national key industries such as shipbuilding, energy equipment, and rail transportation. The welding quality of these plates directly impacts structural safety and service lifespan. Traditional welding methods for medium-thick plates still rely heavily on manual operations or robot-programmed teaching techniques, which suffer from low efficiency and inconsistent quality stability. These limitations make it challenging to meet the demands of modern intelligent manufacturing for

Z. Lin et al. (Eds.): ICIG 2025, LNCS 16161, pp. 51–64, 2026.
https://doi.org/10.1007/978-981-95-3398-5_5

high precision and superior welding efficiency [1–7]. Multi-layer multi-pass welding is a critical process for medium-thick plate welding. However, influenced by factors such as workpiece assembly errors, thermal deformation, and complex groove structures, conventional fixed trajectory and parameter control methods exhibit significant limitations when addressing intricate welding environments [8–12]. Therefore, the development of adaptive multi-layer multi-pass welding technology for medium-thick plates holds substantial engineering value and practical significance in advancing welding automation and intelligentization [13–18].

Shi Hao et al. [19] proposed an automated narrow-gap multi-layer multi-pass laser wire-filling welding method with seam tracking, achieving welding process optimization and trajectory auto-correction, which significantly improved welding quality and efficiency. Wang Tianqi et al. [20] developed a GA-BP neural network-based prediction and optimization method for multi-layer multi-pass welding parameters, enabling intelligent prediction and optimization of welding parameters, thereby enhancing welding quality and process efficiency. Chang Shuhe et al. [21] introduced an online path recognition method for wire arc additive manufacturing using multi-visual information fusion. Their approach integrated directional shadow imaging and structured light fusion technology to achieve precise path tracking for multi-layer multi-pass welding and additive manufacturing, allowing real-time prediction of weld geometry, pass sequence, and torch tip coordinate deviations. Liao Weidong et al. [22] developed an offline programming system for multi-layer multi-pass welding robots based on the OpenCASCADE (OCC) modeling engine. By customizing weld layer/pass quantities and automatically planning torch postures, the system realized precise welding path planning and collision avoidance. Liu Zhaojiang et al. [23] proposed a laser sensor-based adaptive multi-layer multi-pass welding method. Through visual coordinate transformation and real-time pose adjustment, their technique achieved adaptive compensation for workpiece errors and accurate path planning. Ni Monan [24] established a laser monocular vision-based seam tracking technology for arc welding robots in multi-layer multi-pass applications. By optimizing laser vision sensor parameters and developing enhanced image processing algorithms, the method achieved tracking localization errors of less than 0.5 mm for groove boundaries and weld roots.

Current research primarily focuses on individual technological approaches such as visual recognition or adaptive welding, or investigates welding parameters and trajectory postures for single groove types (e.g., standard V-grooves) with specific plate thicknesses. These methods exhibit limited algorithmic generalizability and process adaptability. In practical manufacturing scenarios, however, groove configurations encompass multiple types (e.g., V-groove, single-bevel V-groove, and J-groove), while plate thickness variations span a wide range (8–160 mm). These complexities severely compromise the applicability of existing techniques in workshop environments. To address these challenges, this paper proposes an intelligent multi-layer multi-pass welding system for medium-thick plates, integrating deep learning, computational graphics, and adaptive welding process control. The system comprehensively addresses critical stages including groove-type classification and recognition, three-dimensional reconstruction, welding posture planning, parameter matching, and real-time welding control. Its efficacy has been validated through practical industrial applications.

2 Experimental Methodology

2.1 Automatic Groove Classification and Recognition

Accurate identification of groove types in multi-layer multi-pass welding of medium-thick plates forms the basis for achieving adaptive path planning and welding parameter control, as different groove types necessitate distinct process strategies. For industrial scenarios involving V-groove, single-bevel V-groove, U-groove, and single-bevel U-groove configurations [24–27], this study proposes an intelligent recognition method combining deep neural networks with density clustering. The approach first employs an image classification model to determine groove types, followed by data clustering based on classification results to identify feature points. This enables geometric feature extraction, ultimately obtaining groove characteristic parameters applicable to subsequent processes.

ResNet-101-Based Automatic Classification Algorithm. This chapter employs the resNet-101 network as the classification model. Its deep network architecture and residual connection mechanism effectively enhance the model's perception capability for subtle feature differences in grooves. The core residual block of resNet-101 can be expressed as:

$$y_l = h(x_l) + F(x_l, W_l) \tag{1}$$

$$x_{l+1} = f(y_l) \tag{2}$$

where: x_l and x_{l+1} represent the input and output of the l-th residual block, respectively, F denotes the residual function, $h(x_l)$ is the identity mapping (if the input and output dimensions are inconsistent, the dimensions can be adjusted via a 1×1 convolution), and f is the activation function.

For the welding groove classification task, data augmentation techniques were employed to expand training samples, including random rotation ($\pm 10°$) and horizontal flipping. The following modifications were implemented on ResNet-101:

① Input Layer:The original network's input size is set to 224×224 pixels with a 7×7 convolutional kernel and a stride of 2.

② Activation function employs LeakyReLU to replace the traditional ReLU:

$$LeakyReLU(x) = \begin{cases} x, x \geq 0 \\ 0.01x, x < 0 \end{cases} \tag{3}$$

After encapsulating the module into a general interface, the final pseudocode is shown below:

Algorithm 1. Automated Groove Type Classification

Require: *Input image*
Ensure: *Predicted groove type groove_type*
1 : *model←load_pretrained_resnet101()*
2 : *preprocessed←preprocess(image)*
3 : *prediction←model(preprocessed)*
4 : *groove_type←argmax(prediction)*
5 : *return groove_type*

Feature Extraction Based on GMM. To accurately extract geometric keypoints in weld groove structures, this study proposes a Gaussian Mixture Model (GMM)-based feature point extraction method utilizing point cloud data. The approach constructs multidimensional feature vectors from the structural statistical characteristics of raw point clouds and achieves identification of critical groove boundaries through a probabilistic density clustering model.

First, the point cloud data is defined in two-dimensional coordinate form. Let a frame of data be represented as the point set:

$$\mathcal{P} = \{p_i = (x_i, z_i) \mid i = 1, 2, \ldots, N\} \tag{4}$$

where, x_i represents the lateral coordinate of the laser position and z_i denotes the longitudinal coordinate. To comprehensively characterize spatial distribution variations in the point cloud, this study designs a three-dimensional feature vector:

$$\mathbf{f}_i = \left[x_i, \Delta z_i, \sigma_z^{(i)} \right] \tag{5}$$

where: x_i denotes the lateral position of a point, $z_i = |z_{i+1} - z_i|$ epresents the height difference between adjacent points (reflecting local variations), σ_z represents the standard deviation of local z-values within a window of length w centered at the i-th point, defined as:

$$\sigma_z^{(i)} = \sqrt{\frac{1}{w} \sum_{j=i-w/2}^{i+w/2} \left(z_j - \bar{z}_i \right)^2} \tag{6}$$

where $\bar{z}_i$ represents the mean value of the local region centered at the i-th point:

$$\bar{z}_i = \frac{1}{w} \sum_{j=i-w/2}^{i+w/2} z_j \tag{7}$$

The aforementioned feature vectors are employed to train the Gaussian Mixture Model (GMM), whose probability density function is expressed as:

$$p(\mathbf{f}) = \sum_{k=1}^{K} \pi_k \cdot \mathcal{N}(\mathbf{f}|\boldsymbol{\mu}_k, \Sigma_k) \tag{8}$$

where K denotes the preset number of Gaussian distributions, determined by the groove type and typically equivalent to the number of theoretical line segments constituting the groove geometry (e.g., K = 4 for V-groove and single-bevel V-groove; K = 5 for U-groove and single-bevel U-groove). π_k represents the mixing coefficient of the k-th component, satisfying $\sum_{k=1}^{k} \pi_k = 1$. μ_k and $\sum k$ correspond to the mean vector and covariance matrix, respectively.

Upon completion of clustering, each point is assigned a class label $c_i \in \{1,2,...,K\}$. This study identifies candidate feature points by selecting the maximum and minimum values of lateral position x within each class.

$$x_{\min}^{(k)} = \min_{i:c_i=k} x_i \tag{9}$$

$$x_{\max}^{(k)} = \max_{i:c_i=k} x_i \tag{10}$$

Subsequently, the spatial relationships between adjacent clusters are evaluated. if the following conditions are satisfied:

$$|x_{\min}^{(k+1)} - x_{\max}^{(k)}| < \delta \tag{11}$$

The interval is then recognized as a valid boundary region and recorded as a geometric feature point of the groove. Here, δ denotes the preset minimum effective spacing threshold, which suppresses pseudo-boundary points induced by noise or fitting errors.

2.2 Welding Position, Parameter, and Pose Planning Based on OCC

This paper proposes a method that combines computational graphics and welding parameters to ensure interlayer weld flattening, which guarantees planarization of each weld layer while accommodating groove welding of arbitrary depths. After extracting groove types and cross-sectional feature points, the OCC graphics engine reconstructs three-dimensional groove information (as shown in Fig. 4) by connecting points into lines and lines into surfaces, preserving point-line-surface data for vector calculations and positional transformations. This enables the computation of torch poses for each welding point. For grooves with uniform gaps, linear paths combined with planar fitting are sufficient. For grooves with non-uniform gap variations, Bézier curves or spline curves combined with surface fitting are employed. The groove is then categorized into three processing phases: root pass, fill pass, and cap pass.

The core challenge in root pass treatment lies in achieving variable-gap single-sided welding with double-sided formation. This paper introduces a robotic welding process package that integrates wrist manipulation techniques, crescent weaving, and zigzag weaving patterns to accomplish backing-free variable-gap root pass welding with double-sided formation (Figs. 1 and 2).

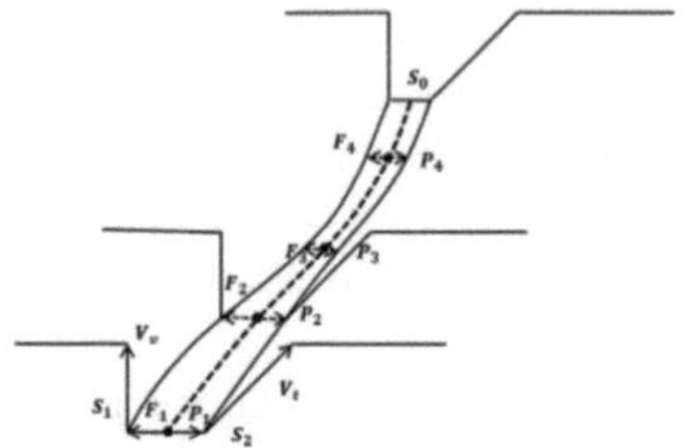

Fig. 1. Variable-gap groove cross-section

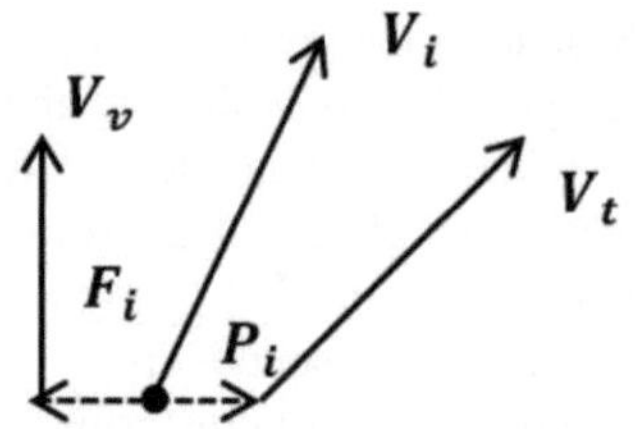

Fig. 2. Point pose and oscillation amplitude calculation

First, scan the cross-sectional dimensions of the groove, calculate the bottom mid-point ($P_1 \ldots P_n$) and the corresponding oscillation amplitude F_i for each midpoint, then derive the angle bisector vector V_i based on the sidewall vectors V_v and V_t.

Then filter adjacent F_i with a specified threshold ($F_i \leq \pm\Delta$), discard intermediate F and corresponding P points, and save the next F_{i+1} that does not meet this threshold until the last set of cross-sectional data. Import the position points, orientations, oscillation amplitudes, and other data into the process package and execute the welding program to complete the root pass welding (Fig. 3 and Table 1).

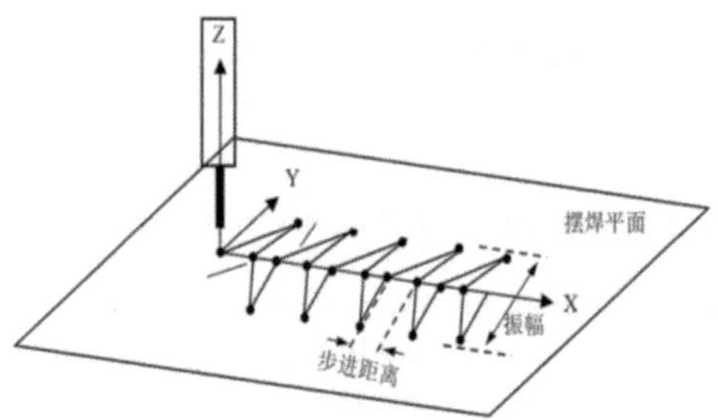

Fig. 3. Crescent oscillation

Table 1. Welding parameters for 5.0–6.0 mm gap range

Current (A)	Step distance (mm)	Dwell time (s)	Speed (cm/min)
110	1.6	1.6	55

The specific steps for filling and capping layer treatment are as follows (taking a single-side V-groove with one layer and two weld passes for filling as an example) (Fig. 5):

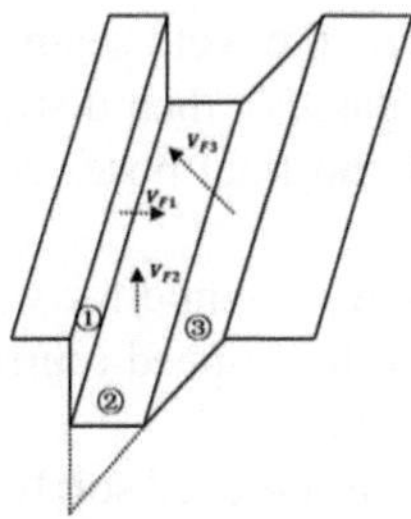

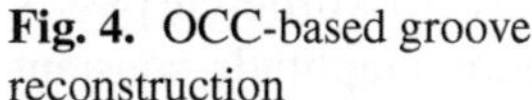

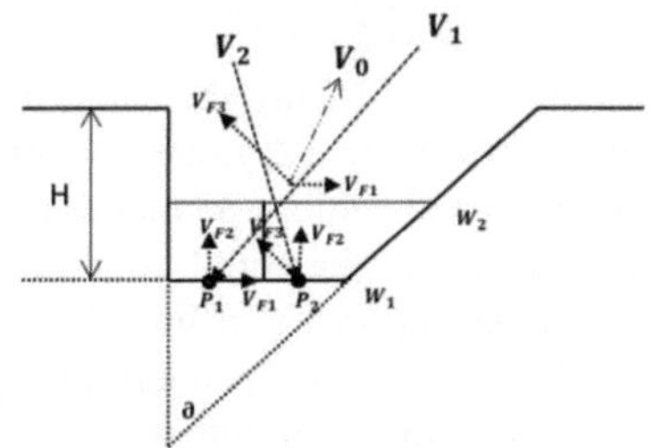

Fig. 4. OCC-based groove reconstruction

Fig. 5. Single-pass weld pose calculation

First, create the fill surfaces for each feature point using the right-hand rule, ensuring the surface normals point toward the side to be filled. Calculate the normals (V_{F1}, V_{F2}, V_{F3}) of the surfaces to be filled. For planar surfaces, use the midpoint normal; if the side-walls are curved, adjust the orientation by calculating normals through the intersection points of W_2 (post-fill bottom width) with curved surfaces ① and ③.

Set the single-pass weld width of the filling layer as w. Calculate the number of weld passes N and oscillation amplitude F required for the layer based on the bottom width W_1. Evenly divide to obtain the torch placement points P_1 and P_2. Using the normal directions of each surface, determine the normal directions V_1 and V_2 at points P_1 and P_2 via the angle bisector. The overall angle bisector normal direction for this groove layer is V_0.

$$N = ceil\left(\frac{W_1}{w}\right) \quad where\ is\ the\ ceiling\ function \tag{12}$$

$$F = \frac{W_1}{2N} - 1 \quad where\ N\ is\ the\ number\ of\ single-layer\ weld\ passes \tag{13}$$

The calculation of the pose of each weld seam through the above method is only the initial path planning. During actual welding, interlayer weld flatness cannot be guaranteed, requiring a secondary adjustment. V_1 must be offset towards side V_v to obtain V_1' (Fig. 7), and V_2 is derived by referencing V_v to obtain V_2' (Fig. 7), with V_1' calculated as follows:

Cross the inverse vector $V_{1'}$ of V_1 with V_0 to obtain $V_{1'0}$, then rotate $V_{1'}$ around $V_{1'0}$ by a specified angle (empirical value $R_A = F$) with P_1 as the origin (as shown in Fig. 6).

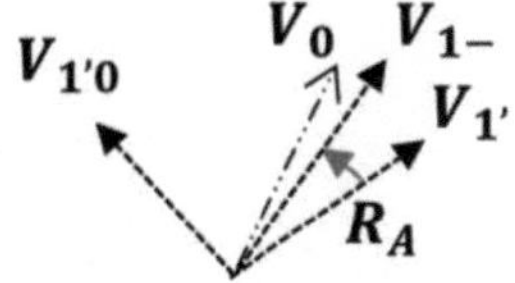

Fig. 6. Reverse vector V_{1-} calculation of V_1'

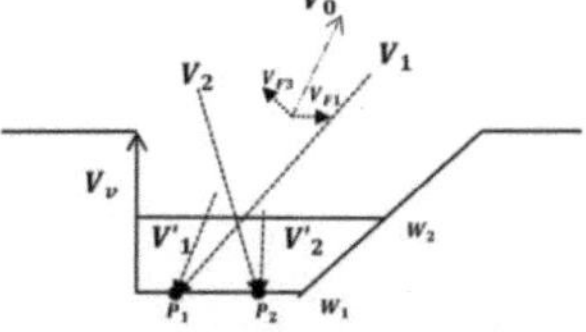

Fig. 7. Optimized welding pose

When the number of weld passes exceeds 2, first calculate the weld seam poses of the first and last passes (using the same method as for two passes), then distribute the angular differences of Δx, Δy, and Δz between the initial and final poses across the intermediate passes to achieve a smooth transition.

This study employs the equal-height method and equal-area method for weld bead filling. The deposition area is primarily correlated with wire feed speed (current) and dwell time, which can be determined through welding experiments.

In multi-pass welding, maintaining weld flatness cannot be achieved solely through pose constraints. Adjustments to welding parameters are required across different passes. For the same filler layer, this study keeps current and oscillation amplitude constant, primarily modifying travel speed (Fig. 8).

$$TheFinalSpeedRatio = \frac{S_1}{S_2 + S_+} = 1 - \frac{h \times \tan\partial}{W_1 + h \times \tan\partial} \tag{14}$$

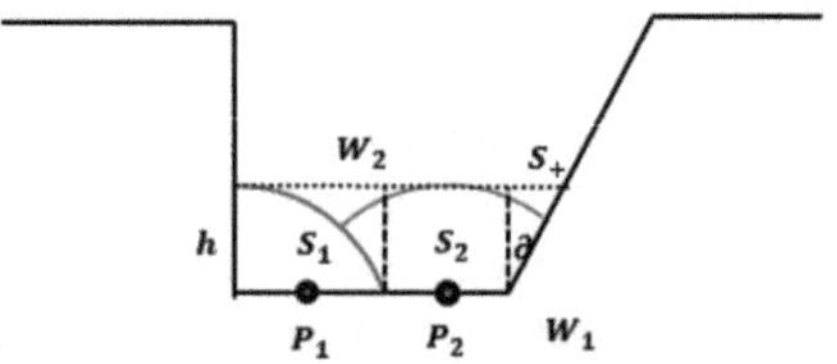

Fig. 8. Speed optimization schematic

2.3 Adaptive Control of Welding Process

To address formability control issues in single-sided V-groove welding, this study proposes an adaptive welding strategy based on geometric feature recognition. The system first acquires groove profile data via laser scanning and determines the welding initiation edge (marked as Boolean variable is_reverse) by analyzing the directional sequence of measurement points. Subsequently, vector space analysis calculates the angles between feature vectors on both groove sides (angles θ_1 and θ_2 between vectors V_1–V_2 and V_3–V_4). Combined with the state of is_reverse, the system dynamically determines the welding sequence: when condition is_reverse $=$ TURE is met, welding prioritizes the steep side (direction V_1) to enhance fusion quality and interlayer flatness; otherwise, welding initiates from the blunt side (direction V_3) to mitigate interlayer depression defects, The non-uniform gap filling surface can also refer to this method (Fig. 9).

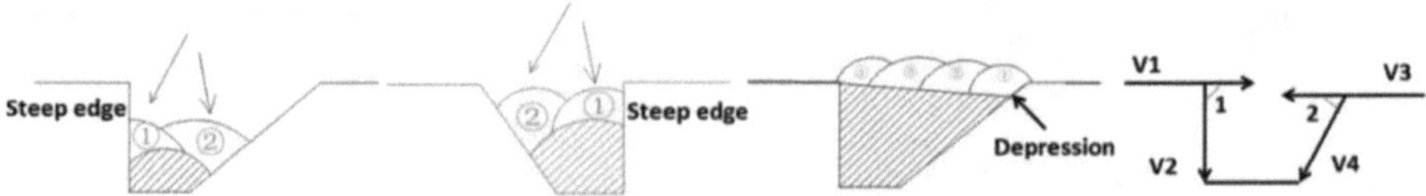

Fig. 9. Welding sequence and pose adaptive adjustment schematic

3   Experimental Results

3.1   Groove Automatic Classification Recognition Experiment

This paper constructs a dataset containing four typical groove configurations: V-groove, single-sided V-groove, U-groove, and single-sided U-groove, comprising 3,000 image samples.

ResNet101-Based Automated Classification Experiment. To validate the performance of the proposed ResNet101-based groove classification model across various groove types, the dataset is partitioned into training set (70%), validation set (15%), and test set (15%). After applying data augmentation to the training set, the expanded dataset contains 12,600 samples (Fig. 10).

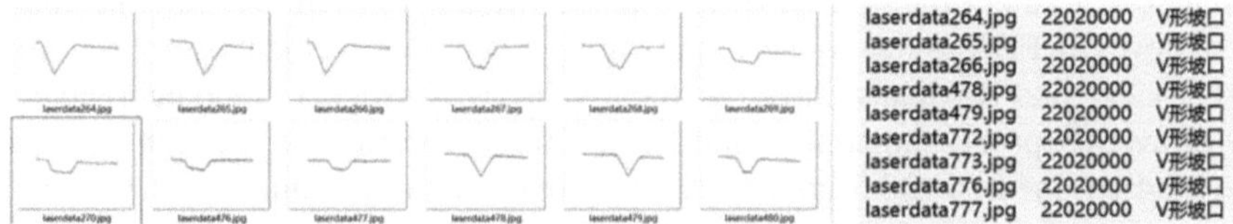

Fig. 10. Sample and annotation diagram

Comparative experiments with classification models VGG16 and MobileNetV2 were conducted. As shown in the table below, the ResNet101-based groove classification model demonstrates a significant advantage in accuracy (Table 2).

Table 2. Groove classification model performance comparison

Model Name	Top-1 Accuracy	Recall	F1 Score
ResNet101	99.8%	99.6%	99.7%
VGG16	92.1%	91.4%	91.7%
MobileNetV2	88.3%	87.1%	87.7%

GMM-Based Feature Extraction Experiment. The relationship between clustering iteration count and measurement accuracy (MAE)/false detection rate (FDR) of the proposed method is shown in the figure. It can be observed that both MAE and FDR stabilize after 13 iterations, demonstrating the method's strong convergence and stability. With fewer iterations required to achieve high precision and low false detection rates, this approach meets practical engineering requirements (Fig. 11).

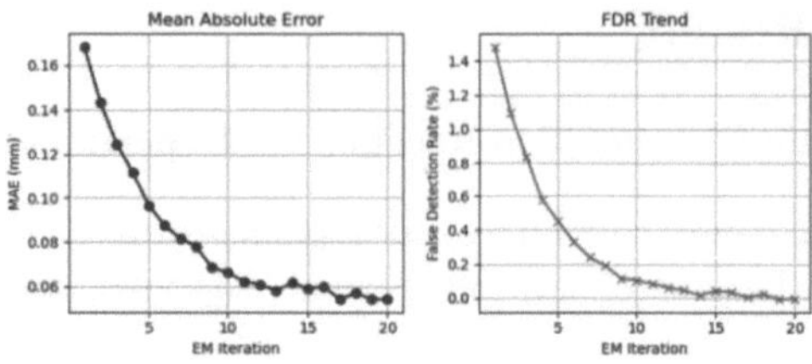

Fig. 11. MAE and FDR of GMM under different iteration numbers

Comparative experiments were conducted on 3,000 sample groups using gradient method, K-Means clustering, and GMM. As shown in the table below, significant differences exist among these methods in MAE, FDR, and computational efficiency. GMM demonstrates superior overall performance with MAE of only 0.06 mm, substantially lower than the gradient method (1.91 mm) and K-Means (0.27 mm). Simultaneously, GMM achieves an FDR as low as 0.4%, showing marked improvement over the gradient method (16.2%) and K-Means (2.6%). Although GMM has higher computational complexity, its average processing time remains at 42.7 ms, comparable to K-Means (36.7 ms) and the gradient method (22.5 ms), all meeting real-time requirements (<200 ms). In conclusion, GMM significantly enhances detection accuracy and reliability while maintaining efficient computation, making it suitable for high-precision real-time applications (Table 3).

Table 3. Comparison of classification algorithm effectiveness

Method	MAE(mm)	FDR (%)	Avg. Processing Time (ms)
Gradient	1.91	16.2	22.5
K-Means	0.27	2.6	36.7
GMM	0.06	0.4	42.7

This method integrates both geometric and statistical attributes of point clouds, naturally delineating regional boundaries through probabilistic modeling to overcome traditional limitations, demonstrating strong adaptability to various groove structures. By linking with groove classification models, the system automatically sets the Gaussian component number K, achieving full-process automation from recognition to parameter extraction.

3.2 Multi-layer Multi-pass Welding Process Experiment

This study employs a 40 mm-deep groove welding process, executing a multi-pass welding operation comprising 7 layers and 16 passes. During welding, the system achieved intelligent layered and pass-by-pass control through adaptive algorithms, effectively compensating for thermal deformation (Fig. 12).

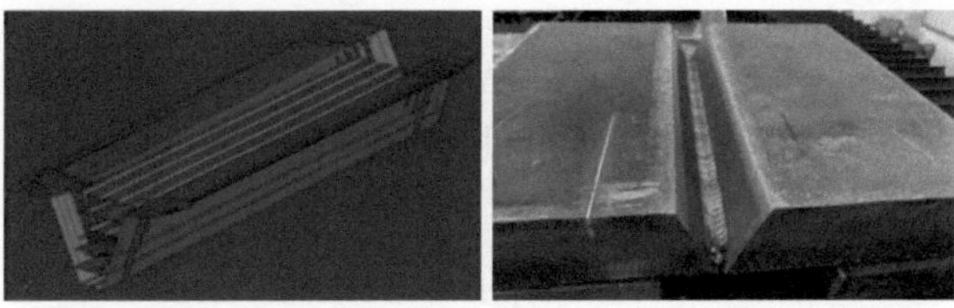

Fig. 12. Schematic of the automatic layer and path arrangement experiment process

Under conditions without anti-deformation fixtures, the workpiece exhibited significant deformation induced by welding thermal cycles, with a longitudinal shrinkage angle of 12° and 5 mm lateral shrinkage at the groove top region. Despite this deformation, the welding process maintained full-process automation control, delivering excellent weld formation quality characterized by a smooth and flat surface. The geometric dimensions conformed to ISO 5817 Class B requirements, with all weld passes free from surface defects and meeting UT1-class inspection criteria per GB/T 11345–2013 (Fig. 13).

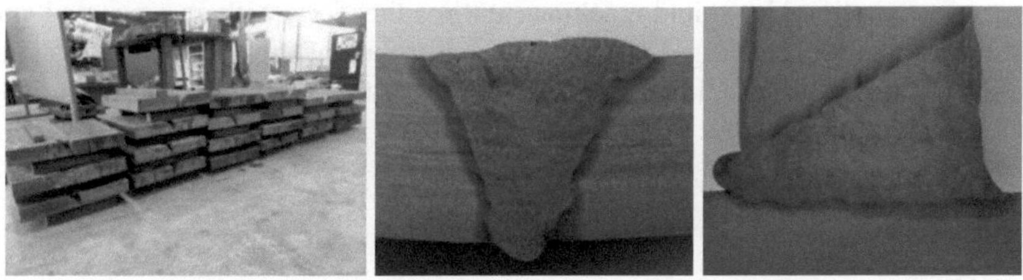

Fig. 13. Weld formation and metallographic diagrams

3.3 Engineering Application

This study demonstrated excellent performance in industrial applications of full-penetration adaptive welding for plates with 20–80 mm thickness and 2–11 mm groove gaps, achieving a 99.89% groove recognition accuracy and an average welding deviation of 0.08 mm. All weld results met UT1-class inspection requirements, with 25% higher welding efficiency compared to manual teaching, a 30% increase in daily welding wire consumption per operator, and significantly amplified efficiency gains as the number of welds per workpiece increased (Fig. 14).

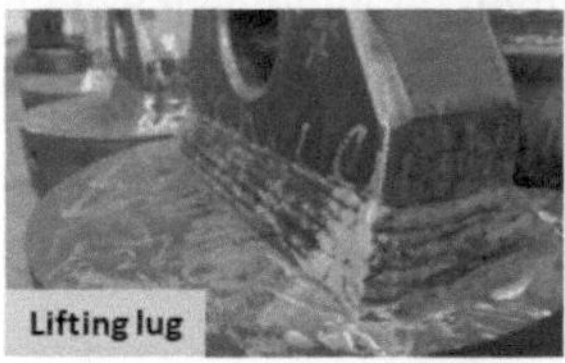

Fig.14. Industrial production application effects

In the case of stirring rod welding, adaptive technology significantly reduced manual teaching time, achieving a 27.8% improvement in efficiency compared to manual teaching welding. The auxiliary operation time was reduced from 116 min to 20 min, demonstrating substantial time savings (Table 4).

Table 4. Field application effectiveness

Working mode	Number of grooves	Number of weld seams	Total operation duration	Auxiliary operation time
Manual teaching	4	104	291 min	116 min
Adaptive welding	4	98	210 min	20 min

This technological breakthrough preliminarily resolves the persistent challenge of unstable welding quality in critical components of high-end underground engineering equipment, exemplified by shield machines and roadheaders, with an estimated annual production capacity exceeding 2,000 units. It will robustly support the manufacturing of megaprojects including China's deepest undersea tunnel shield machines and the world's largest-diameter shaft boring machines.

4 Conclusion

(1) This study proposes an intelligent welding system for medium-thick plate applications, establishing a ResNet101-based deep convolutional neural network model that achieves 99.62% classification accuracy in automatic groove type recognition. Integrated with GMM clustering algorithms, it accomplishes submillimeter-level accuracy in groove feature point extraction and geometric parameter analysis.
(2) A multi-layer multi-pass welding process is developed, incorporating three adaptive strategies: adaptive adjustment of welding sequence and torch pose, dynamic compensation of wire stick-out, and thermal deformation/scanning error compensation, ensuring process stability and welding consistency in industrial environments.
(3) Experimental results demonstrate over 91.3% reduction in manual intervention time and 30% increased welding efficiency, validating engineering feasibility. The system has been deployed in welding production for tunnel boring machines (TBMs) and roadheaders, providing an engineerable solution for intelligent welding transformation under smart manufacturing frameworks.

References

1. Zhou, Q., Wu, J.G., Li, S.C., et al.: Adaptive path and process planning method for multi-layer and multi-pass welding of medium-thick plates with robots. Meas. Sci. Technol. **36**(3), 036202 (2025)

2. Liu, S.J., Lu, H., Liu, S., et al.: A speed adaptive path planning method based on line structured light information for robotic multi-layer/multi-pass welding. J. Phys: Conf. Ser. **2281**, 012001 (2022)
3. Zhang, R., Wang, X.G., Liu, W., et al.: Offline programming and simulation of robot multi-layer multi-pass welding for medium-thick plates based on customized filling strategy. Electric Weld. Mach. **49**(12), 98–103 (2019)
4. Kim, Y.B., Kim, J.G., Jang, W.T., et al.: Development of automatic welding system for multi-layer and multi-pass welding. IFAC Proceedings Vol. **41**(2), 4290–4291 (2008)
5. Li, C., Ji, H., Yan, Z., et al.: Prediction of residual stress and deformation of 316L multi-layer multi-pass welding based on GA-BP neural network. Trans. China Weld. Inst. **45**(5), 20–28 (2024)
6. Sun, X., Yao, J., Mao, C., et al.: Numerical simulation of 50mm thick Q420 steel plate welding with multi-layer and multi-pass welding process. J. Phys: Conf. Ser. **2944**, 012005 (2025)
7. Xu, F., He, L., Hou, Z., et al.: An automatic feature point extraction method based on laser vision for robotic multi-layer multi-pass weld seam tracking. Int. J. Adv. Manuf. Technol. **131**, 5941–5960 (2024)
8. Zhao, B.: Multi-layer and multi-channel welding trajectory control method of welding robot. Jordan J. Mech. Indust. Eng. **16**(1), 153–162 (2022)
9. Trupiano, S., Belardi, V.G., Fanelli, P., et al.: A novel modeling approach for multi-passes butt-welded plates. J. Pressure Vessel Technol. **143**(4), 829–849 (2021)
10. Wang, H., Li, S., Liu, X., et al.: ADAP: adaptive & dynamic arc padding for predicting seam profiles in multi-layer-multi-pass robotic welding
11. Zhang, H., Lu, H., Wang, S., et al.: Welding path planning algorithm for medium-thick plate based on process parameters. In: 2021 IEEE 5th Advanced Information Technology, Electronic and Automation Control Conference (IAEAC), 9390816. IEEE, (2021)
12. Wang, T.Q., Zhang, S.H., Long, B., et al.: Visual measurement and process planning for multi-layer multi-pass welding of medium-thick plates. J. Mech. Eng. **60**(14), 1–10 (2024)
13. Wei, X.P.: Research on adaptive multi-layer multi-pass welding technology for medium-thick plates. Lanzhou University of Technology, Lanzhou (2023)
14. Yang, L.: 3D information extraction of multi-layer multi-pass welds and welding path trajectory planning. Xiangtan University, Xiangtan (2022)
15. Huang, H.: Path planning strategy and experimental research for multi-layer multi-pass welding robot of medium-thick plates. Wuhan University of Technology, Wuhan (2022)
16. Zhang, H.J., Zhang, G.J., Cai, C.B., et al.: Laser vision recognition of multi-layer multi-pass welding seams for robots. J. Mech. Eng. **45**(8), 208–213 (2009)
17. Yu, J.J., Zhou, J.P., Xue, R.L., et al.: Weld surface quality inspection based on structured light vision and illumination model. J. Mech. Eng. **58**(4), 56–63 (2022)
18. Hu, Q.Q., Wu, X.J., Yang, M.X., et al.: A novel weld adaptive path generation method based on 3-D point cloud for robotic multilayer multipass welding. IEEE Trans. Instrum. Meas. **74**, 2513813 (2025)
19. Shi, H., Zhang, K.: Automated laser wire-filling welding and seam tracking for thick-plate narrow-gap multi-layer multi-pass welding. J. Shanghai Jiao Tong Univ. **49**(6), 821–827 (2015)
20. Wang, T.Q., Meng, K.Q., Wang, C.R.: Prediction and optimization of multi-layer multi-pass welding process parameters based on GA-BP neural network. Trans. China Weld. Inst. **45**(5), 1–10 (2024)
21. Chang, S.H., Zhang, H.Y., Xu, H.Y., et al.: Online path recognition for additive manufacturing and arc welding with filler wire based on multi-vision information fusion. J. Mech. Eng. **55**(17), 1–9 (2019)
22. Liao, W.D., Li, J.Y., Huang, X., et al.: Robotic off-line programming path planning for multi-path/multi-layer welding. Mach. Tool Hydraulics **49**(15), 89–94 (2021)

23. Liu, Z.J., Ma, S.L., Dai, H.F., et al.: Adaptive multi-layer multi-pass robotic welding based on laser sensor. Weld. Join. **8**, 23–28 (2020)
24. Ni, M.N.: Research on laser vision seam tracking technology for arc welding robot in multi-layer multi-pass welding. Tiangong University, Tianjin (2019)
25. Zeng, J., Chang, B., Du, D., et al.: A weld position recognition method based on directional and structured light information fusion in multi-layer/multi-pass welding. Sensors **18**(1), 129 (2018)
26. Li, R., Wang, T., Wang, C., et al.: A study of narrow gap laser welding for thick plates using the multi-layer and multi-pass method. Opt. Laser Technol. **62**, 172–183 (2014)
27. Pan, H.H., Li, R.L., Liu, G.L., et al.: Path planning for multi-layer multi-pass welding based on laser vision system. Mach. Build. Autom. **50**(11), 24–29 (2021)

M³E: Mixture of Multi-scale Multi-modal Experts for Time Series Forecasting

Shaobo Xie[1], Han Jiang[2], Chenlin Zhao[3], and Xiaoshan Yang[3(✉)]

[1] Henan Institute of Advanced Technology, Zhengzhou University, Zhengzhou, China
[2] University of Science and Technology of China, Hefei, China
[3] Institute of Automation, Chinese Academy of Sciences, Beijing, China
`xiaoshan.yang@nlpr.ia.ac.cn`

Abstract. Recent research has shown that large language model (LLM) can be effectively used for real-world time series forecasting due to their strong natural language understanding capabilities. However, these approaches face a fundamental challenge that LLM operate on discrete tokens, while time series data is continuous. Meanwhile, recent works leverage pre-trained visual masked autoencoders (visual MAE) to construct time series forecasting foundation models. Nevertheless, converting time series into images disrupts the critical temporal dependencies of time series. Additionally, it is intuitive that different sampling scale time series exhibit distinct patterns, where the microscopic information is reflected in the fine scale, while the macroscopic information is reflected in the coarse scale. Based on these observations, we first generate multi-scale time series through downsampling to capture diverse temporal patterns, then we design a novel dual-modality encoding framework for long-term time series forecasting, consisting of an LLM encoding branch for discrete semantic reasoning and a visual MAE encoding branch for continuous representation learning. To effectively leverage the complementary strengths of both LLM encoding branch and visual MAE encoding branch, we propose a mixture of multi-scale multi-modal experts (M³E) to fuse features from the LLM with features from the visual MAE. Furthermore, M³E adaptively selects key-scale features from multi-scale features from LLM and visual MAE respectively to reduce computational costs, and facilitates multi-scale features interaction, which enables the capture of both short-term details and long-term patterns. Extensive experiments on six real-world datasets demonstrate M³E is a powerful time series model, outperforming state-of-the-art methods.

Keywords: Time series forecasting · Large language models · Multi-scale

1 Introduction

Long-term time series forecasting (LTSF) is an important yet challenging task, which is widely used in various fields, such as demand planning [1], energy load

Z. Lin et al. (Eds.): ICIG 2025, LNCS 16161, pp. 65–76, 2026.
https://doi.org/10.1007/978-981-95-3398-5_6

forecasting [2] and climate modeling [3]. In the past years, many methods based on deep learning have been developed for LTSF. However, the limited number of learnable parameters and the small-scale training data prevent these methods from achieving better performance and being more robust [4].

Recently, to alleviate above limitations, some pre-trained foundation model approaches for LTSF have been introduced. These approaches leverage the abundant knowledge of pre-trained model, which can be classified into two types: (1) The first road is LLM-based methods, which exploit the robust pre-trained knowledge, sophisticated reasoning and pattern recognition capabilities of LLM [5]. They are motivated by the similar sequential formulation of time series and text. Specifically, Zhou et al. [6] fine-tune the weights of LLM which have been pre-trained on text data for LTSF, while Jin et al. [7] focus on introducing prompts with text as additional input to help LLM understand the time series forecasting task. Although these LLM-based models have achieved notable performance, they are challenged by the modality mismatch. In other words, LLM operate on discrete tokens, while time series data is continuous. (2) The seconed road is based on the visual masked autoencoder (visual MAE). Specifically, Chen et al. [8] strive to build time series forecasting foundation model with pre-trained visual MAE. It tries to reformulate time series forecasting as a patch-level image reconstruction task, which is based on the intrinsic similarities between natural images and time series: both time series and images are continuous and observations of real-world physical systems. However, despite these similarities, converting time series into image formats also inevitably incurs substantial information loss, particularly compromising the inherent temporal ordering that is critical for LTSF.

Overall, we observe that while LLM demonstrate strong capabilities in sophisticated reasoning, they face inherent limitations in processing continuous signals. Conversely, visual MAE can effectively handle continuous data but often disregard crucial temporal dependencies when converting time series into image representations. Additionally, time series data has multiple temporal scales, from short-term fluctuations to long-term trends. However, these pre-trained foundation models typically process fixed-length sequences, which means they may only capture short-term dependencies.

To address these challenges, we design **a mixture of multi-scale multimodal experts** (**M^3E**), which dynamically selects and integrates multi-scale features from LLM and visual MAE to leverage the complementary strengths of LLM and visual MAE. Besides, by generating multi-resolution representations and adaptively selecting optimal scales, our model can more effectively capture both short-term details and long-term patterns. Specifically, we propose to organize the multi-scale features from LLM and visual MAE into two distinct groups. To encourage the model to select the optimal scale information, M^3E employs two distinct routers, where each router dynamically selects its Top-K most relevant scale features from each group through gating mechanisms. Moreover, we design a scale-level balance Loss to avoid unbalanced load and a global balance loss to minimize feature divergence between two modalities. To prevent information degradation, we designate the original-scale features as a shared head for each group that remains always activated. Our contributions can be summarized as follows.

(1) We propose M^{3}E, a novel time series forecasting framework that facilitates multi-modal interaction to leverage the complementary strengths of LLM and visual MAE.

(2) To effectively represent complex patterns, our proposed M^{3}E adaptively selects a small number of key-scale features from multiple scale features, and implements multi-scale interactions to capture both short-term details and long-term patterns.

(3) Extensive experiments on six datasets demonstrate that M^{3}E outperforms other baseline models in time series forecasting tasks.

2 Related Work

2.1 Pre-trained Foundation Models

In recent years, several pre-trained foundation models have tried to transfer LLM's capabilities of other modalities to achieve time series forecasting. However, the main challenges lie in discussing the relationship between time series data and text data. Some previous works claim that aligning them is important and useful for multi-modal forecasting. Zhou et al. [9] leverage pre-trained large language models and freezing the parameters of self-attention and feed-forward layers. Jin et al. [7] reprogram the time series with text prototypes before feeding it into the LLM to align the two modalities. However, time series data is continuous, whereas text data is discrete. Encoding time series as text results in the loss of fine-grained temporal information, ultimately degrading forecasting performance.

Simultaneously, VisionTS [8] builds time series forecasting foundation models with visual MAE. It tried to reformulate time series forecasting as a patch-level image reconstruction task based on the intrinsic similarities between time series and image, such as both time series and image are same continuous natural signals. However, although natural images and time series have certain intrinsic similarities, reconstructing time series into image formats still inevitably incurs substantial information loss, particularly compromising the inherent temporal ordering that is critical for time series forcasting. In this paper, we rethink the use of large language models and visual MAE for time series and strive to develop a more robust and effective time series prediction model.

2.2 Mixture-of-Experts Models

The Mixture-of-Experts (MoE) method [10] has emerged as an effective approach to scale up deep neural networks without increasing computational costs. Unlike dense models, In these approaches, only a subset of parameters, known as experts, is activated for each input. Shazeer et al. [11] first propose MoE layer between LSTM layers. Jin et al. [12] strive to further reducing the activation of redundant attention heads. In our paper, we propose M^3E, a novel extension of MoE tailored for time series forecasting, which dynamically activates specialized heads, while enabling multi-scale and multi-modal feature fusion.

3   Methodology

Problem Formulation. Given a lookback window $X_{1:L} \in \mathbb{R}^L$ (where T is the length of history time series), we strive to develop a model that captures temporal dependencies in historical time series to forecast future values $X_{L+1:L+H}$ (H is the forecast length).

Framework Overview. As illustrated in Fig. 1, the M^3E architecture comprises four core components: **(1) Data Pre-processing:** The input time series undergoes normalization and segmentation, followed by multi-scale downsampling through strided mean pooling to generate multi-scale time series data. **(2) Dual-Modality Encoding:** Dual-modality encoding employs two parallel branches for feature extraction. LLM encoding branch transforms time series patches into discrete semantic tokens via scale-specific linear projections, enabling symbolic reasoning through the LLM backbone. Meanwhile, the visual MAE branch preserves continuous temporal dependencies by converting 1D time series into 3D structural representations via grayscale rendering and resizing, followed by masked autoencoding to learn robust spatio-temporal features. **(3) Mixture of Multi-scale Multi-modal Experts:** This module employs dual modality-specific routers that dynamically select Top-K optimal scale features from LLM and Visual MAE groups through gating mechanisms, while maintaining always-activated shared heads of original-scale features to prevent information degradation. **(4) Time Series Forecasting:** Predictions are produced through parallel modality-specific decoders (LLM and visual MAE branches), with their outputs dynamically weighted summed and denormalized to produce the time series forecast.

3.1   Data Pre-processing

Normalization. Data normalization is crucial for pre-trained models across various modalities. Therefore, we adopt a data normalization block to facilitate knowledge transfer. This normalization block simply normalizes the input time series using mean and variance, which will add back to the output.

Segmentation. Following PatchTST [13], we simply divide the normalized time series $X_{norm} \in \mathbb{R}^L$ into $\lfloor L/P \rfloor$ segments, where P denotes the periodicity. These segments are then stacked into a 2D matrix $X_{\text{raw}} \in \mathbb{R}^{P \times Q}$, where $Q = \lfloor L/P \rfloor$.

Multi-scale Time Series. To effectively capture temporal patterns at different resolutions, we develop a multi-scale processing module based on downsampling operation. Specifically, given the normalized 2D time series matrix $X_{\mathrm{raw}} \in \mathbb{R}^{P \times Q}$, we generate multiple downsampled time series X_{raw}^i through strided mean pooling with varying strides $s_i = 2^{i-1}$ for $i \in \{1, \ldots, h\}$.

$$X_{\mathrm{raw}}^i = (\mathrm{MeanPool1D}\ s_i\,(X_{\mathrm{raw}}))^{\top} \in \mathbb{R}^{Q \times \lfloor P/2^{i-1} \rfloor} \tag{1}$$

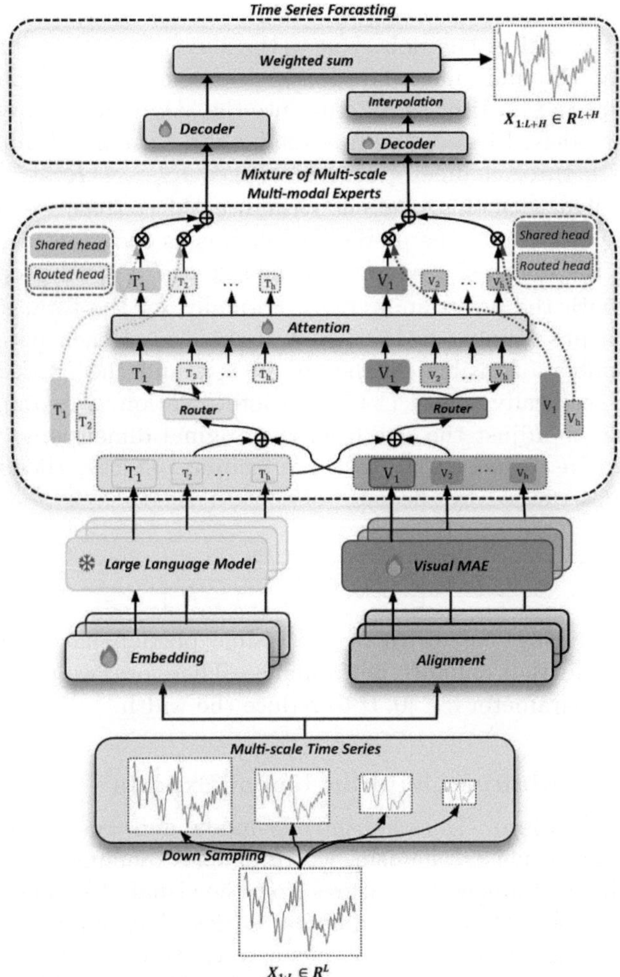

Fig. 1. The model framework of M^{3}E. Given time series $X_{1:L} \in \mathbb{R}^L$, we pre-process and embed them through dual-modality encoding branch. After that, we employ M^{3}E to effectively fuse multi-scale features from LLM and visual MAE. Then the fused features V and T generate prediction sequence respectively. Finally, these sequences are weighted summed and denormalized to predict time series $X_{L:L+H}$.

3.2 Dual-modality Encoding

LLM Encoding Branch. Building on our pre-processing pipeline, which includes normalization, segmentation, and down sampling operation. The LLM encoding branch deploys scale-specific linear projectors W_i to map each time series patch into the LLM's semantic space. Each projector W_i operates on normalized input patches X^i_{raw} from scale i, where $W_i \in \mathbb{R}^{S \times d_{llm}}, S = \lfloor \frac{P}{2^{i-1}} \rfloor$ $(i = 1, 2, \ldots, h)$

$$T_i = X^i_{\text{raw}} W_i + b_i \tag{2}$$

Visual MAE Encoding Branch. Due to the dimensional discrepancy between time series data (1D) and image data (3D), we employ a dimensional alignment strategy to adapt the 1D time series data into the 3D input requirements of pre-trained visual models. First, we simply render the normalized multi-scale time series X^i_{raw} as a three-channel grayscale images $I^i_{\text{grey}} \in R^{3 \times \lfloor P/2^{i-1} \rfloor \times Q}, (i = 1, 2, \ldots, h)$ to align with this inherent structure. After that, we treat I^i_{grey} as the visible left portion and the predicted columns as the masked right portion. However, since the image size not match the size of I^i_{grey}, we propose to resize I^i_{grey} to align with the pre-training data. Formally, let the total number of 2D patches used in pre-training be $N \times N$ and the size of each patch be $S \times S$. We set the number of visible patches to $N \times n$ and the masked patches to $N \times (N - n)$. Specifically, we select bilinear interpolation to resample the multi-scale time series to adjust the size from the original dimensions $(\lfloor P/2^{i-1} \rfloor, Q)$ to$(N \cdot S, n \cdot S)$, where N denotes the total pre-training patches, s denotes the patch size, and n is determined by the ratio of context length $L/2^{i-1}$ and prediction length H.

$$n = \left\lfloor c \cdot N \cdot \frac{L/2^{i-1}}{(L/2^{i-1}) + H} \right\rfloor \tag{3}$$

Moreover, reducing the width of the visible portion has been empirically demonstrated to further enhance performance. Therefore, we propose multiplying n by a hyperparameter $c \in [0, 1]$ to reduce the width.

3.3 Mixture of Multi-scale Multi-modal Experts

Attention Mechanism. To establish cross-modal and cross-scale interactions, we employ the attention mechanism, which enables dynamic focus on relevant input regions. In our framework, features from the visual MAE and features from the LLM are concatenated across different scales. This unified representation enables the attention layer to simultaneously capture: (1) fine-grained cross-modal alignments between features from visual MAE and LLM.(2) hierarchical cross-scale relationships within each modality.

$$X = \text{Concat}\left(\{V^t_i\}^h_{i=1}, \{T^t_i\}^h_{i=1} \right) \tag{4}$$

$$\left[\tilde{V}^t, \tilde{T}^t \right] = \text{Attention}\left(XW_Q, XW_K, XW_V \right) \tag{5}$$

where h denotes the number of scales, $W_Q \in \mathbb{R}^{d_{in} \times d_k}$, $W_K \in \mathbb{R}^{d_{in} \times d_k}$, and $W_V \in \mathbb{R}^{d_{in} \times d_k}$ represent the projection matrices for the query, key, and value, respectively.

Heads as Experts. Inspired by Deepseek-V2 [14], we propose M^{3}E to dynamically select and integrate multi-scale features from visual MAE and LLM. M^{3}E treats each scale-specific feature from visual MAE and LLM as an input. Specifically, M^{3}E consists of $2h$ heads divided into two modality-specific groups $V = \{V_1, V_2, \dots V_h\}$, $T = \{T_1, T_2, \dots T_h\}$ and two dedicated routers that independently select the Top-k heads. Then, these selected heads from both modalities interact through an attention mechanism to enable effective cross-modal interaction and multi-scale fusion. Given input tokens V_i^t and T_i^t (t denote the t_{th} token, i represents the i_{th} head), the output of M^{3}E is the weighted sum of the outputs from the k selected heads, as formulated in Eq. 6

$$V^t = W_O^V \sum_{i=1}^{h} g_i^V \tilde{V}_i^t, T^t = W_O^T \sum_{i=1}^{h} g_i^T \tilde{T}_i^t \tag{6}$$

where $\tilde{V}_i^t$ and $\tilde{T}_i^t$ are the i_{th} scale features of token t_{th} generated by the attention mechanism in Eq. 5, and these features are subsequently transformed through modality-specific projection matrices $W_O^V \in \mathbb{R}^{d_{in} \times (d_{in}/h)}$ and $W_O^T \in \mathbb{R}^{d_{in} \times (d_{in}/h)}$, respectively.

Routed Heads. To dynamically balance the weights of routed heads, we propose a routing strategy. In this routing strategy, the routing scores are determined by both the score of each individual head and the score associated with the head type. Specifically, given the t_{th} input token V^t and T^t, the routing score g_i^M is defined as:

$$g_i^M = \begin{cases} 1, & \text{if } i = 1 \\ \text{softmax}\left(W_r^M(V^t + T^t)\right)_i, & \text{if } g_i^M \in \text{Top-k}\left(\{g_i^M \mid 1 < i < h\}\right) \\ 0, & \text{otherwise} \end{cases} \tag{7}$$

where $M \in \{V, T\}$ denotes the modality type (visual or textual), g_i^M denote the routing score for the i_{th} attention head of modality M, and $W_r^M \in \mathbb{R}^{(h-1) \times d_{in}}$ represent the projection matrices for the routed heads.

Notably, g_i^M take a non-zero value only when the i_{th} attention head is activated and it is computed based on the combined features of visual and textual modalities. The purpose of this design is to perform dynamic scale selection by jointly considering both modalities, thereby effectively bridging the representational gap between them.

Shared Heads. In attention mechanism, some heads may learn common knowledge across diverse contexts, such as language grammatical rules. In our paper, we design two distinct heads for text and vision modalities as shared heads that remains always activated. Specifically, we configure original-scale features from both the LLM and visual MAE as shared heads to preserve fine-grained information and set multiple downsampled scales as routed heads to select and capture coarse-grained information.

Scale-Level Balance Loss. Directly training M^{3}E may cause the majority of tokens to be routed to a small number of experts, leaving the remaining experts insufficiently trained. To avoid unbalanced load while preserving multi-scale granularity, we propose separate scale-level balance losses for each modality. Specifically, for the t_{th} input token x_t^M from modality $M \in \{V, T\}$, the scale-Level Balance Loss L_b is formulated as:

$$L_b = L_b^V + L_b^T, L_b^M = \sum_{i=2}^{h} f_i^M P_i^M \tag{8}$$

$$f_i^M = \frac{1}{Q} \sum_{t=1}^{Q} \mathbb{1} \left(\text{Token } x_t^M \text{ selects Head } i \right) \tag{9}$$

$$P_i^M = \frac{1}{Q} \sum_{t=1}^{Q} \text{softmax} \left(W_r^M x_t^M \right)_i \tag{10}$$

where $\mathbb{1}(\cdot)$ denotes the indicator function, and Q denotes the number of tokens in a sequence.

Global Balance Loss. While the scale-level balance loss effectively regulate expert allocation within each individual modality, their independent optimization may lead to inconsistent feature representations across modalities. To address this problem, we introduce a global balance loss to minimize inter-modal discrepancy by enforcing correlation constraints between visual and textual expert selections. Precisely, given the t_{th} input token $x_t = \{V_2, V_3, \ldots V_h, T_2, T_3, \ldots, T_h\}$, the global balance loss L_g is formulated as:

$$L_g = \sum_{i=2}^{h} \sum_{j=2}^{h} (V_i T_j - 1)^2 \tag{11}$$

3.4   Time Series Forecasting

After processing through M^{3}E, the features from the text modality are decoded to generate segmented time series predictions. These segmented outputs are thenconcatenated to form time seriesprediction X_T. Concurrently, the features from the vision modality undergo decoding to reconstruct the image. After obtaining the reconstructed image, we simply reverse the previous steps for forecasting. Specifically, we average the three channels to obtain a single-channel image, and resize the single-channel image back to the original time series segmentations X_V through the same bilinear interpolation. Finally, both X_V and X_T are weighted summed and denormalized to produce the time series $X_{1:L+H} \in R^{L+H}$, and forecasting window $X_{L:L+H} \in R^H$ can be extracted.

4   Experiment

Datasets. We evaluate our proposed M^{3}E framework on six datasets: ETTm1, ETTm2, ETTh1, ETTh2, Electricity (ECL) and Traffic, which have been commonly used for benchmarking of long-term time series forecasting models. We set the length of time series is 672, and we use four different prediction length, including 96, 192, 336 and 720.

Table 1. Long-term series forecasting results on six datasets. Bold indicates the best.(MSE/MAE metrics)

Method	Metric	M^{3}E		VisionTS		Time-LLM		GPT4TS		DLinear		FEDformer	
		MSE	MAE	MSE	MAE	MSE	MAE	MSE	MAE	MSE	MAE	MSE	MAE
ETTh1	96	**0.344**	**0.373**	0.347	0.376	0.376	0.402	0.370	0.389	0.375	0.399	0.376	0.419
	192	**0.375**	**0.400**	0.385	0.400	0.407	0.421	0.412	0.413	0.405	0.416	0.420	0.448
	336	**0.397**	0.415	0.407	**0.415**	0.430	0.438	0.448	0.431	0.439	0.443	0.459	0.465
	720	**0.406**	**0.435**	0.439	0.442	0.457	0.468	0.441	0.449	0.472	0.490	0.506	0.507
	avg	**0.379**	**0.406**	0.395	0.409	0.418	0.432	0.418	0.421	0.423	0.437	0.440	0.460
ETTh2	96	**0.275**	**0.335**	0.282	0.337	0.286	0.346	0.280	0.335	0.289	0.353	0.358	0.336
	192	**0.333**	**0.378**	0.348	0.383	0.361	0.391	0.348	0.380	0.383	0.418	0.429	0.379
	336	**0.353**	**0.398**	0.365	0.402	0.390	0.414	0.380	0.405	0.448	0.465	0.496	0.439
	720	0.409	0.445	0.412	0.442	**0.405**	**0.434**	0.406	0.436	0.605	0.551	0.463	0.474
	avg	**0.343**	**0.389**	0.352	0.391	0.361	0.396	0.354	**0.389**	0.431	0.447	0.437	0.449
ETTm1	96	**0.279**	**0.320**	0.281	0.322	0.291	0.341	0.300	0.340	0.299	0.343	0.379	0.419
	192	**0.320**	**0.351**	0.322	0.353	0.341	0.369	0.343	0.368	0.335	0.365	0.426	0.441
	336	**0.350**	**0.376**	0.351	0.379	0.359	0.379	0.376	0.386	0.369	0.386	0.445	0.459
	720	**0.382**	**0.410**	0.391	0.413	0.433	0.419	0.431	0.416	0.425	0.421	0.543	0.490
	avg	**0.333**	**0.364**	0.336	0.367	0.356	0.377	0.363	0.378	0.357	0.379	0.448	0.452
ETTm2	96	0.168	0.255	0.169	0.256	**0.162**	0.248	0.163	**0.249**	0.167	0.269	0.203	0.287
	192	0.225	**0.289**	0.225	0.294	0.235	0.304	**0.222**	0.291	0.224	0.303	0.269	0.328
	336	**0.268**	0.333	0.278	0.334	0.280	0.329	0.273	**0.327**	0.281	0.342	0.325	0.366
	720	0.361	0.389	0.372	0.392	0.366	0.382	**0.357**	**0.376**	0.397	0.421	0.421	0.415
	avg	0.256	0.317	0.261	0.319	0.261	0.316	**0.254**	**0.311**	0.267	0.333	0.305	0.349
Electricity	96	**0.125**	**0.216**	0.126	0.218	0.137	0.233	0.141	0.239	0.140	0.237	0.193	0.308
	192	**0.142**	**0.234**	0.144	0.237	0.152	0.247	0.158	0.253	0.153	0.249	0.201	0.315
	336	**0.158**	**0.252**	0.162	0.256	0.169	0.267	0.172	0.266	0.169	0.267	0.214	0.329
	720	0.197	**0.286**	**0.192**	**0.286**	0.200	0.290	0.207	0.293	0.203	0.301	0.246	0.355
	avg	**0.155**	**0.247**	0.156	0.249	0.165	0.259	0.170	0.263	0.166	0.264	0.214	0.327
Traffic	96	**0.339**	**0.234**	0.344	0.236	0.392	0.267	0.410	0.264	0.410	0.282	0.587	0.366
	192	**0.368**	**0.243**	0.372	0.249	0.409	0.271	0.423	0.268	0.423	0.287	0.604	0.373
	336	**0.375**	**0.252**	0.383	0.257	0.434	0.296	0.436	0.296	0.436	0.296	0.621	0.383
	720	**0.414**	**0.277**	0.422	0.280	0.451	0.291	0.466	0.315	0.466	0.315	0.626	0.382
	avg	**0.374**	**0.252**	0.380	0.256	0.422	0.281	0.434	0.295	0.434	0.295	0.610	0.376
1st count		49		3		3		8		0		0	

Baselines and Evaluation. We use visual MAE (Base) with 112M parameters as our vision backbone and Llama (7B) as our LLM backbone. In the following, we will use Llama(K) to represent Llama-backbone with first K layers. This study uses a comprehensive comparative analysis between M^3E model and five mainstream deep learning models, including VisionTS [8] based on visual MAE, GPT4TS [6] and Time-LLM [7] based on large language model (LLM), FEDformer [15] based on the transformer structure,DLinear [16] based on a simple linear model, and TimesNet [17] based on convolutional neural networks (CNNs). We utilize the widely used metrics mean square error (MSE) and mean absolute error (MAE) [13] as evaluation.

Results. The main experimental results are shown in Table 1, which reveals that M^3E significantly outperforms all baselines in most cases. Specifically, compared to the Transformer-based model FEDformer, our approach demonstrates even more substantial gains, achieving over 30% reduction in MSE across most prediction horizons. This significant performance gap highlights the effectiveness of using multi-modal knowledge. By comparing with the LLM-based time series model GPT4TS and Time-LLM, we also have average improvements of 7.17% and 7.2% in terms of MSE.

Ablation Studies. The results in Table 2 show ablation studies of model design. The most impactful variant is w/o M^3E, where removing it demonstrates our experts-based mechanism effectively enables information fusion. Next, w/o visual MAE branch confirms dual branches outperform visual MAE alone. Without the LLM branch, performance drops, highlighting LLM's reasoning capability enhances time series prediction. Notably, for the LLM branch, using only the first transformer block of Llama-7B marginally outperforms deeper architectures on ETTh1, suggesting shallow layers suffice for temporal patterns. Thus, we adopt this single-block setup to reduce computation. Furthermore, we conduct a comprehensive analysis of the impact of the number of scales (h) in the proposed M^3E framework. As illustrated in Fig. 2 (Left), the average mean squared error (MSE) consistently decreases as the number of scales increases, indicating that a multi-scale approach enhances model performance. However, the improvement plateaus when h reaches 5, suggesting diminishing returns beyond this point.

After that, we further conduct comparative experiments to evaluate different downsampling strategies, including average (Avg), maximum (Max), and minimum (Min) pooling. The results, shown in Fig. 2 (Right), demonstrate that average pooling outperforms the others, achieving the lowest MSE. This is consistent with the observation that average pooling tends to preserve more global information across scales compared to max/min pooling, which may focus on localized features. These findings validate our design choices and underscore the importance of selecting appropriate hyperparameters and pooling methods for optimal performance.

Table 2. Ablations study of the proposed model on ETTh1, ETTh2. A lower value indicates better performance. The best results are highlighted in bold.(MSE/MAE metrics)

Variant		Llama (1)		Llama (8)		w/o text branch		w/o visual branch		w/o M^{3}E	
ETTh1	96	**0.344**	**0.373**	0.346	0.375	0.347	0.376	0.367	0.378	0.347	0.376
	192	**0.375**	**0.399**	0.379	0.400	0.385	0.400	0.396	0.405	0.384	0.400
	336	**0.397**	0.415	0.401	0.416	0.407	0.415	0.417	0.425	0.405	**0.413**
	720	**0.406**	**0.435**	0.410	0.436	0.439	0.442	0.445	0.446	0.436	0.440
	Avg	**0.379**	**0.406**	0.384	0.407	0.395	0.409	0.406	0.414	0.393	0.408
ETTh2	96	**0.275**	**0.335**	0.277	**0.335**	0.282	0.337	0.280	0.336	0.282	0.339
	192	**0.333**	**0.378**	0.335	0.380	0.348	0.383	0.348	0.380	0.350	0.384
	336	**0.353**	**0.398**	0.354	0.400	0.365	0.402	0.380	0.405	0.367	0.403
	720	0.409	0.445	0.411	0.439	0.412	0.442	**0.406**	**0.436**	0.415	0.439
	Avg	**0.343**	**0.389**	0.344	**0.389**	0.352	0.391	0.354	0.392	0.354	0.391

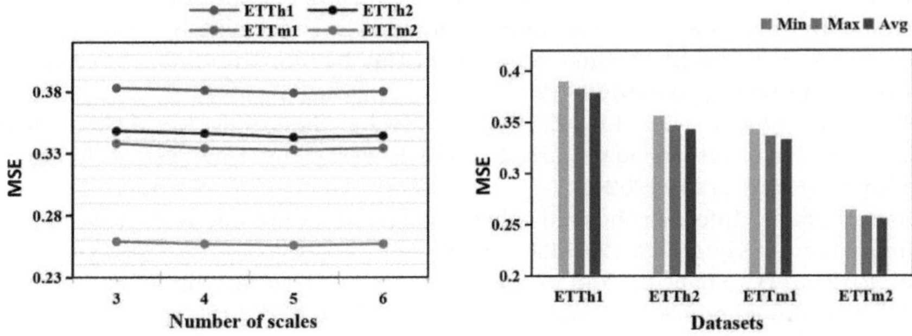

Fig. 2. (Left) Analysis on number of scales. (Right) Effect of different downsampling strategies.

5   Conclusion

This paper presents M^{3}E, a novel model designed to effectively fuse multi-scale features from the visual MAE and LLM. By integrating multi-scale features from visual MAE and LLM, our model effectively leverages the complementary strengths of LLM and visual MAE. In addition, by generating multi-resolution representations and adaptively selecting optimal scales, our model can more effectively capture various patterns. However, although M^{3}E has effectively fused features from visual MAE and LLM, inherent discrepancies between vision and text modalities still persist. Future research could focus on designing more advanced fusion mechanisms to further reduce inter-modal gaps, enabling more robust and effective multi-modal feature fusion.

Acknowledgments. This work was supported by the National Natural Science Foundation of China under Grant 62322212.

References

1. Leonard, M.J.: A practical time series approach, promotional analysis and forecasting for demand planning (2001)
2. Liu, H., et al.: SADI: a self-adaptive decomposed interpretable framework for electric load forecasting under extreme events. In: ICASSP 2023 - 2023 IEEE International Conference on Acoustics, Speech and Signal Processing (ICASSP), pp. 1–5 (2023)
3. Schneider, S.H., Dickinson, R.E.: Climate modeling (2007)
4. Jin, M., et al.: Position: what can large language models tell us about time series analysis. In: International Conference on Machine Learning (2024)
5. Wang, Y., et al.: Enhancing recommender systems with large language model reasoning graphs. ArXiv:abs/2308.10835 (2023)
6. Zhou, T., Niu, P., Wang, X., Sun, L., Jin, R.: One fits all: power general time series analysis by pretrained LM. In: Neural Information Processing Systems (2023)
7. Jin, M., et al.: Time-LLM: time series forecasting by reprogramming large language models. ArXiv:abs/2310.01728 (2023)
8. Chen, M., Shen, L., Li, Z., Wang, X.J., Sun, J., Liu, C.: Visionts: visual masked autoencoders are free-lunch zero-shot time series forecasters. ArXiv:abs/2408.17253 (2024)
9. Zhou, H., et al.: Informer: beyond efficient transformer for long sequence time-series forecasting. ArXiv:abs/2012.07436 (2020)
10. Jin, P., Zhu, B., Yuan, L., Yan, S.: Moe++: accelerating mixture-of-experts methods with zero-computation experts. ArXiv:abs/2410.07348 (2024)
11. Shazeer, N.M., et al.: Outrageously large neural networks: the sparsely-gated mixture-of-experts layer. ArXiv:abs/1701.06538 (2017)
12. Jin, P., Zhu, B., Yuan, L., Yan, S.: MOH: multi-head attention as mixture-of-head attention. ArXiv:abs/2410.11842 (2024)
13. Nie, Y., Nguyen, N.H., Sinthong, P., Kalagnanam, J.: A time series is worth 64 words: long-term forecasting with transformers. ArXiv:abs/2211.14730 (2022)
14. Liu, A., et al.: Deepseek-v2: a strong, economical, and efficient mixture-of-experts language model. arXiv preprint arXiv:2405.04434 (2024)
15. Zhou, T., Ma, Z., Wen, Q., Wang, X., Sun, L., Jin, R.: Fedformer: frequency enhanced decomposed transformer for long-term series forecasting. In: International Conference on Machine Learning (2022)
16. Zeng, A., Chen, M.-H., Zhang, L., Xu, Q.: Are transformers effective for time series forecasting? In: AAAI Conference on Artificial Intelligence (2022)
17. Wu, H., Hu, T., Liu, Y., Zhou, H., Wang, J., Long, M.: Timesnet: temporal 2d-variation modeling for general time series analysis. ArXiv:abs/2210.02186 (2022)

PoseCLR: Bridging 2D and 3D Pose Representations via Contrastive Learning for Action Recognition

Jianlong Lu[1], Weiyu Yu[1]([✉]), Jinquan Chen[2], Dandan Qi[1], and Shuang Gong[1]

[1] South China University of Technology, Guangzhou 510630, China
`yuweiyu@scut.edu.cn`
[2] Guangzhou Liqi Intelligent Technology Co., Ltd., Guangzhou 510630, China

Abstract. Graph Convolutional Network have emerged as a pivotal method in skeleton-based action recognition, demonstrating exceptional performance across multiple benchmarks. However, the inherent measurement errors in skeleton data—particularly the joint position estimation errors caused by occlusion—severely limit the recognition accuracy of existing models. To address this issue, this paper proposes a multimodal contrastive learning framework, PoseCLR, which effectively mitigates the impact of joint errors by leveraging the complementary characteristics of 2D and 3D skeleton data. Specifically, 3D skeleton data provides rich spatial information in three dimensions, while 2D skeleton data preserves more precise two-dimensional joint coordinates. The feature interaction between these two modalities achieves error compensation and information enhancement. Furthermore, this work supplements complete information on joint motion and bone motion, significantly improving the feature representation capability of individual modalities and thereby enhancing the performance of multi-stream score fusion. Experimental results demonstrate that the proposed method achieves breakthrough performance improvements on three mainstream datasets—NTU RGB+D, NTU RGB+D 120, and NW-UCLA—reaching current state-of-the-art methods.

Keywords: Skeleton-based Action Recognition · Contrastive Learning · GCN

1 Introduction

Human action recognition, as a highly valuable research field with extensive application scenarios, spans multiple critical domains including human-computer interaction and video surveillance. In recent years, with the rapid development of depth-sensing technologies, skeleton-based human action recognition techniques [2–7] have emerged as a research hotspot due to their exceptional robustness in complex background environments, garnering widespread attention from both academia and industry.

Existing methods [2, 3, 5, 6] employ Graph Convolutional Network (GCN) to model human skeletal motion sequences. GCN-based approaches suffer from the following limitations: (1) Current skeleton-based action recognition techniques primarily rely on

Z. Lin et al. (Eds.): ICIG 2025, LNCS 16161, pp. 77–88, 2026.
https://doi.org/10.1007/978-981-95-3398-5_7

joint data acquisition systems such as the Microsoft Kinect sensor [14, 15]. This system captures 3D scene information through infrared depth cameras to enable human detection and keypoints localization. In practical applications, when joint occlusion occurs during human motion, depth information in the occluded regions is entirely lost, forcing the system to estimate the positions of occluded joints. Notably, such estimations exhibit significant errors in representing joint depth information, and these systematic measurement biases directly impact the model's action recognition accuracy. (2) In multi-stream fusion frameworks—taking the typical four streams of joints, bones, joint motion, and bone motion as an example—the base joint data and derived bone data demonstrate comparable representation capabilities. However, the recognition accuracy of temporal dynamic features (joint motion and bone motion) is noticeably lower. Analysis reveals that traditional methods [1] inherently lose information when generating dynamic motion features from static joints, preventing the model from fully extracting optimal feature representations across modalities and thereby diminishing the overall performance of multi-stream score fusion.

Inspired by these limitations, this paper proposes the PoseCLR method, which addresses the above issues through contrastive learning between 2D and 3D skeleton data and by supplementing missing modality-transition information. Specifically, 2D skeleton data is obtained using RGB image-based keypoints detection techniques such as HR-Net [27] and YOLOv11 [28], represented as heatmaps indicating the probability distribution of keypoints locations. Although 2D detection also suffers from positional errors due to occlusion, its precision is significantly higher than the 3D joint data predicted by Kinect sensors [26]. By integrating the high-precision positional information of 2D data with the spatial geometric information of 3D data, PoseCLR effectively mitigates the impact of errors in 3D skeletal data. Additionally, by supplementing complete modality information, it resolves the information loss during feature transformation, thereby enhancing single-modality feature extraction and the overall performance of multi-stream fusion.

Extensive experiments on three benchmark datasets—NTU RGB + D, NTU RGB + D 120, and NW-UCLA—demonstrate that PoseCLR significantly achieves mainstream graph convolutional methods in skeleton-based action recognition tasks. The main contributions of this paper are summarized as follows:

- A contrastive learning framework based on 2D and 3D skeletal data is proposed. This method leverages the high precision of 2D skeleton data and the spatial advantages of 3D skeleton data, effectively mitigating the impact of data source errors on recognition performance through their complementary characteristics.
- To address information loss during modality transformation, an improved method of information supplementation is introduced. This approach significantly enhances the representation capability of derived modalities such as joint motion and bone motion, thereby improving the effectiveness of multi-stream score fusion.
- Comprehensive experiments validate the efficacy of the proposed method. Results on multiple standard datasets demonstrate that PoseCLR achieves state-of-the-art skeleton-based action recognition methods.

2 Related Work

2.1 GCN

Skeleton-based action recognition aims to accurately classify sequences of human key-points into specific action categories. Early studies primarily employed Convolutional Neural Network (CNN) [21] and Recurrent Neural Network (RNN) [22] to capture spatiotemporal features of skeleton data. However, due to insufficient modeling of skeletal topology, their recognition performance was notably limited. This limitation was overcome with the introduction of ST-GCN [2], which utilized Graph Neural Network as feature extractors, significantly improving recognition accuracy through manually designed fixed graph structures.

Building upon this foundation, researchers have continuously advanced the capabilities of GCN, proposing methods such as learnable topological graph structures [3], channel-wise decomposition strategies [5], hierarchical graph decomposition [16], multi-modal feature fusion [6], and text-knowledge assistance [17]. Concurrently, Transformer architectures have also been applied to action recognition: SkateFormer [18] enhanced action modeling by integrating spatial-temporal local and global attention mechanisms; MotionBERT [20] learned motion representations through 2D-to-3D pose lifting techniques; and Hyperformer [19] effectively captured high-order kinematic dependencies among joints using hypergraph self-attention mechanisms.

2.2 Contrastive Learning

Contrastive learning improves model performance by pulling the representations of similar samples (positive pairs) closer in the feature space while pushing dissimilar samples (negative pairs) apart [14]. In the field of self-supervised representation learning, SimCLR [24] framework laid the groundwork for subsequent research by employing various data augmentation techniques, such as random cropping, Gaussian blur, and color distortion, to construct positive pairs. For skeleton-based action recognition, researchers have applied contrastive learning during the model pre-training phase. For instance, AimCLR [25] enhanced contrastive learning through extreme data augmentation strategies, while ActCLR [23] utilized the average motion of all action sequences in the dataset as static anchors for contrastive learning.

3 Proposed Method

3.1 Overview of PoseCLR

The proposed PoseCLR network architecture is illustrated in Fig. 1. First, the input skeleton sequences undergo temporal alignment processing, where they are uniformly sampled to T frames to ensure temporal consistency. For each action sample, the data is represented as $X \in R^{C_{in} \times T \times V \times M}$, where V denotes the number of joints, M represents the number of participants, and C_{in} indicates the data dimension of a single joint. Specifically, the 3D skeleton employs $V = 25$ joints ($C_{in} = 3$), while the 2D skeleton uses $V = 17$ joints ($C_{in} = 2$). During training, batch data is reshaped: the input tensor X is transformed from its original shape (N, C, T, V, M) to $(N * M, C, T, V)$. This processing treats each participant as an independent entity, facilitating separate network processing. After reshaping, the data dimension becomes $X \in R^{C_{in} \times T \times V}$.

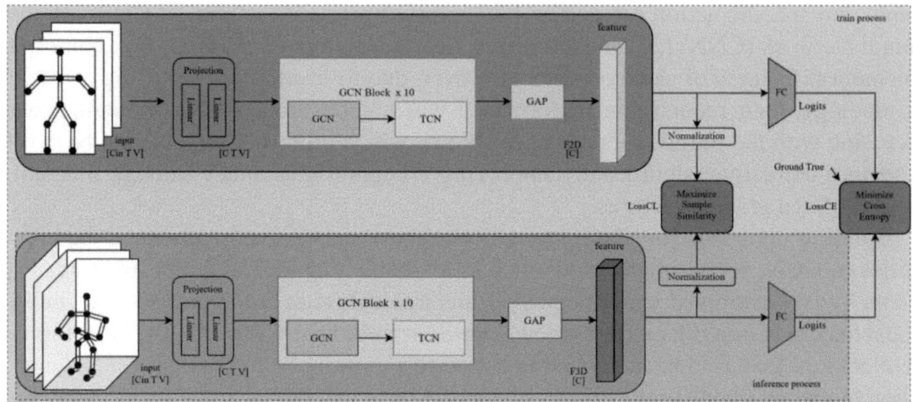

Fig. 1. The overall framework of proposed PoseCLR.

The core processing pipeline of PoseCLR includes:(1) Projecting the skeleton sequence data into a high-dimensional feature space through an initial mapping layer; (2) Performing multi-level feature extraction via 10 GCN Blocks; (3) Applying global average pooling to obtain compact feature representations, yielding feature vectors F_{2D} and F_{3D} for 2D and 3D skeletons, respectively.These feature vectors serve a dual purpose:On one hand, they are used for contrastive learning between samples, calculating feature similarity loss.On the other hand, they serve as inputs to the classification head, computing cross-entropy loss.This dual-objective optimization strategy enables the model to simultaneously learn discriminative features while maintaining inter-modal consistency.

3.2 Sample Contrastive Learning

3D pose data and 2D pose data, as two complementary representations of the same action, collectively form a more comprehensive motion description system. Although these two data types are acquired through different methods, they essentially both characterize human motion patterns and belong to the same pose modality category, exhibiting high semantic consistency. Notably, they can be processed using a unified GCN architecture, requiring only adjustments to the input data dimensions for feature extraction. In the implementation of the contrastive learning method between these two data types, the feature vectors F_{2D} and F_{3D}, obtained after average pooling, undergo L2 normalization to yield $F_{2D-norm}$ and $F_{3D-norm}$. The distance between them is then computed as the contrastive loss $Loss_{CL}$:

$$Loss_{CL} = \frac{1}{N} \sum_{i=0}^{N} \left(F_{2D-norm}^i - F_{3D-norm}^i \right)^2 \tag{1}$$

Here, N represents the batch size, $F_{2D-norm} = \|F_{2D}\|$ and $F_{3D-norm} = \|F_{3D}\|$. This approach establishes a correspondence between 3D and 2D pose features, enabling the model to better learn action representations for samples with occluded joints. Since the contrastive learning loss in this study serves only as an auxiliary loss during the training phase, it does not incur additional computational costs during inference.

3.3 Information Completeness

Existing methods calculate joint motion through simple frame differencing, which captures motion trends but loses critical absolute positional information. This significantly impacts the recognition of actions sensitive to initial positions, such as "two people walking toward each other" and "two people walking away from each other." Similarly, bone motion computation also suffers from inherent limitations: traditional vector differencing methods fail to fully describe composite motion features in three-dimensional space. As illustrated in Fig. 2, the motion of a human arm swing comprises both the rotation angle θ and the displacement x in 3D space, where θ and x represent the angle and displacement in three-dimensional space, respectively.

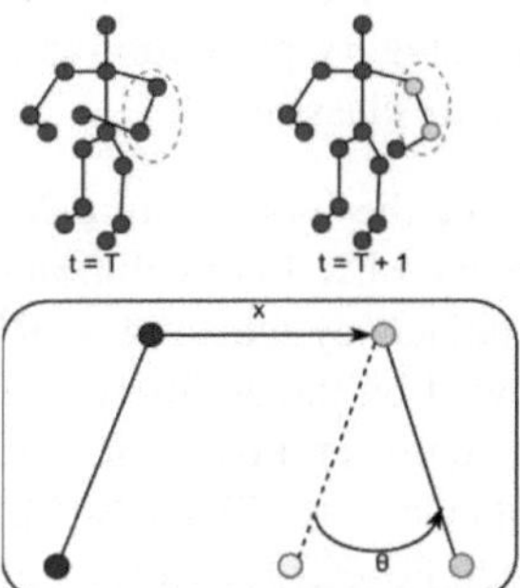

Fig. 2. Arm swing motion from time T to T + 1, where the arm movement incorporates both spatial displacement and rotation of the limb.

This paper proposes a core principle for maintaining information completeness during modality conversion: derived modalities must be fully reversible to their original modalities. Based on this principle, we designed targeted information supplementation schemes:

For the joint-motion modality, the traditional frame differencing approach was enhanced by incorporating initial position information, ensuring the absolute spatial position of actions is preserved.

$$jm = Concat(j_{t=0}, (j_{t=1} - j_{t=0}), (j_{t=2} - j_{t=1}), \ldots, (j_{t=T} - j_{t=T-1})) \tag{2}$$

Here, jm represents the motion sequence of a specific joint, j denotes the joint data, and T indicates the total number of sequence time step.

For the bone-motion modality, more comprehensive improvements are implemented: First, rigid body kinematics is employed to precisely describe bone motion; second, spherical coordinates are adopted to represent bones. Each bone in every frame of bone-motion is represented by a 6-tuple, specifically implemented as:

$$bm_t = (r, \theta, \varphi, \psi, \delta, \phi \tag{3}$$

Here, bm represents the motion of a specific bone at time t,(r, θ, φ) form the spherical coordinate system, describing the radial distance r, polar angle θ, and azimuthal angle φ of the bone. (ψ, δ, ϕ) constitute Euler angles, representing the rotational components about the z, y, and x axes, respectively. The use of spherical coordinates offers dual advantages: it completely preserves the original positional information of bones, and the geometric properties of spherical coordinates better align with the characterization of rotational motion.

3.4 GCN Block

The designed GCN Block consists of two core components: GCN and TCN, which are responsible for modeling joint relationships in the spatial dimension and extracting motion patterns in the temporal dimension, respectively. The entire network architecture comprises 10 isomorphic basic modules, each maintaining a consistent dimensionality of 256 channels. Finally, action category prediction is accomplished through a global average pooling layer and a softmax classifier.

GCN. As illustrated in Fig. 3, for the input feature $\mathbf{X} \in \mathbf{R}^{C_{in}^{\times}T\times V}$, the network first performs feature transformation via a 1×1 convolutional layer. It then conducts matrix multiplication with a learnable adjacency matrix $A \in R^{V\times V\times C}$ to achieve information aggregation among joints, followed by the addition of a residual connection to output the feature. The key distinctions between PoseCLR and existing approaches lie in the design of the adjacency matrix:(1) Unlike CTR-GCN [5], which requires an independent adjacency matrix for each channel, PoseCLR employs an adjacency matrix reuse mechanism. Specifically, the dimension G is repeated n times to match the channel count C, thereby reducing the number of adjacency matrices that need to be learned. This design is based on an important observation: appropriately limiting the number of adjacency matrices helps the model learn topological structures that accurately describe joint relationships more efficiently. (2) Compared to 2s-AGCN [3], which uses only three layers of learnable adjacency matrices, PoseCLR is capable of learning richer joint relationships.

TCN. As shown in Fig. 4, the multi-scale temporal convolution module proposed in this paper is optimized and improved based on the architecture of [29]. The key distinction lies in the addition of an extra branch for feature extraction at a broader temporal scale. The module first preprocesses the input features using a 1×1 convolutional layer, then evenly splits the channel dimension into five sub-branches. The first four branches incorporate temporal convolution layers with varying dilation rates and max-pooling layers, while the fifth branch preserves the original features to maintain information integrity. The outputs of all branches are fused through channel concatenation, and the final result is combined with a residual connection before being output.

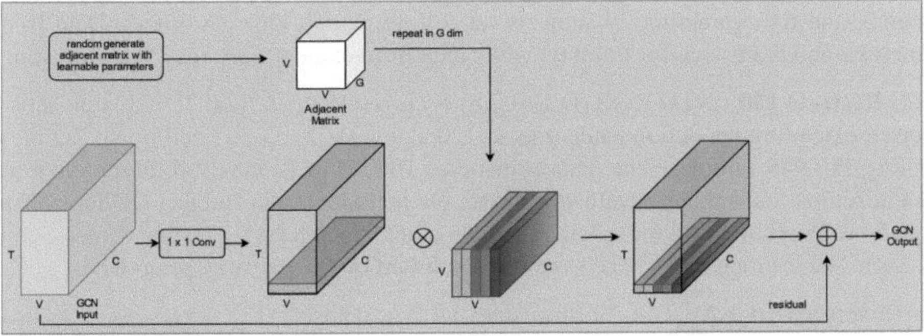

Fig. 3. The architecture of GCN.

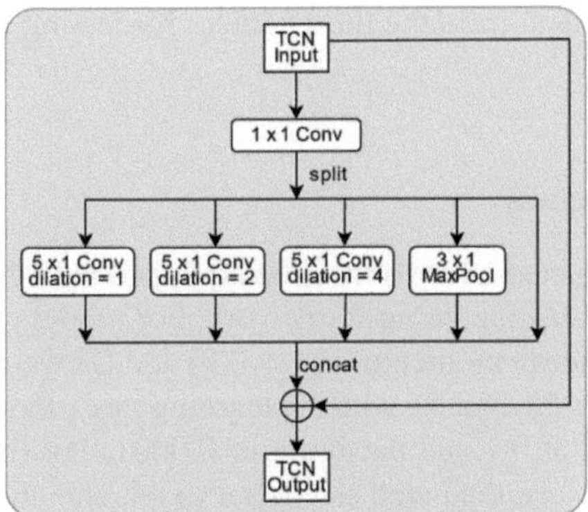

Fig. 4. The architecture of TCN.

4 Experiment

4.1 Dataset

This paper conducts experimental validation on three representative skeleton-based action recognition datasets: NTU RGB+D, NTU RGB+D 120, and Northwestern-UCLA. During data preprocessing, the 2D skeleton data for NTU RGB+D and NTU RGB+D 120 datasets are obtained using the pose extractor HR-Net [27] as provided in [30]. For the NW-UCLA dataset, YOLOv11 [28] is employed for pose extraction by applying the pose estimator to the original RGB images. The final experimental results are evaluated using Top-1 accuracy as the metric.

NTU RGB+D. As a key benchmark in skeleton-based action recognition, the NTU RGB+D dataset [14] contains 56,880 3D skeleton action sequences covering 60 classes of daily activities. The dataset was collected from 40 subjects performing actions under three Kinect v2 cameras with varying viewpoints, with each sample involving up to two interacting individuals. Following the original protocol [14], this paper adopts two standard evaluation settings: Cross-Subject (X-Sub): Data from 20 subjects are used for training, and the remaining 20 subjects for testing. Cross-View (X-View): Data from cameras 2 and 3 are used for training, while data from camera 1 are reserved for testing.

NTU RGB+D 120. NTU RGB+D 120 [15] is currently the largest 3D skeleton action dataset, extending the action categories to 120 classes with 57,367 additional samples, totaling 113,945 samples. The dataset involves 106 subjects and 32 different environmental setups. Its standard evaluation protocols include: Cross-Subject (X-Sub): Data from 53 subjects are used for training, and the other 53 subjects for testing. Cross-Setup (X-Set): The training and test sets are divided based on the parity of setup IDs.

Northwestern-UCLA. The Northwestern-UCLA dataset [13] serves as a critical benchmark for multi-view action recognition, comprising 1,494 video samples across 10 classes of daily activities, with each action performed by 10 different subjects. This paper strictly adheres to the evaluation protocol in [13], using data from the first two cameras for training and data from the third camera for testing, ensuring comparability of experimental results.

4.2 Implementation Details

All experiments are conducted on a workstation equipped with dual NVIDIA RTX 3080 GPUs using the PyTorch deep learning framework. For model optimization, we use the SGD optimizer with Nesterov momentum ($\beta = 0.9$) and L2 weight decay ($\lambda = 0.0004$). The training process spans 55 epochs, with the learning rate following a cosine annealing schedule [12], initialized at 0.1 and decaying to 0.0001. For the NTU RGB + D and NTU RGB + D 120 datasets, the batch size is set to 64, and all skeleton sequences are uniformly adjusted to 96 frames using the preprocessing method from [11]. In contrast, for the Northwestern-UCLA dataset, a smaller batch size of 16 is adopted, following the preprocessing pipeline in [4].

4.3 Ablation Study

This section experimentally validates the effectiveness of the proposed PoseCLR model on the NTU-RGB + D 120 dataset, with a focus on evaluating its action recognition accuracy under the cross-subject (X-Sub) and cross-setup (X-Set) benchmarks.

Validation of Information Completeness Necessity. To investigate the impact of information completeness on model performance, this study compares the baseline joint-motion and bone-motion computation methods from MS-AGCN [1] with the information-completeness-enhanced approach described in Sect. 3.3, using the model architecture outlined in Sect. 3.4. As shown in Table 1, the experimental results demonstrate that enhancing information completeness significantly improves model performance, confirming its necessity for action recognition tasks.

For the joint-motion modality, the first-frame position information of the skeleton sequence is concatenated with joint-motion features. Experiments show that this method markedly enhances motion recognition accuracy. For the bone-motion modality, a rigid-body-motion-based representation is adopted to characterize bone movements.

The optimized bone-motion single modality achieves performance improvements of 5.1% and 5.4% on the two benchmarks, respectively, significantly outperforming traditional joint and bone modalities and validating the effectiveness of the proposed method. Furthermore, this study examines the performance of four-stream score fusion. By supplementing information completeness for joint-motion and bone-motion modalities, the four-stream fusion yields a stable 0.3% improvement on both benchmarks.

Table 1. Accuracy Comparison (%) Before and After Information Completeness Enhancement on the NTU-RGB + D 120 Dataset.

Modality	Method	X-Sub	X-Set
jm	Baseline (w/o start position)	80.6	82.5
	+Start position concatenation	**83.0 (+2.4)**	**84.0 (+1.5)**
bm	Baseline (traditional description)	80.2	81.6
	Rigid-body motion representation	**85.3 (+5.1)**	**87.0 (+5.4)**
4-stream	Baseline (w/o info completeness)	89.3	90.6
	+Information completion	**89.6 (+0.3)**	**90.9 (+0.3)**

Table 2. Accuracy Comparison (%) Before and After Contrastive Learning on NTU-RGB+D 120 Dataset.

Modality	Method	X-Sub	X-Set
j	Baseline (w/o $Loss_{CL}$)	84.5	85.1
	+$Loss_{CL}$	**84.9(+0.4)**	**87.4(+2.3)**
4-stream	Baseline (w/o $Loss_{CL}$)	89.6	90.9
	+$Loss_{CL}$	**89.7(+0.1)**	**91.0(+0.1)**

Validation of Contrastive Learning Effectiveness. To verify the efficacy of the contrastive learning approach, this study conducts ablation experiments by introducing a 2D pose contrastive learning mechanism, using 3D pose skeleton sequences as the baseline. Experimental results based on the model architecture in Sect. 3.4 show that the proposed method significantly enhances single-modality model performance on the NTU-RGB+D 120 dataset, with accuracy improvements of 0.4% (X-Sub) and 2.3% (X-Set), respectively. The four-stream fusion also achieves a stable 0.1% gain. This improvement confirms that 2D pose information effectively compensates for 3D pose estimation errors, particularly in challenging scenarios such as occlusion, where 2D poses provide critical supplementary information for joint position inference. Notably, the additional computational cost is incurred only during training, while inference efficiency remains unchanged, ensuring practical applicability (Table 2).

4.4 Comparison with State-of-the-Arts Methods

Following the framework design in reference [1], this study integrates prediction scores from four modalities: joint, bone, joint motion, and bone motion. The experimental results, as shown in Table 3, demonstrate that PoseCLR achieves the performance of current state-of-the-art approaches across mainstream benchmarks.

Table 3. Comparisons of the top-1 accuracy (%) against state-of-the-art methods on the NTU-RGB+D 60, 120 and Northwestern UCLA datasets. The yellow and green cells respectively indicate the highest and second-highest value.

Methods	Publication	NTU-RGB+D 60		NTU-RGB+D 120		Northwestern UCLA
		X-Sub	X-View	X-Sub	X-Set	
ST-GCN [2]	AAAI 2018	81.5	88.3	70.7	73.2	-
2s-AGCN [3]	CVPR 2019	88.5	95.1	82.5	84.2	-
Shift-GCN [4]	CVPR 2020	90.7	96.5	85.9	87.6	94.6
CTR-GCN [5]	ICCV 2021	92.4	96.8	88.9	90.6	96.5
EfficientGCN [6]	TPAMI 2022	91.7	95.7	88.3	89.1	-
InfoGCN [7]	CVPR 2022	92.7	96.9	89.4	90.7	96.6
FR Head [8]	CVPR 2023	92.8	96.8	89.5	90.9	96.8
TD-GCN [9]	TMM 2024	92.8	96.8	-	-	97.4
MCMT-Net [10]	TCSVT 2024	92.8	96.8	89.3	91.0	97.2
PoseCLR		**93.0**	**96.7**	**89.7**	**91.0**	**97.3**

5 Conclusion

This study proposes a novel PoseCLR framework for skeleton-based action recognition. The framework enhances model robustness through a 2D pose contrastive learning mechanism and improves multimodal representation capability via a modality information completeness enhancement strategy. Experimental results demonstrate that PoseCLR achieves the performance of current state-of-the-art methods on three benchmark datasets.

References

1. Shi, L., Zhang, Y., Cheng, J., Lu, H.: Skeleton-based action recognition with multi-stream adaptive graph convolutional networks. IEEE Trans. Image Process. **29**, 9532–9545 (2020)

2. Yan, S., Xiong, Y., Lin, D.: Spatial temporal graph convolutional networks for skeleton-based action recognition. In: Proceedings of the AAAI Conference on Artificial Intelligence, vol. 32, no. 1 (2018)

3. Shi, L., Zhang, Y., Cheng, J., Lu, H.: Two-stream adaptive graph convolutional networks for skeleton-based action recognition. In: Proceedings of the IEEE/CVF Conference on Computer Vision and Pattern Recognition, pp. 12026–12035 (2019)

4. Cheng, K., Zhang, Y., He, X., Chen, W., Cheng, J., Lu, H.: Skeleton-based action recognition with shift graph convolutional network. In: Proceedings of the IEEE/CVF Conference on Computer Vision and Pattern Recognition, pp. 183–192 (2020)

5. Chen, Y., Zhang, Z., Yuan, C., Li, B., Deng, Y., Hu, W.: Channel-wise topology refinement graph convolution for skeleton-based action recognition. In: Proceedings of the IEEE/CVF International Conference on Computer Vision, pp. 13359–13368 (2021)

6. Song, Y.F., Zhang, Z., Shan, C., Wang, L.: Constructing stronger and faster baselines for skeleton-based action recognition. IEEE Trans. Pattern Anal. Mach. Intell. **45**(2), 1474–1488 (2022)

7. Chi, H., Ha, M.H., Chi, S., et al.: InfoGCN: representation learning for human skeleton-based action recognition. In: Proceedings of the IEEE/CVF Conference on Computer Vision and Pattern Recognition. 2022: 20186–20196

8. Zhou, H., Liu, Q., Wang, Y.: Learning discriminative representations for skeleton based action recognition. In: Proceedings of the IEEE/CVF Conference on Computer Vision and Pattern Recognition, pp. 10608–10617 (2023)

9. Liu, J., Wang, X., Wang, C., Gao, Y., Liu, M.: Temporal decoupling graph convolutional network for skeleton-based gesture recognition. IEEE Trans. Multimedia **26**, 811–823 (2023)

10. Wu, C., Wu, X.J., Xu, T., Shen, Z., Kittler, J.: Motion complement and temporal multifocusing for skeleton-based action recognition. IEEE Trans. Circuits Syst. Video Technol. **34**(1), 34–45 (2023)

11. Ye, F., Pu, S., Zhong, Q., Li, C., Xie, D., Tang, H.: Dynamic GCN: context-enriched topology learning for skeleton-based action recognition. In: Proceedings of the 28th ACM International Conference on Multimedia, pp. 55–63 (2020)

12. Loshchilov, I., Hutter, F.: SGDR: stochastic gradient descent with warm restarts. arXiv preprint arXiv:1608.03983 (2016)

13. Wang, J., Nie, X., Xia, Y., Wu, Y., Zhu, S.C.: Cross-view action modeling, learning and recognition. In: Proceedings of the IEEE Conference on Computer Vision and Pattern Recognition, pp. 2649–2656 (2014)

14. Shahroudy, A., Liu, J., Ng, T.T., Wang, G.: NTU RGB+ D: a large scale dataset for 3d human activity analysis. In: Proceedings of the IEEE Conference on Computer Vision and Pattern Recognition, pp. 1010–1019 (2016)

15. Liu, J., Shahroudy, A., Perez, M., Wang, G., Duan, L.Y., Kot, A.C.: Ntu rgb+ d 120: a large-scale benchmark for 3d human activity understanding. IEEE Trans. Pattern Anal. Mach. Intell. **42**(10), 2684–2701 (2019)

16. Lee, J., Lee, M., Lee, D., Lee, S.: Hierarchically decomposed graph convolutional networks for skeleton-based action recognition. In: Proceedings of the IEEE/CVF International Conference on Computer Vision, pp. 10444–10453 (2023)

17. Xu, H., Gao, Y., Hui, Z., Li, J., Gao, X.: Language knowledge-assisted representation learning for skeleton-based action recognition. arXiv. 2023. arXiv:2305.12398

18. Do, J., Kim, M.: Skateformer: skeletal-temporal transformer for human action recognition. In European Conference on Computer Vision, pp. 401–420. Cham: Springer, Cham (2024)

19. Zhou, Y., et al.: Hypergraph transformer for skeleton-based action recognition. arXiv preprint arXiv:2211.09590 (2022)

20. Zhu, W., Ma, X., Liu, Z., Liu, L., Wu, W., Wang, Y.: MotionBert: a unified perspective on learning human motion representations. In: Proceedings of the IEEE/CVF International Conference on Computer Vision, pp. 15085–15099 (2023)
21. Ding, Z., Wang, P., Ogunbona, P.O., Li, W.: Investigation of different skeleton features for cnn-based 3d action recognition. In: 2017 IEEE International Conference on Multimedia & Expo Workshops (ICMEW), pp. 617–622. IEEE (2017)
22. Zhu, W., et al.: Co-occurrence feature learning for skeleton based action recognition using regularized deep LSTM networks. In: Proceedings of the AAAI Conference on Artificial Intelligence, vol. 30, no. 1 (2016)
23. Lin, L., Zhang, J., Liu, J.: Actionlet-dependent contrastive learning for unsupervised skeleton-based action recognition. In: Proceedings of the IEEE/CVF Conference on Computer Vision and Pattern Recognition, pp. 2363–2372 (2023)
24. Chen, T., Kornblith, S., Norouzi, M., Hinton, G.: A simple framework for contrastive learning of visual representations. In: International Conference on Machine Learning, pp. 1597–1607. PmLR (2020)
25. Guo, T., Liu, H., Chen, Z., Liu, M., Wang, T., Ding, R.: Contrastive learning from extremely augmented skeleton sequences for self-supervised action recognition. In: Proceedings of the AAAI Conference on Artificial Intelligence, vol. 36, No. 1, pp. 762–770 (2022)
26. Duan, H., Zhao, Y., Chen, K., Lin, D., Dai, B.: Revisiting skeleton-based action recognition. In: Proceedings of the IEEE/CVF Conference on Computer Vision and Pattern Recognition, pp. 2969–2978 (2022)
27. Sun, K., et al.: High-resolution representations for labeling pixels and regions. arXiv preprint arXiv:1904.04514 (2019)
28. Khanam, R., Hussain, M.: Yolov11: an overview of the key architectural enhancements. arXiv preprint arXiv:2410.17725 (2024)
29. Liu, Z., Zhang, H., Chen, Z., Wang, Z., Ouyang, W.: Disentangling and unifying graph convolutions for skeleton-based action recognition. In: Proceedings of the IEEE/CVF Conference on Computer Vision and Pattern Recognition, pp. 143–152 {2020)
30. Duan, H., Wang, J., Chen, K., Lin, D.: PYSKL: TGood practices for skeleton action recognition. In: Proceedings of the 30th ACM International Conference on Multimedia, pp. 7351–7354 (2022)

Art3D-Fusion: A Hybrid Framework for Visual Synthesis with Artistic Control

Kohou Wang[1,4], Ping Chen[1,4], Zhaoxiang Liu[1,4,5(✉)], Xiang Liu[1,4],
Zezhou Chen[1,4], Huan Hu[1,4], Xin Wang[2,3], Kai Wang[1,4],
and Shiguo Lian[1,4(✉)]

[1] Data Science and Artificial Intelligence Research Institute, China Unicom,
Beijing, China
{wangzp103,chenp181,liuzx178,liux750,chenzz51,huh30,
wangk115,liansg}@chinaunicom.cn
[2] Guangdong Provincial Key Laboratory of Intelligent Information Processing and
Shenzhen Key Laboratory of Media Security, Shenzhen University, Shenzhen, China
[3] China United Network Communications Group Corporation Limited,
Beijing, China
[4] Unicom Data Intelligence, China Unicom, Beijing, China
[5] Beijing Key Laboratory of Science Fiction Audio and Video Intelligent Processing,
Beijing, China

Abstract. Traditional visual synthesis methods suffer from blurring, ghosting, and significant artistic deprivation due to their sole reliance on physical disparity reconstruction. These methods fail to capture the artistic elements that directors carefully design in classic 3D films. To address these issues, we propose Art3D-Fusion, a hybrid framework combining geometric processing with advanced diffusion models. This framework integrates physical depth information with global artistic control, particularly in 0-plane selection. Through depth estimation and optical flow-based disparity matching, we create a pseudo-realistic disparity map that reflects the director's artistic adjustments. This approach enables precise depth-to-disparity transformation and ensures natural detail restoration and effective occlusion handling. Art3D-Fusion generates high-quality right-view images by driving a diffusion model under an enhanced ControlNet architecture using the artistic disparity map and original left-view image as dual-conditional inputs. This approach accurately represents the director's artistic vision and allows for the transfer of artistic styles from classic 3D films to new scenes, ensuring the consistent reproduction of different directors' artistic styles through the estimation and transfer of camera parameters.

K. Wang and P. Chen—Equal contribution.

This work was supported in part by the Guangdong Provincial Key Laboratory (Grant 2023B1212060076).

1   Introduction

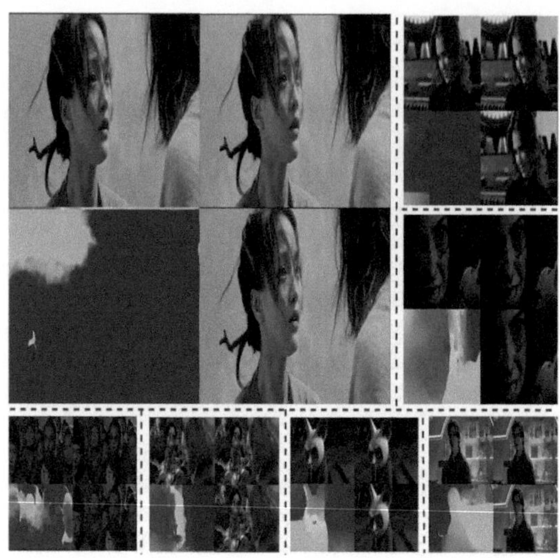

Fig. 1. Generated right-view images using our **Art3D-Fusion**. Each set shows (from top left to bottom right): left view, ground truth right view, disparity map, and our generated right view. The results demonstrate high image quality and spatial reasoning across a wide range of scene depths, highlighting the true conditional adaptability of our approach. The generated right view adapts to varying depths, with corresponding disparity to the left view when depth is rich in the disparity map, and vice versa. We further share a curated dataset of 140,000 triplets, each containing a left-view image, a disparity map, and the corresponding right-view ground truth.

In recent years, the rapid development of immersive experiences such as Augmented Reality (AR) and Virtual Reality (VR) has propelled 2D-to-3D conversion technology to become a focal research area in the digital imaging field. However, traditional approaches, which mainly rely on depth estimation [2,11] and depth-image-based rendering (DIBR) [2], have several significant limitations. These methods often suffer from blurring and ghosting during occlusion handling, detail recovery, and viewpoint transformation, leading to suboptimal results. More importantly, they focus solely on physical disparity reconstruction without incorporating artistic control [16]. This lack of artistic expression is further exacerbated when these methods are trained with non-artistic data, resulting in "artistic deprivation" and the inability to capture and incorporate artistic elements (Fig. 1).

In classic 3D films, directors typically do not use horizontal filming with traditional binocular shooting setups like stereo camera rigs [7]. Instead, they employ more complex filming techniques and meticulously adjust the 0-plane in post-production to craft unique spatial layers and visual impact [12]. This

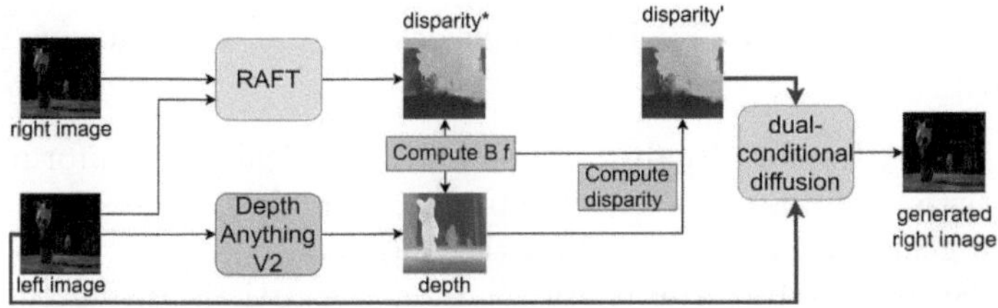

Fig. 2. The training pipeline of our **Art3D-Fusion**. We first use a depth estimator to extract depth maps from left-view images. Then, RAFT is applied to estimate disparities between the left and right views in a right-to-left manner. Using the least squares method [15], we determine baseline (b) and focal length (f), transforming the physical depth maps into disparity maps reflecting global artistic design. Then we drive the diffusion model under the enhanced dual-conditional ControlNet architecture to generate the right-view image.

process endows the image with distinct beauty and enhances the audience's immersive experience. However, existing automated 2D-to-3D methods struggle to replicate this director-level artistic expression, often generating right-view images that lack cinematic visual appeal.

Additionally, traditional methods [2,23] often face coordinate system misalignment issues due to relying solely on the left-view for generation, making it difficult to capture real-world spatial constraints.

To address these limitations, we introduce **Art3D-Fusion**, an innovative hybrid framework that combines traditional geometric processing with advanced diffusion models. This framework enables the fusion of physical depth information with global artistic control, particularly in 0-plane selection.

In the training phase of **Art3D-Fusion**, we first use a state-of-the-art depth estimator (e.g., Depth Anything v2 [24]) to extract depth maps from left-view images. Then, RAFT [22] is applied to estimate disparities between the left and right views in a right-to-left manner. This generates a pseudo-realistic disparity map that aligns with the global artistic adjustments of the director and ensures consistency with the coordinate system of the network's monocular input (left image). Using the least squares method [15], we determine the optimal scaling and translation relationships between the inverse depth map and the artistic disparity map. This process is closely tied to camera parameters, namely baseline (b) and focal length (f), allowing for the precise transformation of physical depth maps into disparity maps that perfectly reflect global artistic design, particularly the 0-plane selection.

Using this artistic depth-to-disparity map and the original left-view image as dual-conditional inputs, we drive the diffusion model under the enhanced ControlNet [26] architecture to generate the right-view image. This approach not only ensures natural detail restoration and occlusion handling but also perfectly showcases the director's carefully designed global artistic effects. Additionally, it solves the coordinate system misalignment issue by constructing an artistic left disparity map that conforms to the real-world physical space. The framework is shown in Fig. 2.

In summary, the **Art3D-Fusion** framework achieves the following significant contributions:

- **Artistic and Physical Fusion**: It combines physical depth information with global artistic control, particularly in 0-plane selection, to generate 3D images with both geometric accuracy and artistic appeal.
- **Precise Spatial Alignment**: By aligning the artistic disparity map with the real-world physical space, it avoids coordinate misalignment and handles occlusions effectively during the generation of the right-view image.
- **Adaptive Artistic Style Transfer**: It allows for the transfer of artistic styles from classic 3D films to new scenes, ensuring the consistent reproduction of different directors' artistic styles through the estimation and transfer of camera parameters.

2   Related Work

The field of stereo synthesis has seen significant advancements in recent years, driven by the growing demand for immersive media experiences in applications such as virtual reality (VR) and augmented reality (AR). Traditional methods in view synthesis generally rely on depth or disparity estimation, followed by the generation of a new viewpoint based on this information [28]. More recently, the rise of generative models, particularly diffusion models, has further pushed the boundaries of what can be achieved in view synthesis [17]. Here, we review relevant literature in depth estimation, disparity-based view synthesis, and diffusion-based generative models.

2.1   Depth Image-Based View Synthesis

Depth estimation has traditionally been approached as an image-to-image translation problem, where a depth map is predicted from a single input image [14,15,25]. Once the depth is estimated, traditional synthesis methods often apply pixel-level warping or stereoscopic generation to create the desired right-view image. Gautier et al. [6] propose an approach utilizing a single reference view and a set of depth maps, which not only deals with small disocclusion filling related to small camera baseline, but also manages to fill in larger disocclusions in distant synthesized views. Solh et al. [21], using a lower resolution estimates of the 3D wrapped image in a pyramid-like structure, introduce a new hole-filling approach for DIBR, which requires no preprocessing of the depth map. Gao et al. [5] implement an improved gaussian mixture model and foreground depth correlation to get more stable backgrounds, which are used for hole filling. They also adopt an adaptive hole-filling method to adaptively fill the holes in virtual views.

2.2   Diffusion Models in Image Generation

In recent years, diffusion models [1,8,17] have witnessed substantial progress in the image generation field, with numerous acceleration strategies emerging.

These models have recently gained traction for high-quality image synthesis. They generate images by iteratively denoising random noise, learning a generative process that can be conditioned on various inputs. Building on this, latent diffusion models (LDMs) [17] introduces efficiency improvements by performing diffusion steps in a compressed latent space. This approach significantly reduces the computational cost while maintaining high fidelity in the generated images. Palette [18] demonstrates the potential of diffusion models for image-to-image translation tasks, achieving impressive results in colorization and super-resolution tasks.

More recent developments in diffusion models, including Conditional Diffusion and Latent Diffusion, have expanded their utility by incorporating additional conditional inputs like text or images. The idea of conditioning diffusion models on multiple data sources has been explored to enhance model performance in tasks such as image inpainting and style transfer. For example, Rombach et al. [17] demonstrates that LDMs could condition the generative process on text or image information to yield contextually rich outputs, capturing fine details and structural coherence. Inspired by these works, our approach conditions the model on both left-view images and disparity maps, providing the diffusion model with explicit depth information to guide the generation of the right-view image. This dual conditioning offers distinct advantages in stereo image synthesis, where precise alignment and occlusion handling are paramount.

Several recent works have attempted to adapt diffusion models for depth-related tasks. For instance, DepthGen [19] extends diffusion models to depth estimation, addressing problems arising due to noisy, incomplete depth maps in training data and enabling applications like text-to-3D scene generation. Similarly, VPD [27] explores using a pretrained diffusion model as an image feature extractor for monocular depth estimation. These methods showcase the ability of diffusion models to capture fine-grained details and generalize across diverse domains, making them particularly well-suited for complex tasks like view synthesis in 3D video.

2.3   Artistic Single-View-to-Stereo Conversion

Previous methods have focused on the physical aspects rather than the artistic elements. However, the artistic aspect is the most important factor in 3D movies. Currently, artistic creation mainly relies on manual work. Although there are conversion tools such as Owl3D [13], they still require human interaction and cannot achieve full automation. Moreover, transferring the artistic intentions of directors from known 3D movies to other 2D films remains a challenge. This paper will detail how to achieve artistic 2D-to-3D stereoscopic image synthesis.

3   Method

Figure 3 illustrates the overall framework, where ControlNet extracts structured features from each input, which are then combined and passed to the Flux model

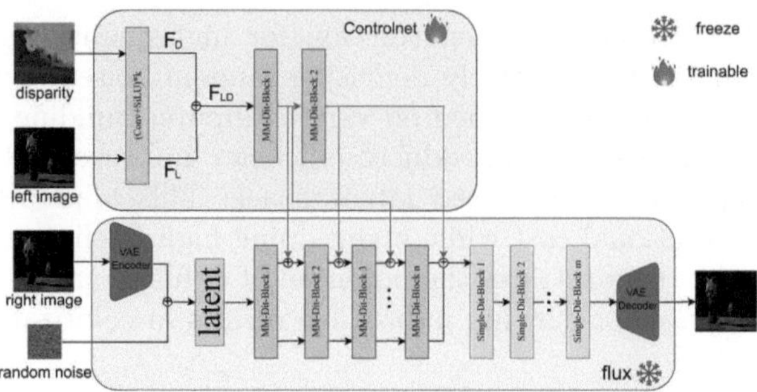

Fig. 3. The training architecture of our proposed dual-conditional diffusion. The model uses left-view and disparity map inputs, processed through ControlNet layers, and then passed to the flux model to guide the generation of accurate right-view images with enhanced structural and depth fidelity.

for generating a coherent right-view image. To maintain the quality and consistency of learned representations, we selectively fine-tune only the parameters within ControlNet, leveraging the pre-trained knowledge embedded within Flux's diffusion layers.

3.1 Input Preparation

To construct the input for our model, we begin by leveraging Depth Anything v2 to estimate depth maps from left-view images. This state-of-the-art depth estimator provides a dense and reliable depth representation, which serves as the foundation for our subsequent processing. Next, we employ the RAFT optical flow estimation scheme to compute disparities between the left and right views. This method aligns the left and right views and generates a pseudo ground truth disparity map that incorporates artistic adjustments. By introducing a least squares transformation between inverse depth and disparity, we link these parameters to camera parameters b (baseline) and f (focal length), effectively adjusting the global zero-disparity plane. Least squares is a statistical method for estimating unknown parameters by minimizing the sum of the squares of residuals:

$$\hat{\beta} = (X^T X)^{-1} X^T y \tag{1}$$

where $\hat{\beta}$ is the vector of estimated parameters, X is the design matrix, y is the vector of observed values. This transformation not only captures the artistic intent but also ensures consistency with the coordinate system of the network's monocular input (left image). The resulting disparity map, enriched with artistic modifications, is then combined with the left-view image to form the dual conditional inputs for our diffusion-based framework.

3.2   Art3D-Fusion Model Design

The core of our architecture lies in the dual-conditional diffusion model, which drives the generation of the right-view image. This model takes the artistic disparity map and the original left-view image as inputs, ensuring that both geometric accuracy and artistic appeal are maintained throughout the generation process. This dual conditioning setup allows our model to produce right-view images that are not only structurally sound but also visually coherent with the artistic vision of the director.

For each input–left-view image and disparity map–ControlNet applies a sequence of convolutional layers with SiLU (Sigmoid Linear Unit) [3] activations, denoted as `conv+SiLU`, to independently extract low-level features. Let F_L represent the feature map extracted from the left-view image and F_D the feature map from the disparity map. These features are computed as follows:

$$F_L = \text{conv+SiLU}(I_L), \quad F_D = \text{conv+SiLU}(D), \tag{2}$$

where I_L is the left-view image and D is the disparity map.

After extracting these features, ControlNet combines the left-view and disparity features through element-wise addition. This combined feature map is then passed through two replicated MM-Dit-Block layers, which are taken from the Flux model's original architecture. These blocks allow ControlNet to integrate the combined features into higher-level representations while preserving pre-trained weights from the Flux model.

To align these features with the corresponding layers in the Flux model, we employ an alternating layer integration strategy within the MM-Dit-Blocks. Specifically, features from the first MM-Dit-Block layer in ControlNet are added to the embeddings from the even-numbered MM-Dit-Block layers of the Flux model, and similarly, features from the second MM-Dit-Block layer in ControlNet are added to the embeddings from the odd-numbered MM-Dit-Block layers of the Flux model. Let $F_{Flux}^{(k)}$ denote the image embedding output from the k-th MM-Dit-Block in the Flux model, and $F_{Control}^{(0)}$ and $F_{Control}^{(1)}$ the output from the first and second MM-Dit-Block layer in ControlNet. The integrated feature for each layer is computed as:

$$F^{(k)} = \begin{cases} F_{Flux}^{(1)} + F_{Control}^{(k)} & \text{if } k \text{ is odd,} \\ F_{Flux}^{(0)} + F_{Control}^{(k)} & \text{if } k \text{ is even.} \end{cases}$$

This alternating integration scheme ensures that each level of features in the synthesized image captures depth cues from the disparity map and structural information from the left view. Through this detailed feature alignment, ControlNet conditions the diffusion process more effectively, overcomes limitations in traditional 3D view synthesis by incorporating artistic control through disparity maps. This alleviates artistic deprivation, ensuring generated right-view images are both geometrically accurate and artistically enhanced.

4   Experiments

4.1   Dataset Preparation

The experiments are conducted on a curated dataset of 140,000 triplets, each containing a left-view image, a disparity map, and the corresponding right-view ground truth. The training dataset was constructed by extracting left-view and right-view image pairs from a collection of 3D movies. Specifically, we downloaded multiple publicly available 3D movies, selecting diverse scenes from each to capture a variety of spatial configurations, occlusions, and depth profiles. For each selected video clip, frames were sampled, and for each frame pair, we obtained:

- **Left-view image** (L): The reference image for generating the corresponding right-view.
- **Right-view image** (R): The ground truth image used for training and evaluation.
- **Disparity map** (D): Estimated using the RAFT model, which provides the disparity between the left-view and right-view images.

The RAFT model was applied to each left-right pair to obtain the disparity map, creating a triplet (L, D, R) for each sampled frame. This approach allowed us to generate a dataset with complex and varied depth characteristics. The final dataset includes 140,000 such triplets, ensuring a robust representation of different scene structures and depths.

4.2   Training Protocol

Our model is trained on a custom dataset of 140,000 triplets of left-view images, disparity maps, and right-view ground truth images. These data samples are extracted from various 3D movies, ensuring diverse content and challenging scenarios. Each movie provides several video clips, from which left-view and right-view frames are selected. Disparity maps are generated using the RAFT model [22], which estimates disparities between the left and right views.

Table 1. Quantitative evaluation of our model's performance on the test dataset. The symbol ↑ means that a higher value is better, while ↓ indicates that a lower value is preferable.

Metric	SSIM ↑	PSNR ↑	FID ↓
Score	0.76 ± 0.12	33.04 ± 2.31	7.16

The specific steps in the training process are as follows:

- Initialize ControlNet by copying the weights from the first two MM-Dit-Block layers of the Flux model, ensuring consistent and aligned feature extraction.

- Feed the left-view image L and disparity map D into ControlNet, applying multiple convolutional layers with SiLU activation to obtain independent feature maps F_L and F_D.
- Combine F_L and F_D by element-wise addition to form a unified feature representation F_{LD}, which is then passed through the two copied MM-Dit-Block layers in ControlNet to produce refined features.
- Integrate F_{LD} into the Flux model by adding the outputs of ControlNet's odd and even MM-Dit-Block layers to the corresponding odd and even MM-Dit-Block layers in the Flux model. Use these enriched embeddings to generate the right-view image prediction $\hat{R}$.
- Compute the loss between the predicted right-view image $\hat{R}$ and the ground truth R.
- Update only the parameters of ControlNet during backpropagation, keeping the rest of the Flux model unchanged to preserve its pre-trained knowledge.

4.3   Evaluation Metrics

To assess the performance of our method, we utilized the following metrics:

- **PSNR (Peak Signal-to-Noise Ratio)** [9]: Measures the fidelity of generated images with respect to the ground truth, capturing pixel-level similarity.
- **SSIM (Structural Similarity Index)** [20]: Evaluates the perceptual similarity between generated and ground truth images, taking into account luminance, contrast, and structure.
- **Fréchet Inception Distance (FID)** [10]: FID evaluates the distributional similarity between the generated images and the ground truth set, focusing on high-level perceptual features. Lower FID values reflect better alignment with the target distribution, indicating more realistic and high-quality synthesis.

These metrics provide a comprehensive evaluation, covering both pixel-level accuracy and perceptual fidelity.

4.4   Quantitative Results

Table 1 presents the quantitative results of our model across the entire test set of more than 5000 left-view and disparity map pairs, which are randomly sampled. The high SSIM and PSNR values demonstrate the model's effectiveness in capturing fine structural details and reducing artifacts, while the low FID score confirms that the synthesized right-view images closely resemble the distribution of ground-truth images. Besides, it's worth noted that the generated right view adapts to varying depths, with corresponding disparity to the left view when depth is rich in the disparity map, and vice versa.

We also present the FID scores of several diffusion models in Table 2. Compared to their results, our model demonstrates strong performance and competitiveness, which to some extent validates the effectiveness of our approach. The experimental results demonstrate that by conditioning on both the left-view

Table 2. FID scores of various models and our Art3D-fusion. Compared to the FID values of these diffusion models, the FID score of our Art3D-fusion can be considered quite good. VQGAN from [4], LDM from [17].

Method	Year	Algorithm Type	FID↓
VQGAN	2020	GAN	26.28
LDM	2021	Diffusion	25.35
ControlNet	2023	Diffusion Control	15.27
Art3D-fusion	–	Hybrid Framework	**7.16**

and disparity map, our method effectively addresses the limitations of traditional right-view generation methods. Specifically, our approach significantly reduces blurriness and fills occluded regions more accurately, leading to a high-quality right-view synthesis.

4.5   Ablation Studies

To evaluate the effectiveness of our proposed approach, we conduct a comparison experiment using three model configurations: 1)conditioning only on the disparity map, 2)conditioning only on the left-view image, 3)conditioning on both the disparity map and left-view image. Each configuration is trained on the same dataset, using identical training parameters and number of training steps, and evaluated on the same test set. The generated right-view images from each model are then assessed using FID, PSNR, and SSIM to compare the performance of each conditioning method.

Table 3. Comparison of model performance with different conditioning inputs on the same test set. The best results are highlighted in bold.

Conditioning Method	FID ↓	PSNR ↑	SSIM ↑
Disparity Only	205.71	27.90 ± 0.07	0.09 ± 0.04
Left View Only	27.43	29.85 ± 1.61	0.63 ± 0.12
Disparity + Left View	**26.23**	**30.32 ± 1.29**	**0.64 ± 0.12**

Table 3 presents the results of this comparison. The model conditioned on both the disparity map and left-view image achieves the best performance across all metrics, demonstrating that combining structural and depth information leads to higher-quality synthesis. Specifically, the FID score is lowest when using both conditions, indicating a closer alignment with the ground-truth distribution. The SSIM and PSNR values are also highest for this configuration, confirming that our proposed method enhances both perceptual quality and structural fidelity in the generated right-view images.

The results suggest that using both the left-view image and disparity map as conditioning inputs provides a significant advantage in synthesizing high-quality right-view images. The *Disparity-only* model benefits from depth information but lacks the structural detail needed to achieve high SSIM and PSNR scores. Conversely, the *Left-view only* model captures structural details but struggles with accurate depth representation, resulting in a moderate FID score. By combining the structural cues from the left-view image with the depth information from the disparity map, our full model achieves superior performance, as evidenced by the highest SSIM and PSNR and the lowest FID.

5   Conclusion

In this paper, we introduced Art3D-Fusion, a novel approach for generating directorial right-view images using diffusion models with a dual-input conditioning framework. Our method integrates left-view images and disparity maps through an enhanced ControlNet structure, addressing common issues like blurriness and incomplete details in traditional synthesis methods. Art3D-Fusion combines physical depth information with global artistic control, generating 3D images that are both geometrically accurate and artistically appealing. We have made publicly available a dataset of over 140,000 high-quality image pairs, providing a valuable resource for further research in 3D view synthesis. Our experiments demonstrate the effectiveness of Art3D-Fusion, achieving high PSNR, SSIM, and FID scores. The results highlight the potential of diffusion models in stereo vision applications, offering a reliable solution for directorial right-view synthesis and paving the way for future innovations in 3D and immersive applications.

References

1. Chen, P., et al.: Optimizing for the shortest path in denoising diffusion model. In: Proceedings of the IEEE/CVF Conference on Computer Vision and Pattern Recognition (CVPR) (2025)
2. Chowdhary, N., Chauhan, M., Bhura, P.: An efficient method of depth map generation and rendering to convert 2D video to 3D. Computer **24**(8) (2024)
3. Elfwing, S., Uchibe, E., Doya, K.: Sigmoid-weighted linear units for neural network function approximation in reinforcement learning. Neural Netw. **107**, 3–11 (2018)
4. Esser, P., Rombach, R., Ommer, B.: Taming transformers for high-resolution image synthesis. In: Proceedings of the IEEE/CVF Conference on Computer Vision and Pattern Recognition, pp. 12873–12883 (2021)
5. Gao, P., Zhu, T., Paul, M.: Disocclusion filling for depth-based view synthesis with adaptive utilization of temporal correlations. J. Vis. Commun. Image Represent. **78**, 103148 (2021)
6. Gautier, J., Le Meur, O., Guillemot, C.: Depth-based image completion for view synthesis. In: 2011 3DTV Conference: The True Vision-Capture, Transmission and Display of 3D Video (3DTV-CON), pp. 1–4. IEEE (2011)

7. Geiger, A., Lenz, P., Urtasun, R.: Are we ready for autonomous driving? The KITTI vision benchmark suite. In: CVPR, pp. 3354–3361 (2012)

8. Ho, J., Jain, A., Abbeel, P.: Denoising diffusion probabilistic models. Adv. Neural. Inf. Process. Syst. **33**, 6840–6851 (2020)

9. Hore, A., Ziou, D.: Image quality metrics: PSNR vs. SSIM. In: 2010 20th International Conference on Pattern Recognition, pp. 2366–2369. IEEE (2010)

10. Jayasumana, S., Ramalingam, S., Veit, A., Glasner, D., Chakrabarti, A., Kumar, S.: Rethinking fid: Towards a better evaluation metric for image generation. In: Proceedings of the IEEE/CVF Conference on Computer Vision and Pattern Recognition, pp. 9307–9315 (2024)

11. Ke, B., Obukhov, A., Huang, S., Metzger, N., Daudt, R.C., Schindler, K.: Repurposing diffusion-based image generators for monocular depth estimation. In: Proceedings of the IEEE/CVF Conference on Computer Vision and Pattern Recognition, pp. 9492–9502 (2024)

12. Kuang, R.: Design and implementation of 3D film and television scene production algorithm based on the internet of things. Wirel. Commun. Mob. Comput. **2021**(1), 1219849 (2021)

13. Owl3D: Owl3D: AI-powered 2D to 3D conversion software (2024). https://www.owl3d.com/. Accessed 15 Nov 2024

14. Ranftl, R., Bochkovskiy, A., Koltun, V.: Vision transformers for dense prediction. In: Proceedings of the IEEE/CVF International Conference on Computer Vision, pp. 12179–12188 (2021)

15. Ranftl, R., Lasinger, K., Hafner, D., Schindler, K., Koltun, V.: Towards robust monocular depth estimation: mixing datasets for zero-shot cross-dataset transfer. IEEE Trans. Pattern Anal. Mach. Intell. **44**(3), 1623–1637 (2020)

16. Ranftl, R., Lasinger, K., Hafner, D., Schindler, K., Koltun, V.: Towards robust monocular depth estimation: mixing datasets for zero-shot cross-dataset transfer. IEEE TPAMI **44**(3), 1623–1637 (2020)

17. Rombach, R., Blattmann, A., Lorenz, D., Esser, P., Ommer, B.: High-resolution image synthesis with latent diffusion models. In: CVPR, pp. 10674–10685 (2022)

18. Saharia, C., et al.: Palette: image-to-image diffusion models. In: ACM SIGGRAPH 2022 Conference Proceedings, pp. 1–10 (2022)

19. Saxena, S., Kar, A., Norouzi, M., Fleet, D.J.: Monocular depth estimation using diffusion models. arXiv preprint arXiv:2302.14816 (2023)

20. Setiadi, D.R.I.M.: PSNR vs SSIM: imperceptibility quality assessment for image steganography. Multimedia Tools Appl. **80**(6), 8423–8444 (2021)

21. Solh, M., AlRegib, G.: Hierarchical hole-filling for depth-based view synthesis in FTV and 3D video. IEEE J. Sel. Top. Signal Process. **6**(5), 495–504 (2012)

22. Teed, Z., Deng, J.: Raft: recurrent all-pairs field transforms for optical flow (extended abstract). In: International Joint Conference on Artificial Intelligence (2021)

23. Xie, J., Girshick, R., Farhadi, A.: Deep3D: fully automatic 2D-to-3D video conversion with deep convolutional neural networks. In: Leibe, B., Matas, J., Sebe, N., Welling, M. (eds.) ECCV 2016. LNCS, vol. 9908, pp. 842–857. Springer, Cham (2016). https://doi.org/10.1007/978-3-319-46493-0_51

24. Yang, L., et al.: Depth anything v2. arXiv preprint arXiv:2406.09414 (2024)

25. Yin, W., et al.: Learning to recover 3D scene shape from a single image. In: Proceedings of the IEEE/CVF Conference on Computer Vision and Pattern Recognition, pp. 204–213 (2021)

26. Zhang, L., Rao, A., Agrawala, M.: Adding conditional control to text-to-image diffusion models. In: Proceedings of the IEEE/CVF International Conference on Computer Vision, pp. 3836–3847 (2023)
27. Zhao, W., Rao, Y., Liu, Z., Liu, B., Zhou, J., Lu, J.: Unleashing text-to-image diffusion models for visual perception. In: Proceedings of the IEEE/CVF International Conference on Computer Vision, pp. 5729–5739 (2023)
28. Zhou, K., Meng, X., Cheng, B.: Review of stereo matching algorithms based on deep learning. Comput. Intell. Neurosci. **2020**(1), 8562323 (2020)

Lesion Localization Prior-Driven Few-Shot Learning for Branch Atheromatous Disease Diagnosis

Kaijun Zhang[1,3], Shengde Li[2], Shengpei Wang[1(✉)], Jie Peng[1], Shangyi Shi[4], Bin Peng[2], Jun Ni[2(✉)], and Huiguang He[1(✉)]

[1] State Key Laboratory of Brain Cognition and Brain-inspired Intelligence Technology, Chinese Academy of Sciences, Institute of Automation, Beijing, China
{wangshengpei2014,huiguang.he}@ia.ac.cn
[2] Department of Neurology, State Key Laboratory of Complex Severe and Rare Diseases, Peking Union Medical College Hospital, Chinese Academy of Medical Science and Peking Union Medical College, Beijing, China
pumchnijun@163.com
[3] School of Future Technology, University of Chinese Academy of Sciences, Beijing, China
[4] State Key Laboratory of Processors, Institute of Computing Technology, Chinese Academy of Sciences, Beijing, China

Abstract. Early diagnosis of Branch Atheromatous Disease is critical for reducing associated disability rates. Recent advancements underscore the potential of deep learning methods in developing automated diagnostic tools. However, the limited availability of clinical data poses a significant challenge to their practical application. Traditional deep learning models, which rely on large-scale datasets, perform poorly in few-shot scenarios, limiting their effectiveness in this context. To address these challenges, we propose a few-shot learning framework for Branch Atheromatous Disease diagnosis that leverages Lesion Localization prior knowledge. This approach incorporates domain expertise to guide data augmentation, effectively mitigating the issue of limited training data. Specifically, our framework is developed based on 251 BAD slices, 51 Non-BAD slices, and 400 lesion-free slices obtained from preprocessed clinical DWI images. Furthermore, we introduce a two-stage training strategy and an adapter module for parameter-efficient fine-tuning, enabling effective model optimization even with constrained data. Our method was evaluated on clinical cases from multiple medical centers, demonstrating superior diagnostic accuracy and robustness compared to various baseline models. These results highlight the potential of our approach to enhance the efficiency and accuracy of early BAD diagnosis and alleviate clinical diagnostic workload.

Keywords: Branch Atheromatous Disease · few-shot · Lesion Localization · data augmentation · two-stage training · parameter-efficient fine-tuning

Z. Lin et al. (Eds.): ICIG 2025, LNCS 16161, pp. 102–112, 2026.
https://doi.org/10.1007/978-981-95-3398-5_9

1   Introduction

Branch Atheromatous Disease (**BAD**) [1] is an ischemic stroke subtype caused by atherosclerotic lesions at the origin of the perforating arteries. Studies have shown that the incidence of early neurological deterioration (END) in patients with BAD ranges from 26.8% to 37.6% [2,3], with a disability rate reaching as high as 61% [4]. Currently, diagnosis relies on clinicians interpreting DWI images to identify BAD-related lesions. This process is highly dependent on the clinician's experience and condition, leading to low efficiency and high risk of misdiagnosis, which may delay treatment. Therefore, developing an efficient and accurate automated diagnostic method has become an urgent and novel research task in this field.

In the field of stroke diagnosis, deep learning methods, particularly Convolutional Neural Networks (CNNs) and Vision Transformers (ViTs), have demonstrated significant effectiveness and outstanding performance [5–8]. However, due to the insufficient early research on BAD, data scarcity has emerged as a critical challenge, limiting the availability of annotated samples and hindering model training. This data scarcity restricts the generalization ability and diagnostic accuracy of models, highlighting the need for innovative methods to enhance model robustness. Data augmentation, a widely used technique in few-shot learning [9], applies random transformations to original images to generate new samples, thereby improving model generalization. However, in BAD diagnosis, the morphological and spatial features of lesions are heavily influenced by underlying anatomical and pathological factors [10], and traditional random augmentation methods often fail to capture these clinical details, resulting in samples that may lack medical validity. This underscores the need for more targeted data augmentation strategies that integrate clinically relevant features to create anatomically meaningful training data and improve model generalization. Additionally, Parameter-Efficient Fine-Tuning (PEFT) [11], which fine-tunes only a subset of pre-trained model parameters, has proven effective in improving performance with limited data [12]. Recent advancements, such as adapters [13,14], have further enhanced the efficiency of fine-tuning, enabling effective parameter adaptation without sacrificing performance. However, these techniques have yet to be fully explored in the context of stroke diagnosis, particularly for BAD, indicating the need for further research into their potential applications.

To address these challenges, we propose a novel Lesion Localization prior knowledge-driven few-shot learning framework for BAD diagnosis. We first analyzed clinical insights from medical professionals and redefined lesion categories based on spatial localization. Using this foundation, we generated synthetic data by simulating lesion locations and synthesized real pathological images. A vision encoder was initially trained on the synthetic data to capture prior knowledge of lesion localization. The encoder parameters were then frozen, and the model was fine-tuned using real pathological images with a parameter-efficient fine-tuning module, adapter, preserving lesion localization knowledge while learning detailed

---

K. Zhang and S. Li—Contributed equally to this work.

pathological features. Our results, evaluated on clinical data from multiple centers, demonstrate that our model outperforms existing methods, achieving an AUC of 86.8% ± 1.7% and significantly improving diagnostic accuracy.

The main contributions of this work are four-fold as follows:

- We propose the first automated diagnostic method for Branch Atheromatous Disease, addressing the challenge of data scarcity.
- We analyze clinical knowledge and incorporate lesion localization into data augmentation to effectively enhance model performance.
- We design a two-stage training framework and introduce a parameter-efficient fine-tuning module, allowing the model to learn both spatial localization and fine-grained pathological features.
- We test our approach on extensive clinical datasets, demonstrating that it outperforms existing baseline models, achieving superior diagnostic accuracy.

2   Clinical Knowledge in BAD Diagnosis

Recent clinical studies, including work from the Peking Union Medical College Hospital (PUMCH) team, have established indirect imaging-based diagnostic criteria for Branch Atheromatous Disease (BAD), emphasizing lesion shape, location, and axial distribution [10,15]. These criteria have become foundational for constructing high-quality BAD cohorts and advancing mechanistic research. Among BAD subtypes, lesions in the paramedian pontine arteries (PPA) region are particularly significant due to their clinical severity and distinct imaging characteristics.

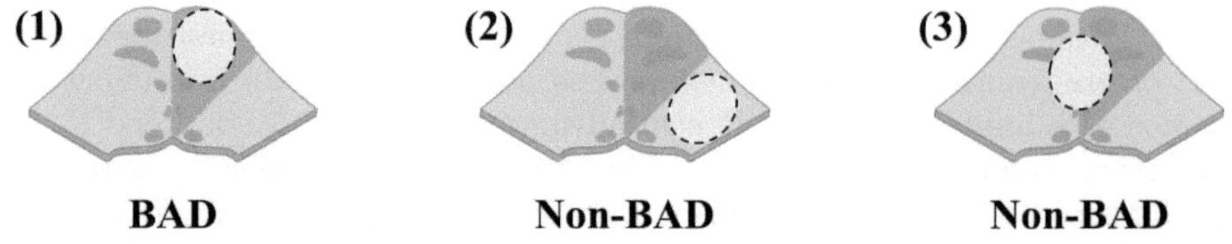

Fig. 1. PPA region slices corresponding to BAD and Non-BAD cases, shadows representing BAD lesion areas and white ellipses indicating lesions. (2) Lesion far from the midline; (3) Lesion crossing the midline.

This study focuses on the PPA region, a critical blood supply area located deep within the pons, which is commonly affected in BAD cases [16]. As summarized by Zhou et al. [10], lesion localization within the PPA plays a pivotal role in diagnosis: infarcts typically appear near the midline without crossing it and often involve the ventral surface of the pontine base (see Fig. 1). These imaging features align closely with the anatomical distribution of the PPA.

3   Methodology

Our goal is to address the challenge of limited training samples and develop a robust BAD diagnosis model. We approach this by focusing on both data augmentation and model fine-tuning. Leveraging lesion localization prior knowledge, we redefine lesion categories based on their location, which serves as the foundation for our data augmentation strategy. During training, we employ a two-stage process, incorporating a parameter-efficient fine-tuning module to enhance model performance and improve efficiency. After obtaining the classification results, we set a threshold to reclassify the four categories into BAD and Non-BAD, completing the diagnostic process. The overview of the proposed framework is shown in Fig. 2. In this section, we introduce the two steps in detail.

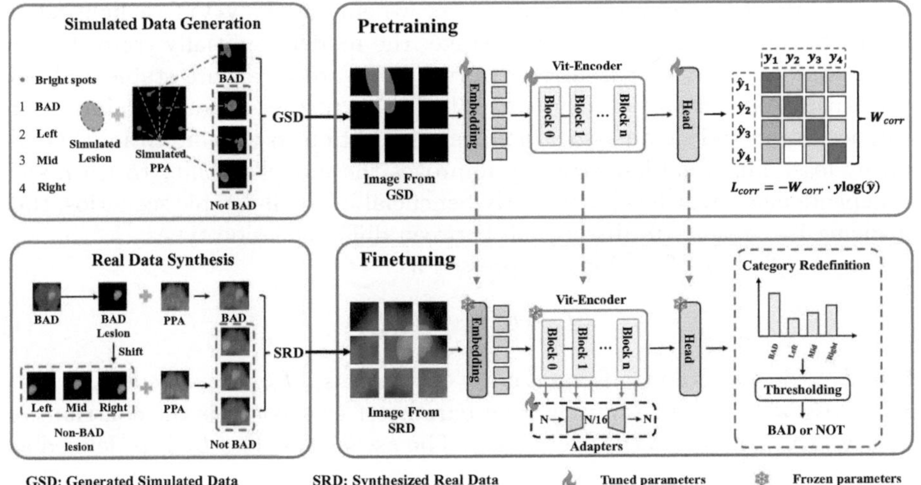

Fig. 2. Overview of few-shot BAD diagnosis framework. **Phase 1:** A large amount of Simulated data (GSD) is generated based on lesion localization prior knowledge. This data is used to train a ViT encoder to capture lesion location information. **Phase 2:** A certain amount of real data (SRD) is synthesized. The model's ViT encoder parameters are frozen, and an adapter module is used to fine-tune the model based on this data, ensuring efficient adaptation to real-world scenarios.

3.1   Pretraining with GSD

Simulated Data Generation. In the first phase, we aim for the model to learn the lesion localization prior knowledge typically provided by doctors. Referring to clinical knowledge and diagnostic criteria for BAD, as illustrated in Fig. 1, the spatial location of lesions within the PPA region plays a critical role in BAD diagnosis. Based on this insight, we directly classify the lesions into four categories: **BAD, Left, Mid, and Right** (as shown in Fig. 2).

Based on the redefinition of lesions, we adopted a simulation-based data generation approach to efficiently create large-scale simulated datasets. Specifically, we simulated PPA perfusion areas by using a completely black background, subdivided into predefined spatial regions corresponding to different lesion categories. Within these regions, white elliptical spots of varying sizes and shapes were randomly generated to simulate diverse lesion patterns. This process does not require meticulous annotation and repeated validation by medical experts, allowing for the rapid generation of a large amount of data that meets the required standards, overcoming the complexity and time consumption associated with traditional methods. This systematic generation process enabled us to construct a comprehensive generated simulated dataset (GSD), providing the model with a rich set of training samples.

Pretraining. For the model architecture, we employ Tiny-ViT, a lightweight Vision Transformer [17]. During this stage, the model is initially trained using simulated data, with its parameters frozen afterward to ensure stable and efficient feature extraction for downstream tasks. To further enhance training performance, we introduce an association loss in addition to the conventional cross-entropy loss. This dual-loss strategy improves the model's ability to learn spatial dependencies, which is particularly beneficial in small-sample scenarios, thus enhancing its capacity to distinguish between different lesion types.

The modified loss function is expressed as:

$$L = L_{\mathrm{CE}} + \lambda L_{\mathrm{corr}}, \tag{1}$$

where L_{CE} denotes the traditional cross-entropy loss, L_{corr} represents the association loss, and $\lambda = 0.1$ is a weighting parameter that controls the contribution of the association loss to the overall loss. The association loss L_{corr} is defined as:

$$L_{\mathrm{corr}} = -\sum_{i=1}^{C} \sum_{j=1}^{C} w_{ij} \cdot y_i \log(\hat{y}_j), \tag{2}$$

where $C = 4$ indicates the number of lesion categories, y_i and $\hat{y}_j$ denote the ground truth and predicted probabilities for categories i and j, respectively, and w_{ij} is derived from the association matrix, capturing the correlation between categories i and j. This formulation integrates spatial correlations into the loss function, enabling the model to better capture inter-class dependencies and improving classification performance in small-sample settings.

3.2 Finetuning with SRD

Real Data Synthesis. In the second phase, we aim for the model to acquire genuine diagnostic capabilities. Due to variations in lesion shapes, sizes, and internal characteristics within the PPA region, generating real data is crucial to further improve the model's accuracy and reliability. To achieve this, we propose a data synthesis method that combines PPA region images with extracted lesion images to generate synthetic stroke images. The method consists of three key steps: clustering segmentation, random lesion translation, and linear weighting fusion.

An unsupervised clustering algorithm [18] is applied to segment the PPA region slices into distinct areas: background, perfusion region, and lesion region. This step establishes clear boundaries for subsequent processing. Within the defined lesion regions, random shifts are introduced to lesion positions, generating diverse lesion distribution samples, including left shift, right shift, midline crossing, and BAD. Finally, linear weighting fusion is used to seamlessly integrate the lesions with the surrounding tissues, ensuring a smooth and realistic transition. The resulting synthesized real dataset is referred to as SRD, as shown in Fig. 2.

Finetuing. In the fine-tuning stage, we design a lightweight **Adapter module** [14,19], inspired by residual learning. This module efficiently captures task-specific information while introducing minimal parameter overhead. The structure consists of two main operations: dimensionality reduction and dimensionality expansion, separated by a ReLU activation. A residual connection is incorporated to preserve original features while introducing task-specific adjustments. Prior to fine-tuning, the model parameters are frozen to ensure stable feature extraction, and only the parameters of the Adapter module are updated during training.

3.3 Limitations of Segmentation-Based Diagnosis

While infarct lesion segmentation followed by rule-based classification may appear to be a straightforward strategy for diagnosing BAD in the PPA region, this approach faces several critical limitations in real-world clinical practice. In our study, we applied the widely used segmentation framework nnU-Net [20] to clinical DWI data and observed unsatisfactory performance. This is largely due to the domain shift introduced by scanner heterogeneity and variations in acquisition protocols, which significantly degrade the model's generalization ability outside of curated benchmark datasets. Moreover, obtaining accurate pixel-level annotations for BAD lesions is extremely resource-intensive, requiring extensive manual effort by experienced neurologists. Lastly, the diagnosis of BAD in the PPA region often depends on nuanced spatial features–such as lesion proximity to the midline or axial extension–which are difficult to encode using rigid geometric rules, limiting the applicability of rule-based classification schemes.

To address these challenges, our method avoids explicit lesion segmentation. Instead, it incorporates lesion distribution priors directly into data augmentation and fine-tuning processes, allowing effective few-shot diagnosis without relying on pixel-wise annotations.

4   Experiments

4.1   Experimental Setup

Dataset. In this study, we used three types of datasets: clinical data, GSD, and SRD. The clinical data was collected from the BAD-study [21] and SMART-study [22]. We annotated the PPA region from raw DWI images, resulting in 251 BAD slices, 51 Non-BAD slices, and 400 slices without lesions. Among them, 151 BAD slices and slices without lesions were used for data synthesis, while the remaining data were reserved for model training and testing. GSD for pre-training: 1,800 BAD slices and 2,250 Non-BAD slices, including 900 left, 450 middle, and 900 right. SRD for fine-tuning: 300 BAD slices and 375 Non-BAD slices, including 150 left, 75 middle, and 150 right slices. Ethical approval for clinical imaging data was granted by the Ethics Committee of Peking Union Medical College Hospital (PUMCH). All data were fully anonymized to protect patient privacy.

Evaluation Metrics. To evaluate the model performance, we use Sensitivity (SE), Specificity (SP), Accuracy (ACC), and AUC. Given the limited dataset, all experiments are repeated 7 times with different data splits for training and testing. The highest and lowest AUC values are excluded, and the average of the remaining 5 runs is reported to improve the robustness of the results. Although the dataset is imbalanced, the selected evaluation metrics–especially AUC and Specificity–are less sensitive to class imbalance, thereby providing a more reliable performance assessment.

Training Details. Our method is implemented using the PyTorch framework on an NVIDIA A100-PCIE-40GB GPU. The model is optimized using the Adam optimizer [23] with a learning rate of 0.0001 and a mini-batch size of 8. Pre-training is performed for 20 epochs, followed by 10 epochs for fine-tuning.

While the clinical data cannot be shared due to privacy constraints, the code and synthetic data generation scripts will be made publicly available upon publication.

4.2   Comparison Study

We compared our novel approach based on Tiny-ViT with several widely-used baseline models, including ResNet18, VGG16, and ViT-Base. Since no direct SOTA exists for this specific task, we selected these models as reasonable baselines for comparison. We used 60% of the clinical data to train the baseline models, while our method did not rely on clinical data for training. The remaining 40% of the clinical data was used to evaluate all models.

As illustrated in Table 1, our method consistently outperforms baseline models, achieving the highest AUC (86.0% $\pm$ 1.8%) and accuracy (83.7%). To assess the statistical significance of these results, we conducted a one-way ANOVA analysis, which revealed that the AUC and accuracy differences between our method and the baseline models are statistically significant ($p < 0.05$). Compared to other models, our approach effectively balances sensitivity (93.3%) and

Table 1. Experimental Results of Comparison Study: Comparison of Our Method with Tiny-ViT, ViT-Base, ResNet18, and VGG16 for BAD Diagnosis, Using AUC, ACC, Sensitivity (Se), and Specificity (Sp) Metrics.

Method	AUC	ACC	Se	Sp
Tiny-ViT	83.0 $\pm$ 1.7	67.3	**100.0**	1.9
ViT-Base	63.4 $\pm$ 4.8	66.7	**100.0**	0.0
ResNet18	81.8 $\pm$ 1.9	76.7	92.9	44.8
VGG16	77.4 $\pm$ 3.0	75.0	89.0	46.7
Ours	**86.0 $\pm$ 1.8**	**83.7**	93.3	**65.2**

specificity (65.2%), demonstrating superior overall diagnostic performance. In contrast, Tiny-ViT and ViT-Base exhibit extreme sensitivity (100.0%) but suffer from extremely low specificity (1.9% and 0.0%, respectively), making them unreliable for practical diagnosis. Meanwhile, ResNet18 and VGG16 perform moderately but still fall short of our method, particularly in terms of AUC and specificity. These results indicate that our approach delivers more reliable and stable predictions, especially in complex data conditions.

Segmentation-based baselines were not included due to the limited dataset size and the lack of lesion-level mask annotations. Existing pretrained segmentation models were also ineffective on our clinical DWI data, failing to detect lesion regions likely due to domain differences and subtle lesion appearance. Therefore, we focus on classification approaches guided by lesion localization priors, which are more suitable for our few-shot, weakly-supervised setting.

4.3   Ablation Study

We conducted an ablation study to evaluate the effectiveness and rationale of each component in our method. To systematically analyze the impact of different components on model performance, we designed several training configurations:

- **Full training pipeline**: Pre-train with GSD, fine-tune with SRD, and introduce the Adapter module for parameter-efficient fine-tuning.
- **Without Adapter module**: Pre-train with GSD and fine-tune with SRD, but without using the Adapter module.
- **SRD only**: Pre-train using only SRD.
- **GSD only**: Pre-train using only GSD.

As shown in Table 2, the model using both the GSD and SRD datasets performs the best, with an AUC of 86.8% $\pm$ 1.7% and accuracy (ACC) of 82.3%. In contrast, when the Adapter module is removed during fine-tuning, the model's performance decreases, with an AUC of 79.1% $\pm$ 4.5% and accuracy of 76.8%. This result highlights the crucial role of the Adapter module in improving model performance.

Table 2. Experimental Results of Ablation Study: Analyzing the Impact of Two-Stage Training with GSD, SRD, and the Adapter Module on Diagnosis Performance, Evaluated on All Clinical Data Using AUC, ACC, Sensitivity (Se), and Specificity (Sp) Metrics.

Method	Training Data	AUC	ACC	Se	Sp
Ours	GSD + SRD	**86.8 ± 1.7**	**82.3**	90.1	67.1
Ours w/o Adapter	GSD + SRD	79.1 ± 4.5	76.8	**92.4**	46.3
Ours w/o Adapter w/o GSD	SRD	75.1 ± 4.5	74.2	87.4	48.2
Ours w/o Adapter w/o SRD	GSD	70.8 ± 5.3	60.4	56.8	**67.5**

When only the SRD dataset is used, the AUC is 75.1% ± 4.5% and accuracy is 74.2%, whereas using only the GSD dataset yields an AUC of 70.8% ± 5.3% and accuracy of 60.4%. These results indicate that training on both datasets (GSD and SRD) sequentially better captures lesion spatial distribution and morphological features, thereby improving the overall model performance. The SRD dataset, by generating synthetic real data, effectively supplements the contextual information lacking in the GSD dataset, while the GSD dataset improves specificity (Sp) by providing clear lesion location data.

In summary, our approach significantly enhances diagnostic capability by combining simulated data for pre-training to learn lesion locations, followed by fine-tuning with synthetic real data and the use of the Adapter module. Each module contributes effectively: the GSD dataset enhances the model's specificity by focusing on lesion location, while the SRD dataset improves the model's recognition of different lesion types by supplementing contextual information. The inclusion of the Adapter module further optimizes task-specific feature learning, resulting in an overall improvement in model performance.

5   Conclusion and Discussion

In this work, we propose a lesion localization prior knowledge-driven few-shot learning framework for Branch Atheromatous Disease (BAD) diagnosis. By integrating an expert-driven data augmentation method and a parameter-efficient fine-tuning strategy, we effectively address the challenge of limited medical imaging data. Our framework leverages simulated data and realistic synthetic data to enhance model performance, demonstrating strong generalization ability and diagnostic accuracy. Through rigorous evaluation on clinical datasets, we show that our approach surpasses multiple baseline models, achieving an AUC of 86.8% ± 1.7% and ACC of 82.3%. We believe that this method can significantly enhance the diagnostic efficiency of clinicians, reduce their workload, and help lower the disability rate associated with BAD. Future work will focus on refining the model, broadening its applicability, and further integrating clinical insights to improve performance.

Acknowledgment. This work was supported in part by the National Natural Science Foundation of China (NSFC) under Grant Nos. 62201569 and 62020106015, and in part by the Noncommunicable Chronic Diseases-National Science and Technology Major Project under Grant No. 2023ZD0515700.

References

1. Caplan, L.R.: Intracranial branch atheromatous disease: a neglected, understudied, and underused concept. Neurology **39**(9), 1246–1246 (1989)
2. Duan, Z., et al.: Lesion patterns of single small subcortical infarct and its association with early neurological deterioration. Neurol. Sci. **36**(10), 1851–1857 (2015). https://doi.org/10.1007/s10072-015-2267-1
3. Jeong, H.-G., Kim, B.J., Yang, M.H., Han, M.-K., Bae, H.-J.: Neuroimaging markers for early neurologic deterioration in single small subcortical infarction. Stroke **46**(3), 687–691 (2015)
4. Kwan, M.W.-M., Mak, W., Cheung, R.T.-F., Ho, S.-L.: Ischemic stroke related to intracranial branch atheromatous disease and comparison with large and small artery diseases. J. Neurol. Sci. **303**(1–2), 80–84 (2011)
5. Gautam, A., Raman, B.: Towards effective classification of brain hemorrhagic and ischemic stroke using cnn. Biomed. Signal Process. Control **63**, 102178 (2021)
6. Marbun, J., Andayani, U., et al.: Classification of stroke disease using convolutional neural network. J. Phys. Conf. Ser. **978**(1), 012092 (2018)
7. Raj, R., Mathew, J., Kannath, S.K., Rajan, J.: StrokeViT with AutoML for brain stroke classification. Eng. Appl. Artif. Intell. **119**, 105772 (2023)
8. Bivard, A., Churilov, L., Parsons, M.: Artificial intelligence for decision support in acute stroke-current roles and potential. Nat. Rev. Neurol. **16**(10), 575–585 (2020)
9. Shorten, C., Khoshgoftaar, T.M.: A survey on image data augmentation for deep learning. J. Big Data **6**(1), 1–48 (2019)
10. Zhou, L., Yao, M., Peng, B., Zhu, Y., Ni, J., Cui, L.: Atherosclerosis might be responsible for branch artery disease: evidence from white matter hyperintensity burden in acute isolated pontine infarction. Front. Neurol. **9**, 840 (2018)
11. Nakamura, A., Harada, T.: Revisiting fine-tuning for few-shot learning. arXiv preprint arXiv:1910.00216 (2019)
12. Shen, Z., Liu, Z., Qin, J., Savvides, M., Cheng, K.-T.: Partial is better than all: revisiting fine-tuning strategy for few-shot learning. In: Proceedings of the AAAI Conference on Artificial Intelligence, vol. 35, no. 11, pp. 9594–9602 (2021)
13. Houlsby, N., et al.: Parameter-efficient transfer learning for NLP. In: International Conference on Machine Learning, pp. 2790–2799. PMLR (2019)
14. Wang, R., et al.: K-adapter: infusing knowledge into pre-trained models with adapters. arXiv preprint arXiv:2002.01808 (2020)
15. Petrone, L., Nannoni, S., Del Bene, A., Palumbo, V., Inzitari, D.: Branch atheromatous disease: a clinically meaningful, yet unproven concept. Cerebrovasc. Dis. **41**(1–2), 87–95 (2016)
16. Kataoka, S., Hori, A., Shirakawa, T., Hirose, G.: Paramedian pontine infarction: neurological/topographical correlation. Stroke **28**(4), 809–815 (1997)
17. Wu, K., et al.: TinyvIT: fast pretraining distillation for small vision transformers. In: European Conference on Computer Vision, pp. 68–85. Springer (2022)
18. Krishna, K., Murty, M.N.: Genetic k-means algorithm. IEEE Trans. Syst. Man Cybernet. Part B (Cybernetics) **29**(3), 433–439 (1999)

19. Chen, Z., et al.: Vision transformer adapter for dense predictions. arXiv preprint arXiv:2205.08534 (2022)
20. Soliman, A., et al.: Brain stroke segmentation using deep learning models: a comparative study. arXiv e-prints, pp. arXiv–2403 (2024)
21. Li, S., et al.: Clinical and prognostic characteristics of acute bad-related stroke: a multicenter MRI-based prospective study. Stroke **55**(10), 2431–2438 (2024)
22. Peng, B., et al.: Implementation of a structured guideline-based program for the secondary prevention of ischemic stroke in China. Stroke **45**(2), 515–519 (2014)
23. Kingma, D.P.: Adam: a method for stochastic optimization. arXiv preprint arXiv:1412.6980 (2014)

Deep Multi-sentence Aligned Cross-Modal Retrieval

Zhijian Lin[1], Sihan Gong[2], and Xueliang Liu[3]($\boxtimes$)

[1] Hefei University of Technology, Hefei, China
`2023170739@mail.hfut.edu.cn`
[2] Hefei Comprehensive National Science Center, Institute of Artificial Intelligence,
Hefei, China
`gongsh@iai.ustc.edu.cn`
[3] Hefei University of Technology, Hefei, China
`liuxueliang1982@gmail.com`

Abstract. Current cross-modal retrieval models predominantly rely on one-to-one image-text pairs for training, with most approaches projecting each sample into a single embedding vector. However, recent studies indicate that this single-vector representation fails to capture the inherent complexity of images and texts, resulting in the loss of critical semantic information during the embedding process. Consequently, these models often struggle to effectively learn the nuanced features of both modalities. In this paper, we propose a novel training strategy that transitions from traditional one-to-one image-text pairing to a one-to-many framework and introduce an innovative Set Prediction Module with Weight to better capture the diverse semantics of the input data. By incorporating a more diverse set of textual representations during training, our method significantly enhances the performance of cross-modal retrieval models. Extensive evaluations across various backbone networks on the COCO and Flickr30K datasets demonstrate that our approach consistently outperforms most existing methods.

Keywords: cross-modal retrieval · multiple matching relations · set prediction module with weight · ambiguity issue

1 Introduction

Cross-modal retrieval, an emerging information retrieval technology, aligns semantic information across modalities. Traditional approaches employ single embedding vectors, either projecting modalities into a shared latent space [4,10] or computing direct similarity [15,25,27], but struggle with inherent ambiguity as complex visual content often exceeds text captions' descriptive capacity (e.g., Fig. 1). Recent solutions include computationally intensive cross-attention networks [31] that improve alignment at the cost of scalability, and oversimplified shared space projections [4,10], with both paradigms limited by single-vector representations that cannot fully resolve multimodal ambiguity.

Fig. 1. The figure demonstrates cross-modal retrieval ambiguity, where color-coded alignments show how one image matches multiple valid captions (e.g., focusing on tram, scenery, or car), while each caption only partially describes the full visual content.

Recent work [11,15,25,27] tackles ambiguity by using dual encoders to represent text and images as sets of embedding vectors, preserving more semantic information. While multiple vectors capture additional nuances (Fig. 1), they remain insufficient as single captions cannot fully describe images. Consequently, we posit that employing multiple embedding vectors in cross-modal retrieval is insufficient to fully mitigate inherent semantic ambiguity. To effectively address this challenge, additional textual information should be incorporated during the training process.

We propose a novel cross-modal retrieval method using multiple matching relationships. Our approach projects single modalities into embedding sets via a Weighted Set Prediction Module, preserving richer semantics. We also replace one-to-one matching with one-to-many training to overcome single-text limitations, achieving better retrieval performance.

The proposed method has been evaluated and compared with previous work using two realistic cross-modal retrieval benchmarks: COCO [17] and Flickr30K [23]. Our method outperforms previous methods in most settings, and experiments demonstrate its effectiveness. Our contributions are summarized as follows:

- We propose a training strategy with multiple matching relations to address the issue that a single caption or a set of embedding vectors cannot fully represent images in cross-modal retrieval;
- We propose a novel Set Prediction Module with Weight that generates an embedding set whose elements can not only encode essentially different semantics but also retain the weighted global context of the input data;
- We conducted extensive experiments on COCO and Flick30K datasets and demonstrated the effectiveness of our proposed model.

2   Related Work

Cross-modal Retrieval. Image-text retrieval matches queries of one modality to corresponding images or text [13,28]. Existing methods mainly use either independent encoders or cross-attention networks. Independent encoders project visual and text data into a shared embedding space (e.g., VSE++ [8] with ranking loss, GXN [10] with generative embeddings), enabling efficient retrieval but facing modality gaps. Cross-attention networks (e.g., SCAN [27], SGM [15]) model inter-modal interactions better but are computationally costly [18,20,21,29], motivating our focus on improving independent encoders.

Multiple Embedding Vectors. Most existing methods focus on projecting samples into a single embedding vector [10]. However, studies have shown that a single embedding vector is inadequate for representing samples with inherent ambiguity. To address this challenge, novel feature representation approaches have been proposed, such as PVSE [26], DivE [15], and PCME [6].

PCME proposed to use **probabilistic embeddings** to represent the image and its corresponding captions as a probability distribution in a common embedded space suitable for cross-modal retrieval. These distributions effectively capture the uncertainty caused by multiple concepts in the visual scene and implicitly realize the many-to-many matching between these concepts. PVSE introduced **Polysemous Instance Embedding Networks** (PIE-Nets), which generate varied and multiple representations of an instance by integrating global context with locally-guided features through the use of multi-head self-attention and residual learning. While these methods capture a broader range of semantic information through diverse embeddings, they still fail to fully address the limited information in individual texts.

3   Proposed Method

This section consists of four parts. We will begin by describing the overall model architecture and the Backbone network for feature extraction. Next, we will provide a detailed explanation of the set prediction module with weight. After that, we will elaborate on the proposed method for multiple matching between image and texts and how it resolves the ambiguity issue. Finally, we will outline our training objectives.

3.1   Overall Model Framework

Our method architecture, illustrated in Fig. 2, consists of three core components working in sequence. The visual and textual feature extractors, implemented following established designs [3,25,26], process input image-text groups to extract both local and global features. These extracted features then feed into modality-specific set prediction modules that generate the final embedding sets IG^V and IG^T. The model optimizes these representations through carefully designed loss functions that simultaneously minimize distances within groups while maximizing separation between different groups, ensuring effective feature learning for the retrieval task.

Feature Extractor. We employ two types of feature extractors for both visual and textual modalities. For visual features, one approach uses flat convolution

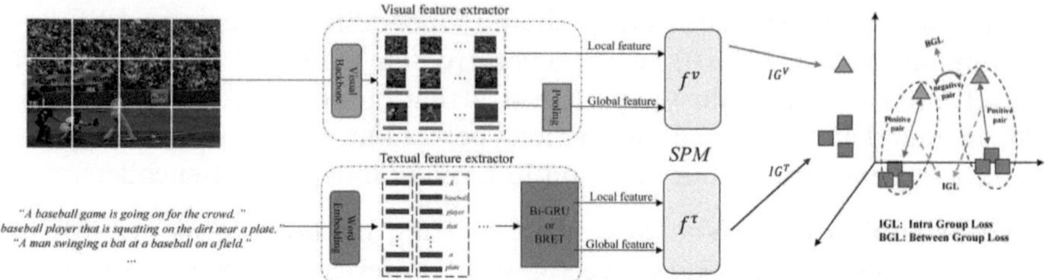

Fig. 2. The overview architecture of our proposed framework. The model consists of three parts: visual feature extractor, textual feature extractor, and set-prediction modules f^v and f^τ. First, the feature extractors of each modality extract local and global features from input samples. The input sample contains an image and multiple texts. Then, the features are fed to the set prediction modules with weight to produce embedding sets IG^V and IG^T. Then we combine IG^V and IG^T to a Group. The model is trained with the Between Group Loss and the Intra Group Loss.

features as local features and their average pooling as global features, while the other utilizes ROI features [1] with max pooling, both yielding $\psi^V(x) \in \mathbb{R}^{N \times D}$ and $\phi^V(x) \in \mathbb{R}^D$ for an input image x. For text, we adopt either bi-GRU [5] with GloVe embeddings [22] or BERT [7], processing multiple captions per image for training.

3.2 Set Prediction Module with Weight

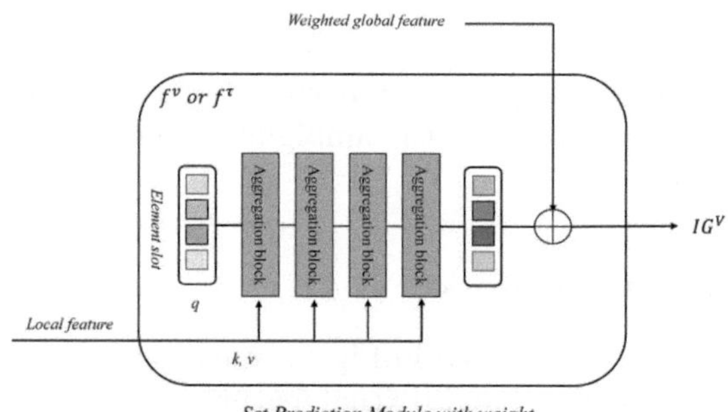

Set Prediction Module with weight

Fig. 3. Take image processing as an example—the overview architecture of the Set Prediction Module with weight. Initially, local features and weighted global features are integrated with element slots, serving as the key, value, and query for the attention mechanisms. These inputs are then processed through multiple stacked aggregation blocks, ultimately producing the output IG^V

To resolve input ambiguity, we propose an aggregation module combining slot attention [19] and DivE's SPM [15]. Through iterative updates, it fuses diverse semantics with weighted global features, producing distinct yet context-aware embeddings. We detail the visual module f^V the textual counterpart f^T follows the same design.

As shown in Fig. 3, the Set Prediction Module with Weights consists of multiple aggregation blocks that share their weights. Moreover, the module includes local features, weighted global features, and element slots as input. The initial element slots is a learnable embedding vector $F^0 \in R^{k \times D}$, where K is the cardinality of the embedding set. The module sends local features and element slots as inputs to the Aggregation blocks and gets F^t after t iterations:

$$F^T = AggBlock\left(\psi^V(x); F^{T-1}\right) \in R^{k \times D}. \tag{1}$$

The inputs after normalized, the aggregation block projects the input local feature $\psi^V(x)$ to $k \in R^{N \times D_h}$ and $v \in R^{N \times D_h}$, and the last aggregation block F^{t-1} to $q \in R^{K \times D_h}$. The attention map B between $\psi^V(x)$ and F^{t-1} is obtained using the following process:

$$B_{i.j} = \frac{exp(M_{i,j})}{\sum_{j=1}^{J} exp(M_{i,j})}, \ where \ M = \frac{1}{\sqrt{D_h}}kq^T. \tag{2}$$

After iterative processing through multiple aggregation blocks, each element slot will be refined to aggregate local features with distinct semantics.

Then, to further highlight important information, we aggregate image representation with text as the condition. In detail, we calculate the inner product between the text representation $T = \{t_1, t_2, \ldots, t_n\}$ and image representation v. We get the weight of the images by:

$$\alpha_i = \frac{exp(\frac{v^T t_i}{\tau})}{\sum_{j=1}^{N} exp(\frac{v^T t_j}{\tau})}, \tag{3}$$

where τ is the trade-off hyper-parameter. The smaller τ allows visual features to take more textual conditions into account during aggregation. The final visual global feature is defined as

$$\phi^V(x) = \sum_{j=1}^{N} \alpha_i v. \tag{4}$$

Finally, the model predicts an embedding set IG by adding the global feature $\phi^V(x)$ to each element slot F^T:

$$IG = LN\left(F^t\right) + [LN\left(\phi^V(x)\right)^{\times k}], \tag{5}$$

where LN is a layer normalization, and $\phi^V(x)^{\times k}$ is K repetitions of $\phi^V(x)$. The module utilizes the weighted global feature to effectively process samples with little ambiguity because the weighted global feature enables these samples to be represented by a set of embeddings with low variance within the set.

3.3   Multiple Matching Between Image and Texts

We propose **Multiple Matching Between Image and Texts** to address the limitation of single-caption representations, we propose direct multiple correspondences between images and diverse texts, fundamentally improving retrieval performance. Unlike PVSE and PCME that use multiple embeddings but single captions, our method processes image-caption groups through the Weighted Set Prediction Module, calculating intra-group similarities to bring matching pairs closer in the embedding space. In detail, we calculate the similarity between the image feature IG^V and the matching captions features $IG^T = \{IG^{t_1}, IG^{t_2}, \ldots, IG^{t_n}\}$, where t_n is the number of captions that match the same image. We get the similarity S_1 by:

$$
\begin{aligned}
S_1\left(IG^T, IG^V\right) = &\frac{1}{2\alpha\left|IG^T\right|} \sum_{x \in IG^T} LSE_{y \in IG^V}\left(\alpha c\left(x, y\right)\right)+ \\
&\frac{1}{2\alpha\left|IG^V\right|} \sum_{y \in IG^V} LSE_{x \in IG^T}\left(\alpha c\left(x, y\right)\right),
\end{aligned}
\tag{6}
$$

where $\alpha > 0$ is a scaling parameter, LSE indicates Log-Sum-Exp, Since the property of LSE, such similarity softly assigns elements in one group to those in the other group, it also can provide dense supervision but without the collapsing issue [15].

Besides, we aim to increase the dissimilarity between different groups G and minimize the similarity S within each group by reducing the similarity value during the training process:

$$
\begin{aligned}
S_2\left(G_1, G_2\right) = &\frac{1}{2\alpha\left|G_1\right|} \sum_{x \in G_1} \log\left(\sum_{y \in G_2} e^{\alpha c(x, y)}\right)+ \\
&\frac{1}{2\alpha\left|G_2\right|} \sum_{y \in G_2} \log\left(\sum_{x \in G_1} e^{\alpha c(x, y)}\right).
\end{aligned}
\tag{7}
$$

Both of the above similar functions can be clearly demonstrated by the gradient with respect to $c(x, y)$, which is given by:

$$
\begin{aligned}
\frac{1}{\partial c(x', y')} \partial S(S_1, S_2) = &\frac{1}{2|S_1|} \frac{e^{\alpha c(x', y')}}{\sum_{y \in S_2} e^{\alpha c(x', y)}}+ \\
&\frac{1}{2|S_2|} \frac{e^{\alpha c(x', y')}}{\sum_{x \in S_1} e^{\alpha c(x, y')}}.
\end{aligned}
\tag{8}
$$

The gradient is the combination of two relative similarity scores. This means that the gradient for $c(x', y')$ is given more importance when x' and y' are close to each other. Using a weighting scheme based on their relative proximity, we can provide denser supervision during training while maintaining enough variation within the set.

3.4 Training Objective

Following common practice [26], we leverage triplet loss, diversity regularizer, and Maximum Mean Discrepancy (MMD) [9] to optimize our model. We adopt the triplet loss with hard negative mining. In a batch $B = \{IG_i^V, IG_i^{t_1}, IG_i^{t_2}, \ldots, IG_i^{t_n}\}_{i=1}^N$, the triplet loss is given by:

$$L_{IGL} = \sum_{i=1}^N \max_j \left[\gamma + S_1\left(IG_i^V, IG_j^T\right) - S_1\left(IG_i^V, IG_i^T\right)\right] + \\ \sum_{i=1}^N \max_j \left[\gamma + S_1\left(IG_i^T, IG_j^V\right) - S_1\left(IG_i^T, IG_i^V\right)\right], \tag{9}$$

where margin $\gamma > 0$. The MMD regularizer reduces the MMD between the embedding sets of images and text, ensuring that embeddings from different modalities stay aligned during the early phases of training. Meanwhile, the diversity regularizer discourages the model from creating too many similar embeddings, promoting a set of diverse embeddings. The two regularizers are formulated as $L_{mmd} = MMD\left(B^V, B^T\right)$ and $L_{div} = \sum_{x,x' \in FT} e^{-2\|x-x'\|^2}$, where B^V and B^T refer to subsets of batch B consisting of each modality embeddings.

Additionally, to increase the separation between different groups, we apply a between group loss function that minimizes the similarity between them. The function is given by:

$$L_{BGL} = -log(1 - U), \tag{10}$$

where U is the similarity between different groups. In conclusion, the training objectives can be established as $L = L_{IGL} + L_{BGL} + \alpha\, L_{mmd} + \beta\, L_{div}$, where α and β are the trade-off hyper-parameters.

4 Experiments

4.1 Experiment Setup

Datasets. We evaluate on two standard benchmarks: (1) COCO [14] (123K images, 5 texts each) with 113K/5K/5K train/val/test split, reporting both 1K (5-fold average) and 5K test results; (2) Flickr30K [23] (30K images) using 28K/1K/1K splits, with evaluation on the 1K test set.

Metrics. We selected Recall@K which represents the percentage of queries with matching samples in the top-K retrieval results. Following reference [3], we also report the RSUM, which is the sum of the Recall@K at $K \in \{1, 5, 10\}$ in the image-to-text and text-to-image retrieval settings.

Table 1. The results of Recall@K and RSUM on COCO dataset. Evaluation results for both the 1K test setting (average of 5-fold test dataset) and the 5K test setting. The best scores are highlighted in bold. * denotes that the experimental results are reproduced in our experimental environment.

Method	1K Test Images			5K Test Images		
	Image-to-Text R@1 R@5 R@10	Text-to-Image R@1 R@5 R@10	RSUM	Image-to-Text R@1 R@5 R@10	Text-to-Image R@1 R@5 R@10	RSUM
ResNet-152+Bi-GRU						
VSE++ [8]	64.6 90.0 95.7	52.0 84.3 95.7	478.6	41.3 71.1 81.2	30.3 59.4 72.4	355.7
PVSE [26]	69.2 91.6 96.6	55.2 86.5 93.7	492.8	32.4 74.3 84.5	32.4 63.0 75.0	374.4
PCME [25]	68.8 —— ——	54.6 —— ——	——	44.2 —— ——	31.9 —— ——	——
DivE* [15]	70.6 91.8 96.6	56.0 87.1 94.4	496.5	47.5 75.4 84.7	33.0 63.3 75.8	379.6
Ours	**71.0 92.2 96.9**	**56.0 87.1 94.1**	**497.5**	47.1 **76.6 85.5**	**33.2 63.4 75.9**	**381.7**
Faster R-CNN+Bi-GRU						
SCAN [27]	72.7 94.8 98.4	58.8 88.4 94.8	507.9	50.4 82.2 90.0	38.6 69.3 80.4	410.9
VSRN [16]	76.2 94.8 98.2	62.8 89.7 95.1	516.8	53.0 81.1 89.4	40.5 70.6 81.1	415.9
CAAN [31]	75.5 95.4 98.5	61.3 89.7 95.2	515.6	52.5 83.3 90.9	41.2 70.3 82.9	421.1
IMRAM [2]	76.7 95.6 98.5	61.7 89.1 95.0	516.6	53.7 83.2 91.0	39.7 69.1 79.8	416.5
DivE* [15]	79.7 95.4 98.3	63.0 90.3 95.6	522.3	59.3 84.4 90.9	40.5 71.1 81.8	428.0
Ours	79.6 **95.9 98.4**	**63.1** 90.2 **95.6**	**522.9**	**59.3 84.8 92.2**	**40.7 71.3 81.8**	**430.0**
ResNeXt-101+BERT						
DivE* [15]	84.1 97.8 99.3	69.9 93.4 97.4	541.9	66.2 89.6 94.7	48.8 77.6 86.4	463.3
Ours	**84.4** 97.6 **99.4**	69.3 93.3 97.4	541.4	**67.2 89.7 94.7**	47.8 77.3 86.3	463.0

4.2 Implementation Details

Feature Extractor. For the visual feature extractor, convolutional visual features are derived by applying a 1×1 convolution to the final feature map of the CNN. The ROI visual features are obtained by passing the pre-extracted features from Faster R-CNN [24] through a 2-layer MLP with residual connections, as described in [3]. In all models, the dimensionality D is set to 1024, and the number of regions K is set to 4. For a fair comparison with previous work, our method is evaluated using three different visual extractors: ResNet-152 [12], pre-trained on ImageNet; ROI features [1], pre-extracted by Faster R-CNN [24]; and ResNeXt-101 [30], pre-trained on the Instagram dataset. The implementation details of training settings vary based on the previous work [6,15,26].

4.3 Comparisons with Other Methods

Following [3,26], we use 224×224 resolution for ResNet-152 and 512×512 for ResNeXt-101. Text features are extracted using either bi-GRU or BERT. Ensemble results combine predictions from two differently-initialized models. Performance on COCO and Flickr30K is reported in Tables 1 and 2 respectively.

Table 2. The results of Recall@K and RSUM on Flickr30K dataset. Evaluation results for both the 1K test setting and the best scores are highlighted in bold. * denotes that the experimental results are reproduced in our experimental environment.

Method	Image-to-Text			Text-to-Image			RSUM
	R@1	R@5	R@10	R@1	R@5	R@10	
ResNet-152+Bi-GRU							
VSE++	52.9	80.5	87.2	39.6	70.1	79.5	409.8
PVSE	59.1	84.5	91.0	43.4	73.1	81.5	432.6
PCME	58.5	81.4	89.3	44.3	72.7	81.9	428.1
DivE*	61.2	86.5	92.7	46.9	76.4	84.5	448.1
Ours	**63.1**	**88.5**	**92.8**	**47.2**	75.7	83.8	**451.0**
Faster R-CNN+Bi-GRU							
SCAN	67.4	90.3	95.8	48.6	77.7	85.2	465.0
VSRN	71.3	90.6	96.0	54.7	81.8	88.2	482.6
CAAN	70.1	91.6	97.2	52.8	79.0	87.9	478.6
IMRAM	74.1	93.0	96.6	53.9	79.4	87.2	484.2
DivE*	77.3	94.0	96.6	56.1	83.1	89.7	496.8
Ours	**78.1**	**94.1**	**97.2**	**56.3**	82.5	88.9	**497.0**
ResNeXt-101+BERT							
DivE*	89.1	98.7	99.5	71.7	92.8	96.4	548.2
Ours	**89.2**	98.6	**99.8**	**71.8**	92.8	96.2	**548.4**

Our method outperforms most models in terms of the RSUM, demonstrating significant improvements of 7.3 % on COCO 5K and 18.4% on Flickr30K compared to existing approaches. The ResNet152+Bi-GRU combination consistently outperforms all baselines, with particularly notable gains in image-text retrieval. Our multi-matching framework shows clear advantages over PVSE and PCME across all test scenarios, validating the effectiveness of leveraging additional textual information during training.

Our method achieves the highest Recall@K scores on both COCO and Flickr30K datasets, particularly excelling in the Faster R-CNN+Bi-GRU architecture. It demonstrates superior performance in both retrieval directions, with R@1 scores of 78.1 (image-to-text) and 56.3 (text-to-image) on Flickr30K, while also attaining the highest RSUM scores across all settings.

5   Ablation Study

We conducted ablation studies to evaluate the importance of the Multi-Matching strategy and the impact of the two proposed loss functions L_{IGL} and L_{BGL} on RSUM performance.

Effectiveness of Multi-Matching strategy. Our experiments across multiple datasets demonstrate that using one-to-five (M = 5) image-text matching significantly outperforms traditional one-to-one (M = 1) matching. As shown in Table 3, the M = 5 configuration achieves superior results across all evaluation metrics, clearly validating that our Multi-Matching strategy effectively enhances cross-modal retrieval performance.

Importance of loss function. We propose two loss functions to regulate similarity: an intra-group loss that increases similarity between related texts and images within the same group, and a between-group loss that reduces similarity across different groups. As shown in Fig. 4, both functions significantly enhance cross-modal retrieval performance, with the between-group loss contributing more substantially to the improvement.

Table 3. The ablation study evaluates the effect of Multi-Matching strategy. The image to text retrieval results of Recall@K and RSUM on various datasets and feature extraction networks. The best scores are highlighted in bold.

One to M	Image-to-Text			
	R@1	R@5	R@10	RSUM
Flickr30K/Faster R-CNN+Bi-GRU				
M = 1	77.2	93.6	96.5	267.3
M = 5	**78.1**	**94.1**	**97.2**	**269.4**
COCO/ResNet-152+Bi-GRU				
M = 1	70.6	91.8	96.5	258.9
M = 5	**71.0**	**92.1**	**96.9**	**260.0**

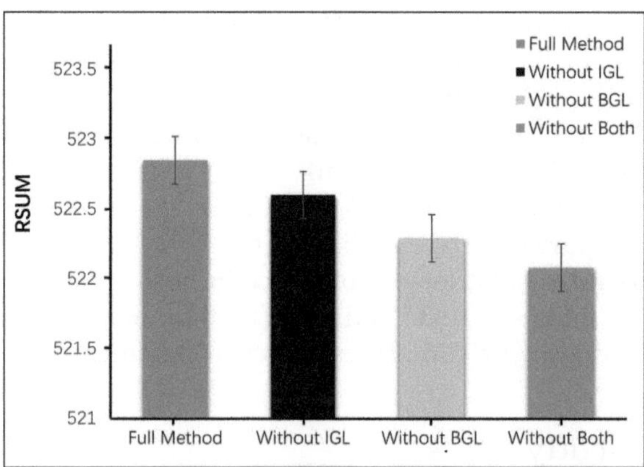

Fig. 4. The ablation study evaluates the effect of two loss functions, L_{IGL} and L_{BGL}, on RSUM. The blue bar shows the best RSUM score when both are used. The red bar, with neither loss function, results in the lowest score.

6   Conclusion

We propose a novel cross-modal retrieval training strategy that replaces the conventional one-to-one approach with a one-to-many method to mitigate poor matching caused by limited textual information. Our Set Prediction Module with Weight encodes diverse semantics while preserving weighted global context. Experiments on COCO and Flickr30K show superior performance over prior models. The strategy is adaptable and integrable into other frameworks. Future work will explore broader domain applications.

Acknowledgements. This work is supported by National Natural Science Foundation of China (No. 62372151).

References

1. Anderson, P., et al.: Bottom-up and top-down attention for image captioning and visual question answering. In: Proceedings of the IEEE Conference on Computer Vision and Pattern Recognition, pp. 6077–6086 (2018)
2. Chen, H., Ding, G., Liu, X., Lin, Z., Liu, J., Han, J.: Imram: iterative matching with recurrent attention memory for cross-modal image-text retrieval. In: Proceedings of the IEEE/CVF Conference on Computer Vision and Pattern Recognition, pp. 12655–12663 (2020)
3. Chen, J., Hu, H., Wu, H., Jiang, Y., Wang, C.: Learning the best pooling strategy for visual semantic embedding. In: Proceedings of the IEEE/CVF Conference on Computer Vision and Pattern Recognition, pp. 15789–15798 (2021)
4. Chen, Y.C., et al.: Uniter: universal image-text representation learning. In: European Conference on Computer Vision, pp. 104–120. Springer (2020)
5. Cho, K.: Learning phrase representations using rnn encoder-decoder for statistical machine translation. arXiv preprint arXiv:1406.1078 (2014)
6. Chun, S., Oh, S.J., De Rezende, R.S., Kalantidis, Y., Larlus, D.: Probabilistic embeddings for cross-modal retrieval. In: Proceedings of the IEEE/CVF Conference on Computer Vision and Pattern Recognition, pp. 8415–8424 (2021)
7. Devlin, J.: Bert: Pre-training of deep bidirectional transformers for language understanding. arXiv preprint arXiv:1810.04805 (2018)
8. Faghri, F., Flect, D.J., Kiros, J.R., Fidler, S.: Vse++: Improving visual-semantic embeddings with hard negatives. arXiv preprint arXiv:1707.05612 (2017)
9. Gretton, A., Borgwardt, K., Rasch, M., Schölkopf, B., Smola, A.: A kernel method for the two-sample-problem. Advances in neural information processing systems **19** (2006)
10. Gu, J., Cai, J., Joty, S.R., Niu, L., Wang, G.: Look, imagine and match: improving textual-visual cross-modal retrieval with generative models. In: Proceedings of the IEEE Conference on Computer Vision and Pattern Recognition, pp. 7181–7189 (2018)
11. Han, H., Zheng, Q., Dai, G., Luo, M., Wang, J.: Learning to rematch mismatched pairs for robust cross-modal retrieval. In: Proceedings of the IEEE/CVF Conference on Computer Vision and Pattern Recognition, pp. 26679–26688 (2024)

12. He, K., Zhang, X., Ren, S., Sun, J.: Deep residual learning for image recognition. In: Proceedings of the IEEE Conference on Computer Vision and Pattern Recognition, pp. 770–778 (2016)
13. Jabri, A., Joulin, A., Van Der Maaten, L.: Revisiting visual question answering baselines. In: European Conference on Computer Vision, pp. 727–739. Springer (2016)
14. Karpathy, A., Fei-Fei, L.: Deep visual-semantic alignments for generating image descriptions. In: Proceedings of the IEEE Conference on Computer Vision and Pattern Recognition, pp. 3128–3137 (2015)
15. Kim, D., Kim, N., Kwak, S.: Improving cross-modal retrieval with set of diverse embeddings. In: Proceedings of the IEEE/CVF Conference on Computer Vision and Pattern Recognition, pp. 23422–23431 (2023)
16. Li, K., Zhang, Y., Li, K., Li, Y., Fu, Y.: Visual semantic reasoning for image-text matching. In: Proceedings of the IEEE/CVF International Conference on Computer Vision, pp. 4654–4662 (2019)
17. Lin, T.-Y., et al.: Microsoft COCO: common Objects in Context. In: Fleet, D., Pajdla, T., Schiele, B., Tuytelaars, T. (eds.) ECCV 2014. LNCS, vol. 8693, pp. 740–755. Springer, Cham (2014). https://doi.org/10.1007/978-3-319-10602-1_48
18. Liu, C., Mao, Z., Liu, A.A., Zhang, T., Wang, B., Zhang, Y.: Focus your attention: a bidirectional focal attention network for image-text matching. In: Proceedings of the 27th ACM International Conference on Multimedia, pp. 3–11 (2019)
19. Locatello, F., et al.: Object-centric learning with slot attention. Adv. Neural. Inf. Process. Syst. **33**, 11525–11538 (2020)
20. Lu, J., Batra, D., Parikh, D., Lee, S.: Vilbert: pretraining task-agnostic visiolinguistic representations for vision-and-language tasks. Advances in neural information processing systems **32** (2019)
21. Nam, H., Ha, J.W., Kim, J.: Dual attention networks for multimodal reasoning and matching. In: Proceedings of the IEEE Conference on Computer Vision and Pattern Recognition, pp. 299–307 (2017)
22. Pennington, J., Socher, R., Manning, C.D.: Glove: Global vectors for word representation. In: Proceedings of the 2014 Conference on Empirical Methods in Natural Language Processing (EMNLP), pp. 1532–1543 (2014)
23. Plummer, B.A., Wang, L., Cervantes, C.M., Caicedo, J.C., Hockenmaier, J., Lazebnik, S.: Flickr30k entities: collecting region-to-phrase correspondences for richer image-to-sentence models. In: Proceedings of the IEEE International Conference on Computer Vision, pp. 2641–2649 (2015)
24. Ren, S., He, K., Girshick, R., Sun, J.: Faster r-cnn: towards real-time object detection with region proposal networks. IEEE Trans. Pattern Anal. Mach. Intell. **39**(6), 1137–1149 (2016)
25. Shi, Y., Jain, A.K.: Probabilistic face embeddings. In: Proceedings of the IEEE/CVF International Conference on Computer Vision, pp. 6902–6911 (2019)
26. Song, Y., Soleymani, M.: Polysemous visual-semantic embedding for cross-modal retrieval. In: Proceedings of the IEEE/CVF Conference on Computer Vision and Pattern Recognition, pp. 1979–1988 (2019)
27. Van Gansbeke, W., Vandenhende, S., Georgoulis, S., Proesmans, M., Van Gool, L.: Scan: Learning to classify images without labels. In: European Conference on Computer Vision, pp. 268–285. Springer (2020)
28. Wang, L., Li, Y., Huang, J., Lazebnik, S.: Learning two-branch neural networks for image-text matching tasks. IEEE Trans. Pattern Anal. Mach. Intell. **41**(2), 394–407 (2018)

29. Wei, X., Zhang, T., Li, Y., Zhang, Y., Wu, F.: Multi-modality cross attention network for image and sentence matching. In: Proceedings of the IEEE/CVF Conference on Computer Vision and Pattern Recognition, pp. 10941–10950 (2020)
30. Xie, S., Girshick, R., Dollár, P., Tu, Z., He, K.: Aggregated residual transformations for deep neural networks. In: Proceedings of the IEEE Conference on Computer Vision and Pattern Recognition, pp. 1492–1500 (2017)
31. Zhang, Q., Lei, Z., Zhang, Z., Li, S.Z.: Context-aware attention network for image-text retrieval. In: Proceedings of the IEEE/CVF Conference on Computer Vision and Pattern Recognition, pp. 3536–3545 (2020)

Single-Layer Denoising Taylorformer for UAV Nighttime Tracking

Zihao Su, Haijun Wang$^{(\boxtimes)}$, and Lihua Qi

Aviation Information Technology Research and Development, Shandong University of Aeronautics, BinZhou, China
`whjkyx@163.com`

Abstract. The automation of unmanned aerial vehicles (UAVs) has been driven in large part by vision object tracking methods with onboard cameras. However, random and complex real-world noise in captured imagery severely degrades the performance of state-of-the-art (SOTA) UAV trackers, especially under low-illumination conditions. To address this challenge, we propose a prompt-guided Taylorformer and design a plug-and-play, single-layer denoising network (SDT) aimed at suppressing heterogeneous noise and thereby improving UAV tracking performance. Specifically, our lightweight single-layer architecture employs minimal network depth to reduce computational overhead. We introduce prompt-guided Taylor self-attention (PTSA) and prompt-guided Taylor cross-attention (PTCA) to form a raw feature extraction (RFE) encoder and a multi-feature fusion (MFF) decoder, respectively, enhancing both feature extraction and fusion capabilities. In addition, we develop a multi-scale feed-forward network (MSFN) that more effectively leverages noise information across multiple receptive fields to further optimize network performance. Extensive experiments demonstrate that our proposed SDT achieves significantly denoising efficacy and substantially enhances UAV nighttime object tracking accuracy.

Keywords: Unmanned aerial vehicle · Object tracking · Image denoising · Low-illumination environments

1 Introduction

Object tracking remains a critical research focus in computer vision, showcasing substantial practical value in unmanned aerial vehicle (UAV). With continued advancements in foundational research, numerous state-of-the-art (SOTA) UAV trackers have been developed, and recent studies have increasingly concentrated on low-light tracking scenarios [1–3]. Due to the inherent limitations of onboard cameras in low-light conditions, images often suffer from cluttered and severe real-world noise. Therefore, addressing the noise challenges encountered in UAV tracking under low-light conditions has become an urgent and imperative research goal.

© The Author(s), under exclusive license to Springer Nature Singapore Pte Ltd. 2026
Z. Lin et al. (Eds.): ICIG 2025, LNCS 16161, pp. 126–137, 2026.
https://doi.org/10.1007/978-981-95-3398-5_11

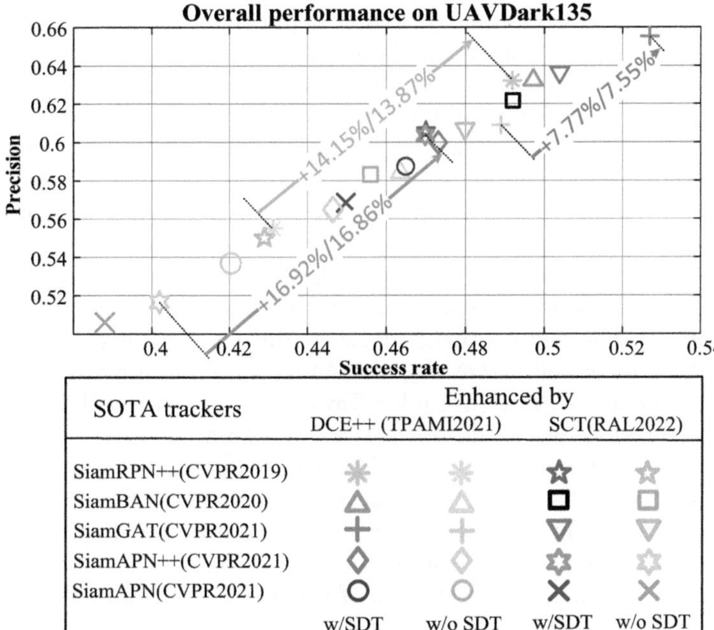

SOTA trackers	Enhanced by			
	DCE++ (TPAMI2021)		SCT(RAL2022)	
SiamRPN++(CVPR2019)	✳	✳	☆	☆
SiamBAN(CVPR2020)	△	△	◻	◻
SiamGAT(CVPR2021)	+	+	▽	▽
SiamAPN++(CVPR2021)	◇	◇	✪	✪
SiamAPN(CVPR2021)	◯	◯	✕	✕
	w/SDT	w/o SDT	w/SDT	w/o SDT

Fig. 1. Overall performance improvement of leading-edge trackers [1,4–6] with SDT on the UAVDark135 [2] benchmark. Symbols with light color represent the original trackers and dark-colored ones denote trackers denoised by SDT.

Siamese UAV trackers [1,4,7] leverage the feature extraction capabilities of their dual-branch backbone network to demonstrate robust performance in low-light UAV tracking tasks. However, under uneven illumination, noise captured by onboard cameras severely disrupts feature extraction. To mitigate the adverse effects of insufficient lighting, many trackers [3,7] are typically integrated with low-light enhancers to improve their ability to extract discriminative features. Unfortunately, while enhancing image brightness, these enhancers also amplify image noise levels, further degrading feature quality. To further enhance tracker performance, we propose an efficient denoiser that eliminates noise interference from enhanced nighttime images, thereby enhancing UAV tracking performance in nighttime environments.

Denoising, as a core task in image restoration, aims to estimate the underlying clean image from its noisy observation. In real-world UAV scenarios, image noise often deviates from a Gaussian distribution. These non-Gaussian characteristics substantially increase the difficulty of denoising. Compared to traditional denoising methods that rely on physical modeling, deep learning-based denoising algorithms demonstrate superior generalization capability and robustness through massive data-driven training. With the rise of Transformer [8] and the proposal of U-Net structures, deep learning-based denoising methods have achieved continuous performance improvements [9,10]. However, the inherent complexity of U-Net hinders its lightweight deployment, and the quadratic computational complexity of Transformer's self-attention mechanism makes existing algorithms difficult to adapt to computationally constrained UAV platforms. Therefore, simplifying U-Net architectures and optimizing Transformer computations, which holds significant importance for enabling real-time, efficient denoising on UAVs.

As mentioned above, UAV nighttime tracking performance remains suboptimal in the presence of chaotic and complex noise. To mitigate the impact of real-world noise on UAV tracking, we design a single-layer denoising network (SDT) which uses a prompt-guided Taylorformer to provide a novel solution for object tracking under challenging nocturnal noise conditions. Specifically, we introduce prompt-guided Taylor self-attention (PTSA) to construct a raw feature extraction (RFE) encoder and prompt-guided Taylor cross-attention (PTCA) to build a multi-feature fusion (MFF) decoder. Moreover, to accommodate the diversity of features across different receptive fields, we design a multi-scale feed-forward network (MSFN) that adaptively extracts and aggregates features at multiple scales. As shown in Fig. 1, SDT can assist trackers in significantly improving performance in severe noise environments.

In summary, the main contributions of this work are as follows:

1) We propose a single-layer denoising network architecture with a novel prompt-guided Taylorformer to restore noisy images with reduced computational cost, thereby significantly enhancing UAV nighttime tracking performance.
2) We design novel RFE encoder and MFF decoder modules whose synergistic integration enables interactive feature fusion, improving the model's robustness to complex noise environments.
3) We develop a novel MSFN that employs dilated convolutions to expand the receptive field, adaptively extracting multi-scale spatial features across varying receptive fields.
4) Extensive results demonstrate that, even with a simplified architecture, our proposed SDT can achieve expected tracking performance when integrated with various trackers, thereby exhibiting substantial application value in the field of UAV nighttime tracking.

2   Related Work

2.1   Object Tracking Algorithms

In recent years, the adoption of Siamese networks in visual tracking has achieved significant performance improvements [1,4,5,11,12]. Due to their balance of efficiency and accuracy, Siamese networks have been widely applied in UAV tracking tasks [1,4]. Siamese trackers can be categorized into anchor-based and anchor-free methods depending on the target localization approach [13]. Anchor-based trackers [5,12] employ predefined anchors to distinguish foreground from background and predict target positions and scales through regression using a Region Proposal Network (RPN). In contrast, anchor-free trackers eliminate the use of predefined anchors and directly regress target offsets to improve generalization. Building on the strengths of these two approaches, SiamAPN++ [5] demonstrates its effectiveness as a UAV tracker by generating a minimal set of high-quality anchor boxes to achieve more precise tracking performance. Recent research in UAV nighttime tracking have mainly focused on employing image enhancers to improve the quality of nighttime images [3,14]. However, most approaches do not address the adverse impact of complex noise on tracking performance, which can lead to unstable target localization and reduced tracking accuracy.

2.2 Image Denoising

As a crucial component of image restoration, image denoising task aims to reconstruct high-quality, clean images from noisy observations. Recent studies have demonstrated that deep learning-based denoising methods exhibit significant advantages over traditional handcrafted prior-based approaches [9,10,15]. Through data-driven large-scale training combined with prompt parameter optimization strategies, the performance and robustness of denoising models can be substantially enhanced, particularly in complex noise scenarios such as UAV low-light imaging. The classical U-Net architecture employs an encoder-decoder design, which hierarchically extracts and fuses multi-scale features to capture global and local information [9,10,15]. Its residual learning mechanism fully exploits inter-layer feature residuals, enabling efficient feature propagation in image restoration and super-resolution tasks [16]. However, existing U-Net [17] structures face parameter redundancy during downsampling and upsampling operations, as well as error accumulation effects during feature propagation. These limitations not only constrain further performance improvement but also result in persistently high computational resource consumption.

2.3 Vision Transformer

With the rapid advancement of computational technologies, the emergence of the Vision Transformer (ViT) [8] has introduced novel solutions for image analysis tasks. Benefiting from the global self-attention mechanism's ability to efficiently model long-range dependencies, ViT has demonstrated exceptional performance in numerous computer vision tasks, such as image segmentation and object detection. In recent years, the applications of ViT have expanded into domains like object tracking and image restoration. However, unlike traditional convolutional neural networks (CNNs), the computational complexity of ViT increases quadratically with the spatial resolution of feature maps, making it challenging to deploy on lightweight platforms such as UAVs. To fully leverage the advantages of self-attention while minimizing computational burdens, Qiu et al. [18] proposed Taylor-expanded multi-head self-attention (T-MSA), which integrates Taylor expansion with ViT to alleviate computational demands. Nevertheless, the highly complex and unpredictable noise distributions in real-world scenarios require the network to focus on multi-receptive field and multi-frequency feature representations. Sole reliance on self-attention mechanisms struggles to achieve ideal denoising performance under such conditions.

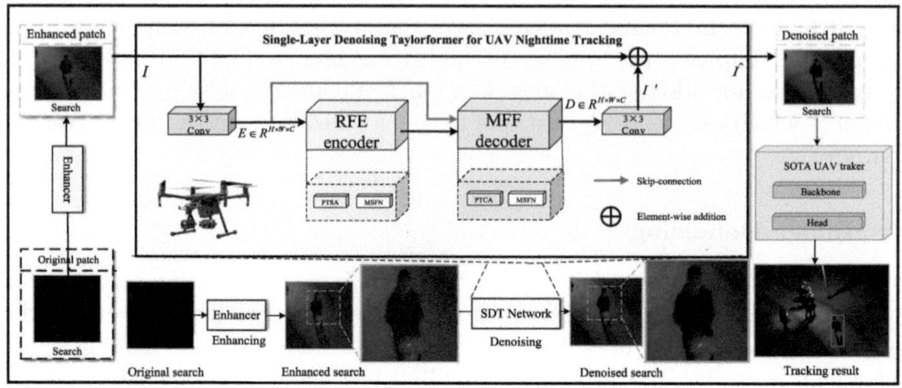

Fig. 2. The framework of single-layer denoising Taylorformer.

3   Proposed Method

3.1   Overall Structure

As shown in Fig. 2, given an image patch $I \in \mathbb{R}^{H \times W \times 3}$ from the search region, SDT first applies a 3×3 convolution operation to extract the initial feature map $E \in \mathbb{R}^{H \times W \times C}$, where H, W, and C denote height, width, and channel number, respectively. The initial feature map E is then sequentially processed by the RFE encoder and the MFF decoder, yielding the decoded features $D \in \mathbb{R}^{H \times W \times C}$. To assist the recovery process, a skip-connection is introduced to preserve the image's structural and textural details. Additionally, a cross-attention is employed in the decoder to facilitate the fusion of features. Finally, a convolution layer is applied to the decoded features D to generate the residual image $I' \in \mathbb{R}^{H \times W \times 3}$, which is then added to the degraded input image to obtain the restored image $\hat{I} = I' + I$. The following section presents the core components of the proposed SDT.

3.2   Prompt-Guided Taylorformer

In order to address the high computational cost and limited sensitivity to noisy features inherent in conventional self-attention mechanisms, we propose PTSA and PTCA, as illustrated in Fig. 3. These modules are integrated into the RFE encoder and MFF decoder, respectively. By incorporating prompt information [19] and leveraging Taylor-series approximations, the proposed mechanism can enhance noise awareness while preserving linear computational complexity.

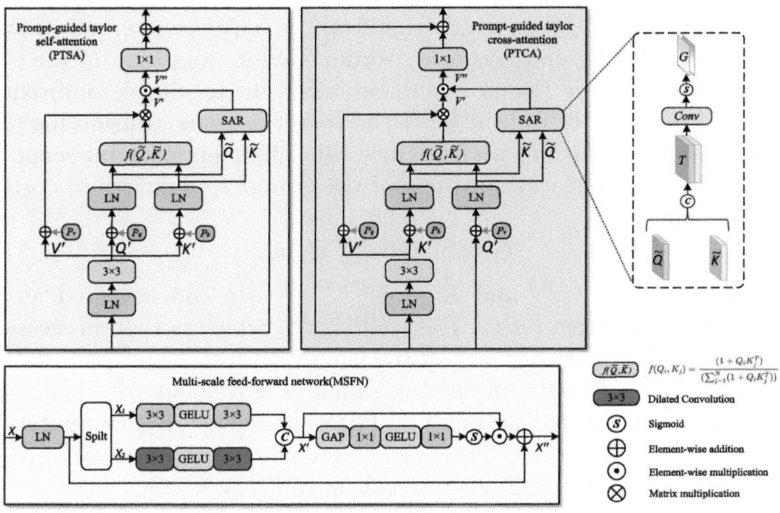

Fig. 3. Illustration of each component in Taylorformer blocks.

Specifically, given an input feature with spatial resolution $H \times W$ and channels C, PTSA first generates matrix query(Q), key(K) and value(V) through point convolution and depth-wise convolution operations. The original matrices $Q, K, V \in \mathbb{R}^{H \times W \times C}$ are then reshaped into $Q', K', V' \in \mathbb{R}^{HW \times C}$ to accommodate prompt injection. Next, the learnable prompt vectors $P_q, P_k, P_v \in \mathbb{R}^{1 \times C}$ are injected into their corresponding feature matrices via element-wise addition, yielding enhanced feature representations:

$$\tilde{Q} = Q' + P_q$$
$$\tilde{K} = K' + P_k \tag{1}$$
$$\tilde{V} = V' + P_v$$

Here $\tilde{Q}, \tilde{K}, \tilde{V}$ represent the enhanced versions of Q', K', V' matrices after prompt adjustments. By injecting prompt information into these matrices, we introduce semantic-space shifts that explicitly guide the model to focus on processing specific types of noise features. Inspired by T-MSA [18], we approximate the softmax in the standard self-attention using a first-order Taylor series expansion, thereby generalizing it into the Taylor-Attention formulation:

$$V_i' = \text{Taylor-Attention}(\tilde{Q}_i, \tilde{K}_i, \tilde{V}_i)$$
$$= \frac{\sum_{j=1}^{N} \tilde{V}_j^T + \tilde{Q}_i^T \sum_{j=1}^{N} \tilde{K}_j \tilde{V}_j^T}{N + \tilde{Q}_i^T \sum_{j=1}^{N} \tilde{K}_j}. \tag{2}$$

This approach preserves the semantic modeling capacity of the core self-attention while reducing the computational complexity of conventional self-attention from

$\mathcal{O}(H^2W^2)$ to linear $\mathcal{O}(HW)$, which significantly improves computational efficacy. However, as PTSA employs a first-order Taylor expansion of the softmax function and neglects the Peano remainder term, an inevitable approximation error is introduced into the output V'. To address this issue, considering that the images have local correlation, we introduce the self-attention refinement (SAR) to extract the local correlation features of the $\tilde{Q}$ and $\tilde{K}$ matrices to correct the inaccurate output V'.

$$G = \mathrm{Sigmoid}(TW_l), \tag{3}$$

Specifically, $\tilde{Q} \in \mathbb{R}^{D \times H \times W}$ and $\tilde{K} \in \mathbb{R}^{D \times H \times W}$ are concatenated along the channel dimension to form tensor $T \in \mathbb{R}^{2D \times H \times W}$, which is then processed by a 3×3 convolution W_l to extract local correlation features and generate the gating signal $G \in \mathbb{R}^{1 \times H \times W}$. Finally, the gating signal G is element-wise multiplied by V' to generate the corrected output V''. The enhanced PTSA computation can be expressed as:

$$\begin{aligned}
V' &= \text{Taylor-Attention } (\tilde{Q}, \tilde{K}, \tilde{V}), \\
V'' &= X + \mathrm{Concat}(V' \odot G)W^p,
\end{aligned} \tag{4}$$

where X and V'' denote the input and output feature maps. Correspondingly, PTCA is built upon the PTSA. To overcome the limitation of self-attention in handling only single-source features, this work introduces cross-attention in the MFF decoder and proposes the PTCA module. Unlike traditional methods that rely on complex feature concatenation and channel adjustment, PTCA directly uses the network's full input feature map as the query. This design eliminates additional computational overhead while preserving semantic integrity. As demonstrated in Sect. 4, the proposed Taylorformer significantly improves UAV tracking performance under nighttime conditions.

3.3 Multi-scale Feed-Forward Network

Inspired by the multi-scale principle, we propose a multi-scale feed-forward network (MSFN) to effectively capture fine-grained image details complementary to the self-attention. As illustrated in Fig. 3, MSFN first evenly splits the input feature $X \in \mathbb{R}^{H \times W \times C}$ along the channel dimension into two sub-feature maps $X_1, X_2 \in \mathbb{R}^{H \times W \times C/2}$. Next, we apply a differentiated convolution strategies $\mathcal{F}$ to the two sub-feature maps: standard convolution is applied to X_1 to extract conventional local features, while dilated convolution is applied to X_2 to capture broader receptive field information. Finally, the parallel outputs are concatenated and passed through multiple residual structures to enhance sensitivity to high-frequency noise. The entire process can be expressed as:

$$\begin{aligned}
X'' &= G(X') \cdot X' + \mathrm{LN}(X), \\
X' &= \mathcal{F}(X_1, X_2) = \mathrm{Cat}[W_g(\mathrm{GELU}(W_g(X_1))), W_d(\mathrm{GELU}(W_d(X_2)))], \\
G(X) &= W_f(\mathrm{GELU}(W_f(\mathrm{GAP}(X)))),
\end{aligned} \tag{5}$$

where $\mathrm{Cat}(\cdot)$ denotes the channel-wise concatenation, $\mathrm{GAP}(\cdot)$ performs global average pooling, and W_f, W_g, W_d correspond to 1×1 convolution, 3×3 convolution, and 3×3 dilated convolution.

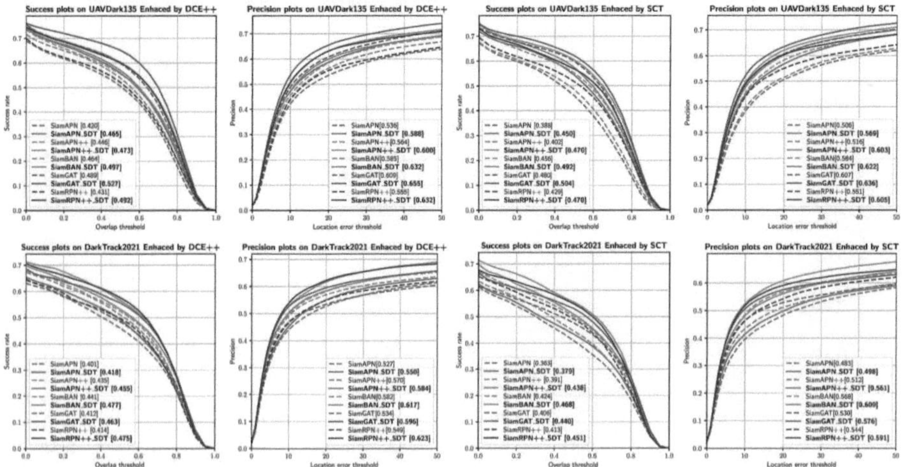

Fig. 4. Overall performance of SOTA trackers on UAVDark135 and DarkTrack2021, using various enhancers deployed with (plots with solid lines) or not (plots with dashed lines).

4   Experiments

4.1   Implementation Details

The proposed SDT adopts an encoder-decoder architecture, in which both the encoder and decoder consist of a single Taylorformer block. The channel expansion factor in the MSFN is configured as $\gamma = 2.66$. During training, the SIDD dataset [20] is utilized. Two authoritative low-light UAV tracking benchmark datasets, UAVDark135 [2] and DarkTrack2021 [14] are used to evaluate the effectiveness of SDT for UAV nighttime object tracking. All training experiments are conducted on a workstation equipped with four NVIDIA GeForce RTX 3080 GPUs, while inference tests are performed using three Tesla P100 GPUs.

4.2   Combination of SDT with Trackers and Low-Light Enhancers

To validate the performance of SDT when integrated with different trackers and low-light enhancers, this section selects five SOTA trackers including SiamAPN [1], SiamAPN++ [4], SiamRPN++ [5], SiamBAN [6] and SiamGAT [21] along with two widely used low-light enhancers, SCT [14] and DCE++ [22], for evaluation. As shown in Fig. 4, the performance comparison of SDT is demonstrated on two low-light UAV benchmark datasets: UAVDark135 [2] and DarkTrack2021 [14]. On UAVDark135, when combining SCT with SiamAPN++, SDT achieves 16.92% and 16.86% improvements in success rate and precision, respectively.

On DarkTrack2021, SiamRPN++ enhanced by DCE++ exhibits 14.73% and 13.84% gains in success rate and precision with SDT assistance. Although the

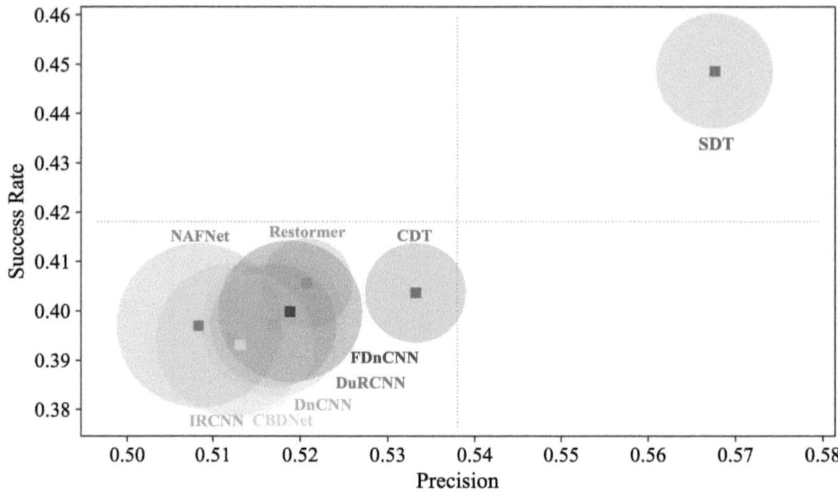

Fig. 5. Tracking performance comparison with different denoisers applied. The area of the circle represents the running speed of the denoiser. The larger, the faster.

extent of performance improvement varies across different trackers, the effectiveness of noise suppression in enhancing the overall tracking performance is conclusively validated.

4.3   Comparison With SOTA Denoisers

To further assess the effectiveness of SDT in improving UAV object tracking performance under low-light conditions, we conduct a comparative study involving eight SOTA denoising methods: Restormer [9], NAFNet [15], DRUNet [23], CBDNet [24], FDnCNN [25,26], DnCNN [26], IRCNN [27], and CDT [28]. As illustrated in Fig. 5, our proposed SDT demonstrates performance improvements in both accuracy and efficiency on the enhanced UAVDark135. Specifically, SDT requires approximately one-eighth the training time of Restormer, while achieving a 9.42% increase in precision and an 11.11% improvement in success rate. These results confirm that SDT can effectively enhance UAV tracking performance.

4.4   Ablation Study

In this subsection, we analyze the performance of various SDT variant models. We use SiamAPN combined with SCT as the tracking baseline and evaluate performance on the UAVDark135 dataset, with detailed results summarized in Table 1. Single refers to the single-layer encoder-decoder architecture, Prec. denotes precision, and Δ indicates the performance improvement margin relative to the baseline method. The best results are highlighted in bold.

Table 1. Comparison of SDT with different components on UAVDark135.

	Proto.			+SDT
Single	–	✓	✓	✓
PTSA+PTCA	–	–	✓	✓
MSFN	–	–	–	✓
Prec. (CLE = 20)	0.506	0.535	0.556	**0.569**
Δ (%)	–	+5.73	+9.88	**+12.45**

Table 2. Comparison of SDT with different number of levels on UAVDark135.

n (Levels)	1	2	3	4
Prec. (CLE = 20)	**0.569**	0.546	0.549	0.556
Δ (%)	–	−4.54	−3.95	−2.57

Single-Layer Encoder-Decoder Architecture: To address the limitations of the traditional four-stage U-Net, we design a single-layer encoder-decoder that streamlines the network and dramatically reduces the denoiser's computational demands. With only a minimal number of modules, this architecture improves tracking accuracy by 5.73%.

PTSA and PTCA: Instead of using self-attention throughout the network, cross-attention is introduced into the decoder structure. Combined with the single-layer backbone, these modules yield a 9.88% gain in tracking precision.

MSFN: MSFN enhances sensitivity to high-frequency noise by employing differentiated convolution operations across multiple receptive fields and embedding residual structures. While maintaining a lightweight design, this module boosts the network's performance by 12.45%.

4.5 Parametric Analysis

To evaluate the impact of network depth on UAV nighttime tracking performance, we conducted an ablation study by varying the number of layers. As presented in Table 2, using the single-layer model ($n = 1$) as the baseline, we tested on the UAVDark135 dataset in conjunction with SiamAPN and SCT. When $n > 1$, the network suffered both degraded feature representation and amplified noise, leading to reduced tracking accuracy and increased computational cost. In contrast, reducing the depth to $n = 1$ improved the precision rate by 2.57% and reduced the training time by approximately 25%. These findings suggest that a single-layer architecture is more effective in achieving high-quality features for UAV nighttime tracking.

5   Conclusion

In this work, we propose a efficient denoising network (SDT) to enhance noise resistance in UAV nighttime tracking. Built on a single-layer encoder-decoder architecture integrated with Taylorformer, SDT reduces overall computational complexity while maintaining efficient feature capture capabilities. PTSA focuses on extracting low-level texture features from raw image patches, while PTCA enables effective fusion between raw features and encoded features. After acquiring enriched feature representations, MSFN further extracts multi-receptive field features in parallel, combined with residual structures to reinforce high-frequency noise suppression. Extensive experiments demonstrate that SDT effectively mitigates low-light noise interference in UAV nighttime object tracking.

References

1. Fu, C., Cao, Z., Li, Y., Ye, J., Feng, C.: Siamese anchor proposal network for high-speed aerial tracking. In: 2021 IEEE International Conference on Robotics and Automation (ICRA), pp. 510–516 (2021)
2. Li, B., Fu, C., Ding, F., Ye, J., Lin, F.: All-day object tracking for unmanned aerial vehicle. IEEE Trans. Mob. Comput. **22**(8), 4515–4529 (2023)
3. Ye, J., Fu, C., Zheng, G., Cao, Z., Li, B.: Darklighter: Light up the darkness for uav tracking. In: 2021 IEEE/RSJ International Conference on Intelligent Robots and Systems (IROS), pp. 3079–3085 (2021)
4. Cao, Z., Fu, C., Ye, J., Li, B., Li, Y.: Siamapn++: Siamese attentional aggregation network for real-time uav tracking. In: 2021 IEEE/RSJ International Conference on Intelligent Robots and Systems (IROS), pp. 3086–3092 (2021)
5. Li, B., Wu, W., Wang, Q., Zhang, F., Xing, J., Yan, J.: Siamrpn++: Evolution of siamese visual tracking with very deep networks. In: Proceedings of the IEEE/CVF Conference on Computer Vision and Pattern Recognition, pp. 4282–4291 (2019)
6. Chen, Z., Zhong, B., Li, G., Zhang, S., Ji, R.: Siamese box adaptive network for visual tracking. In: Proceedings of the IEEE/CVF Conference on Computer Vision and Pattern Recognition, pp. 6668–6677 (2020)
7. Fu, C., Dong, H., Ye, J., Zheng, G., Li, S., Zhao, J.: Highlightnet: Highlighting low-light potential features for real-time uav tracking. In: 2022 IEEE/RSJ International Conference on Intelligent Robots and Systems (IROS), pp. 12146–12153 (2022)
8. Dosovitskiy, A., et al.: An image is worth 16x16 words: Transformers for image recognition at scale. arXiv preprint arXiv:2010.11929 (2020)
9. Zamir, S.W., Arora, A., Khan, S., Hayat, M., Khan, F.S., Yang, M.H.: Restormer: Efficient transformer for high-resolution image restoration. In: Proceedings of the IEEE/CVF Conference on Computer Vision and Pattern Recognition, pp. 5728–5739 (2022)
10. Wang, Z., Cun, X., Bao, J., Zhou, W., Liu, J., Li, H.: Uformer: a general u-shaped transformer for image restoration. In: Proceedings of the IEEE/CVF Conference on Computer Vision and Pattern Recognition, pp. 17683–17693 (2022)
11. Bertinetto, L., Valmadre, J., Henriques, J.F., Vedaldi, A., Torr, P.H.S.: Fully-Convolutional Siamese Networks for Object Tracking. In: Hua, G., Jégou, H. (eds.) ECCV 2016. LNCS, vol. 9914, pp. 850–865. Springer, Cham (2016). https://doi.org/10.1007/978-3-319-48881-3_56

12. Li, B., Yan, J., Wu, W., Zhu, Z., Hu, X.: High performance visual tracking with siamese region proposal network. In: Proceedings of the IEEE Conference on Computer Vision and Pattern Recognition, pp. 8971–8980 (2018)
13. Fu, C., Lu, K., Zheng, G., Ye, J., Cao, Z., Li, B., Lu, G.: Siamese object tracking for unmanned aerial vehicle: a review and comprehensive analysis. arxiv 2022. arXiv preprint arXiv:2205.04281
14. Ye, J., Fu, C., Cao, Z., An, S., Zheng, G., Li, B.: Tracker meets night: a transformer enhancer for uav tracking. IEEE Robot. Automation Lett. **7**(2), 3866–3873 (2022)
15. Chen, L., Chu, X., Zhang, X., Sun, J.: Simple baselines for image restoration. In: European conference on computer vision. pp. 17–33. Springer (2022)
16. Zhang, Y., Li, K., Li, K., Wang, L., Zhong, B., Fu, Y.: Image super-resolution using very deep residual channel attention networks. In: Proceedings of the European Conference on Computer Vision (ECCV), pp. 286–301 (2018)
17. Ronneberger, O., Fischer, P., Brox, T.: U-Net: Convolutional Networks for Biomedical Image Segmentation. In: Navab, N., Hornegger, J., Wells, W.M., Frangi, A.F. (eds.) MICCAI 2015. LNCS, vol. 9351, pp. 234–241. Springer, Cham (2015). https://doi.org/10.1007/978-3-319-24574-4_28
18. Qiu, Y., Zhang, K., Wang, C., Luo, W., Li, H., Jin, Z.: Mb-taylorformer: Multi-branch efficient transformer expanded by taylor formula for image dehazing. In: Proceedings of the IEEE/CVF International Conference on Computer Vision, pp. 12802–12813 (2023)
19. Gao, H., Yang, J., Zhang, Y., Wang, N., Yang, J., Dang, D.: Prompt-based ingredient-oriented all-in-one image restoration. IEEE Trans. Circuits Syst. Video Technol. (2024)
20. Abdelhamed, A., Lin, S., Brown, M.S.: A high-quality denoising dataset for smartphone cameras. In: Proceedings of the IEEE Conference on Computer Vision and Pattern Recognition, pp. 1692–1700 (2018)
21. Guo, D., Shao, Y., Cui, Y., Wang, Z., Zhang, L., Shen, C.: Graph attention tracking. In: Proceedings of the IEEE/CVF Conference on Computer Vision and Pattern Recognition, pp. 9543–9552 (2021)
22. Li, C., Guo, C., Loy, C.C.: Learning to enhance low-light image via zero-reference deep curve estimation. IEEE Trans. Pattern Anal. Mach. Intell. **44**(8), 4225–4238 (2021)
23. Zhang, K., Li, Y., Zuo, W., Zhang, L., Van Gool, L., Timofte, R.: Plug-and-play image restoration with deep denoiser prior. IEEE Trans. Pattern Anal. Mach. Intell. **44**(10), 6360–6376 (2021)
24. Guo, S., Yan, Z., Zhang, K., Zuo, W., Zhang, L.: Toward convolutional blind denoising of real photographs. In: Proceedings of the IEEE/CVF Conference on Computer Vision and Pattern Recognition, pp. 1712–1722 (2019)
25. Zhang, K., Zuo, W., Zhang, L.: Ffdnet: toward a fast and flexible solution for cnn-based image denoising. IEEE Trans. Image Process. **27**(9), 4608–4622 (2018)
26. Zhang, K., Zuo, W., Chen, Y., Meng, D., Zhang, L.: Beyond a gaussian denoiser: residual learning of deep cnn for image denoising. IEEE Trans. Image Process. **26**(7), 3142–3155 (2017)
27. Zhang, K., Zuo, W., Gu, S., Zhang, L.: Learning deep cnn denoiser prior for image restoration. In: Proceedings of the IEEE Conference on Computer Vision and Pattern Recognition, pp. 3929–3938 (2017)
28. Lu, K., Fu, C., Wang, Y., Zuo, H., Zheng, G., Pan, J.: Cascaded denoising transformer for uav nighttime tracking. IEEE Robot. Automation Lett. **8**(6), 3142–3149 (2023)

Position-Aware Text-to-Image Generation with Efficient Controllability

Junchao Gu[✉], Xiangyu Wang, Yuchen Du, and Hao Chen

School of Artificial Intelligence, Xidian University, Xi'an, China
`23171214627@stu.xidian.edu.cn`

Abstract. In recent years, Stable Diffusion has significantly advanced the quality of text-to-image generation. However, accurately interpreting and representing Spatial Layouts specified by text prompts remains challenging. Existing approaches typically rely either on extra grounding information or utilize LLMs (large language models) combined with layout-controllable models which suffer from high computational costs. To address these limitations, we propose a novel method SamLayGe, a lightweight and efficient layout generation model designed for seamless integration into existing text-to-image pipelines. SamLayGe autonomously generates comprehensive layouts without requiring explicit user inputs, thus surpassing current LLM-based and layout-controllable approaches in terms of versatility and efficiency. Furthermore, we propose LayGeBench, a benchmark dataset addressing ambiguities in spatial descriptions of prior datasets. Extensive evaluations demonstrate that SamLayGe consistently produces images that accurately adhere to textual layout descriptions, achieving superior performance in terms of both accuracy and computational efficiency. Code is available at https://github.com/shenlanzhuanshu/caption-to-positional-layout. Position-Aware Text-to-Image Generation with Efficient Controllability.

Keywords: Text-to-image · Text-to-layout · Efficient Controllability · Positional Relationship

1 Introduction

Text-to-Image (T2I) models, represented by the rise of Stable Diffusion, allow users to generate high-quality images through simple text descriptions, revolutionizing the field of generative AI. Especially, Stable Diffusion demonstrates exceptional performance in generating single-object images. These technological advancements have established T2I models as an important cornerstone for AI-driven creation and visual content generation.

Although the Stable Diffusion series of models have demonstrated excellent performance, they still face significant challenges in comprehensively understanding and generating layout information and positional relationships between objects described

---

This work was supported by the Fundamental Research Funds for the Centra Universities and Natural Science Basic Research Program of Shaanxi (Program No. 2023-JC-QN-0736).

in text prompts (i.e., the Better Prompt [29] problem). To address this issue, controllable text-to-image generation techniques have gradually become a new research focus. Methods such as ControlNet [14], GLIGEN [15], and ReCo [18] employ LoRA fine-tuning [21] to embed modules in Stable Diffusion that specifically receive user-input layout information, enabling the model to generate images that match the provided layout requirements. However, these approaches still rely on additional user input and fail to fundamentally solve the core challenge of T2I models automatically generating images consistent with caption descriptions—ultimately failing to resolve the Better Prompt [29] problem at its root.

Recently, a new paradigm utilizing LLMs to generate layout information has gradually emerged. Methods such as Ranni [32] and Attention Refocusing [33] leverage LLMs to produce structured layouts, which are seamlessly integrated into layout-controllable T2I models (e.g., BoxDiff [10] or GLIGEN [15]) to generate high-quality images. While these approaches demonstrate excellent performance in generation effects, they incur substantial computational overhead: users need not only deploy LLMs but also run resource-intensive T2I models, making it difficult to support their operation on consumer-grade GPUs.

We propose SamLayGe, a lightweight end-to-end framework for text-to-image generation. It extracts positional cues from captions to build accurate layouts, then renders high-quality images that faithfully match the original description. Our model can seamlessly integrate into any layout-controllable T2I model. Unlike existing methods that rely on high-computational LLMs or additional user input, the proposed method SamLayGe directly incorporates layout generation into the T2I generation pipeline, offering a lightweight and resource-efficient solution. By eliminating the need for standalone LLM deployment, this approach makes layout-controllable T2I technology more accessible to scenarios with limited computational resources. Compared to previous methods, SamLayGe uses a supervised training approach to generate more accurate layout information, enabling seamless integration with any layout-controllable T2I model. As shown in Fig. 1, the predicted layout steers the layout-to-image stage step by step, yielding high-quality images that strictly match the caption.

The main contributions of this work are as follow:

- We propose SamLayGe, a novel lightweight end-to-end framework for Text-to-Layout generation that directly extracts positional cues from captions to create accurate layouts, enhancing the fidelity of generated images.
- We develop an end-to-end architecture for layout controllable T2I generation, which effectively integrates layout generation into the T2I pipeline, eliminating the need for high computational LLMs and additional user input.
- We conduct LayGeBench, a benchmark dataset specifically designed to assess the effectiveness of layout-controllable T2I models, facilitating consistent performance evaluation and advancing research in the field.

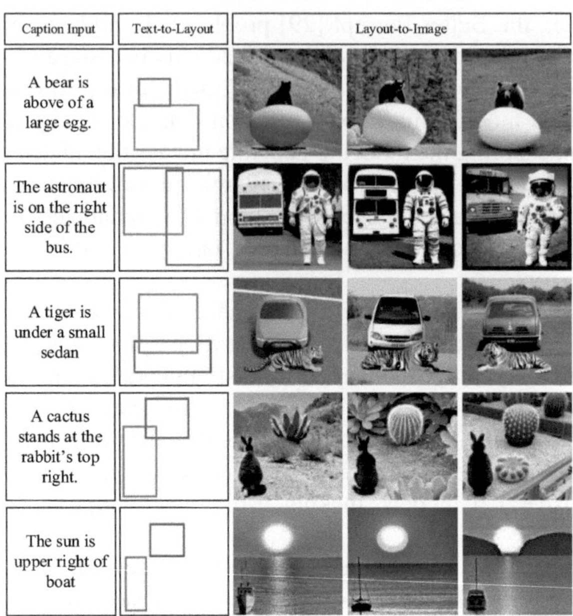

Fig. 1. The text-to-image architecture. First stage SamLayGe generates layout information incorporating positional expressions from text (second column), and then further generates image group outputs.

2 Related Work

2.1 Text-to-Image Generation

T2I technology has advanced rapidly in recent years. Early approaches relied on GAN (Generative Adversarial Networks), such as StackGAN and AttnGAN, which improved image quality and text-semantic consistency via multi-stage generation and attention mechanisms. However, GANs faced challenges in high-resolution image synthesis and complex scene modeling. VAEs (Variational AutoEncoders) offered an alternative for data distribution modeling and diverse outputs but lagged in image sharpness and detail compared to GANs, limiting realism.

Diffusion models have revolutionized T2I, with DALL-E2 [5] and Stable Diffusion achieving [25, 27–29] superior quality through text-guided iterative denoising, enabling high-fidelity, semantically rich images. Stable Diffusion, as an open-source model, has become pivotal for generating diverse, detailed visuals from text prompts, impacting fields like advertising design, 3D modeling, and virtual reality. Unlike earlier methods, diffusion models use sequential noise adjustment to progressively refine outputs, balancing complexity and realism in modern T2I research.

2.2 Conditional Image Generation

Despite their exceptional capabilities, Stable Diffusion text-to-image models face limitations in handling layout and quantitative caption information. Recent efforts address this through LoRA fine-tuning, training modules to integrate user inputs (e.g., layout, style, object placement) as conditional constraints during denoising [10, 13–17]. Models like ControlNet, GLIGEN, and ReCo exemplify this approach: ControlNet uses LoRA to accept bounding boxes or segmentation maps for spatial alignment; GLIGEN leverages structured layout prompts; and ReCo enhances controllability for detailed synthesis. Alternatives include full fine-tuning on large datasets [18, 19], though this incurs high computational costs and yields limited gains due to incomplete caption descriptions. Cross-attention loss calculations also enable layout control [10, 20].

While these techniques improve precision, they require explicit user layout inputs, limiting scalability. Spatial layout-guided generation still risks hallucinations and inherent constraints [22, 23]. Collectively, these methods advance conditional image generation but highlight ongoing trade-offs between control, usability, and computational efficiency in refining text-to-image models.

2.3 Layout Generation with LLM Free Training

Conventional text-to-image models have focused on aligning textual embeddings with visual representations via frameworks like CLIP [30] and Vision Transformers [31], but struggle to capture complex spatial semantics and fine-grained positional details in prompts. Integrating LLMs [24–26] has emerged as a key innovation, with works like Ranni [32] and Attention Refocusing [33] using LLMs to generate hierarchical layout blueprints as intermediate layers. These frameworks leverage LLMs to semantically decompose text into bounding box parametrizations (encoding x, y, width, height), offering compact yet rich spatial specifications.

However, LLMs face limitations in accurately modeling object dimensions and proportional scaling within layouts. Computationally, even a 7B-parameter LLM requires over 20GB GPU memory, hindering widespread deployment in consumer settings. Additionally, relying on discrete bounding boxes constrains spatial expressivity, imposing rigid geometric limits that may reduce generative diversity and structural complexity in images. While LLMs enhance semantic parsing, their trade-offs in accuracy, computational cost, and representational flexibility highlight ongoing challenges in merging language and vision for precise spatial control in text-to-image generation.

2.4 Evaluation Benchmarks for T2I Models

Robust evaluation benchmarks are critical for quantifying T2I models' capabilities in understanding complex layouts and spatial relationships. However, existing benchmarks like ComposeBench [34] and HRS [16] fall short in assessing intricate positional dynamics.

ComposeBench [34] evaluates positional relationships using object center coordinates and strict IoU(Intersection over Union) thresholds (e.g., IoU < 0.1), which works for non-overlapping scenarios but fails with partial overlaps. For example, two symmetrically intersecting rectangles (IoU $= 0.33$) with clear left-right orientation are misjudged as invalid due to exceeding the IoU limit, despite human visual clarity. HRS [16] adopts a lenient framework, requiring only polar coordinate thresholds (e.g., an object's max/min coordinate exceeding another's to validate "above"). While mitigating ComposeBench's strictness for overlaps, HRS ignores horizontal distances in relations like "above," causing mismatches between human perception and automated metrics. Both benchmarks also focus on basic positional terms ("above," "below," etc.) rather than complex 2D descriptions (e.g., "upper-left," "lower-right").

3 Methodology

During training, SamLayGe parses each caption for spatial cues, estimates the size of every mentioned object, and outputs bounding boxes whose positions and scales reproduce the described layout. The overall SamLayGe architecture is structured into two sequential stages as illustrated in Fig. 2.

Stage 1: Text-to-Layout. The input caption is processed end-to-end by the pre-trained SamLayGe model, which generates a set of bounding boxes representing the correct spatial layout. These bounding boxes serve as grounded positional constraints for the subsequent image generation stage.

Stage 2: Layout-to-Image. The original caption and the layout features derived from Stage 1 are seamlessly integrated into controllable T2I models such as GLIGEN [15], BoxDiff [10], or LayoutDiffusion. This integration enables the generation of an image whose spatial arrangement precisely aligns with the semantic description provided in the original caption.The complete workflow of SamLayGe is illustrated in Fig. 2.

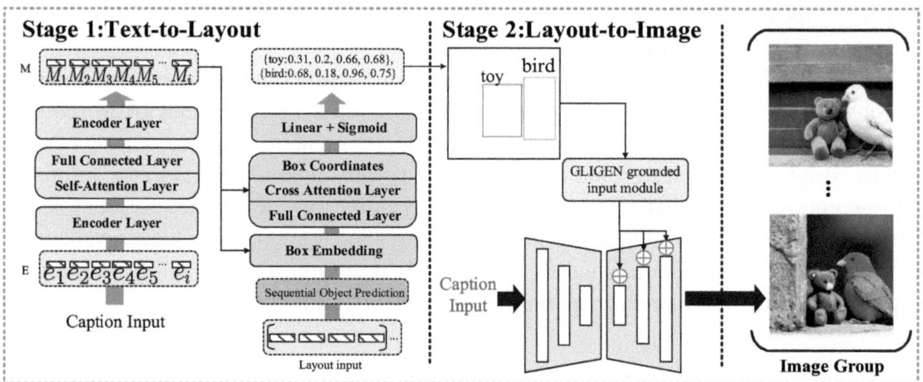

Fig. 2. The architecture of our proposed method is divided into two stages. In the first stage, the SamLayGe model generates layout information that captures the relative positional relationships. In the second stage, this layout information, which accurately reflects the intended spatial relationships, serves as grounded input for a controllable text-to-image generation model. This process results in an image that accurately represents the spatial relationships described in the input text.

3.1 Two-Stage Box Decoder

First Box. SamLayGe is trained using teacher forcing, the input for the first stage directly uses the vector representation of the actual first box $\hat{b}_1$. After passing through a linear mapping layer (or several network layers), the hidden vector representation h_1 of the first target is obtained. Subsequently, the output head $\hat{b}_1 = FC_{out}(h_1)$ regresses to predict the boundaries of the bounding box:

$$\hat{b}_1 = FC_{out}(h_1) \tag{1}$$

in the inference mode, the actual bounding box cannot be used. Therefore, the model extracts features from the encoder output M to predict h_2, achieving the first step of autoregressive decoding.

Second Box. To generate the bounding box for the second target, the information of the predicted bounding box from the first stage is integrated with the global textual semantics and concatenated with the hidden vector and predicted box $\hat{b}_1$ from the previous stage. After linear projection, a new feature representation h_2 is obtained. Next, h_2 is fed into the decoder to perform cross-attention with M, and a subsequent mask ensures that the second stage can only access information from the first stage. Finally, the second target bounding box $\hat{b}_2$ is decoded through the output layer.

3.2 Relationship Prediction

In addition to predicting the absolute positions of the two targets, to better capture the relative positional relationships described in the text (e.g., "left," "above," "lower right," etc.), we adopted a multi-task learning approach for our model. Specifically, we added a relationship prediction head to the feature vector h_1 generated in the first stage:

$$\hat{r} = FC_{relation}(h_1) \in R^S \tag{2}$$

where S represents the number of relationship categories. The model applies a softmax function to transform the outputs into a multi-class probability distribution, which is used to predict the relative positional category between the two targets.

3.3 Training Loss

To enable the model to correctly fit the relative positional relationships and absolute positions implied in the target descriptions, we introduce two types of losses and combine them with weighted summation to form the total loss:

Relative Positional Loss. Relationship prediction is formulated as a multi-class classification problem, where cross-entropy loss is used to measure the relative positional loss $\mathscr{L}_{rel}$ between the predicted distribution and the ground truth labels:

$$\mathscr{L}_{rel} = -\sum_{n=1}^{N} r_c \log(\hat{r}_c) \tag{3}$$

where c represents the number of relationship categories, r_c denotes the ground truth distribution vector, and $\hat{r}_c$ represents the probability in the predicted distribution.

Absolute Positional Loss. We design an absolute position loss $\mathcal{L}_{abs}$ to measure the overlap between the predicted bounding box and the ground truth bounding box, using IoU as the basis for the regression loss:

$$\mathcal{L}_{abs} = 1 - \text{IoU}(\hat{b}, b) \tag{4}$$

Where b denotes the ground-truth layout, and $\hat{b}$ denotes the layout produced by the model.

For external tasks, the IoU Loss for each target object needs to be calculated separately, and the average is then taken.

Total Loss. After comprehensively considering the different impacts of the two parts of the loss, we use hyperparameters λ_1 and λ_2 to control their weights. Then, the total loss $\mathcal{L}_{total}$ is computed as:

$$\mathcal{L}_{total} = \lambda_1 \mathcal{L}_{rel} + \lambda_2 \frac{1}{n} \sum_{i=1}^{n} \mathcal{L}_{abs}^i \tag{5}$$

where $\mathcal{L}_{rel}$ converges relatively quickly, while $\mathcal{L}_{abs}$ converges more slowly. To address this, a dynamic loss training strategy is used. During the first half of the training process, λ_1 and λ_2 are set to 0.5. In the second half of the training process, λ_1 is set to 0.3 and λ_2 is set to 0.7.

3.4 LayGeBench

Existing benchmarks in the T2I domain primarily focus on basic spatial relationships such as above, below, left, and right. LayGeBench is designed to more comprehensively evaluate T2I models performance under complex layout relationships. Additionally, we develop automated evaluation methods to systematically assess the consistency between text descriptions and generated layouts. For example, "A is left of B", we define the spatial relationship as $\{x_{min}, y_{min}, x_{max}, y_{max}\}$, and our positional relationship evaluation must satisfy the following conditions:

$$x_{1center} < x_{2\,min} \text{ and } x_{2center} > x_{1\,max} \tag{6}$$

$$y_{1center} > y_{2\,max} \text{ and } y_{2center} > y_{1\,min} \tag{7}$$

where x_{center} or y_{center} represents the coordinates of the center of a box.

Given a textual input T, our goal is to measure the consistency of the generated layout L to the caption as shown in Eq. (8). Specifically, we design a systematic evaluation process that considers the semantic and spatial relationships described in T and verifies whether L faithfully represents these relationships. The proposed framework ensures a comprehensive and automated assessment of how well the layout reflects the text, providing a robust measure of fidelity.

$$\text{Consistency(T,L)} = \frac{\sum_{i=1}^{N} w_i \cdot (pred_i = target_i)}{\sum_{i=1}^{N} w_i} \tag{8}$$

where w_i will be set to 1 when the position prompts refer to left / right / up / bellow and w_i will be set to 0.7 when the position prompts refer to upper left / lower right / upper right / lower left.

4 Experiments

The experiments conduct evaluations from two dimensions: text-to-image generation and text-to-layout generation. For the T2I task, we integrate our model into GLIGEN [15] and follow the evaluation protocols of ComposeBench [34] datasets to assess performance. In the T2I domain, we compare with the Ranni [32] approach, an existing method aligned with our task objectives and utilize the LayGeBench benchmark to test layout generation under complex positional relationship descriptions. Additionally, the LayGeBench dataset is employed to evaluate the generation efficiency of our model against Llama [24], a representative large language model.

4.1 Training Dataset Construction

Constructing a robust training dataset is pivotal for training the SamLayGe model. Our objective is to enable SamLayGe not only to generate accurate layout information containing positional relationships but also to correctly model the actual size and spatial information of target objects. Leveraging the COCO instance dataset [35] as a foundation, we perform data augmentation on its images and corresponding text descriptions, with a particular focus on incorporating explicit "relative positional relationship" descriptions. The process is detailed as follows:

Data Cleaning. We initiate by filtering the original captions to exclude those that are ambiguous or lack clear references to visible objects. Specifically, we remove captions that fail to unambiguously identify objects or their spatial relationships within the image. This cleaning step ensures that the remaining data is more precise, facilitating accurate extraction and enhancement of positional relationship information.

Positional Relationship Calculation. Using the bounding box annotations provided in the COCO dataset, we compute the relative spatial positions between objects. For example, relationships such as "A is to the left of B" or "C is above D" are identified. Specifically, for each image, we randomly select pairs of target objects and determine their relative positions based on their bounding box coordinates (x, y, width, height). The original caption and corresponding positional labels are recorded, generating structured relative position descriptions for each sample. These descriptions serve as critical inputs for subsequent text augmentation.

Data Augmentation with LLM. The cleaned captions, associated bounding box information, and computed relative position descriptions are fed into a LLM. Leveraging the LLM's generative capabilities, the original captions are rewritten and expanded to explicitly include spatial relationships (e.g., "left," "upper-right") between the target objects. The augmented text not only retains visual features but also explicitly encodes relative positional attributes, enriching the semantic dimensionality of the training data and enhancing the model's ability to parse and predict precise bounding boxes from text inputs.

Dataset Processing Results. Following these steps, we compiled a final dataset consisting of 50,000 augmented training samples and 6,000 test samples. The spatial relationship categories within the training and validation sets were evenly distributed, ensuring coverage of diverse relative position configurations. This balanced distribution is crucial for the model's generalization ability, enabling it to accurately predict bounding boxes across different spatial relationship scenarios. Additionally, all generated data has been made publicly available.

4.2 Implement Details

For the Text-to-Image Task, we use different datasets to validate the effectiveness of the SamLayGe model. We employ ComposeBench [34] to assess the model's generation performance on diverse object categories and traditional simple positional relations, such as "above" and "left". Additionally, we use our proposed LayGeBench benchmark to measure SamLayGe's ability to handle complex positional relationships, including intricate spatial descriptions like "upper-left" and "lower-right".

For the Text-to-Layout Task, LayGeBench serves as the core evaluation framework. This benchmark is specifically designed for assessing spatial layout generation, suitable for testing layout generation capabilities under complex positional constraints such as descriptions involving relative directional terms like "upper-left" and "lower-right".

For the text-to-image evaluation, we followed the protocols outlined in ComposeBench [34] to calculate spatial layout accuracy. We used LayGeBench to verify the effectiveness of our model in text-to-layout generation tasks. Generation accuracy was employed as our evaluation metric. SamLayGe adopts an end-to-end training approach, enabling single-step generation during the inference phase. Our experiments were conducted on a machine equipped with four NVIDIA RTX 4090 GPUs.

4.3 Results and Discussion

As shown in Fig. 3, our model demonstrates superior performance compared to LLMs. During the training phase, our model incorporates both relative position loss and absolute position loss. As a result, our model not only accurately captures the relative positional relationships between target objects but also correctly fits the shapes of the targets.

As shown in Table 1, the Spatial Score indicates the effectiveness of the model in aligning discrete textual features with layout features in generating images. Our model aligns discrete textual features with discrete layout features through supervised training, enabling it to effectively extract layout information from captions and integrate with existing controllable text-to-image capabilities to generate spatially controllable images. On the ComposeBench [34] dataset, our model SamLayGe achieves a Spatial Score of 0.32 significantly higher than the "free train" approach based on Llama [24]. When compared with the Ranni [32] model, which fine-tunes Llama [24] for similar tasks, our supervised training framework demonstrates superior generation performance, highlighting its robust capacity to translate semantic descriptions into precise layout configurations.

As shown in Table 2, the Base Score denotes the overall evaluation of positional relationships such as above, below, left, and right. The Complex Score denotes the scores for positional relationships such as top-left, bottom-left, top-right, and bottom-right. The Overall Score denotes the comprehensive score of all positional relationships. While traditional text-to-image models Ranni [32] and ChatGPT-4o [26] primarily evaluate intuitive positional relationships, such as above, below, left, and right, user descriptions

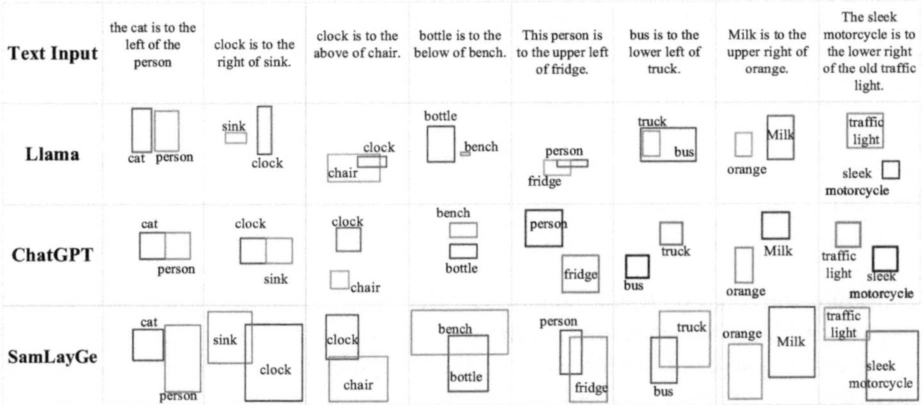

Fig. 3. Architecture of our proposed method. SamLayGe generates layout information with relative positions in the first stage, which is then used as grounded input in the second stage to produce an image with accurate spatial relationships.

Table 1. Results of our model on the ComposeBench dataset

Model	Spatial Score
SDV1	0.1246
SDV2	0.1342
Composable v2	0.0800
Structured v2	0.1386
Attn-Exct v2	0.1455
Ranni	0.2720
SamLayGe	0.3200

often include more nuanced spatial relationships, such as upper left, lower left, upper right, and lower right.

Our model has been specifically trained to handle these types of layouts, and the results demonstrate its effectiveness in capturing and generating complex spatial relationships accurately. This specialized training methodology enhances our model's performance in contexts that necessitate the generation of precise and intricate layouts derived from textual descriptions.

As shown in Table 3, we conducted a comparative evaluation of inference efficiency between our model and Ranni (fine-tuned on Llama). The evaluation was performed on the LayGeBench dataset using a single NVIDIA RTX 4090 GPU. Inference time (excluding model loading time) was recorded in milliseconds.

The results demonstrate that our model outperforms Ranni in both parameter scale and inference speed, showcasing greater reliability and practicality. This is primarily attributed to our model's supervised training approach and its end-to-end lightweight

Table 2. Evaluation results on the LayGeBench dataset

Spatial Score	Base Score	Complex Score	Overall Score
Ranni	32.73	18.60	32.46
ChatGPT-4o	86.25	58.75	72.50
SamLayGe	66.24	36.13	60.18

architecture. In contrast, Ranni employs a "free train" architecture with multi-stage inference on Llama, which results in relatively lower efficiency.

The evaluation results further validate the exceptional performance of our model, both in terms of computational efficiency and practical usability.

Table 3. Comparison of model performance

Model	LayGeBench	Parameter Count	Speed
GPT3 [26]	-	175B	-
Lallma7B [24]	32.46	7B	1372.87
SamLayGe	55.54	170M	6.67

5 Conclusion

This paper presents SamLayGe, a lightweight model enhancing controllability in text-to-image generation. Unlike methods requiring explicit layouts or heavy language models, it integrates seamlessly to generate precise spatial relationships from text alone. Experiments ComposeBench, and the LayGeBench dataset demonstrate superior layout accuracy and semantic alignment over baselines like Ranni, with reduced computational overhead and better generalization on ambiguous prompts. LayGeBench addresses limitations in existing benchmarks by evaluating complex 2D relationships. However, SamLayGe struggles with highly complex layouts (>5 objects) and depth-dependent descriptions. Future work will focus on multi-modal extensions (e.g., 3D scenes), high-resolution outputs, and architectural optimizations. The model and dataset advance research in controllable text-to-image generation, balancing efficiency and spatial precision.

References

1. Goodfellow, I.J., et al.: Generative adversarial nets. In: Proceedings of the NeurIPS, vol. 2 (2014)
2. Zhang, H., Xu, T., Li, H., et al.: StackGAN: text to photo-realistic image synthesis with stacked generative adversarial networks. In: Proceedings of the IEEE International Conference on Computer Vision, pp. 5907–5915 (2017)

3. Xu, T., Zhang, P., Huang, Q., et al.: AttnGAN: fine-grained text to image generation with attentional generative adversarial networks. In: Proceedings of the IEEE Conference on Computer Vision and Pattern Recognition, pp. 1316–1324 (2018)

4. Tomczak, J., Welling, M.: VAE with a VampPrior. In: International Conference on Artificial Intelligence and Statistics, pp.1214–1223. PMLR (2018)

5. Ramesh, A., Dhariwal, P., Nichol, A., et al.: Hierarchical text-conditional image generation with clip latents. arXiv preprint arXiv:2204.06125 (2022)

6. Rombach, R., Blattmann, A., Lorenz, D., et al.: High-resolution image synthesis with latent diffusion models. In: Proceedings of the IEEE/CVF Conference on Computer Vision and Pattern Recognition, pp. 10684–10695 (2022)

7. Singh, J., Gould, S., Zheng, L.: High-fidelity guided image synthesis with latent diffusion models. In: 2023 IEEE/CVF Conference on Computer Vision and Pattern Recognition (CVPR), pp. 5997–6006. IEEE (2023)

8. Mou, C., Wang, X., Xie, L., et al.: T2i-adapter: learning adapters to dig out more controllable ability for text-to-image diffusion models. In: Proceedings of the AAAI Conference on Artificial Intelligence, vol. 38, no.5, pp. 4296–4304 (2024)

9. Bussell, C., Ehab, A., Hartle-Ryan, D., Kapsalis, T.: Generative AI for immersive experiences: integrating text-to-image models in VR-mediated co-design workflows. In: International Conference on Human-Computer Interaction, vol. 2, pp. 380–388 (2023)

10. Xie, J., Li, Y., Huang, Y., et al.: Boxdiff: text-to-image synthesis with training-free box-constrained diffusion. In: Proceedings of the IEEE/CVF International Conference on Computer Vision, pp. 7452–7461 (2023)

11. Lin, C.-H., et al.: Magic3D: high-resolution text-to-3D content creation. In: Proceedings of the IEEE/CVF Conference on Computer Vision and Pattern Recognition, vol. 2, pp. 300–309 (2023)

12. Poole, B., Jain, A., Barron, J.T., Mildenhall, B.: DreamFusion: Text-to-3D using 2D diffusion. In: Proceedings of the International Conference on Learning Representations, vol. 2 (2023)

13. Laina, C.M, Vedaldi, I.A.: Training-free layout control with cross-attention guidance. In: Proceedings of the IEEE/CVF Winter Conference on Applications of Computer Vision, pp. 5343–5353 (2024)

14. Zhang, L., Rao, A., Agrawala, M.: Adding conditional control to text-to-image diffusion models. In: Proceedings of the IEEE/CVF International Conference on Computer Vision, pp. 3836–3847 (2023)

15. Li, Y., Liu, H., Wu, Q., et al.: GLIGEN: open-set grounded text-to-image generation. In: Proceedings of the IEEE/CVF Conference on Computer Vision and Pattern Recognition, pp. 22511–22521 (2023)

16. Lin, T.-Y., et al.: Microsoft coco: common objects in context. In: Proceedings of the European Conference on Computer Vision (ECCV), vol. 2, no. 6 (2014)

17. Zheng, G., Zhou, X., Li, X, et al.: Layoutdiffusion: controllable diffusion model for layout-to-image generation. In: Proceedings of the IEEE/CVF Conference on Computer Vision and Pattern Recognition, pp. 22490–22499 (2023)

18. Yang, Z., Wang, J., Gan, Z., et al.: Reco: region-controlled text-to-image generation. In: Proceedings of the IEEE/CVF Conference on Computer Vision and Pattern Recognition, pp. 14246–14255 (2023)

19. Zheng, G., Zhou, X., Li, X., et al.: Layoutdiffusion: controllable diffusion model for layout-to-image generation. In: Proceedings of the IEEE/CVF Conference on Computer Vision and Pattern Recognition, pp. 22490–22499 (2023)

20. Couairon, G., Careil, M., Cord, M., et al.: Zero-shot spatial layout conditioning for text-to-image diffusion models. In: Proceedings of the IEEE/CVF International Conference on Computer Vision, pp. 2174–2183 (2023)

21. Devalal, S., Karthikeyan, A.: LoRa technology-an overview. In: 2018 Second International Conference on Electronics, Communication and Aerospace Technology (ICECA), pp. 284–290. IEEE (2018)

22. Gunjal, A., Yin, J., Bas, E.: Detecting and preventing hallucinations in large vision language models. arXiv preprint arXiv:2308.06394 (2023)

23. Zhou, Y., et al.: Analyzing and mitigating object hallucination in large vision-language models. arXiv preprint arXiv:2310.00754 (2023)

24. Dubey, A., Jauhri, A., Pandey, A., et al.: The llama 3 herd of models. arXiv preprint arXiv:2407.21783 (2024)

25. Bakr, E.M., Sun, P., Shen, X., et al.: Hrs-bench: holistic, reliable and scalable benchmark for text-to-image models. In: Proceedings of the IEEE/CVF International Conference on Computer Vision, pp. 20041–20053 (2023)

26. Kalyan, K.S.: A survey of GPT-3 family large language models including ChatGPT and GPT-4. Nat. Lang. Process. J. **6**, 100048 (2024)

27. Nichol, A., et al.: Glide: towards photorealistic image generation and editing with text-guided diffusion models. arXiv preprint arXiv:2112.10741 (2021)

28. Ding, M., Zheng, W., Hong, W., Tang, J.: Cogview2: faster and better text-to-image generation via hierarchical transformers. arXiv preprint arXiv:2204.14217 (2022)

29. Rampas, D., Pernias, P., Zhong, E., Aubreville, M. Fast text-conditional discrete denoising on vector-quantized latent spaces. arXiv preprint arXiv:2211.07292 (2022)

30. Hou, Y., Dong, H., Wang, X., et al.: MetaPrompting: learning to learn better prompts. In: Proceedings of the 29th International Conference on Computational Linguistics, pp. 3251–3262 (2022)

31. Radford, A., Kim, J.W., Hallacy, C., et al.: Learning transferable visual models from natural language supervision. In: International Conference on Machine Learning, pp. 8748–8763. PMLR (2021)

32. Dosovitskiy, A., Beyer, L., Kolesnikov, A., et al.: An image is worth 16x16 words: transformers for image recognition at scale. In: International Conference on Learning Representations (2020)

33. Feng, Y., Gong, B., Chen, D., et al.: Ranni: taming text-to-image diffusion for accurate instruction following. In: Proceedings of the IEEE/CVF Conference on Computer Vision and Pattern Recognition, pp. 4744–4753 (2024)

34. Phung, Q., Ge, S., Huang, J.B.: Grounded text-to-image synthesis with attention refocusing. In: Proceedings of the IEEE/CVF Conference on Computer Vision and Pattern Recognition, pp. 7932–7942 (2024)

35. Huang, K., Sun, K., Xie, E., et al.: T2i-compbench: a comprehensive benchmark for open-world compositional text-to-image generation. Adv. Neural. Inf. Process. Syst. **36**, 78723–78747 (2023)

Introducing DINOv2 for Medical Image Boundary Tracking

Jing Chen[1], Gangming Zhao[1], Jun Wu[1,2], Chong Tian[1], Chao Liu[1], and Lei Qu[1,3(✉)]

[1] Information Materials and Intelligent Sensing Laboratory of Anhui Province, Anhui University, Hefei, China
`qulei@ahu.edu.cn`
[2] The 38th Research Institute of China Electronics Technology Group Corporation, Hefei, China
[3] The SEU-ALLEN Joint Center, Institute for Brain and Intelligence, Southeast University, Nanjing, China

Abstract. Medical image segmentation task plays an important role in areas such as clinical care and medical atlas construction, but existing 2D segmentation models often face challenges in 3D organ or tissue segmentation tasks, and 3D models account for a large computing resource proportion. Therefore, we consider 3D tissue organs as video sequences and use the given first layer of tissue organ boundaries as a sequence of query points to predict matching points on subsequent slices. Based on this idea, we propose a point tracking architecture optimised based on the joint point tracking model CoTracker, which compensates for the shortcomings of CNN-based architectures in global feature information extraction and improves the robustness of the overall image features by incorporating the robust, strongly generalisable DINOv2 encoder. The model uses semantic features extracted by the self-supervised learning foundational model DINOv2-ViT for feature fusion with ResNet, and optimises them with a fine-tuning strategy based on the CoTracker weights. Specifically, we introduce the channel attention mechanism to make full use of Vision Transformer's feature recognition capability, and achieve feature optimisation by filtering high-weighted channels, thus improving the accuracy of several evaluation metrics in the point tracking domain. Extensive evaluation results show that our approach not only greatly saves training resources, but also efficiently improves tracking accuracy and has good generalisation in the field of medical image segmentation.

Keywords: DINOv2 · CoTracker · Feature fusion · Medical image processing

1 Introduction

Medical image segmentation has significant research value in areas such as medical diagnosis, treatment planning, and image-guided surgery, and models for

Z. Lin et al. (Eds.): ICIG 2025, LNCS 16161, pp. 151–160, 2026.
https://doi.org/10.1007/978-981-95-3398-5_13

medical image segmentation task are being proposed. Common segmentation backbone networks are U-Net [14], the recent SoTA architecture SAM [11], and SAM 2 [13]. Improved models can consistently achieve superior performance by incorporating adapters for fine-tuned training of downstream tasks, or by designing an optimised image encoder. However, these segmentation tasks are often performed on 2D medical images, and the lack of capturing 3D spatial information makes the task of segmenting 3D medical images difficult. Therefore, we propose a novel method for acquiring image masks called "boundary tracking", which converts the task of target object segmentation to boundary point tracking by introducing a video point tracking model that treats 3D medical images as spatio-temporal videos.

In recent years, the study of dense point correspondence in video sequences has made significant progress, and has been extended to long-time point tracking tasks as the research progresses. Benefited from the introduction of novel network architectures such as Transformer and the development of synthetic datasets with long-term trajectory annotations, tracking algorithms based on supervised learning have demonstrated excellent performance. CoTracker [10] is a model based on Transformer [17] that allows for the joint tracking of densely-packed points in a frame across video sequences. By calculating the correlation between the query points, CoTracker is able to achieve tracking multiple points jointly, thus improving the prediction accuracy of the points on subsequent frames more effectively. Experiments demonstrate that joint tracking results in higher tracking accuracy compared to tracking each point independently. Even when the points are occluded or out of the field of view, tracking can be performed for a long period of time. From a quantitative point of view, CoTracker outperforms all recent trackers on the standard dataset. However, the training and validation of CoTracker is done on natural images. When task comes to the field of medical images processing, CoTracker is often not well suited to the task of tracking objects with biological significance due to the significant differences in the features of natural and medical-biological images.

It has been shown that feature extraction and fusion strategies are key factors in improving the performance of point tracking models. Notably, the recently proposed self-supervised learning model DINOv2, a visual foundation model based on Vision Transformer [4] which is trained on an enormous number of natural image datasets. This kind of foundation model can be directly used for robust feature extraction without fine-tuning, and has demonstrated strong feature representation capabilities in several downstream tasks. For example, DINO-Tracker [16] combines the self-supervised framework of RAFT [15] to design a lightweight CNN network to predict the feature residuals of DINOv2, and achieves long-time tracking through similarity computation with a CNN-based optimiser; RoMa [5] integrates the features of VGG19_bn and DINOv2, and optimises global feature representations to improve the performance of dense matching. To further enhance the model for feature discrimination, we introduce foundation model DINOv2 [12] as a global feature extractor. However, the above methods are usually limited to video-specific optimisation task, while the ambiguity in the spatial distribution of DINOv2 features makes it difficult to accurately locate individual points, limiting the application in point tracking tasks.

To address the above limitations, we propose a fine-tuned optimisation framework based on the current state-of-the-art tracking model CoTracker, which is shown experimentally to outperform the original model performance in several evaluation metrics, and the improved model is verified to be good migratory on medical image datasets. The main contributions of this work include:

1. We design a novel framework-specific feature fusion module based on the channel attention mechanism, which optimises the feature channels through attention weight screening, and innovatively combines the sensitivity of ResNet encoded features to pixel-level displacements with the robust characterisation capability of DINOv2 to achieve a significant improvement in point tracking accuracy;
2. We test on publicly available medical segmentation datasets to achieve the effect of class segmentation by predicting the boundary of the segmentation target, and use medical image segmentation evaluation metrics to validate the transferability of the improved model for cross-domain tasks;
3. We validate the computational efficiency of the approach by completing training on only a single A100 80G GPU without fine-tuning the pretrained foundation model.

2   Methods

Given an RGB video $\{I_t\}_{t=1}^{T}$ of any duration and the query points N_0 in the first frame, our goal is to predict the pixel positions $\delta_{t=2}^{T}$ and visibility $Occ_{t=2}^{T}$ of the query points $N_{t=2}^{T}$ in all remaining frames $\{I_t\}_{t=2}^{T}$. The training dataset uses annotations generated from Google Kubric MOVI-f dataset as query points and query frames.

2.1   Architecture

Feature Fusion Module. The video resolution of the input model $\{I_t\}_{t=1}^{T}$ was uniformly sampled as H $\times$ W $= 384 \times 512$, stride $= 4$, via a convolutional neural network consisting of an initial feature extraction convolutional layer, eight 3×3 residual blocks and a fusion feature convolutional layer to obtain CNN features $\phi_{CNN}(I)$ of size $R^{B \times T \times C \times H \times W}$, where the number of feature channels is C $= 128$.

DINOv2 Encoder Branch. For the DINOv2 encoder branch, DINOv2 receives the input image and divides it into blocks of size 14×14, encoded as image block feature vectors. The sample effect of this resolution will greatly affect the accuracy of the image features, so we first use bilinear interpolation on the video, after the DINOv2 encoder we get the features that are aligned to the direct space of $\phi_{CNN}(I)$, the interpolation multiplicity is s = 1.75. The 384-dimensional features $\phi_{DINO}(I)$ are extracted from the DINOv2 ViT-S model, here we use the default feature layer, i.e., tokens head, 12_{th} layer, stride = 7. The resolution of the interpolated video is increased to $H' \times W' = 672 \times 896$. The ablation experiments in Sect. 3.4 demonstrate that up-sampling the input DINOv2 video frames is beneficial in improving the model prediction accuracy compared to interpolating the features directly.

Feature Fusion Module. We adopt SENet as the base module for feature fusion. This is done by applying channel attention to DINOv2 features and obtaining an importance score for each channel, which is used as a basis for selecting features on a merit basis. The top 128-dimensional features $\phi'_{DINO}(I)$ with the highest scores in SENet are further fused with $\phi_{CNN}(I)$ to obtain the final optimised image coding features $\phi(I) \in R^{B \times T \times C \times H \times W}$, calculated as:

$$\phi(I) = \phi_{CNN}(I) + \phi'_{DINO}(I) \tag{1}$$

The feature fusion module architecture is shown in Fig. 1.

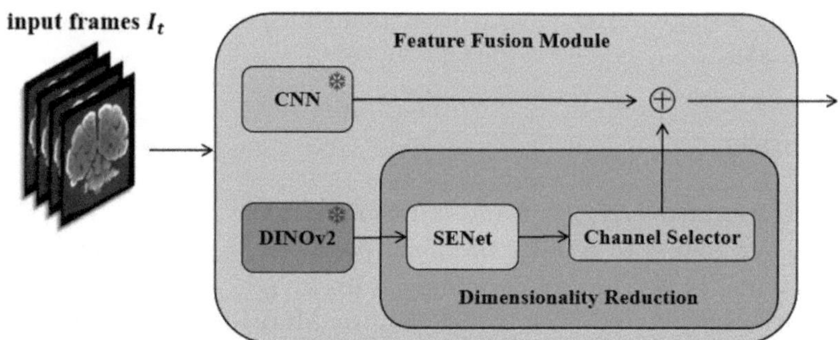

Fig. 1. Feature Fusion Module. We calculate the CNN features $\phi_{CNN}(I)$ of each video frame, and the input DINOv2 video up-sampling 1.75 times to extract the features $\phi_{DINO}(I)$. After SENet and Channel Selector to get the dimensionality reduction of the high score features $\phi'_{DINO}(I)$, and the result of the fusion of the two summed up as the final image coding features.

Transformer-Based Tracks Updater. The query point trajectories are computed by the cross-trajectory/temporal attention module. This module is based on the Transformer architecture and is designed to perform operations on the attention operators across trajectories and temporal dimensions [1]. The flow embedding, correlation features, track features, and track masks are concatenated over the channel, added with sampled position embedding and time embedding, and then fed into the cross attention module for computation. The optical flow embedding was calculated from the relative displacement obtained from the last iteration of the trajectory and represented as a two-dimensional embedding using the sine and cosine functions transformation. The track features are initialised based on the image features and are computed again with each trajectory iteration update. Correlation features are used to match the trajectory to the image, using the RAFT [15] method to optical flow estimation, and the correlation feature is computed by comparing the track features during the current iteration cycle to the image features around the trajectory location. The visibility mask is initialised before the start of the current iteration, propagates the query points over all remaining frames, and are not updated by the Transformer.

The output of the cross-attention module is the relative displacement of the trajectory point with respect to the previous frame, which is used to update the computed tracking features and provide the input coordinates for the next iteration. The coordinates of the predicted points for each frame within this window are obtained by accumulating the relative displacements, and the visibility predictions for all points are obtained at the end of all iterations by linear projection based on the last trajectory feature map.

The overall architecture is shown in Fig. 2

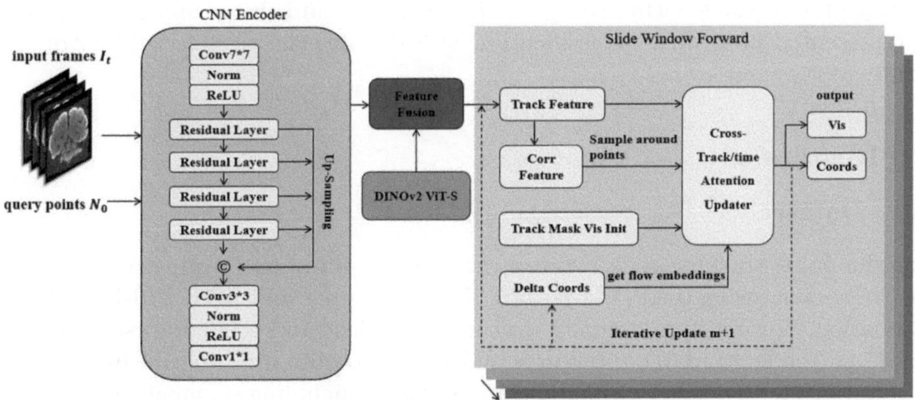

Fig. 2. Method Overview. Training and inference for the entire video is propagated through semi-overlapping sliding windows. The length of the window is 8, with the semi-overlapping sliding window implemented in an unrolled fashion, and the trajectory in each window undergoes M iterations. The obtained $\phi(I)$ after feature fusion is used to compute the track feature and subsequently the correlation feature. The track visibility mask and optical flow embedding are used as inputs to the Transformer and spatio-temporal embedding information is added as a hint. The output of the cross-attention module is the relative displacement of the trajectory point with respect to the previous frame, which is used to update the computation of the track feature and provide the input coordinates for the next iteration. The coordinates of the predicted points for each frame within this window are obtained by accumulating the relative displacements, and the visibility of each point on the corresponding frame is predicted based on the track feature obtained at the end of the iteration.

2.2   Objective

The predominant loss function L_1 is used for track regression, which performs a weighted summation of all past windows and trajectories generated by the iterative process, expressed by the formula:

$$L_1(\hat{P}, P) = \sum_{j=1}^{J} \sum_{m=1}^{M} \alpha^{M-m} \left\| \hat{P}^{(m,j)} - P^{(j)} \right\|$$

(2)

where $\alpha = 0.8$ is used to attenuate the weights of the results of previous Transformer iterations. $\hat{P}^{(m,j)}$ denotes the predicted trajectory within the current iteration m of the current window j. $P^{(j)}$ denotes the ground truth trajectory.

The second loss function L_2 predicts the cross entropy of the visibility flags, expressed by the formula:

$$L_2(\hat{P}, P) = \sum_{j=1}^{J} CE \left(\hat{v}^{(M,j)}, v^{(j)} \right)$$

(3)

where $\hat{v}^{(M,j)}$ denotes the final visibility prediction of all query points after completing all iterations within the j_{th} sliding window, and this visibility prediction is represented in a binary classification. $v^{(j)}$ denotes the actual visibility of the point.

3   Results

3.1   Dataset

For the point tracking task, we use the same training and evaluation datasets as CoTracker, using TAP-Vid-Kubric [7] for training and TAP-Vid-DAVIS for evaluation. Kubric is a virtually synthesised object and scene dataset, synthesised and rendered in 3D animation by Blender to obtain a range of images and annotations for a variety of model training tasks, including segmentation masks, depth maps, point tracking, etc. We use the compositing dataset MOVi-F 512 × 512, each batch of which contains 24 video frames and the corresponding annotations for multiple tasks. Here we choose the annotation for the point tracking task. We use the same evaluation dataset as in [10] for comparison, including TAP-Vid-First, TAP-Vid-Strided, and Dynamic Replica [9], where TAP-Vid-First and Strided are distinguished by the fact that "first" only predicts only temporally subsequent frames, whereas the prediction of "strided" is temporally bidirectional and is queried every five frames.

For the medical image boundary tracking task, we use the BTCV dataset from MICCAI 2015 [6]. This is a commonly used abdominal organ segmentation dataset, provided by Vanderbilt University Medical Center, containing 50 abdominal CTs, of which the test set includes 6. Specific organs or tissues include liver, stomach, aorta, inferior vena cava, and right & left kidneys.

3.2   Evaluation Metrics

The point tracking accuracy evaluation metrics are classified into OA, δ_{avg} and AJ, using metrics given by TAP-Vid [2]. OA (Occlusion Accuracy) is a simple dichotomous judgement of point occlusion prediction on each frame. δ_{avg} only evaluates the positional accuracy of the point visible frame. It is first assumed that the image is resized to 256×256 and measured in pixels. For a given threshold δ, it measures the ratio of points within that threshold to all points, and is the average of 5 thresholds: 1, 2, 4, 8, and 16 pixels. AJ is used to evaluate occlusion and positional accuracy jointly, and is the average of Jaccard's values for the same thresholds in δ_{avg}.

For the segmentation task of the model on the BTCV dataset, we extracted the first frame mask of each target organ, and used OpenCV's findContours function to extract the boundary points of this mask as the query points, and took 20 consecutive slices as the query frames. For the predicted boundary points, we use OpenCV's fillPoly function to fit all the predicted boundary points as 2D closed curves and fill the inner region of the boundary as the prediction mask. We use the terms of Dice similarity coefficient(DSC) scores as the evaluation metric, calculated as:

$$DSC = \frac{2|M_{\text{Pre}} \cap M_{\text{GT}}|}{|M_{\text{Pre}}| + |M_{\text{GT}}|} \tag{4}$$

where M_{Pre} is the prediction mask and M_{Pre} is the ground truth mask.

3.3   Settings

Our training experiment was completed in 3.275 days running on a single NVIDIA A100 80GB GPU using 10,000 TAP-Vid-Kubirc sequences of $T' = 24$ frames, one batch per video, with 50,000 iterations. The optimiser used to update the weights was chosen to be AdamW, which uses OneCycleLR's "linear" approach to rise and fall in a linear fashion, with the learning rate set to 0.00005.

3.4   Experiment Results

We compare CoTracker and the methods mentioned in [10], and the results are displayed in Table 1. Our proposed optimisation method achieves an overall improvement in the TAP-Vid-First and TAP-Vid-Strided evaluation methods, and achieves superior performance in the Dynamic Replica dataset. The evaluation experiments are done on a single A100 80G GPU. We reloaded and tested the CoTracker weights(this version is released in 2023.12) which our approach is optimised based on.

The ablation experiment given in Table 2 aims to demonstrate that video interpolation amplification of the input DINOv2 is effective in improving the model accuracy, and here we use the test set TAP-Vid-First used during training.

We evaluate the effectiveness of CoTracker with the improved model for boundary tracking on six test samples of major organs from the BTCV dataset.

Table 1. Comparison with related methods on datasets

Method	TAP-Vid-First			TAP-Vid-Strided			Dynamic Replica		
	AJ	δ_{avg}^{vis}	OA	AJ	δ_{avg}^{vis}	OA	δ_{avg}	δ_{avg}^{vis}	δ_{avg}^{occ}
TAP-Net [2]	33.0	48.6	78.8	38.4	53.1	82.3	45.5	53.3	20.0
OmniMotion [18]	-	-	-	51.7	67.5	85.3	-	-	-
PIPs [8]	42.2	64.8	77.7	52.4	70.0	83.6	41.0	47.1	21.0
MFT [8]	47.3	66.8	77.8	56.1	70.8	86.9	-	-	-
PIPs++ [19]	-	69.1	-	-	73.7	-	55.5	64.0	28.5
TAPIR [3]	56.2	70.0	86.5	61.3	73.6	88.8	56.8	66.1	27.2
CoTracker [10]	60.9	74.6	88.6	63.1	79.5	87.3	80.0	82.2	59.8
Ours	**61.1**	**75.0**	**88.7**	**63.4**	**79.6**	**87.5**	**80.6**	**82.9**	58.8

Table 2. Ablation results

Method	TAP-Vid-First		
	AJ	δ_{avg}^{occ}	OA
Feature interpolate	58.0	73.3	87.6
Video interpolate	**61.1**	**75.0**	**88.7**

Table 3. Comparison with CoTracker on BTCV dataset

Validation	Method	Liver	L.kid	R.kid	Stom.	IVC	Aorta	Ave
Img0003	CoTracker	0.6895	0.6718	0.7051	0.6718	0.7521	0.7313	0.7036
	ours	0.6963	0.6772	0.7063	0.6772	0.7630	0.7422	**0.7104**
Img0007	CoTracker	0.8418	0.5741	0.6823	0.7156	0.7086	0.7237	0.7077
	ours	0.8190	0.5789	0.7116	0.7354	0.7387	0.7488	**0.7221**
Img0009	CoTracker	0.7598	0.7203	0.6992	0.9090	0.6508	0.7779	0.7528
	ours	0.8041	0.7224	0.7247	0.9044	0.6910	0.7924	**0.7732**
Img0032	CoTracker	0.6691	0.6521	0.6897	0.5647	0.6720	0.7856	0.6722
	ours	0.6703	0.6781	0.7422	0.5236	0.6625	0.7774	**0.6757**
Img0036	CoTracker	0.8209	0.8620	0.7232	0.5246	0.5143	0.7862	0.7052
	ours	0.7991	0.8568	0.7881	0.4910	0.6381	0.8040	**0.7295**
Img0040	CoTracker	0.7443	0.7871	0.6787	0.5768	0.5397	0.8421	0.6948
	ours	0.7632	0.8268	0.6873	0.6223	0.5475	0.8467	**0.7156**

The evaluation results in Table 3 show that our segmentation accuracy is higher than the evaluated segmentation effect of the original model CoTracker in each test sample, validating the effectiveness of the improved model.

4 Conclusion

In this paper, we propose a novel boundary tracking method to achieve efficient and accurate extraction of medical image masks. The model is a CoTracker-based point tracking model, which incorporates the visual foundation model DINOv2. It has acquired a rich priori knowledge into the original CoTracker, which effectively improves the model's generalisation and robustness. Experiment results show that our method performs well on point tracking dataset. Moreover, the fine-tuning method we adopt greatly saves training resources. Compared with training a CoTracker model from scratch, we complete the training on a single A100 80G GPU, which is 3.13% of the original model's training resource usage. Meanwhile, we test on a publicly available medical segmentation dataset to achieve the effect of class segmentation by predicting the boundary of the segmentation target, and use a medical image segmentation evaluation metric to validate the generalisability of the improved model for cross-domain tasks. In the future, we will continue to optimise the existing work to further improve the model performance.

Acknowledgment. This study was funded by the National Natural Science Foundation of China (62271003 and 62201008), the Sci-Tech Innovation 2030 Agenda (2022ZD0205200 and 2022ZD0205204), the Natural Science Foundation of Education Department of Anhui Province (KJ2021A0017), and the University Synergy Innovation Program of Anhui Province (GXXT-2021-001).

Compliance with ethical standards

Disclosure of Funding. The authors have no competing interests to declare that are relevant to the content of this article.

References

1. Bertasius, G., Wang, H., Torresani, L.: Is space-time attention all you need for video understanding? In: ICML, vol. 2, p. 4 (2021)
2. Doersch, C., et al.: Tap-vid: a benchmark for tracking any point in a video. Adv. Neural. Inf. Process. Syst. **35**, 13610–13626 (2022)
3. Doersch, C., et al.: Tapir: tracking any point with per-frame initialization and temporal refinement. In: Proceedings of the IEEE/CVF International Conference on Computer Vision, pp. 10061–10072 (2023)
4. Dosovitskiy, A., et al.: An image is worth 16x16 words: Transformers for image recognition at scale. arXiv preprint arXiv:2010.11929 (2020)
5. Edstedt, J., Sun, Q., Bökman, G., Wadenbäck, M., Felsberg, M.: Roma: Robust dense feature matching. In: Proceedings of the IEEE/CVF Conference on Computer Vision and Pattern Recognition, pp. 19790–19800 (2024)
6. Fang, X., Yan, P.: Multi-organ segmentation over partially labeled datasets with multi-scale feature abstraction. IEEE Trans. Med. Imaging **39**(11), 3619–3629 (2020)

7. Greff, K., et al.: Kubric: a scalable dataset generator. In: Proceedings of the IEEE/CVF Conference on Computer Vision and Pattern Recognition, pp. 3749–3761 (2022)
8. Harley, A.W., Fang, Z., Fragkiadaki, K.: Particle video revisited: tracking through occlusions using point trajectories. In: European Conference on Computer Vision, pp. 59–75. Springer (2022)
9. Karaev, N., Rocco, I., Graham, B., Neverova, N., Vedaldi, A., Rupprecht, C.: Dynamicstereo: consistent dynamic depth from stereo videos. In: Proceedings of the IEEE/CVF Conference on Computer Vision and Pattern Recognition, pp. 13229–13239 (2023)
10. Karaev, N., Rocco, I., Graham, B., Neverova, N., Vedaldi, A., Rupprecht, C.: Cotracker: it is better to track together. In: European Conference on Computer Vision, pp. 18–35. Springer (2024)
11. Kirillov, A., et al.: Segment anything. In: Proceedings of the IEEE/CVF International Conference on Computer Vision, pp. 4015–4026 (2023)
12. Oquab, M., et al.: Dinov2: learning robust visual features without supervision. arXiv preprint arXiv:2304.07193 (2023)
13. Ravi, N., et al.: Sam 2: segment anything in images and videos. arXiv preprint arXiv:2408.00714 (2024)
14. Ronneberger, O., Fischer, P., Brox, T.: U-Net: convolutional networks for biomedical image segmentation. In: Navab, N., Hornegger, J., Wells, W.M., Frangi, A.F. (eds.) MICCAI 2015. LNCS, vol. 9351, pp. 234–241. Springer, Cham (2015). https://doi.org/10.1007/978-3-319-24574-4_28
15. Teed, Z., Deng, J.: RAFT: recurrent all-pairs field transforms for optical flow. In: Vedaldi, A., Bischof, H., Brox, T., Frahm, J.-M. (eds.) ECCV 2020. LNCS, vol. 12347, pp. 402–419. Springer, Cham (2020). https://doi.org/10.1007/978-3-030-58536-5_24
16. Tumanyan, N., Singer, A., Bagon, S., Dekel, T.: Dino-tracker: taming dino for self-supervised point tracking in a single video. In: European Conference on Computer Vision, pp. 367–385. Springer (2024)
17. Vaswani, A., et al.: Attention is all you need. Advances in neural information processing systems **30** (2017)
18. Wang, Q., et al.: Tracking everything everywhere all at once. In: Proceedings of the IEEE/CVF International Conference on Computer Vision, pp. 19795–19806 (2023)
19. Zheng, Y., Harley, A.W., Shen, B., Wetzstein, G., Guibas, L.J.: Pointodyssey: a large-scale synthetic dataset for long-term point tracking. In: Proceedings of the IEEE/CVF International Conference on Computer Vision, pp. 19855–19865 (2023)

Adaptive Pruning and Cross-Domain Feature Fusion for Robust Object Tracking

Jing Wen[1,2]([✉]), Xufeng Li[1,2], Songsong Zhang[1,2], and Yujun Wu[1,2]

[1] Shanxi University, Taiyuan 030006, China
`wjing@sxu.edu.cn`
[2] Key Laboratory of Computer Intelligence and Chinese Processing of Ministry of Education, Taiyuan, China

Abstract. Although Transformer-based methods have become the mainstream solution for single object tracking tasks, their lack of spatial inductive bias makes it difficult for them to effectively distinguish between targets and background in complex scenes. Moreover, relying on positional correlations between patches often causes the model to attend to local regions instead of the entire target, resulting in tracking box drift. To address these issues, we propose a coarse-to-fine target localization approach for object tracking, named Adaptive Pruning Cross-domain Fusion (AdaCF) Tracking. Firstly, The last-rank elimination attention selection strategy, called Routing Attention, is employed to adaptively prune background information that is dissimilar to the target features. This mechanism not only enhances the model's ability to distinguish the target from the background by reducing background noise interference, but also significantly improves inference efficiency by eliminating redundant computations. Secondly, in the cross-domain fusion module, we first apply the Discrete Cosine Transform (DCT) to map spatial information into the frequency domain. Then, we implement joint spatial-frequency enhancement. This enables the model to further distinguish between the target and interfering information, such as accompanying objects, similar backgrounds, or look-alike objects. Thirdly, we introduce the Efficient Intersection over Union Loss (EIOU), which significantly accelerates model convergence and improves the localization accuracy of anchor boxes. The experimental results on the GOT-10k dataset demonstrate that our method significantly improves tracking performance, with AO increased by 3.3% and $SR_{0.5}$ by 4.1%, validating its enhanced stability and adaptability in complex scenes.

Keywords: Single-Object Tracking · Frequency Domain · Transformer

1 Introduction

In recent years, object tracking has remained a fundamental task in computer vision, with applications spanning autonomous driving, surveillance, and human-computer interaction. Single object tracking aims to continuously locate a specific target across video frames, given the initial bounding box of the target in the first frame.

© The Author(s), under exclusive license to Springer Nature Singapore Pte Ltd. 2026
Z. Lin et al. (Eds.): ICIG 2025, LNCS 16161, pp. 161–173, 2026.
https://doi.org/10.1007/978-981-95-3398-5_14

With the advent of deep learning, SiamFC [1] reformulated tracking as a similarity learning problem via a template matching framework, introducing deep features into the field. Successive methods such as SiamRPN [12] followed this paradigm but were constrained by limited receptive fields, hindering global context modeling.

Transformer-based methods [17] have recently emerged as powerful alternatives due to their ability to model global dependencies and perform efficient parallel computation. However, VIT [7], despite having made notable progress in various aspects of the tracking field, still suffers from inherent limitations that cannot be ignored. On one hand, the Transformer model inherently lacks inductive bias, requiring a large amount of training data to learn the ability to distinguish between targets and backgrounds. As a result, it often struggles to accurately identify the target in complex scenes, where it can be easily disturbed by environmental interference. On the other hand, ViT's self-attention mechanism relies solely on spatial domain features. This single-domain feature extraction approach makes it challenging to fully capture the subtle differences between targets and distractors, thereby limiting its performance in complex tracking scenarios.

To address the above issues, we propose a tracking method called Adaptive Pruning Cross-domain Fusion (AdaCF), which implements a coarse-to-fine target localization strategy through two core modules:

- **Adaptive Pruning (Coarse Stage)**: Based on a last-rank elimination strategy using Routing Attention, the model adaptively prunes tokens unrelated to the target. This helps suppress redundant background information, enhances the ViT-based tracker's ability to distinguish between the target and background, and enforces sparse feature interactions to better focus on the target region.
- **Cross-Domain Feature Fusion (Fine Stage)**: By integrating spatial and frequency-domain features, this module captures complementary cues that enhance robustness in complex scenarios involving occlusion, clutter, and appearance changes.
- **EIoU Loss Optimization**: We adopt the EIoU [24] loss to improve localization accuracy and accelerate model convergence by optimizing the aspect ratio and position of predicted bounding boxes.

2   Related Work

Before the rise of deep learning, mainstream object tracking methods primarily relied on correlation filters [3,10], which were vulnerable to scale variations and background clutter. The advent of deep Siamese networks, such as SiamFC [1] and SiamRPN [12], reformulated tracking as a similarity learning problem between template and search regions, introducing region proposal networks (RPN) and depth-wise convolutions to enhance performance. However, due to the inherently local receptive fields of CNNs, these methods struggle to model long-range dependencies, making them prone to errors in complex environments.

The Transformer architecture has recently gained prominence in object tracking due to its strong global modeling capabilities. However, because the Transformer lacks inductive bias, it is difficult to distinguish targets from cluttered backgrounds. To address this, TransT [5] a introduces cross-attention mechanisms to enable feature interaction, while MixFormer's [6] asymmetric hybrid attention module unifies feature extraction and integration. OSTrack [23] further improves robustness by early pruning of irrelevant background blocks. Interestingly, studies have shown that not all attention heads are equally important—many can be pruned without significantly affecting performance [15,18], offering promising insights for relevance-aware adaptive pruning of patch tokens.

Moreover, traditional self-attention focuses only on spatial correlations, limiting the ability to distinguish subtle differences between targets and distractors. Some works, like SwinTrack [13] and ARTrack [19], have introduced temporal cues or trajectory modeling to address this. AQATrack [21] further enhances feature learning via autoregressive spatial queries. These insights show that integrating spatial and temporal dynamics is key to robust tracking. From another perspective, object tracking, as a sequential prediction task, shares strong similarities with Time Series Forecasting (TSF). While TSF models [9,20] leverage Fourier transforms for frequency-domain learning, they often suffer from boundary artifacts (Gibbs phenomenon) and high computational overhead due to inverse operations. DCTnet [22] constructs a frequency representation framework using the Discrete Cosine Transform (DCT), effectively avoiding inverse computation and providing a novel technical solution.

3   Method

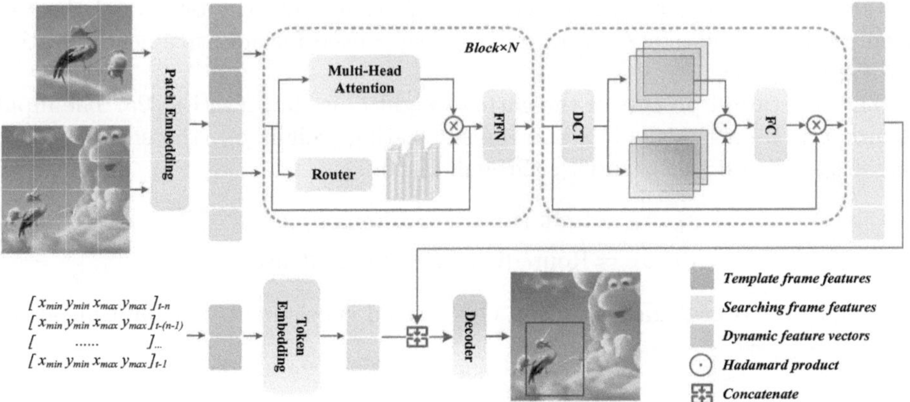

Fig. 1. Overall architecture diagram of AdaCF Tracking.

3.1 Overview

The overall network architecture, as illustrated in Fig. 1, comprises three core components: Adaptive Pruning, Cross-Domain Fusion, and the Enhanced Decoder. First, the ViT encoder extracts features from both the template and search images. In the coarse stage, the Adaptive Pruning module removes background information irrelevant to the target. In the fine stage, the Cross-Domain Fusion module enhances the discriminability between the target and distractors such as similar backgrounds, interfering objects, and accompanying objects. Finally, in the decoder, trajectory-based positional encoding is fused with image features via attention to construct input vectors, and iterative optimization is applied to predict target positions and generate bounding box coordinates.

3.2 Adaptive Pruning

After extracting features from the template and search images using a Vision Transformer (ViT), we introduce an Adaptive Pruning (AP) module to coarsely remove non-essential regions, such as irrelevant backgrounds and distractors. Specifically, the AP module incorporates a dynamic multi-head selection mechanism, as illustrated in Fig. 2a, dividing the attention process into two distinct stages:

Shared Attention: Responsible for learning and capturing common background knowledge across all tokens.

Routed Attention: Dynamically selects the most relevant attention heads for each token, improving computational efficiency by reducing redundancy among attention heads.

The final output feature for each token O is computed as:

$$O = \mathrm{Concat}\left(H^i g_i\right)_{i=1}^{h_R+h_S} = \mathrm{Concat}(H^1, \cdots, H^{h_R}, H^{h_R+1}, \cdots, H^{h_R+h_S})G \quad (1)$$

where $i = 1, \cdots, h_R, h_R+1, \cdots h_R+h_S$, h_R and h_S denote the number of routed and shared attention heads, respectively, H^i represents the output of the i-th attention head, and $g_i \in G$ is the gating weight used for adaptive head selection at different stages.

The generation process of the gating weight G is shown in Fig. 2a. The input feature x is used to calculate the routing gating weight g_R, the shared gating weight g_S, as well as x_R and x_S through Eq. 2.

$$\begin{aligned}
x_R, x_S &= \mathrm{Split}\left(\mathrm{Linear}\left(\mathrm{Softmax}\left(x\right)\right)\right) \\
g_R, g_S &= \mathrm{RoutedGate}\left(x\right), \mathrm{SharedGate}\left(x\right)
\end{aligned} \quad (2)$$

Finally, the overall gating output G is formed via element-wise multiplication:

$$G = \mathrm{Concat}(x_R \odot g_R, x_S \odot g_S) \quad (3)$$

where $\odot$ denotes element-wise multiplication. Notably, the gating mechanism ensures that a token contributes only if it exhibits strong correlation with either the always-activated shared attention heads or its most relevant routed attention heads. Otherwise, the corresponding weight g_i is adaptively suppressed to zero, thereby enforcing sparsity in feature interactions.

During inference, the AP module dynamically prunes tokens that are irrelevant to the target based on the routing attention and gating strategy. This guides the model to focus on salient local features near the target while preserving essential global contextual information. The design effectively balances fine-grained local perception with global scene understanding. Furthermore, it introduces sparsity into feature interactions, significantly reducing computational redundancy and accelerating inference. As a result, the model achieves enhanced target-background discrimination, improved inference efficiency, and superior tracking accuracy.

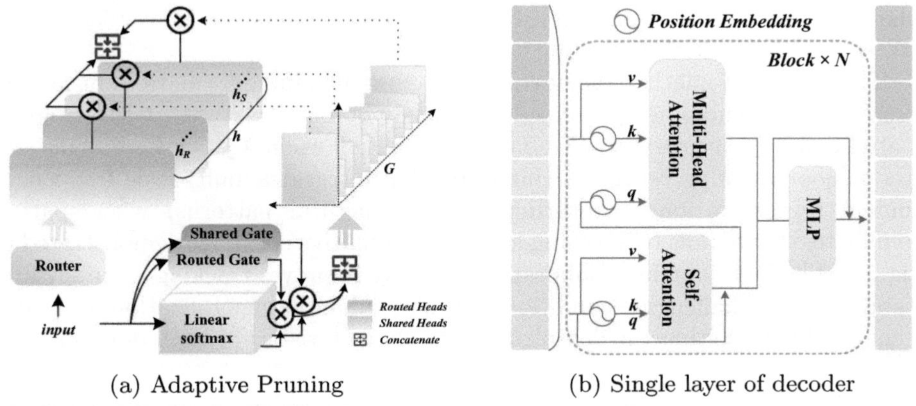

(a) Adaptive Pruning   (b) Single layer of decoder

Fig. 2. Detailed structure diagram of the core module.

3.3   Cross-domain Feature Fusion

In the fine stage, we introduce the Discrete Cosine Transform (DCT) to map the spatial information into the frequency domain, thereby enhancing the model's representation of the target. By modeling in the frequency domain, the model can more effectively distinguish the target from distractors from multiple perspectives. The standard formula of DCT is as follows:

$$\text{DCT}\,(X) = \sum_{n=0}^{N-1} X_n \cdot cos\left(\frac{\pi(2n+1)k}{2N}\right) \tag{4}$$

where $k = 0, 1 \cdots, N-1$.

Taking the template image feature $X \in \mathbb{R}^{N \times C}$ as an example, where N represents the number of patches and C represents the feature dimension of each patch. Specifically, the input feature map is first divided into C subgroups $[v_0, v_1, \ldots, v_{C-1}]$ along the channel dimension, where $v_c \in \mathbb{R}^{N \times 1}$,

$c \in \{0, 1, \ldots, C - 1\}$. Subsequently, the DCT operation is performed on each subgroup:

$$Freq_c = F_c v_c = \mathrm{DCT}\,(v_c)\,v_c \tag{5}$$

At this point, $Freq_c \in \mathbb{R}^N$ is the N-dimensional vector obtained after the DCT transformation of the subgroup v_c. The overall frequency component $Freq \in \mathbb{R}^{N \times C}$ of the image can be obtained through a stack operation:

$$Freq = \mathrm{DCT}\,(X) \odot X = \mathrm{stack}\,(\{Freq_0, Freq_1, \cdots, Freq_{c-1}\}) \tag{6}$$

Subsequently, the frequency domain feature $Freq$ is fed into Fully Connected layer, and a channel feature $F_w \in \mathbb{R}^{N \times C}$ with enhanced representation ability is generated through nonlinear mapping:

$$F_w = \sigma(W_2(\sigma(W_1(LN(Freq))))) \tag{7}$$

where σ represents the activation function, W represents the Linear layer, and LN is the LayerNorm operation.

The proposed method achieves deep cross-domain information fusion by strategically combining processed frequency-domain features with original spatial-domain features through adaptive weighted fusion $X_{\mathrm{out}} = F_w X$. This creates a cooperative perception architecture that integrates multi-scale frequency-domain representations (capturing global structural patterns) with spatial-domain texture details (preserving local discriminative cues). As demonstrated in Fig. 3a, this dual-domain collaboration not only improves tracking accuracy and stability under challenging conditions but also enhances generalization to unseen scenarios by exploiting the complementary characteristics of both domains.

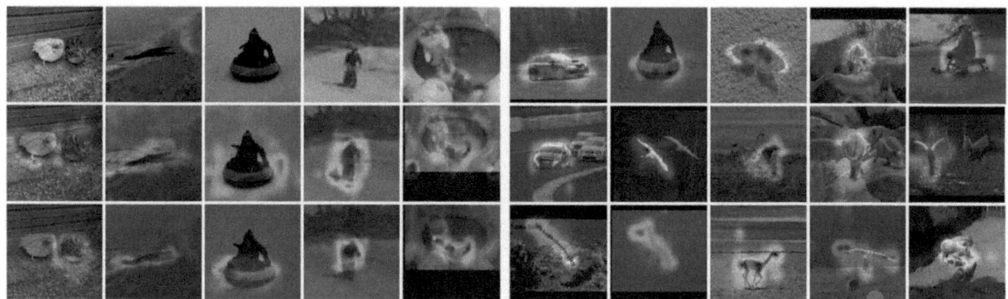

<table>
<tr><td>(a) Cross-Domain Feature Fusion.</td><td>(b) Last layer of decoder.</td></tr>
</table>

Fig. 3. (a) The top row displays the search image of the current frame. The middle and bottom rows show the attention results before and after cross-domain feature fusion, respectively. (b) Attention map of the last layer of the decoder.

3.4   Decoder

The decoder first embeds the original trajectory coordinates into high-dimensional semantic vectors using the marker embedding module, which are then fused with the encoder's multi-scale visual features for further processing.

As shown in Fig. 2b, the decoder adopts a cascaded attention architecture. The trajectory token serves as the query, while the template and search region features serve as keys and values to facilitate cross-modal interaction. An iterative refinement process reuses attention outputs as queries across stages, progressively enhancing feature representation through residual connections.

In the final stage, a response parsing module estimates the bounding box coordinates through spatial extremum detection on the attention map. The decoder performs four iterative refinements, progressively narrowing the search space in a coarse-to-fine manner. This design effectively integrates trajectory cues with visual features, enabling robust localization under occlusion, clutter, and deformation through repeated self-attention refinement. As illustrated in Fig. 3b, the attention-focused regions show strong alignment with the actual location of the target object, further validating the effectiveness of the attention mechanism in achieving precise localization.

3.5   Loss Function

The EIoU [24] loss function consists of three components: overlap loss, center distance loss, and width-height loss. By independently computing the differences in width and height between the predicted box and the ground truth, EIoU eliminates the influence of aspect ratio and accelerates the convergence process. The loss function is defined as follows:

$$L_{EIoU} = 1 - IoU + \frac{\rho^2(b, b^{bt})}{c_w^2 + c_h^2} + \frac{\rho^2(w, w^{bt})}{c_w^2} + \frac{\rho^2(h, h^{gt})}{c_h^2} \tag{8}$$

where c_w and c_h denote the width and height of the smallest enclosing box that covers both the predicted and ground truth boxes.

The final loss L is obtained by combining the EIoU loss L_{EIoU} with the cross-entropy loss L_{ce} :

$$L = L_{ce} + \lambda L_{EIoU} \tag{9}$$

Here, λ is a hyperparameter used to balance the contribution of the two components.

4   Experiments

The experiments were conducted on a server equipped with a 40 GB NVIDIA A100 GPU for training, while validation was performed on an RTX 4070. The input search and template images were sized at 256×256 and 128×128, respectively. The model was optimized using AdamW [14] with a weight decay of 5×10^{-2}. The learning rate was set to 8×10^{-6} for the backbone network and 8×10^{-5} for other parameters. A two-stage training strategy was employed: the first stage involved 240 epochs to thoroughly extract features, followed by a second stage of 60 epochs for fine-tuning.

Table 1. The best is **bold**, the second best is <u>underlined</u>, and the third best is underlined.

Methods	GOT-10k			LaSOT			TrackingNet		
	AO(%)	$SR_{0.5}$(%)	$SR_{0.75}$(%)	AUC(%)	P_{Norm}(%)	P(%)	AUC(%)	P_{Norm}(%)	P(%)
MixFormer-22k [6]	70.7	80.0	67.8	69.1	78.7	74.7	83.1	88.1	81.6
TransT [5]	72.0	82.0	68.0	64.9	73.8	69.0	81.4	86.7	80.3
SwinTrack [13]	72.4	80.5	67.8	70.5	79.7	70.8	-	-	-
ROMTrack [4]	72.9	82.9	70.2	69.3	78.8	75.6	83.6	88.4	82.7
ARTrack$_{256}$ [19]	73.6	82.2	70.9	70.4	79.5	76.2	84.2	88.7	83.5
OSTrack [23]	73.7	83.2	70.8	71.1	81.1	77.6	83.9	88.5	83.2
AQATrack$_{256}$ [21]	73.8	83.2	72.1	**71.4**	**81.9**	**78.6**	84.8	88.6	83.1
our	**76.9**	**86.3**	**74.8**	71	80.2	77.3	84.5	**89.2**	**84.1**

4.1 Performance Comparison

As shown in Table 1, we evaluate our method on three widely used benchmark
datasets: GOT-10k [11], LaSOT [8], and TrackingNet [16]. Our method consistently outperforms the baseline across three mainstream benchmarks. Except for
LaSOT, it surpasses all compared trackers in the other datasets. These results
highlight the model's effectiveness in capturing dynamic target changes and handling complex scenarios. Moreover, the proposed method exhibits strong adaptability to targets with diverse attributes, ranging from fast-moving small objects
to structurally complex large targets.

4.2 Ablation Experiment

To evaluate the individual contributions of Adaptive Pruning, Cross-Domain
Feature Fusion, and EIoU loss function, we conducted ablation studies on the
GOT-10k dataset. As shown in Table 2, the experiments are grouped as follows: The first row presents the baseline model, serving as the reference point
for comparison. The second row evaluates the impact of the adaptive pruning module, which reduces redundancy by dynamically filtering low-information
tokens, thereby enhancing computational efficiency. The third row assesses the
frequency-domain feature module, which emphasizes key signals in the frequency
spectrum to improve the model's discriminative capacity. The fourth row replaces
the original SIoU loss with EIoU loss, aiming to enhance localization precision.
The full model, integrating all modules, achieves the best performance, demonstrating that each component contributes positively to the overall system. The
combined effect of these improvements yields a significant boost in tracking accuracy and robustness.

4.3 Qualitative Analysis

To qualitatively evaluate the performance of the proposed method, we selected
four representative challenging scenarios from the GOT-10k test set for compar-

Table 2. Results of ablation experiment.

BL	AP	CD	EIoU	GOT-10k		
				AO (%)	$SR_{0.5}$ (%)	$SR_{0.75}$ (%)
✓				72.6	81.1	70.1
✓	✓			73.3	82.4	71.3
✓		✓		74.6	84.2	73.4
✓			✓	73.8	82.2	71.9
✓	✓	✓	✓	**76.9**	**86.3**	**74.8**

ison. As illustrated in Fig. 4, we compare our method with three state-of-the-art trackers across typical interference conditions, including occlusion, accompanying objects, complex backgrounds, and similar distractors. The first column displays the initial frame of each video sequence, where the target is marked with a green bounding box; the remaining columns show tracking results on four randomly selected frames from the same sequence. As shown in the Fig. 4, our method consistently demonstrates superior tracking stability and accuracy under various types of interference, primarily due to its strong capability to suppress environmental noise, thereby ensuring precise target localization.

4.4   Quantitative Analysis

GOT-10k. we compared our proposed method against the original ARTrack baseline and several other state-of-the-art trackers [2,4,6,13,19,21,23,25,26]. As shown in Fig. 5a, our method achieves substantial improvements of 3.3%, 4.1%, and 3.9% on Average Overlap (AO), Success Rate at threshold 0.5 ($SR_{0.5}$), and 0.75 ($SR_{0.75}$), respectively, over the baseline. Furthermore, compared with other competing methods, our approach demonstrates strong robustness in complex scenarios involving significant appearance variations, occlusions, and cluttered backgrounds, highlighting the effectiveness of the proposed frequency-domain feature fusion and adaptive pruning mechanisms.

LaSOT. we compared our method with the ARTrack baseline and several other state-of-the-art trackers [2,4,6,13,19,21,23,25,26]. As shown in Fig. 5, although our method does not outperform all competing trackers across every metric, it achieves improvements of 0.6%, 0.7%, and 1.1% over the baseline in AUC, P_{norm}, and P, respectively. These results demonstrate that our model offers greater stability and accuracy in long-term tracking scenarios, particularly under challenging conditions such as significant appearance changes, occlusions, and background distractions. This further validates the effectiveness of our design in enhancing tracking robustness.

Additionally, we analyze the primary limitation of our model: the lack of an effective mechanism for updating or adapting the template features over time. When the target disappears or is completely occluded, the template features

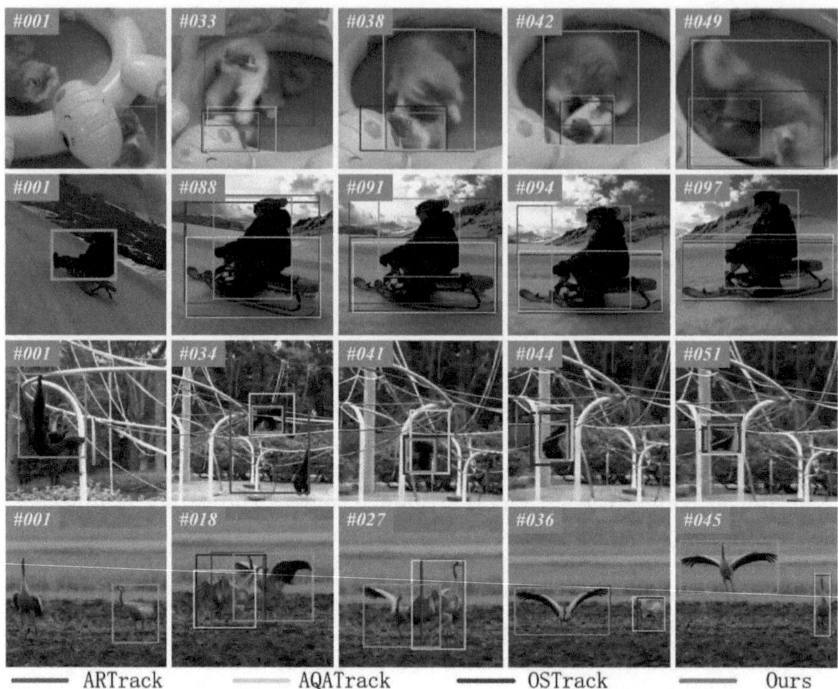

Fig. 4. Tracking effect of selected video sequences in GOT-10k.

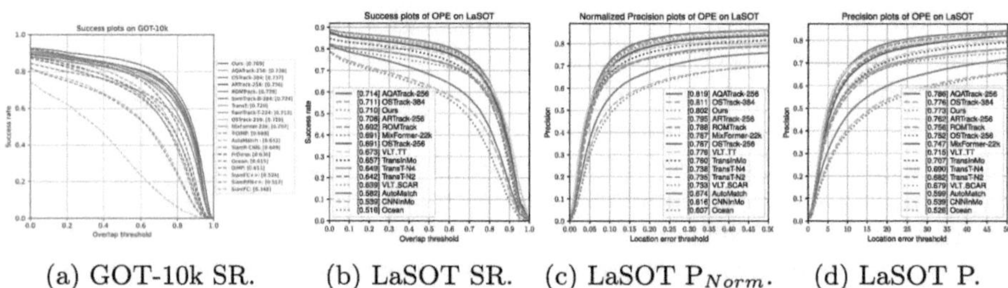

(a) GOT-10k SR. (b) LaSOT SR. (c) LaSOT P_{Norm}. (d) LaSOT P.

Fig. 5. GOT-10k and LaSOT tracking result evaluation curve.

can become outdated or corrupted by background clutter or distractor content. This corruption impairs the feature matching accuracy in subsequent frames, leading to tracking drift or erroneous association with distractors. This issue is further illustrated in Fig. 6.

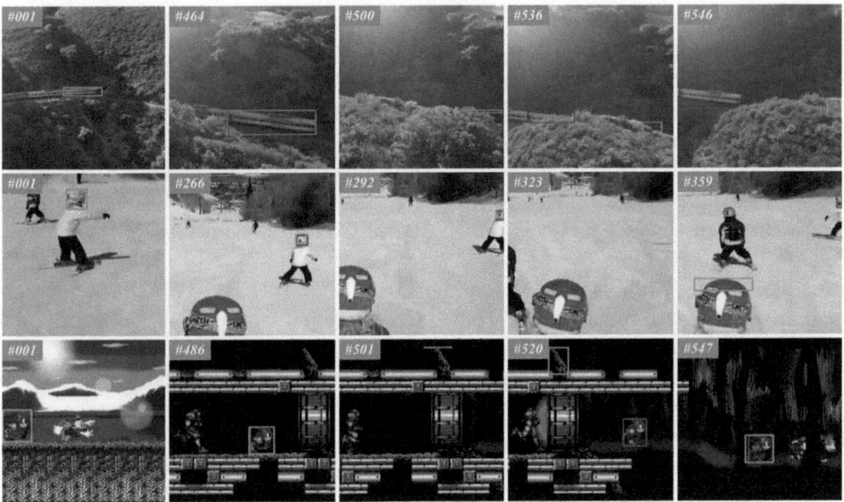

Fig. 6. Failure cases on the LaSOT benchmark, where green is our tracking result and red is ground truth. (Color fugure online)

5 Conclusion

This paper presents AdaCF Tracking, a novel transformer-based object tracking framework designed to tackle environmental interference in complex scenes. The model incorporates two key components—Adaptive Pruning and Cross-Domain Feature Fusion—which together enhance robustness, accuracy, and overall tracking performance.

The Adaptive Pruning module dynamically filters irrelevance tokens using a last-rank elimination strategy, effectively suppressing background noise and redundant features. Meanwhile, Cross-Domain Feature Fusion leverages both spatial and frequency domain cues to strengthen target representation under challenging conditions. Future work will explore trajectory-aware modeling and adaptive template update strategies to enhance long-term tracking stability.

Acknowledgements. This Research Project Supported by Shanxi Scholarship Council of China(No. 2022-008) "Research on Multi-context Propagation and Multi-task Learning based Object Tracking".

References

1. Bertinetto, L., Valmadre, J., Henriques, J.F., Vedaldi, A., Torr, P.H.S.: Fully-Convolutional Siamese Networks for Object Tracking. In: Hua, G., Jégou, H. (eds.) ECCV 2016. LNCS, vol. 9914, pp. 850–865. Springer, Cham (2016). https://doi.org/10.1007/978-3-319-48881-3_56

2. Bhat, G., Danelljan, M., Gool, L.V., Timofte, R.: Learning discriminative model prediction for tracking. In: Proceedings of the IEEE/CVF International Conference on Computer Vision, pp. 6182–6191 (2019)
3. Bolme, D.S., Beveridge, J.R., Draper, B.A., Lui, Y.M.: Visual object tracking using adaptive correlation filters. In: 2010 IEEE Computer Society Conference on Computer Vision and Pattern Recognition, pp. 2544–2550. IEEE (2010)
4. Cai, Y., Liu, J., Tang, J., Wu, G.: Robust object modeling for visual tracking. In: Proceedings of the IEEE/CVF International Conference on Computer Vision, pp. 9589–9600 (2023)
5. Chen, X., Yan, B., Zhu, J., Wang, D., Yang, X., Lu, H.: Transformer tracking. In: Proceedings of the IEEE/CVF Conference on Computer Vision and Pattern Recognition, pp. 8126–8135 (2021)
6. Cui, Y., Jiang, C., Wang, L., Wu, G.: Mixformer: End-to-end tracking with iterative mixed attention. In: Proceedings of the IEEE/CVF Conference on Computer Vision and Pattern Recognition, pp. 13608–13618 (2022)
7. Dosovitskiy, A., et al.: An image is worth 16x16 words: Transformers for image recognition at scale. arXiv preprint arXiv:2010.11929, pp. 1–22 (2020)
8. Fan, H., et al.: Lasot: a high-quality benchmark for large-scale single object tracking. In: Proceedings of the IEEE/CVF Conference on Computer Vision and Pattern Recognition, pp. 5374–5383 (2019)
9. Gupta, G., Xiao, X., Bogdan, P.: Multiwavelet-based operator learning for differential equations. Adv. Neural. Inf. Process. Syst. **34**, 24048–24062 (2021)
10. Henriques, J.F., Caseiro, R., Martins, P., Batista, J.: High-speed tracking with kernelized correlation filters. IEEE Trans. Pattern Anal. Mach. Intell. **37**(3), 583–596 (2014)
11. Huang, L., Zhao, X., Huang, K.: Got-10k: a large high-diversity benchmark for generic object tracking in the wild. IEEE Trans. Pattern Anal. Mach. Intell. **43**(5), 1562–1577 (2019)
12. Li, B., Yan, J., Wu, W., Zhu, Z., Hu, X.: High performance visual tracking with siamese region proposal network. In: Proceedings of the IEEE Conference on Computer Vision and Pattern Recognition, pp. 8971–8980 (2018)
13. Lin, L., Fan, H., Zhang, Z., Xu, Y., Ling, H.: Swintrack: a simple and strong baseline for transformer tracking. Adv. Neural. Inf. Process. Syst. **35**, 16743–16754 (2022)
14. Loshchilov, I., Hutter, F.: Decoupled weight decay regularization. arXiv preprint arXiv:1711.05101 (2017)
15. Michel, P., Levy, O., Neubig, G.: Are sixteen heads really better than one? Advances in neural information processing systems **32** (2019)
16. Muller, M., Bibi, A., Giancola, S., Alsubaihi, S., Ghanem, B.: Trackingnet: A large-scale dataset and benchmark for object tracking in the wild. In: Proceedings of the European conference on computer vision (ECCV), pp. 300–317 (2018)
17. Vaswani, A., et al.: Attention is all you need. Advances in neural information processing systems **30** (2017)
18. Voita, E., Talbot, D., Moiseev, F., Sennrich, R., Titov, I.: Analyzing multi-head self-attention: Specialized heads do the heavy lifting, the rest can be pruned. arXiv preprint arXiv:1905.09418 (2019)
19. Wei, X., Bai, Y., Zheng, Y., Shi, D., Gong, Y.: Autoregressive visual tracking. In: Proceedings of the IEEE/CVF Conference on Computer Vision and Pattern Recognition, pp. 9697–9706 (2023)

20. Wu, H., Xu, J., Wang, J., Long, M.: Autoformer: decomposition transformers with auto-correlation for long-term series forecasting. Adv. Neural. Inf. Process. Syst. **34**, 22419–22430 (2021)
21. Xie, J., Zhong, B., Mo, Z., Zhang, S., Shi, L., Song, S., Ji, R.: Autoregressive queries for adaptive tracking with spatio-temporal transformers. In: Proceedings of the IEEE/CVF Conference on Computer Vision and Pattern Recognition, pp. 19300–19309 (2024)
22. Xu, K., Qin, M., Sun, F., Wang, Y., Chen, Y., Ren, F.: Learning in the frequency domain. CoRR **abs/2002.12416** (2020)
23. Ye, B., Chang, H., Ma, B., Shan, S., Chen, X.: Joint feature learning and relation modeling for tracking: A one-stream framework. In: European Conference on Computer Vision, pp. 341–357. Springer (2022)
24. Zhang, Y.F., Ren, W., Zhang, Z., Jia, Z., Wang, L., Tan, T.: Focal and efficient iou loss for accurate bounding box regression. Neurocomputing **506**, 146–157 (2022)
25. Zhang, Z., Liu, Y., Wang, X., Li, B., Hu, W.: Learn to match: Automatic matching network design for visual tracking. In: Proceedings of the IEEE/CVF International Conference on Computer Vision, pp. 13339–13348 (2021)
26. Zhang, Z., Peng, H., Fu, J., Li, B., Hu, W.: Ocean: Object-aware anchor-free tracking. In: European Conference on Computer Vision, pp. 771–787. Springer (2020)

Data Leakage Detection in Large Vision-Language Models via Multimodal Perturbation

Xin Wang[1,2,3](✉), Zhaoxiang Liu[3], Yue Zhan[4], Kaikai Zhao[3], Kai Wang[3], and Shiguo Lian[3](✉)

[1] China United Network Communications Group Corporation Limited, Beijing, China
`wangxin6735@163.com`
[2] Beijing University of Posts and Telecommunications, Beijing, China
[3] Unicom Data Intelligence China Unicom, Beijing, China
`{liuzx178,zhaokk3,wangk115,liansg}@chinaunicom.cn`
[4] Beijing Jiaotong University, Beijing, China
`zhanyue@bjtu.edu.cn`

Abstract. The training data for large vision-language models (LVLMs) is typically sourced from large-scale corpora, which may inadvertently include copyrighted or sensitive content, raising concerns about private data leakage. However, detecting such leakage remains challenging due to the opaque internal mechanisms of LVLMs. We observe that memorization in large language models (LLMs) can cause LVLMs to generate distinct responses to seen versus unseen inputs. This discrepancy offers a viable signal for privacy leakage detection. In this paper, we propose DLD-MP, a novel framework for Data Leakage Detection in LVLMs through Multimodal Perturbation. DLD-MP comprises three components: Multi-Level Image Perturbation (MLIP), Key Semantic Mask-based Text Perturbation (KSMTP), and a Leakage Evaluator (LE). Given an image-text pair, MLIP applies perturbations to the image at multiple semantic levels, while KSMTP selectively masks key semantic tokens within the corresponding text. The perturbed inputs are then fed into the target LVLM to perform masked text prediction and vision-language understanding tasks. LE assesses the model's responses against predefined rules to determine whether the input is used during training. Extensive experiments on multiple benchmarks demonstrate the effectiveness of DLD-MP.

Keywords: Data leakage detection · Large vision-language model · Membership inference

1 Introduction

Large vision-language models (LVLMs) [1,17,26] recently attracted significant attention for their strong capabilities in understanding both visual and textual modalities. Leveraging these strengths, LVLMs have emerged as foundational components of

Z. Lin et al. (Eds.): ICIG 2025, LNCS 16161, pp. 174–186, 2026.
https://doi.org/10.1007/978-981-95-3398-5_15

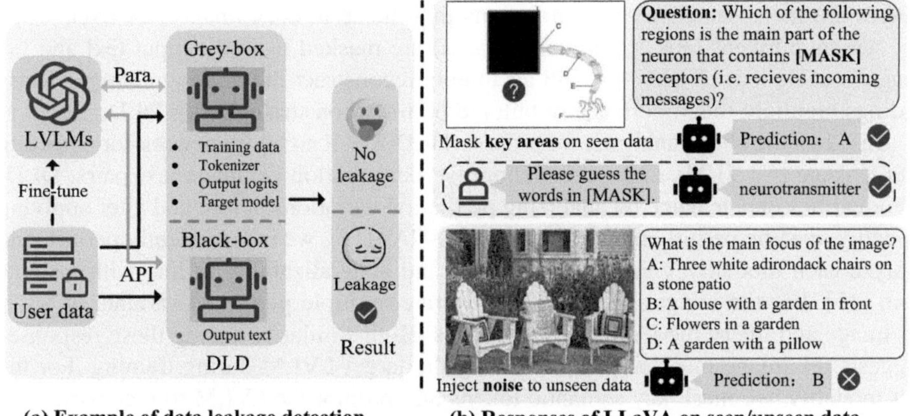

(a) Example of data leakage detection   (b) Responses of LLaVA on seen/unseen data

Fig. 1. An illustrative example of data leakage detection (DLD) in large vision-language models (LVLMs), and the motivation of this work. (a) depicts the DLD process under grey-box and black-box settings. (b) shows the responses of LLaVA [17] to seen and unseen data, where key areas in the seen image are masked and noise is injected into the unseen image. (Color figure online)

various applications, including intelligent assistants and visual question answering systems. The training of LVLMs typically involves two stages: pre-training and instruction tuning. Pre-training uses publicly available datasets to achieve initial cross-modal feature alignment. Instruction tuning requires high-quality, domain-specific data to adapt the model to downstream tasks. These instruction-tuning datasets often include proprietary or copyrighted information, exemplified by commercial medical models trained on unauthorized medical images or diagnostic records. Furthermore, the memorization tendencies of LLMs [11] may lead LVLMs to inadvertently leak training data, raising data security concerns [6]. Consequently, developing a data leakage detection (DLD) pipeline is imperative to assess if private data was used by LVLMs (see Fig. 1 (a)).

DLD aims to identify whether a user's private data was used during model training. This task is closely related to membership inference attacks (MIAs) [19], which exploit the overfitting behavior of models to identify differences in responses to seen (member) versus unseen (non-member) data. Existing MIAs infer membership by analyzing output-level signals, such as perplexity [14] or token-level statistics [21,25]. While extensively studied in LLMs, these techniques remain underexplored in LVLMs, with only limited works [12,15]. Moreover, most existing methods require access to internal model components (e.g., tokenizers or output logits), which are unavailable in real-world black-box scenarios. To overcome this limitation, we consider a practical yet challenging setting: *detecting data leakage in LVLMs based on their generated outputs, without relying on token-level logits or internal access.*

Large models tend to memorize training data, particularly when instruction-tuning data is scarce. Therefore, we conduct an exploratory experiment to investigate how LVLMs (e.g., LLaVA [17]) respond to input perturbations for seen and unseen samples. As illustrated in Fig. 1(b), we observe two key behaviors: 1) Responses to unseen images are more sensitive to perturbations than those to seen images. 2) Even when key semantic tokens (e.g., core noun phrases) are masked from the input text and the image is occluded, LVLMs can still accurately reconstruct the missing content. These findings highlight the importance of tailored perturbation strategies for DLD.

Based on the above analysis, we propose DLD-MP, a novel framework for detecting data leakage in LVLMs through collaborative perturbation of image-text pairs. DLD-MP identifies data leakage by analyzing prediction variations before and after applying modality-specific perturbations. Unlike prior MIAs [12], we independently perturb and analyze each modality, enhancing flexibility and generalizability in line with insights from [15]. For the image modality, we generate multiple perturbed variants of a target image and query the LVLM for responses. High similarity among these responses suggests the image may have been seen by the target LVLM during training. For the text modality, we mask key semantic tokens and prompt the LVLM to reconstruct the missing tokens using only the textual input. Accurate reconstruction from a large vocabulary indicates a high likelihood that the text was included in the training set. The final leakage decision is made by jointly assessing membership signals from both modalities. Experimental results on the VL-MIA benchmark [15] and custom leak detection scenarios validate the effectiveness of DLD-MP, especially in fully black-box settings.

The contributions of this paper can be summarized as follows:

- We propose DLD-MP, a novel DLD framework to detect private data leakage in LVLMs under a fully black-box scenario.
- We design modality-specific perturbation strategies and a rule-based evaluator to achieve DLD in LVLMs, by analyzing prediction changes under perturbations.
- We validate the effectiveness and robustness of DLD-MP through extensive experiments across multiple benchmarks.

2 Related Works

2.1 Large Vision-Language Models (LVLMs)

LVLMs integrate visual content into LLMs to enable multimodal understanding and reasoning. Most LVLMs [1,17] focus on aligning visual features with language embeddings. A common strategy is to employ pre-trained vision encoders and connect them to LLMs via learnable transformation modules, which fall into two categories: 1) Query-based methods [5,27] use learnable query tokens and cross-attention mechanisms to integrate visual features into LLMs; 2) Projection-based methods [17] utilize linear projection layers or multi-layer perceptrons to align visual and language representations. Alternatively, models such as Gemini [23] adopt an end-to-end training paradigm that jointly optimizes all components on large-scale multimodal data. While this method is effective, it incurs significantly higher computational costs. In addition, since LVLM's performance depends on the quality of instruction-tuning data, recent efforts [3] have focused on generating high-quality multimodal datasets to improve LVLMs.

2.2 Membership Inference Attacks of Large Models

MIAs are widely used to assess privacy risks in machine learning models. Existing MIAs can be broadly categorized into reference-based [18,22] and metric-based methods [4,24]. Reference-based MIAs train shadow models to mimic the target model's behavior, which is computationally prohibitive for large models (LMs). In contrast, metric-based methods bypass this cost by leveraging output-level statistics, such as perplexity [2,14] or probabilistic variations [9,21,25], to infer membership via thresholding. Similar techniques have also been adopted for benchmark contamination detection in LLMs [8,20]. Despite rising concerns over privacy in multimodal settings, MIAs against LVLMs remain relatively underexplored. A few recent studies [10,12,15] have attempted to bridge this gap. Ko et al. [12] inferred membership of image-text pairs by measuring cosine similarity between modality-specific features extracted by CLIP. Li et al. [15] introduced a VLA-MI benchmark along with the MaxRényi-K% metric, which operates on output token logits. Hu et al. [10] extended classical MIAs to LVLMs across various scenarios, revealing potential privacy risks. However, these approaches assume access to internal components (e.g., tokenizers, embeddings, or logits), limiting their applicability in black-box scenarios. In this paper, our method infers data leakage solely from the generated outputs of LVLMs, making it suitable for API-based settings.

3 Method

3.1 Problem Setup

DLD aims to determine whether a given sample was included in the training data of LVLMs. Formally, let $\mathbf{M}$ be an LVLM trained on a dataset $\mathcal{D}_m$ (member data), with $\mathcal{D}_{nm}$ denoting non-member data, where $\mathcal{D}_m \cap \mathcal{D}_{nm} = \emptyset$. Given a target sample $X = (X^v, X^q) \in \mathcal{D}_m \cup \mathcal{D}_{nm}$, where X^v and X^q are image and text data of an image-text pair, respectively. The goal of DLD is to design a scoring function $\mathbf{S}(\cdot)$ to support binary classification:

$$\mathbf{A}_d(X, \mathbf{M}) = \begin{cases} 1, & X \in \mathcal{D}_m \quad and \quad \mathbf{S}(X; \mathbf{M}) \geq \tau \\ 0, & X \in \mathcal{D}_{nm} \quad and \quad \mathbf{S}(X; \mathbf{M}) < \tau \end{cases}, \tag{1}$$

where τ denotes a threshold. $\mathbf{A}_d(\cdot)$ outputs 1 if X is predicted to be a member sample, and 0 otherwise. In practice, $\mathbf{A}_d(\cdot)$ can be applied to a set of sample $\mathcal{X} = \{X_i^v, X_i^q\}_{i=1}^{|\mathcal{X}|}$ to improve robustness, since individual samples may yield weak membership signals.

3.2 Overview

Figure 2 illustrates the overall framework of DLD-MP, which is designed to detect data leakage across both image and text modalities. Given an image-text pair (X^v, X^q), the detection process proceeds as follows. For the image modality X^v, we first apply K perturbations to generate a set of perturbed images, denoted as $\mathcal{X}_p^v = \{\hat{X}_i^v\}_{i=1}^K$. Each perturbed image $\hat{X}_i^v$, together with the instruction text X^q, is fed into the LVLM to

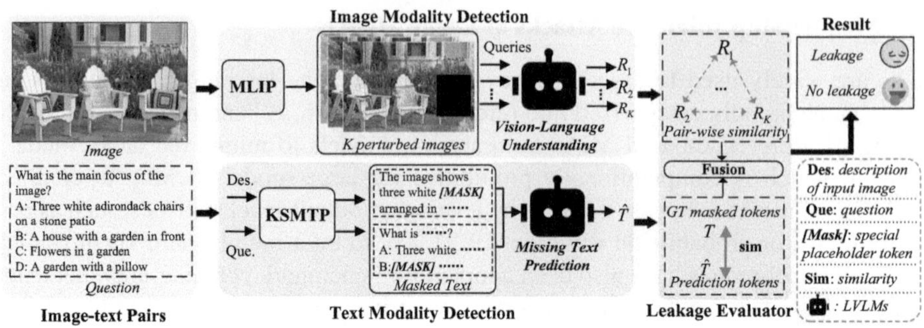

Fig. 2. Overview of the proposed DLD-MP framework. The framework consists of three components: (1) Multi-Level Image Perturbation (MLIP), which perturbs the input image at multiple semantic granularities; (2) Key Semantic Mask-based Text Perturbation (KSMTP), which selectively masks text tokens based on key semantic content; (3) Leakage Evaluator (LE), which quantifies data leakage from the input image-text pair by analyzing modality-specific responses.

produce a corresponding response. The resulting K responses are then passed to the Leakage Evaluator (LE), which computes the pairwise similarity among them. If the aggregated similarity score exceeds a predefined threshold, X^v is identified as member data, indicating a potential image data leakage. For the text modality X^q, we mask a set of keywords $\mathcal{T}$ within both X^q and the LVLM-generated initial image description. The LVLM is prompted to recover the masked content $\hat{\mathcal{T}}$ from a large-scale vocabulary. A high semantic similarity between $\hat{\mathcal{T}}$ and the ground-truth $\mathcal{T}$ suggests that the model has likely memorized the input text during training. Finally, LE aggregates the modality-specific membership signals to provide a comprehensive assessment of the LVLM's leakage risk for the given image-text pair. Detailed descriptions of the core components are provided in the following sections.

3.3 Multi-level Image Perturbation

Intuition. LVLMs tend to generate responses more aligned with the ground truth for training images than for unseen ones. As a result, perturbed versions of the same training image often yield highly similar responses. Inspired by this, we infer whether an image was used during training by measuring the consistency of model predictions across its perturbed variants, under the assumption that LVLMs overfit their training data. In practice, extensive data augmentations are used to improve generalization, making LVLMs robust to common input variations. Consequently, minor perturbations may fail to distinguish training images from unseen ones, increasing the risk of false positives. To address this, we design a multi-level image perturbation (MLIP) strategy that integrates low-level augmentations with high-level semantic transformations, as illustrated in Fig. 3.

Low-level augmentations, such as random noise, color jittering, and grayscale, are used to perform pixel-level perturbations to the input image X^v. In contrast, high-level semantic transformations apply localized modifications at the semantic level, while preserving the image's global structure and contextual coherence. To perform semantic transformations, we randomly generate two rectangular boxes $R_1 = (x_1, y_1, w, h)$ and $R_2 = (x_2, y_2, w, h)$ within X^v, where (x, y) denotes the center coordinates, and (w, h) represents the width and height of each box, set at 20%–40% of the original image size. The images within R_1 and R_2 are then perturbed using the following two techniques:

1) *Region masking.* The pixel values within R_1 and R_2 are set to zero, resulting in the perturbed image $\hat{X}^v$:

$$\hat{X}^v(x, y) = \begin{cases} 0, & \text{if}(x, y) \in R_1 \cup R_2, \\ X^v(x, y), & \text{otherwise,} \end{cases} \tag{2}$$

where $X^v(x, y)$ denotes the pixel value at coordinate (x, y).

2) *Region mixing.* The pixel values within regions R_1 and R_2 are mixed using a weighted combination:

$$\hat{X}^v_{r_1}(x, y) = \lambda \cdot X^v_{r_1}(x, y) + (1 - \lambda) \cdot X^v_{r_2}(x, y), \tag{3}$$

where $X^v_{r_1}$ and $X^v_{r_2}$ denote the pixel values at coordinate (x, y) within R_1 and R_2 of the original image X^v, respectively. The mixing weight $\lambda \in [0, 1]$ determines the relative contribution of each region to the mixed content. In practice, either region masking or region mixing is randomly applied to each image.

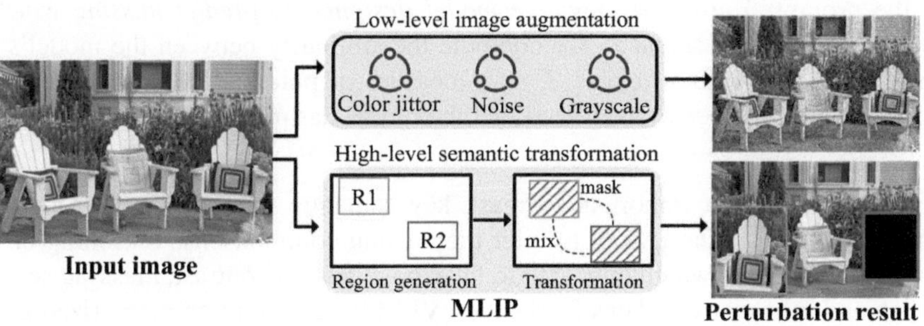

Fig. 3. Illustration of multi-level image perturbation (MLIP).

3.4   Key Semantic Mask-Based Text Perturbation

Intuition. Accurate reconstruction of masked text often implies prior exposure [7] during training, as LVLMs recover missing content more reliably when they have seen similar data. We extend the intuition to DLD in LVLMs by comparing the reconstructed text with the original ground truth. To enable this, we design a key semantic mask-based text perturbation (KSMTP) strategy, as illustrated in Fig. 4.

The question text X^q in image-text pairs is typically generic and short (e.g., < 30 words). This makes it easy for the LVLM to reconstruct the masked content, thereby increasing the risk of false positives in leakage detection. To mitigate this issue, we first prompt the target LVLM to generate a detailed description X^d for each input image X^v

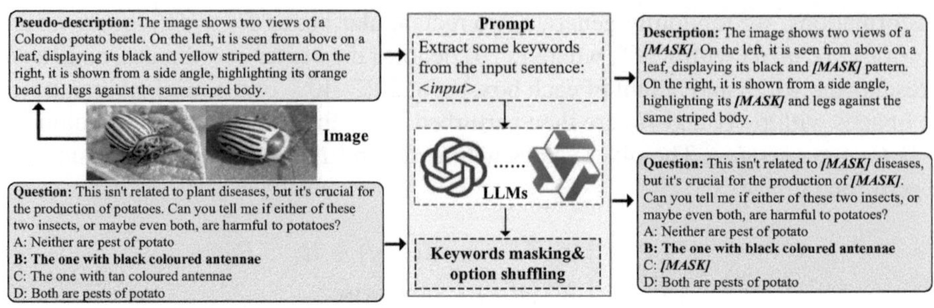

Fig. 4. Illustration of the key semantic mask-based text perturbation (KSMTP).

using the instruction: *Describe this image concisely.* We then apply targeted masking to the key semantics of the combined text $X^t = (X^q, X^d)$, constructing a challenging reconstruction task. Specifically, given the input text $X^t = (t_1, t_2, \ldots, t_N)$, we employ a strong LLM (e.g., GPT-4o), denoted as $\mathbf{LM}(\cdot)$, to extract N_{mt} key semantic tokens $\mathcal{T} = \mathbf{LM}(X^t)$. These tokens are replaced with the *[MASK]* token to construct the perturbed text $\hat{X}^t = (t_1, \ldots, [MASK], \ldots, t_N)$. For multiple-choice questions (MCQs), we further increase perturbation difficulty by randomly shuffling answer choices and masking one incorrect option. The perturbed text $\hat{X}^t$ is then input to the target LVLM using the prompt: *You are a language model designed to predict missing words or phrases in sentences: <input>.* We compute the similarity between the model's prediction $\hat{\mathcal{T}}$ and the original tokens $\mathcal{T}$ as a measure of potential data leakage. Higher similarity suggests a greater likelihood that the model has memorized the text X^q.

Discussion. Why is it important to mask key semantic tokens? Masking trivial or generic tokens allows the LVLM to infer them using commonsense reasoning or general world knowledge, which may lead to false positives. In contrast, masking semantically rich and informative tokens forces the LVLM to rely more on memorized knowledge rather than reasoning, thereby improving the reliability and accuracy of DLD.

3.5   Leakage Evaluator

The overall leakage signal for an image-text pair is computed by aggregating modality-specific leakage indicators, as defined below:

Image Modality. Training images typically yield responses that are more consistent with the ground truth than unseen images. To determine whether an image X^v is likely included in the training set, we evaluate the consistency of model predictions under K perturbed versions of X^v. Specifically, we compute $0.5 \times (K^2 - K)$ pairwise similarity scores among the K responses. Similarity is measured using the ROUGE metric [16] for image description tasks, and exact match for multiple-choice and yes/no questions. If the mean similarity score exceeds a threshold τ_1, the image X^v is flagged as leaked.

Text Modality. Reconstructing masked tokens from a large vocabulary is generally difficult without prior exposure. Therefore, if an LVLM successfully reconstructs the masked tokens, it may indicate that the input text was seen during training. Given the original masked tokens $\mathcal{T}$ and the prediction tokens $\hat{\mathcal{T}}$, we assess semantic similarity using an LLM-based judgment, which outputs a score in the range $[0, 10]$. If this similarity score exceeds a predefined score τ_2, the text is considered leaked.

Overall Leakage. To ensure comprehensive detection, we adopt a conservative decision rule: an image-text pair is classified as leaked if either the image or text modality is flagged as leaked based on the above criteria. To provide a robust and comprehensive evaluation of our method, we use the AUC score as a threshold-independent metric in our experiments.

4   Experiments

4.1   Dataset and Evaluation Metric

We evaluate our method on the VL-MIA benchmark [9], which targets membership inference in vision-language models. Two splits in VL-MIA are used: VL-MIA/Flickr and VL-MIA/DALL-E, each containing 600 samples, with an equal number of member and non-member samples. In VL-MIA/Flickr, member samples are collected from MS-COCO (pre-2014), and non-members are crawled from Flickr (post-2024). In VL-MIA/DALL-E, member images come from LAION-CCS, and non-members are generated by DALL-E using the same captions as the members. Following [9], we use AUC score and TPR@5%FPR as evaluation metrics, where higher values indicate better performance. For ablation studies, we simulate data leakage in LVLMs by splitting the *LLaVA-Instruction-158K* dataset [17] into two disjoint subsets: $\mathcal{D}_m$ (used for instruction-tuning) and $\mathcal{D}_{nm}$ (excluded from training), using an 8:2 ratio.

4.2   Implementation Details

For each image-text pair, we apply modality-specific perturbations by using MLIP for images and KSMTP for text. In MLIP, each image is randomly perturbed by low-level image augmentations and high-level semantic transformations. In KSMTP, we employ GPT-4o to extract key semantic tokens from input text (both the user query and image description). For short questions (fewer than 10 words) or generic prompts, KSMTP is applied only to the image description. In LE, we employ QWQ-32-Preview as the judgment model due to its strong reasoning capabilities. We evaluate our method on the VL-MIA benchmark, using three representative LVLMs: MiniGPT [27], LLaVA-v1.5-7B [17], and LLaVA-OV-7B [13], all with full access to training data and parameters. Performance is measured using the threshold-free AUC score. Hyperparameters are selected via grid search: $K = 10$ and $\lambda = 0.7$ for MLIP, and $N_{mt} \leq 5$ for KSMTP. Although threshold-free metrics are used for evaluation, practical deployment may require setting thresholds (e.g., $\tau_1 = 0.5, \tau_2 = 6$) based on a reference dataset. Experiments are conducted on a single H100 GPU.

Table 1. Performance comparison of different methods on the VL-MIA/DALL-E and VL-MIA/Flickr benchmarks using three LVLMs: LLaVA-1.5-7B [17], LLaVA-OV-7B [13], and MiniGPT-4 [27]. *inst*, *desp* denote the instruction and description slice of the output tokens, respectively. **Bold** and <u>underline</u> indicate the best and second-best results, respectively.

Dataset	Method		LLaVA-v1.5-7B		LLaVA-OV-7B		MiniGPT-4	
			AUC	TPR	AUC	TPR	AUC	TPR
Flickr	Perplexity [2]	inst+desp	56.1%	7.1%	16.3%	0.1%	49.7%	7.3%
	Min-20% [21]	inst+desp	37.0%	0.3%	41.2%	6.3%	57.3%	9.2%
	Min-20%++ [25]	inst+desp	61.3%	<u>18.4%</u>	46.7%	8.9%	62.8%	<u>12.9%</u>
	Image-only [10]	img	61.9%	9.6%	26.4%	6.8%	53.8%	6.2%
	MaxRényi-10% [9]	inst+desp	<u>71.2%</u>	11.4%	**71.3%**	**32.7%**	<u>69.3%</u>	12.1%
		img	62.3%	8.7%	68.1%	29.3%	48.9%	7.0%
	DLD-MP(ours)	inst+desp+img	**74.7%**	**18.9%**	<u>70.9%</u>	<u>30.5%</u>	**72.5%**	**15.8%**
DALL-E	Perplexity [2]	inst+desp	44.8%	5.1%	58.4%	17.0%	42.1%	3.3%
	Min-20% [21]	inst+desp	35.3%	7.8%	61.3%	18.9%	39.3%	5.4%
	Min-20%++ [25]	inst+desp	51.4%	9.2%	57.3%	11.2%	45.2%	5.9%
	Image-only [10]	img	50.5%	5.2%	65.1%	13.1%	51.8%	6.7%
	MaxRényi-10% [9]	inst+desp	65.3%	12.3%	71.2%	<u>21.3%</u>	47.2%	3.9%
		img	63.8%	**19.1%**	68.2%	18.2%	<u>55.1%</u>	<u>7.6%</u>
	DLD-MP(ours)	inst+desp+img	**68.7%**	<u>17.5%</u>	**72.1%**	**22.9%**	**57.9%**	**9.2%**

4.3 Overall Performance

To evaluate the effectiveness of the proposed DLD-MP, we compare it with several recent MIA methods on the VL-MIA benchmark, including Perplexity [2], Min-K% [21], Min-K%++ [25], MaxRényi-K% [9], and Image-only inference [10]. For token-level MIA baselines, we follow the configuration in [10]. Specifically, we fix the instruction X^q to *Describe this image concisely* and prompt the LVLM to generate a textual description X^{des} for the image X^v. The concatenated input sequence $[X^v, X^q, X^{des}]$ is then fed into the LVLM, and we compute statistics from different slices of output logits, including the image embedding slice, instruction slice, and description slice.

Table 1 presents the AUC and TPR@5%FPR results across various methods. Despite having access to token-level output logits, token-based MIA methods often exhibit subpar performance. Notably, methods such as Perplexity [2] and Min-K% [21] even perform worse than random guessing (AUC = 50%). For MIA methods originally designed for LLMs, the image in an image-text pair must be converted into a textual description. This process may discard essential visual details and degrade performance. Similarly, Image-only inference [10], which relies solely on the image modality, also yields suboptimal results. In contrast, our proposed DLD-MP exploits both text and image modalities through a collective perturbation strategy, consistently outperforming other methods across most settings. Even when limited to output text alone, DLD-MP achieves performance comparable to MaxRényi-K% [15], a strong baseline that operates with full access to token-level logits. These results demonstrate the robustness and effectiveness of our method.

4.4   Ablation Study

We conduct ablation studies under a customized data leakage setting, where 2K member and 2K non-member samples are randomly selected from $\mathcal{D}_m$ and $\mathcal{D}_{nm}$, respectively, both derived from *LLaVa-Instruction-158K*. Unless otherwise specified, all experiments are conducted on the LLaVA-v1.5-7B model [17].

Table 2. Ablation of text and image perturbations on the custom data leakage scenario.

Text Perturbation		Image Perturbation		AUC	TPR
des.	que.	low	high		
✓	✗	–	–	57.1%	10.7%
✗	✓	–	–	51.4%	7.6%
✓	✓	–	–	60.3%	12.8%
–	–	✓	✗	59.4%	9.7%
–	–	✗	✓	61.9%	13.1%
–	–	✓	✓	63.1%	15.2%
✓	✓	✓	✓	69.1%	18.7%

Table 3. Effect of memorization level on data leakage detection.

Target model	epoch = 1	epoch = 2	epoch = 3	epoch = 4	epoch = 5
LLaVA-v1.5-7B [17]	69.1%	70.5%	70.9%	71.8%	73.1%
Qwen2.5-VL-7B [1]	70.5%	71.3%	72.6%	74.1%	74.5%

Effect of Different Perturbations. To simulate data leakage while ensuring fairness, we fine-tune the pre-trained LLaVA-v1.5-7B [17] (without instruction tuning) on $\mathcal{D}_m$. After tuning, we evaluate DLD-MP and its variants on the combined set $\mathcal{D}_m \cup \mathcal{D}_{nm}$, as shown in Table 2. Removing either KSMTP or MLIP results in a notable drop in AUC, highlighting the complementary advantages of multimodal perturbation. Additionally, simplifying text or image perturbation further degrades performance, indicating the importance of perturbation diversity. The full version of DLD-MP, which integrates both KSMTP and MLIP, achieves the highest AUC among all variants, validating the effectiveness of the proposed perturbation strategy.

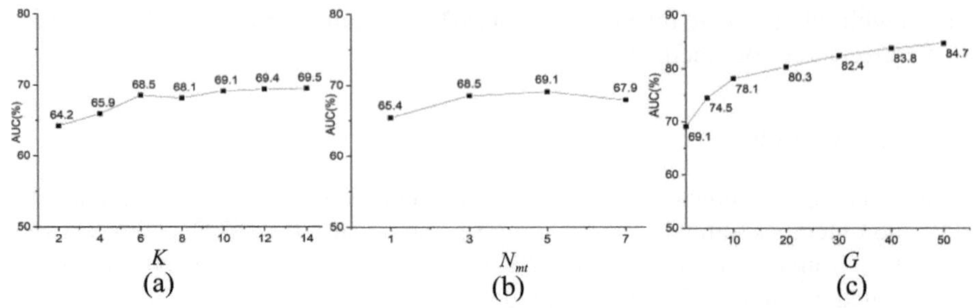

Fig. 5. Impact of key hyperparameters on detection performance: (a) image perturbation steps K, (b) the number of masked text tokens N_{mt}, and (c) the size of the sample set G.

Effect of Training Data Memorization. To evaluate the impact of LMM memorization on DLD, we train LVLMs for different numbers of epochs, simulating varying levels of memorization. As shown in Table 3, LVLMs exhibit limited overfitting during early training stages. This makes it harder to distinguish between member and non-member samples and results in relatively low AUC scores. As training progresses, LVLMs gradually memorize more details from the training data. This increased memorization leads to more distinguishable responses between perturbed and unperturbed inputs. Consequently, DLD performance improves steadily. These results suggest that DLD-MP is more effective when an LVLM has a stronger memorization of private data.

Hyperparameter Analysis. Figure 5 illustrates the impact of different hyperparameter settings on the performance of DLD-MP. As shown in Fig. 5 (a), increasing the number of perturbations K improves AUC scores. However, the marginal benefits diminish with larger K, while the computational cost scales linearly. In Fig. 5 (b), we observe that small values of N_{mt} may introduce false positives, since LVLMs can often infer masked tokens from contextual cues. In contrast, large N_{mt} values degrade the model's ability to reconstruct the original input, thereby compromising detection accuracy. Figure 5(c) shows that aggregating leakage signals over a set of samples outperforms per-sample detection, as it enhances the underlying membership signal and improves detection robustness.

5   Conclusion

This paper proposes DLD-MP, a novel framework for detecting data leakage in large vision-language models (LVLMs) by measuring prediction variance under multimodal perturbations. DLD-MP integrates three key components: multi-level image perturbation, keyword masking-based text perturbation, and a rule-based leakage evaluator. Extensive experiments on multiple benchmarks validate the effectiveness and generality of the proposed DLD-MP in identifying training data misuse. In future work, we plan to explore more robust, scalable, and generalizable detection mechanisms to support privacy auditing in LVLMs.

References

1. Bai, S., et al.: Qwen2.5-VL technical report. arXiv preprint arXiv:2502.13923 (2025)
2. Carlini, N., et al.: Extracting training data from large language models. In: 30th USENIX Security Symposium, pp. 2633–2650 (2021)
3. Chen, L., Li, J., Dong, X., Zhang, P., He, C., Wang, J., Zhao, F., Lin, D.: ShareGPT4V: improving large multi-modal models with better captions. In: European Conference on Computer Vision, pp. 370–387. Springer (2024)
4. Choquette-Choo, C.A., Tramer, F., Carlini, N., Papernot, N.: Label-only membership inference attacks. In: ICML, pp. 1964–1974. PMLR (2021)
5. Dai, W., et al.: InstructBLIP: towards general-purpose vision-language models with instruction tuning. In: Thirty-seventh Conference on Neural Information Processing Systems (2023)
6. Das, B.C., Amini, M.H., Wu, Y.: Security and privacy challenges of large language models: a survey. ACM Comput. Surv. **57**(6), 1–39 (2025)
7. Deng, C., Zhao, Y., Tang, X., Gerstein, M., Cohan, A.: Investigating data contamination in modern benchmarks for large language models. In: NAACL, pp. 8706–8719 (2024)
8. Dong, Y., Jiang, X., Liu, H., Jin, Z., Gu, B., Yang, M., Li, G.: Generalization or memorization: Data contamination and trustworthy evaluation for large language models. arXiv preprint arXiv:2402.15938 (2024)
9. Fu, W., Wang, H., Gao, C., Liu, G., Li, Y., Jiang, T.: Membership inference attacks against fine-tuned large language models via self-prompt calibration. Adv. Neural. Inf. Process. Syst. **37**, 134981–135010 (2025)
10. Hu, Y., Li, Z., Liu, Z., Zhang, Y., Qin, Z., Ren, K., Chen, C.: Membership inference attacks against vision-language models. arXiv preprint arXiv:2501.18624 (2025)
11. Kiyomaru, H., Sugiura, I., Kawahara, D., Kurohashi, S.: A comprehensive analysis of memorization in large language models. In: Proceedings of the 17th International Natural Language Generation Conference, pp. 584–596 (2024)
12. Ko, M., Jin, M., Wang, C., Jia, R.: Practical membership inference attacks against large-scale multi-modal models: a pilot study. In: Proceedings of the IEEE/CVF International Conference on Computer Vision, pp. 4871–4881 (2023)
13. Li, B., et al.: LLaVA-OneVision: easy visual task transfer. Transactions on Machine Learning Research (2025)
14. Li, Y.: Estimating contamination via perplexity: Quantifying memorisation in language model evaluation. arXiv preprint arXiv:2309.10677 (2023)
15. Li, Z., Wu, Y., Chen, Y., Tonin, F., Abad Rocamora, E., Cevher, V.: Membership inference attacks against large vision-language models. Adv. Neural. Inf. Process. Syst. **37**, 98645–98674 (2025)
16. Lin, C.Y.: ROUGE: a package for automatic evaluation of summaries. In: Text summarization branches out, pp. 74–81 (2004)
17. Liu, H., Li, C., Li, Y., Lee, Y.J.: Improved baselines with visual instruction tuning. In: CVPR, pp. 26296–26306 (2024)
18. Mireshghallah, F., Goyal, K., Uniyal, A., Berg-Kirkpatrick, T., Shokri, R.: Quantifying privacy risks of masked language models using membership inference attacks. In: EMNLP, pp. 8332–8347 (2022)
19. Niu, J., et al.: Comparing different membership inference attacks with a comprehensive benchmark. IEEE Transactions on Information Forensics and Security (2025)
20. Oren, Y., Meister, N., Chatterji, N.S., Ladhak, F., Hashimoto, T.: Proving test set contamination in black-box language models. In: The Twelfth International Conference on Learning Representations (2023)

21. Shi, W., et al.: Detecting pretraining data from large language models. In: The Twelfth International Conference on Learning Representations, pp. 1–13 (2024)
22. Shokri, R., Stronati, M., Song, C., Shmatikov, V.: Membership inference attacks against machine learning models. In: 2017 IEEE Symposium on Security and Privacy (SP), pp. 3–18. IEEE (2017)
23. Team, G., et al.: Gemini: a family of highly capable multimodal models. arXiv preprint arXiv:2312.11805 (2023)
24. Yeom, S., Giacomelli, I., Fredrikson, M., Jha, S.: Privacy risk in machine learning: analyzing the connection to overfitting. In: 2018 IEEE 31st Computer Security Foundations Symposium (CSF), pp. 268–282. IEEE (2018)
25. Zhang, J., et al.: Min-K%++: improved baseline for pre-training data detection from large language models. In: ICLR (2025)
26. Zhang, J., Huang, J., Jin, S., Lu, S.: Vision-language models for vision tasks: a survey. IEEE Trans. Pattern Anal. Mach. Intell. **46**(8), 5625–5644 (2024)
27. Zhu, D., Chen, J., Shen, X., Li, X., Elhoseiny, M.: MiniGPT-4: enhancing vision-language understanding with advanced large language models. In: ICLR (2024)

A Novel Dual-Branch Cross-Attention Transformer Network for Low-Dose CT Denoising

Yuqin Li, Mengcheng Huang, Xu Wang, Fei He$^{(\boxtimes)}$, and Zhengang Jiang

Changchun University of Science and Technology, Changchun, China
reechand@cust.edu.cn

Abstract. Low-dose computed tomography (LDCT) has attracted widespread attention in medical imaging due to its significant reduction in radiation exposure. However, compared to normal-dose CT (NDCT) images, LDCT images often contain considerable noise and artifacts, which severely affect diagnostic accuracy. In this paper, a novel dual-branch cross-attention transformer denoising network (DCANet) is proposed for LDCT denoising, which decouples and models the input images in different feature spaces through two complementary branching structures, and achieves feature complementarity and synergistic optimization through the fusion mechanism to improve overall characterization capability. The proposed DCANet includes Residual Triple Attention Blocks (RTAB) and a Cross-Attention Transformer module (CAformer), applied to the upper and lower branches respectively, effectively enabling the synergistic fusion of local detail enhancement and global structural modeling. Additionally, a joint optimization strategy using perceptual loss and Charbonnier loss is adopted, enabling the method to efficiently suppress noise while accurately preserving key structural and textural information in the images. Experimental results on the Mayo LDCT dataset demonstrate that the proposed DCANet achieves significant improvements in both quantitative metrics and perceptual quality.

Keywords: Low-dose computed tomography · Dual-branch · Transformer

1 Introduction

Computed tomography (CT) is widely used in clinical diagnosis due to its rapid imaging, high spatial resolution, and low cost. However, to reduce radiation exposure risks, low-dose CT (LDCT) often suffers from increased noise, which compromises diagnostic accuracy [1]. Therefore, LDCT denoising has become a crucial area of research.

Traditional denoising methods include spatial filtering, transform-domain techniques, and sparse representation. Spatial filters [2, 3], such as the Non-Local Means (NLM) algorithm [4], reduce noise by averaging similar patches, but may blur fine details. Transform-based methods [5, 6], including DCT, DFT, and Wavelet Transform, separate noise in the frequency domain. BM3D [7] effectively combines transform-domain sparsity with non-local self-similarity priors, achieving strong noise suppression while

Z. Lin et al. (Eds.): ICIG 2025, LNCS 16161, pp. 187–198, 2026.
https://doi.org/10.1007/978-981-95-3398-5_16

preserving structural features. Sparse coding methods [8, 9] model images as sparse combinations of dictionary atoms to retain important structures. However, these methods often perform poorly when dealing with complex backgrounds or spatially varying noise.

Deep learning methods have shown great potential for LDCT denoising by learning end-to-end mappings from paired LDCT and NDCT images. Early CNN-based models such as RED-CNN [10], DnCNN [11], Q-AE [12], and EDCNN [13] improve reconstruction by incorporating residual learning, batch normalization, nonlinear activation, and edge enhancement. However, due to their inherently local receptive fields, Convolutional Neural Networks (CNNs) often struggle to model long-range dependencies, leading to detail loss and blurred boundaries in CT images. Transformer-based architectures, such as TransCT [14], SwinIR [15], and CTformer [16], commonly exploit global self-attention to capture long-range dependencies and contextual semantics, offering clear advantages over CNNs in modeling complex image structures. These models typically incorporate frequency-aware components, hierarchical attention, or positional encoding to enhance reconstruction quality. However, they share a common limitation: the lack of sensitivity to local texture variations, making it challenging to preserve fine details crucial for clinical image interpretation.

Dual-branch architectures have recently emerged to address these limitations by learning complementary features through parallel branches. DualCNN [17] s consists of two independent CNN networks, which respectively extract the structural and detailed information in the image. By comparing and combining the two feature vectors, it can more effectively represent and distinguish the differences between image pairs. DRANet [18] introduces residual learning and attention mechanism in the dual branches, respectively capturing rich local features and discarding unimportant features, thereby achieving more comprehensive feature extraction and fusion. LDMANet [19] employs a multi-scale residual attention mechanism to integrate local details and structural information, enhancing denoising performance and model generalization. This method demonstrates superior denoising capability on LDCT images. Thus, designing effective dual-branch feature extraction and fusion mechanisms remains a key research frontier with promising clinical and scientific value.

This paper proposes an innovative dual-branch cross-attention transformer denoising network (DCANet), which aims to achieve more accurate denoising and structure preservation for the noise problem in medical images. DCANet consists of two branches with complementary functions, which model and decouple different feature spaces in the image respectively. Through the CAformer module, the network enables cross-fertilization and complementary integration of two types of feature information, effectively enhancing the ability to capture detailed textures and structural information, and achieving the preservation of image textures and key anatomical structures during denoising. The main contributions of this work are as follows:

(1) A novel dual-branch cross-attention transformer denoising network (DCANet) is proposed for LDCT image denoising, which effectively preserves image details and structural information.

(2) The network includes Residual Triple Attention Blocks (RTAB) and a Cross-Attention Transformer (CAformer) module, which extract complementary features and enable collaborative optimization.

(3) Combined optimization of Charbonnier loss and perceptual loss is used to achieve pixel-level denoising and align denoised images with NDCT images in deep semantic feature space, thereby enhancing visual perception quality.

The remainder of this paper is organized as follows: the Methods section details the proposed DCANet; the Experiments and Discussion section presents the experimental results; finally, the Conclusion summarizes the contributions of this paper.

2 Methods

Conventional methods or single-branch networks often face a trade-off between effective noise suppression and the preservation of structural and textural details. As a result, the denoised images may appear over-smoothed or lack fine anatomical features. To overcome these limitations, we propose a two-branch denoising network, as illustrated in Fig. 1. The upper branch adopts a RTAB to capture localized representations through cross-dimensional attention mechanisms. Meanwhile, the CAformer module in the lower branch aggregates global contextual information and effectively fuses them with the features extracted from the upper branch. This dual-branch architecture enables more effective noise suppression while better preserving the structural integrity and fine-grained textures of low-dose CT images.

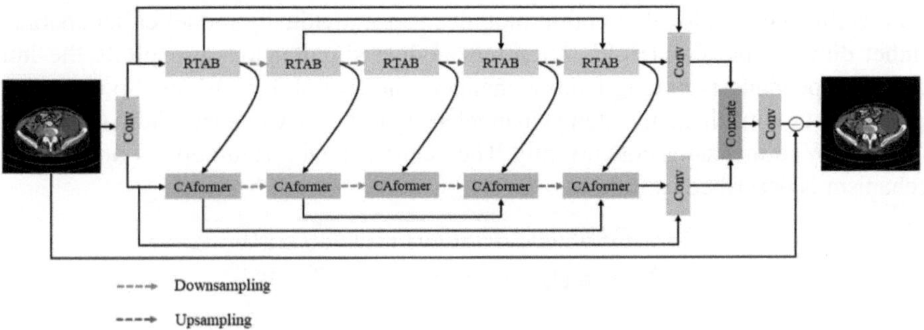

Fig. 1. The overall framework of the proposed DCANet

2.1 Residual Triplet Attention Block, RTAB

To effectively extract and capture rich local feature information from images, we propose RTAB, which comprises two essential components: Residual Block (RB) and Triplet Attention Block (TAB). The detailed architecture is illustrated in Fig. 2.

$$O_{RTAB} = RTAB(I_N) = TAB(RB(I_N)) + I_N \tag{1}$$

The RB is designed to leverage the advantages of CNNs in capturing local texture and edge details by stacking multiple convolutional operations, significantly enhancing the feature representation capability of the network. Each convolutional operation within the RB consists of two sequential steps: a combination of convolution and Rectified Linear Unit (Conv + ReLU) followed by a standalone Conv. Specifically, Conv + ReLU is conbination of linearity and non-linearity as the first convolution to extract rich features, and Conv is responsible for mining linear features, enabling the network to model complex features more effectively. Moreover, residual connections are employed to integrate multi-level convolutional features, effectively alleviating gradient vanishing problems in deep network training and enhancing the transmission of shallow-layer features into deeper layers. Formally, the residual block operation can be defined as:

$$O_{CB}^1 = CB(I_{RB}) = Conv(Relu(Conv(I_{RB})))$$

$$O_{CB}^2 = CB\left(I_{CB}^2\right) = CB\left(I_{RB} + O_{CB}^1\right)$$

$$O_{CB}^3 = CB\left(I_{CB}^3\right) = CB\left(I_{RB} + O_{CB}^1 + O_{CB}^2\right) \tag{2}$$

$$O_{CB}^4 = CB\left(I_{CB}^3\right) = CB\left(2I_{RB} + O_{CB}^1 + O_{CB}^2 + O_{CB}^3\right)$$

$$O_{RB} = O_{CB}^4 + I_{CB}^4 + I_{RB} = 3I_{RB} + 2O_{CB}^1 + O_{CB}^2 + O_{CB}^3 + O_{CB}^4$$

where I_{CB}^n and $O_{CB}^n (n \in \{1, 2, 3, 4\})$ denote the input and output of the n-th residual layer respectively, and I_{RB} 、 O_{RB} denote the input and output of the Residual Block respectively.

To further enhance the capacity of the model in emphasizing critical features while suppressing noise and redundant information, we incorporate the Triplet Attention mechanism. Unlike conventional attention modules that individually model either spatial or channel dimensions, the Triplet Attention module simultaneously exploits the intricate interdependencies among feature channels and spatial dimensions. Specifically, it applies attention mechanisms along Channel-Height (C-H), Channel-Width (C-W), and Spatial (H-W) dimensions concurrently. The mathematical formulation of this attention mechanism is described as follows:

$$O_d = Permute(Attention(Permute(I_{TAB})) \cdot$$
$$Permute(I_{TAB})), d = C - H, C - W \tag{3}$$

$$O_{H-W} = Attention(Permute(I_{TAB})) \cdot I_{TAB} \tag{4}$$

$$Attention = BN(Conv(Z - pool(I))) \tag{5}$$

where I_{TAB} denotes the input feature map to the Triplet Attention module, *Permute* represents tensor permutation operations that rearrange the feature dimensions to facilitate specific attention calculations, and "·" denotes element-wise multi-plication that integrates the attention weights with the original features. After completing attention modeling separately along the C-H, C-W, and H-W dimensions, the outputs from these three paths are integrated via element-wise addition to obtain the final output representation.

$$O_{TAB} = AVG(O_{C-H} + O_{C-W} + O_{H-W}) \tag{6}$$

where O_{TAB} denotes the output feature, and AVG represents the average operation.

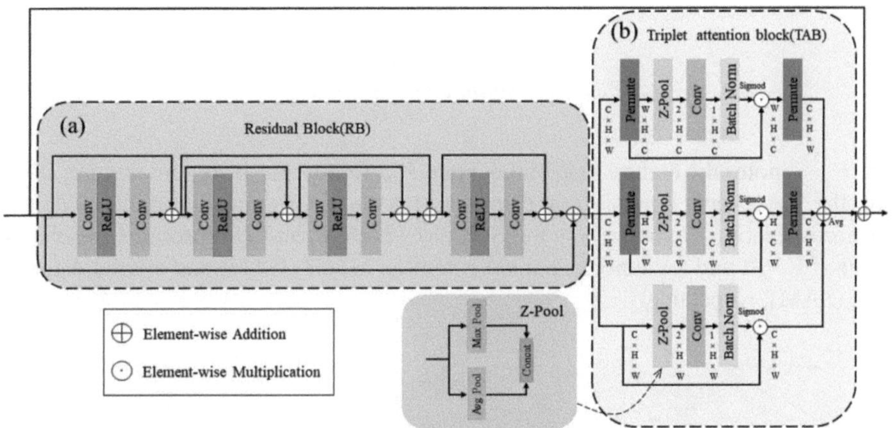

Fig. 2. Structure of the Residual Triplet Attention Block (RTAB), (a) structure of the Residual Block (RB), (b)Schematic diagram of the Triplet Attention Block (TAB)

2.2 Cross-Attention Transformer, CAformer

In the image reconstruction process, CNNs exhibit inherent limitations in capturing long-range spatial dependencies and global contextual information due to their localized receptive fields. In contrast, Transformers, benefiting from their self-attention mechanism, possess strong global modeling capabilities, enabling them to effectively capture long-distance dependencies across different regions of an image. However, Transformers tend to be less effective at modeling fine-grained local details compared to CNNs. To address the aforementioned challenges, we adopt a CAformer module, which is capable of jointly modeling both local and non-local features. As illustrated in Fig. 3, the CAformer begins by processing the local input feature map $F_{in}^x \in R^{h \times w \times c}$ through layer normalization, a 1×1 convolution, and a 3×3 depthwise convolution to generate a query tensor Q. Similarly, another input feature map $F_{in}^y \in R^{h \times w \times c}$ undergoes the same operations and is then split (chunked) into two tensors: the key K and the value V. The tensors Q, K, and V are reshaped into the size of C $\times$ HW, The key tensor K is transposed to HW $\times$ C, and a matrix multiplication between Q and K is performed. A softmax function is then applied to the result to generate an attention map of size C $\times$ C, which captures the dependencies between local details and global contextual information. This attention map is subsequently multiplied with the value tensor V, and the result is reshaped back into the original spatial dimensions, C $\times$ H $\times$ W. The output is element-wise added to the original local feature map F_{in}^x, producing an intermediate feature F_x. To further enhance feature representation, F_x is passed through the Convolutional Block Attention Module (CBAM), which integrates both channel and spatial attention. Finally, the CBAM output is added to F_x to produce the final output feature

F_{out}. This process can be represented as:

$$F_{out} = F_x + SA(CA(LN(F_x))) \tag{7}$$

$$F_x = V \cdot Softmax(\frac{K^T Q}{\sqrt{D}}) + F_{in}^x \tag{8}$$

where $F_{in}^{(\cdot)}$ denotes the feature map of the input, F_{out} represents the output feature, $DW(\cdot)$ means the 3×3 depth convolution, $Conv_{1 \times 1}(\cdot)$ is the 1×1 convolution, $LN(\cdot)$ denotes layer normalization, $Softmax(\cdot)$ is the Softmax function, and D represents the channel number of V. CA and SA denote Channel Attention Moule (CAM) and Spatial Attention Moule (SAM), respectively.

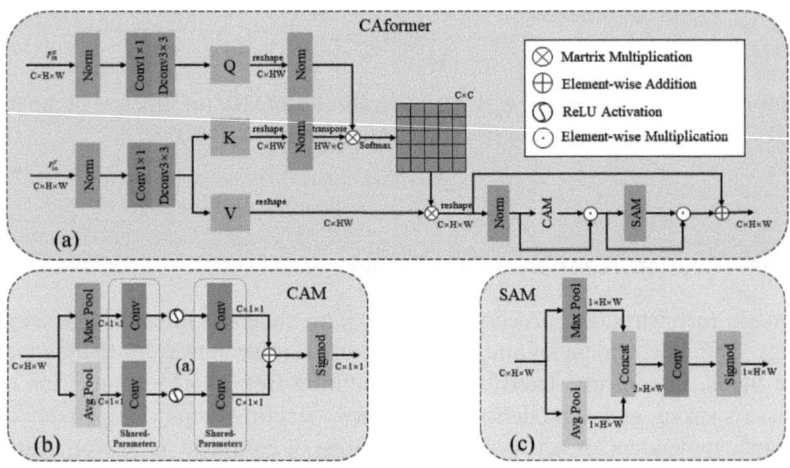

Fig. 3. (a) structure of the Cross-Attention Transformer (CAformer), (b) Channel Attention Module (CAM), (c) Spatial Attention Module (SAM)

2.3 Loss Function

To simultaneously enhance both pixel-level accuracy and structural fidelity in low-dose CT reconstruction, we propose a hybrid loss function that combines the Charbonnier loss and a perceptual loss. The Charbonnier loss, a differentiable approximation of the L1 norm, offers strong robustness and numerical stability, encouraging accurate reconstruction in pixel space and improving quantitative metrics such as PSNR and RMSE. In contrast, perceptual loss captures discrepancies in the feature space, improving the structural integrity and perceptual realism of the output.

Since the VGG network is originally trained on natural images (e.g., ImageNet), it may not generalize well to CT images due to domain shift. To mitigate this problem, we finetune the VGG network on a CT-specific dataset, enabling it to better capture the anatomical features and textures of CT scans. The finetuned model is then employed as a feature extractor for computing the perceptual loss. The overall loss function is formulated as:

$$L_{total} = \lambda_1 L_{charbonnier} + \lambda_2 L_{perceptual} \tag{9}$$

where $\lambda 1$ and $\lambda 2$ are hyperparameters used to balance the contribution of the Charbonnier loss and the perceptual loss, respectively. The Charbonnier loss is defined as:

$$L_{charbonnier}(x, y) = \sqrt{(x - x)^2 + \epsilon^2} \tag{10}$$

where x is the predicted pixel value, x is the ground truth pixel value, and ϵ is a small constant added for numerical stability. The perceptual loss is computed as the L2 distance between deep feature representations extracted from selected layers of the finetuned VGG network:

$$L_{perceptual}(x, y) = \sum_{l \in L} ||\varphi_l(x) - \varphi_l(y)||_2^2 \tag{11}$$

where $\varphi_l(\bullet)$ denotes the feature map from the l-th layer of the VGG network, L denotes the selected layers of the VGG network used for perceptual feature extraction.

3 Experiments

3.1 Dataset

To evaluate the effectiveness of the proposed DCANet, we conduct experiments on the 2016 NIH-AAPM-Mayo Clinic Low Dose CT Grand Challenge dataset [20] and the QIN_LUNG_CT dataset from TCIA. The NIH-AAPM-Mayo dataset includes abdominal LDCT and NDCT images from 10 patients with an image resolution of 512×512 and slice thicknesses of 1 mm and 3 mm. Quarter-dose LDCT images are simulated by adding Poisson noise to full-dose projections. Data from patient L506 are used for testing, and the remaining data are used for training. The QIN_LUNG_CT dataset contains 3,841 normal-dose CT images from 46 patients with a resolution of 512×512. Gaussian noise with a standard deviation of 60 is added to create a noisy subset, and data from patient R0274 are used for testing.

3.2 Experimental Setting

The proposed methodology and all experiments were conducted on an NVIDIA A100 GPU with 40 GB of memory. The implementation was carried out using PyTorch 1.1.0 and Python 3.7.10. To optimize the performance of the proposed DCANet network, the Adam optimizer was employed. The batch size was set to 16 for each training iteration. The initial learning rate was set to 0.0001 and gradually decayed throughout the training process. The network was trained for 400 epochs to ensure convergence.

3.3 Experimental Results and Analysis

This paper compares the proposed method with several classical and state-of-the-art approaches in low-dose CT and natural image denoising. All models are re-trained using publicly available code and evaluated on the 1 mm and 3 mm Mayo datasets. To comprehensively assess denoising performance, three widely used image quality metrics are adopted: Peak Signal-to-Noise Ratio (PSNR) for overall distortion, Structural Similarity Index Measure (SSIM) for structural fidelity, and Root Mean Squared Error (RMSE) for pixel-level accuracy. Tables 1 and 2 respectively summarize the quantitative performance of different models on the 1 mm and 3 mm Mayo datasets. Table 3 shows the denoising performance of each method after introducing noise levels $\sigma = 60$ on the Qin_LUNG_CT dataset. Figure 4 presents denoising results of various models on 1 mm slices, along with magnified regions of interest (ROIs) to highlight their effectiveness in structure preservation and detail restoration. Figure 5 shows the denoising results of the models on 3 mm slices.

Table 1. The average PSNR, SSIM, and RMSE values of different models on the 1 mm Mayodataset.

Method	PSNR	SSIM	RMSE
LDCT	24.4688	0.8246	26.6370
RED-CNN [10]	28.5956	0.8504	15.1572
DNCNN [11]	28.5250	0.8500	15.3026
EDCNN [13]	28.6658	0.8646	15.1129
LDMANet [19]	29.0474	0.8603	14.4259
DRANet [18]	29.1986	0.8638	14.1848
CTformer [16]	28.6373	0.8628	15.2101
Ours	**29.3618**	**0.8665**	**13.9296**

Table 2. The average PSNR, SSIM, and RMSE values of different models on the 1 mm Mayodataset.

Method	PSNR	SSIM	RMSE
LDCT	29.2489	0.8759	14.2416
RED-CNN [10]	32.5046	0.9052	9.6539
DNCNN [11]	32.2443	0.9061	9.9498
EDCNN [13]	32.8197	0.9121	9.3300
LDMANet [19]	33.2180	0.9149	8.9207
DRANet [18]	33.2810	0.9136	8.8963
CTformer [16]	32.6976	0.9064	9.4826
Ours	**33.7275**	**0.9196**	**8.4272**

Table 3. The average PSNR, SSIM, and RMSE values of different models on the Qin_LUNG_CT dataset

Method	$\sigma = 60$		
	PSNR	SSIM	RMSE
LDCT	21.8638	0.7558	32.6669
RED-CNN [10]	31.9511	0.8914	10.1959
DNCNN [11]	31.6938	0.8861	10.5464
EDCNN [13]	32.2389	0.8952	9.7591
LDMANet [19]	33.0703	0.9011	8.9005
DRANet [18]	33.1111	0.9016	8.9506
CTformer [16]	31.4688	0.8802	10.6354
Ours	**33.4089**	**0.9045**	**8.6563**

As shown in Table 1, Table 2 and Table 3 methods like DnCNN [11] and RED-CNN [10] significantly improve PSNR and RMSE by stacking convolutional layers to learn an end-to-end mapping from low-dose to high-quality images. However, their fixed local receptive fields limit the capture of long-range dependencies, leading to weaker modeling of structural consistency. To address this, EDCNN [13] incorporates an edge-guided mechanism within the convolutional framework, enhancing structural information modeling and achieving superior performance in the structural similarity index measure (SSIM). Both LDMANet [19] and DRANet [18] use dual-branch architectures that combine contextual semantics with fine details to boost reconstruction quality. LDMANet [19] merges dynamic convolution with multi-scale edge-guided attention and employs residual blocks for efficient cross-branch fusion, strengthening detail representation. Building on this, DRANet [18] introduces residual attention blocks and hybrid dilated residual attention blocks with multi-hop intra-branch and long-range inter-branch connections, effectively modeling local details and global structures, resulting in stable and superior metrics. The proposed DCANet advances this design with a refined dual-branch structure: the upper branch applies RTAB to coordinate attention across channel, height, and width dimensions, effectively enhancing local details and structural features. The lower branch employs the CAformer module for dynamic inter-branch interaction and fusion, collaboratively modeling global context and local structure. This design greatly improves feature representation robustness and achieves state-of-the-art quantitative results.

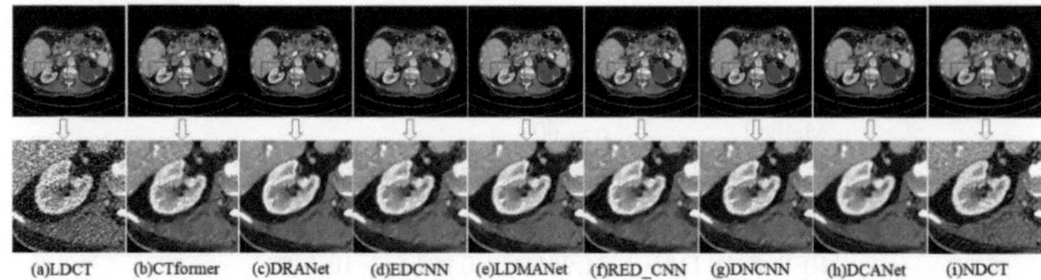

Fig. 4. Denoising results and magnified ROIs of different models on L506 with sample1

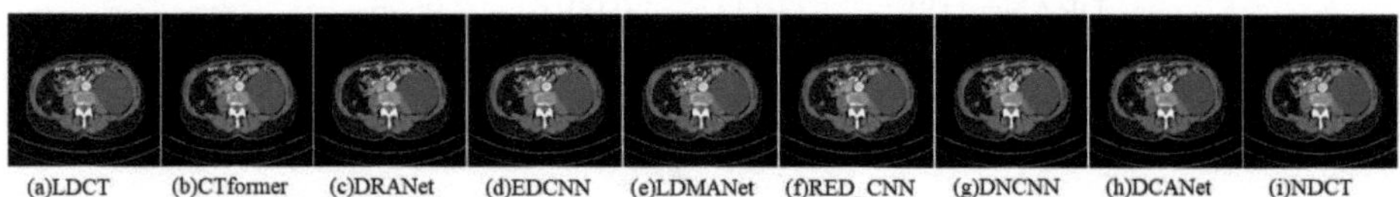

Fig. 5. The denoised results of different models on L506 with sample2

As observed in Fig. 4 and Fig. 5, the LDCT image exhibits a high level of quantum noise and loss of fine anatomical details, particularly in soft tissue regions. Among the compared methods, RED-CNN [10] and EDCNN [13] exhibit good noise suppression but tend to over-smooth the image, thereby compromising subtle structural information. CTformer [16] achieves a relatively better balance between noise removal and detail preservation, though it still suffers from slight residual artifacts.

In contrast, DRANet [18] and LDMANet [19] demonstrate enhanced structure recovery capabilities due to their dual-branch designs, retaining more details in both organ contours and texture regions. Notably, the proposed DCANet yields the best visual result, most closely resembling the NDCT reference. It not only effectively suppresses the noise but also preserves anatomical structures such as liver boundaries, kidney edges, and vascular details with high fidelity. Moreover, DCANet avoids the introduction of artifacts that are occasionally observed in other methods.

Overall, the visual comparison confirms the superior capability of the proposed method in denoising low-dose CT images while maintaining structural integrity, which is crucial for subsequent clinical diagnosis and interpretation.

3.4 Ablation Experiments

In this section, We perform ablation studies to assess the contribution of each DCANet component. Baseline 1 integrates the RTAB into U-Net, enhancing local feature extraction and noise suppression (Fig. 6a). Baseline 2 adds the CAformer, forming a dual-branch structure that improves detail restoration and texture continuity (Fig. 6b). Baseline 3 incorporates a compound loss (Charbonnier + Perceptual), further improving perceptual quality and structural fidelity, especially in soft tissue regions (Fig. 6c). As shown in Table 4 and Fig. 6, these components collectively boost DCANet denoising performance on low-dose CT images.

Table 4. Ablation study of DCANet on the Mayo LDCT dataset in terms of PSNR, SSIM, and RMSE.

Method	PSNR	SSIM	RMSE
LDCT	29.2489	0.8759	14.2416
Baseline1	32.8436	0.9102	9.2103
Baseline2	33.4795	0.9166	8.6694
Baseline3	**33.7275**	**0.9196**	**8.4272**

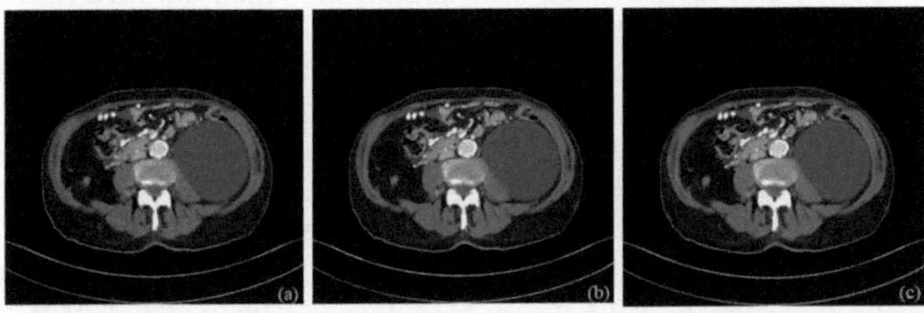

Fig. 6. Visual comparison of ablation experiments (a) baseline1, (b) baseline2, (c) baseline3

4 Conclusion

This study proposes DCANet, a novel LDCT image denoising model that addresses the limitations of single-branch CNNs, which struggle to capture long-range dependencies due to constrained local receptive fields, resulting in structural blurring and detail loss. While Transformer architectures excel at global modeling, they often overlook critical local pathological details. DCANet adopts a dual-branch architecture: the upper branch incorporates RTAB to effectively enhance local feature extraction and noise suppression, while the lower branch employs CAformer to jointly model local and global information. A compound loss combining Charbonnier and perceptual losses is used to balance pixel-level accuracy and perceptual quality. DCANet achieves an effective balance between structural preservation and noise suppression, demonstrating superior performance.

Acknowledgment. This work is supported by the National Natural Science Foundation of China (YDZJ202401620ZYTS).

References

1. Brenner, D.J., Hall, E.J.: Computed tomography—an increasing source of radiation exposure. N. Engl. J. Med. **357**(22), 2277–2284 (2007)
2. Schaller, S., Wildberger, J.E., Raupach, R., et al.: Spatial domain filtering for fast modification of the tradeoff between image sharpness and pixel noise in computed tomography. IEEE Trans. Med. Imaging **22**(7), 846–853 (2003)

3. Manduca, A., Yu, L., Trzasko, J.D., et al.: Projection space denoising with bilateral filtering and CT noise modeling for dose reduction in CT. Med. Phys. **36**(11), 4911–4919 (2009)
4. Buades, A., Coll, B., Morel, J.M.: A non-local algorithm for image denoising. In: 2005 IEEE Computer Society Conference on Computer Vision and Pattern Recognition (CVPR'05), vol. 2, pp. 60–65. IEEE (2005)
5. Liu, Y., Gui, Z., Zhang, Q.: Noise reduction for low-dose X-ray CT based on fuzzy logical in stationary wavelet domain. Optik-Int. J. Light Electron Optics **124**(18), 3348–3352 (2013)
6. Deng, J., Li, H., Wu, H.: A CT image denoise method using curvelet transform. In: Communication Systems and Information Technology: Selected Papers from the 2011 International Conference on Electric and Electronics (EEIC 2011) in Nanchang, China on June 20–22, 2011, Volume 4. Springer Berlin Heidelberg, pp. 681–687 (2011)
7. Kang, D., Slomka, P., Nakazato, R., et al.: Image denoising of low-radiation dose coronary CT angiography by an adaptive block-matching 3D algorithm. In: Medical Imaging 2013: Image Processing. SPIE, vol. 8669, pp. 671–676 (2013)
8. Chen, Y., Shi, L., Feng, Q., et al.: Artifact suppressed dictionary learning for low-dose CT image processing. IEEE Trans. Med. Imaging **33**(12), 2271–2292 (2014)
9. Yu, N.N., Qiu, T.S., Liu, W.: Medical image fusion based on sparse representation with KSVD. In: World Congress on Medical Physics and Biomedical Engineering May 26-31, 2012, Beijing, China. Springer Berlin Heidelberg, pp. 550–553 (2013)
10. Chen, H., Zhang, Y., Kalra, M.K., et al.: Low-dose CT with a residual encoder-decoder convolutional neural network. IEEE Trans. Med. Imaging **36**(12), 2524–2535 (2017)
11. Zhang, K., Zuo, W., Chen, Y., et al.: Beyond a gaussian denoiser: residual learning of deep CNN for image denoising. IEEE Trans. Image Process. **26**(7), 3142–3155 (2017)
12. Fan, F., Shan, H., Kalra, M.K., et al.: Quadratic autoencoder (Q-AE) for low-dose CT denoising. IEEE Trans. Med. Imaging **39**(6), 2035–2050 (2019)
13. Liang, T., Jin, Y., Li, Y., et al.: EDCNN: edge enhancement-based densely connected network with compound loss for low-dose CT denoising. In: 2020 15th IEEE International conference on signal processing (ICSP). IEEE, vol. 1, pp. 193–198 (2020)
14. Zhang, Z., Yu, L., Liang, X., et al.: TransCT: dual-path transformer for low dose computed tomography. In: Medical Image Computing and Computer Assisted Intervention–MICCAI 2021: 24th International Conference, Strasbourg, France, September 27–October 1, 2021, Proceedings, Part VI 24. Springer International Publishing, pp. 55–64 (2021)
15. Liang, J., Cao, J., Sun, G., et al.: SwinIR: image restoration using swin transformer. In: Proceedings of the IEEE/CVF International Conference on Computer Vision, pp. 1833–1844 (2021)
16. Wang, D., Fan, F., Wu, Z., et al.: CTformer: convolution-free Token2Token dilated vision transformer for low-dose CT denoising. Phys. Med. Biol. **68**(6), 065012 (2023)
17. Pan, J., Liu, S., Sun, D., et al.: Learning dual convolutional neural networks for low-level vision. In: Proceedings of the IEEE Conference on Computer Vision and Pattern Recognition, pp. 3070–3079 (2018)
18. Wu, W., Liu, S., Xia, Y., et al.: Dual residual attention network for image denoising. Pattern Recogn. **149**, 110291 (2024)
19. Zhang, J., Ye, L., Gong, W., et al.: A novel network for low-dose CT denoising based on dual-branch structure and multi-scale residual attention. J. Imaging Inf. Med. 1–20 (2024)
20. McCollough, C.H., Bartley, A.C., Carter, R.E., et al.: Low-dose CT for the detection and classification of metastatic liver lesions: results of the 2016 low dose CT grand challenge. Med. Phys. **44**(10), e339–e352 (2017)

TCGFNet: Multi-scale Transformer-Convolution with Geometry-Guided Feedback for Robust Point Cloud Denoising

Kekun Jin, Xiwu Shang$^{(\boxtimes)}$, Guoping Li, and Guozhong Wang

Shanghai University of Engineering Science, Shanghai, China
dxsxw@126.com, liguoping@sues.edu.cn, wanggz@sues.edu.cn
https://www.sues.edu.cn

Abstract. Point-cloud denoising should suppress noise without harming geometry, classical approaches often oversmooth complex object surfaces, erasing fine details. Although recent learning-based techniques alleviate these shortcomings, they still face two critical limitations: (i) single-scale feature extractors without explicit positional encodings struggle to capture long-range dependencies, and (ii) stage-wise pipelines that update normals and coordinates separately accumulate errors. We propose an end-to-end framework that fuses multi-scale convolutions with a position-encoded Transformer and a geometry-guided feedback loop. Convolutions capture local detail, the Transformer models global relations, and residual fusion unifies their features. A key-point selector, driven by normal orthogonality and cross-scale agreement, retains only high-confidence points, while a bidirectional module jointly refines coordinates and normals under a geometric-consistency loss. On synthetic CAD and non-CAD datasets corrupted with 0.6–2.0 % Gaussian noise, the method achieves lower Chamfer and point-to-surface distances than five state-of-the-art baselines. Ablations confirm each component's value, and qualitative results preserve sharp edges and high curvature, providing an efficient, practical solution for point-cloud denoising.

Keywords: Point-cloud denoising · Multi-scale transformer–convolution hybrid · Geometry-guided key-point selection · Bidirectional feedback · Geometric consistency

1 Introduction

Point clouds constitute a fundamental representation of three-dimensional geometry widely employed in autonomous driving, robotic navigation, and digital-twin applications. Due to physical noise in LiDAR and depth cameras and deficiencies in reconstruction algorithms, acquired point clouds contain Gaussian noise and outliers, degrading the accuracy of subsequent tasks. Eliminating noise while

Z. Lin et al. (Eds.): ICIG 2025, LNCS 16161, pp. 199–211, 2026.
https://doi.org/10.1007/978-981-95-3398-5_17

preserving geometric details has become a central challenge in point-cloud processing.

Conventional denoising techniques rely on hand-crafted geometric priors, such as local planar fitting based on principal component analysis (PCA) [13] and normal estimation via Voronoi diagrams [1]. Although effective under mild noise, these methods show limitations with complex geometries: PCA yields biased normal estimates near sharp features, while Voronoi-based approaches are sensitive to outliers. Both require multiple parameter-tuning rounds, hindering automation.

Driven by advances in deep learning, research has shifted toward data-driven paradigms with two architectural families. Single-stage approaches—e.g., Point-CleanNet [15]and TotalDenoising [5]—directly regress point-wise displacement vectors but ignore geometric coupling between normals and coordinates, resulting in blurred features. Two-stage approaches, exemplified by GeoDualCNN [20] and PCDNF [11], first refine normals then update coordinates for enhanced geometric fidelity. However, they suffer from: (i) error accumulation during coordinate updates and (ii) static feature fusion that disregards confidence disparities in noisy regions. Most existing methods also extract features at a single scale, complicating the balance between noise suppression and geometric-dependency modeling. In summary, the main contributions of this paper are as follows:

1. Multiscale Transformer-convolution hybrid: convolutions gather local geometry, the Transformer encodes global context, boosting denoising and long-range modeling.
2. Geometry-guided multiscale key-point selector: uses normal orthogonality and cross-scale consistency to retain only high-confidence points for robust feature fusion.
3. End-to-end bidirectional feedback: simultaneously refines coordinates and normals via a unified geometric-consistency loss, averting error accumulation.

2   Related Work

Contemporary point-cloud denoising techniques fall into two major categories: traditional optimization-based methods, which iteratively adjust parameters to obtain a noise-free point cloud that matches the input, and deep-learning methods, which employ purpose-built architectures with constraint-aware loss functions to generate high-quality denoised results.

2.1   Traditional Methods

Traditional 3-D point-cloud denoising updates point positions through local geometric relationships and can be summarized along two technical lines. The first comprises filtering-based approaches: the bilateral filter proposed by Digne [3] simultaneously considers the Euclidean distance between neighboring and central points as well as the distance along the normal direction, whereas the rolling-guided normal filter introduced by Sun et al. preserves prominent structures but may discard salient semantic points near sharp features. Such methods are sensitive to normal quality and struggle with noise around edges and corners.

The second line consists of sparsity-based representation and optimization schemes inspired by 2-D image denoising. Avron [2]employs sparse regularization to reconstruct piecewise-smooth surfaces, and Leal [8]combines median filtering with sparse priors to move noisy points along normals; the MLS family [9]iteratively projects points onto an approximated base surface but often oversmooths geometric details owing to its piecewise-smooth assumption; Lipman's locally optimal projection (LOP) and its variants [10]aim to produce uniformly distributed points that describe the underlying surface, achieving robust denoising yet failing to retain fine geometry under heavy noise. Sparsity-driven optimization preserves sharp details, while dictionary-learning techniques maintain repetitive surface structures; the feature-map learning method of Hu [7], which uses both coordinates and normals as descriptors, further demonstrates promising results. These traditional methods require labor-intensive parameter tuning and their reliance on geometric priors can compromise non-geometric features.

2.2   Learning-Based Methods

Deep-learning-based point-cloud denoising uses encoderdecoder neural networks to suppress noise while preserving geometry, with methods divided into supervised and unsupervised paradigms. Since Qi *et al.*'s pioneering PointNet, [14], derivatives like PCPNet, [4]—the first to adapt PointNet [14] for normal estimation on noisy point clouds—have laid the groundwork for learning-based normal filtering. Supervised methods rely on paired cleannoisy data (often with synthetic Gaussian noise) to learn mappings from corrupted to pristine point sets.

Early work PointProNet, [16] projects point clouds to 2-D height maps, denoises via 2-D CNNs, and back-projects, suffering from projection-induced information loss. PointCleanNet, [15] uses a two-stage pipeline (outlier removal followed by displacement regression) to mitigate overfitting but poorly preserves sharp features. Subsequent encoderdecoder models like PointFilter, [23] predict displacements from local neighborhoods, excelling at retaining edges but struggling with fine details. Edge-aware designs such as EC-Net, [22] strengthen boundaries but leave residual noise, while DMRDenoise, [12] integrates denoising with downsampling, suppressing noise at the cost of blurred geometry.CMDC-PCQA [21] achieves cross-modal deep coupling by fusing point cloud and projected image features with dual-stage attention, inspiring multi-modal fusion in point cloud processing. The contrastive-learning framework CLJ, [18] uses noise perturbation as data augmentation to learn patch-level representations, enhancing global consistency but failing to preserve local sharp features and suffering from normal-sign ambiguity. PCDNF, [11] introduces end-to-end joint optimization with a shape-aware selector and feature-refinement module, but incurs high computational cost and depends on high-quality initial normals.

3   Methods

This chapter introduces a point-cloud processing framework that integrates a multi-scale Transformerconvolution hybrid module, a geometry-guided multi-scale key-point consistency selection mechanism, and a bidirectional feedback strategy enabling end-to-end joint optimization. Working in concert, these components provide noise-robust geometric feature extraction while simultaneously refining point coordinates and normals. The overall architecture is illustrated in Fig. 1.

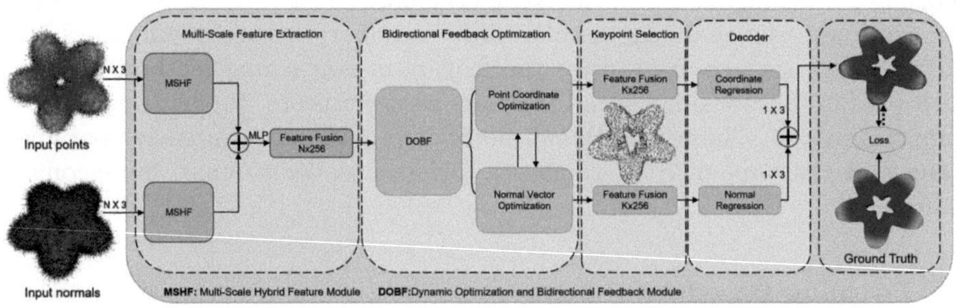

Fig. 1. The overall network architecture of point cloud denoising.

3.1   Multi-scale Hybrid Feature Module

To address the limitation of pure convolutional or Transformer architectures in jointly capturing fine-grained local details and long-range global dependencies, we introduce a multi-scale Transformer–convolution hybrid architecture that significantly enhances feature expressiveness under high noise levels. As illustrated in Fig. 2, the framework employs a hierarchical convolutional branch with progressively increasing kernel sizes ($k_1 < k_2 < k_3$) to extract geometric features at multiple resolutions: the k_1-neighborhood convolution focuses on high-frequency details (e.g., sharp edges and corners), generating fine-grained features

$$F_1 = \text{ReLU}\left(\text{BN}\left(\text{Conv1d}(X, k_1)\right)\right) \in \mathbb{R}^{N \times 128}, \tag{1}$$

the k_2- and k_3-neighborhood convolutions capture coarse-scale structures and suppress high-frequency noise, producing intermediate and low-frequency feature maps, respectively. The activated features from all scales are concatenated to form

$$F_{\text{conv}} \in \mathbb{R}^{N \times 384}, \tag{2}$$

encoding multi-resolution local geometry.

In parallel, the Transformer branch utilizes sinusoidal positional encoding to address permutation invariance of point sets and employs multi-head self-attention to model global point-to-point contextual dependencies, yielding

$$F_{\text{attn}} \in \mathbb{R}^{N \times 256}. \tag{3}$$

This attention feature is further processed by a feedforward network (F_{ffn}) to refine global representations.

Local and global cues are integrated via residual aggregation:

$$F_{\text{hybrid}} = F_{\text{conv}} + F_{\text{ffn}} \in \mathbb{R}^{N \times 256}, \tag{4}$$

where the residual connection facilitates the fusion of multi-scale local details and global contextual information. This hybrid design enables robust noise representation by preserving fine-grained structures while modeling long-range geometric dependencies, providing rich feature inputs for subsequent keypoint selection and optimization modules.

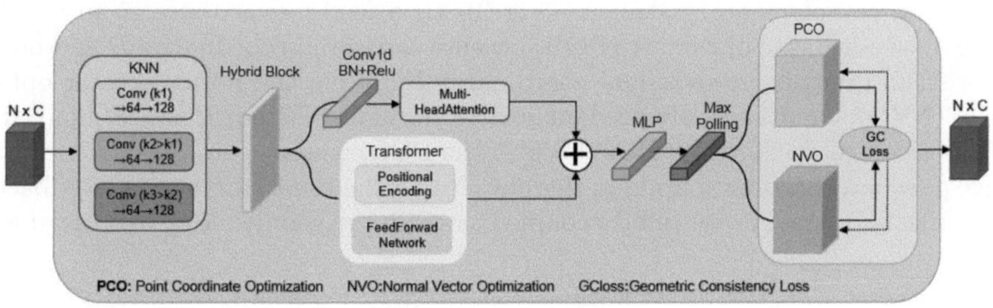

Fig. 2. End-to-End Point-Cloud Denoising Framework.

3.2   Geometry-Guided Keypoint Selector

To improve keypoint reliability in noisy point clouds, we combine a normal-alignment prior with cross-scale saliency verification.

Normal-Alignment Prior. For each candidate keypoint p_i, we compute the mean angle α_i between its unit normal $\hat{\mathbf{n}}_i$ and those of its k nearest neighbours. Points with $\alpha_i < \theta$ are considered geometrically stable and assigned high confidence, while outliers with inconsistent normals are discarded. Following the normal-smoothness analyses in [6,15], we set $\theta = 30°$, which falls within the commonly used $20°$–$45°$ interval for surface stability and empirically balances detail preservation and noise suppression.

Cross-scale Consistency. The multi-scale encoder (Sect. 3.1) produces fine, medium, and coarse feature maps, which are fused into $F_{\text{hybrid}} \in \mathbb{R}^{N \times 256}$. From F_{hybrid}, we select K salient points by $F_{\text{key}} = \text{Attention}(F_{\text{hybrid}}, K)$, where the attention mechanism favours responses that persist across scales.

Joint Criterion. A point is retained as a keypoint only if it satisfies both: (i) normal coherence, i.e., $|\hat{\mathbf{n}}_i \cdot \hat{\mathbf{n}}_j| \geq 1 - \varepsilon$ for its neighbours, and (ii) cross-scale agreement, i.e., its saliency ranks within the top K at all three scales. The resulting keypoints form a noise-resilient geometric skeleton, which anchors subsequent feature fusion and enhances both coordinate and normal regression during decoding.

3.3   Dynamic OptimizationBidirectional Feedback Module

To curb the error accumulation characteristic of stage-wise optimisation, we propose a bidirectional feedback mechanism that jointly refines point coordinates and normals, as depicted by the DOBF module in Fig. 1. The mechanism comprises two complementary streams (Fig. 2): (i) a feed-forward stream in which the point-coordinate optimiser (PCO) accepts the initial coordinates P and normals N and outputs provisional coordinates P', while the normal-vector optimiser (NVO) simultaneously predicts revised normals N' from P and P'; and (ii) a feedback stream that routes N' back to the PCO, where geometric constraints drive a second coordinate update, thereby closing the *coordinatenormal* feedback loop. The two streams are tightly coupled through the geometric consistency loss

$$L_{\text{geo}} = \lambda_1 L_{\text{smooth}} + \lambda_2 L_{\text{normal}} + \lambda_3 L_{\text{compat}} \tag{5}$$

where L_{smooth} enforces local smoothness via the squared distance between neighbouring coordinates, $L_{\text{normal}} = 1 - \hat{n}_i \cdot \hat{n}_j$ encourages alignment of adjacent normals, and L_{compat} penalises the angle between a point and the normal of its neighbourhood plane to preserve geometric compatibility. End-to-end minimisation of L_{geo} jointly optimises coordinates and normals, effectively suppressing the error propagation that typically afflicts staged pipelines.

The weights λ_1, λ_2, and λ_3 in Eq. 5 balance the influence of each term in the joint optimization process. Through extensive empirical evaluation, we determined optimal values of $\lambda_1 = 1.0$, $\lambda_2 = 0.5$, and $\lambda_3 = 0.1$. This weighting scheme prioritizes the smoothness constraint (L_{smooth}) to ensure regular point distribution, while the normal alignment (L_{normal}) and geometric compatibility (L_{compat}) terms act as regularizers that guide the optimization toward solutions that respect the underlying surface geometry.

We ablated these weights through a series of experiments on our validation dataset, testing configurations where we systematically varied each weight while holding others constant. Our analysis revealed that increasing λ_1 beyond 1.0 tends to over-smooth fine-scale surface details, while decreasing it below 0.5 results in insufficient regularization of point positions. Similarly, λ_2 values above

0.8 over-emphasize normal consistency at the expense of accurate point positioning, while values below 0.3 lead to inconsistent normal fields. For λ_3, we found that even small values (0.05–0.2) provide sufficient guidance to enforce compatibility between points and normals, while larger values can introduce instability during training.

In our implementation, these weights are dynamically adjusted during the first 10 epochs of training using a warm-up schedule to improve convergence stability, after which they remain fixed at the aforementioned values for the remainder of the training process.

4 Experiment

4.1 Datasets

The dataset follows the protocol of PointFilter [23], comprising a training set (22 synthetic point clouds: 11 CAD and 11 non-CAD objects), a validation set (3 objects), and a test set (23 objects). Each object is represented by a 100 K-point cloud from uniform random sampling. Training data is augmented with five Gaussian noise levels (from 0.25% to 2.5% of bounding-box diagonal), yielding 132 point clouds. The test set evaluates robustness using five unseen noise levels (0.6% to 2.0%), totaling 115 point clouds.

4.2 Implementation Details

All experiments were conducted on a single NVIDIA V100 GPU with 32 GB of memory using the PyTorch framework. Stochastic gradient descent was employed with an initial learning rate of 1×10^{-4}, a momentum factor of 0.9, and no weight decay. The network was trained for 100 epochs with a mini-batch size of 64. For each point-cloud shape, we randomly sampled 8 000 patches with a normalised radius of 0.05. Data loading was parallelized with four `num workers`, and cuDNN benchmarking was enabled to accelerate training.

4.3 Result

To comprehensively assess our approach to 3-D point-cloud denoising, we conducted quantitative and qualitative comparisons across a spectrum of noise levels, employing two widely adopted metrics. (i) The Chamfer distance (CD) between the denoised set $\widehat{\mathcal{P}}$ and the ground-truth set $\mathcal{P}$ is given by

$$\mathrm{CD}(\widehat{\mathcal{P}}, \mathcal{P}) = \frac{1}{N} \sum_{p_i \in \widehat{\mathcal{P}}} \min_{p_j \in \mathcal{P}} \|p_i - p_j\|_2^2 + \frac{1}{M} \sum_{p_j \in \mathcal{P}} \min_{p_i \in \widehat{\mathcal{P}}} \|p_i - p_j\|_2^2, \qquad (6)$$

where $N = |\widehat{\mathcal{P}}|$ and $M = |\mathcal{P}|$ denote the numbers of points in the denoised and reference sets, respectively. (ii) The point-to-surface distance (P2S) computes, for each denoised point, the shortest Euclidean distance to the underlying mesh surface.

Table 1. Comparison of Chamfer Distance ($\times 10^{-5}$) and Point-to-Surface Distance ($\times 10^{-3}$) under Different Noise Levels.

Chamfer dist ($\times 10^{-5}$)

Noise (σ)	Noisy	TD	PCN	PF	CLJ	PCDNF	Ours
0.6%	4.762	4.638	1.467	1.444	1.241	1.288	1.271
0.8%	7.517	4.038	1.752	1.749	1.545	1.573	1.322
1.1%	12.746	3.508	2.572	2.355	1.987	2.161	1.965
1.5%	21.637	7.472	5.787	3.544	3.244	2.847	2.544
2.0%	35.906	22.838	17.658	5.307	8.055	3.993	3.811
Average	16.514	8.499	5.847	2.880	3.214	2.372	2.102

Point-to-Surface dist ($\times 10^{-3}$)

Noise (σ)	Noisy	TD	PCN	PF	CLJ	PCDNF	Ours
0.6%	4.658	3.195	1.380	1.141	1.067	1.083	1.014
0.8%	6.143	3.078	1.592	1.386	1.324	1.337	1.217
1.1%	8.306	3.063	2.108	1.810	1.807	1.846	1.884
1.5%	11.073	5.471	3.100	2.472	2.937	2.310	2.176
2.0%	14.432	11.282	5.124	3.440	5.020	3.241	3.157
Average	8.922	5.218	2.661	2.050	2.431	1.963	1.870

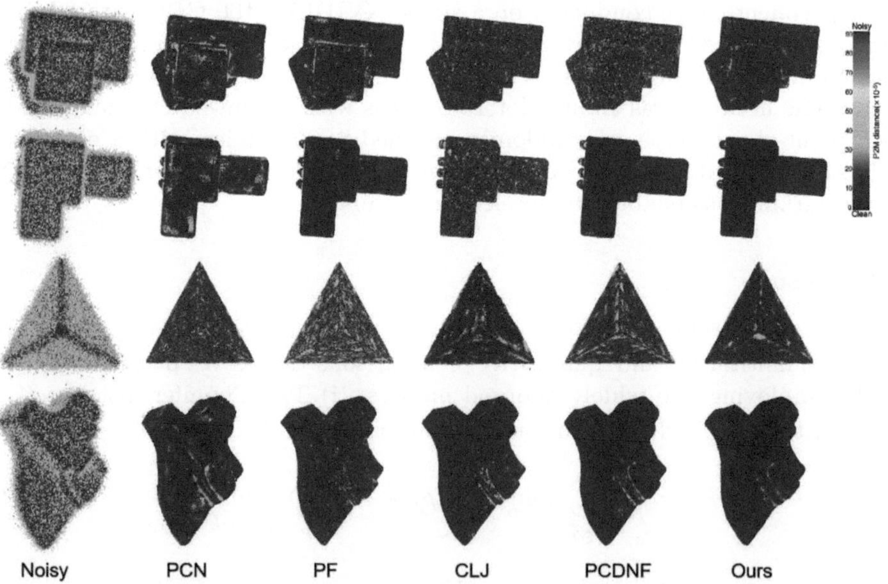

Fig. 3. Visual results of point-wise P2M distance for CAD models of 10K-resolution shapes with 2% Gaussian noise applied to the bounding sphere radius.

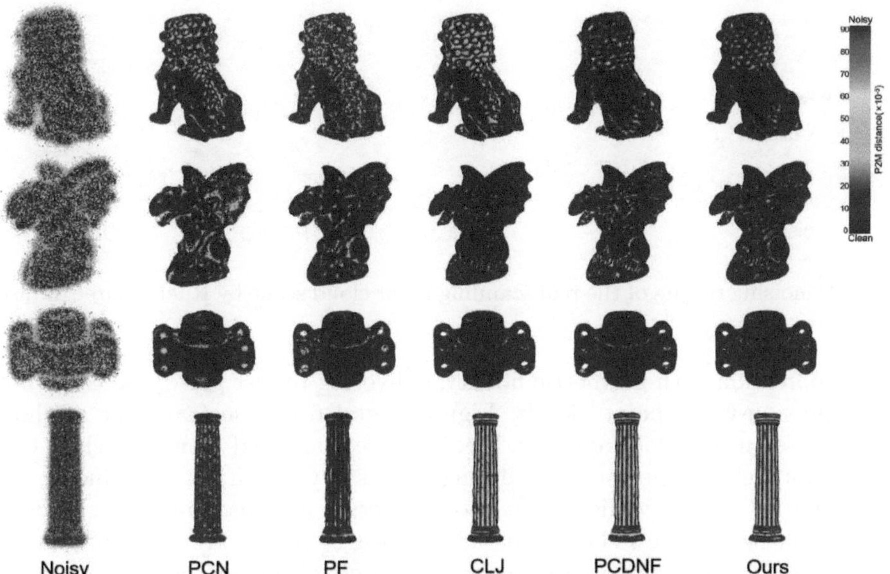

Fig. 4. Visual results of point-wise P2M distance for non-CAD models of 10K-resolution shapes with 2% Gaussian noise applied to the bounding sphere radius.

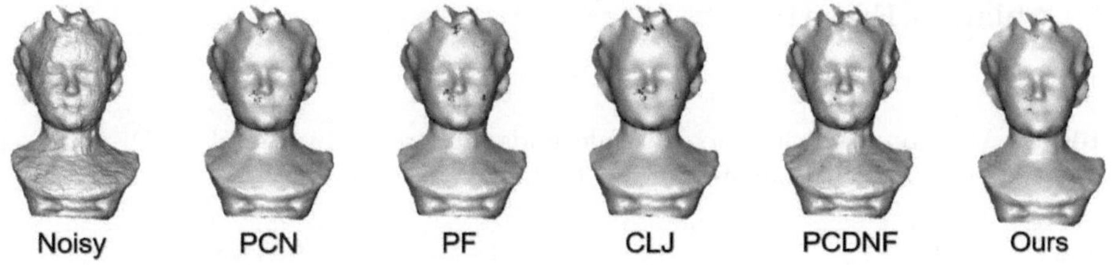

Fig. 5. Denoising results of data captured by Kinect. From left to right: noisy input, results produced by PCN, PF, CLJ, PCDNF, and our method.

Table 1 reports quantitative results over five Gaussian noise levels. Our model achieves the best average Chamfer distance (CD) of 2.102×10^{-5} and consistently ranks first at $\sigma = 0.8\,\%, 1.1\,\%, 1.5\,\%, 2.0\,\%$, while remaining competitive at the mild setting $\sigma = 0.6\,\%$. For point-to-surface distance (P2S) we likewise obtain the lowest error across the spectrum, with an overall mean of 1.87×10^{-3}, demonstrating the effectiveness of the multi-scale transformerconvolution hybrid and the bidirectional feedback optimisation.

Figures 34 visually confirm these findings. Compared with PCN, PF and PCDNF, which leave blurred or fragmented edges, our *local-to-global* strategy removes noise while preserving sharp CAD edges and high-curvature details such as the lion's mane and column flutes. This evidence shows that the geometry-guided key-point scheme and the end-to-end feedback framework jointly balance

Fig. 6. Denoising results of the real scanning point cloud scene by RueMadame dataset.

noise suppression with geometric fidelity, delivering robust performance on both CAD and non-CAD point clouds. Figures 5 and 6 demonstrate our method's effectiveness on real-world data. In Fig. 5, Kinect-captured scans [19] show competing approaches either oversimplifying details (PCN, PF) or introducing artifacts (CLJ, PCDNF), while our method preserves architectural elements while removing noise. Figure 6 shows similar advantages on the RueMadame dataset [17], where our local-to-global framework recovers clean surfaces and maintains structural boundaries despite challenging environmental noise, outperforming other methods that struggle with the noise-detail balance.

4.4 Ablation Experiments

Table 2. Ablation study of each module under different noise levels. CD: Chamfer Distance ($\times 10^{-5}$), P2S: Point-to-Surface Distance ($\times 10^{-3}$).

Model Variant	CD		P2S	
	$\sigma = 0.6\%$	$\sigma = 2.0\%$	$\sigma = 0.6\%$	$\sigma = 2.0\%$
Baseline (Single-scale Convolution)	2.152	5.127	1.683	3.440
+ Multi-scale Convolution Module	1.936	4.389	1.415	3.341
+ Hybrid Architecture	1.547	3.993	1.232	3.257
+ Keypoint Selector	1.549	3.855	1.127	3.202
+ Bidirectional Feedback Framework (Ours)	1.271	3.811	1.014	3.157

To evaluate the contribution of each core component at different noise levels, we performed an ablation study on the synthetic dataset. Starting from a baseline that contains only single-scale convolutions, we successively incorporated (i) a multi-scale convolutional module, (ii) global modelling via a transformer (Hybrid Arch), (iii) a geometry-guided key-point consistency scheme, and (iv) an end-to-end bidirectional feedback framework. Chamfer distance (CD) and point-to-surface distance (P2S) were measured over noise levels ranging from $\sigma = 0.6\,\%$ to $2.0\,\%$.

As summarised in Table 2, the baseline yields a CD of 5.127×10^{-5} and a P2S of 3.440×10^{-3} at $\sigma = 2.0\%$, indicating severe geometric distortion under high noise. Introducing the multi-scale convolutions reduces these errors to 4.389×10^{-5} (14.4% relative improvement) and 3.341×10^{-3} (2.9%), confirming the adaptability gained by aggregating receptive fields of different sizes. Adding the transformer further lowers CD to 3.993×10^{-5} (8.9%) and P2S to 3.257×10^{-3} (2.5%), demonstrating that global context mitigates local feature ambiguity. Incorporating the key-point consistency mechanism improves P2S from 1.232×10^{-3} to 1.127×10^{-3} (8.5%) at $\sigma = 0.6\%$ and to 3.202×10^{-3} (1.7%) at $\sigma = 2.0\%$, validating the effectiveness of normal-orthogonality constraints in selecting high-confidence key points. Finally, the bidirectional feedback framework attains the best overall results: at $\sigma = 0.6\%$, CD and P2S drop to 1.271×10^{-5} (40.9%) and 1.014×10^{-3} (39.7%), whereas at $\sigma = 2.0\%$ they reach 3.811×10^{-5} (25.7%) and 3.157×10^{-3} (8.2%). The end-to-end joint optimisation of coordinates and normals, enforced by a geometric-consistency loss, prevents error accumulation across stages and corroborates the synergistic gains of the proposed components.

5   Conclusion

In this paper, we present an end-to-end multi-scale transformer–convolution denoising framework equipped with a geometry-guided bidirectional feedback loop. The convolutional branches extract fine-to-coarse local shape cues, the transformer encoder models long-range context, and the feedback mechanism jointly refines point coordinates and normals under a unified geometric-consistency loss. This unified design effectively resolves the long-standing trade-off between noise suppression and edge preservation: existing denoisers blur sharp features because they treat high-frequency details and noise indiscriminately and rely on sequential pipelines that accumulate errors. Experiments on synthetic and real-scan datasets corrupted by 0.6%–2.0% Gaussian noise show that our method lowers the average Chamfer distance and point-to-surface error by 14% and 17%, respectively, compared with five state-of-the-art baselines.

Acknowledgments. This work was supported by the Shanghai Natural Science Foundation (25ZR1401152; Research on Point Cloud Coding Method Based on Human Visual Perception).

References

1. Amenta, N., Bern, M.: Surface reconstruction by voronoi filtering. In: Proceedings of the Fourteenth Annual Symposium on Computational Geometry, pp. 39–48 (1998)
2. Avron, H., Sharf, A., Greif, C., Cohen-Or, D.: ℓ1-sparse reconstruction of sharp point set surfaces. ACM Trans. Graph. (TOG) **29**(5), 1–12 (2010)

3. Digne, J., Franchis, C.: The bilateral filter for point clouds. Image Process. Line **7**, 278–287 (2017)
4. Guerrero, P., Kleiman, Y., Ovsjanikov, M., Mitra, N.J.: Pcpnet learning local shape properties from raw point clouds. In: Computer graphics forum. vol. 37, pp. 75–85. Wiley Online Library (2018)
5. Hermosilla, P., Ritschel, T., Ropinski, T.: Total denoising: unsupervised learning of 3d point cloud cleaning. In: Proceedings of the IEEE/CVF International Conference on Computer Vision, pp. 52–60 (2019)
6. Hoppe, H., DeRose, T., Duchamp, T., McDonald, J., Stuetzle, W.: Surface reconstruction from unorganized points. In: Proceedings of the 19th Annual Conference on Computer Graphics and Interactive Techniques, pp. 71–78 (1992)
7. Hu, W., Gao, X., Cheung, G., Guo, Z.: Feature graph learning for 3d point cloud denoising. IEEE Trans. Signal Process. **68**, 2841–2856 (2020)
8. Leal, E., Sanchez-Torres, G., Branch, J.W.: Sparse regularization-based approach for point cloud denoising and sharp features enhancement. Sensors **20**(11), 3206 (2020)
9. Levin, D.: The approximation power of moving least-squares. Math. Comput. **67**(224), 1517–1531 (1998)
10. Lipman, Y., Cohen-Or, D., Levin, D., Tal-Ezer, H.: Parameterization-free projection for geometry reconstruction. ACM Trans. Graph. (ToG) **26**(3), 22–es (2007)
11. Liu, Z., Zhao, Y., Zhan, S., Liu, Y., Chen, R., He, Y.: Pcdnf: revisiting learning-based point cloud denoising via joint normal filtering. IEEE Trans. Visualizat. Comput. Graph. (2023)
12. Luo, S., Hu, W.: Differentiable manifold reconstruction for point cloud denoising. In: Proceedings of the 28th ACM International Conference on Multimedia, pp. 1330–1338 (2020)
13. Mitra, N.J., Nguyen, A.: Estimating surface normals in noisy point cloud data. In: Proceedings of the Nineteenth Annual Symposium on Computational Geometry, pp. 322–328 (2003)
14. Qi, C.R., Su, H., Mo, K., Guibas, L.J.: Pointnet: deep learning on point sets for 3d classification and segmentation. In: Proceedings of the IEEE Conference on Computer Vision and Pattern Recognition, pp. 652–660 (2017)
15. Rakotosaona, M.J., La Barbera, V., Guerrero, P., Mitra, N.J., Ovsjanikov, M.: Pointcleannet: learning to denoise and remove outliers from dense point clouds. In: Computer Graphics Forum, vol. 39, pp. 185–203. Wiley Online Library (2020)
16. Roveri, R., Öztireli, A.C., Pandele, I., Gross, M.: Pointpronets: consolidation of point clouds with convolutional neural networks. In: Computer Graphics Forum, vol. 37, pp. 87–99. Wiley Online Library (2018)
17. Serna, A., Marcotegui, B., Goulette, F., Deschaud, J.E.: Paris-rue-madame database: a 3d mobile laser scanner dataset for benchmarking urban detection, segmentation and classification methods. In: 4th International Conference on Pattern Recognition, Applications and Methods ICPRAM 2014 (2014)
18. de Silva Edirimuni, D., Lu, X., Li, G., Robles-Kelly, A.: Contrastive learning for joint normal estimation and point cloud filtering. IEEE Trans. Visualizat. Comput. Graph. (2023)
19. Wang, P.S., Liu, Y., Tong, X.: Mesh denoising via cascaded normal regression. ACM Trans. Graph. **35**(6), 232–1 (2016)
20. Wei, M., Chen, H., Zhang, Y., Xie, H., Guo, Y., Wang, J.: Geodualcnn: geometry-supporting dual convolutional neural network for noisy point clouds. IEEE Trans. Visual Comput. Graph. **29**(2), 1357–1370 (2021)

21. Wu, B., Shang, X., Zhao, X., Shen, L., An, P., Ma, S.: Cmdc-pcqa: no-reference point cloud quality assessment via a cross-modal deep-coupling framework. IEEE Trans. Instrument. Meas. (2025)
22. Yu, L., Li, X., Fu, C.W., Cohen-Or, D., Heng, P.A.: Ec-net: an edge-aware point set consolidation network. In: Proceedings of the European Conference on Computer Vision (ECCV), pp. 386–402 (2018)
23. Zhang, D., Lu, X., Qin, H., He, Y.: Pointfilter: point cloud filtering via encoder-decoder modeling. IEEE Trans. Visual Comput. Graph. **27**(3), 2015–2027 (2020)

Adversarial Iterative Pre-enactment Framework for Air Combat Based on Mental Simulation Theory

Songde Han, Xiao Zhang, Tianyu Hu$^{(\boxtimes)}$, and Huimin Ma

University of Science and Technology, Beijing, China
`tianyu@ustb.edu.cn`

Abstract. Current air combat decision methods mostly lack structured adversarial validation and adaptive reflection mechanisms, limiting their robustness and reliability when facing deceptive or unfamiliar enemy strategies. To address this, we propose the Adversarial Iterative Pre-Enactment (AIP) framework, which integrates cognitive mental simulation with a large language model. First, we design a self-adversarial pre-enactmentfeedback loop that enables the model to simulate and evaluate both friendly and enemy actions before execution. Second, we introduce a multiscale segmented evaluation mechanism that analyzes tactical effectiveness across different time horizons and perspectives. Third, we build a high-fidelity simulation environment with scenario rewind capability, enabling real-time dual-strategy execution and supporting structured adversarial evaluation. Experimental results demonstrate the superiority of AIP over standard LLM baselines in terms of both tactical score and stability under complex adversarial conditions.

Keywords: Air combat · Adversarial pre-enactment · Multiscale evaluation · Strategy optimization

1 Introduction

Existing air combat decision-making methods fall mainly into two categories: symbolic rule-based reasoning and numerical optimization models. Both suffer from significant limitations [8,10]. Symbolic methods (e.g., expert systems, knowledge reasoning) rely on manually crafted rule bases, which struggle with poor adaptability and limited knowledge boundaries in complex dynamic battlefields. For example, traditional expert systems require pre-defining all possible situational templates but often fail against deceptive maneuvers or novel enemy tactics, with rule updates lagging behind battlefield changes. Numerical methods (e.g., reinforcement learning, game theory) can dynamically optimize strategies, but often face slow convergence and risk of overfitting [15]. Reinforcement learning demands massive confrontation data, and large action spaces cause algorithms to fall into local optima.

Z. Lin et al. (Eds.): ICIG 2025, LNCS 16161, pp. 212–223, 2026.
https://doi.org/10.1007/978-981-95-3398-5_18

Large language models (LLMs), with their multimodal understanding and dynamic strategy generation capabilities, provide a new direction to overcome these limitations [4,11]. Preliminary applications of LLMs in air combat decision-making include: drone swarm control based on natural language instruction parsing, mapping semantic understanding to tactical actions; hybrid architectures combining reinforcement learning with LLMs to generate candidate action sets and improve exploration efficiency; multi-agent game-theoretic intention reasoning simulating enemy mental states via textual interaction. However, current LLM-based air combat decision methods mostly lack structured adversarial validation and adaptive reflection mechanisms. When confronting atypical or deceptive enemy behaviors, the absence of feedback loops often causes misjudgments. LLM-driven air combat agents can generate "reasonable" strategy actions based on semantics but lack human-like "preset outcome anticipation," failing to systematically verify and revise the potential game consequences of their generated strategies. For instance, MITRE's systematic air combat agents [1] produce tactical advice but do not implement adversarial pre-enactment modules simulating enemy counter-strategies, risking tactical loopholes.

To address this challenge, we propose an Adversarial Iterative Pre-Enactment (AIP) framework, grounded in the mental simulation theory from cognitive science [5,14], as shown in Fig. 1. AIP emulates the human cognitive process of "presetting one's own actions and anticipating adversary responses" to construct adaptive decision-correction pathways [16]. By incorporating a self-adversarial pre-enactment loop, the framework enhances the robustness of strategy generation.

While the self-adversarial pre-enactment loop enables dynamic reflection and refinement at the strategic level, it lacks an explicit mechanism to evaluate decision quality at fine-grained temporal resolutions. Without structured intermediate feedback, the model may struggle to identify which aspects of a strategy contribute to success or failure over time. To address this limitation, we further introduce a segmented multiscale evaluation and iterative refinement mechanism within the pre-enactment process.

To support the implementation of AIP framework, we develop a high-fidelity simulation environment that enables real-time dual-strategy execution and structured adversarial evaluation. This environment incorporates scenario rewind capabilities, multi-agent control protocols, and customizable engagement settings, allowing the model to iteratively simulate, reflect, and refine its decisions under complex and deceptive conditions. It serves not only as a testbed for cognitive reasoning mechanisms, but also as a critical component for enabling the self-adversarial pre-enactmentfeedback loop central to AIP.

Empirical results in 4v4 combats show that our framework significantly outperforms standard LLM-based baselines. Specifically, AIP achieves higher tactical scores and exhibits greater decision stability across diverse adversarial scenarios. These improvements validate the effectiveness of combining mental simulation theory with large-scale language models under high-pressure, multi-agent conditions. The key innovations of AIP are as follows:

- We propose an LLM-based strategy optimization framework that integrates a self-adversarial pre-enactmentfeedback loop, enabling the model to simulate enemy responses and refine reasoning paths through adversarial feedback [18].
- We design a multiscale segmented evaluation mechanism that periodically assesses tactical effectiveness and drives iterative strategy refinement via simulation-guided reflection.
- We develop a high-fidelity air combat simulation platform based on Harfang3D to support real-time pre-enactment, self-play, and robust validation of decision-making under adversarial scenarios.

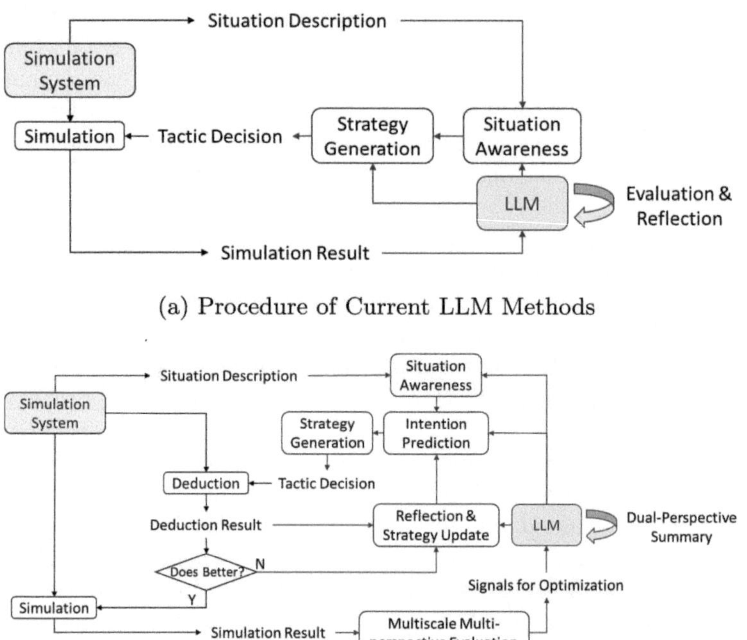

(a) Procedure of Current LLM Methods

(b) Procedure of AIP

Fig. 1. The Contrast Between Procedures of Current LLM Methods and AIP. (a) Current LLM Methods: The LLM receives a situational description from the simulation system, returns a tactical decision, and evaluates the resulting simulation outcome. (b) AIP Procedure: The LLM first switches perspective to predict the enemy's strategy before formulating the friendly-side response. Both strategies then undergo a series of deductions, and the friendly-side strategy is selected as final strategy if the new outcome does not surpass the previous deduction; otherwise, the LLM reflects and revises the tactic. AIP computes multi-scale tactical scores from both friendly and enemy viewpoints. The LLM then synthesizes both perspectives to generate final advice and summary.

2 Related Work

With the widespread adoption of LLMs in complex reasoning and decision tasks, multi-stage reasoning and dynamic feedback techniques have rapidly developed in intelligent aerial combat [9,13,24]. Key research directions include task-driven Chain-of-Thought (CoT) [19], Thought-of-Thought (ToT) [21], Graph-of-Thought (GoT) [2], and Action-Oriented Thought (AoT) [7], all contributing theoretical and practical support for efficient and robust air combat agent decision-making systems. CoT improves multi-step reasoning by decomposing complex tactics into ordered steps, enhancing coherence and interpretability. However, it relies on single-path reasoning and lacks adaptability to dynamic, uncertain air combat scenarios. ToT introduces multi-level, multi-perspective reasoning with recursive reflection and dynamic path adjustment, improving robustness under ambiguity. GoT structures reasoning as a graph, where nodes represent thought units and edges encode causal and strategic interactions. AoT tightly couples reasoning with action, driving the model to generate executable commands and interact with the environment in a closed loop, greatly improving real-time responsiveness in drone-based confrontations.

In summary, CoT, ToT, GoT, and AoT represent four core directions enriching agents' cognitive depth and action capabilities from different dimensions. However, most existing approaches are isolated [7,22,23], lacking systematic integration and insufficiently addressing robustness and adaptability demands in air combat agent confrontation. To overcome this challenge, we proposes the AIP framework, combining advantages of the aforementioned reasoning paradigms. It innovatively introduces multiscale, multi-perspective evaluation, capturing both friendly and enemy strategy effects comprehensively to avoid bias. It also incorporates segmented evaluation across different time scales to balance immediate tactical response and global strategic planning, preventing shortsighted local optima. The framework establishes a closed-loop mechanism encompassing pre-enactment self-play, feedback reflection, and multiscale multi-perspective evaluation, significantly improving decision reliability and practical value of air combat agents in complex dynamic environments.

3 Methodology

3.1 Problem Definition and Challenges

Air combat is a typical dynamic non-zero-sum game where agents must devise strategies based on the current battlefield state to maximize tactical advantage. Enemy strategies dynamically adjust in response to friendly actions, creating highly nonlinear and uncertain situation evolution. Traditional rule-based and language model methods struggle to balance robustness and adaptability, especially against deceptive or novel enemy tactics, easily falling into decision blind spots.

The core challenge is enabling agents with human-like "pre-enactment" ability, i.e., simulating continuous game processes of own actions and enemy reactions before making decisions, iteratively optimizing strategies based on simulation results to realize proactive adjustment and self-reflection. Formally, at each timestep t, the agent observes the current battlefield state s_t and selects an action $a_t \in A$ according to a policy $\pi_\theta(a_t|s_t)$. Simultaneously, the adversary selects its action $b_t \in B$ with policy $\pi_\phi(b_t|s_t, a_t)$. The environment then transitions to a new state s_{t+1} and returns a feedback signal r_t. The objective is to optimize θ such that the expected cumulative reward $\mathbb{E}[r_t]$ is maximized, while ensuring the reasoning path remains credible and adaptive in adversarial settings.

3.2 Framework Description

To address the limitations of static and isolated decision-making in aerial combat, we propose AIP framework, which consists of two key modules: the strategy generation module and the multiscale multi-perspective evaluation module, as shown in Fig. 2. The strategy generation module uses a pre-trained large language model to generate both friendly and simulated adversary strategies, which are executed in a high-fidelity simulation environment to obtain tactical feedback. The multiscale multi-perspective evaluation module assesses performance across different time windows and from both sides' viewpoints, providing fine-grained signals to guide iterative optimization. Together, the two modules form a closed-loop mechanism that enhances the robustness, adaptability, and interpretability of decision-making in complex air combat scenarios.

3.3 Strategy Generation Module

This module addresses the core limitations of current LLM-based air combat decision-making methods: the lack of structured adversarial validation and adaptive reflection mechanisms. To overcome these issues, it introduces a dual-perspective, multi-stage decision loop inspired by human-like mental simulation, forming the foundation for structured adversarial reasoning and iterative self-correction. As shown in Fig. 3, the module consists of five tightly integrated stages: situation awareness, intention prediction and strategy generation, tactical decision and simulation, reflection and strategy update, and adversarial self-play with dual-perspective summary.

Situation Awareness. The situation awareness stage equips the model with a comprehensive understanding of the current tactical landscape. The LLM parses raw battlefield inputs, including position, velocity, and attitude (roll, pitch, yaw), formalized as six degrees of freedom (6-DoF) data:

$$s_t = (x_t, y_t, z_t, \theta_t, \psi_t, \phi_t) \tag{1}$$

where (x, y, z) represents spatial coordinates, and (θ, ψ, ϕ) represent roll, pitch, and yaw, respectively. This structured representation supports robust downstream reasoning and enhances the agent's perception under dynamic conditions.

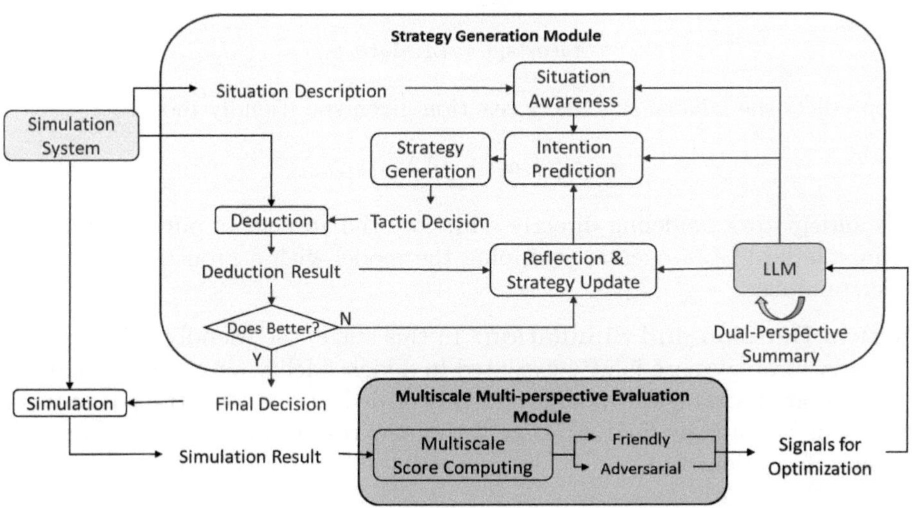

Fig. 2. Key Modules of AIP Framework. The strategy module employs a pre-trained language model to generate both friendly and adversary strategies. The evaluation module analyzes performance across timescales and perspectives, offering fine-grained feedback for iterative optimization.

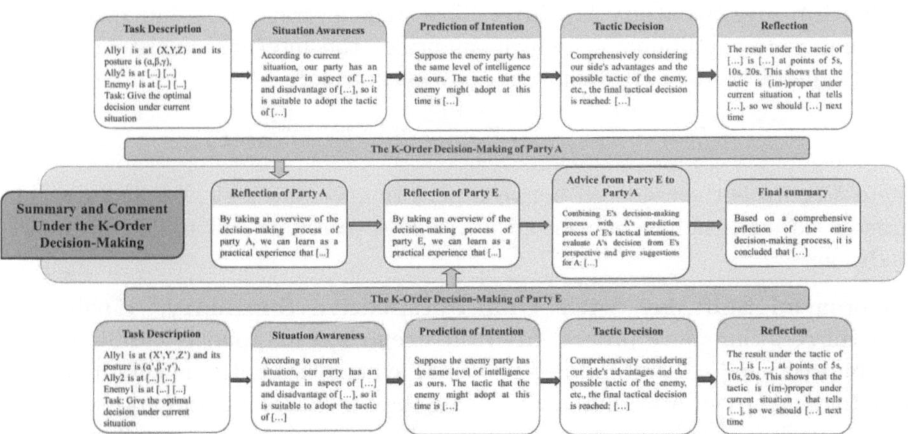

Fig. 3. Steps of K-Order Decision Making in AIP. K-order decision denotes the k-th tactical decision in a deduction sequence. The LLM first acts as the friendly side (party A), analyzes the situation, predicts the enemy's move, and reflects on simulation feedback at the 5th, 10th, and 20th seconds. It then switches roles to simulate the enemy (party E), repeating the same reasoning steps. Finally, the LLM reflects from both perspectives, provides advice from party E to party A, and produces a summary of the entire k-order decision process.

Intention Prediction and Strategy Generation. In this stage, the LLM generates the friendly action policy [3]:

$$\pi_\theta(a_t|s_t) = \text{LLM}_\theta(s_t) \tag{2}$$

and predicts the adversary's likely reaction given the friendly move:

$$\pi_\phi(b_t|s_t, a_t) = \text{LLM}_\phi(s_t, a_t) \tag{3}$$

This anticipatory modeling directly addresses the absence of outcome forecasting in standard LLM agents, equipping the model with a proactive adversarial understanding.

Tactical Decision and Simulation. In this stage, the friendly and predicted adversary strategies are jointly executed in a high-fidelity air combat simulator. The generated strategies undergo a series of deductions, and the friendly-side strategy is adopted as final strategy if the new result does not outperform the previous deduction:

$$s_{t+1} = \text{Simulate}(s_t, a_t, b_t), \quad r_t = f(s_{t+1}) \tag{4}$$

with feedback signals of damage level collected at key timestamps (5 s, 10 s, 20 s) from multiscale multi-perspective evaluation module. This multi-turn simulation directly tackles the issue of LLMs' lack of "preset outcome anticipation," revealing long-term effects of strategies.

Reflection and Strategy Update. This stage leverages outcome metrics and reasoning path credibility c_t, which quantifies the internal consistency of the model's inference steps, to refine strategy generation:

$$L(\theta) = \mathbb{E}[r_t] + \lambda \cdot \mathbb{E}[c_t], \quad \theta \leftarrow \theta - \eta \nabla_\theta L(\theta) \tag{5}$$

where λ controls the trade-off between performance and logical coherence. This targeted adjustment mechanism ensures adaptive refinement under adversarial conditions.

Adversarial Self-play with Dual-Perspective Summary. Finally, this stage mirrors the above process from the enemy's standpoint, yielding a reflective, bidirectional understanding. The LLM synthesizes both viewpoints to generate tactical advice and summary, closing the feedback loop and addressing the lack of structured validation in traditional LLM-based decision pipelines [12].

3.4   Multiscale Multi-perspective Evaluation Module

As shown in Fig. 4, the multiscale multi-perspective evaluation module computes tactical scores across multiple time scales $T = \{5\text{s}, 10\text{s}, 20\text{s}\}$, capturing both immediate reactions and extended planning horizons. These evaluations are conducted from both friendly and adversarial perspectives and, together with the final combat outcomes, are provided to the LLM, which enables LLM to comprehensively quantify the agent's short-term responsiveness and long-term strategic effectiveness in adversarial environments. This dual-view, multiscale assessment provides a more comprehensive understanding of tactical quality under dynamic and adversarial conditions. Let S_T denote the tactical score at time point T, then:

$$S_T = \text{Survival}_{\text{friendly}}(t) - \text{Survival}_{\text{enemy}}(t) \tag{6}$$

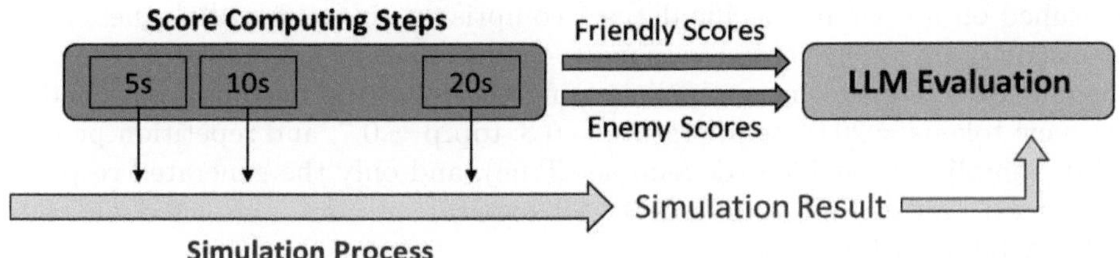

Fig. 4. Key Process of Multiscale Multi-perspective Evaluation. The module collects tactical scores at the 5 s, 10 s, and 20 s marks during the simulation process, and provides them, together with the final outcome, to the LLM for evaluation and reflection.

In summary, AIP innovates by modeling human cognitive mental simulation for decision-making to form a self-adversarial pre-enactment loop that helps preemptively identify and mitigate risks [17], and incorporating reasoning path credibility and multiscale multi-perspective evaluations to ensure logical, stable, and deeply aware strategy generation and iterative improvement.

This design effectively overcomes traditional methods' adaptability shortcomings, substantially improving robustness, adaptability, and interpretability of agents in complex dynamic air combat.

4 Experiments

4.1 Experimental Setup

Experiments were conducted on a high-fidelity air combat simulation platform capable of modeling realistic dynamic maneuvers, radar detection, and weapon interactions within multi-agent complex game scenarios. To ensure realism, enemy agents utilize reinforcement learning models trained on historical combat data, simulating diverse and deceptive tactics to enhance experimental challenge and credibility.

Based on the Harfang3D platform, we developed a trace-back system to support AIP's pre-enactment, along with a real-time data exchange module for interaction between the simulation and the LLM. A dual-level finite state machine was designed to control friendly unmanned aerial vehicle (UAV) behavior, with individual states (e.g., takeoff, engagement) and team-level tactics (e.g., encompass, distract), while exposing interfaces for LLM-driven decisions. Adversary UAVs were governed via a separate RL-based control module.

A multiscale evaluation mechanism was designed [20], measuring key tactical indicators within 5 s, 10 s, and 20 s windows after engagement initiation (combat begins around 30 s in simulation). Results report average segmented tactical scores over 210 simulated 4v4 confrontations.

We employ DeepSeek-R1-Distill-Qwen-32B, a distilled 32-billion-parameter bilingual large language model developed by DeepSeek [6]. The model is further fine-tuned on a domain-specific dataset comprising air combat dialogues, tactical instructions, and decision reasoning chains. Inference is performed via the Hugging Face Transformers pipeline using the following decoding parameters: max_new_tokens = 2048, temperature = 0.3, top_p = 0.7, and repetition_penalty = 1.0. Sampling is enabled (do_sample=True), and only the generated response is returned (return_full_text=False). All experiments are conducted on eight NVIDIA RTX 4090 GPUs.

4.2   Comparative Experiments

Table 1 compares average segmented tactical scores over 210 runs for different methods at 5 s, 10 s, and 20 s scales. Higher scores indicate stronger survival advantage. Table 2 presents the average win rates.

Table 1. Comparison of average segmented tactical scores over 210 simulations.

Method	5 s Avg Score	10 s Avg Score	20 s Avg Score
Direct LLM Strategy	0.05	–0.14	–0.13
LLM + CoT	0.10	0.59	0.55
LLM + GoT	0.10	0.60	0.58
LLM + ToT	-0.02	-0.01	0.51
LLM + AoT	-0.02	-0.01	0.50
Proposed AIP	**-0.02**	**0.31**	**0.62**

Table 1 presents a detailed comparison of average tactical scores across 210 simulations at different temporal segments (5 s, 10 s, and 20 s). As shown, the direct LLM strategy performs poorly across all intervals, particularly at longer time horizons, indicating its limited planning capability and instability over extended engagements. Among the baseline enhancement methods, both CoT and GoT significantly improve mid- and long-term tactical scores, showing their effectiveness in structured multi-step reasoning. Notably, GoT slightly outperforms CoT at the 20-second mark, likely due to its graph-based representation allowing more flexible information reuse. Surprisingly, ToT and AoT—despite showing high win rates in Table 2—exhibit negative or near-zero scores at early stages (5 s and 10 s). This suggests that their planning benefits emerge primarily

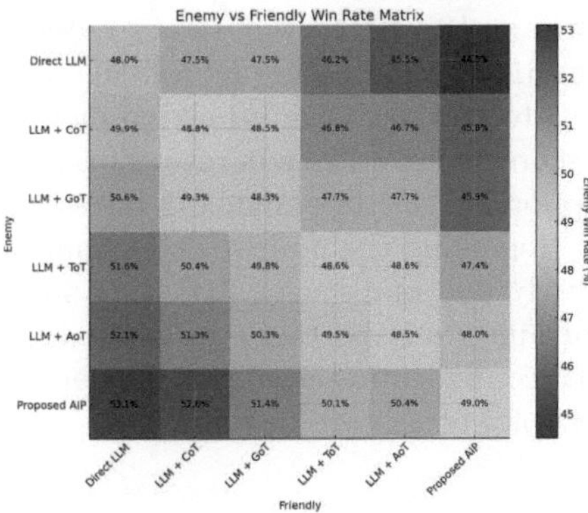

Fig. 5. Average Win Rate Matrix.

Table 2. Average win rate comparison.

Method	Average Win Rate
Direct LLM Strategy	58.6%
LLM + CoT	61.4%
LLM + GoT	62.9%
LLM + ToT	65.2%
LLM + AoT	67.1%
Proposed AIP	**69.8%**

in the later stages of engagement, where longer-term reasoning and feedback take effect. The proposed AIP framework demonstrates the best overall tactical performance, achieving the highest score (0.62) at the 20 s mark while maintaining a balanced score (0.31) at the 10 s interval. Interestingly, it also avoids early-stage degradation (–0.02 at 5 s), indicating that AIP not only facilitates long-horizon planning but also suppresses initial instability observed in other feedback-based methods. These results show AIP's advantage in maintaining consistent performance via iterative pre-enactment and segmented evaluation.

As shown in Fig. 5, AIP achieves the highest enemy win rates and the lowest loss rates as a friendly agent, confirming its superiority in both offense and defense. In contrast, ToT and AoT perform well against weaker baselines but struggle against AIP.

4.3 Ablation Studies

Ablation experiments evaluated contributions of the mental simulation module, enemy role-switching mechanism, and multiscale evaluation module (Table 3).

Table 3. Ablation study results over 210 simulations.

Method	5 s Avg Score	10 s Avg Score	20 s Avg Score	Avg Win Rate
Pure LLM Strategy	0.05	–0.14	–0.13	58.6%
W/O Mental Deduction	0.08	0.59	0.52	61.2%
W/O Adversarial Decision-Making	–0.02	0.32	0.57	68.1%
W/O Multiscale Eval	–0.03	–0.03	0.31	68.5%
Full AIP	**–0.02**	**0.31**	**0.62**	**69.8%**

Table 3 shows the ablation results over 210 simulations, evaluating the impact of removing each core module from the AIP framework. Without the mental deduction, the model maintains strong scores at 10 s (0.59) but shows reduced long-term performance and a lower win rate (61.2%), indicating its role in stabilizing extended engagements. Removing the adversarial decision-making module results in a slight drop in long-term tactical score and average win rate. This indicates that adversarial reasoning plays a supportive role in enhancing late-stage decision robustness and outcome reliability. Removing the multiscale evaluation leads to clear performance degradation at early and mid stages (0.03 at 5 s and 10 s) and a reduced win rate (68.5%), confirming its importance for short-term feedback and planning stability. The full AIP configuration performs best across all metrics, highlighting the complementary roles of its core components.

5   Conclusion

This paper presents AIP, an iterative air combat framework addressing key weaknesses of LLM-based methods, notably the lack of structured adversarial validation and adaptive feedback. Inspired by mental simulation theory, AIP couples a strategy generator with multiscale evaluation to simulate and assess outcomes over time. This closed loop supports realistic feedback and fine-grained optimization. Experiments show AIP outperforms standard LLM baselines in tactical score and win rate. Future work will focus on real-time performance, multi-agent coordination, and causal reasoning for enhanced interpretability.

Acknowledgments. This study was funded by National Natural Science Foundation of China (grant number 62172036).

References

1. Abdali, S., Anarfi, R., Barberan, C., He, J.: Securing large language models: threats, vulnerabilities and responsible practices (2024)
2. Besta, M., et al.: Graph of thoughts: solving elaborate problems with large language models. In: Proceedings of the AAAI Conference on Artificial Intelligence, vol. 38, pp. 17682–17690 (2024)
3. Brown, T., et al.: Language models are few-shot learners. Adv. Neural. Inf. Process. Syst. **33**, 1877–1901 (2020)
4. Caffagni, D., et al.: The revolution of multimodal large language models: a survey. arXiv preprint arXiv:2402.12451 (2024)
5. Collerton, D., Mosimann, U.: Wiley interdisciplinary reviews: cognitive science (2010)
6. DeepSeek-AI, Guo, D., Yang, D., et al.: Deepseek-r1: incentivizing reasoning capability in llms via reinforcement learning (2025)
7. Gao, C., et al.: Large language models empowered agent-based modeling and simulation: a survey and perspectives. Human. Soc. Sci. Commun. **11**(1), 1–24 (2024)
8. Guo, J., et al.: Formation cooperative intelligent tactical decision making based on bayesian network model. Drones (2504-446X) **8**(9) (2024)
9. Huang, J., Chang, K.C.C.: Towards reasoning in large language models: a survey. arXiv preprint arXiv:2212.10403 (2022)

10. Huo, L., Wang, C., Han, Y.: Autonomous air combat decision making via graph neural networks and reinforcement learning. Sci. Rep. **15**(1), 1–21 (2025)
11. Liang, Z., et al.: A survey of multimodel large language models. In: Proceedings of the 3rd International Conference on Computer, Artificial Intelligence and Control Engineering, pp. 405–409 (2024)
12. Madaan, A., et al.: Self-refine: iterative refinement with self-feedback. Adv. Neural. Inf. Process. Syst. **36**, 46534–46594 (2023)
13. Nie, Q., Liu, T.: Large language models: tools for new environmental decision-making. J. Environ. Manag. **375**, 124373 (2025)
14. Rafid, A.H.M., Sandu, A.: Adversarial training using feedback loops. arXiv preprint arXiv:2308.11881 (2023)
15. Sarıkaya, B.S., Bahtiyar, Ş.: A survey on security of uav and deep reinforcement learning. Ad Hoc Netw. 103642 (2024)
16. Senaratne, H., et al.: A framework for dynamic situational awareness in human robot teams: an interview study (2025)
17. Shanton, K., Goldman, A.: Simulation theory. Wiley Interdisc. Rev. Cogn. Sci. **1**(4), 527–538 (2010)
18. Silver, D., et al.: Mastering the game of go without human knowledge. Nature **550**(7676), 354–359 (2017)
19. Wei, J., et al.: Chain-of-thought prompting elicits reasoning in large language models. Adv. Neural. Inf. Process. Syst. **35**, 24824–24837 (2022)
20. Xi, Z., Kou, Y., Li, Y., Li, Z., Lv, Y.: A dynamic air combat situation assessment model based on situation knowledge extraction and weight optimization. Aerospace **10**(12), 994 (2023)
21. Yao, S., et al.: Tree of thoughts: deliberate problem solving with large language models. Adv. Neural. Inf. Process. Syst. **36**, 11809–11822 (2023)
22. Yao, Y., Li, Z., Zhao, H.: Beyond chain-of-thought, effective graph-of-thought reasoning in language models. arXiv preprint arXiv:2305.16582 (2023)
23. Yu, Y., et al.: Chain-of-reasoning: towards unified mathematical reasoning in large language models via a multi-paradigm perspective (2025)
24. Zhou, K., Wei, R., Zhang, Q., Xu, Z.: Learning system for air combat decision inspired by cognitive mechanisms of the brain. IEEE Access (2020)

SA-Pillar: Structure-Aware Feature Learning for Real-Time 3D Object Detection

Shanshan Huang[1], Wenkang Chen[2], Zhengrong Xu[1], and Xuejun Zhang[1,3(✉)]

[1] School of Computer, Electronics and Information, Guangxi University, Nanning, Guangxi, China
[2] School of Electrical Engineering, Guangxi University, Nanning, Guangxi, China
[3] Guangxi Key Laboratory of Multimedia Communications and Network Technology, Guangxi University, Nanning, Guangxi, China
xjzhang@gxu.edu.cn

Abstract. Single-stage 3D object detection based on pillar structures has gained attention for its high inference efficiency in autonomous driving. However, the quantization of point clouds into pillars often leads to the loss of fine-grained structural details, limiting performance in detecting small objects under sparse scenarios. To overcome this challenge, we propose an efficient LiDAR-based detection algorithm that incorporates multi-source feature encoding and structure-aware enhancement. Specifically, we design a Structure-Aware Feature Encoding (SAFE) module that integrates intra-pillar attention, inter-pillar structural modeling, and height histogram encoding to improve the geometric representation of pillar features. The backbone further incorporates a large kernel attention mechanism to capture long-range dependencies, along with an atrous spatial pyramid pooling module and a weighted dual-scale feature fusion module to strengthen semantic expressiveness and detection accuracy. The proposed method is evaluated on the KITTI dataset, with extensive visualizations and ablation studies. Results show an improvement of 3.9% in mean 3D average precision (mAP) over the baseline, including 3.66% and 4.59% gains for pedestrian and cyclist categories. The model runs at 34.2 FPS, demonstrating both accuracy and efficiency for real-time applications.

Keywords: 3D object detection · Attention mechanism · Structure-aware representation

1 Introduction

With the rapid development of intelligent transportation, autonomous driving has attracted increasing attention from both academia and industry for its potential to reduce driver workload and improve traffic safety [1,15]. A core component of autonomous systems is the perception module, which is tasked with accurately sensing the dynamic environment and identifying multiple objects, thereby supplying crucial inputs for path planning, decision-making, and motion control [16,22]. Within this pipeline, 3D object detection plays a pivotal role by modeling object position, size, and orientation to generate structured semantic information for downstream tasks [12]. However, 3D point clouds often exhibit irregular distributions and local sparsity, which pose significant challenges for deep learning models in capturing robust spatial features—especially when detecting small or distant objects [8,9].

In recent years, fueled by advances in deep learning, LiDAR-based 3D object detection has made significant progress. To address the unordered and sparse nature of point cloud data, three main paradigms have emerged: point-based [3,20,25], voxel-based [4,5,7,24], and projection-based methods [10,11,14,19]. Among them, projection-based approaches convert 3D point clouds into structured 2D representations such as Bird's Eye View (BEV) or Front View (FV), allowing efficient feature extraction using mature 2D CNNs. Due to their computational efficiency and simplicity, they are widely adopted in real-time applications. PointPillars [10], a representative projection-based method, encodes point clouds into BEV pillars and applies 2D convolutions to balance accuracy and speed. However, in sparse scenes, especially when detecting distant or small-scale objects [13], max pooling within pillars tends to overlook local geometric relationships, leading to loss of fine-grained structural information. In addition, many backbones and fusion strategies focus on global semantics while neglecting local detail, limiting robustness under occlusion and sparsity [2,17]. Although recent works introduce 3D sparse convolutions, Transformers, or multi-head attention to enhance representation [6], they often bring high computational overhead and deployment challenges [18,23]. Therefore, achieving accurate detection of small objects in sparse point clouds under lightweight and deployable constraints remains a key challenge in 3D object detection.

To address this, we propose SA-Pillar, a structure-aware pillar-based 3D object detection framework designed for sparse LiDAR point clouds.

(1) We design a structure-aware feature encoding module that integrates intra-pillar attention, inter-pillar structural modeling, and height histogram encoding, overcoming the limitations of max pooling and enhancing feature expressiveness.
(2) We devise a lightweight detection architecture combining large kernel attention with dual-path multi-scale fusion, integrating atrous spatial pyramid pooling and weighted dual-scale fusion for accurate multi-scale representation and small-object detection, while ensuring real-time efficiency.
(3) Extensive experiments on the KITTI benchmark show that our method outperforms baselines in detecting small and distant objects under sparse conditions, with high inference efficiency suitable for practical deployment.

2   Method

This section presents the SA-Pillar 3D object detection network, illustrated in Fig. 1. SA-Pillar is an end-to-end convolutional framework designed to enhance small object detection in sparse point cloud scenarios by integrating multi-source

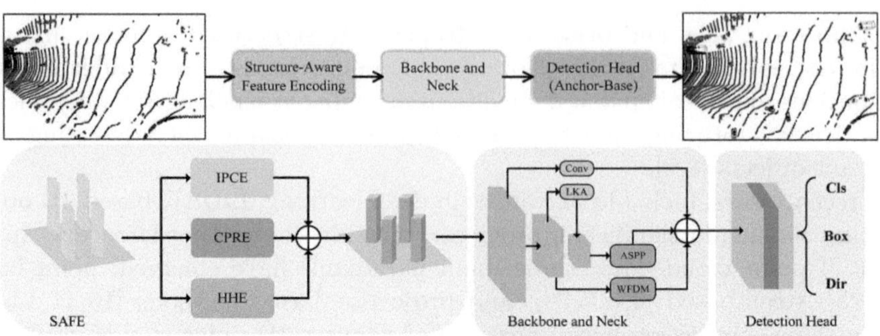

Fig. 1. Overall network framework structure.

feature perception and structure-aware strategies. The following subsections provide a detailed description of each module.

2.1 Structure-Aware Feature Encoding

When encoding point clouds as voxels or pillars, effective intra-unit feature extraction is critical for detection accuracy. PointPillars uses max pooling for efficiency but often discards fine-grained structure, limiting the representation of complex local patterns. To address this, we propose the Structure-Aware Feature Encoding (SAFE), which enhances point cloud representation by modeling both intra- and inter-pillar relationships. As illustrated in Fig. 1, SAFE includes: (1) Intra-Pillar Context Encoding (IPCE) to capture contextual dependencies within each pillar and recover local detail; (2) Cross-Pillar Relation Encoding (CPRE) to model spatial relationships across neighboring pillars in BEV space; and (3) Height Histogram Encoding(HHE) to capture vertical distribution of points. Together, these components provide a structure-aware representation that improves detection, particularly for small or occluded objects.

Intra-Pillar Context Encoding (IPCE). The input point cloud P is projected onto the X-Y plane and divided into a regular grid, where each cell (pillar) aggregates its contained points into a tensor of shape (M, T, C). To enhance intra-pillar feature representation, we augment each point $p_n = (x_n, y_n, z_n)$ with relative offsets to both the pillar centroid $[x_n^g, y_n^g, z_n^g]$ and grid center $[x_n^c, y_n^c, z_n^c]$, forming a 10D input feature:

$$p_n' = [x_n, y_n, z_n, r_n, x_n - x_n^g, y_n - y_n^g, z_n - z_n^g, x_n - x_n^c, y_n - y_n^c, z_n - z_n^c] \in \mathbb{R}^{10} \quad (1)$$

To model local dependencies, we introduce an Intra-Pillar Context Encoding (IPCE) module (Fig. 2). First, a point-wise MLP encodes each point feature into a higher-dimensional space:

$$\hat{p}_n^j = C(p_n'^j; \omega_c), \quad \hat{p}_n^j \in \mathbb{R}^C \quad (2)$$

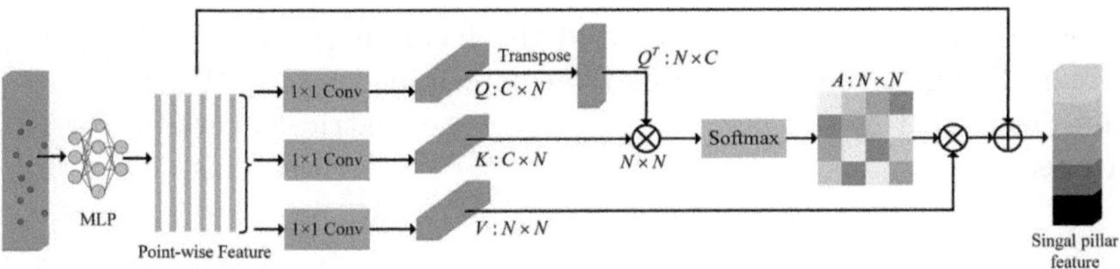

Fig. 2. The structure of IPCE module.

where $C(\cdot)$ denotes a shared 1D convolution, and ω_c are learnable parameters. The encoded pillar features $\hat{P}^j \in \mathbb{R}^{C \times T'}$ are used to compute Query, Key, and Value representations:

$$Q = W_q \hat{P}^j, \quad K = W_k \hat{P}^j, \quad V = W_v \hat{P}^j \tag{3}$$

with $W_q, W_k \in \mathbb{R}^{C' \times C_r}$, $W_v \in \mathbb{R}^{C \times C'}$, and $C_r = C'/r$. Then, a dot-product attention mechanism captures the similarity between point features:

$$A_{i,j} = \frac{\exp(q_i^\top k_j)}{\sum_{l=1}^{T'} \exp(q_i^\top k_l)}, \quad A \in \mathbb{R}^{T' \times T'} \tag{4}$$

The final output is computed by applying the attention to V with a residual connection:

$$F = A \cdot V + P_{input} \tag{5}$$

This structure-aware encoding enhances feature expressiveness by incorporating local context and preserving fine-grained geometry, boosting detection robustness in sparse point cloud scenarios (Fig. 2).

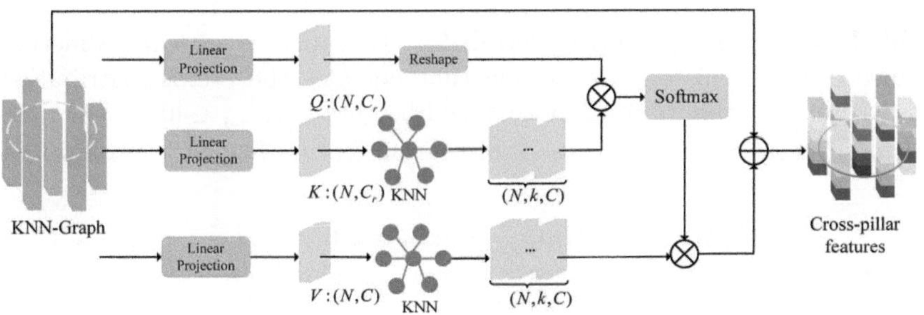

Fig. 3. The structure of CPRE module.

Cross-Pillar Relation Encoding (CPRE). Let the total number of points be N, and the i-th pillar's points be $V_i = \{v_{i,n} \in \mathbb{R}^3\}_{n=1}^{T_i}$. We first compute the global centroid $\bar{g} = \frac{1}{N}\sum_{i,n} v_{i,n}$ and the local centroid $g_i = \frac{1}{T_i}\sum_n v_{i,n}$ for each pillar. The grid center c_i of pillar i is determined by its BEV index (u_i, v_i), and the mean grid center is $\bar{c} = \frac{1}{M}\sum_i c_i$. A geometric feature vector is then constructed as:

$$f_i = [\bar{g}, \bar{c}, g_i - \bar{g}, c_i - \bar{c}] \in \mathbb{R}^{12} \tag{6}$$

This captures both global and local spatial structure. A two-layer MLP further maps f_i into a high-dimensional space. To encode inter-pillar relations, we treat each pillar as a graph node and construct a KNN-like receptive field based on spatial proximity in BEV space, using a square region of radius r with up to $\hat{k} = 8$ neighbors. A hash-based lookup is applied to efficiently retrieve neighbors. Given input features $F = [f_1, \ldots, f_N] \in \mathbb{R}^{N \times C}$ and positions $P = [p_1, \ldots, p_N]$, the attention vectors are computed as:

$$q_i = W_q f_i, \quad k_j = W_k f_j, \quad v_j = W_v f_j \tag{7}$$

with $W_q, W_k, W_v \in \mathbb{R}^{C \times d}$. The attention weight between i and its neighbor j is:

$$\alpha_{ij} = \frac{\exp\left(q_i^\top k_j / \sqrt{d}\right)}{\sum_{j \in N_i} \exp\left(q_i^\top k_j / \sqrt{d}\right)} \tag{8}$$

The final feature is updated via weighted aggregation and residual fusion:

$$\hat{f}_i = f_i + \sum_{j \in N_i} \alpha_{ij} v_j \tag{9}$$

In summary, the pillar-to-pillar attention models geometric context across pillars, enhancing spatial awareness beyond local encoding. When combined with intra-pillar attention, it significantly improves the structural expressiveness and detection accuracy, especially in cluttered or sparse scenes.

Height Histogram Encoding Module. To capture vertical geometry, we introduce a height histogram module that encodes the z-axis distribution of points within each pillar. For T normalized heights $\{z_j\}_{j=1}^T \in [0, 1]$, the range is uniformly divided into B bins, and a histogram feature $h_i \in \mathbb{R}^B$ is computed as:

$$h_i[b] = \sum_{j=1}^T \mathbb{I}(bin(z_j) = b), \quad b = 0, \ldots, B - 1 \tag{10}$$

This histogram is then projected via a two-layer MLP:

$$\hat{h}_i = \phi(W_h h_i + b_h) \tag{11}$$

where $\phi(\cdot)$ is ReLU, and W_h, b_h are learnable parameters. $\hat{h}_i \in \mathbb{R}^C$ provides vertical structural cues, complementing semantic and geometric features. Finally, we concatenate intra-pillar, inter-pillar, and histogram features, and apply a lightweight MLP to obtain the final fused representation $\tilde{f}_i$ (Fig. 4).

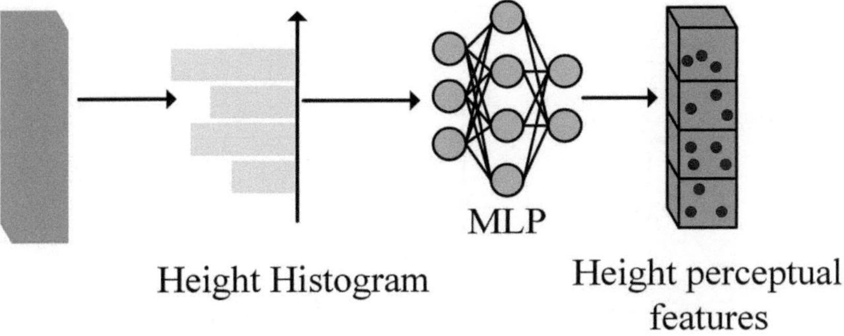

Fig. 4. The structure of HHE module.

2.2 Backbone and Neck Design

To enhance multi-scale contextual modeling, we adopt a hierarchical feature extraction network. The first two layers use standard residual blocks to capture local geometry and mid-level semantics in BEV space, while the third layer incorporates a Large Kernel Attention (LKA) module to enlarge the receptive field and improve structural perception and long-range dependency modeling (Fig. 5). The LKA stacks depthwise separable, dilated, and pointwise convolutions, significantly improving deep feature expressiveness for small-object detection in complex 3D environments.

To further enrich semantic information across scales, we design a lightweight multi-branch fusion architecture that integrates Atrous Spatial Pyramid Pooling (ASPP), a Weighted Dual-direction Feature Fusion Module (WDFM), and a shallow feature enhancement strategy. ASPP expands the receptive field via parallel convolution branches with varying dilation rates and global pooling, alleviating the semantic sparsity of deep features. The WDFM then aligns and fuses ASPP-enhanced deep features with mid-level features using learnable weights, followed by convolution and nonlinear activation for synergistic integration. In parallel, shallow features—rich in edge and spatial detail—are projected to higher dimensions and fused with the mid-deep features, generating a unified representation that combines high-resolution spatial cues with deep semantic context. This hierarchical and cross-level fusion enhances the network's ability to detect objects at varying scales and improves overall robustness in diverse driving scenes.

2.3 Detection Head Design

To enable accurate 3D object detection, we adopt an anchor-based detection head inspired by SECOND [21] and PointPillars [10], comprising three parallel branches for classification, bounding box regression, and orientation estimation. The classification branch predicts category probabilities for each anchor, while

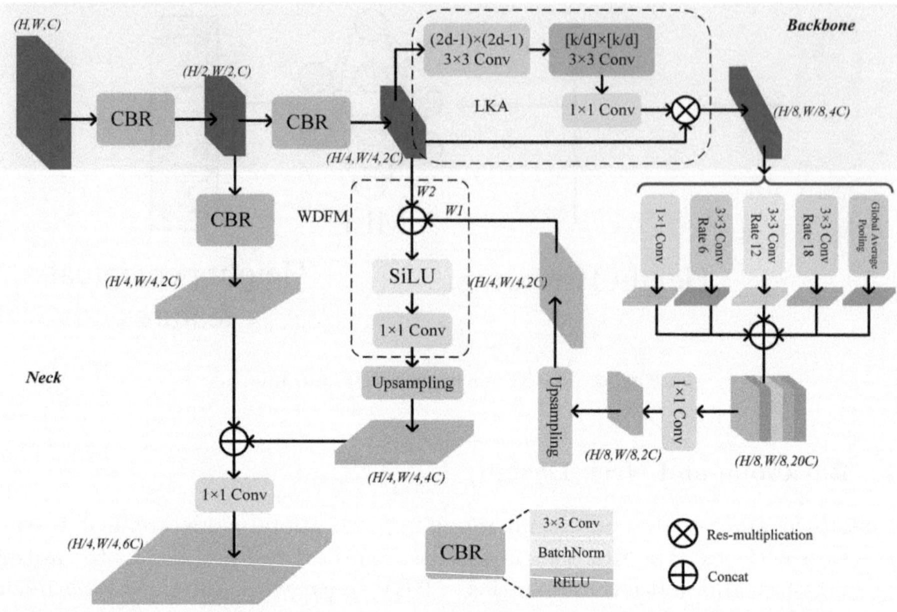

Fig. 5. The structure of backbone and neck.

the regression branch estimates offsets for object center, size, and heading. To address angle periodicity, the direction classification branch applies a binary strategy to distinguish orientation bins. All branches are implemented with 1×1 convolutions, differing only in output channels. Additionally, we apply bias initialization to the classification branch to favor background predictions at early stages, mitigating class imbalance and improving training stability.

2.4   Loss Function

To supervise accurate 3D object localization and classification, we employ a multi-task joint loss consisting of three terms: classification loss L_{cls}, bounding box regression loss L_{reg}, and direction classification loss L_{dir}.

For classification, we adopt Focal Loss to address foreground-background imbalance:

$$L_{cls} = -\alpha(1 - p)^\gamma \log(p) \tag{12}$$

The regression targets are computed as normalized geometric differences between anchors and ground truth:

$$\begin{cases} \Delta x = \dfrac{x^{gt} - x^j}{d^a}, \quad \Delta y = \dfrac{y^{gt} - y^j}{d^a}, \quad \Delta z = \dfrac{z^{gt} - z^j}{h^j} \\[2ex] \Delta \omega = \log \dfrac{\omega^{gt}}{\omega^j}, \quad \Delta l = \log \dfrac{l^{gt}}{l^j}, \quad \Delta h = \log \dfrac{h^{gt}}{h^j}, \quad \Delta \theta = \sin(\theta^{gt} - \theta^j) \end{cases} \tag{13}$$

with $d^a = \sqrt{(\omega^j)^2 + (l^j)^2}$ as a scale normalization term. The regression loss is computed using Smooth L1 loss:

$$L_{reg} = \sum_{b \in \{x,y,z,\omega,l,h,\theta\}} \text{SmoothL1}(\omega_b \Delta b) \tag{14}$$

where weights $\omega_{x,y,z,\omega,h,\theta} = 1.0$ and $\omega_t = 1.1$ are used for balancing.

For orientation, we adopt a binary classification strategy over discretized direction bins:

$$L_{dir} = \text{CE}(\hat{\theta}_{bin}, \theta_{bin}^{gt})$$

The final loss is the weighted sum:

$$L = \frac{1}{N_{pos}}(\lambda_{cls}L_{cls} + \lambda_{reg}L_{reg} + \lambda_{dir}L_{dir}) \tag{15}$$

with $\lambda_{cls} = 1$, $\lambda_{reg} = 2$, and $\lambda_{dir} = 0.2$.

3   Experiment and Result

3.1   Experimental Datasets and Evaluation Metrics

We conduct experiments on the KITTI 3D object detection benchmark, following the official split in [10], with 3712 samples for training and 3769 for validation. KITTI includes three categories: Car, Pedestrian, and Cyclist, each with Easy, Moderate, and Hard levels defined by object size, occlusion, and truncation. To improve generalization, we apply various data augmentation strategies, including database sampling, global transformations (rotation, scaling, translation, flipping), bounding box perturbation, and range filtering of point clouds and objects. Detection performance is evaluated using Average Precision (AP), with IoU thresholds of 0.7 for Car and 0.5 for Pedestrian and Cyclist.

3.2   Implementation Details

All experiments are conducted on an Ubuntu 22.04 system with an NVIDIA RTX 4090 GPU and PyTorch 1.8.1. Point clouds are cropped to $x \in [0, 69.12]$m, $y \in [-39.68, 39.68]$m, and $z \in [-3, 1]$m, and voxelized into pillars of size $[0.16, 0.16, 4]$m, each containing up to 32 points. A maximum of 16,000/40,000 non-empty pillars are generated during training/testing. We train the model for 160 epochs using Adam optimizer with a batch size of 6, an initial learning rate of 0.00025, and weight decay of 0.01. The learning rate is scheduled by the OneCycleLR policy, which employs a 40% warm-up phase followed by cosine annealing. Momentum is dynamically adjusted between 0.85 and 0.95.

3.3   Experimental Results Analysis

3D object detection is conducted on Car, Pedestrian, and Cyclist categories in the test set. For fair comparison, all compared methods are trained on the same hardware using identical training configurations.

Table 1. Average precision of 3D detection on KITTI dataset.

Algorithm	Car (IoU $=0.7$)			Pedestrian (IoU $=0.5$)			Cyclist (IoU $=0.5$)			mAP/% (middle)	FPS (frame$\cdot$ s^{-1})
	easy	middle	hard	easy	middle	hard	easy	middle	hard		
VoxelNet [26]	81.97	65.46	62.85	49.48	43.69	40.51	67.17	48.36	44.37	52.83	5.11
SECOND [21]	83.13	73.66	66.20	51.07	42.56	41.29	70.51	53.85	46.90	56.69	22.47
Pointpillars [10]	85.41	73.98	67.76	51.46	46.40	42.48	78.72	59.95	57.25	60.11	**41.48**
TANet [14]	**87.97**	76.67	73.61	51.80	45.06	40.41	83.39	62.71	58.60	61.49	36.0
PiFENet [11]	86.96	73.61	62.02	**56.39**	48.89	44.09	76.96	59.99	55.84	61.16	18.9
Ours	85.74	**77.19**	**74.57**	54.97	**50.72**	**45.64**	**83.69**	**64.43**	**61.56**	64.11	34.2

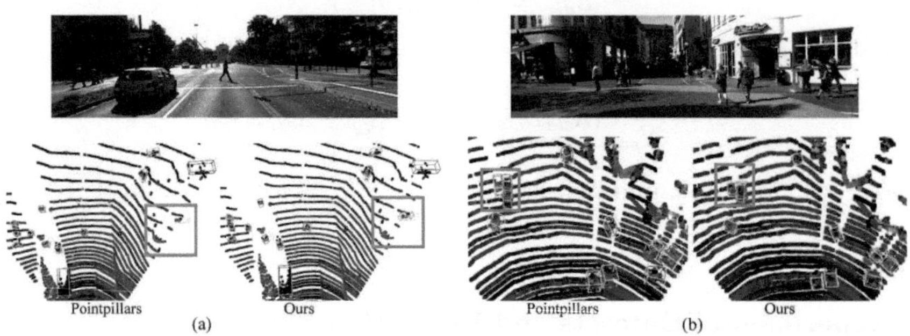

Fig. 6. Visual comparison results. The red 3D box represents pedestrians, the green 3D box represents cyclists, the blue 3D box represents cars, and the yellow 3D box represents the ground truth. In (a), Pointpillars fails to detect the cyclist who only appears halfway on the right side of the image, and misdetects the roadside sign post as a pedestrian, while the proposed algorithm not only correctly detects the incomplete cyclist, but also avoids misdetection. In (b), Pointpillars also misdetects the pedestrian at a distance, while the proposed algorithm can accurately detect both the pedestrian and the cyclist.

Quantitative Analysis. For 3D object detection, we use mean Average Precision (mAP) and inference speed as evaluation metrics. As shown in Table 1, our method achieves the highest mAP across all three object categories under the Moderate difficulty level. Specifically, compared with PointPillars, mAP improves by 3.51%, 4.32%, and 3.16% for Pedestrian, 4.97%, 4.48%, and 4.31% for Cyclist, and 0.33%, 3.21%, and 7.01% for Car across Easy, Moderate, and Hard levels, respectively. On average, our method surpasses PointPillars, TANet, and PiFENet by 4.0%, 2.62%, and 2.95%, respectively. Despite a 7.28 fps drop in inference speed compared to PointPillars, the proposed approach significantly improves detection performance, especially for sparse and small-scale targets, demonstrating superior robustness in complex point cloud scenarios. To further verify its effectiveness, visual comparisons with the PointPillars baseline are conducted in multi-object scenes with varying occlusion levels, as shown in Fig. 6. Our method accurately detects small and partially occluded objects while reducing false positives, highlighting its enhanced perception capability in crowded and challenging environments.

Ablation Studies. To assess the effectiveness of the proposed components, we conduct ablation experiments under the same settings as Sect. 3.3, and summarize the results in Table 2. Based on the baseline model from [10], Experiment 1 adds the structure-aware feature encoding module (SAFE), resulting in mAP improvements of 4.46% for pedestrians, 1.62% for cyclists, and 3.26% for cars. Experiment 2 further integrates the enhanced backbone with LKA, WDFM, and ASPP, achieving additional gains of 1.92%, 1.35%, and 3.44% across the three categories. These results confirm that SAFE improves feature representation, while the enhanced backbone boosts multi-scale fusion and structural perception, leading to better performance on small and distant objects.

Table 2. 3D detection ablation experimental results.

Algorithm	Car (IoU = 0.7)			Pedestrian (IoU = 0.5)			Cyclist (IoU = 0.5)		
	easy	middle	hard	easy	middle	hard	easy	middle	hard
Baseline	85.41	73.98	67.76	51.46	46.40	42.48	78.72	59.95	57.25
Baseline+(1)	85.93	76.99	74.01	**56.23**	**51.18**	**46.30**	78.89	62.93	58.95
Baseline+(2)	**85.99**	77.07	74.41	53.18	48.55	44.23	80.40	61.36	58.21
Ours	85.74	**77.19**	**74.57**	54.97	50.72	45.64	**83.69**	**64.43**	**61.56**

4   Conclusion

This paper presents an efficient 3D object detection framework tailored for sparse point cloud scenarios, with a focus on small-object recognition. A structure-aware feature encoding module is designed to capture intra-pillar geometric cues, inter-pillar structural dependencies, and vertical distribution information, significantly enhancing representation quality. Additionally, a large-kernel attention module and a multi-scale fusion strategy incorporating ASPP and weighted bidirectional fusion improve the model's spatial perception and context modeling capabilities. Experiments on the KITTI dataset demonstrate that the proposed method achieves superior detection accuracy, particularly for sparse and small targets like pedestrians and cyclists. Despite the performance gains, the introduced structural modules increase computational overhead. Future work will focus on optimizing the network architecture for real-time deployment in applications such as autonomous driving.

References

1. Badue, C., et al.: Self-driving cars: a survey. Expert Syst. Appl. **165**, 113816 (2021)
2. Bai, Z., Wu, G., Barth, M.J., Liu, Y., Sisbot, E.A., Oguchi, K.: Vinet: lightweight, scalable, and heterogeneous cooperative perception for 3d object detection. Mech. Syst. Signal Process. **204**, 110723 (2023)

3. Chen, C., Chen, Z., Zhang, J., Tao, D.: Sasa: semantics-augmented set abstraction for point-based 3d object detection. In: Proceedings of the AAAI Conference on Artificial Intelligence, vol. 36, pp. 221–229 (2022)

4. Chen, Y., Liu, J., Zhang, X., Qi, X., Jia, J.: Voxelnext: fully sparse voxelnet for 3d object detection and tracking. In: Proceedings of the IEEE/CVF Conference on Computer Vision and Pattern Recognition, pp. 21674–21683 (2023)

5. Deng, J., Shi, S., Li, P., Zhou, W., Zhang, Y., Li, H.: Voxel r-cnn: towards high performance voxel-based 3d object detection. In: Proceedings of the AAAI Conference on Artificial Intelligence, vol. 35, pp. 1201–1209 (2021)

6. Gorschlüter, F., Rojtberg, P., Pöllabauer, T.: A survey of 6d object detection based on 3d models for industrial applications. J. Imaging **8**(3), 53 (2022)

7. He, C., Zeng, H., Huang, J., Hua, X.S., Zhang, L.: Structure aware single-stage 3d object detection from point cloud. In: Proceedings of the IEEE/CVF Conference on Computer Vision and Pattern Recognition, pp. 11873–11882 (2020)

8. Hsu, W.Y., Chen, P.C.: Pedestrian detection using stationary wavelet dilated residual super-resolution. IEEE Trans. Instrum. Meas. **71**, 1–11 (2022)

9. Kharroubi, A., Poux, F., Ballouch, Z., Hajji, R., Billen, R.: Three dimensional change detection using point clouds: a review. Geomatics **2**(4), 457–485 (2022)

10. Lang, A.H., Vora, S., Caesar, H., Zhou, L., Yang, J., Beijbom, O.: Pointpillars: fast encoders for object detection from point clouds. In: Proceedings of the IEEE/CVF Conference on Computer Vision and Pattern Recognition, pp. 12697–12705 (2019)

11. Le, D.T., Shi, H., Rezatofighi, H., Cai, J.: Accurate and real-time 3d pedestrian detection using an efficient attentive pillar network. IEEE Rob. Autom. Lett. **8**(2), 1159–1166 (2022)

12. Li, H., et al.: Delving into the devils of bird's-eye-view perception: a review, evaluation and recipe. IEEE Trans. Pattern Anal. Mach. Intell. **46**(4), 2151–2170 (2023)

13. Liu, M., Ma, J., Zheng, Q., Liu, Y., Shi, G.: 3d object detection based on attention and multi-scale feature fusion. Sensors **22**(10), 3935 (2022)

14. Liu, Z., Zhao, X., Huang, T., Hu, R., Zhou, Y., Bai, X.: Tanet: robust 3d object detection from point clouds with triple attention. In: Proceedings of the AAAI Conference on Artificial Intelligence, vol. 34, pp. 11677–11684 (2020)

15. Mao, J., Shi, S., Wang, X., Li, H.: 3d object detection for autonomous driving: a comprehensive survey. Int. J. Comput. Vision **131**(8), 1909–1963 (2023)

16. Mozaffari, S., Al-Jarrah, O.Y., Dianati, M., Jennings, P., Mouzakitis, A.: Deep learning-based vehicle behavior prediction for autonomous driving applications: a review. IEEE Trans. Intell. Transp. Syst. **23**(1), 33–47 (2020)

17. Pan, X., Xia, Z., Song, S., Li, L.E., Huang, G.: 3d object detection with point-former. In: Proceedings of the IEEE/CVF Conference on Computer Vision and Pattern Recognition, pp. 7463–7472 (2021)

18. Qi, C.R., Su, H., Mo, K., Guibas, L.J.: Pointnet: deep learning on point sets for 3d classification and segmentation. In: Proceedings of the IEEE Conference on Computer Vision and Pattern Recognition, pp. 652–660 (2017)

19. Shi, G., Li, R., Ma, C.: Pillarnet: real-time and high-performance pillar-based 3d object detection. In: European Conference on Computer Vision, pp. 35–52. Springer, Heidelberg (2022). https://doi.org/10.1007/978-3-031-20080-9_3

20. Vora, S., Lang, A.H., Helou, B., Beijbom, O.: Pointpainting: sequential fusion for 3d object detection. In: Proceedings of the IEEE/CVF Conference on Computer Vision and Pattern Recognition, pp. 4604–4612 (2020)

21. Yan, Y., Mao, Y., Li, B.: Second: sparsely embedded convolutional detection. Sensors **18**(10), 3337 (2018)

22. Yang, B., Li, J., Zeng, T.: A review of environmental perception technology based on multi-sensor information fusion in autonomous driving. World Electr. Veh. J. **16**(1), 20 (2025)
23. Ye, T., Qin, W., Zhao, Z., Gao, X., Deng, X., Ouyang, Y.: Real-time object detection network in UAV-vision based on CNN and transformer. IEEE Trans. Instrum. Meas. **72**, 1–13 (2023)
24. Yin, T., Zhou, X., Krahenbuhl, P.: Center-based 3d object detection and tracking. In: Proceedings of the IEEE/CVF Conference on Computer Vision and Pattern Recognition, pp. 11784–11793 (2021)
25. Zhang, Y., Hu, Q., Xu, G., Ma, Y., Wan, J., Guo, Y.: Not all points are equal: learning highly efficient point-based detectors for 3d lidar point clouds. In: Proceedings of the IEEE/CVF Conference on Computer Vision and Pattern Recognition, pp. 18953–18962 (2022)
26. Zhou, Y., Tuzel, O.: Voxelnet: end-to-end learning for point cloud based 3d object detection. In: Proceedings of the IEEE Conference on Computer Vision and Pattern Recognition, pp. 4490–4499 (2018)

Knowledge-Aware Intent Subgraph Learning for Recommendation

Langchen Lang[1], Meng Jian[1(✉)] (iD), and Wei Zhou[2]

[1] Beijing University of Technology, Beijing 100124, China
jianmeng648@163.com
[2] Naval Aviation University, Yantai 264001, China

Abstract. The Knowledge Graph (KG) augmented recommendation mitigates the cold start issue by exploiting complex semantic clues in users' behaviors. However, existing methods focus on bringing these auxiliary knowledge into the user-item interaction space, ignoring the gap between different sources. In this study, we propose a knowledge-aware intent subgraph learning (KISL) which mines users' intents with KG to promote fine-grained interest learning for personalized recommendation. We model each intent representation as an attentive combination of KG relations on the knowledge graph. Guided by the intents, KISL devises a dimensional disentanglement to divide the interaction graph into several augmented intent-aware subgraphs. Fine-grained personalized embedding is learned during subgraph message propagation to predict users' interactions. Extensive experiments on two public datasets demonstrate the effectiveness of KISL by knowledge-aware intent modeling over baselines.

Keywords: Recommender system · knowledge graph · intent subgraph · interest disentangling

1 Introduction

In today's digital ecosystem, the recommender system (RS) has evolved into a pivotal component in shaping online experiences. RS inherently suffered from the cold start problem. Many approaches integrate auxiliary domain knowledge through knowledge graphs (KGs) into the recommender system to mitigate these limitations. Knowledge graphs are heterogeneous graphs that encode real-world (objects/concepts/instances), their attributes, and relational semantics. The auxiliary information in KGs is incorporated in recommender models to alleviate the cold start problem in recommendations. By combining user-item interaction information with representations learned from knowledge graphs of users and items, KG-enhanced recommendation methods model complex high-order relationships between them. Some methods [1] have already proved the effectiveness of incorporating KG into the recommender system. These methods can be categorized into two primary approaches: path-based methods [8] and

Z. Lin et al. (Eds.): ICIG 2025, LNCS 16161, pp. 236–248, 2026.
https://doi.org/10.1007/978-981-95-3398-5_20

embedding-based methods. Path-based methods focus on extracting meta-paths from knowledge graphs beyond local information to capture high-order relationships. Embedding-based methods consider additional knowledge beyond user-item interactions, incorporating attributes and relationships into the embedding process for richer recommendations. Despite the demonstrated effectiveness of existing KG-aware recommendation methods, these methods directly bring KG as side information into users and items modeling without further selection and filtering. However, in the real world, knowledge graphs often suffer from noise that is irrelevant to user preference. Directly incorporating knowledge graph into user-item interactions will cause the model to be unable to represent users' interests accurately.

To address these issues, this model proposed a novel framework known as KISL. Drawing inspiration from recent disentangle methods, we propose a knowledge graph derived intent disentangle subgraph learning paradigm that effectively captures fine-grained users' interest. Our approach consists of two components to solve the foregoing limitations: (1) Intention modeling: since each user makes a decision based on multiple intentions, how to semantically express these intentions as latent representations can be a problem. Given that the knowledge graph has rich semantic meaning, we use an attention mechanism to combine the KG relations into intent; the higher the attention score, the greater the proportion of the relation in one intention. (2). Intent-aware disentanglement: Unlike other KG-aware methods incorporating KG information into embedding spaces, we endeavor to learn fine-grained embeddings by disentangling representations into multiple intent spaces. In each intent space, we augment the subgraph based on the similarity of intent-aware node features. We obtain different perspectives' node embeddings through subgraph learning, which can capture latent users' interests. In summary, this work makes the following contributions:

- Mining users' intents within the knowledge graph to bring semantic information into the embedding space, mitigating sparse interaction data.
- Proposing a new KISL model, which disentangles user-item interaction graphs into intent-aware subgraphs and learns fine-grained interest representations through recursive message propagation.
- Empirical studies on two benchmark datasets demonstrate the effectiveness of intent learning and intent-guided interest prediction in KISL.

2   Related Work

2.1   GCN-Based Recommendation Methods

Based on how the convolution operation is used [1], GCN models can be categorized as spectral and spatial models. Due to simplicity and lower computation cost compared with spectral-GCNs, spatial-GCNs are widely adopted in recommender systems, but they suffer from scalability issues, causing over-smoothing. To address these challenges, researchers have developed a range of improvements.

GraphSAGE [2] uses a sampled, fixed-sized neighborhood for aggregation. To further reduce time complexity, LightGCN [3] removes the complicated transformation and activation functions that have been proven ineffective in recommendation tasks. To avoid over-smoothing, UltraGCN [7] replaces GCN layers with constraint losses. However, it only captures first-order interactions and fails in high data sparsity scenarios. Therefore, we argue that using LightGCN as an embedding encoder is a balance of time complexity and task expressiveness.

2.2 Knowledge-Based Recommendation Methods

In knowledge-based methods, items are recommended based on explicit knowledge about the user's preferences and the items' characteristics. KGCL [12], MCCLK [13] introduce cross-view CL paradigms between the knowledge graph and user-item graph. However, these methods rely on random augmentation or contrastive views, overlooking the noise in the knowledge graph that will bring bias to users' preference learning. KGCN [5], KGIN [9] extend the GCN approach onto KG by using selective neighborhood aggregation to learn structural and semantic information about the KG and users' personalized and potential preferences. Although these approaches bring knowledge graph into graph structure, they still fail to model fine-grained representations since they mix semantic and structural information in a single representation space. Based on the drawbacks above, we propose the following idea: extract intent signals from the semantic information in knowledge graphs to guide the learning of subgraphs, thereby disentangling user interests into fine-grained representations using distinct intents.

2.3 Disentangle-Based Recommendation Methods

Disentangle representation learning methods endeavor to learn disentangled user preference features such that any feature is relatively independent and not influenced by changes in other features. The concept of disentanglement has been widely adopted in various fields, including images, multimedia, and graphs. MacridVAE [6] disentangles user preferences into micro- and macro-perspectives without explicit guidance. DGCF [10] aggregates node representations across different subgraphs based on intent distribution possibilities. However, these methods did not fully consider explicit semantic information within the data. Our work differs from these previous methods, where we incorporate external information and design an intent mining mechanism to disentangle users' intentions, which are more explainable than other disentangle-based methods.

3 Methodology

In this section, we detail the technical design of our method. Our framework comprises three core components: (1) intent mining within the knowledge graph, (2) disentangled subgraph construction, and (3) intent-aware subgraph learning module. These components synergistically capture latent intent signals from the KG while ensuring robust intent-aware subgraph learning through hierarchical feature disentanglement and adaptive graph refinement. The overall framework is present in Fig. 1.

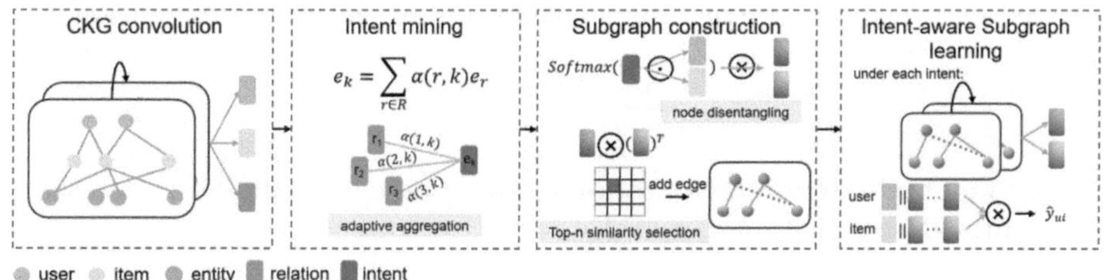

Fig. 1. Illustration of the proposed KISL framework.

3.1 Intent Mining Within the KG

To capture fine-grained user preferences, we conduct pre-training on the Collaborative Knowledge Graph (CKG) to derive KG-enriched user and item representations for subsequent subgraph construction. Specifically, we employ attention mechanisms to dynamically aggregate relational information through weighted summation, generating relation-aware intent signals. The technical implementation involves performing graph convolution operations on the CKG to obtain enhanced user and item embeddings that intrinsically encode both collaborative filtering patterns and knowledge graph semantics.

Collaborative Knowledge Graph Convolution. First, we perform relation-aware aggregation over the KG to derive expressive representations for users, items, and KG relations. Specifically, we formulate KG relations as multi-head attention weights to dynamically quantify relational significance when updating head and tail entity embeddings. The formal implementation involves a linear transformation matrix that enhances representation capacity by projecting head entities into query vectors while treating relation-specific tail entities as keys for query-key matching. The resultant relation-adjusted tail entities then serve as value vectors for attentive aggregation. The core operation can be expressed as:

$$Q = e_h \cdot W_Q, K = (e_t \cdot W_Q) \odot e_r[r], \qquad V = e_t \odot e_r[r] \qquad (1)$$

where e_h and e_t are the head and tail entity representations in the knowledge graph separately. e_r is the representation of the knowledge graph's relation. W_Q is a learnable linear transformation matrix to add more explainability. Then we calculate the similarity between Q and K to obtain the multi-head attention weight:

$$Attention_{edge} = softmax\left(\frac{\mathbf{Q} \cdot K}{\sqrt{d_k}}\right), \tag{2}$$

Use attention weight to (further explanation) obtain entity representation.

$$e_{entity} = \sum_{e \in \varepsilon(h)} Attention_{edge} \cdot V[e] \tag{3}$$

Next, we obtain item representation e_i based on e_{entity} and user representation e_u through aggregation of e_i:

$$e_i = e_{\text{entity}}[i_e], \quad e_u = \sum_{e \in \varepsilon(u)} e_i[e] \tag{4}$$

After L layers of CKG propagation, we obtain the final representations E_i and E_u.

$$E_i = \frac{1}{L}\sum_{l=0}^{L-1} e_i^l, \quad E_u = \frac{1}{L}\sum_{l=0}^{L-1} e_u^l \tag{5}$$

Representation Learning of Intents. Intuitively, users' intents could be entangled within KG relations that have rich semantic information. Therefore, we designed an attention strategy to combine KG relations with several intents. Each intent $k \in K$ will be a combination of multiple KG relations to capture fine-grained intent representation. Technically, the intent embedding will be calculated as follows:

$$e_k = \sum_{r \in R} \alpha(r, k) e_r \tag{6}$$

where e_r is the KG relation embedding we acquired from the above CKG-GCN training stage. $\alpha(r, k)$ is the attention score for intent k, which is calculated using $Softmax$ with a trainable weight matrix W:

$$\alpha(r, k) = \frac{exp(w_{rk})}{\sum_{r' \in R} exp(w_{r'k})} \tag{7}$$

where w_{rk} is a specific weight between relation r and intent k.

Optimize Pre-train Model. In this pre-training stage, we optimize the CKG-GCN model parameters with BPR loss to reconstruct the historical data. The function can be formulated as follows:

$$L_{BPR} = \sum_{(u,i,j) \in O} -ln\sigma(\hat{y}_{ui} - \hat{y}_{uj}), \tag{8}$$

where $O = \{(u, i, j)|(u, i) \in O^+, (u, j) \in O^-\}$ is the training dataset, O^+ are the observed interactions and O^- is the unobserved counterpart. $\sigma(\cdot)$ is the sigmoid function.

$$L = L_{BPR} + \lambda\|\Theta\|_2^2, \tag{9}$$

where $\Theta = \{E_U, E_I, W\}$ is the set of model parameters; λ is the hyperparameter to control the L_2 regularization term.

3.2 Disentangled Subgraph Construction

Disentangle Node Representation. After acquiring user and item embeddings enriched with CKG information, we disentangle these representations via intent embeddings. Recognizing that each dimension of the node embeddings captures distinct semantic features, we propose a dimension-wise attention mechanism to align knowledge graph relations with user/item embedding dimensions. Concretely, we compute the similarity between each intent representation e_k and the user/item embeddings on each dimension. This operation dynamically reorganizes the dimensions, ultimately generating intent-aware user/item embeddings. In technical details, we apply $\odot$ operation to achieve this dimensional-level attention:

$$\beta_{i,k} = Softmax(e_k \odot E_i), \quad \beta_{u,k} = Softmax(e_k \odot E_u) \tag{10}$$

Then we use the dimensional-level attention score β_k to disentangle user/item embedding into K intent-aware user/item embeddings, while keeping each of their representation dimension as same as the original user/item embedding E_u and E_i:

$$e_i^k = \beta_{i,k} E_i, \quad e_u^k = \beta_{u,k} E_u \tag{11}$$

Subgraph Construction. To ensure fairness for each user, we calculate the similarity between user and item nodes, select the top-n most similar items for each user, and augment the original user-item adjacency matrix by adding these edges. In specific, we create K masks M_k and apply it on the original adjacent matrix A:

$$M_k = select[e_u^k \cdot (e_i^k)^T] \tag{12}$$
$$A_k = A + M_k \tag{13}$$

Subgraph Learning. After obtaining the augmented subgraph adjacent matrix A_k, we perform information propagation on it to update the intent-aware representation:

$$E_{i,k} = D_I^{-\frac{1}{2}} A_k D_U^{-\frac{1}{2}} e_i^k, \quad E_{u,k} = D_U^{-\frac{1}{2}} A_k D_I^{-\frac{1}{2}} e_u^k \tag{14}$$

3.3 Model Prediction and Optimization

Since we perform learning on each subgraph separately, to preserve the discriminative intent view information maximally, we concatenate these multi-view representations instead of pooling them into a unified embedding:

$$E_I = E_i\|E_{i,1}...\|E_{i,K}, \quad E_U = E_u\|E_{u,1}...\|E_{u,K} \tag{15}$$

Thereafter, we employ the inner product on the user and item representations to predict how likely the user would adopt the item:

$$\hat{y}_{ui} = E_U \cdot (E_I)^T \tag{16}$$

For optimization, we optimize the model parameter with Eq. 9.

4 Experiments

4.1 Experimental Settings

Dataset Description. We use two benchmark datasets: movieLens-1M, LastFM in the experiments. Detailed statistics for the two datasets and their corresponding KGs can be found in Table 1. Following previous studies, we adopt the same data split. During the training phase, each observed user-item interaction serves as a positive instance, while a randomly sampled item that the user has not previously adopted is paired with the user as a negative instance.

Table 1. Statistics of the datasets.

		MovieLens-1M	Last-FM
User-Item Interaction	#Users	6,036	1,872
	#Items	2,445	3,846
	#Interactions	753,772	42,346
	#Density	5.1e-2	5.9e-3
Knowledge Graph	#Entities	182,011	9,366
	#Relations	12	60
	#Triplets	1,241,996	15,518

Evaluation Metrics. In the evaluation phase, we conduct the all-ranking strategy, meaning for each user, all non-interacted items are defined as negative samples, and the items with observed interactions in the test set serve as positive samples. We utilize Recall@K and NDCG@K as top-K recommendation metrics, where K is set as 20 by default. We report the average metrics for all users in the testing set.

Baselines. We compare our method with the state-of-the-art methods, covering KG-free (LightGCN) and GNN-based (KGIN, KGRec, DiffKG) methods: LightGCN [3] is a GCN-based method, which leverages user-item interactions for neighborhood message aggregation. It removes the transform matrix and the nonlinear activation for computational costs. KGIN [9] is a GCN-based method aggregating semantics through relational paths. It considers user-item relationships from a finer-grained perspective. KGRec [11] is a KG-based method that aligns collaborative signal and knowledge graph semantics via contrastive learning. DiffKG [4] is a KG diffusion model that integrates generative diffusion and data augmentation to iteratively corrupt and reconstruct KG structures, thereby filtering noise and improving robustness in modeling user-item interactions.

Parameter Settings. We implement our model on PyTorch. For a fair comparison, we fixed the embedding dimension to 64, used Adam optimizer, and initialized model parameters using Xavier. All the comparison methods take the default setting. We adjust learning rate between $\{10^{-5}, 10^{-4}, 10^{-3}, 10^{-2}\}$. The L_2 regularization strength is searched in $\{10^{-6}, 10^{-5}, ..., 10^{-2}\}$ to prevent overfitting. The number of subgraphs is searched in $\{1, 2, 4, 8\}$. The number of subgraph convolution layers is tuned in $1, 2, 3$. The number of top-N similar edges for subgraph augmentation is tuned in $\{1, 5, 10\}$. Without specification, we fixed the subgraph convolution layer $L = 1$, the regularization strength $\lambda = 10^{-4}$.

4.2   Performance Comparison

We report the performance of all methods on two datasets in Table 2. Based on the results, we make the following observations:

- Our method KISL consistently outperforms all baselines across two datasets. This demonstrates the effectiveness of KISL. We attribute the improvements to two factors: (1). KISL extracts practical semantic information from the knowledge graph by modeling the abstract intent. In comparison, baseline methods (except KGIN) treat user-item interactions uniformly by representing them as undifferentiated pathways for information aggregation, while failing to account for latent user motivations; (2). Under the guidance of latent intent signals, KISL constructs a subgraph disentangling module, enabling CF signals to propagate more flexibly across diverse fine-grained perspectives. However, existing approaches do not consider the heterogeneity of user-item representations across distinct spaces; even those (e.g., KGIN) that attempt to aggregate cross-space representations via learnable attention mechanisms risk diluting the discriminative power of individual intent-specific subspaces.
- A cross-dataset evaluation reveals that KISL performance gains on LastFM surpass those observed on MovieLens-1M. This discrepancy can be attributed to two key factors: (1). LastFM's interaction data and knowledge graph exhibit lower density and semantic noise than MovieLens-1M; (2). The KG structure of MovieLens-1M is dominated by first-order connectivity patterns

(e.g., fashion outfit composition), limiting the potential benefits of modeling long-range dependencies.

- KGIN, KGRec, and DiffKG achieve comparable performance and outperform LightGCN. Although LightGCN is a GNN-based model specially tailored for recommendation tasks, it does not incorporate auxiliary information like other KG-based methods, restricting its capacity to exploit enriched semantic relationships in collaborative filtering. This finding is consistent with previous studies, indicating the effectiveness of side information such as KG.
- GNN-based methods (i.e., LightGCN, KGIN) show stable performance across two datasets compared to DiffKG. Diffusion models impose a strong continuity assumption on the underlying data distribution. At the same time, user-item interactions in recommendation tasks are high-dimensional and sparse, exhibiting long-tailed distributions, which significantly hinders the stable modeling of diffusion processes. Moreover, diffusion models are sensitive to hyperparameters and need manual tuning across different datasets.

Table 2. Overall Performance Comparison.

	MovieLens-1M		Last-FM	
	Recall@20	NDCG@20	Recall@20	NDCG@20
LightGCN	0.2767	0.2506	0.2711	0.1686
KGIN	0.3115	<u>0.2853</u>	<u>0.3358</u>	<u>0.2113</u>
KGRec	<u>0.3207</u>	0.2793	0.3055	0.1867
DiffKG	0.2996	0.2832	0.3111	0.1955
KISL	**0.3295**	**0.2951**	**0.3559**	**0.2173**
%Imp	2.67%	3.32%	5.65%	2.84%

4.3 Ablation Studies

We conduct ablation studies to evaluate the contribution of critical components within the proposed KISL framework, specifically, how the intent mining and disentangled subgraph modules influence our model. We constructed three variants to benchmark against the baseline methodology:

- w/o intent: removing intent mining and the disentangled subgraph module.
- w/o intent-knowledge: replacing the intent mining module with randomly initialized intents.
- w/o subgraph: keeping the intent mining module and removing the subgraph module.

We report the ablation study result in Table 3 and make the following observations: (1). The proposed intent mining and disentangled subgraph module positively influence performance. This demonstrates that subgraph disentanglement is an effective way to exploit knowledge graph for recommendation. (2). The random intent guidance is not beneficial to empirical results, given that random guidance without auxiliary information does not incorporate semantic meaning. (3). The disentangled subgraph mechanism can further improve the performance by selecting valuable information and constructing diverse fine-grained views for users.

Table 3. Ablation Study.

	MovieLens-1M		Last-FM	
	Recall@20	NDCG@20	Recall@20	NDCG@20
w/o intent	0.2600	0.2351	0.2736	0.1699
w/o intent-knowledge	0.2558	0.2282	0.2821	0.1734
w/o subgraph	0.3003	0.2874	0.3244	0.1943

4.4 Sensitivity to Key Hyperparameters

In this study, we investigate the sensitivity of KISL to changes in key hyperparameters, including the number of intents (k) and the number of top-n selection(n) in Fig. 2.

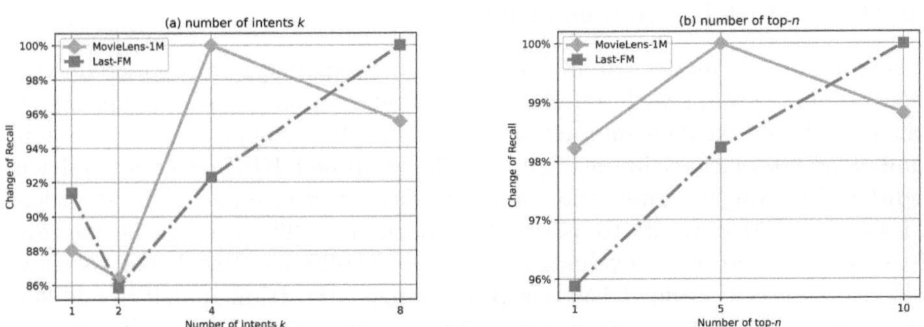

Fig. 2. Impact of Hyperparameters.

Impact of Intent Modeling. We tune the number of intents between $[1, 2, 4, 8]$. Specifically, we find that: (1). Increasing the number of intents generally enhances performance. $k = 4$ is ideal for MovieLens-1M, while $k = 8$

is optimal for Last-FM. Notably, setting $k = 1$ leads to performance degradation, which indicates that modeling fine-grained representations and constructing subgraphs are critical. This suggests that a single, undifferentiated intent fails to capture the complexity of interaction patterns, highlighting the necessity of decomposing interactions into distinct intents.(2). In MovieLens-1M, performance deteriorates when k exceeds 4. A reasonable explanation is that while independent intent modeling disentangles correlations between intents, excessive partitioning results in overly granular intents that lack semantic coherence. Specifically, highly detailed intents may become too sparse or contextually irrelevant, failing to encode meaningful behavioral patterns and instead introducing noise into the representation learning process.

Impact of Subgraph Top-N Selection. We tune the number of top-n between $[1, 5, 10]$, through which we find that: (1). For Last-FM, the performance exhibits a consistent upward trend as the subgraph edge count increases. The augmentation of edges within its subgraph yields a more pronounced performance improvement. Given that this dataset is smaller and sparser compared to MovieLens-1M. This can be attributed to the relatively limited interactions, where additional connections enrich the structural information more effectively. (2). In the case for MovieLens-1M, Recall@20 peaks at $n = 5$ and subsequently declines. A plausible explanation is that this dataset already contains a sufficient number of user-item interactions. Directly increasing edges may introduce noise or irrelevant connections, which disrupt the model's ability to learn meaningful patterns and thus degrade performance.

4.5   Cold Start Recommendation

To investigate the model's ability to address data sparsity, we conducted experiments on user groups with differing levels of interaction sparsity. In specific, we split users based on their interaction volume into five groups, ensuring an equal number of interactions in each group. The proposed KISL is compared with LightGCN on varying interaction sparsity of the user groups on the Movielens-1M and LastFM datasets to assess its performance. The average performance of users in each group is evaluated using NDCG@20 and Recall@20, as shown in Fig. 3. In Fig. 3, group 1 has relatively higher interaction sparsity (cold start users), increasing progressively across subsequent groups. Our analysis reveals that KISL effectively tackles the cold-start problem for a diverse user base compared with LightGCN. This superior performance can be attributed to its innovative design, incorporating KG-derived intents with subgraph learning scheme, effectively capturing valuable knowledge for fine-grained representation learning.

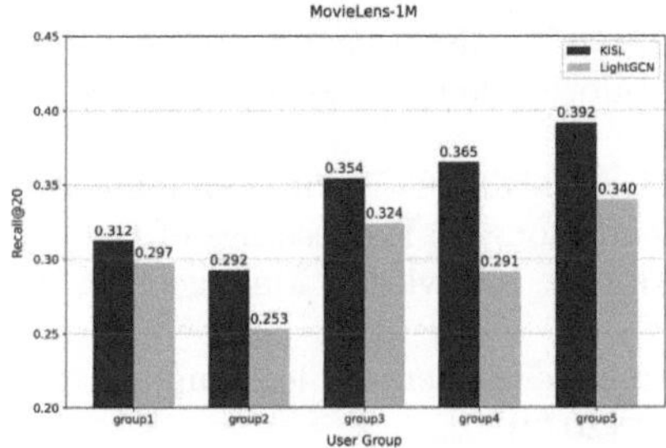
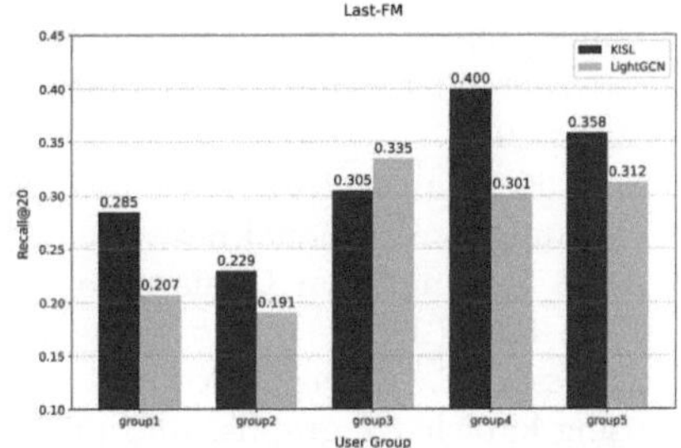

Fig. 3. Cold Start Study.

5   Conclusion

In this work, we introduced a novel knowledge-aware recommendation framework KISL, that addresses cold start in KG-augmented recommender systems by mining intents from KG relations and learning disentangled intent-aware subgraphs. By modeling fine-grained user intents through KG relations and constructing disentangled intent-aware subgraphs, KISL effectively captures nuanced user preferences in KG-augmented recommendation systems. In future work, incorporating self-supervised learning to generate auxiliary supervision signals can be a direction to enhance robustness in sparse data scenarios.

Acknowledgments. This work was supported by the Beijing Natural Science Foundation under Grant No. L241053, and the National Natural Science Foundation of China under Grant No. 62176011.

Disclosure of Interests. The authors have no competing interests to declare that are relevant to the content of this article.

References

1. Anand, V., Maurya, A.K.: A survey on recommender systems using graph neural network. ACM Trans. Inf. Syst. **43**(1), 1–49 (2025)
2. Hamilton, W., Ying, Z., Leskovec, J.: Inductive representation learning on large graphs. In: Advances in Neural Information Processing Systems, vol. 30 (2017)
3. He, X., Deng, K., Wang, X., Li, Y., Zhang, Y., Wang, M.: LightGCN: simplifying and powering graph convolution network for recommendation. In: Proceedings of the 43rd International ACM SIGIR Conference on Research and Development in Information Retrieval, pp. 639–648 (2020)
4. Jiang, Y., Yang, Y., Xia, L., Huang, C.: DIFFKG: knowledge graph diffusion model for recommendation. In: Proceedings of the 17th ACM International Conference on Web Search and Data Mining, pp. 313–321 (2024)
5. Kojima, R., Ishida, S., Ohta, M., Iwata, H., Honma, T., Okuno, Y.: KGCN: a graph-based deep learning framework for chemical structures. J. Cheminf. **12**, 1–10 (2020)

6. Ma, J., Zhou, C., Cui, P., Yang, H., Zhu, W.: Learning disentangled representations for recommendation. In: Advances in Neural Information Processing Systems, vol. 32 (2019)
7. Mao, K., Zhu, J., Xiao, X., Lu, B., Wang, Z., He, X.: UltraGCN: ultra simplification of graph convolutional networks for recommendation. In: Proceedings of the 30th ACM International Conference on Information & Knowledge Management, pp. 1253–1262 (2021)
8. Troussas, C., Krouska, A.: Path-based recommender system for learning activities using knowledge graphs. Information 14(1), 9 (2022)
9. Wang, X., et al.: Learning intents behind interactions with knowledge graph for recommendation. In: Proceedings of the Web Conference 2021, pp. 878–887 (2021)
10. Wang, X., Jin, H., Zhang, A., He, X., Xu, T., Chua, T.S.: Disentangled graph collaborative filtering. In: Proceedings of the 43rd International ACM SIGIR Conference on Research and Development in Information Retrieval, pp. 1001–1010 (2020)
11. Yang, Y., Huang, C., Xia, L., Huang, C.: Knowledge graph self-supervised rationalization for recommendation. In: Proceedings of the 29th ACM SIGKDD Conference on Knowledge Discovery and Data Mining, pp. 3046–3056 (2023)
12. Zhang, X., Ma, H., Yang, F., Li, Z., Chang, L.: KGCL: a knowledge-enhanced graph contrastive learning framework for session-based recommendation. Eng. Appl. Artif. Intell. 124, 106512 (2023)
13. Zou, D., et al.: Multi-level cross-view contrastive learning for knowledge-aware recommender system. In: Proceedings of the 45th International ACM SIGIR Conference on Research and Development in Information Retrieval, pp. 1358–1368 (2022)

PF-DETR:Enhanced DETR with Pre-encoded Feature Fusion for Small and Multi-scale Object Detection in UAV Imagery

Lina Huo, Jianing Qian, Wei Wang$^{(\boxtimes)}$, and Benchao Guo

Hebei Normal University, Shijiazhuang, Hebei, China
`wangwei2021@hebtu.edu.cn`

Abstract. Object detection in UAV imagery presents a significant challenge due to low image resolution, complex visual backgrounds, and substantial inter-object scale variation. Detection Transformer (DETR)-based models often underperform in such scenarios. This paper proposes Pre-Fusion Guided DETR (PF-DETR), a refined and enhanced extension of the D-FINE model, specifically designed for robust small-object detection in UAV imagery. PF-DETR introduces a novel Pre-Encoded Feature Fusion (PEFF) module, which employs a unidirectional fusion strategy to integrate low-level spatial features into high-level semantic features, thereby improving the model's ability to capture fine-grained details of small objects. Additionally, a Feature Enhancement Attention (FEA) mechanism is incorporated to strengthen feature representation and reduce background interference. To address information loss during multi-scale processing, a Haar Wavelet Downsampling (HWD) module is proposed, combining Haar wavelet transforms with convolutional downsampling to better preserve critical features. Furthermore, the original GIoU loss is replaced with an Enhanced IoU (EIoU) loss function to improve localization accuracy and training efficiency. Experimental results on the challenging VisDrone2019 benchmark demonstrate that PF-DETR outperforms state-of-the-art detectors, including DEIM, D-FINE, YOLOv10, and YOLOv11, in both detection accuracy and robustness. Specifically, PF-DETR achieves an AP50 of 40.6% and an AP of 23.6%, representing improvements of 2.0% and 1.5% over D-FINE, 2.7% and 1.8% over DEIM, and notable gains of 7.6% and 8.3% in AP50 compared to YOLOv11n and YOLOv10s, respectively. These results underscore the strong potential of PF-DETR for real-world UAV applications requiring precise small-object detection under challenging conditions.

Keywords: DETR · Multi-Scale Feature Enhancement and Fusion · UAV Imagery

1 Introduction

Object detection continues to be a fundamental task in computer vision due to its widespread applications in military reconnaissance [1], autonomous driving [2],

© The Author(s), under exclusive license to Springer Nature Singapore Pte Ltd. 2026
Z. Lin et al. (Eds.): ICIG 2025, LNCS 16161, pp. 249–264, 2026.
https://doi.org/10.1007/978-981-95-3398-5_21

surveillance [3], and remote sensing [4]. With the growing use of UAVs, object detection based on aerial images has attracted increasing attention, owing to its broad coverage and high resolution. Detecting small targets—such as people, vehicles, and infrastructure—is essential for tasks like environmental monitoring and facility protection. However, the small size of these objects, combined with complex backgrounds and large scale variations, poses a significant challenge for accurate detection in UAV imagery.

The field of object detection is predominantly divided into two paradigms: one-stage and two-stage detection frameworks, which differ significantly in terms of efficiency, accuracy, and computational complexity.

Two-stage algorithms (e.g., R-CNN [24], Fast R-CNN [16], Faster R-CNN [15]) first generate candidate regions (region proposals) and then perform object classification and bounding box regression. This sequential pipeline allows them to achieve high accuracy, especially for small or complex objects, but comes with significant computational costs. The redundancy in generating and processing numerous proposals often leads to slow inference speeds, making them less suitable for real-time applications, particularly in dense object scenarios.

In contrast, one-stage algorithms (e.g., YOLO [1,20], SSD [13], EfficientDet [19]) directly predict object categories and locations from input images in a single pass, eliminating the need for region proposal generation. This design enables much faster inference, making them ideal for real-time tasks like drone surveillance or autonomous driving. However, they typically rely on non-maximum suppression (NMS) to resolve overlapping bounding boxes, which introduces inefficiencies due to its sequential nature and sensitivity to threshold settings. Additionally, their CNN-based architectures often struggle to model long-range dependencies in images, potentially affecting detection accuracy in complex scenes.

Compared to traditional CNN-based models like PANet [12], SSD [13], and Faster R-CNN [15], Transformer-based architectures have shown better ability to capture long-range dependencies, leading to stronger performance in object detection tasks. DETR [27](Detection Transformer) was the first to use Transformer architecture in computer vision. It changes the object detection problem into a set prediction problem, removing the need for anchor boxes and non-maximum suppression (NMS), which makes the detection process simpler. However, DETR has some downsides, like slow training and high computational requirements, which make it less suitable for real-time applications. To solve these problems, many improvements have been proposed.

For example, DN-DETR [9], developed by Li et al., introduces a de-noising training strategy that makes the matching process in DETR's decoder more stable, speeding up training. Deformable DETR [30], by Zhu et al., adds a deformable attention mechanism to lower training costs and improve accuracy, bringing us closer to real-time DETR-based detectors. RT-DETR [28], created by Zhao et al., takes this further by offering an end-to-end real-time object detection model that maintains high accuracy, beating YOLO models of similar size in both speed and precision. D-FINE improves the bounding box regression task in DETR by adding Fine-grained Distribution Refinement (FDR) and Global Optimal Localization Self-Distillation (GO-LSD) [14,22], which greatly improves location accuracy while keeping real-time performance. Lastly, the DEIM [6] framework adds even more improvements with Dense One-to-One Matching and a Matchability-Aware Loss function, which helps speed up training and maintain detection quality.

Collectively, these advancements highlight the growing potential of Transformer-based architectures in achieving a favorable trade-off between detection accuracy and computational efficiency for real-time object detection.

Despite significant advancements in the field of object detection, UAV-based object detection still faces several critical challenges. First, the usual convolutional methods used in object detection struggle because they can't look at the bigger picture. They have a limited view, making it hard to capture the full spatial relationships and tiny details of objects in aerial images.

Second, because the scale of objects in UAV images can vary a lot and many objects are small, it's much harder to extract features and learn good representations of these objects. Compared with YOLO series models, adding small object detection heads to Transformer series models leads to substantial computational and memory overhead. Additionally, traditional strided convolutions and down-sampling operations are prone to information loss during feature extraction or fusion for small objects, leading to suboptimal detection performance. Finally, the combination of complex backgrounds, lighting changes, and weather factors in aerial images generates substantial interference, which significantly degrades detection accuracy.

To address these challenges, we propose PF-DETR, an improved version of D-Fine [14],first, we constructed a novel network component—the Pre-Encoding Feature Fusion Module (PEFF). By performing unidirectional fusion of small-object information before feature fusion and encoding, PEFF ensures that small-object information is fused as much as possible at an early stage without adding detection heads. This enhances the model's ability to capture fine-grained details of complex-shaped objects. Second, to reduce the abundant background noise in low-level feature maps, we developed a Multi-Branch Feature Refinement Attention Module (FEA). Finally, we introduced a Hierarchical Wavelet Downsampling (HWD) [23]module into the multi-scale feature fusion [22] module. The Haar wavelet transform is applied to reduce the spatial resolution of feature maps while preserving as much information as possible. The key innovations and contributions of this study are synthesized as follows:

The PEFF module is proposed to address the need for enhanced small object detection without introducing additional detection heads. It adopts a unidirectional bottom-up fusion path combined with element-wise addition to efficiently integrate multi-scale features before feature encoding, thereby mitigating the limitations of traditional top-down fusion methods in capturing fine-grained details. This design not only preserves computational efficiency but also significantly improves the model's sensitivity to small objects by retaining low-level spatial information in the early stages of feature extraction.

The Lightweight FEA Module is proposed to suppress background noise and enhance small object features. By applying spatial separable convolutions to capture long-range dependencies, it combines channel and spatial attention mechanisms to first filter channel-wise features and then focus on critical spatial regions, effectively strengthening small object representations while reducing interference from complex backgrounds.

The HWD Module is introduced to address detail loss in downsampling. Using learnable Haar wavelet bases, it decomposes feature maps into low-frequency (approximate) and high-frequency (detail) components, enabling dual-path processing during downsampling. This approach avoids information loss caused by traditional pooling or strided convolutions, preserving fine-grained details and improving the model's ability to detect small objects with subtle spatial features.

To enhance localization accuracy, especially for small and irregular objects, this study employs the EIoU [26] loss function in place of the traditional GIoU [17] loss. EIOU innovatively decouples bounding box regression into two geometric components—centroid alignment and dimension regularization—establishing a more precise and geometry-aware constraint mechanism. This decomposition strategy significantly enhances the model's ability to represent object shapes, resulting in notable improvements in localization accuracy under challenging conditions.

2   Method

In this section, the proposed PF-DETR model is introduced in detail. The overall architecture diagram of PF-DETR is shown in Fig. 1.

The PF-DETR network comprises four core modules: the backbone feature extractor, the pre-encoding feature fusion module, the hybrid encoder fusion module, and the prediction decoder. Initially, the backbone network extracts multi-scale feature maps—P4, P8, P16, and P32—which correspond to spatial resolutions of 1/4, 1/8, 1/16, and 1/32 of the input image, respectively. This module generates fused feature maps of P8, P16, and P32 through unidirectional cross-layer fusion. The fused feature maps are subsequently fed into the Hybrid Wavelet Fusion Module (HWFM), which facilitates comprehensive cross-scale information interaction. Unlike conventional downsampling-based architectures, HWFM leverages wavelet-based decomposition to preserve both spatial detail and frequency-domain information across scales. This hybrid mechanism integrates multi-scale feature aggregation with attention mechanisms, thereby capturing both fine-grained local features and global contextual relationships.

During decoding, the model outputs a set of object queries containing predicted bounding boxes and class probabilities. The Hungarian matching algorithm is employed to assign predictions to ground-truth objects based on a combined classification and localization cost. This assignment guides the computation of the loss function, typically composed of cross-entropy and box regression terms.

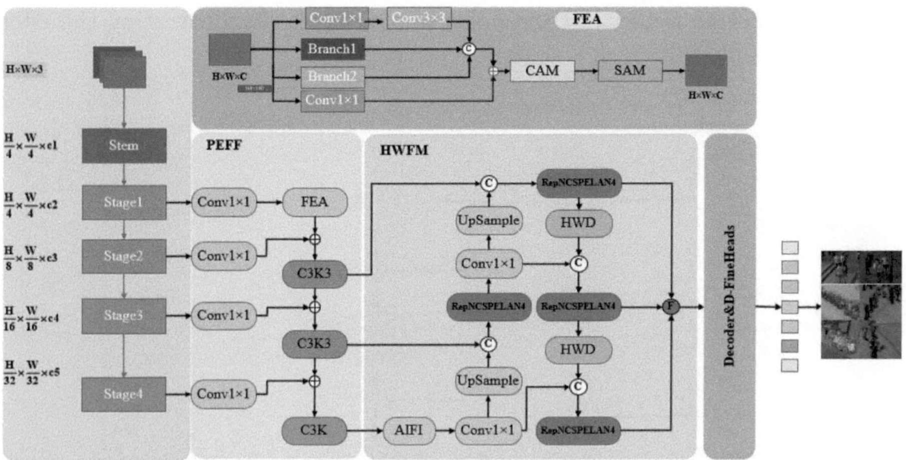

Fig. 1. Network structure diagram of PF-DETR.

2.1 Pre-encoding Feature Fusion Module

Unlike the YOLO series [1,20,21], which enhances small object detection by adding dedicated detection heads, directly introducing additional heads in DETR-based models significantly increases memory consumption and degrades inference efficiency. Moreover, conventional strided convolutions or aggressive downsampling operations tend to discard fine-grained details and introduce noise—particularly detrimental for small object representation.

To address these issues, PF-DETR introduces a hierarchical unidirectional fusion strategy within its Pre-Encoding Fusion Module. First, a multi-branch feature refinement attention module is applied to low-level features (e.g., P4) to enhance edge and texture details while suppressing irrelevant background activations.

These refined features are then passed through a C3K3 module, which builds upon the lightweight C3K structure [8,20,29] by integrating a 3×3 convolution with stride 2. The C3K component facilitates cross-stage feature interaction, while the subsequent mild downsampling preserves spatial integrity and reduces the risk of information loss typically associated with large-stride operations.

Finally, the downsampled features are fused with higher-level features (e.g., P16 and P32) via point-wise addition rather than channel concatenation, effectively preserving multi-scale consistency while reducing computational overhead. As illustrated in Fig. 2, this fusion design ensures that small-object features are continuously preserved and propagated across scales. These enriched representations are subsequently passed to the hybrid fusion encoder, providing semantically rich and detail-preserving multi-scale inputs for robust object detection.

As shown in Fig. 3, before using the PEFF module, as depicted in Fig. 3(b), the density distribution of the heatmap was concentrated and detailed information was obscured. After using the module, as shown in Fig. 3(c), the detailed information became richer and the noise was reduced, demonstrating the effectiveness of this module.

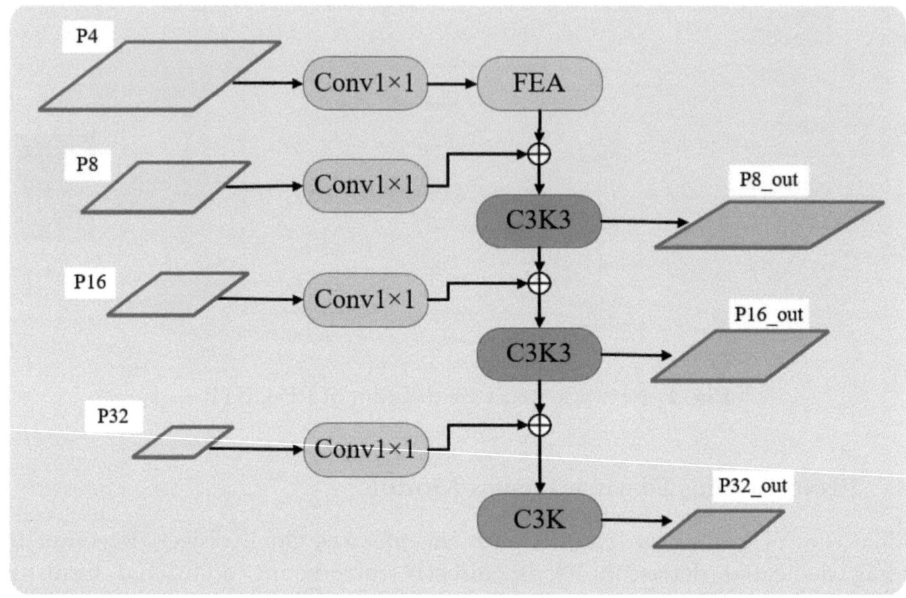

Fig. 2. Network structure diagram of PEFF.

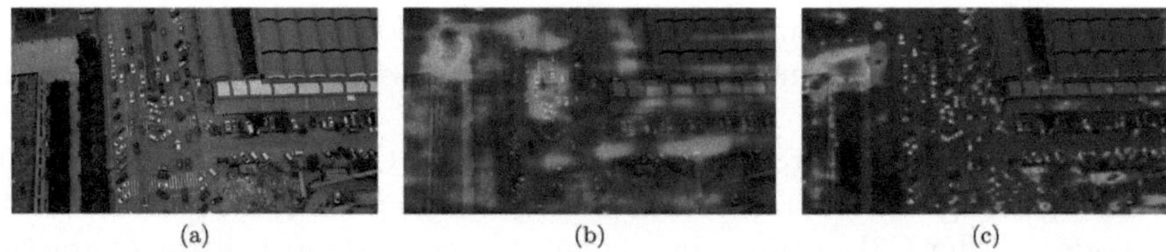

Fig. 3. The comparison of heatmaps before and after processing by the PDFF module, (a) represents the original image, (b) represents the heatmap without PDFF module processing, (c) represents the heatmap processed by the PDFF module.

2.2 Feature Enhancement Attention Module

The Feature Refinement Attention Module addresses the challenges of insufficient feature representation and background noise in small-object detection with a lightweight design, enhancing feature representation through a fusion of multi-branch multi-scale feature extraction and channel-spatial attention mechanisms. It includes three core branches: Branch 1 uses two convolutional layers with a stride of 1 and kernel sizes of 3×3 and 1×1 to extract local features and adjust channel dimensions; Branch 2 employs an asymmetric convolutional path with four layers (stride = 1, kernels = 3×1, 1×3, and standard 1×1) to capture horizontal and vertical features for adaptability to irregular objects; Branch 3 combines 3×3, 1×1, 3×1, and 1×3 convolutions (four layers, stride=1) to supplement multi-scale feature information. After concatenating the output feature maps of the three branches, their intensities are adjusted via scale coefficients, added to the original features through residual connections, and activated by ReLU [8] to generate discriminative representations. Additionally, a spatial-channel attention mechanism is introduced for secondary enhancement: channel-wise global pooling and shared MLP generate attention weights to capture semantic information, while spatial pooling and convolution focus on target positions, jointly enhancing small-object features, suppressing noise, and synergizing with the feature refinement module to improve detail-capturing ability efficiently under lightweight constraints.

As shown in Fig. 4, after passing through the FEA module, the input feature map further strengthens the target features and suppresses background interference, demonstrating the effectiveness of the module.

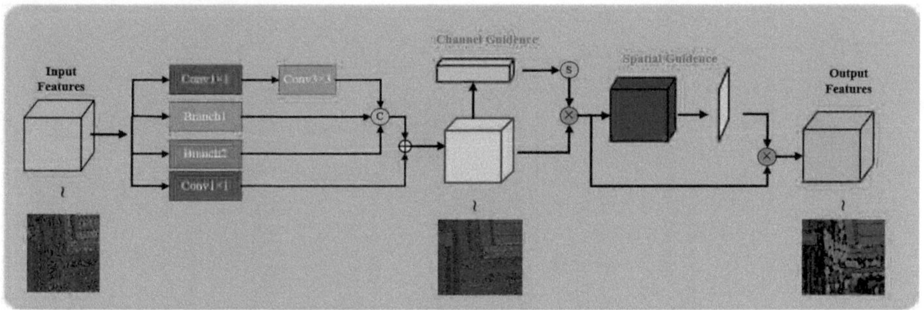

Fig. 4. Network structure model of FEA.

2.3   Haar Wavelet Downsampling Fusion Module

To effectively address the issue of information loss in small targets caused by traditional downsampling methods or strided convolutions, this paper proposes a novel Haar Wavelet Downsampling Module (HWD) [23]. Unlike conventional approaches that may discard critical spatial details during downsampling, the HWD module leverages frequency domain analysis to decompose feature maps into multiple components, thereby preserving both global semantic information and local detailed features.

As illustrated in Fig. 5, the input feature map with spatial dimensions of $H \times W \times C$ is first processed through the Haar Wavelet Transform (HWT) module. This operation decomposes the feature map into four sub-bands: one low-frequency component (LL), which captures the coarse approximation of the original signal, and three high-frequency components—horizontal (LH), vertical (HL), and diagonal (HH)—which retain detailed edge and texture information in different orientations. Such multi-directional decomposition enables the module to comprehensively capture multi-scale structural information within the feature map.

$$(y_L, y_{HL}, y_{LH}, y_{HH}) = \text{HWT}(x) \quad x \in \mathbb{R}^{H \times W \times C} \tag{1}$$

$$x' = \text{CBR}(\text{Concat}(y_L, y_{HL}, y_{LH}, y_{HH})) \quad x' \in \mathbb{R}^{\frac{H}{2} \times \frac{W}{2} \times C_{out}} \tag{2}$$

Subsequently, As shown in Eq. 1 and Eq. 2 above,these four components are concatenated along the channel dimension to form a fused feature representation. Finally, a Convolution-Batch Normalization-ReLU (CBR) [5,18] block is applied to refine the features and reduce the number of channels, yielding the final downsampled feature map. This design not only achieves effective spatial downsampling but also significantly mitigates the loss of critical information, especially for small objects.

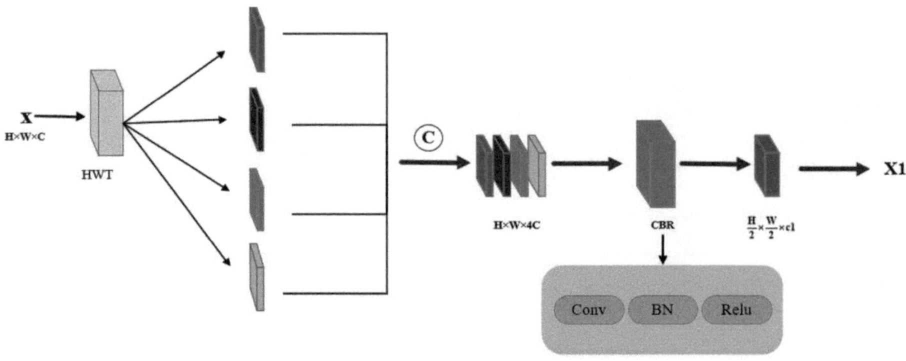

Fig. 5. Network structure diagram of HWD.

2.4   The Optimization Of Loss Functions

In the task of object detection, to improve the localization accuracy and convergence efficiency of the model for small objects, this study replaces the original GIoU [17] loss function with the EIoU loss function. The EIoU loss explicitly decomposes the loss into three independent components, which enables fine-grained optimization of bounding box geometry:

1. **Base term**: $1 - \text{IoU}$ (traditional IoU loss), which measures the overlap between the predicted and ground-truth boxes;

2. **Center distance term**: $\dfrac{\rho^2(\mathbf{b}_{\mathrm{gt}}, \mathbf{b}_{\mathrm{pred}})}{c^2}$ (normalized center distance), which penalizes the displacement of the predicted box's center from the ground-truth center, with c denoting the diagonal length of the smallest enclosing rectangle of the two boxes;

3. **Aspect ratio term**: $\dfrac{\rho^2(w_{\mathrm{gt}}, w_{\mathrm{pred}})}{c_w^2} + \dfrac{\rho^2(h_{\mathrm{gt}}, h_{\mathrm{pred}})}{c_h^2}$ (decoupled aspect ratio constraint), which separately constrains the width and height differences between the predicted and ground-truth boxes, where c_w and c_h represent the width and height of the smallest enclosing rectangle.

By introducing these decompositions, EIoU effectively addresses the slow optimization issue of GIoU under box inclusion scenarios and enhances the model's capability to model object shapes, particularly for small objects with high aspect ratio variation. The complete EIoU loss is shown in Eq. 1.

$$L_{\mathrm{EIoU}} = 1 - \mathrm{IoU} + \frac{\rho^2(\mathbf{b}_{\mathrm{gt}}, \mathbf{b}_{\mathrm{pred}})}{c^2} + \frac{\rho^2(w_{\mathrm{gt}}, w_{\mathrm{pred}})}{c_w^2} + \frac{\rho^2(h_{\mathrm{gt}}, h_{\mathrm{pred}})}{c_h^2} \qquad (3)$$

3   Experiments and Analysis

3.1   Implementation Details

All experiments are conducted on 4 NVIDIA GeForce RTX 3080 GPUs with CUDA 11.6, using Python 3.10.8 and PyTorch 2.0.1. To leverage multi-scale training, image sizes are dynamically adjusted rather than fixed; before model input, images undergo resizing with flexible dimensions to capture multi-scale features. The training and test batch sizes are both set to 8, and the AdamW optimizer is used with a weight decay of 0.0001, enabling efficient training across varying input resolutions.

3.2   Introduction to Datasets

This paper used three publicly available drone target detection datasets: Vis-Drone2019, CODrone, and HazyDet for experiments.

VisDrone2019. VisDrone2019 [3] is a large drone - perspective dataset open - sourced by Tianjin University and other teams, covering cities, rural areas, pedestrians, vehicles, and scenes of different densities. Its training set has 6,471 images, validation set 548 images, and test set 1,610 images.

HazyDet. HazyDet [4] is a dataset collected by teams including the Army Engineering University of the Chinese People's Liberation Army, containing 383,000 real - world instances. It uses a large amount of annotated data under normal weather conditions and simulates and generates drone detection datasets under hazy conditions via the Atmospheric Scattering Model (ASM).

CODrone. CODrone [24] is a drone-based object detection dataset that increases task difficulty through multi-dimensional variations, including six perspective combinations of three flight altitudes (30 m, 60 m, and 100 m) and two camera angles (30° tilt and 90° vertical top-down). The dataset covers diverse environments such as parks, urban streets, and rural roads under varying lighting and weather conditions. It employs a high-resolution 3840×2160 pixel onboard camera to ensure small-object detection precision, extends target categories beyond vehicle-centric types to richer ones, and provides annotations of flight altitude and camera angle to support pose-aware research. Comprising 5,002 training images, 2,000 validation images, and 3,002 test images, CODrone addresses real-world complexities to advance aerial perception tasks.

3.3 Evaluation Metrics

This paper comprehensively evaluates the detection performance of the algorithm using Average Precision (AP). According to the classification criteria of the COCO dataset [11], objects with an area smaller than 32×32 pixels are defined as small objects, with their average precision denoted as APs; objects with an area between 32×32 and 64×64 pixels are medium objects (average precision: APm); and objects with an area larger than 64×64 pixels are large objects (average precision: APl). All results are evaluated using the standard COCO Average Precision (AP) metrics. The relevant formulas are as follows:

$$P = \frac{TP}{TP + FP} \tag{4}$$

$$R = \frac{TP}{TP + FN} \tag{5}$$

$$AP = \int_0^1 P(R)\, dR \tag{6}$$

3.4 Quantitative Analysis

As shown in Table 1, the baseline model D-Fine demonstrates excellent performance, achieving an AP50 of 38.6% and an AP of 22.1% on the VisDrone2019 dataset. In comparison, classical methods such as YOLOv9 and YOLOv8 yield relatively lower results in these metrics. Among the YOLO series, YOLOv11 performs the best but still lags behind the baseline D-Fine. Another emerging method from the DETR series, DEIM, also achieves high detection accuracy, with an AP50 of 37.9% and an AP of 21.8% on the VisDrone2019 dataset.

The proposed method, PF-DETR, exhibits superior overall performance across all key metrics. On the VisDrone2019 dataset, PF-DETR achieves an AP50 of 40.6% and an AP of 23.6%, outperforming all other models. In small-object detection, PF-DETR achieves an AP of 13.8%, slightly lower than the PANet method but significantly better than other series of models. This highlights the remarkable advantage of the proposed method in UAV-based object detection tasks (Fig. 6).

As shown in Fig. 7, we selected three different scenarios for visualization. By comparing with YOLOv9, YOLOv11, and the baseline model, our model demonstrates superior performance in scenarios with occlusions and dense objects.

Table 1. Detection results on the VisDrone2019 test set.

Model	AP	AP_{50}	AP_{75}	AP_s	AP_m	AP_l
YOLOv8s [25]	0.181	0.318	0.183	0.081	0.280	0.411
YOLOv9s [8]	0.187	0.329	0.188	0.084	0.293	0.470
YOLOv10s [20]	0.182	0.323	0.184	0.085	0.282	0.417
YOLOv11s [7]	0.188	0.330	0.190	0.086	0.287	0.460
YOLOv11n [7]	0.154	0.280	0.151	0.064	0.239	0.355
RetinaNet [10]	0.176	0.296	0.181	0.081	0.294	0.368
YOLOF [1]	0.151	0.263	0.154	0.061	0.252	0.324
PANet [12]	0.230	0.381	0.242	**0.139**	0.346	0.390
RT-DETR-R18 [28]	0.206	0.371	0.205	0.113	0.303	0.424
EF-DETR [2]	0.132	0.242	0.123	0.081	0.184	0.357
DEIM [6]	0.218	0.379	0.218	0.122	0.320	0.412
D-Fine [14]	0.221	0.386	0.220	0.122	0.323	0.431
PF-DETR(Ours)	**0.236**	**0.406**	**0.239**	0.138	**0.338**	**0.488**

3.5 Generalization Experiment

In this section, we empirically demonstrate the effectiveness of our methodology on two additional datasets, HayDet and CODrone, and rigorously verify its flexibility in adapting to diverse detection scenarios. As shown in Table 2, our PF-DETR achieves state-of-the-art performance on the HayDet test set with 61.2% AP, demonstrating clear improvements over existing methods. The model shows a 1.6% higher AP than D-Fine, a 3.0% improvement over YOLOv11m, and a 3.9% advantage compared to YOLOv9m.

Table 2. Detection results on the HayDet test set.

Model	AP	AP_{50}	AP_{75}	AP_s	AP_m	AP_l
YOLOv8s	0.542	0.769	0.632	0.196	0.549	0.732
YOLOv9s	0.543	0.773	0.631	0.188	0.554	0.739
YOLOv8m	0.565	0.790	0.661	0.230	0.578	0.747
YOLOv9m	0.573	0.799	0.667	0.236	0.588	0.757
YOLOv10m	0.568	0.787	0.663	0.233	0.583	0.748
YOLOv11m	0.582	0.805	0.680	0.252	0.594	0.762
D-Fine	0.596	0.800	0.683	0.264	0.602	0.775
PF-DETR(Ours)	**0.612**	**0.811**	**0.703**	**0.292**	**0.623**	0.773

For small object detection, PF-DETR achieves 29.2% APs, outperforming D-Fine by 2.8% and YOLOv11m by 4.0%. In medium object detection, the

Fig. 6. Visual comparison of detection results across four methods.

model maintains a 2.1% superiority over D-Fine, while showing comparable performance in large object detection while still exceeding all YOLO variants.

These results highlight PF-DETR's balanced detection capability across all object scales, with particularly strong performance in small object detection. The comprehensive improvements validate our model's effectiveness for diverse detection scenarios.

Table 3. Detection results on the CODrone test set.

Model	AP	AP_{50}	AP_{75}	AP_s	AP_m	AP_l
YOLOv9m	0.142	0.284	0.127	0.018	0.133	0.257
YOLOv10m	0.160	0.312	0.145	0.025	0.150	0.277
YOLOv11s	0.144	0.292	0.127	0.019	0.133	0.264
RT-DETR	0.167	0.334	0.151	0.032	0.160	0.287
DEIM	0.168	0.326	0.154	0.038	0.168	0.279
D-Fine	0.180	0.349	0.166	0.037	0.174	0.304
PF-DETR	**0.191**	**0.368**	**0.177**	**0.047**	**0.189**	**0.303**

As shown in Table 3, when compared with DEIM, a model specifically optimized for DETR-based architectures, PF-DETR demonstrates significant improvements. It achieves a 0.9% increase in APs(small objects)and a 2.3% enhancement in overall AP, highlighting its superior capability in capturing fine-grained details of small targets.In benchmarks against the latest YOLO-series models, PF-DETR exhibits distinct advantages. It outperforms YOLOv10m by

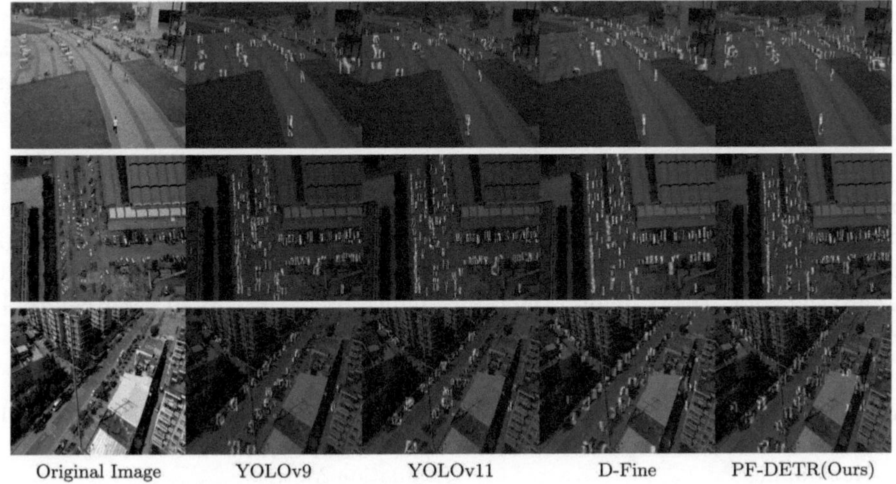

Fig. 7. Comparison of heatmaps from different models.

3.1% in AP and surpasses YOLOv9m by 4.7% in AP, underscoring its effectiveness in multi-scale object representation. Notably, when evaluated against the Transformer-based RT-DETR, PF-DETR achieves a 2.4% improvement in AP and a 3.4% boost in AP50. These results rigorously validate the efficacy of PF-DETR's architectural innovations for object detection tasks in complex aerial scenarios.

3.6 Ablation Experiments

In this study, D-Fine was used as the baseline model, and a series of ablation experiments were conducted on the VisDrone2019 dataset to validate the effectiveness of the proposed improvements. First, EIoU [26] and PEFF were gradually introduced, and the performance changes were evaluated. Subsequently, innovative techniques such as the FEA model and the HWD module were gradually integrated to further enhance the model's performance. (In Table 4, "✓" indicates whether a module is activated, showing how each component contributes to performance improvement.).

Using the VisDrone2019 test set as the benchmark, the study systematically evaluated the independent contributions of key components in the PF-DETR model. The results show that the baseline D-Fine achieved an AP of 22.1% and an AP50 of 38.6%. After introducing the PEFF module combined with EIoU [26], the model's accuracy increased to 23.3%, the AP50 reached 40.4%, and the AP for small objects increased to 13.3%. This significant improvement is attributed to the efficient cross-scale feature fusion performed by the Pre-Encoding Feature Fusion module (PEFF).

When the HWFM module was subsequently introduced, the model's AP was 22.8% and the AP50 was 39.4%, which was inferior to the performance when only the PEFF module was introduced, possibly due to excessive noise. Finally, based on the original three modules, the Feature Refinement Attention module (FEA) was introduced, resulting in the highest overall model accuracy, with an AP of 23.6%, an AP50 of 40.6%, and an AP for large objects reaching 48.8%, representing a substantial increase.

These findings fully demonstrate that the innovative components do not function in isolation. The combination of the PEFF module and EIoU lays the foundation, while the FEA module further exploits the model's potential through refined feature processing. The synergy and complementarity among these modules are the core drivers behind the performance breakthrough of the PF-DETR model.

Table 4. Comprehensive ablation study on VisDrone test set (optimal results in bold)

No.	Modules					Evaluation Metrics					
	Baseline	EIOU	PEFF	HWFM	FEA	AP	AP_{50}	AP_{75}	AP_s	AP_m	AP_l
1	✓					0.221	0.386	0.220	0.122	0.323	0.431
2	✓	✓				0.218	0.381	0.219	0.119	0.320	0.463
3	✓	✓	✓			0.233	0.404	0.233	0.133	0.336	0.441
4	✓	✓	✓	✓		0.228	0.394	0.228	0.127	0.330	0.431
5	✓	✓	✓	✓	✓	**0.236**	**0.406**	**0.239**	**0.138**	**0.338**	**0.488**

4　Conclusion

To address the challenges of weak small-target features and complex background interference in UAV object detection, this paper proposed the PF-DETR algorithm based on D-Fine model. The solution incorporated three key technical contributions: the PEFF module for early small-target feature capture, the FRA module for background noise filtering and feature refinement, and the HWFM with HWD to reduce information loss during fusion. Extensive experiments on three UAV datasets verified that the proposed method outperforms existing state-of-the-art approaches in both detection accuracy and recall rate, demonstrating its effectiveness and robustness for UAV-based detection tasks. These results suggest that PF-DETR could serve as a valuable solution for practical UAV applications requiring reliable small-target detection.

Acknowledgments. This work is partially supported by Natural Science Foundation of Hebei F2024205028, the Central Guidance on Local Science and Technology Development Fund of Hebei Province (236Z0102G, 226Z1808G), the Science Foundation of Hebei Normal University (L2024ZD15, L2024J01, L2022B22).

Disclosure of Interests. The authors declare no competing interests.

References

1. Chen, Q., Wang, Y., Yang, T., Zhang, X., Cheng, J., Sun, J.: You only look one-level feature. In: Proceedings of the IEEE Conference on Computer Vision and Pattern Recognition (CVPR), pp. 13039–13048, Nashville, TN, USA (2021)
2. Cheng, S., et al.: EF-DETR: a lightweight transformer-based object detector with an encoder-free neck. IEEE Trans. Ind. Inf. **20**(11), 12994–13002 (2024). https://doi.org/10.1109/TII.2024.3431044
3. Du, D., et al.: VisDrone-det2019: the vision meets drone object detection in image challenge results. In: Proceedings of the IEEE/CVF International Conference on Computer Vision Workshops (ICCVW), pp. 213–226, Seattle, WA, USA (2019)
4. Feng, C., et al.: HAZYDET: open-source benchmark for drone-view object detection with depth-cues in hazy scenes. arXiv preprint arXiv:2409.19833 (2024). https://arxiv.org/abs/2409.19833
5. Ghiasi, G., Lin, T.-Y., Le, Q.V.: NAS-FPN: learning scalable feature pyramid architecture for object detection. In: Proceedings of the IEEE/CVF Conference on Computer Vision and Pattern Recognition (CVPR), pp. 7036–7045, Long Beach, CA, USA (2019). Computer Vision Foundation
6. Huang, S., Lu, Z., Cun, X., Yu, Y., Zhou, X., Shen, X.: DEIM: DETR with improved matching for fast convergence. In: Proceedings of the IEEE/CVF Conference on Computer Vision and Pattern Recognition (CVPR), Nashville, TN, USA, June 11–15 2025 (2025)
7. Khanam, R., Hussain, M.: YOLOv11: an overview of the key architectural enhancements. arXiv preprint arXiv:2410.17725 (2024)
8. Li, C., et al.: YOLOv6: a single-stage object detection framework for industrial applications. arXiv preprint arXiv:2209.02976 (2022)
9. Li, F., Zhang, H., Liu, S., Guo, J., Ni, L.M., Zhang, L.: DN-DETR: accelerate DETR training by introducing query denoising (2022)
10. Lin, T.Y., Goyal, P., Girshick, R., He, K., Dollár, P.: Focal loss for dense object detection. arXiv preprint arXiv:1708.02002 (2018)
11. Lin, T.Y., et al.: Microsoft COCO: common objects in context. arXiv preprint arXiv:1405.0312 (2015)
12. Liu, S., Qi, L., Qin, H., Shi, J., Jia, J.: Path aggregation network for instance segmentation. arXiv preprint arXiv:1803.01534 (2018)
13. W. Liu, D. Anguelov, D. Erhan, C. Szegedy, S. Reed, C.-Y. Fu, and A. C. Berg. *SSD: Single Shot MultiBox Detector*, pages 21–37. Springer International Publishing, 2016. Lecture Notes in Computer Science, vol 9905
14. Peng, Y., Li, H., Wu, P., Zhang, Y., Sun, X., Wu, F.: D-FINE: redefine regression task in DETRS as fine-grained distribution refinement. arXiv preprint arXiv:2410.13842 (2024)
15. Ren, S., He, K., Girshick, R., Sun, J.: Faster R-CNN: towards real-time object detection with region proposal networks. In: Advances in Neural Information Processing Systems (NeurIPS), vol. 28, pp. 91–99 (2015)
16. Ren, S., He, K., Girshick, R., Sun, J.: Faster R-CNN: towards real-time object detection with region proposal networks. arXiv preprint arXiv:1506.01497 (2016)
17. Rezatofighi, H., Tsoi, N., Gwak, J., Sadeghian, A., Reid, I., Savarese, S.: Generalized intersection over union: a metric and a loss for bounding box regression. arXiv preprint arXiv:1902.09630 (2019)
18. Song, J., et al.: Boundary-aware feature fusion with dual-stream attention for remote sensing small object detection. IEEE Trans. Geosci. Remote Sens. **63**(5600213), 1–13 (2025)

19. Tan, M., Pang, R., Le, Q.V.: EfficientDet: scalable and efficient object detection. In: Proceedings of the IEEE/CVF Conference on Computer Vision and Pattern Recognition (CVPR), pp. 10781–10790 (2020)
20. Wang, A., et al.: YOLOv10: real-time end-to-end object detection. arXiv preprint arXiv:2405.14458 (2024)
21. Wang, C.Y., Bochkovskiy, A., Liao, H.Y.M.: YOLOv7: trainable bag-of-freebies sets new state-of-the-art for real-time object detectors. In: Proceedings of the Computer Vision and Pattern Recognition (CVPR), pp. 7464–7475, Vancouver, BC, Canada, June 17–24 2023 (2023)
22. Wei, C., Wang, W.: RFAG-YOLO: a receptive field attention-guided yolo network for small-object detection in UAV images. Sensors **25**(7), 2193 (2025)
23. Xu, G., Liao, W., Zhang, X., Li, C., He, X., Wu, X.: HAAR wavelet downsampling: a simple but effective downsampling module for semantic segmentation. Pattern Recogn. **143**, 109819 (2023)
24. Ye, K., Tang, H., Liu, B., Dai, P., Cao, L., Ji, R.: More clear, more flexible, more precise: a comprehensive oriented object detection benchmark for UAV. arXiv preprint arXiv:2504.20032 (2025)
25. Zeng, S., Yang, W., Jiao, Y.: SCA-YOLO: a new small object detection model for UAV images. Vis. Comput. **40**, 1787–1803 (2024)
26. Zhang, Y.-F., Ren, W., Zhang, Z., Jia, Z., Wang, L., Tan, T.: Focal and efficient IOU loss for accurate bounding box regression. arXiv preprint arXiv:2101.08158 (2022)
27. Zhao, Y., et al.: DETRS beat YOLOs on real-time object detection. In: Proceedings of the IEEE/CVF Conference on Computer Vision and Pattern Recognition (CVPR), pp. 16965–16974, Seattle, WA, USA (2024)
28. Zhao, Y., et al.: DETRs beat YOLOs on real-time object detection. arXiv preprint arXiv:2304.08069, https://arxiv.org/abs/2304.08069 (2024)
29. Zhu, X., Lyu, S., Wang, X., Zhao, Q.: TPH-YOLOv5: improved YOLOv5 based on transformer prediction head for object detection on drone-captured scenarios. In: Proceedings of the International Conference on Computer Vision (ICCV), pp. 2778–2788, Montreal, QC, Canada, October 10–17 2021 (2021)
30. Zhu, X., Su, W., Lu, L., Li, B., Wang, X., Dai, J.: Deformable DETR: deformable transformers for end-to-end object detection. arXiv preprint arXiv:2010.04159 (2021)

Selective Labeling for 3D Shape Label Transfer Based on Local-Global Features

Zhigeng Pan[1,2,3(✉)], Xin Zheng[1], Nenglun Chen[1], and Rongjin Zou[2]

[1] Nanjing University of Information Science and Technology, Nanjing, China
zgpan@nuist.edu.cn
[2] AI Lab, Nanjing MUST Science and Technology Research Institute, Nanjing, China
[3] Jiangsu Provincial Key Laboratory of Culture and Tourism for Research on the Application Technology of Metaverse Cultural Tourism Scenarios, Nanjing, China

Abstract. For deep learning models, the selection of samples for annotation has a profound impact on the training results, particularly when working with limited annotation budgets. This problem is challenging and underexplored. Our goal is to identify the most important data for annotation that can be used for transferring shape labels for 3D point clouds. Intuitively, the selected 3D shapes should be representative and cover local and global shape structure variations. Towards this goal, we introduce a stochastic optimization strategy that uses both local and global features to select the most relevant 3D shapes for annotation. Our method is effective, extensive experiments have demonstrated that our method can achieve superior performance compared with the state-of-the-art methods on two 3D shape label transfer tasks, namely 3D shape segmentation label transfer and key point transfer.

Keywords: Selective labeling · Label transfer · 3d point cloud · Shape Segmentation · Key Point

1 Introduction

Deep learning technology has advanced 3D shape research in the past decade, achieving great success in tasks such as classification, segmentation, and label transfer, etc. However, due to the complex three-dimensional structure of 3D shapes, it is time-consuming and laborious to annotate 3D shapes. There exist a lot of works focusing on learning with a small amount of labeled data, including semi-supervised learning and few-shot learning. The information of labels are either transferred implicitly during training or explicitly during inference. Despite its benefits, learning with a small amount of labeled data poses a challenge that has received little attention: the selection of different data for labeling will have a great impact on the training results. For 3D shapes, due to the complexity of 3D shape structures, how to select appropriate shape for labeling is a complex problem, which is challenge and under explored.

As illustrated in Fig. 1, our work mainly focuses on selecting the most worthy 3D shapes for annotation within the scenario of 3D shape label transfer. 3d shape label transfer uses a self-supervised model to extract features of 3d

Z. Lin et al. (Eds.): ICIG 2025, LNCS 16161, pp. 265–277, 2026.
https://doi.org/10.1007/978-981-95-3398-5_22

shapes, and uses the relative position of 3D shape in the feature space to transfer labels to unlabeled 3d shapes. Compared with the pretrain-finetune method, label transfer does not require any additional training and can be applied to different tasks. As shown in Fig. 1(b), different label sources will produce different transfer results, and this process does not require any fine-tuning.

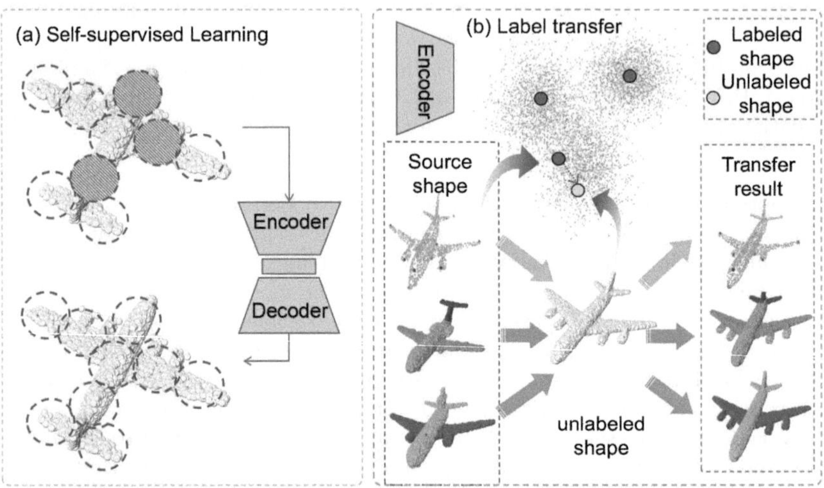

Fig. 1. Flow of 3D shape label transfer: (a) 3D shape self-supervised Learning; (b) Label Transfer. This process utilizes the semantic relations between 3D shapes, and can transfer any labels in different downstream tasks without fine-tuning.

For selecting the most worthy data to label, active learning [16] has provided a possible solution. However, active learning is not appropriate in our scenario due to the following reasons: Firstly, it requires a set of randomly sampled labeled data before the first training session, which is sample-inefficient. Secondly, active learning methods usually require multiple labeling and training rounds, which is tedious and labor-intensive, and is not suitable in the scenarios where labeling budget is limited. Besides, some researchers have also discussed this phenomenon in semi-supervised learning. Unsupervised Selective Labeling (USL) [17] selects data from self-supervised data sets based on data representativeness and diversity to annotate, thereby improving the performance of semi-supervised learning in many downstream tasks; Sample Choosing Policy (SCP) [14] selects the most valuable data from the data set to annotate, which can reduce the mean radial errors of the medical landmark detection task. However, none of these studies have delved into the issue of selective labeling for 3D shape label transfer.

To address the above-mentioned issues, we propose a framework for selecting the most important 3D shapes to annotation from a set of unlabeled 3D shapes. Intuitively, the selected samples should be representative and can cover different structure variations among all the 3D shapes. Unlike existing works

[17] which mainly use global features for selecting 3D shapes, in our work, we also take local features into consideration, as local features are also very important for label transfer tasks. To make the selected 3D shapes able to cover local and global structure variations, we propose a stochastic optimization strategy to select 3D shapes based on local and global features. Our method is simple and quite effective. Extensive experiments have verified the superiority of our proposed method. Our key contributions are summarized as follows:

- A novel framework for selecting the most worthy 3D shapes to label for 3D shape label transfer tasks based on local and global features.
- A novel stochastic optimization strategy for efficient and effective optimization of our proposed objective function based on local and global features.
- Our proposed method is beneficial for various downstream tasks, including segmentation label transfer and key point label transfer.

2   Related Work

2.1   Selective Labeling

Selective labeling is a task for selecting the most worthy data to annotate for deep learning g models. Wang et al. (2022) [17] proposed a novel sampling method called Unsupervised Selective Labeling (USL), which exploits the representativeness and diversity of samples from the unlabeled dataset to filter out suitable data to annotation. This approach enables better adaptation to various downstream tasks, enhancing the performance and stability of semi-supervised learning. Quan et al. (2021) [14] presented a novel sampling strategy called Sample Choosing Policy (SCP), which optimizes the selection process by evaluating the performance of multiple random sampling and choosing the most representative samples for annotation. In the context of few-shot learning medical landmark detection, this approach significantly enhances the accuracy of prediction results.

2.2   Activate Learning

Active learning, also known as query learning, is a technique that can select appropriate data from an unlabeled data set for annotation and training, in order to save labeling costs [16]. The workflow of active learning is as follows: Firstly, active learning selects a batch of data from the unlabeled data set for annotation [1,6,9]. Active learning can be divided into membership query synthesis [7], stream-based selective sampling [8], and pool-based sampling [10], where membership query synthesis can select suitable data for annotation directly from the sample space, while stream-based selective sampling evaluates all samples in sequential order, and pool-based selective sampling evaluates the entire dataset.

2.3   Self-supervised 3D Point Cloud Representation Learning

Self-supervised point cloud representation learning aims to capture the structural information of the data in point cloud format. Existing methods can be classified into the following categories: The first category uses reconstruction or generation, that learns the latent features by training a network with an encoder and a decoder to reconstruct or generate the input point clouds [4,5,19]. The second category is based on context-based methods, that use the contextual information of point clouds, including the similarity and spatial-temporal structure of the context, to learn the structural information of point clouds.

2.4   Label Transfer

Label transfer is a task for transferring labels from labeled source data to unlabeled targets. Douze et al. [3] used label transfer on image datasets and achieved few-shot learning on large-scale datasets. Suichan Li et al. [11] analyzed the clustering characteristics of the semantic space under unsupervised learning and proposed the Target-aware Unsupervised Pretraining method, which improved the performance of few-label transfer under unsupervised learning. For 3D shape label transfer, Chen et al. [2] proposed an unsupervised model based on the intrinsic structural information of 3D shape, which can extract local features of point clouds, and transfer 3D shape segmentation labels accordingly.

3   Method

3.1   Problem Statement

Given a dataset of unlabeled 3D shapes represented as $\mathbb{D} = \{x_i\}_{i=1}^{n}$, our objective is to automatically select and annotate s 3D shapes instances within a specified annotation budget. By considering the selected instances as the labeled source set $\mathbb{S} = \{s_i\}_{i=1}^{s}$, our goal is to achieve optimal performance in transferring 3D shape labels. This includes transferring segmentation labels and key points from the labeled instances to the remaining unlabeled shapes in the dataset.

3.2   3D Shape Label Transfer

3D shape label transfer tasks primarily focus on transferring point-wise labels from a set of labeled 3D point cloud shapes $\mathbb{S} = \{s_i\}_{i=1}^{s}$ to a set of unlabeled ones $\mathbb{U} = \{u_i\}_{i=1}^{u}$. The label transfer process relies on establishing point-wise correspondences between the source and target 3D shapes. These correspondences are induced using self-supervised pre-trained point cloud representations [2,13,15]. It is important to note that in our work, we do not require manual annotations during the training phase, and it enables the transfer of arbitrary labels. To transfer labels between 3D shapes, we use a 3D self-supervised model to embed shapes and generate a feature vector for each point. Then, the similarity between the feature vectors is utilized to transfer the labels corresponding to the points with the highest similarity to the target shape. Figure 3 gives an illustration of 3D shape label transfer tasks. In 3D shape segmentation label transfer task, the segmentation label of a specific point on a target shape is transferred from the point on source shapes whose feature is the most similar to the target point. To

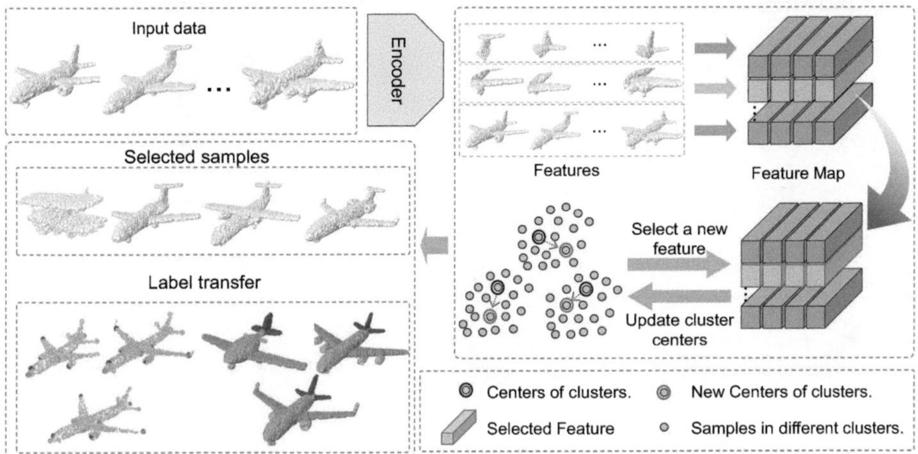

Fig. 2. Pipeline of our method: Given a set of unlabeled 3D shapes, a pre-trained 3D shape encoder is first applied to extract local and global features. Then, a stochastic optimization strategy is used to choose the 3D shapes for annotation.

identify the locations of the key points on a target shape in 3D key points label transfer task, we first find the source shape from the labeled set whose feature is the most similar with the target one and the key points are transferred according to the local feature similarity between source and target.

3.3 Objective Function

The problem of selective labeling for 3D shape label transfer tasks is challenging because we lack prior knowledge of the specific labels that need to be transferred before the selection process. To select the 3D point cloud shapes that will significantly benefit the label transfer tasks, our main focus is on choosing samples that are highly representative of the entire dataset. For label transfer tasks, both global and local features play crucial roles, making it essential for the selected samples to be both globally and locally representative. To assess the representativeness of a selected subset $\mathbb{S}$, we introduce an objective function denoted as L. This function calculates the similarity between each 3D shapes in the dataset $\mathbb{D}$ and the selected subset $\mathbb{S}$. It achieves this by evaluating the feature distances between their local and global features. A smaller value of the objective function L indicates a more effective representation of the dataset $\mathbb{D}$ by the subset $\mathbb{S}$. Here, we give the formula of our objective function:

$$L(\mathbb{S}, \mathbb{D}) = \lambda_g L_{global}(\mathbb{S}, \mathbb{D}) + \lambda_l L_{local}(\mathbb{S}, \mathbb{D}) \tag{1}$$

where λ_g and λ_l denote the weight of the corresponding terms. The global feature representativeness L_{global} of the selected 3D shapes can be defined as follows:

$$L_{\mathrm{global}} = \frac{1}{|\mathbb{D}|} \sum_{x_i \in \mathbb{D}} \left\| f^g(x_i) - f^g(s_k) \right\|^2 \tag{2}$$

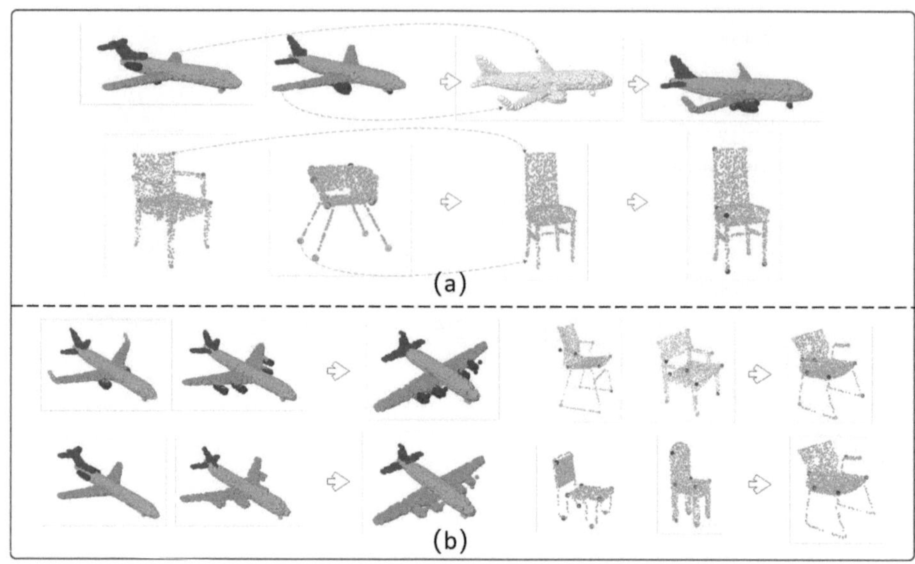

Fig. 3. Illustration of 3D shape label transfer tasks. (a) The label transfer tasks mainly aim at transferring labels from labeled source 3D shapes to unlabeled target ones based on point-wise correspondence. (b) Transferring labels from different source labeled data to the same target one will lead to different results.

where $s_k \in \mathbb{S}$ denotes the 3D shapes in the selected subset $\mathbb{S}$ which is closest to x_i in global feature space. $f^g(s_k)$ and $f^g(x_i)$ are the global feature vectors of s_k and x_i respectively. $|\mathbb{D}|$ denotes the size of the dataset $\mathbb{D}$. Assuming that for each 3D shape, we extract m local features using pre-trained point cloud encoders. The local feature representativeness L_{local} of the selected shapes are defined as:

$$L_{\text{local}} = \frac{1}{|\mathbb{D}| \times m} \sum_{x_i \in \mathbb{D}} \sum_{j=1}^{m} \left\| f_j^l(x_i) - f_j^l(s_k) \right\|^2 \tag{3}$$

where $s_k \in \mathbb{S}$ denotes the 3D shapes in $\mathbb{S}$ which is closest to x_i in local feature space. $f_j^l(s_k)$ and $f_j^l(x_i)$ are the jth local feature vectors of s_k and x_i respectively, and m denotes the number of local feature points on each 3D shape. The above optimization is of combinatorial nature, involving a vast number of possible combinations, which can become extremely challenging to solve in practice. In the following (Sect. 3.4), we will provide our stochastic optimization strategy for solving the above optimization problem approximately.

3.4   Stochastic Optimization Based on Local and Global Features

We propose a stochastic optimization strategy to approximately solve the optimization problem that is mentioned above. Generally, given a collection of feature vectors that from the same feature space, the representativeness of the feature vectors can be evaluated by applying a clustering algorithm, like k-means, on the feature space. And the feature vectors that belong to the cluster centers are usually more representative than others. Unlike previous works, we take into account the feature representativeness of both global and local features. And, we cannot directly apply the clustering method on both global and local features. Inspired by [12], we propose a stochastic optimization strategy by randomly selecting and optimizing specific local or global features step by step.

Our method can be regarded as a variant of the k-means clustering method. For 3D shape data x_i, we have $m + 1$ features $\{f_j(x_i)\}_{j=1}^{m+1}$, consisting of one global feature and m local features. Given a collection of unlabeled 3D point clouds $\mathbb{D}$ and an annotation budget s, we initially select s 3D shapes randomly as the initial cluster centers and compute the initial score based on Eq. 1. Subsequently, we apply random feature selection and update the cluster centers iteratively. We randomly pick a feature in each iteration t, for example, the jth feature $f_j(x_i)$ of each 3D shape x_i. Then, similar to the k-means method, we update the cluster centers using the following steps:

(1) For each 3D shape x_i, calculate its distance to each of the s cluster centers according to their jth features. And assign each 3D shape to the cluster whose cluster center is closest to it.
(2) Estimate the new cluster center for each cluster. And the new cluster center is the 3D shape with the minimum distance to the mean of that cluster.
(3) Calculate the score by substituting the cluster centers into Eq. 1, and update the cluster centers if the current score is smaller than previous ones.

The above steps are applied iteratively until convergence. And the pseudo code is shown in Algorithm 1. Note that, the calculation of Eq. 1 is time-consuming, and we apply the farthest point sampling algorithm on the corresponding feature space to accelerate the speed.

3.5   Overview of Our Method

Given a dataset of unlabeled 3D point cloud shapes. We first pre-train a point cloud encoder in a self-supervised learning way, and for each 3D shape, the pre-trained point cloud encoder is further used to extract the global feature together with a set of local features. And then we use a stochastic optimization strategy to select the 3D shapes for annotation with a given annotation budget by applying random feature selection and clustering center updating in an iterative manner. Finally, as shown in Fig. 2, the quality of the selected 3D shapes is evaluated by conducting label transfer tasks.

4   Experiment

4.1   Implementation Details

All experiments were conducted on a Linux server with an NVIDIA RTX 3090Ti GPU. For training self-supervised models [2,13,15], we used default parameters

---

Algorithm 1: Algorithmic Flow

Input: Dataset $\mathbb{D}$, number of target budget s, feature set
$F = \{f_j(x_i), x_i \subseteq \mathbb{D}, j \subseteq (1, t); f_j(x_i)$: the j-th feature of the i-th data point.$\}$, objective function L (see Equ. 1)

Output: *Labeled subset*

1 *best score* $\leftarrow$ Infinity
2 $\mathbb{C} \leftarrow$ Randomly select s 3D shapes from the $\mathbb{D}$ as the initial cluster centers.
3 **repeat**
4   **foreach** j *in range(1, t)* **do**
5       $\mathbb{T} \leftarrow$ Apply clustering on $\mathbb{D}$ based on the location of $\mathbb{C}$ using the j-th feature, and obtain the clusters.
6       $\mathbb{C}' \leftarrow$ Calculate the mean of each cluster, and return the 3D shapes closest to the mean as the new cluster center.
7   *score* $\leftarrow L(\mathbb{D}, \mathbb{C}')$
8   **if** *best score* $>$ *score* **then**
9 | *best score*, $\mathbb{C} \leftarrow$ *score*, $\mathbb{C}'$
10   **end**
11   **end**
12 **until** $\mathbb{C}$ *does not change*;
13 **return** $\mathbb{C}$;

---

that were used in their original papers. During optimization, we set the weights of the global and local terms in Eq. 1 to $\lambda_g = 1$ and $\lambda_l = 1$ respectively. For implementing Eq. 1, we use farthest point sample algorithm to sample 4096 features. In order to mitigate the impact of randomness during the experiments, each of the methods underwent testing across 10 randomized repetitions.

4.2 Self-supervised Learning Models

In our experiments, we opted for three self-supervised learning models designed for 3D point clouds, employing them as feature extractors. These models include Point-MAE [13], Point-GLR [15], and Structural-Points model [2]. Importantly, it's worth noting that we utilized the same feature extractor for both selective labeling and label transfer tasks.

4.3 Comparison Methods

In our experiment, we compared our method with four different selective labeling methods, including: random sampling, Sample Choosing Policy (SCP) [14], Unsupervised Selective Labeling (USL) [17], and K-means sampling. Random sampling selects 3D shapes randomly from the dataset for labeling. SCP first obtains 10,000 3D shapes group by sampling the dataset multiple times. After that, the similarity between all the samples in each group and the dataset is calculated and summed as the score of the group. USL selects 3D shapes that are both representative and diverse from the dataset. K-means sampling selects the 3D shapes closest to the cluster centers for labeling.

Table 1. Selective labeling results for segmentation label transfer task on ShapeNet part dataset under annotation budget 4, 6, and 10. We report the $mIOU$ with mean and standard deviation.

Model	Budget	Method				
		random	scp	usl	kmeans	ours
Structural-Point	4	72.77 ± 3.8	72.77 ± 3.6	74.62 ± 0.6	74.36 ± 0.8	**76.98 ± 0.5**
	6	74.22 ± 3.4	74.31 ± 2.8	76.65 ± 0.5	77.32 ± 0.7	**78.39 ± 0.7**
	10	75.82 ± 2.3	75.87 ± 2.0	77.60 ± 0.8	77.40 ± 1.2	**79.10 ± 0.0**
Point-MAE	4	71.99 ± 3.4	72.49 ± 3.5	72.22 ± 1.4	74.32 ± 1.1	**76.06 ± 0.7**
	6	73.42 ± 2.8	73.24 ± 2.8	72.68 ± 1.5	75.53 ± 1.7	**78.21 ± 0.9**
	10	74.15 ± 2.4	74.96 ± 2.3	74.58 ± 0.8	76.15 ± 2.1	**78.05 ± 1.0**
Point-GLR	4	65.61 ± 3.2	65.19 ± 3.5	67.99 ± 0.8	68.41 ± 1.5	**68.99 ± 0.6**
	6	67.20 ± 2.4	66.57 ± 0.2	69.98 ± 0.8	69.73 ± 1.5	**70.29 ± 0.6**
	10	68.88 ± 1.6	68.82 ± 1.3	71.14 ± 0.8	70.60 ± 1.5	**71.69 ± 0.7**

4.4 3D Segmentation Label Transfer

We evaluated the effectiveness of our proposed selective labeling method by checking the quality of the 3D shapes we selected for the 3D shape segmentation label transfer task. And labeling budgets 4, 6, and 10 were used in our experiments. We used the **ShapeNet part** [18] dataset for the shape segmentation label transfer. The dataset consists of 16 categories with different numbers of training samples for each category. In our experiment, we selected six categories that have more than 500 in 3D shapes, including airplane, car, chair, lamp, table, and guitar. To assess how well our method works, we tested selective labeling methods on the training sets under a transductive setting. The quality of the transferred labels was measured by mean Intersection over Union ($mIOU$).

Results. We present the quantitative results of the label transfer task for segmenting 3D shapes in Table 1. For each method, we provide both the mean and standard deviation values of $mIOU$ across 10 randomized repetitions. Our method clearly outperforms other existing state-of-the-art techniques.

4.5 3D Key Point Label Transfer

We further evaluated the effectiveness of our proposed selective labeling method by measuring the quality of the chosen 3D shape through the 3D shape key point label transfer task. Like the task of segmentation label transfer, labeling budgets 4, 6, and 10 were used. We used the **KeypointNet dataset**, which has 16 categories, each with a different number of training 3D shapes. We selected five categories that have more than 500 3D shapes, including airplane, car, chair,

Table 2. Selective labeling results for key point label transfer task on KeypointNet dataset under annotation budget 4, 6, and 10. The mean and standard deviation of the PCK (Percentage of Correct Keypoints) are reported.

Model	Budget	Method				
		random	scp	usl	kmeans	ours
Struct Point	4	73.96 ± 3.5	75.15 ± 2.1	75.32 ± 1.9	76.26 ± 1.8	**78.12 ± 1.4**
	6	71.79 ± 3.3	74.31 ± 2.8	75.94 ± 1.6	**77.31 ± 2.1**	77.21 ± 2.0
	10	73.96 ± 2.9	73.87 ± 2.6	77.11 ± 1.2	77.63 ± 2.7	**80.85 ± 1.7**
Point-MAE	4	74.44 ± 4.9	74.49 ± 4.1	77.73 ± 2.7	77.90 ± 2.6	**79.81 ± 2.0**
	6	73.95 ± 4.4	74.18 ± 2.8	**79.12 ± 2.0**	78.29 ± 1.9	78.57 ± 2.3
	10	76.75 ± 2.3	77.15 ± 1.3	79.74 ± 1.6	79.39 ± 2.5	**79.92 ± 2.1**
Point-GLR	4	55.86 ± 4.1	57.91 ± 4.0	61.47 ± 1.9	61.79 ± 1.0	**62.17 ± 1.6**
	6	57.92 ± 3.0	60.05 ± 2.1	61.46 ± 1.5	**63.98 ± 1.2**	62.67 ± 1.9
	10	60.04 ± 2.4	62.08 ± 2.0	62.52 ± 1.4	63.58 ± 1.8	**64.60 ± 1.2**

table, and guitar. Percentage of Correct Keypoints (PCK) was used for evaluating the quality of the transferred 3D key points, which refers to the percentage of all transferred keypoints that fall within a threshold of correct keypoints. Different selective labeling methods are compared in terms of their effects on the task of 3D shapes key points label transfer at a threshold of 0.1.

Results. Table 2 illustrates the quantitative results. For each method, we also report both the mean and standard deviation values of PCK (Percentage of Correct Keypoints) at thresholds 0.1 across 10 randomized repetitions. Our method clearly surpasses other methods in most scenarios.

Table 3. The result of considering both local and global information versus the result of considering only local or global information.

Model	Structural-Point			Point-MAE			Point-GLR		
Target budget	local + global	local	global	local + global	local	global	local + global	local	global
4	**76.98**	75.96	75.56	**76.06**	74.39	75.47	**68.99**	68.31	67.98
5	**77.89**	76.75	75.67	**77.24**	74.57	76.13	**70.05**	69.18	68.88
6	**78.39**	77.29	76.02	**78.21**	74.84	76.75	**70.29**	69.51	69.97
7	**77.97**	77.43	77.19	**77.68**	76.17	76.59	**70.06**	69.97	69.53
8	**78.24**	77.86	77.56	**77.97**	75.11	76.67	**70.42**	70.09	70.16
9	**78.02**	77.94	77.79	**77.24**	76.21	76.89	**70.90**	70.36	70.18
10	**78.88**	78.06	77.86	**78.05**	76.18	77.03	**71.69**	70.29	70.21
Average	**78.05**	77.33	76.81	**77.49**	75.35	76.50	**70.34**	69.67	69.55

4.6   Ablation Study

Effectiveness of Global and Local Features. Our stochastic optimization strategy can comprehensively consider the global and local information of shape data. In the experiment, we assume that global and local features play the same role in sampling. We performed experiments in the scenarios considering local information or global information only to test the effectiveness of global and local features. We keep the experiment settings the same as Sect. 4.4 by default. We present a summary of the results in Table 3. Compared to others, considering both global and local features leads to the best performance when testing with three feature extraction models.

Effectiveness of Farthest Point Sampling. As described in Sect. 3.4, the farthest point sampling algorithm is used to accelerate the speed in computing the score. Here we evaluated the effectiveness of the farthest point sampling strategy by comparing it with the random sampling strategy. Specifically, we used Point-MAE as the feature extractor and conducted the experiments with a labeling budget of 4. The comparison results are shown in Fig. 4. Using the farthest point sampling strategy will lead to significantly better performance than using the random sampling strategy. Note that, it can be extremely time-consuming without using any sampling strategy.

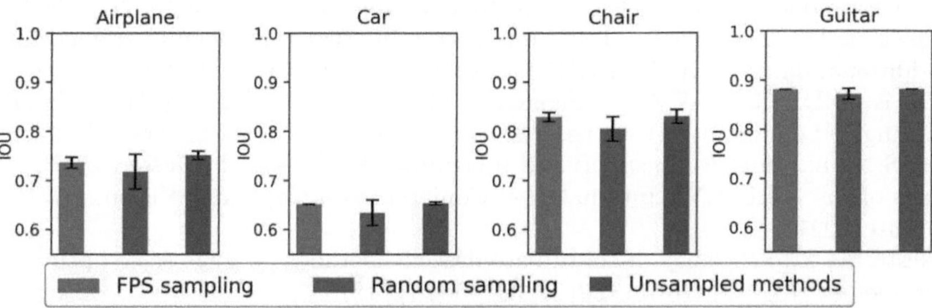

Fig. 4. Effectiveness of farthest point sampling(FPS). Different colors indicate different sampling strategies.

5   Conclusions

In this paper, we have studied the problem of selective labeling for 3D shape label transfer, and have proposed a stochastic optimization strategy that can select a subset from the unlabeled dataset for labeling and use it as the source of label transfer. Under different self-supervised point cloud feature extraction models, we have verified the superiority and reliability of our stochastic optimization strategy compared with other state-of-the-art methods for 3d shape segmentation label transfer and 3d shape key point label transfer tasks.

References

1. Beluch, W.H., Genewein, T., Nürnberger, A., Köhler, J.M.: The power of ensembles for active learning in image classification. In: Proceedings of the IEEE Conference on Computer Vision and Pattern Recognition, pp. 9368–9377 (2018)
2. Chen, N., et al.: Unsupervised learning of intrinsic structural representation points. In: Proceedings of the IEEE/CVF Conference on Computer Vision and Pattern Recognition, pp. 9121–9130 (2020)
3. Douze, M., Szlam, A., Hariharan, B., Jégou, H.: Low-shot learning with large-scale diffusion. In: Proceedings of the IEEE Conference on Computer Vision and Pattern Recognition, pp. 3349–3358 (2018)
4. Gao, X., Hu, W., Qi, G.J.: Graphter: unsupervised learning of graph transformation equivariant representations via auto-encoding node-wise transformations. In: Proceedings of the IEEE/CVF Conference on Computer Vision and Pattern Recognition, pp. 7163–7172 (2020)
5. Girdhar, R., Fouhey, D.F., Rodriguez, M., Gupta, A.: Learning a predictable and generative vector representation for objects. In: Leibe, B., Matas, J., Sebe, N., Welling, M. (eds.) ECCV 2016. LNCS, vol. 9910, pp. 484–499. Springer, Cham (2016). https://doi.org/10.1007/978-3-319-46466-4_29
6. Joshi, A.J., Porikli, F., Papanikolopoulos, N.: Multi-class active learning for image classification. In: 2009 IEEE Conference on Computer Vision and Pattern Recognition, pp. 2372–2379 (2009)
7. King, R.D., et al.: Functional genomic hypothesis generation and experimentation by a robot scientist. Nature **427**(6971), 247–252 (2004)
8. Krishnamurthy, V.: Algorithms for optimal scheduling and management of hidden Markov model sensors. IEEE Trans. Signal Process. **50**(6), 1382–1397 (2002)
9. Lewis, D.D.: A sequential algorithm for training text classifiers: Corrigendum and additional data. In: ACM SIGIR Forum, vol. 29, pp. 13–19 (1995)
10. Lewis, D.D., Gale, W.A.: A Sequential Algorithm for Training Text Classifiers. Springer, London (1994). https://doi.org/10.1007/978-1-4471-2099-5_1
11. Li, S., et al.: Improve unsupervised pretraining for few-label transfer. In: Proceedings of the IEEE/CVF International Conference on Computer Vision, pp. 10201–10210 (2021)
12. Nesterov, Y.: Efficiency of coordinate descent methods on huge-scale optimization problems. SIAM J. Optim. **22**(2), 341–362 (2012)
13. Pang, Y., Wang, W., Tay, F.E., Liu, W., Tian, Y., Yuan, L.: Masked autoencoders for point cloud self-supervised learning. In: Computer Vision–ECCV 2022: 17th European Conference, Tel Aviv, Israel, 23–27 October 2022, Proceedings, Part II, pp. 604–621 (2022)
14. Quan, Q., Yao, Q., Li, J., Zhou, S.K.: Which images to label for few-shot medical landmark detection? In: Proceedings of the IEEE/CVF Conference on Computer Vision and Pattern Recognition, pp. 20606–20616 (2022)
15. Rao, Y., Lu, J., Zhou, J.: Global-local bidirectional reasoning for unsupervised representation learning of 3D point clouds. In: Proceedings of the IEEE/CVF Conference on Computer Vision and Pattern Recognition, pp. 5376–5385 (2020)
16. Settles, B.: Active learning literature survey. University of Wisconsinmadison (2009)
17. Wang, X., Lian, L., Yu, S.X.: Unsupervised selective labeling for more effective semi-supervised learning. In: Avidan, S., Brostow, G., Cissé, M., Farinella, G.M., Hassner, T. (eds.) European Conference on Computer Vision, pp. 427–445. Springer, Cham (2022). https://doi.org/10.1007/978-3-031-20056-4_25

18. Yi, L., et al.: A scalable active framework for region annotation in 3D shape collections. ACM Trans. Graph. (TOG) **35**(6cd), 210.1–210.12 (2016)
19. Zhang, X., Zhang, S., Yan, J.: PCP-MAE: learning to predict centers for point masked autoencoders. Adv. Neural. Inf. Process. Syst. **37**, 80303–80327 (2024)

Biological and Medical Image Processing

MAA-Net: A Multi-attention Aggregation Network for Segmentation of Key Structures in Microvascular Decompression

Jinghua Yue[1], Fugen Zhou[1,2], Qinglong Yao[1], Bo Liu[1,2(✉)], Yulian Zhang[3], Xueke Zhen[3], and Yanbing Yu[3]

[1] Image Processing Center, Beihang University, Beijing 102206, China
bo.liu@buaa.edu.cn

[2] State Key Laboratory of High-Efficiency Reusable Aerospace Transportation Technology, Beijing 102206, China

[3] Department of Neurosurgery, China-Japan Friendship Hospital, Beijing 100029, China

Abstract. Microvascular decompression (MVD) plays a critical role in the treatment of neurovascular compression-related diseases, with its success heavily dependent on the precise preoperative identification of key anatomical structures, especially small-volume and densely distributed tissues like nerves and vessels. To address this challenge, we propose a multi-attention aggregation network (MAA-Net), for the segmentation of MVD-related structures in MRI images. The method is based on the U-Net architecture and incorporates two attention mechanisms. A spatial-channel parallel attention module at the bottleneck jointly models spatial and channel dependencies to better capture complex interwoven anatomical structures, particularly in regions where nerves and cerebral vessels are intertwined. In addition, a lightweight gated attention module is inserted between the encoder and decoder to improve the perception of small-volume nerve targets by promoting feature selectivity and suppressing background noise, especially when processing fine nerve structures. We evaluated the proposed method on a private clinical dataset covering the brainstem, nerves, cerebral vessels, and cerebellum. The results demonstrate that our method achieves superior performance in volume overlap metrics (e.g., Dice score), delivers precise boundary delineation in distance-based metrics (HD95 and ASD), and exhibits strong recognition ability for elongated structures as reflected in the clDice score, confirming its practical value for preoperative MVD localization.

Keywords: Attention Mechanism · Microvascular Decompression · Nerve Structure Segmentation

1 Introduction

Microvascular decompression (MVD) is a crucial surgical technique for treating functional neurological disorders caused by neurovascular compression, such as trigeminal neuralgia and hemifacial spasm [1–3]. By relieving abnormal vascular pressure on cranial nerves, MVD can significantly alleviate symptoms and improve patient outcomes,

Z. Lin et al. (Eds.): ICIG 2025, LNCS 16161, pp. 281–293, 2026.
https://doi.org/10.1007/978-981-95-3398-5_23

making it an essential procedure in neurosurgical practice [4]. However, MVD is performed within the cerebellopontine angle (CPA), an anatomically complex and spatially constrained region where multiple nerves and cerebral vessels are densely distributed [5]. Even for experienced surgeons, limited intraoperative visualization and complex neurovascular anatomy post significant challenges, potentially leading to complications such as intracranial hemorrhage and cranial nerve dysfunction [6]. Consequently, accurate preoperative identification of cranial nerves, compressed cerebral vessels, and surrounding brain structures is essential to improving both the safety and efficacy of MVD.

At present, preoperative planning for MVD primarily relies on manual identification of nerves and vessels on MRI or CT images, supplemented by traditional segmentation techniques [7, 8]. However, due to limited resolution, low tissue contrast, and structural ambiguity in medical images, these conventional methods often struggle with low accuracy and require time-consuming manual corrections, limiting their clinical utility [9].

In recent years, deep learning, particularly convolutional neural networks (CNNs) based on U-Net [10] and its variants, has achieved remarkable success in the automatic segmentation of various organs such as the liver, lungs, and brain tumors [11–14]. Nevertheless, segmentation of the key neurovascular structures for MVD planning remains highly challenging. Small-volume cranial nerves like the trigeminal and facial nerves present blurred boundaries and low contrast with adjacent tissues while cerebral vessels follow complex, tortuous paths intertwined with the brainstem and cerebellum [15], leading to frequent segmentation errors.

A large body of research has targeted automatic segmentation of tubular structures, including cerebral vessels, coronary arteries, and airways [15–18]. However, these methods generally focus on single vascular systems and are not well adapted to anatomical regions where nerves and cerebral vessels are densely intertwined. Relative few studies have explored the segmentation of structures relevant to MVD on 3D MRI. Lin et al.[19] designed a coarse-to-fine strategy to refine segmentation of the trigeminal nerve and responsible cerebral vessels. Although this approach has yielded certain progress, there is still room to further improve segmentation performance, particularly in capturing small peripheral nerves and vessels and accurately modeling their complex spatial relationships.

To further advance segmentation performance in this domain, this study proposes a multi-attention aggregation network (MAA-Net) for accurate segmentation of critical brain structures in MVD preoperative planning. Leveraging dual-modal MRI data, comprising 3D FIESTA and 3D TOF-MRA, MAA-Net enhances the visibility of critical structures such as nerves and cerebral vessels. In terms of network architecture, a spatial-channel parallel attention (SCPA) module is embedded at the bottleneck to jointly capture key anatomical features across spatial and channel dimensions, enhancing the model's ability to focus on complex, interwoven structures. Additionally, a lightweight gated attention (LGA) module is introduced between the encoder and decoder to dynamically fuse features and guide selective information flow, thereby improving sensitivity to small-volume nerves. Through the synergistic design of these modules, the proposed method achieves superior multi-class segmentation of critical brain structures, providing a more accurate and reliable imaging foundation for MVD.

2 Methodology

To achieve precise and synchronized segmentation of key anatomical structures for pre-operative planning of MVD, we propose a multi-attention aggregation segmentation network. This model combines dual-modal imaging and incorporates attention mechanisms specifically designed for small-volume nerves and complex cerebral vessels. The overall network adopts a classic encoder-decoder framework, with two key modules introduced to enhance segmentation accuracy: the spatial-channel parallel attention module and the lightweight gated attention module. The following sections will detail the network architecture and the design specifics of these modules.

2.1 Network Architecture Overview

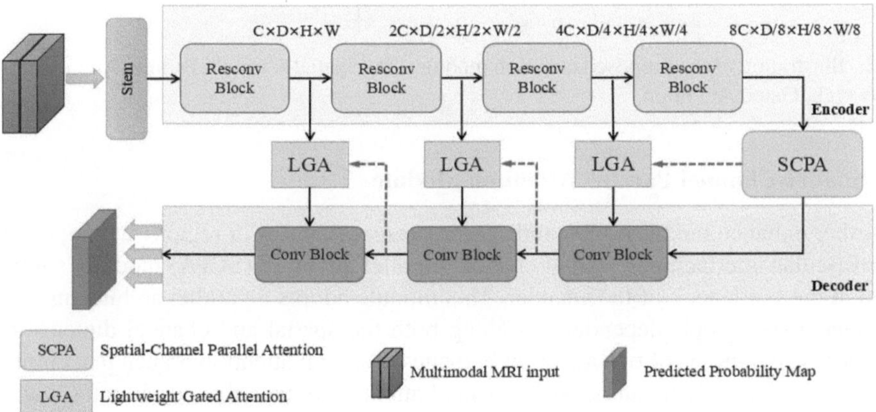

Fig. 1. Overall workflow of the proposed multi-attention aggregation network.

The MAA-Net is based on the U-Net architecture. As shown in Fig. 1, the encoder consists of four convolution layers, each implemented with residual convolution blocks to facilitate stable feature extraction and improve gradient flow during training. The first layer does not perform downsampling to retain spatial information of small vessels and fine nerves, preventing details loss from early downsampling. Starting from the second layer, three downsampling operations are performed to balance the retention of spatial information and computational efficiency. The decoder fuses the feature maps of the encoder and decoder through skip connections, progressively restoring spatial resolution to generate the final segmentation result. At the bottleneck, an SCPA module is embedded to enhance the representation of complex and interwoven anatomical structures by jointly modeling spatial and channel dimensions in parallel. Additionally, to improve the sensitivity of the model to small targets, an LGA module is introduced at each skip connection, selectively filtering relevant features and suppressing background noise during feature fusion.

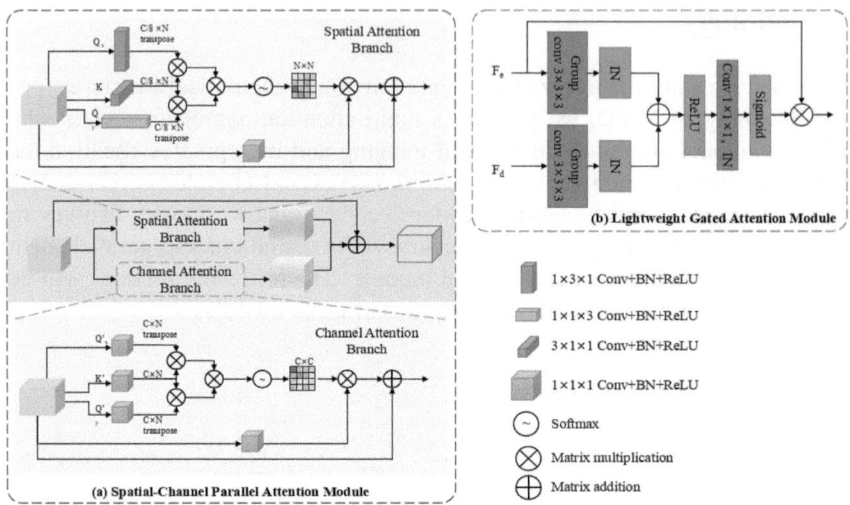

Fig. 2. Illustration of the proposed attention modules: (a) Spatial-Channel Parallel Attention; (b) Lightweight Gated Attention.

2.2 Spatial-Channel Parallel Attention Module

To further enhance the network's ability to represent features in regions with complex neurovascular interlacing, a spatial-channel parallel attention (SCPA) module is introduced at the bottleneck of the encoder. This module adopts a parallel architecture that simultaneously models dependencies along both the spatial and channel dimensions. Specifically, it consists of two attention branches: a spatial attention branch that emphasizes location-specific features, and a channel attention branch that recalibrates feature responses across channels. By integrating the outputs from both branches in parallel, the SCPA module is designed to more effectively capture the complementary information between spatial and channel contexts, thereby improving the sensitivity to small-volume and poorly defined structures, supporting more accurate segmentation of the trigeminal nerve, facial nerve, and intricate cerebral vessels.

Spatial Attention Branch. As illustrated in Fig. 2 (a), the input feature map $F \in \mathbb{R}^{C \times D \times H \times W}$ is first processed through three direction-specific convolutional layers with kernel sizes of $3 \times 1 \times 1$, $1 \times 3 \times 1$, and $1 \times 1 \times 3$, respectively. This design explicitly captures boundary-sensitive features along the z-axis, x-axis, and y-axis, which is crucial for delineating fine, elongated structures. Batch normalization and ReLU activation follow each convolution to enhance non-linear feature representational. The resulting features K, Q_x, and Q_y are reshaped into matrices of size $\mathbb{R}^{C \times N}$ (where $N = D \times H \times W$) for spatial affinity modeling. Cross-dimensional dependencies are then encoded via matrix multiplications:

$$S_1 = Q_x \times K^T \tag{1}$$

$$S_2 = Q_y \times K^T \tag{2}$$

Here, S_1 captures dependencies in the height and depth dimensions, while S_2 captures those in the width and depth, both essential for distinguishing intertwined neurovascular structures in 3D space. These two matrices are then combined via matrix multiplication, and a Softmax function is applied to obtain the final voxel-wise spatial affinity matrix S.

Meanwhile, a separate $1 \times 1 \times 1$ convolution is applied to the input feature F to obtain a reduced representation $V \in \mathbb{R}^{C \times D \times H \times W}$, which is reshaped to $\mathbb{R}^{C \times N}$. The attention-enhanced spatial feature F_S is then computed via:

$$F_S = V \times S \tag{3}$$

This result is reshaped back to its original 3D size and fused with the input via a residual connection, ensuring both refined spatial attention and retention of the original feature information. This process enables the network to better localize small-volume, spatially entangled structures, enhancing segmentation precision in challenging regions.

Channel Attention Branch. For the channel attention pathway, four parallel $1 \times 1 \times 1$ convolutions are applied to obtain channel-wise feature representations K', Q'_x, Q'_y, and $V' \in \mathbb{R}^{C \times D \times H \times W}$. These are reshaped into matrices of size $\mathbb{R}^{C \times N}$ to facilitate affinity computation. The channel affinity matrix S' is constructed as:

$$S' = \left(Q'_x \times (K')^T \right) \times \left(Q'_y \times (K')^T \right) \tag{4}$$

This operation captures inter-channel dependencies, allowing the network to recalibrate feature responses across channels based on their global relationships. This is particularly beneficial for distinguishing nerve and vessel tissues, which often share similar spatial patterns but differ in texture and intensity profiles. Subsequently, the reduced feature V' is then multiplied by the channel affinity matrix S' to obtain the enhanced channel feature F_C:

$$F_C = V' \times S' \tag{5}$$

The result is reshaped back to $\mathbb{R}^{C \times D \times H \times W}$ and refined through a residual connection, yielding the final output of the channel attention branch.

2.3 Lightweight Gated Attention Module

To better integrate the semantic features from the encoder and decoder and alleviate the semantic gap [20] often introduced by conventional skip connections, a lightweight gated attention (LGA) module is introduced between the encoding and decoding stages. By combining feature maps with attention weights, the module enables the network to selectively emphasize features of critical structures (such as small nerves and intricate vessels) while suppressing irrelevant background information, thereby enhancing segmentation accuracy. The gating mechanism generates guidance signals based on high-level features to regulate information flow across different stages, which is particularly beneficial for accurately modeling the complex neurovascular anatomy in MVD preoperative planning.

Specifically, as illustrated in Fig. 2 (b), the LGA module takes the encoded features and the upsampled decoded features as inputs. First, both inputs are processed independently through 3×3 grouped convolutions, which extract representative information while keeping computational cost low. The resulting feature maps are then normalized via instance normalization and fused via element-wise addition, followed by a ReLU activation to introduce non-linearity. Next, a 1×1 convolution and another instance normalization layer are applied to produce a single-channel feature map, which is then activated by a Sigmoid activation function to generate attention coefficients. Finally, these attention coefficients are used to scale the original encoded features through element-wise multiplication, producing gated features that are subsequently used in the decoding stage.

2.4 Loss Function

To optimize the segmentation performance, we employ a composite loss function that combines Dice loss and cross-entropy loss. This design encourages both accurate voxel-wise classification and region-level overlap, which is particularly beneficial for small structures such as cranial nerves and fine vessels. The overall loss is computed as:

$$L = \alpha \cdot L_{dice} + \beta \cdot L_{ce} \tag{6}$$

where both weighting coefficients α and β are set to 1. The Dice loss L_{dice} and the cross-entropy loss L_{ce} are defined as:

$$L_{dice} = -\frac{2}{N} \sum_{n \in N} \frac{\sum_{i \in I} y_i^n p_i^n}{\sum_{i \in I} y_i^n + \sum_{i \in I} p_i^n} \tag{7}$$

$$L_{ce} = -\frac{1}{I} \sum_{I} \sum_{n=1}^{N} y_i^n \log p_i^n \tag{8}$$

Here, y_i^n and p_i^n denote the ground truth label and predicted probability for class n at voxel i, respectively. I and N represent the total number of voxels and target classes. To facilitate gradient flow and guide feature learning at multiple scales, auxiliary outputs are generated at intermediate decoding layers during training, and their losses are aggregated into the final optimization objective.

3 Experiments

3.1 Dataset

The dataset used in this study was collected from the China-Japan Friendship Hospital in Beijing and consists of 47 paired MRI cases. Each case includes co-registered 3D FIESTA and 3D TOF-MRA images, providing complementary anatomical and vascular information. All data were manually annotated by two experienced radiologists using the ITK-SNAP software, with cross-verification to ensure annotation consistency and accuracy. The labeled structures include the brainstem, cranial nerves (trigeminal and facial nerves), cerebral vessels, and cerebellum, which are critical targets for MVD preoperative planning.

3.2 Implementation Detail

We adopted the open-source nnU-Net v2 [21] framework to facilitate model training and evaluation, leveraging its standardized data pre-processing and post-processing pipelines. The input data were automatically preprocessed by nnU-Net, including resampling to a target spacing of $0.5 \times 0.39 \times 0.39$ mm, z-score normalization, and foreground cropping. Model optimization was conducted using stochastic gradient descent (SGD) with Nesterov momentum ($\mu = 0.99$). The initial learning rate was set to 0.01 and decayed using a polynomial learning rate schedule with power 0.9. A batch size of 2 was used, with each epoch comprising 250 iterations. To ensure stable convergence and enough training for all experiments, the training process was allowed to run for up to 500 epochs. The loss function combined Dice loss and cross-entropy loss, as implemented in the nnU-Net default configuration. The input patch size for the network was set to $32 \times 256 \times 224$. Default data augmentation strategies, such as rotation, scaling, elastic deformation, and gamma correction, were applied during training. All experiments were conducted using a single NVIDIA RTX 3090 GPU.

3.3 Evaluation Metrics

We adopted five commonly used metrics to quantitatively evaluate the segmentation performance: Dice coefficient, Jaccard index, Hausdorff Distance at the 95th percentile (HD95), Average Surface Distance (ASD), and centerline Dice (clDice) [22]. Among them, Dice, Jaccard, and clDice are overlap-based metrics, where higher values indicate better performance. HD95 and ASD are distance-based metrics, and lower values reflect more accurate boundary localization. The formulas for the overlap-based metrics are:

$$\text{Dice} = \frac{2|P \cap G|}{|P| + |G|}, \ \text{Jaccard} = \frac{|P \cap G|}{|P \cup G|} \tag{9}$$

Here, P and G denote the predicted and ground truth voxel sets, respectively. HD95 measures the 95th percentile of the distances from boundary points of the prediction to the closest points on the ground truth boundary, helping to reduce the influence of outliers. ASD computes the average of all distances between the boundaries of the prediction and ground truth, reflecting overall surface discrepancy. They are defined as:

$$\text{HD95} = \frac{K_{95}\left(\min_{p \in P} D(g,p)\right) + K_{95}\left(\min_{g \in G} D(p,g)\right)}{2} \tag{10}$$

$$\text{ASD} = \frac{1}{2}\left(\frac{\sum_{y \in Y} \min_{p \in P} D(g,p)}{G} + \frac{\sum_{p \in P} \min_{g \in G} D(p,g)}{P}\right) \tag{11}$$

where $D(g, p)$ is the Euclidean distance and K_{95} means the 95th percentile. clDice is designed to assess the quality of long and thin structures by combining spatial overlap with topological consistency, and is mainly applied to evaluate nerve and cerebral vessel segmentation in our experiments. It is defined as:

$$\text{clDice} = \frac{2 \bullet |C(P) \cap G| \bullet |C(G) \cap P|}{|C(P) \cap G| + |C(G) \cap P|} \tag{12}$$

where $C()$ represents the centerline extraction operator.

3.4 Performance Comparisons

To comprehensively evaluate the effectiveness of the proposed MAA-Net, we compared it with several representative segmentation methods. These include the widely adopted V-Net [23] and nnU-Net [21], as well as two transformer-based models, UNETR [24] and Swin UNETR [25], which have shown promising results in various medical segmentation tasks. Additionally, we included CS2-Net [26], a method specifically designed for tubular structure segmentation, and the approach proposed by Lin et al. [19], which was tailored for anatomical segmentation in the context of MVD surgery.

Table 1. Performance comparison of MAA-Net with other segmentation models on four key anatomical structures for MVD preoperative planning. The best and second-best scores are indicated in bold and underlined. Results are reported as mean $\pm$ standard deviation.

Models	Dice (%) ↑	Jaccard (%) ↑	HD95 (mm) ↓	ASD (mm) ↓
V-Net [23]	88.32 ± 1.28	80.25 ± 1.86	1.89 ± 0.93	0.35 ± 0.14
nnU-Net [21]	88.36 ± 0.98	80.42 ± 1.46	2.01 ± 0.75	**0.29 ± 0.10**
UNETR [24]	87.93 ± 1.33	79.70 ± 1.90	1.99 ± 0.85	0.38 ± 0.13
Swin UNETR [25]	88.00 ± 1.04	79.84 ± 1.49	2.33 ± 1.00	<u>0.32 ± 0.08</u>
CS2-Net [26]	<u>88.70 ± 1.03</u>	**80.85 ± 1.48**	<u>1.85 ± 1.09</u>	0.34 ± 0.14
Lin et al. [19]	88.06 ± 0.90	79.80 ± 1.32	2.20 ± 1.00	0.45 ± 0.12
MAA-Net (Ours)	**88.73 ± 0.79**	<u>80.84 ± 1.16</u>	**1.81 ± 0.36**	**0.29 ± 0.04**

Table 2. Comparative evaluation of nerve and cerebral vessel segmentation accuracy for MAA-Net and other segmentation models.

Models	Nerves			Cerebral vessels		
	clDice (%) ↑	HD95 (mm) ↓	ASD (mm) ↓	clDice (%) ↑	HD95 (mm) ↓	ASD (mm) ↓
V-Net [23]	82.60 ± 5.74	1.07 ± 0.27	0.20 ± 0.03	84.40 ± 3.02	3.32 ± 4.02	0.59 ± 0.59
nnU-Net [21]	83.57 ± 4.14	1.03 ± 0.12	0.20 ± 0.02	83.90 ± 2.03	4.07 ± 3.04	0.48 ± 0.43
UNETR [24]	82.02 ± 4.40	1.12 ± 0.12	0.26 ± 0.06	80.73 ± 4.66	3.74 ± 3.43	0.65 ± 0.54
Swin UNETR [25]	81.45 ± 3.42	1.24 ± 0.22	0.21 ± 0.03	81.55 ± 5.38	4.82 ± 4.33	**0.37** ± 0.34
CS2-Net [26]	83.30 ± 4.15	1.04 ± 0.12	**0.19** ± 0.03	84.19 ± 2.90	3.63 ± 4.42	0.64 ± 0.59
Lin et al. [19]	**86.27** ± 4.61	**0.85** ± 0.15	0.30 ± 0.03	83.13 ± 3.03	4.73 ± 4.30	0.85 ± 0.59
MAA-Net (Ours)	86.09 ± 3.40	0.97 ± 0.04	0.20 ± 0.02	**84.78** ± 2.29	3.19 ± 1.83	0.44 ± 0.20

As shown in Table 1, our proposed MAA-Net achieves the best average performance across all evaluation metrics. For instance, it obtains the highest Dice score of 0.8873, reflecting superior overlap accuracy. In terms of boundary precision, our method reduces HD95 to 1.81mm, which is noticeably lower than Lin et al.'s 2.20 mm. These results highlight the balanced advantage of our method in both region-level accuracy and boundary delineation. Moreover, MAA-Net achieves the lowest standard deviations across all evaluated metrics, indicating statistically stable performance and improved generalization. Table 2 further presents detailed results for nerve and cerebral vessel segmentation. While Lin et al.'s method slightly surpasses ours in nerve segmentation on clDice and HD95, this is achieved by using heavily weighted loss functions that emphasize nerves but lead to significantly worse cerebral vessel results. In contrast, our method delivers a balanced and robust performance, ranking first or second on nerve and cerebral vessel metrics and maintaining overall superiority across all structures.

As shown in Fig. 3, our method provides more complete vessel segmentation and more precise nerve delineation with reduced adhesion. Benefiting from the SCPA and LGA modules, small and fine structures are better preserved, and the separation between nerves and surrounding vessels appears clearer compared to other methods. Moreover, more extensive and continuous peripheral branches are visible in our results. Compared with the blue regions of the figure, more small vessel structures are captured by our method than by other methods. These visual improvements are consistent with our quantitative results, confirming the effectiveness of our approach in enhancing both completeness and anatomical clarity.

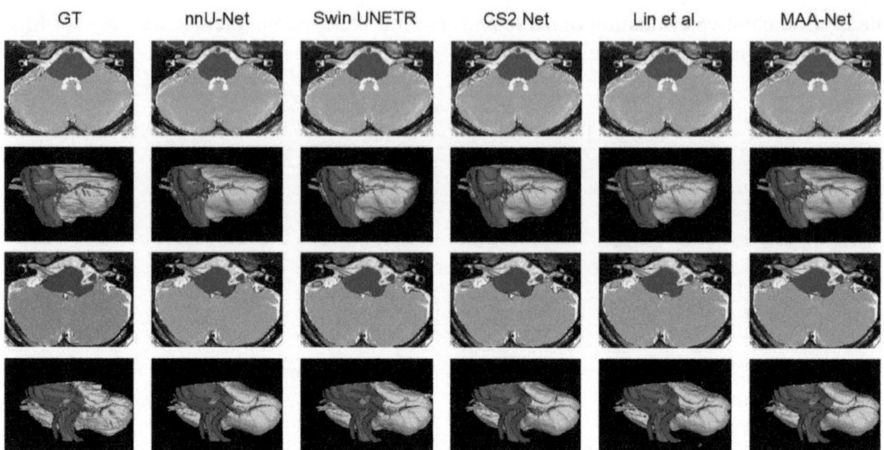

Fig. 3. Visual comparison of segmentation results: Brainstem (Red), Vessels (Blue), Nerves (Green), and Cerebellum (Yellow). (Color Figure Online)

3.5 Ablation Study

To evaluate the contribution of each proposed module, we conducted ablation experiments on nerve and vessel segmentation. Table 3 presents the ablation study results. Compared to the baseline model without any module, adding the LGA module alone improves the distance-based metrics consistently for both nerves and vessels, although a slight decrease in clDice is observed for nerves. This suggests that the LGA module is particularly effective in enhancing boundary precision and reducing segmentation errors around complex structures. Introducing the SCPA module individually also leads to performance gains, particularly in vessel segmentation, where clDice rises from 82.65% to 84.10%. Additionally, we experimented with connecting the spatial and channel attention branches in series (SCSA). While SCSA shows certain improvements over the single-module settings (Row 2 vs. Row 4), our parallel design (Row 5) demonstrates overall superior performance. This confirms that the parallel structure of SCPA more effectively captures the complementary information from spatial and channel dimensions by allowing simultaneous and independent modeling, whereas the serial configuration may lead to information bottlenecks and reduced flexibility in feature interaction.

Table 3. Ablation study on nerves and cerebral vessels with different module settings. SCSA refers to connecting the spatial and channel branches in series.

Modules	Nerves			Cerebral vessels		
	clDice (%) ↑	HD95 (mm) ↓	ASD (mm) ↓	clDice (%) ↑	HD95 (mm) ↓	ASD (mm) ↓
None	85.10 ± 3.03	1.07 ± 0.17	0.20 ± 0.03	82.65 ± 1.54	4.55 ± 2.56	0.59 ± 0.47
+LGA	84.11 ± 3.63	1.01 ± 1.00	0.20 ± 0.03	83.65 ± 2.33	4.33 ± 3.50	0.56 ± 0.48
+SCPA	84.97 ± 3.45	0.99 ± 0.03	0.19 ± 0.03	84.10 ± 1.09	4.08 ± 2.85	0.51 ± 0.37

(continued)

Table 3. (*continued*)

Modules	Nerves			Cerebral vessels		
	clDice (%) ↑	HD95 (mm) ↓	ASD (mm) ↓	clDice (%) ↑	HD95 (mm) ↓	ASD (mm) ↓
+LGA + SCSA	85.14 ± 3.52	0.98 ± 0.06	0.20 ± 0.03	84.07 ± 2.65	4.08 ± 3.54	0.56 ± 0.50
+LGA+SCPA	86.09 ± 3.40	0.97 ± 0.04	0.20 ± 0.02	84.78 ± 2.29	3.19 ± 1.83	0.44 ± 0.20

4 Conclusion

In this study, we proposed MAA-Net, a multi-attention aggregation network for accurate segmentation of key neurovascular structures in MVD planning. By incorporating a spatial-channel parallel attention module and a lightweight gated attention module, our method enhances the representation of small-volume nerves and complex cerebral vessels, achieving superior performance across multiple evaluation metrics. Experiments on dual-modal MRI datasets demonstrate that our approach outperforms existing methods, offering improved accuracy and reliability for preoperative localization in MVD procedures. In future work, we aim to further validate the generalization ability of our method on larger, multi-center datasets, and explore its extension to other neurovascular compression syndromes and neurosurgical applications.

Acknowledgments. This study was funded by Beijing Natural Science Foundation under Grant L222034, Grant L232037, and Grant L242112; in part by the National Natural Science Foundation of China under Grant 12375359.

References

1. Ko, A.L., Ozpinar, A., Lee, A., Raslan, A.M., McCartney, S., Burchiel, K.J.: Long-term efficacy and safety of internal neurolysis for trigeminal neuralgia without neurovascular compression. J. Neurosurg. **122**, 1048–1057 (2015)
2. Heinskou, T.B., et al.: Prognostic factors for outcome of microvascular decompression in trigeminal neuralgia: a prospective systematic study using independent assessors. Cephalalgia **39**, 197–208 (2019)
3. Kong, C.-C., et al.: Delayed facial palsy after microvascular decompression for hemifacial spasm. World Neurosurg. **134**, e12–e15 (2020)
4. Cheng, J.S., Lim, D.A., Chang, E.F., Barbaro, N.M.: A review of percutaneous treatments for trigeminal neuralgia. Operative Neurosurgery **10**, 25–33 (2014)
5. Greve, T., Tonn, J.-C., Mehrkens, J.-H.: Microvascular decompression for trigeminal neuralgia in the elderly: efficacy and safety. J. Neurol. **268**, 532–540 (2021)
6. Sade, B., Lee, J.H.: Microvascular decompression for trigeminal neuralgia. Neurosurg. Clin. N. Am. **25**, 743–749 (2014)

7. Sultana, S., Blatt, J.E., Gilles, B., Rashid, T., Audette, M.A.: MRI-based medial axis extraction and boundary segmentation of cranial nerves through discrete deformable 3D contour and surface models. IEEE Trans. Med. Imaging **36**, 1711–1721 (2017)

8. Sultana, S., et al.: Medial axis segmentation of cranial nerves using shape statistics-aware discrete deformable models. Int. J. Comput. Assist. Radiol. Surg. **14**, 1955–1967 (2019)

9. Li, H., Tang, Z., Nan, Y., Yang, G.: Human treelike tubular structure segmentation: a comprehensive review and future perspectives. Comput. Biol. Med. **151**, 106241 (2022)

10. Ronneberger, O., Fischer, P., Brox, T.: U-net: convolutional networks for biomedical image segmentation. In: Medical Image Computing and Computer-Assisted Intervention–MICCAI 2015: 18th International Conference, Munich, Germany, 5–9 October 2015, Proceedings, Part III 18, pp. 234–241. Springer, Cham (2015). https://doi.org/10.1007/978-3-319-24574-4_28

11. Azad, R., et al.: Medical image segmentation review: the success of u-net. IEEE Trans. Pattern Anal. Mach. Intell. **46**, 10076–10095 (2024)

12. Wang, B., Yang, C.: Liver tumor segmentation method based on U-Net architecture: a review. EAI Endorsed Trans. e-Learn. **10** (2024)

13. Liu, W., Luo, J., Yang, Y., Wang, W., Deng, J., Yu, L.: Automatic lung segmentation in chest X-ray images using improved U-Net. Sci. Rep. **12**, 8649 (2022)

14. Walsh, J., Othmani, A., Jain, M., Dev, S.: Using U-Net network for efficient brain tumor segmentation in MRI images. Healthc. Anal. **2**, 100098 (2022)

15. Goni, M.R., Ruhaiyem, N.I.R., Mustapha, M., Achuthan, A., Nassir, C.M.N.C.M.: Brain vessel segmentation using deep learning—a review. IEEE Access **10**, 111322–111336 (2022)

16. Yang, X., et al.: airway segmentation based on topological structure enhancement using multi-task learning. In: Linguraru, M.G., et al. (eds.) International Conference on Medical Image Computing and Computer-Assisted Intervention, pp. 86–95. Springer (2024). https://doi.org/10.1007/978-3-031-72114-4_9

17. Wu, J., et al.: Segmentation of carotid artery vessel wall and diagnosis of carotid atherosclerosis on black blood magnetic resonance imaging with multi-task learning. Med. Phys. **51**, 1775–1797 (2023)

18. Kirchhoff, Y., et al.: Skeleton recall loss for connectivity conserving and resource efficient segmentation of thin tubular structures. In: Leonardis, A., Ricci, E., Roth, S., Russakovsky, O., Sattler, T., Varol, G. (eds.) European Conference on Computer Vision, pp. 218–234. Springer, Cham (2024). https://doi.org/10.1007/978-3-031-72980-5_13

19. Lin, J., et al.: Automated segmentation of trigeminal nerve and cerebrovasculature in MR-angiography images by deep learning. Front. Neurosci. **15**, 744967 (2021)

20. Wang, R., Lei, T., Cui, R., Zhang, B., Meng, H., Nandi, A.K.: Medical image segmentation using deep learning: a survey. IET Image Proc. **16**, 1243–1267 (2022)

21. Isensee, F., Jaeger, P.F., Kohl, S.A., Petersen, J., Maier-Hein, K.H.: NnU-Net: a self-configuring method for deep learning-based biomedical image segmentation. Nat. Methods **18**, 203–211 (2021)

22. Shit, S., et al.: clDice-a novel topology-preserving loss function for tubular structure segmentation. In: Proceedings of the IEEE/CVF Conference on Computer Vision and Pattern Recognition, pp. 16560–16569. IEEE (2021)

23. Milletari, F., Navab, N., Ahmadi, S.-A.: V-Net: fully convolutional neural networks for volumetric medical image segmentation. In: 2016 Fourth International Conference on 3D Vision (3DV), pp. 565–571. IEEE (2016)

24. Hatamizadeh, A., et al.: UNETR: transformers for 3D medical image segmentation. In: Proceedings of the IEEE/CVF Winter Conference on Applications of Computer Vision, pp. 574–584. IEEE (2022)

25. Hatamizadeh, A., Nath, V., Tang, Y., Yang, D., Roth, H.R., Xu, D.: Swin UNETR: swin transformers for semantic segmentation of brain tumors in MRI images. In: International MICCAI Brainlesion Workshop, pp. 272–284. Springer (2021). https://doi.org/10.1007/978-3-031-08999-2_22
26. Mou, L., et al.: CS2-Net: deep learning segmentation of curvilinear structures in medical imaging. Med. Image Anal. **67**, 101874 (2021)

Contrastive Hierarchical Graph Based Multiple Instance Learning for Fundus Screening

Yubo Tan[1], Shiye Wang[2], Wenda Shen[3], and Yong-Jie Li[1(✉)]

[1] University of Electronic Science and Technology of China, Chengdu 610054, China
`ybt@std.uestc.edu.cn, liyj@uestc.edu.cn`
[2] Henan Kaifeng College of Science Technology and Communication, Kaifeng 475001, China
[3] Changchun University of Science and Technology, Changchun 130022, China

Abstract. Fundus imaging techniques, such as Fundus Fluorescein Angiography (FFA) and Optical Coherence Tomography (OCT), serve as pivotal diagnostic tools for retinal disease detection. These modalities reveal intricate variations in retinal tissue structure, thereby aiding clinicians in accurate diagnosis and treatment planning. Recent advancements in Multiple Instance Learning (MIL) have transformed the analysis of fundus images datasets by effectively extracting discriminative features from image-level key instances. However, a critical limitation of conventional MIL methods lies in their neglect of region-level key instances (e.g., localized lesions) within the 2-D spatial domain, particularly in fundus imaging where pathological regions are often sparse. To address this gap, we propose a Contrastive Hierarchical Graph based Multiple Instance Learning (CHG-MIL) framework, which integrates three novel components: (1) a Spatial Instance Graph (SIG) module that preserves 2-D spatial topology and mines contextual relationships among neighboring region-level instances; (2) a Hierarchical Instance Interaction (HII) module that utilizes deeper semantic representations to refine shallow-layer features through cross-hierarchy guidance; and (3) a Hierarchical Contrastive Loss (HCL) designed to suppress redundant, non-disease-related features in nodes and instances. Extensive experiments on the APTOS2023 and GAMMA datasets demonstrate the superiority of our proposed method over existing state-of-the-art MIL methods.

Keywords: Fundus Fluorescein Angiography · Optical Coherence Tomography · Multiple Instance Learning · Contrastive Hierarchical Graph

1 Introduction

Fundus Fluorescein Angiography (FFA) and Optical Coherence Tomography (OCT) play a pivotal role in ophthalmic diagnostics [1,2], providing clinicians

Z. Lin et al. (Eds.): ICIG 2025, LNCS 16161, pp. 294–305, 2026.
https://doi.org/10.1007/978-981-95-3398-5_24

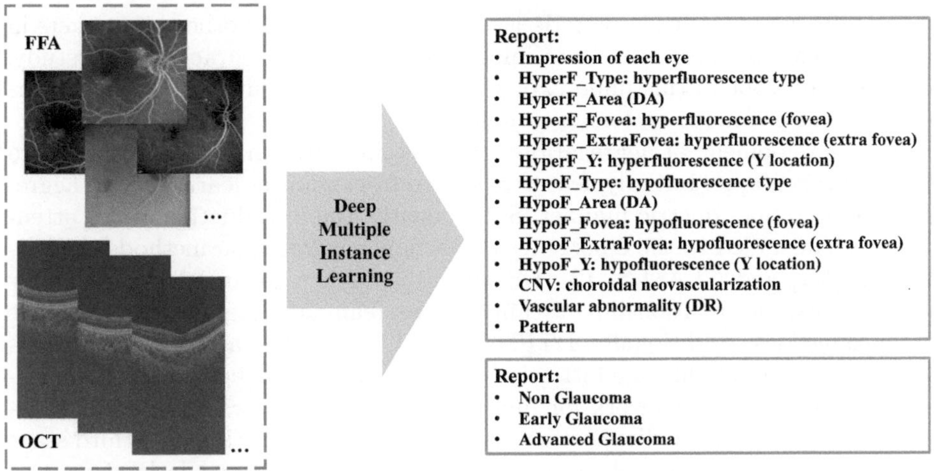

Fig. 1. Illustrating the prediction of ophthalmic reports from fundus images.

with in-depth insights into pathological changes in the retina. These invaluable imaging modalities allow for the meticulous examination of the retinal microvasculature and retinal layers, thereby facilitating the detection of various ocular conditions, such as glaucoma, diabetic retinopathy [3], and retinal vascular leakage [4]. Accurate interpretation of fundus images is of utmost importance for the early diagnosis [5] and timely intervention of retinal diseases, which is crucial for preventing vision loss [6]. Given the critical significance of FFA and OCT in ophthalmic diagnostics, there is a pressing need to develop deep learning models that can automatically report different retinal morphologies, abnormalities, and blood flow statuses in FFA or OCT images, as depicted in Fig. 1. Such models would greatly streamline the generation of comprehensive fundus examination reports for patients, saving ophthalmologists a substantial amount of time and significantly improving the overall quality of medical care. This initiative is in line with the broader goal of leveraging advanced technological solutions to enhance diagnostic accuracy and efficiency in ophthalmology.

Unlike image segmentation tasks [7], which rely on detailed pixel-level segmentation labels [8], image classification tasks typically assign a single image-level label to each image. In clinical diagnosis, the analysis of medical images often involves examining multiple images from a single examination. The Multiple Instance Learning (MIL) paradigm treats each image as an instance, with multiple instances sharing a common bag-level label [9–11].

The objective of fundus screening is to accurately predict patient-specific diagnostic parameters using a diverse set of FFA or OCT images captured during a single examination. However, the scarcity of FFA datasets poses a significant challenge to the progress of this field. Moreover, despite the development of numerous state-of-the-art MIL algorithms for image-level analysis, there is a lack of research on region-level features and their inter-relationships. It is essential to carefully analyze the characteristics of lesion regions and other biomarkers in fundus images, as these are key to improving diagnostic accuracy. In this study, we aim to set foot in this underexplored area and contribute to the continuous development of fundus screening techniques.

The development of aggregation strategies in MIL can be categorized into three distinct stages. Initially, features derived from transfer learning were aggregated in a non-parametric manner. Subsequently, the introduction of the attention mechanism led to the emergence of learnable aggregation methods, such as AB-MIL [11] and CLAM-S [12]. DS-MIL [13] further advanced this trend by modeling instance relationships within a dual-stream architecture with trainable distance metrics. Additionally, DTFD-MIL [14] established a double-tier framework that effectively utilizes intrinsic features. SGMF, a structure-aware hierarchical graph-based framework for multi-instance learning, was proposed, drawing inspiration from the diagnostic workflow of pathologists [15]. The third stage witnessed the integration of more sophisticated self-attention mechanisms and transformers, resulting in high-performing models. For example, TransMIL [9] capitalized on both morphological and spatial information through its multi-head self-attention (MHSA) component. To address the computational complexities associated with transformers, ILRA-MIL [16] proposed low-rank learnable aggregation methods. While contrastive learning [1] and graph networks [17] are established tools in medical image analysis, we investigate their potential for advancing multi-instance learning tasks.

Despite the maturity of the design of aggregation operators, there is a lack of research on other crucial aspects of network architecture. Notably, two critical aspects remain underexplored: (1) the comprehensive utilization of multi-scale features from the backbone network, and (2) the exploration of spatial relationships among instance features across regions. In this work, we make progress in these directions by extracting multi-scale features from Convolutional Neural Networks (CNNs). We then use Graph Neural Networks (GNNs) to capture the topological relationships among instances in 2-D space. By imposing contrastive constraints and facilitating cross-scale feature interactions, we achieve superior performance, thus contributing to the broader understanding and advancement of MIL techniques. Our contributions are four-fold:

- To enhance the learning of region-level instances and their inter-relationships in the MIL framework, a Spatial Instance Graph (**SIG**) module is employed to process the features obtained from transfer learning.
- A Hierarchical Instance Interaction (**HII**) module is proposed to guide the network to learn features at different levels in a top-down manner.
- To eliminate the disease-irrelevant individual differences in the embeddings of graph nodes, instances, and bag-level representations, a Hierarchical Contrastive Loss (**HCL**) is introduced to constrain the model.
- Extensive experiments on the APTOS2023 and GAMMA datasets demonstrate that the proposed Contrastive Hierarchical Graph based Multiple Instance Learning (**CHG-MIL**) model achieves state-of-the-art performance.

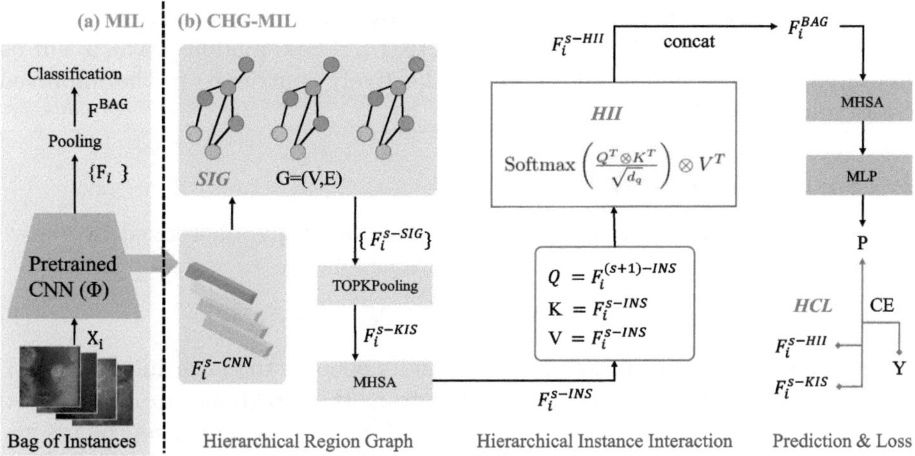

Fig. 2. The architectures of (a) common MIL method, and (b) the proposed CHG-MIL. CHG-MIL extracts finer-grained image features, performs relationship extraction via the Spatial Instance Graph (SIG), integrates features through the Hierarchical Instance Interaction (HII) module, and applies constraints using the Hierarchical Contrastive Loss (HCL) to generate predictions.

2 Methodology

2.1 The Overall Framework

As shown in Fig. 2-(a), within the MIL framework, we consider a bag of instances $X_i = \{x_1, x_2, \ldots, x_N\}$, where each instance x_i resides in the feature space $\mathbb{R}^{B \times 1 \times H_0 \times W_0}$. Here, B represents the batch size, N denotes the number of instances per bag, and H_0 and W_0 represent the height and width of each image instance, respectively. Each bag X_i is associated with a bag-level label Y_i.

To extract instance-aware 2-D features, common MIL methods utilize a pretrained backbone model (e.g., ResNet34) along with average pooling. Subsequently, these features are reshaped into a set $F_i = \{f_1, f_2, \ldots, f_N\}$, where each $f_i \in \mathbb{R}^{B \times 1 \times L}$ and $F_i \in \mathbb{R}^{B \times N \times L}$. The set of instance-aware features F_i is then aggregated into a bag-level representation F^{BAG}. This aggregated representation is then fed into a linear layer to generate a bag-level prediction.

The aggregation of instance-aware features into a bag-level representation can be accomplished through various aggregation operations, including max-pooling, avg-pooling, and attention weighting modules. Each of these aggregation techniques provides a unique perspective on combining individual instance features to form a comprehensive bag-level representation.

Figure 2-(b) illustrates the architecture of our proposed Contrastive Hierarchical Graph based Multiple Instance Learning (CHG-MIL) framework. Different from traditional MIL approaches, our method extracts CNN features from multiple levels and feeds them into subsequent modules, namely the Spatial Instance

Graph (SIG) and Hierarchical Instance Interaction (HII), which are regularized by the Hierarchical Contrastive Loss (HCL). These modules, which will be elaborated on in the following sections, collectively contribute to the improved performance of our CHG-MIL framework.

2.2 Spatial Instance Graph

Using the four layers of the backbone (e.g., ResNet34, parameterized by Φ), we extract features from a bag of fundus images as follows:

$$F_i^{s-\mathrm{CNN}} = \Phi(X_i), \quad i \in [1, N], \quad s \in [1, 4] \tag{1}$$

where i indexes the N instances in a bag, and s denotes the layer index (1 to 4).

The four-layer feature maps extracted from the backbone are represented as 2-D tensors, denoted as $F_i^{s-\mathrm{CNN}} \in \mathbb{R}^{(BN)\times L\times H\times W}$, where L represents the number of feature channels, and H and W refer to the height and width of $F_i^{4-\mathrm{CNN}}$, respectively. To reduce computational complexity, we resize the 2-D feature map of each scale to a fixed size $H \times W$. Interpreting $F_i^{s-\mathrm{CNN}}$ as a collection of features corresponding to region instances, we reorganize it into $F_i^{s-\mathrm{CNN}} \in \mathbb{R}^{(BN)\times(HW)\times L}$. For convenient processing, a linear layer is used to transform $F_i^{s-\mathrm{CNN}}$ into $F_i^s \in \mathbb{R}^{(BN)\times(HW)\times D}$, where $D = 256$. This transformation ensures that the feature representation remains computationally manageable while retaining relevant information for subsequent analysis.

Given that the regional instance representations F_i^s extracted by the backbone inherently have a 2-D structure, they naturally encode positional priors among each instance. However, in the context of MIL, it is necessary to flatten these 2-D instance features into a 1-D representation. This flattening process unfortunately leads to the loss of the original spatial relationships among the instances, which is crucial for accurate learning. To address this limitation, we introduce the Spatial Instance Graph (SIG), a novel approach that effectively models the spatial relationships within the instance features. By leveraging the graph G, we can preserve critical spatial information, thereby enhancing the learning capabilities of our framework.

SIG is defined as $G(V, E)$, where each node $v \in V$ corresponds to a spatial position in F_i^s, and edges E connect nodes within their 8-neighborhood. Node embeddings are $\{F_i^s\}$, with edge weights set to 1. The adjacency matrix A is:

$$A_{m,n} = \begin{cases} 1 & \text{if } n \in N_8(m), \\ 0 & \text{otherwise.} \end{cases} \tag{2}$$

Subsequently, the node feature F_i^s and the adjacency matrix A are input into three layers of GNNs. Within each GNN layer, the following computation is carried out:

$$F_i^{s-\mathrm{SIG}} = F_i + \mathrm{ReLU}(\mathrm{LN}(\mathrm{GENConv}(F_i^s, A))). \tag{3}$$

Here, ReLU is the rectified linear unit, LN represents layer normalization, and GENConv denotes the generalized graph convolution operation as introduced in

[18]. This equation aggregates feature information from neighboring nodes, followed by the application of nonlinear activation and normalization, resulting in an updated node representation $F_i^{s-\mathrm{SIG}}$.

Since the diagnosis of diseases often mainly depends on specific key areas, such as diseased regions, while other irrelevant regions only increase the workload of film screening, it is essential to effectively identify the characteristics of relevant examples before proceeding to subsequent steps. Key instances are selected via TOPKPooling:

$$F_i^{s-\mathrm{KIS}} = \mathrm{TOPKPooling}(F_i^{s-\mathrm{SIG}}), \tag{4}$$

Subsequently, the derived key instance representation $F_i^{s-\mathrm{KIS}}$ is transmitted to the MHSA module. Initially, $F_i^{s-\mathrm{KIS}} \in \mathbb{R}^{BND}$ is concatenated with a class token $cls_i^S \in \mathbb{R}^{B \times 1 \times D}$ to mark the location of the aggregated instance representation $F_i^{s-\mathrm{CLS}}$ within the sequence. This token serves as a reference point for the instance representation.

Next, $F_i^{s-\mathrm{CLS}}$ is processed by a MHSA block, which models the interdependencies among the sequence elements. Then, a position encoding (PE) block is used to restore the original order of the instances, ensuring that the sequential information is preserved. A second MHSA block is then applied to further aggregate and enrich the features.

Mathematically, this process can be expressed as follows:

$$\begin{cases} F_i^{s-\mathrm{CLS}} & = \mathrm{concat}(cls_i^S, F_i^{s-\mathrm{KIS}}), \\ F_i^{s-\mathrm{MHSA1}} & = \mathrm{MHSA}(F_i^{s-\mathrm{CLS}}), \\ F_i^{s-\mathrm{PE}} & = \mathrm{PE}(F_i^{s-\mathrm{MHSA1}}), \\ F_i^{s-\mathrm{MHSA2}} & = \mathrm{MHSA}(F_i^{s-\mathrm{PE}}), \\ F_i^{s-\mathrm{INS}} & = \mathrm{LN}(F_i^{s-\mathrm{MHSA2}}). \end{cases} \tag{5}$$

Here, $F_i^{s-\mathrm{INS}}$ represents the i-th instance-level representation corresponding to the s-th layer of the network.

2.3   Hierarchical Instance Interaction

Deep neural networks are well-known for generating deep features with a broadened receptive field, while shallow features retain richer image details. Our proposed method carefully exploits the multi-scale characteristics inherent in the backbone network to minimize potential information loss. Additionally, we propose a Hierarchical Instance Interaction (HII) module, which uses global semantic information to guide the learning of shallow features in a top-down manner.

The HII framework is formalized as follows:

$$F_i^{s-\mathrm{INS}} = \mathrm{HII}(F_i^{(s+1)-\mathrm{INS}}, F_i^{s-\mathrm{INS}}). \tag{6}$$

Within each HII block, inspired by the Q, K, V concept in self-attention, the guiding feature is set as $Q = F_i^{(s+1)-\mathrm{INS}}$, and K and V are set as $F_i^{s-\mathrm{INS}}$, serving as the guided features. The HII block operates as follows:

$$
\begin{cases}
F_i^{s-\text{Att}} = \text{Softmax}\left(\dfrac{QK^T}{\sqrt{d_q}}\right)V, \\
F_i^{s-\text{RES}} = Q + \text{Dropout}(F_i^{s-\text{Att}})^T, \\
F_i^{s-\text{LN}} = \text{LN}(F_i^{s-\text{RES}}), \\
F_i^{s-\text{MLP}} = F_i^{s-\text{LN}} + \text{MLP}(\text{Dropout}(\text{ReLU}(\text{MLP}(F_i^{s-\text{LN}})))), \\
F_i^{s-\text{HII}} = \text{LN}(F_i^{s-\text{MLP}}).
\end{cases}
\tag{7}
$$

Here, d_q represents the last dimension of Q, $F_i^{s-\text{Att}}$ represents the attention-weighted features, which are then combined with the original features $F_i^{(s+1)-\text{INS}}$ through residual connections to form $F_i^{s-\text{RES}}$. LN is applied to generate $F_i^{s-\text{LN}}$. Subsequently, a multi-layer perceptron (MLP) with Dropout and ReLU activation is used to further enrich the features, resulting in $F_i^{s-\text{MLP}}$. Finally, another LN is applied to obtain $F_i^{s-\text{HII}}$. This comprehensive HII framework enables the effective integration of multi-scale information, enhancing the overall feature representation.

Subsequently, the hierarchical bags of features are concatenated to form a unified representation.

$$
F_i^{BAG} = \text{concat}(F_i^{2-\text{HII}}, F_i^{3-\text{HII}}, F_i^{4-\text{HII}}).
\tag{8}
$$

F_i^{BAG}, is then aggregated into a bag-level representation through another MHSA block. Finally, a linear layer is applied to derive the ultimate prediction P. In this work, we adopt the cross-entropy loss function.

$$
L_{\text{cls}}(P, Y) = -\sum_{i=1}^{C}[Y_i \log(P_i) + (1 - Y_i)\log(1 - P_i)].
\tag{9}
$$

2.4 Hierarchical Contrastive Loss

Aggregating representations of global spatial nodes is a challenging task, and it is crucial to effectively integrate different tissues and pathological features in FFA or OCT images. In addition to designing a GNN for node aggregation, we have designed a Hierarchical Contrastive Loss (HCL). HCL constrains the model to improve its learning ability of node embeddings by measuring the similarity between node embeddings and bag representations. The loss function is designed as follows:

$$
L_{\text{hcl-node}} = 1 - \frac{1}{|G|}\sum_{k=1}^{|G|}\left(\frac{F_i^{BAG} \cdot F_i^{s-\text{KIS}}}{\|F_i^{BAG}\| \cdot \|F_i^{s-\text{KIS}}\|}\right)
\tag{10}
$$

where $|G|$ is the number of nodes of G. Cascaded networks may suffer from constrained feature extraction capabilities in shallow layers due to their long gradient backpropagation paths. The proposed CHG-MIL inherently adopts such a structure. Therefore, it is necessary to impose node-level regularization during training. $L_{\text{hcl-node}}$ enforces SIG to strengthen the representational capacity of individual nodes, aligning them with the final bag-level representations.

Representing the bags of different instances is also extremely difficult. Besides extracting important instance information through modules like MHSA and HII, we have also designed a contrastive loss for instance embeddings and bag representations. Its definition is as follows:

$$L_{\text{hcl-ins}} = 1 - \frac{1}{N} \sum_{i=1}^{N} \left(\frac{F_i^{BAG} \cdot F_i^{s-\text{HII}}}{\|F_i^{BAG}\| \cdot \|F_i^{s-\text{HII}}\|} \right) \tag{11}$$

Applying contrastive constraints solely to the SIG can only regulate the model's ability to extract regional features, which is insufficient. Since feature extraction across multiple instances is equally critical, we introduce $L_{\text{hcl-ins}}$ to address this limitation. The overall loss is given by:

$$L_{\text{all}} = L_{\text{ce}} + \lambda_1 \cdot L_{\text{hcl-node}} + \lambda_2 \cdot L_{\text{hcl-ins}} \tag{12}$$

where $\lambda_1 = 1$ and $\lambda_2 = 1$ are the coefficients for $L_{\text{hcl-node}}$ and $L_{\text{hcl-ins}}$.

3   Experiments

3.1   Experiment Setup

To demonstrate the superiority of the proposed CHG-MIL approach in FFA and OCT images, we conducted a comprehensive comparison with various state-of-the-art MIL methods using two competition datasets.

APTOS2023[1] Dataset. Derived from the Asia Pacific Academy of Ophthalmology Big Data Competition 2023, the APTOS2023 dataset aims to develop machine learning models capable of automatically generating FFA reports for patients. This dataset comprises FFA images from 1,921 eyes. In this work, it is partitioned into training, validation, and test sets in a 3:1:1 ratio. Notably, it encompasses 14 multi-label symptoms, which are disaggregated into 116 binary labels, providing a rich ground for analysis.

GAMMA[2] Dataset [19]. The GAMMA Challenge is dedicated to glaucoma grading using multi-modal imaging. The 100 publicly available 3D OCT volumes are adopted in this work. These volumes were provided by the Sun Yat-sen Ophthalmic Center at Sun Yat-sen University (Guangzhou, China) and acquired with a Topcon DRI OCT Triton scanner. Each 3D OCT scan is centered on the macula, covers a 3×3 mm scan area, and comprises 256 cross-sectional OCT images with a resolution of 992×512 pixels. The dataset categorizes patients into early, intermediate, and advanced glaucoma stages, with 80% of cases allocated to the training set and the remaining 20% reserved for test.

---

[1] https://tianchi.aliyun.com/competition/entrance/532160.
[2] https://aistudio.baidu.com/competition/detail/90/0/introduction.

Implementation Details. During preprocessing, all images were normalized to a pixel range of [0, 1] and uniformly resized to 128×128 pixels after cropping to minimize computational demands. To address variability in the number of images per case, we implemented a random sampling strategy, selecting 8 images per case for the APTOS2023 dataset and 16 images per case for the GAMMA dataset as the inputs. Backbone architectures were tailored to each dataset: ResNet34 for APTOS2023 and ResNet18 for GAMMA. The Adadelta optimizer was employed with an initial learning rate of 0.01, dynamically adjusted using the PolyLR scheduler. Training spanned 200 epochs with a batch size of 64 to balance convergence speed and memory constraints.

Evaluation Metrics. To assess the classification performance, we utilized a comprehensive set of evaluation metrics, including Accuracy (acc), Sensitivity (sen), Precision (prc), Specificity (spe), F1-Score (f1s), balanced Accuracy (bac), Kappa (kap), and Matthews Correlation Coefficient (mcc). These metrics were calculated using a threshold of 0.5.

3.2   Ablation Study

To evaluate the individual contributions of the proposed modules, we conducted a series of ablation studies, as summarized in Table 1. The baseline (BL) refers to a method that employs only the backbone network, without incorporating modules or loss functions such as SIG, HII, HCL.

Table 1. Ablation study on GAMMA dataset. (Unit:%)

BL	SIG	HII	HCL	acc	sen	prc	spe	f1s	bac	kap	mcc
✓	✗	✗	✗	60.00	46.67	41.41	81.11	43.87	46.67	72.88	35.14
✓	✓	✗	✗	65.00	56.67	57.78	83.33	56.94	56.67	73.08	44.18
✓	✓	✓	✗	70.00	60.00	58.89	84.44	58.64	60.00	78.95	50.94
✓	✓	✓	✓	75.00	66.67	66.67	88.89	66.33	66.67	80.77	60.24

The SIG module improves performance by effectively modeling the spatial relationships among instances within the same layer. Furthermore, the HII module, which introduces top-down instance interaction, further enhances performance. When the HCL module is added to constrain the similarity between node embeddings (or instance-aware features) and the bag-level representation, the classification performance improves significantly. Each module contributes uniquely to the improvement in classification performance, and their combination leads to a notable enhancement in overall model effectiveness.

3.3   Comparison with State-of-the-Art Methods

We present a quantitative comparison between the proposed method CHG-MIL and state-of-the-art approaches on GAMMA and APTOS dataset. The comparison includes various MIL methods: those based on simple aggregation techniques such as Avg-Pooling and Max-Pooling, as well as more sophisticated approaches that employ attention mechanisms for instance aggregation, like AB-MIL. Additionally, recent state-of-the-art methods including CLAM-S/M, MIL-RNN, DTFD-MIL, TransMIL, SGMF, and ILRA-MIL are included for comparison.

Table 2. Comparison with state-of-the-arts on GAMMA dataset. The highest scores are in bold and red. (Unit:%)

Method	acc	sen	prc	spe	f1s	bac	kap	mcc
Avg-Pooling	65.00	53.33	52.53	83.33	52.20	53.33	72.00	43.41
Max-Pooling	65.00	56.66	54.99	83.33	55.59	56.66	75.86	44.18
AB-MIL [11]	60.00	46.67	45.56	80.00	45.30	46.67	68.63	33.96
CLAM-S [12]	65.00	53.33	52.53	83.33	52.20	53.33	72.00	43.41
CLAM-M [12]	70.00	60.00	60.30	85.56	59.89	60.00	77.36	51.25
DS-MIL [13]	65.00	53.33	55.56	82.22	51.95	53.33	70.83	43.03
MIL-RNN [10]	50.00	33.33	16.67	66.67	22.22	33.33	0.00	0.00
DTFD-MIL [14]	70.00	60.00	61.11	84.44	59.93	60.00	66.67	50.71
TransMIL [9]	70.00	60.00	61.26	85.56	57.94	60.00	74.47	52.59
ILRA-MIL [16]	50.00	33.33	16.67	66.67	22.22	33.33	0.00	0.00
SGMF [15]	65.00	53.33	55.56	82.22	51.95	53.33	70.83	43.03
CHG-MIL (Ours)	**75.00**	**66.67**	**66.67**	**88.89**	**66.33**	**66.67**	**80.77**	**60.24**

As shown in Table 2, MIL methods using Avg-Pooling and Max-Pooling achieve respectable performance, with acc of 65%, even outperforming AB-MIL, MIL-RNN, and ILRA-MIL. However, their performance remains inferior to methods employing learnable instance aggregation, such as CLAM-M, Trans-MIL, and DTFD-MIL.

The proposed CHG-MIL achieves an acc of 75%, sen of 66.67%, f1s of 66.33%, bac of 66.67%, kap of 80.77%, and mcc of 60.24%, significantly outperforming the second-best method. Notably, CHG-MIL achieves the highest scores across all metrics, demonstrating its overall superiority for this task compared to other considered approaches.

In Table 3, it can be observed that attention-based and transformer-based MIL methods generally achieve better results than Avg-Pooling or Max-Pooling, particularly in terms of bac, kap, and mcc. This suggests that individual image instances in FFA images contain more significant pathological information, making them more amenable to methods utilizing learnable aggregation strategies. CHG-MIL achieves the best performance among all compared methods, with acc of 89.65%, prc of 57.21%, kap of 59.55%, and mcc of 60.42%. Except for a slightly lower sen score of 76.56%, which ranks below DS-MIL, CHG-MIL outperforms all other methods on the remaining seven evaluation metrics.

Table 3. Comparison with state-of-the-arts on APTOS2023 dataset. The highest scores are in bold and red. (Unit:%)

Method	acc	sen	prc	spe	f1s	bac	kap	mcc
Avg-Pooling	87.19	75.15	50.03	88.96	76.22	82.05	52.80	54.35
Max-Pooling	87.04	75.00	49.65	88.81	76.01	81.91	52.40	53.99
AB-MIL [11]	87.74	74.78	51.51	89.64	76.86	82.21	54.02	55.34
CLAM-S [12]	88.76	75.08	54.46	90.77	78.25	82.92	56.69	57.71
CLAM-M [12]	88.96	75.50	55.07	90.94	78.59	83.22	57.36	58.36
DS-MIL [13]	87.95	**77.50**	52.01	89.48	77.54	83.49	55.40	56.97
MIL-RNN [10]	86.05	74.08	47.19	87.81	74.65	80.95	49.79	51.61
DTFD-MIL [14]	89.32	77.14	56.08	91.11	79.32	84.13	58.83	59.87
TransMIL [9]	87.73	74.80	51.47	89.63	76.85	82.21	53.99	55.32
ILRA-MIL [16]	82.52	71.24	39.83	84.17	70.23	77.71	41.47	44.07
SGMF [15]	88.96	75.14	55.36	91.01	78.62	83.08	57.42	58.35
CHG-MIL (Ours)	**89.65**	76.56	**57.21**	**91.58**	**79.70**	**84.07**	**59.55**	**60.42**

3.4   Conclusion

In this study, we introduce a contrastive hierarchical graph based multiple instance learning (CHG-MIL) framework specifically designed for fundus images screening. To capture the intricate topological relationships among regional instances, we design a spatial instance graph (SIG) module. The sampled features, extracted at various levels, undergo hierarchical instance interaction (HII) from top to down. Ultimately, this leads to a prediction of the bag-level category. Furthermore, the hierarchical contrastive loss functions are adopted to remove the disease-irrelevant features in graph nodes and instances. Our proposed CHG-MIL demonstrates superior performance on the APTOS2023 and GAMMA datasets, outperforming numerous state-of-the-art methods. Looking ahead, we aim to further explore the interpretability of multiple instance learning within the context of medical applications.

Acknowledgments. This work was supported by the Huzhou Science and Technology Program under Grant 2023GZ13.

References

1. Zhou, W., Ji, J., Cui, W., Yi, Y.: Pseudo-label clustering-driven dual-level contrast learning based source-free domain adaptation for fundus image segmentation, pp. 492–503. Springer Nature Singapore (2023). https://doi.org/10.1007/978-981-99-8469-5_39
2. Feng, Y., Zhou, S., Wang, Y., Li, Z., Liu, H.: Edge-prior contrastive transformer for optic cup and optic disc segmentation. In: Liu, Q., et al. (eds.), pp. 443–455. Springer Nature Singapore (2023). https://doi.org/10.1007/978-981-99-8469-5_35

3. Zhao, P.Y., Bommakanti, N., Yu, G., et al.: Deep learning for automated detection of neovascular leakage on ultra-widefield fluorescein angiography in diabetic retinopathy. Sci. Rep. **13**(1), 9162 (2023)
4. Ebrahimiadib, N., Kianzad, Z., Zarei, M., Davoudi, S., et al.: Non-cystic macular thickening on optical coherence tomography as an alternative to fluorescein angiography for predicting retinal vascular leakage in early stages of uveitis. Sci. Rep. **12**(1), 13473 (2022)
5. Tavakoli, M., Shahri, R.P., Pourreza, H., Mehdizadeh, A., et al.: A complementary method for automated detection of microaneurysms in fluorescein angiography fundus images to assess diabetic retinopathy. Pattern Recognit. **46**(10), 2740–2753 (2013)
6. Shen, S., Jin, S., Li, F., Zhao, J.: Optical coherence tomography parameters as prognostic factors for stereopsis after vitrectomy for unilateral epiretinal membrane: a cohort study. Sci. Rep. **14**(1), 6715 (2024)
7. Tan, Y., Yang, K.-F., Zhao, S.-X., Wang, J., et al.: Deep matched filtering for retinal vessel segmentation. Knowl. Based Syst. **283**, 111185 (2024)
8. Tan, Y., Shen, W.-D., Ming-Yuan, W., Liu, G.-N., et al.: Retinal layer segmentation in oct images with boundary regression and feature polarization. IEEE Trans. Med. Imaging **43**(2), 686–700 (2024)
9. Shao, Z., Bian, H., Chen, Y., Wang, Y., et al.: TRANSMIL: transformer based correlated multiple instance learning for whole slide image classification. Proc. NeuIPS **34**, 2136–2147 (2021)
10. Campanella, G., Hanna, M.G., Geneslaw, L., Miraflor, A., et al.: Clinical-grade computational pathology using weakly supervised deep learning on whole slide images. Nat. Med. **25**(8), 1301–1309 (2019)
11. Ilse, M., Tomczak, J., Welling, M.: Attention-based deep multiple instance learning. In: Dy, J., Krause, A. (eds.) Proceedings of the ICML, Machine Learning Research, vol. 80 , pp. 2127–2136. PMLR 10–15 (2018)
12. Lu, M.Y., Williamson, D.F., Chen, T.Y., Chen, R.J., et al.: Data-efficient and weakly supervised computational pathology on whole-slide images. Nat. Biomed. Eng. **5**(6), 555–570 (2021)
13. Li, B., Li, Y., Eliceiri, K.W.: Dual-stream multiple instance learning network for whole slide image classification with self-supervised contrastive learning. In: Proceedings of the CVPR, pp. 14318–14328 (2021)
14. Zhang, H., Meng, Y., Zhao, Y., Qiao, Y., et al.: DTFD-MIL: double-tier feature distillation multiple instance learning for histopathology whole slide image classification. In: Proceedings of the CVPR, pp. 18802–18812 (2022)
15. Shi, J., et al.: A structure-aware hierarchical graph-based multiple instance learning framework for PT staging in histopathological image. IEEE Trans. Med. Imaging **42**(10), 3000–3011 (2023)
16. Xiang, J., Zhang, J.: Exploring low-rank property in multiple instance learning for whole slide image classification. In: Proceedings of the ICLR (2022)
17. Xue, J., et al.: HGCL: hierarchical graph contrastive learning for user-item recommendation (2025)
18. Li, G., Xiong, C., Thabet, A., Ghanem, B.: DeeperGCN: all you need to train deeper GCNs. arXiv preprint arXiv:2006.07739 (2020)
19. Junde, W., Fang, H., Li, F., Huazhu, F., et al.: GAMMA challenge: glaucoma grading from multi-modality images. Medical Image Anal. **90**, 102938 (2023)

Polyp Segmentation Based on Edge Guidance

Yulong Bai[1,2], Xiuhong Li[1,2(✉)], Kuan Wang[1,2], Boyuan Li[1,2], Haodong Zeng[1,2], and Wenjing Guo[1,2]

[1] School of Computer Science and Technology, Xinjiang University, Urumqi, China
`xjulxh@xju.edu.cn`
[2] Xinjiang Key Laboratory of Signal Detection and Processing, Urumqi, China

Abstract. Accurate segmentation of polyps in colonoscopy images is of vital importance for the early diagnosis and treatment of colorectal cancer (CRC). However, accurate segmentation is a challenge due to the diversity of polyps in size and shape as well as unclear boundaries. To this end, we propose a novel edge-guided network (EGNet) for polyp segmentation, which achieves cross-level feature fusion by effectively utilizing edge information and enhances the focus on polyp edges. Specifically, we first propose a multi-scale enhancement module (MSEM), which strengthens the feature representation capability through the interaction between convolutional kernels of different sizes. Next, we propose an edge-aware guided module (EAGM), which extracts more discriminative edge features and enhances the model's sensitivity to edge details. Finally, we propose a cross-level fusion module (CLFM) that integrates contextual cues from different levels to enhance the semantic perception of target regions in complex backgrounds. Our experimental results on four benchmark datasets show that EGNet outperforms other state-of-the-art methods.

Keywords: Polyp segmentation · Edge-aware guidance · Cross-level fusion

1 Introduction

Colorectal cancer (CRC) is one of the malignant tumors with high morbidity and mortality rates worldwide [1]. Its occurrence is usually closely related to the precancerous lesions of adenomatous polyps. If effective intervention is not performed in the early stages, polyps may gradually develop into malignant tumors within a few years. At present, colonoscopy is considered to be the "gold standard" for clinical diagnosis of such lesions, which can provide key information such as the morphological characteristics of polyps and their spatial location. However, this technology is highly dependent on the operator's experience and

Supported by the Xinjiang Uygur Autonomous Region Graduate Research Innovation Project (XJ2024G088), the Central Guidance Local Science and Technology Development Fund (No. ZYYD2025JD10), the Tianshan Talent Training Project - Xinjiang Science and Technology Innovation Team Program (2023TSYCTD) and National Natural Science Foundation of China (No. 62261053).

judgment in practical applications, and there is a certain degree of subjectivity and risk of missed diagnosis. In addition, manual identification and labeling of polyp areas are not only inefficient, but also easily affected by factors such as visual fatigue, which limits the consistency and accuracy of diagnosis. Therefore, it is urgent to develop an efficient automatic polyp segmentation method to assist doctors in achieving accurate positioning and quantitative analysis of polyp areas, thereby improving the efficiency and accuracy of diagnosis and treatment.

In recent years, researchers have proposed a variety of deep learning-based solutions to address the challenges of polyp segmentation. Fang *et al.* [2] proposed SFANet, which effectively improved the model's recognition accuracy of polyp regions by introducing regional constraints and boundary constraints in the selective feature aggregation network. Fan *et al.* [3] designed PraNet, which uses parallel partial decoders to generate initial positioning regions and combines the reverse attention mechanism to mine edge clues, thereby significantly enhancing boundary perception. CFANet proposed by Zhou *et al.* [4] improves the model's sensitivity to polyp boundaries by fusing multi-scale and multi-level feature information and combining boundary prediction and aggregation modules. NPDNet developed by Guo *et al.* [5] uses a non-pre-training strategy for deep supervision and introduces a parallel dual-attention mechanism to improve the model's generalization performance and segmentation accuracy without relying on large-scale pre-training. In addition, Zhou *et al.* [6] also proposed EFANet, which embeds edge information into multi-level feature representations, thereby further optimizing the overall effect of polyp segmentation.

Although certain results have been achieved in the field of automatic polyp segmentation, there are still some challenges in existing methods. First, polyps show significant morphological differences at different stages of development, and their sizes range from tiny lesions to large lesions. Existing models have certain limitations in dealing with scale changes, especially when dealing with small-sized polyps, which is prone to insufficient feature representation, resulting in decreased segmentation accuracy or even information loss. Secondly, shallow features usually contain rich spatial structural information, while deep features have stronger semantic expression capabilities, which help to accurately locate the polyp area. However, how to effectively fuse these two different levels of features to achieve accurate modeling of the polyp area is still one of the difficulties in current research. Finally, since the edge between polyps and their surrounding mucosal tissues is often unclear, it is difficult to achieve accurate edge positioning relying solely on global semantic information. Therefore, introducing a edge perception mechanism to establish an association between the polyp body and edge cues helps to improve the model's sensitivity to edge details and segmentation consistency.

To this end, we propose a new edge-guided network (EGNet) for polyp segmentation, which achieves cross-level feature fusion by effectively utilizing edge cues and enhances the model's ability to identify polyp boundaries. Specifically, we first propose a multi-scale enhancement module (MSEM), which strengthens the feature expression ability and improves the model's adaptability to the multi-scale characteristics of polyps through the synergy between convolutional kernels of various sizes. Secondly, we propose a edge-aware guided module (EAGM) to extract discriminative edge information, thereby enhancing the model's sensitivity to edge details. Finally, we propose a cross-level fusion module (CLFM), which enhances the model's stability and accuracy in dealing with polyp areas with fuzzy boundaries and complex structures by integrating contextual features from different levels.

We summarize our main contributions as follows:

- We proposed a novel polyp segmentation framework EGNet, which significantly improved the model's ability to recognize polyp areas and their boundaries by introducing a edge-aware mechanism and a cross-level feature fusion strategy.
- We propose a multi-scale enhancement module (MSEM), which enhances the model's ability to model the diversity of polyp morphology through the interaction between convolution kernels of different sizes, enabling it to better cope with polyps of different sizes and shapes.
- We conduct comparative experiments on four benchmark colonoscopy datasets and show that our EGNet achieves superior results compared to seventeen state-of-the-art segmentation methods.

2 Methodology

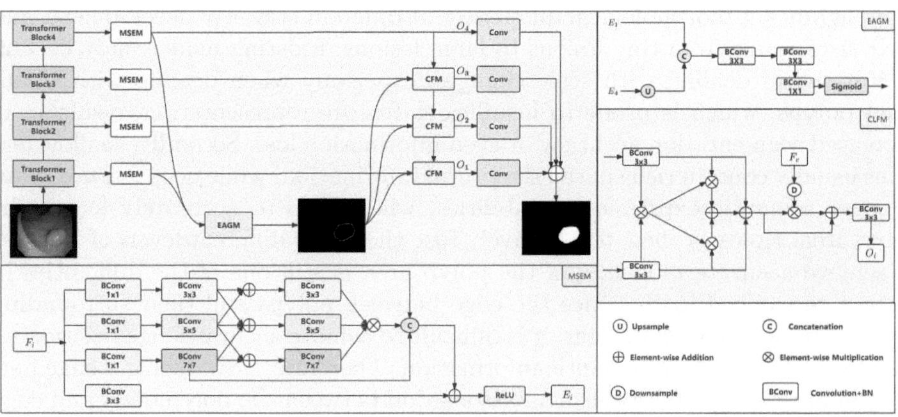

Fig. 1. The architecture of the proposed EGNet, which consists of multi-scale enhancement module (MSEM), edge-aware guided module (EAGM), and cross-level fusion module (CLFM).

2.1 Overview of the Architecture

The overall architecture of the edge-guided polyp segmentation network (EGNet) proposed in this paper is shown in Fig. 1, which consists of three parts: pyramid visual transformer (PVT) encoder, multi-scale enhancement module (MSEM), edge-aware guided module (EAGM), and cross-level fusion module (CLFM).

Specifically, the colonoscopy images are first fed into the encoder network (PVTv2 [7] as the backbone) to extract multi-level features, which are represented as F_i ($i = 1, 2, 3, 4, 5$). Subsequently, these features are sent to MSEM for further processing to obtain multi-scale feature representations E_i to ensure that information at different levels of detail is fully captured. Next, E_1 and E_4 are sent to EAGM to obtain edge map F_e. After that, CLFM is used to fuse features at different levels and edge-aware features F_e to capture local and global contextual information, and the processed features are passed to the prediction head to generate a preliminary prediction map O_i. Finally, by weighting the four preliminary prediction maps, a final segmentation map with higher accuracy is formed.

2.2 Multi-scale Enhancement Module

Due to polyps of different scales differ in morphology, learning scale-related feature representations is crucial to improving the performance of polyp segmentation models. To effectively capture rich contextual information while reducing the number of channels, we propose a MSEM to enhance feature representations using different scale-dependent information. Specifically, as shown in Fig. 1, we first pass the original feature F_i through three parallel 1×1 convolutions, followed by a batch normalization. Subsequently, three convolutional layers with varying kernel sizes are employed to facilitate information sharing and capture multi-scale features. The feature maps F_1, F_2, and F_3 are processed by convolutional layers with kernel sizes 3×3, 5×5, and 7×7, respectively, resulting in F_{31}, F_{51}, and F_{71}. Next, we use element-wise addition operations to fuse adjacent features and then feed them to convolutional layers with different convolutional kernels, which can be represented as follows:

$$\begin{cases} F_{32} = BConv_{3\times3}(F_{31} \oplus F_{51}) \\ F_{52} = BConv_{5\times5}(F_{31} \oplus F_{51} \oplus F_{71}) \\ F_{72} = BConv_{7\times7}(F_{51} \oplus F_{71}) \end{cases} \tag{1}$$

where $\oplus$ denotes element-wise addition. Next, we perform element-wise multiplication on the obtained F_{32}, F_{72}, and F_{52}, and then concatenate them with F_{31}, and F_{71} to obtain F_m, which is obtained as follows:

$$F_m = Concat(F_{31}, F_{71}, F_{32} \otimes F_{52} \otimes F_{72}) \tag{2}$$

where $Concat(\cdot)$ denotes the concatenation operation. Subsequently, the concatenated features are added element-wise to the original features after a 3×3 convolution, which can be expressed as:

$$E_i = ReLU(BConv_{3\times3}(F_m) \oplus BConv_{3\times3}(F_i)) \tag{3}$$

where $BConv_{3\times3}(\cdot)$ denotes the operation of a 3×3 convolution followed by batch normalization, and $ReLU(\cdot)$ denotes ReLU activation function.

2.3   Edge-Aware Guided Module

Edge information has shown significant advantages in segmentation and detection tasks. Low-level features can effectively capture edge details, and current models usually integrate these low-level features to learn the semantics of edges. Sun *et al.* [8] proposed that edge semantic information can be extracted more accurately by utilizing high-level features. Therefore, we propose an EAGM, which combines low-level features E_1 and high-level features E_4 to extract more effective edge information. Specifically, as shown in Fig. 1, we first upsample E_4 to the same size as E_1, then concatenate them, and then through 3×3 convolution to get E_c, which can be represented as:

$$E_c = BConv_{3\times3}(Concat(E_1, Up(E_4))) \tag{4}$$

Next, E_c is processed sequentially by a 3×3 convolution followed by a 1×1 convolution, then passed through a Sigmoid activation function. Thus, the resulting edge-aware feature F_e can be represented as:

$$F_e = S(BConv_{3\times3}(BConv_{1\times1}(E_c))) \tag{5}$$

where $S(\cdot)$ denotes the Sigmoid function. In addition, considering the significant imbalance in pixel distribution between the polyp area and the background, we use Dice loss to solve it. It optimizes the overlap between the predicted area and the true label, enhances the model's ability to recognize the polyp edge on a global scale, and effectively improves the edge clarity and consistency of the segmentation result.

2.4   Cross-Level Fusion Module

In order to make full use of cross-level contextual semantic information and edge-aware features to improve segmentation results, we propose a CLFM to achieve effective integration of contextual clues at different levels. Specifically, as shown in Fig. 1, taking F_a and F_b as examples, we first pass them through a 3×3 convolution, then perform element-wise multiplication on them, and then send them to the Sigmoid activation function, which can be depicted by

$$\mathcal{H} = S(BConv_{3\times3}(F_a) \otimes BConv_{3\times3}(F_b)) \tag{6}$$

where $\otimes$ denotes element-wise multiplication. Next, we perform element-wise multiplication on them and the original features, and then perform element-wise addition to obtain F_g, which can be expressed as follows:

$$F_g = \mathcal{H} \otimes BConv_{3\times3}(F_a) \oplus (1 - \mathcal{H}) \otimes BConv_{3\times3}(F_b) \tag{7}$$

Subsequently, F_g is added to the original features element by element to obtain F_h, which ensures that the model retains the original features while fusing the cross-enhancement information. Next, we first downsample the edge map F_e to the same resolution as F_h. Then, skip connections and 3×3 convolutions are used to perform element-wise multiplication on F_e and F_h, which is obtained as follows:

$$O_i = BConv_{3\times3}(F_h \otimes D(F_e) \oplus F_h) \tag{8}$$

where $\otimes$ denotes element-wise multiplication, $\oplus$ denotes element-wise addition, and $D(\cdot)$ denotes the downsampling operation.

2.5   Loss Function

Our model makes five predictions, including the edge map (F_e) and $O_i(i \in (1, \cdots, 4))$. All prediction maps are adjusted to the same resolution as the input. During model training, we used a combination of weighted binary cross entropy loss $(\mathcal{L}_{wBCE})$ [9] and weighted intersection-over-union loss $(\mathcal{L}_{wIoU})$ [9]. $\mathcal{L}_{wBCE}$ effectively alleviates the class imbalance problem by assigning higher weights to difficult-to-segment areas, especially improving the segmentation accuracy of polyp boundaries. $\mathcal{L}_{wIoU}$ enhances the model's ability to model global structures by optimizing the overlap between the predicted area and the true label. Combining these two loss functions enables the model to strike a balance between local details and global semantic information, thereby achieving more accurate polyp segmentation. Therefore, the basic loss function $\mathcal{L}_{basic}$ is as follows:

$$\mathcal{L}_{basic} = \mathcal{L}_{wBCE}(P, G) + \mathcal{L}_{wIoU}(P, G) \tag{9}$$

In addition, we use dice loss [8] to supervise the generation process of the edge map. Therefore, the overall loss function $\mathcal{L}_{total}$ is as follows:

$$\mathcal{L}_{total} = \alpha \mathcal{L}_{dice}(F_e, G_e) + \sum_{i=1}^{4} \mathcal{L}_b(O_i, G) \tag{10}$$

The hyperparameter α is set to 5, G denotes the ground truth map, and G_e denotes the ground truth map of the edge.

3   Experiment

3.1   Experimental Settings

Datasets. In order to verify the performance of the model in the polyp segmentation task, we conducted comparative experiments on four widely used public datasets. The details of each dataset are as follows:

· CVC-ClinicDB [10]: This dataset contains a total of 612 colonoscopy images with an image size of 288×384.

· Kvasir [11]: This dataset was collected by the Vestre-Viken Health Trust in Norway and contains 1,000 images from inside the digestive tract.

· CVC-300 [12]: This dataset contains 60 high-resolution images with an image size of 500×574.

· CVC-ColonDB [13]: This dataset contains 380 images with an image size of 500×570.

In terms of training and testing division, we refer to the division strategy in PraNet [3], randomly select 550 images from CVC-ClinicDB, and combine them with 900 images from the Kvasir dataset to form a training set, totaling 1450 images. The remaining data not used for training, including the remaining images in CVC-ClinicDB, Kvasir, and the entire CVC-300 and CVC-ColonDB datasets, are used as test sets.

Evaluation Metrics. To comprehensively evaluate the model performance, we adopt five widely recognized evaluation metrics, namely, mean dice score (mDice) [14], mean Intersection over Union (mIoU) [14], S-measure (S_α) [15], F-measure (F_β^ω) [16], and E_ϕ^{max} [17].

Implementation Details. In our model, we use the pre-trained PVTv2 as the backbone network. Our proposed framework is implemented in PyTorch and trained using an NVDIA RTX 4090 GPU with 24 GB memory. We use the Adam algorithm to optimize the proposed model and the learning rate is set to 1e-4. During training and testing, we resize the images to 352*352 and apply operations such as random flipping, scaling, and rotation as data augmentation. The batch size is set to 16, the training epoch is 100, and the entire training process takes about three hours.

3.2 Comparison to State-of-the-Art Methods

Comparison Methods. To verify the effectiveness of the proposed model, we compared EGNet with seventeen state-of-the-art segmentation methods, namely UNet [18], UNet++ [19], Atten-Unet [20], SFA [2], PraNet [3], UTNet [21], TranUnet [22], MSNet [23], M^{2}SNet [24], HiFormer [25], SAM-Adapter [26], SAM-L [27], CFANet [4], MedSAM [28], PRCNet [29], NPDNet [5], and EFANet [6]. We obtained the predicted segmentation maps from the original papers or retrained the models using the authors' open source code for fair comparison. In addition, we evaluated all the predicted segmentation maps using the evaluation code provided by PraNet.

Quantitative Comparison. Table 1 shows the quantitative comparison results of our model with 17 state-of-the-art methods on four benchmark datasets using five evaluation metrics. The results show that our model performs better than other segmentation methods, mainly due to its effective integration of cross-level contextual information with multi-scale feature representations, and dynamically optimizing the feature fusion process through a edge-aware guidance mechanism, which significantly improves the segmentation performance. Specifically, compared with the state-of-the-art model EFANet, our model improves

Table 1. Four polyp datasets were quantitatively evaluated. Five indicators were used in this study, namely mDice, mIou, S_α, F_β^ω, E_ϕ^{max}. The best results are highlighted in bold.

Methods	CVC-ClinicDB [10]					Kvasir [11]					CVC-300 [12]					CVC-ColonDB [13]				
	mDice	mIou	S_α	F_β^ω	E_ϕ^{max}	mDice	mIou	S_α	F_β^ω	E_ϕ^{max}	mDice	mIou	S_α	F_β^ω	E_ϕ^{max}	mDice	mIou	S_α	F_β^ω	E_ϕ^{max}
UNet [18]	0.824	0.767	0.889	0.811	0.917	0.821	0.756	0.858	0.794	0.901	0.717	0.639	0.842	0.684	0.867	0.519	0.449	0.711	0.498	0.763
UNet++ [19]	0.797	0.741	0.872	0.785	0.898	0.824	0.753	0.862	0.808	0.907	0.714	0.636	0.838	0.687	0.884	0.490	0.413	0.691	0.467	0.762
Atten-Unet [20]	0.866	0.809	0.908	0.856	0.960	0.769	0.683	0.828	0.730	0.859	0.603	0.511	0.760	0.554	0.819	0.466	0.385	0.670	0.431	0.724
SFA [2]	0.698	0.615	0.793	0.647	0.816	0.725	0.619	0.782	0.670	0.828	0.465	0.332	0.640	0.341	0.604	0.467	0.351	0.634	0.379	0.648
PraNet [3]	0.902	0.858	0.935	0.896	0.958	0.901	0.848	0.915	0.885	0.943	0.873	0.804	0.924	0.843	0.938	0.716	0.645	0.820	0.699	0.847
UTNet [21]	0.860	0.818	0.910	0.856	0.963	0.862	0.803	0.886	0.843	0.911	0.806	0.733	0.882	0.778	0.924	0.676	0.600	0.799	0.656	0.855
TranUnet [22]	0.847	0.798	0.907	0.831	0.920	0.869	0.816	0.899	0.847	0.920	0.828	0.757	0.906	0.785	0.901	0.717	0.645	0.824	0.685	0.841
MSNet [23]	0.921	0.879	0.941	0.914	0.972	0.907	0.862	0.922	0.893	0.944	0.869	0.807	0.925	0.849	0.943	0.755	0.678	0.836	0.737	0.883
M²SNet [24]	0.918	0.869	0.942	0.917	0.970	0.912	0.861	0.922	0.901	0.953	0.876	0.805	0.926	0.848	0.965	0.758	0.685	0.842	0.737	0.869
HiFormer [25]	0.891	0.837	0.895	0.888	0.961	0.881	0.823	0.846	0.873	0.939	0.847	0.775	0.897	0.832	0.940	0.676	0.605	0.786	0.669	0.812
SAM-Adpter [26]	0.774	0.673	–	–	–	0.847	0.763	–	–	–	0.815	0.725	–	–	–	0.671	0.568	–	–	–
SAM-L [27]	0.578	0.526	0.744	0.563	0.683	0.782	0.710	0.832	0.773	0.834	0.726	0.676	0.849	0.729	0.824	0.468	0.422	0.690	0.463	0.607
CFANet [4]	0.932	0.883	0.950	0.924	0.981	0.915	0.861	0.924	0.903	0.956	0.893	0.827	0.938	0.875	0.962	0.743	0.665	0.835	0.728	0.869
MedSAM [28]	0.867	0.803	–	–	–	0.862	0.795	–	–	–	0.870	0.798	–	–	–	0.734	0.651	–	–	–
PRCNet [29]	0.925	0.869	0.943	0.916	0.980	0.799	0.716	0.837	0.763	0.886	0.819	0.736	0.891	0.777	0.909	0.688	0.599	0.800	0.660	0.843
NPDNet [5]	0.928	0.878	0.946	0.926	0.982	0.910	0.855	0.921	0.899	0.958	0.876	0.803	0.925	0.848	0.971	**0.812**	**0.729**	**0.869**	0.795	**0.923**
EFANet [6]	0.919	0.871	0.943	0.916	–	0.914	0.861	**0.929**	0.906	–	0.894	0.830	**0.941**	0.878	–	0.774	0.696	0.855	0.753	–
Ours	**0.940**	**0.895**	**0.952**	**0.941**	**0.989**	**0.922**	**0.870**	0.926	**0.912**	**0.962**	**0.898**	**0.831**	0.932	**0.881**	**0.973**	0.811	0.728	0.863	**0.797**	0.919

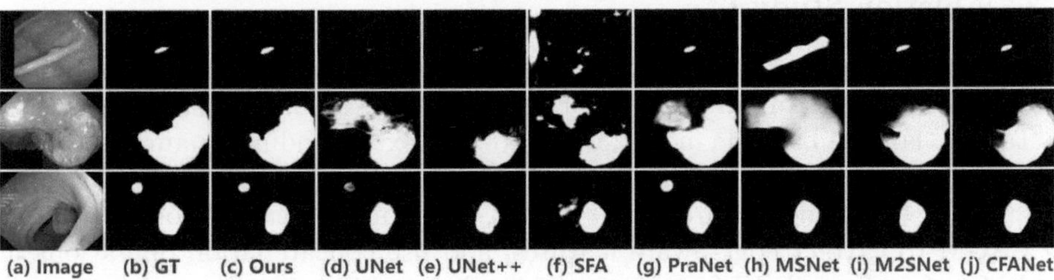

Fig. 2. Visual comparisons between our model and seven state-of-the-art models demonstrate its superior performance.

by 2.1%, 2.4%, 0.9%, and 2.5% in mDice, mIoU, S_α, and F_β^ω on CVC-ClinicDB, respectively. On the Kvasir dataset, our model improves by 1.2%, 1.5%, 5%, 1.3%, and 4% in mDice, mIoU, S_α, F_β^ω, and E_ϕ^{max}, respectively, over NPDNet. These results show that our model has stronger generalization ability and significantly improves the performance of polyp segmentation.

Qualitative Comparison. Figure 2 depicts the segmentation results of our model compared with eight state-of-the-art polyp segmentation methods. According to the visualization results, the prediction results of our model are closest to the ground truth map, and our model outperforms other polyp segmentation methods in different challenging scenarios. Specifically, in the first row, the size of the polyp is very small, and our model can still accurately segment the small polyp. In the second row, the size of the polyp is relatively large, our model can accurately segment the polyp, while other models almost fail. In the third row, the image contains multiple polyp targets, our model is

Table 2. Results of ablation study on the CVC-ClinicDB and Kvasir datasets. The best results are highlighted in bold.

Methods	CVC-ClinicDB [10]					Kvasir [11]				
	mDice	mIou	S_α	F_β^ω	E_ϕ^{max}	mDice	mIou	S_α	F_β^ω	E_ϕ^{max}
(a)Baseline	0.897	0.837	0.921	0.897	0.975	0.897	0.840	0.910	0.890	0.955
(b)w/o MSEM	0.916	0.863	0.938	0.911	0.970	0.910	0.860	0.918	0.903	0.954
(c)w/o EAGM	0.916	0.865	0.938	0.916	0.973	0.910	0.859	0.919	0.903	**0.964**
(d)w/o CLFM	0.919	0.873	0.940	0.919	0.977	0.909	0.858	0.913	0.899	0.953
Ours	**0.940**	**0.895**	**0.952**	**0.941**	**0.989**	**0.922**	**0.870**	**0.926**	**0.912**	0.962

able to effectively distinguish each polyp area and suppress background interference, while other models generally have problems with incomplete recognition or blurred boundaries.

3.3   Ablation Study

We conduct comprehensive ablation experiments to demonstrate the importance of different modules in our proposed EGNet, and the ablation results are shown in Table 2. For the baseline model, we remove all extra modules (namely MSEM, EAGM, and CLFM), use 1×1 convolution instead of MSEM to reduce the channels of backbone features ($F_i, i \in \{1, \ldots, 4\}$), use concatenation operations in EAGM to extract edge-aware features, and use concatenation operations in CLFM to fuse cross-level features and edge features in a top-down manner.

Effectiveness of MSEM. To verify the importance of MSEM, we adopt 1×1 convolution to replace it, namely "w/o MSEM". As shown in Table 2, we can see that the performance decreases without using the proposed MSEM, which indicates that MSEM can effectively enhance the feature expression ability and enhance the model's recognition ability for complex morphology polyps, thereby improving the model's adaptability and stability to polyps of different scales.

Effectiveness of EAGM. To study the contribution of EAGM, we use a concatenation operation to extract edge-aware features, namely "w/o EAGM". As shown in Table 2, we observe a performance degradation of "w/o EGAM" on both datasets. The results show that EGAM can effectively model the edge features of polyps, thereby improving the model's ability to perceive edge details.

Effectiveness of CLFM. To study the importance of CLFM, we directly use the concatenation operation to fuse the two features, namely "w/o CLFM". As shown in Table 2, we can observe that the performance decreases without using CLFM. The experimental results verify the effectiveness of CLFM, which can effectively fuse semantic information from different levels, effectively alleviate the information gap between high-level semantics and low-level details, and better capture the global structure and local details of polyps.

4   Conclusion

In this work, we propose a novel edge-guided network (EGNet) for polyp segmentation, which significantly enhances the recognition ability of polyp edges by effectively utilizing edge information for cross-level feature fusion. Specifically, we first propose a multi-scale enhancement module (MSEM) to strengthen the feature representation through the interaction between convolution kernels of different sizes, improving the model's adaptability to the diversity and complexity of polyps. In addition, we propose a edge-aware guidance module (EAGM) to extract more discriminative edge features and improve the model's sensitivity to polyp edge details. Finally, the cross-level fusion module (CLFM) integrates contextual information from different levels to enhance the semantic understanding of target regions in complex backgrounds. Extensive experimental results on four benchmark datasets verify the effectiveness of our EGNet in accurately segmenting polyps, providing strong support for the early diagnosis and treatment of colorectal cancer (CRC). In future work, we will focus on further optimizing the model structure and exploring its potential for application across a broader range of medical image analysis tasks.

References

1. Constantinou, V., Constantinou, C.: Focusing on colorectal cancer in young adults. Molecular Clin. Oncol. **20**(1), 1–10 (2024)
2. Fang, Y., Chen, C., Yuan, Y., Tong, K.: Selective feature aggregation network with area-boundary constraints for polyp segmentation. In: Shen, D., et al. (eds.) MICCAI 2019. LNCS, vol. 11764, pp. 302–310. Springer, Cham (2019). https://doi.org/10.1007/978-3-030-32239-7_34
3. Fan, D.-P., et al.: PraNet: parallel reverse attention network for polyp segmentation. In: Martel, A.L., et al. (eds.) MICCAI 2020. LNCS, vol. 12266, pp. 263–273. Springer, Cham (2020). https://doi.org/10.1007/978-3-030-59725-2_26
4. Zhou, T., et al.: Cross-level feature aggregation network for polyp segmentation. Pattern Recogn. **140**, 109555 (2023)
5. Yu, Z., Zhao, L., Liao, T., Zhang, X., Chen, G., Xiao, G.: A novel non-pretrained deep supervision network for polyp segmentation. Pattern Recogn. **154**, 110554 (2024)
6. Zhou, T., Zhang, Y., Chen, G., Zhou, Y., Wu, Y., Fan, D.-P.: Edge-aware feature aggregation network for polyp segmentation. Mach. Intell. Res. **22**(1), 101–116 (2025)
7. Wang, W., et al.: Pvt v2: improved baselines with pyramid vision transformer. Comput. Vis. Media **8**(3), 415–424 (2022)
8. Sun, Y., Wang, S., Chen, C., Xiang, T.-Z.: Boundary-guided camouflaged object detection. In: IJCAI 2022: 31st International Joint Conference on Artificial Intelligence, pp. 1335–1341 (2022)
9. Wei, J., Wang, S., Huang, Q.: F^{3}Net: fusion, feedback and focus for salient object detection. In: AAAI Conference on Artificial Intelligence 2020, vol. 34(07), pp. 12321–12328 (2020)

10. Bernal, J., Sánchez, F.J., Fernández-Esparrach, G., Gil, D., Rodríguez, C., Vilariño, F.: WM-DOVA maps for accurate polyp highlighting in colonoscopy: validation vs. saliency maps from physicians. Comput. Med. Imaging Graph. **43**, 99–111 (2015)
11. Jha, D., et al.: Kvasir-SEG: a segmented polyp dataset. In: Ro, Y.M., et al. (eds.) MMM 2020. LNCS, vol. 11962, pp. 451–462. Springer, Cham (2020). https://doi.org/10.1007/978-3-030-37734-2_37
12. Vázquez, D., et al.: A benchmark for endoluminal scene segmentation of colonoscopy images. J. Healthcare Eng. **2017**(1), 4037190 (2017)
13. Tajbakhsh, N., Gurudu, S.R., Liang, J.: Automated polyp detection in colonoscopy videos using shape and context information. IEEE Trans. Med. Imaging **35**(2), 630–644 (2015)
14. Yang, C., Guo, X., Zhu, M., Ibragimov, B., Yuan, Y.: Mutual-prototype adaptation for cross-domain polyp segmentation. IEEE J. Biomed. Health Inform. **25**(10), 3886–3897 (2021)
15. Fan, D.-P., Cheng, M.-M., Liu, Y., Li, T., Borji, A.: Structure-measure: A new way to evaluate foreground maps. In: IEEE International Conference on Computer Vision, pp. 4548–4557 (2017)
16. Achanta, R., Hemami, S., Estrada, F., Susstrunk, S.: Frequency-tuned salient region detection. In: IEEE Conference on Computer Vision and Pattern Recognition, pp. 1597–1604 (2009)
17. Fan, D.-P., Gong, C., Cao, Y., Ren, B., Cheng, M.-M., Borji, A.: Enhanced-alignment measure for binary foreground map evaluation. arXiv preprint arXiv:1805.10421 (2018)
18. Ronneberger, O., Fischer, P., Brox, T.: U-Net: convolutional networks for biomedical image segmentation. In: Navab, N., Hornegger, J., Wells, W.M., Frangi, A.F. (eds.) MICCAI 2015. LNCS, vol. 9351, pp. 234–241. Springer, Cham (2015). https://doi.org/10.1007/978-3-319-24574-4_28
19. Zhou, Z., Rahman Siddiquee, M.M., Tajbakhsh, N., Liang, J.: UNet++: a nested U-Net architecture for medical image segmentation. In: Stoyanov, D., et al. (eds.) DLMIA/ML-CDS -2018. LNCS, vol. 11045, pp. 3–11. Springer, Cham (2018). https://doi.org/10.1007/978-3-030-00889-5_1
20. Oktay, O., et al.: Attention u-net: Learning where to look for the pancreas. arXiv preprint arXiv:1804.03999 (2018)
21. Gao, Y., Zhou, M., Metaxas, D.N.: UTNet: a hybrid transformer architecture for medical image segmentation. In: de Bruijne, M., et al. (eds.) MICCAI 2021. LNCS, vol. 12903, pp. 61–71. Springer, Cham (2021). https://doi.org/10.1007/978-3-030-87199-4_6
22. Chen, J., et al.: Transunet: transformers make strong encoders for medical image segmentation. arXiv preprint arXiv:2102.04306 (2021)
23. Zhao, X., Zhang, L., Lu, H.: Automatic polyp segmentation via multi-scale subtraction network. In: de Bruijne, M., Cattin, P.C., Cotin, S., Padoy, N., Speidel, S., Zheng, Y., Essert, C. (eds.) MICCAI 2021. LNCS, vol. 12901, pp. 120–130. Springer, Cham (2021). https://doi.org/10.1007/978-3-030-87193-2_12
24. Zhao, X., et al.: M^2SNet: multi-scale in multi-scale subtraction network for medical image segmentation. arXiv preprint arXiv:2303.10894 (2023)
25. Heidari, M., et al.: Hiformer: hierarchical multi-scale representations using transformers for medical image segmentation. In: IEEE/CVF Winter Conference on Applications of Computer Vision, pp. 6202–6212 (2023)

26. Chen, T., et al.: Sam-adapter: adapting segment anything in underperformed scenes. In: IEEE/CVF International Conference on Computer Vision, pp. 3367–3375 (2023)
27. Zhou, T., Zhang, Y., Zhou, Y., Wu, Y., Gong, C.: Can sam segment polyps? arXiv preprint arXiv:2304.07583 (2023)
28. Ma, J., He, Y., Li, F., Han, L., You, C., Wang, B.: Segment anything in medical images. Nat. Commun. 15(1), 654 (2024)
29. Li, J., Wang, J., Lin, F., Heidari, A.A., Chen, Y., Chen, H., Wu, W.: PRCNet: a parallel reverse convolutional attention network for colorectal polyp segmentation. Biomed. Signal Process. Control 95, 106336 (2024)

A Deep Unfolding Based on U-Net Graph-Guided Hybrid Regularization Method for Bioluminescence Tomography

Wei Lyu[1(✉)] and Mengxiang Chu[2]

[1] School of Science, Xi'an Shiyou University, Xi'an 710065, China
`lvweixiann@163.com`
[2] School of Information Sciences and Technology, Northwest University, Xi'an 710127, China

Abstract. Due to the strong scattering and low absorption of light in biological tissues, the inverse problem of bioluminescence tomography (BLT) is ill-posed. Hybrid regularization constraints can effectively alleviate the inherent ill-posedness of the BLT inverse problem. However, the hybrid regularization of traditional algorithms involves multiple parameter determinations, and it is difficult to select parameters manually. This paper proposes deep unfolding based on U-Net graph-guided hybrid regularization (DUnet-GGHR) method for BLT. The gradient update step in the traditional GGHR algorithm is reformulated as a flexible gradient descent update module for automatic learning. At the same time, the soft threshold calculation step in the traditional GGHR algorithm solution process is expanded into a proximal mapping module for training. A series of reconstruction experiments have verified that the proposed DUnet-GGHR model performs better than other end-to-end deep unrolling comparison methods in tumor localization, morphology restoration, and energy recovery. At the same time, the mathematical process is combined with the deep neural network to improve the interpretability and generalization of the network, reduce training data, and speed up the calculation.

Keywords: Bioluminescence Tomography · Ill-Posed · Deep Unfolding · U-Net · Graph-Guided Hybrid Regularization

1 Introduction

The main purpose of bioluminescence tomography (BLT) research is to reconstruct the parameter distribution inside the organism, namely the location, shape and light flux distribution of the tumor, by measuring the luminous signal from the inside of the organism. Due to the complexity and heterogeneity of the interior of the organism, various effects will occur during the transmission of light inside the organism, such as serpentine transmission, reflection, absorption, scattering, refraction, etc. [4], which makes the inverse problem of BLT ill-posed [3] and significantly affects the performance of BLT. In practical applications, regularization terms are used to alleviate its ill-posedness [2].

W. Lyu and M. Chu—Co-first authors.

© The Author(s), under exclusive license to Springer Nature Singapore Pte Ltd. 2026
Z. Lin et al. (Eds.): ICIG 2025, LNCS 16161, pp. 318–329, 2026.
https://doi.org/10.1007/978-981-95-3398-5_26

In traditional algorithms, the forward operator models the physical relationship between the measured data and the target, ensuring stability and generalizability in model-based approaches [10]. However, hybrid regularization typically involves multiple manually tuned parameters, making optimization challenging [6]. Deep unfolding bridges traditional iterative algorithms and deep learning by mapping each iteration step (e.g., gradient descent, thresholding) to a corresponding neural network layer [5]. This design enables automatic parameter learning while preserving the interpretability of the original algorithmic structure [9]. Unlike black-box models, each network component retains a clear mathematical meaning, improving transparency and generalization. Although techniques such as generalized cross-validation can assist with parameter tuning, they still require manual range setting and are computationally expensive. Therefore, deep unfolding offers a more efficient and interpretable strategy for regularized inverse problems in BLT.

The deep unfolding of the algorithm has achieved superior performance and higher efficiency in many practical fields. Zhang et al. developed a model-driven deep unfolding network named GAICN, which integrates graph attention mechanisms and iterative contraction within a finite element mesh framework to enhance the stability, generalizability, and interpretability of bioluminescence tomography reconstruction [11]. The interpretable model-driven network based on fast iterative shrinkage thresholding algorithm (FISTA) named FISTA-NET was proposed for BLT reconstruction, which unfolds the FISTA algorithm into a deep network and expands the iterative process into the network model for BLT reconstruction [12]. Zhang et al. converted the iterative thresholding algorithm (ISTA) iterative process into a deep network module ISTA-NET and developed an effective strategy to solve the proximal mapping using nonlinear transformations [13]. Additionally, Ronneberger et al. observed the architectural similarities between the popular U-Net and the unfolded ISTA network, combined FBP with U-Net, and constructed a deep network called FBPConvNet that combines physical iterative processes and deep learning for better CT reconstruction [8]. Compared with conventional black-box deep networks, deep unfolding maintains a clear mathematical correspondence to the original optimization steps (e.g., gradient descent and soft-thresholding), enabling better insight into the model's behavior and decisions.

In view of previous studies, this study proposes a deep unfolding based on U-Net graph guided hybrid regularization (DUnet-GGHR) method for BLT, which uses the deep unfolding method to more effectively determine the automatic parameter selection of the inverse problem of BLT. The gradient iteration step and soft threshold update step in the solution process of our proposed GGHR algorithm are unfolded into two corresponding convolutional neural network modules respectively. The gradient iteration step is unfolded into a flexible gradient descent update module (GDUM) to automatically calculate the gradient update. First, the surface measurement is passed to the GDUM, and then the gradient of this update is output after feature extraction and feature fusion for calculating the gradient descent update; soft threshold calculation is one of the core steps of the FISTA algorithm. The soft threshold update step is unfolded into a proximal mapping module (PMM) for training the next iteration. Therefore, the DUnet-GGHR method can connect the physical iteration process with the deep learning, inherit the underlying physical structure and prior information, improve the generalization and interpretability of the model, and speed up the calculation. Finally, a series of simulation experiments are conducted to verify and evaluate the performance of the proposed DUnet-GGHR.

2   Materials and Methods

2.1   Traditional GGHR Method

The GGHR was proposed the graph-guided penalty term previously and fuse it with the L_1-L_2 regularization penalty term to construct a hybrid regularized BLT reconstruction algorithm to restore the bioluminescent source:

$$\begin{cases} \hat{x} = \arg\min_x \frac{1}{2}\|b - Ax\|_2^2 + \lambda|x|_1 + \phi\|x\|_2^2 + \xi\Phi_G(x) \\[2mm] \Phi_G(x) = \sum_{e=\{m,l\}\in E, m<l} \omega_{ml}|x_m - x_l| \\[2mm] \omega_{ml} = \exp\left(-\frac{\|p_m - p_l\|_2^2}{2\sigma^2}\right) \end{cases} \tag{1}$$

where $\Phi_G(x)$ is the graph-guided penalty. A represents an M×N system matrix that depends on geometric and optical parameters; x is an N×1 vector that represents the distribution of unknown bioluminescent light sources; b is an M×1 vector that represents boundary observations. λ, ϕ, and ξ is penalty term weight parameter, x_m, x_l, p_m and p_l represent the bioluminescent energy and spatial coordinates of nodes m and l respectively, σ is a parameter for adjusting the weight matrix.

The dual decomposition and Nesterov smoothing techniques are used to decouple the inseparable and non-smooth $\Phi_G(x)$ term and transform into their differentially smooth approximate forms [2,7]:

$$f_\mu = \max_{\|\alpha\|\leq 1} \left(\alpha^T C x - \mu d(\alpha)\right) \tag{2}$$

where $\alpha \in \mathbb{R}^K$ is an auxiliary dual variable constrained by $\|\alpha\| \leq 1$, $C \in \mathbb{R}^{K \times N}$ is the incidence matrix encoding the graph structure, and $d(\alpha) = \frac{1}{2}\|\alpha\|^2$ is a smooth convex function introduced via Nesterov smoothing [7]. Let $h(x) = \frac{1}{2}\|b - Ax\|_2^2 + \phi\|x\|_2^2 + \xi f_\mu$, this function is smooth and differentiable [2]. Therefore, the final optimization equation is obtained is:

$$\hat{x} = \arg\min_x h(x) + \lambda|x|_1 \tag{3}$$

Since the above formula only involves a very simple non-smooth term, in the process of solving the problem through the FISTA algorithm [1], the following iterative functions are required:

$$x^{(i+1)} = \arg\min_x \frac{L}{2}\left\|x - \left(x^{(i)} - \frac{1}{L}\nabla h(x^{(i)})\right)\right\|^2 + \lambda|x|_1 \tag{4}$$

where $x^{(i+1)}$ represents the output of the $i+1$ iteration, ∇h represents the data fidelity term in the graph-guided hybrid regularization algorithm formula, and ∇ is a differential operator. Mathematically speaking, the above iterative function mainly involves the gradient descent operation step and the soft threshold update step. The soft threshold update can be solved by the proximal operator through mapping. Therefore, the GGHR solution mainly considers three sub-problems, namely the gradient descent problem, the proximal mapping problem and the momentum acceleration problem:

$$h(x^{(i)}) = x^{(i)} - A^T(Ax^{(i)} - b) + 2x^{(i)} + C^T\alpha^* \tag{5}$$

$$y^{(i+1)} = \Gamma_{\theta^{(i)}}(h(x^{(i)})) \tag{6}$$

$$x^{(i+1)} = y^{(i+1)} + \eta^{(i)}(y^{(i+1)} - x^{(i)}) \tag{7}$$

where $\Gamma_{\theta^{(i)}}$ represents the nonlinear proximal operator and $\eta^{(i)}$ represents the momentum update weight.

2.2 DUnet-GGHR Model

The DUnet-GGHR architecture is shown in Fig. 1, and consists of multiple identical stages, each of which contains a flexible GDUM and a PMM, corresponding to the theoretical basis of interpretability, as equations (5) and (6) directly stem from the mathematical formulation of the FISTA algorithm. By explicitly modeling the gradient descent and proximal mapping operations through neural network modules (GDUM and PMM), the proposed architecture preserves the algorithmic transparency of traditional solvers, thus enabling interpretability in terms of optimization logic. This structure allows us to trace each output to a corresponding optimization component, ensuring that the network's actions can be understood and verified against known mathematical principles. The cascade order is set to n=10 by default. It is a learnable parameter, and more flexible parameters are automatically learned from training data in DUnet-GGHR.

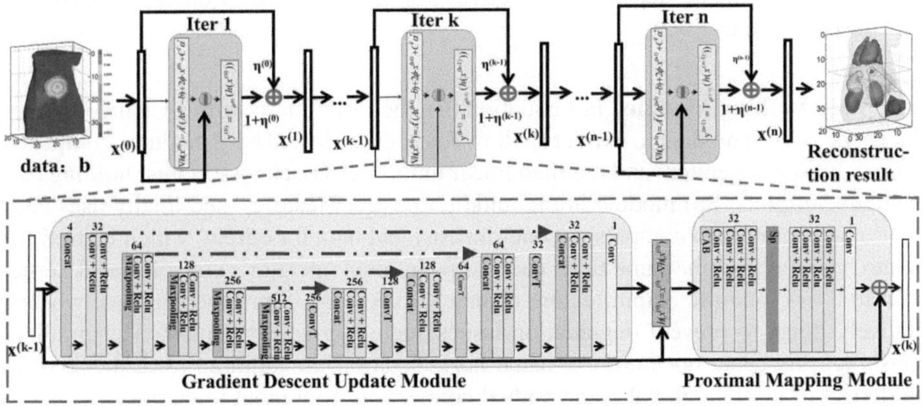

Fig. 1. The overall structure of the DUnet-GGHR model. It includes the gradient descent update module (GDUM) and the proximal mapping module (PMM).

Gradient Descent Update Module. The GDUM is a U-Net-like hourglass architecture, where the left path performs feature extraction and the right path handles feature fusion. Each scale includes double convolutional layers with ReLU activation, and pooling operations on the left side enhance hierarchical feature representation while mitigating overfitting. In the fusion stage, each scale applies deconvolution followed by concatenation with corresponding features from the left side to preserve spatial information and avoid reconstruction artifacts. Finally, convolutional layers compress the output to one-dimensional gradient values used for the descent update. The convolutional and pooling kernels are set to 3×1 and 2×1, respectively. The GDUM is designed to retain traditional optimization structure while enabling learnable, data-driven gradient updates for enhanced generalization and interpretability.

Since the finite element mesh of the mouse after discretization in each experiment is determined, the image corresponding to the graph regularization in this study and the system matrix are determined, and the exact gradient can be directly calculated using:

$$\nabla h(x^{(i)}) = \left(A^T \left(Ax^{(i)} - b \right) + 2x^{(i)} + C^T \alpha^* \right) \tag{8}$$

where $A^T \left(Ax^{(i)} - b \right)$ is the basic data fidelity gradient operator, $C^T \alpha^*$ is the approximate gradient operator of the graph-guided regularization term, for ease of notation, the input and output sets of the network at each scale are:

$$\nabla h(x^{(i)}) = \left\{ x^{(i)},\ A^T(Ax^{(i)} - b), 2x^{(i)}, C^T \alpha^* \right\} \tag{9}$$

Then calculate the gradient descent update:

$$h(x^{(i)}) = x^{(i)} - \nabla h(x^{(i)}) \tag{10}$$

The gradient update step size parameter is implicitly learned by the network parameters during training.

Proximal Mapping Module. For equation (6), the PMM starts with a Channel Attention Block (CAB) module to extract shallow features, followed by 8 modules composed of convolutional operators and rectified linear units (ReLU), and a soft thresholding calculation (Softpluts: Sp) module in the middle to extract features, and finally uses convolutional operators to compress to one-dimensional data for output, which is used for the next iteration. At the same time, each convolutional operator's convolutional kernel is set to 3×1, and the output feature channel is set to 32. Since the entire network is relatively deep, to prevent degradation issues such as gradient explosion or gradient vanishing, this paper does not use batch normalization. In addition, to further reduce the impact of noise, a global path residual connection from input to output is added to prevent network degradation issues.

In the PMM module, the $\theta^{(i)}$ is set as a learnable parameter, to adapt to different noise environments, and is not globally shared in different iterations. In addition, the momentum acceleration weight parameter $\eta^{(i)}$ is also set as learnable. To ensure their correct convergence, this paper introduces additional constraints to ensure that the threshold is always positive and the momentum acceleration step update weight increases monotonically:

$$\theta^{(i)} = \mathrm{sp}(a_1 i + a_2), a_1 < 0 \tag{11}$$

$$\eta^{(i)} = \frac{\mathrm{sp}(a_3 i + a_4) - \mathrm{sp}(a_1 + a_2)}{\mathrm{sp}(a_1 i + a_2)}, a_3 > 0 \tag{12}$$

where $\mathrm{sp}(x) = \ln(1 + \exp(x)); \eta^{(i)} \in (0, 1)$.

Loss Function. In the GDUM, during the learned iterative reconstruction process, the neural network is coupled with the evaluations of the system matrix, its adjoint, and the graph-guided regularization term. More precisely, given supervised training data $(x_i, b_i) \in X \times Y$, and denoting the gradient update function as: $h(x^i) = x^i - \nabla(h(x^i)) = x^i - \nabla((A^T(Ax^i - b) + 2x^i + C^T \alpha^*))$, the optimal parameters are obtained by solving:

$$\min_{\rho} \frac{1}{m} \sum_{i=1}^{n} L_\rho(x^{(i)}, b^{(i)}) \tag{13}$$

Thus, the loss function for the GDUM module in this paper is determined to be:

$$L_1 = \lambda_1 \sum_{i=1}^{n} |h(x^{(i+1)}) - (x^{(i)} - \nabla(h(x^{(i)})))|_1 \tag{14}$$

For the PMM module, in mathematical theory, sparse transformation is a reversible operation, the loss of the sparse transformation F is defined as follows:

$$L_2 = \lambda_2 L_{\mathrm{syml}} + \lambda_3 L_{\mathrm{spal}}$$
$$= \lambda_2 \sum_{i=1}^{n} \left\| F'(F(x^{(i)}) - x^{(i)} \right\|_2^2 + \lambda_3 \sum_{i=1}^{n} |F(x^{(i)}|_1 \tag{15}$$

where L_{syml} represents the inverse transformation loss, L_{spal} represents the sparsity constraint, and F' denotes the pseudo-inverse matrix of F.

Thus, the total loss function is defined as follows:

$$L = L_1 + L_2 + \lambda_4 L_{\mathrm{mse}} = \lambda_1 L_1 + \lambda_2 L_{\mathrm{sym}} + \lambda_3 L_{\mathrm{spal}} + \lambda_4 L_{\mathrm{mse}}$$
$$= \lambda_1 \sum_{i=1}^{n} |h(x^{(i+1)} - (x^{(i)} - \nabla(h(x^{(i)}))|_1$$
$$+ \lambda_2 \sum_{i=1}^{n} \left\| F'(F(x^{(i)}) - x^{(i)} \right\|_2^2$$
$$+ \lambda_3 \sum_{i=1}^{n} |F(x^{(i)}|_1 + \lambda_4 |x^{(n)} - x|_1 \tag{16}$$

This paper uses a fixed hyper-parameter training network model, with default values $\lambda_1 = 1, \lambda_2 = 0.1, \lambda_3 = 0.01, \lambda_4 = 1, x^{(0)} = XB^T(BB^T)^{-1}b$, where X represents the label data of the training data, and B represents the surface measurement data of the training data.

3   Experiments and Results

3.1   Experiment Setup

Three sets of numerical simulation experiments were designed to verify the generalization ability of the DUnet-GGHR model. In the single-target reconstruction experiment, three single light sources of different shapes (a sphere with a radius of 0.8 mm, a cube with a side length of 2 mm, and a cylinder with a radius of 0.8 mm and a height of 2 mm) were set, as shown in Fig. 2(a). The dual-target reconstruction experiment was set to consider the influence of the light source size and shape on the model reconstruction performance, as shown in Fig. 2(b). In addition, considering that in the preclinical application of BLT, the reconstruction of multiple targets with sharp boundaries and close distances is a great challenge, two cube dual light source experiments with different EEDs were set to verify the model reconstruction performance, as shown in Fig. 2(c).

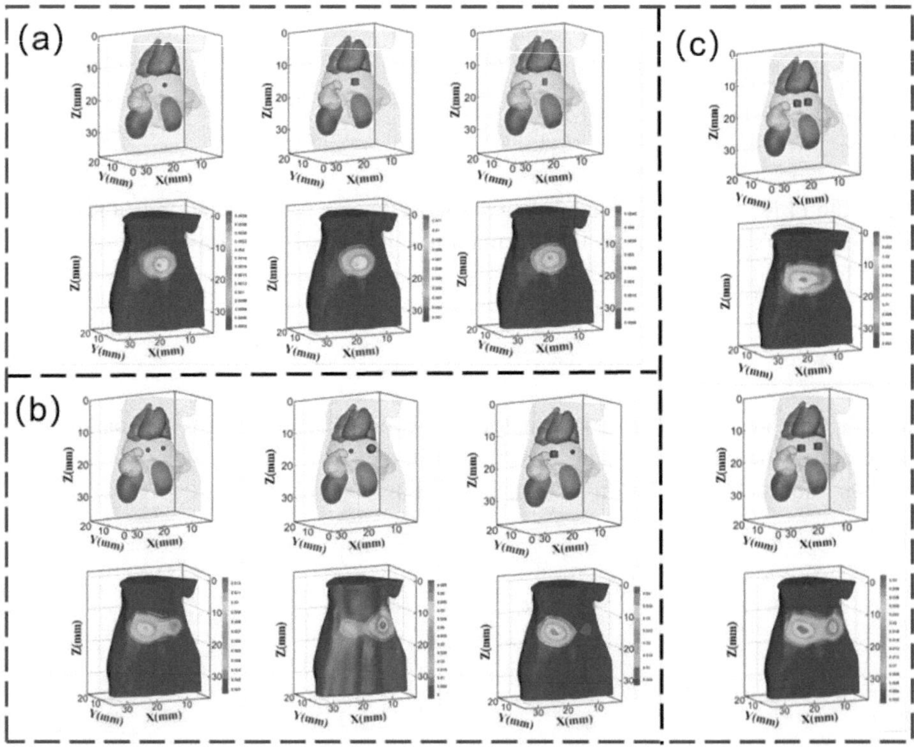

Fig. 2. Simulation experiment settings and corresponding surface luminous flux distribution. (a) Single source, spherical light source with a radius of 0.8mm; cube light source with a side length of 2 mm; cylindrical light source with a radius of 0.8 mm and a height of 2 mm. (b) Dual sources of different shapes, spherical dual sources with a radius of 0.8 mm; spherical dual sources with a radius of 0.8mm and a radius of 1.8; a cube with a side length of 2 mm and a sphere with a radius of 0.8mm. (c) Dual sources with different EEDs, EED = 2 mm, EED = 4 mm.

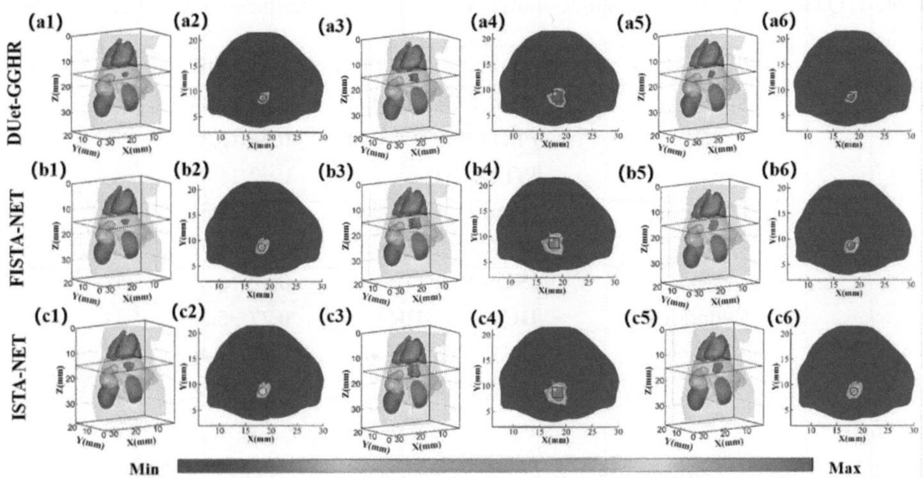

Fig. 3. The 3D and lateral views of the reconstruction results for a single light source, where the lateral view is indicated by the black dashed line in the 3D view. The green region in the 3D view represents the reconstructed area, and the black circle in the 2D slice denotes the actual area of the bioluminescent light source. (Color figure online)

FISTA-NET [12] and ISTA-NET [13] are selected for comparison with the GUnet-GGHR to verify the performance. Dice, LE and CNR are used to quantitatively evaluate the reconstruction performance of the DUnet-GGHR model. All models are optimized using the Adam algorithm, and each network is trained for 1,000 iterations, with the batch-size set to 32 and the initial learning rate set to 1e-3.

3.2 Experimental Results

Figure 3 and Table 1 show the results of single light source reconstruction. The FISTA-NET and ISTA-NET methods have a large reconstruction area, blurred boundaries, poor energy recovery, small Dice values, and weak positioning effects. In contrast, the reconstructed shape of the DUnet-GGHR model proposed in this paper is closer to the shape of the real light source, especially for spherical and cylindrical light sources. At the same time, for cube light sources with sharp edges, the DUnet-GGHR method has a stronger shape recovery ability than the other two deep unfolding methods. The quantitative results of light source reconstruction of three different shapes have obtained the largest Dice value, low LE value (<0.5) and larger CNR.

Figure 4 and Table 2 indicate the reconstruction results of dual light sources of different sizes. The three deep unfolding methods can distinguish dual light sources. However, ISTA-NET has poor energy recovery and unstable positioning. FISTA-NET has fewer artifacts and better positioning, but it is still unstable for different shapes. DUnet-GGHR has the best fitting effect for high-energy areas of different sizes, the least artifacts, the largest Dice value, the highest CNR of 38.47, the low LE value, and superior performance.

Table 1. Quantitative results for single-source reconstruction experiments with different shapes.

Light Source's Shape	Method	LE (mm)	Dice	CNR
Spherical	**DUnet-GGHR**	**0.40**	**0.63**	**21.17**
	FISTA-NET	0.88	0.46	18.33
	ISTA-NET	1.03	0.42	15.70
Cubic	**DUnet-GGHR**	**0.46**	**0.70**	**28.50**
	FISTA-NET	0.91	0.57	22.73
	ISTA-NET	1.06	0.40	16.32
Cylindrical	**DUnet-GGHR**	**0.49**	**0.77**	**35.32**
	FISTA-NET	0.72	0.52	27.46
	ISTA-NET	0.99	0.43	18.86

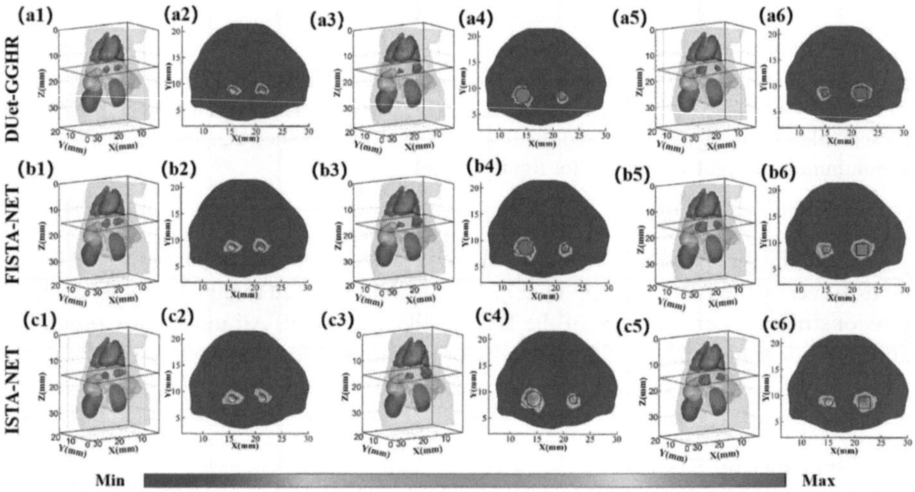

Fig. 4. The 3D view and lateral view of the reconstruction results of dual light sources of different sizes.

Figure 5 and Table 3 reveal that the dual-light source reconstruction results at different EEDs. ISTA-NET loses boundary information and has many artifacts, resulting in poor positioning and shape recovery. FISTA-NET has obvious artifacts and adhesions at 2 mm EED, and positioning is improved at 4 mm EED. DUnet-GGHR performs well at different EEDs. The reconstructed area is closer to the real cube light source shape, and the high light source area better fits the real luminous flux distribution. The quantitative results have the smallest LE, the largest Dice and CNR, which also show that the DUnet-GGHR method has high positioning accuracy and strong light source shape and energy recovery capabilities.

Table 2. Quantitative results for dual-source reconstruction experiments with different sizes.

Sources	Shape	Method	LE (mm)	Dice	CNR
Spherical(0.8 mm)	Spherical(0.8 mm)	**DUnet-GGHR**	**0.60**	**0.66**	30.73
			0.45	**0.57**	
		FISTA-NET	0.61	0.57	25.88
			0.62	0.43	
		ISTA-NET	0.96	0.50	20.91
			0.99	0.43	
Spherical(1.5 mm)	Spherical(0.8 mm)	**DUnet-GGHR**	**0.53**	**0.71**	**36.05**
			0.46	**0.59**	
		FISTA-NET	0.67	0.60	33.72
			0.38	0.47	
		ISTA-NET	1.70	0.42	20.56
			0.92	0.38	
Spherical(0.8 mm)	Cubic(2.0 mm)	**DUnet-GGHR**	**0.49**	**0.74**	**38.47**
			0.49	**0.51**	
		FISTA-NET	0.46	0.57	30.05
			1.25	0.46	
		ISTA-NET	0.79	0.67	20.14
			1.06	0.50	

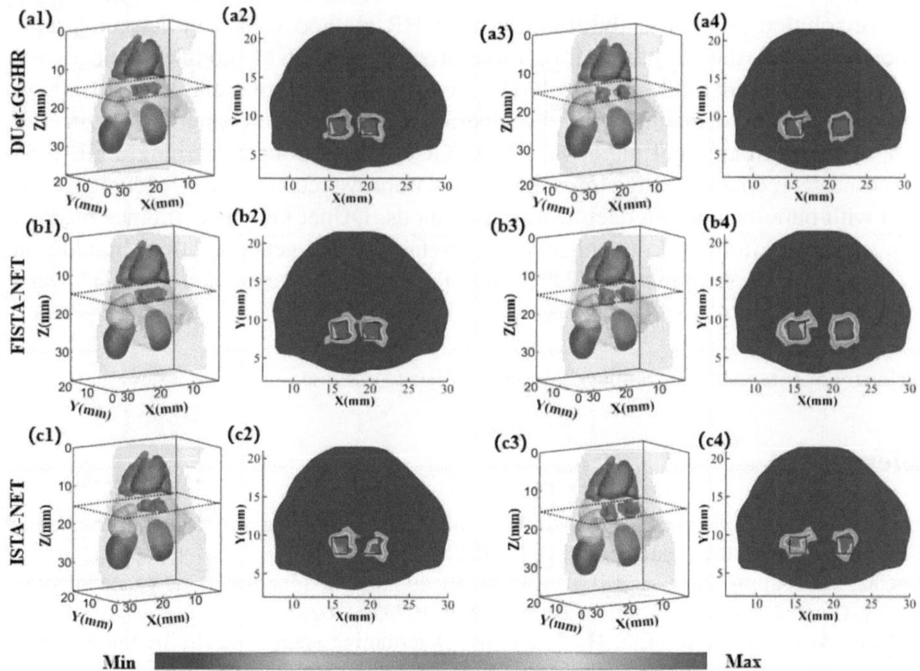

Fig. 5. The 3D view and lateral view of the dual light source reconstruction results with different EEDs.

Table 3. Quantitative results for dual-source reconstruction experiments with different EEDs.

Sources' Shape	Method	LE (mm)	Dice	CNR
EED=2mm	**DUnet-GGHR**	**0.55**	**0.59**	40.90
		0.36	**0.71**	
	FISTA-NET	0.92	0.43	37.87
		0.90	0.52	
	ISTA-NET	1.43	0.37	22.82
		0.99	0.46	
EED=4mm	**DUnet-GGHR**	**0.46**	**0.68**	37.31
		0.17	**0.65**	
	FISTA-NET	0.47	0.50	36.04
		0.22	0.57	
	ISTA-NET	1.19	0.40	20.76
		0.98	0.49	

4   Discussion and Conclusion

This paper proposes DUnet-GGHR for BLT. The DUnet-GGHR model combines the iterative solution process of the traditional GGHR method with deep learning, automatically updates the gradient information through the GDUM module, achieves soft threshold convergence through the PMM module, and performs end-to-end training. Data simulation experiments verify the superior performance of DUnet-GGHR in BLT. Compared with traditional methods, DUnet-GGHR has stronger learning ability, can remove noise, reconstruct edge information, and improve reconstruction accuracy; compared with pure data-driven deep learning methods, DUnet-GGHR combines physical logic and prior information to enhance interpretability and generalization. In addition, by changing the system matrix, DUnet-GGHR can be easily extended to other inverse problems.

Disclosure of Interests. The authors have no conflicts to disclose.

References

1. Chen, X., Lin, Q., Kim, S., Carbonell, J.G., Xing, E.P.: Smoothing proximal gradient method for general structured sparse regression (2012)
2. Chu, M., et al.: A graph-guided hybrid regularization method for bioluminescence tomography. Comput. Methods Programs Biomed. **230**, 107329 (2023)
3. Ding, M.H., Gong, R., Liu, H., Lo, C.W.: Determining sources in the bioluminescence tomography problem. Inverse Prob. **40**(12), 125022 (2024)
4. Hang, Y., Boryczka, J., Wu, N.: Visible-light and near-infrared fluorescence and surface-enhanced raman scattering point-of-care sensing and bio-imaging: A review. Chem. Soc. Rev. **51**(1), 329–375 (2022)

5. Li, T., Yan, Q., Zou, Q., Dai, Q.: Gates-controlled deep unfolding network for image compressed sensing. IEEE Trans. Comput. Imaging (2024)
6. Mao, D., et al.: Angular super resolution of real aperture radar for target scale measurement using a generalized hybrid regularization approach. IEEE Trans. Geosci. Remote Sensing (2023)
7. Nesterov, Y.: Smooth minimization of non-smooth functions. Math. Program. **103**, 127–152 (2005)
8. Ronneberger, O., Fischer, P., Brox, T.: U-Net: Convolutional Networks for Biomedical Image Segmentation. In: Navab, N., Hornegger, J., Wells, W.M., Frangi, A.F. (eds.) MICCAI 2015. LNCS, vol. 9351, pp. 234–241. Springer, Cham (2015). https://doi.org/10.1007/978-3-319-24574-4_28
9. Wang, J., Shao, Z., Huang, X., Lu, T., Zhang, R.: A deep unfolding method for satellite super resolution. IEEE Trans. Compu. Imaging **8**, 933–944 (2022)
10. Xiang, J., Dong, Y., Yang, Y.: Fista-net: learning a fast iterative shrinkage thresholding network for inverse problems in imaging. IEEE Trans. Med. Imaging **40**(5), 1329–1339 (2021)
11. Zhang, H., et al.: Gaicn: graph attention iterative contraction network for bioluminescence tomography. IEEE Trans. Med. Imaging (2024)
12. Zhang, H., et al.: Based on model-driven fast iterative shrinkage thresholding network for bioluminescence tomography reconstruction. In: Medical Imaging 2023: Image Processing, vol. 12464, pp. 911–916. SPIE (2023)
13. Zhang, J., Ghanem, B.: Ista-net: interpretable optimization-inspired deep network for image compressive sensing. In: Proceedings of the IEEE Conference on Computer Vision and Pattern Recognition, pp. 1828–1837 (2018)

CMambaR: Cardiac Phase Embedded Vision Mamba for Accelerating Cardiac MRI Reconstruction

Bangjun Li, Jingchuan Wang, Mengli Xue, Yujun Li[✉], and Zhi Liu[✉]

School of Information Science and Engineering, Shandong University, Qingdao, China
{liyujun,liuzhi}@sdu.edu.cn

Abstract. Cardiac Magnetic Resonance Imaging (CMR) is a crucial clinical imaging modality for assessing cardiac morphology and function, and it has become the gold standard for diagnosing cardiovascular diseases. However, its widespread clinical adoption is hindered by long acquisition times and high costs—challenges that are particularly acute in dynamic imaging, where both high spatial and temporal resolutions must be achieved within a limited timeframe. In this paper, we propose a novel dynamic deep unrolling method, CMambaR, a cardiac phase-embedded Vision Mamba architecture designed to accelerate cardiac MRI reconstruction. The proposed method integrates the strengths of unfolded iterative optimization with a spatiotemporal dynamic reconstruction network, enabling it to effectively capture complementary information embedded in dynamic sequences while leveraging physics-based priors to deliver high-quality reconstruction. Inspired by structured state space models, we design a local enhanced vision Mamba module as the core building block of our network, capable of capturing both local details and long-range dependencies. Furthermore, we introduce a cardiac phase fusion mechanism that incorporates cardiac phase prior into the reconstruction process, further enhancing reconstruction performance. Extensive experiments on two cardiac datasets demonstrate that our method achieves high-fidelity image reconstruction and consistently outperforms existing approaches.

Keywords: Cardiac MRI · Accelerated Reconstruction · Deep Unrolling · Space State Model · Cardiac Phase Fusion

1 Introduction

Cardiac Magnetic Resonance Imaging (CMR) plays an important role in revealing cardiac evolving phenomena and has become the gold standard for cardiovascular diseases (CVDs) diagnosis [9]. However, long time clinical scanning challenges this dynamic imaging technique due to hardware limitations and physiological constraints, making it expensive and struggle to achieve the required spatial and temporal resolution simultaneously in clinical routine [12,14]. K-space undersampling is an variable solution while the resulting aliasing artefacts

Z. Lin et al. (Eds.): ICIG 2025, LNCS 16161, pp. 330–340, 2026.
https://doi.org/10.1007/978-981-95-3398-5_27

severely degrade the imaging quality, recovering high-fidelity anatomical information from limited acquired data remains an ill-posed inverse problem [3,23]. Classical reconstruction methods mainly adopt compressed sensing (CS) and parallel imaging (PI) techniques, where the CS technique assumes that the measurements must be compressible by sparse coding in some transform domain [24], while the PI technique mainly relies on the sensitivity encoding information of multiple receiver coils to reduce the scan time [4]. However, these traditional methods suffered from high sensitivity to the chosen hyper-parameters [21]. Current learning-based MRI reconstruction methods mainly classified two main branches. The first one is the pure data driven end-to-end learning, which adaptively learn a mapping from the undersampled data to the high-quality images without relying on other physical priors [2,10,17,20]. The second one is deep unfolding learning methods which combine the merits of physics model based iterative algorithms and the learning based models, they typically unrolled the neural network into the physics defined models and also acquire promising performance for reconstruction [5,11,19]. In addition, current CMR reconstruction still faces several special unique challenges. First, most existing methods suitable for static slices reconstruction, while the significant gap between static and dynamic imaging makes it different to directly apply conventional static reconstruction methods to CMR reconstruction. It is necessitating to effectively extract the compensation knowledge hidden in whole sequences [15,18]. Second, MRI scanning measurements are achieved in the k-space domain, and therefore the resulting aliasing artifacts exhibit long-range spatial distribution in the reconstructed images [22]. Recent proposed space state models [6] excel in their ability to model global relationships, but their effectiveness in cardiac MRI reconstruction remains to be investigated. Third, the cardiac alternatively undergoes diastole phase and systole phase, an important domain knowledge that often used for diagnosis of cardiac function, which provides additional temporal information reflecting the cycle of cardiac motion, but rarely explored.

To address these challenges, we propose a novel deep unfolding-based dynamic reconstruction method to accelerate cardiac MRI reconstruction. Furthermore, by incorporating a cardiac phase-aware Vision Mamba, our method effectively captures spatiotemporal dependencies both within and across MRI slices. In summary, the main contributions of this work are as follows:

- We propose CMambaR, a cardiac phase-embedded vision Mamba-based method for accelerating cardiac MRI reconstruction. It adopts a deep unfolding architecture that enables comprehensive spatiotemporal feature extraction and achieves high-quality reconstruction performance.
- We design a locally enhanced vision Mamba (LeVM) module as the fundamental building block of the reconstruction network, which facilitates global feature modeling while preserving fine structural details.
- We incorporate cardiac phase information as additional temporal prior knowledge into the reconstruction process. Extensive experiments show that the proposed method achieves superior performance compared to the state-of-the-art methods.

2 Methodology

2.1 Preliminary

MRI Reconstruction. Let $y \in \mathbb{C}^N$ denote the observed complex-valued full sampled k-space measurement and $x \in \mathbb{C}^N$ is the corresponding full sampled images, $y_u \in \mathbb{C}^M$ represents the under-sampled k-space measurement. The aim of reconstruction is to reconstruct x from y_u,

$$y_u = F_u x + \epsilon, \tag{1}$$

where F_u denotes the undersampled Fourier encoding matrix, ϵ represents the acquisition noise. In addition, F_u can be further represented by the concatenation of two operations $F_u = FM$, where F represents the Fourier transform, and M denotes the undersampled matrix. Typically, MRI reconstruction can be formulated as an unconstrained optimization problem as follows:

$$\operatorname*{argmin}_{x} = \lambda \|y_u - F_u(x)\|_2^2 + \mathcal{R}(x), \tag{2}$$

where $\mathcal{R}$ represents the regularisation terms on x, λ is the learnable parameter that allows adjustment the contribution of data fidelity. Moreover, for learning based approaches, one can force x to be approximated by the neural network reconstruction, and this optimization problem can be expressed as:

$$\min_{x} \|x - f_{nn}(x_u|\theta)\|_2^2 + \lambda \|F_u x - y\|_2^2, \tag{3}$$

where f_{nn} denotes the forward pass of the network parameterized by θ, and x_u denotes the zero-filled input image.

State Space Model. As a type of the linear time-invariant systems, State Space Models (SSM) could map the 1D input simulation $x(t) \in \mathbb{R}$ to the output response $y(t) \in \mathbb{R}$ through a hidden state $h(t) \in \mathbb{R}^N$. Typically, This process can be formulated by the following linear ordinary differential equation (ODE) [6]:

$$\begin{aligned} h'(t) &= \mathbf{A}h(t) + \mathbf{B}x(t), \\ y(t) &= \mathbf{C}h'(t), \end{aligned} \tag{4}$$

where system parameters include, evolution matrix $\mathbf{A} \in \mathbb{R}^{N \times N}$, projection matrices $\mathbf{B} \in \mathbb{R}^{N \times 1}$ and $\mathbf{C} \in \mathbb{R}^{N \times 1}$. Furthermore, the continuous ODE needs to be discretized to integrate with modern deep learning frameworks [25]. The Selective Scan SSM (referred to as Mamba or S6) is a discrete system derived from a continuous one using the zero-order hold (ZOH) method. Specifically, it employs a timescale parameter Δ to sample the continuous parameter $\mathbf{A}, \mathbf{B}$ into discreted one:

$$\begin{aligned} \bar{\mathbf{A}} &= exp(\Delta\mathbf{A}), \\ \bar{\mathbf{B}} &= (\Delta\mathbf{A})^{-1}(exp(\Delta\mathbf{A}) - I) \cdot \Delta\mathbf{B}, \end{aligned} \tag{5}$$

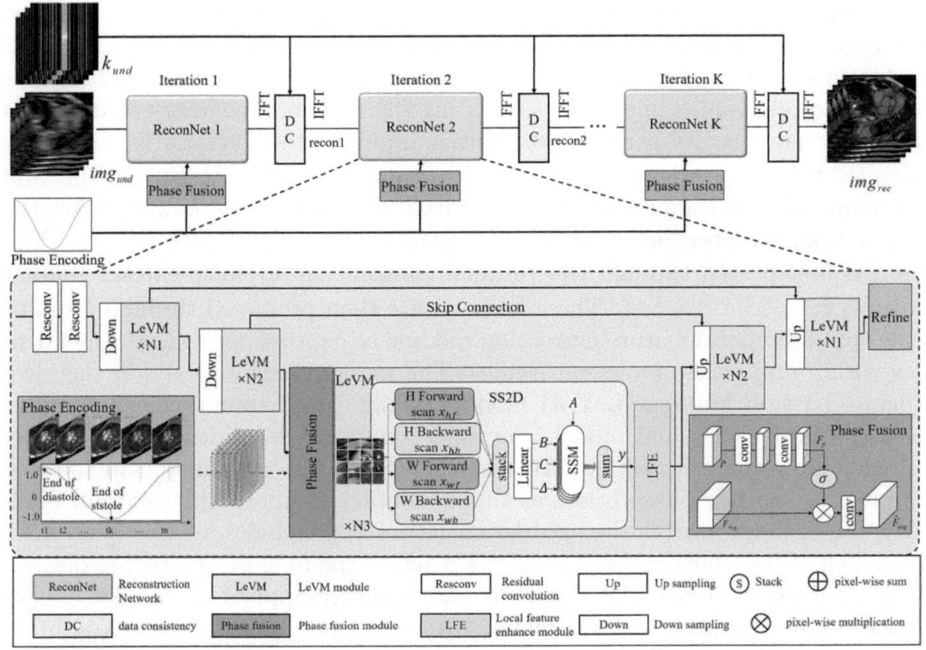

Fig. 1. Illustration of the proposed CMambaR. It adopts deep unfolding structure and recover complete data alternatively between image domain and k-space domain.

where I represents the identity matrix. Hence, the continuous transformation can be reformulated as discreted one:

$$
\begin{aligned}
h[k] &= \bar{\mathbf{A}}h[k-1] + \bar{\mathbf{B}}x[k], \\
y[k] &= \mathbf{C}h[k].
\end{aligned}
\tag{6}
$$

To faciliate the practical parallelized training, the recursive process can be achieved by a global convolutional as follows:

$$
\begin{aligned}
\bar{\mathbf{K}} &= (\mathbf{C}\bar{\mathbf{B}}, \mathbf{C}\bar{\mathbf{A}}\bar{\mathbf{B}}, \ldots, \mathbf{C}\bar{\mathbf{A}}^{M-1}\bar{\mathbf{B}}), \\
y &= x * \bar{\mathbf{K}},
\end{aligned}
\tag{7}
$$

where M denotes the length of the input sequence x, $\bar{K} \in \mathbb{R}^M$ repesents a structured convolutional kernel. The Mamba adopts the selective scan mechanism that makes the learnable parameters input dependent, *i.e.*, $(\mathbf{B}, \mathbf{C}, \Delta)$ are derived from the input sequence x through the linear projection.

2.2 CMambaR

The overall architecture of the proposed Cardiac MRI reconstruction method is illustrated in Fig. 1. It adopts the deep unfolding structure and recover complete data alternatively between image domain and k-space domain, where each iteration comprises a reconstruction network followed by a data consistency layer.

Given a zero filled complex-valued input cardiac MRI sequence, we first convert it into real-valued images by separating the real and imaginary components into two channels. As a result, the initial input to the network is defined as $x_u \in \mathbb{R}^{W \times H \times T \times 2}$, where W, H, and T denote the spatial width, height, and the temporal dimension, respectively. At each iteration i, the network takes the output from the previous iteration x^{i-1} as its current input, with $x^0 = x_u$. The input is first passed through two residual convolution layers to extract shallow features $x_s \in \mathbb{R}^{W \times H \times T \times 2}$. These features are then processed through a multi-scale spatiotemporal feature extraction module to capture contextual dependencies within and across temporal frames. The model is mainly rely on the local enhanced vision Mamba (LeVM) module, which could simultaneously extract local spatial features and model long-range temporal dependencies. To further enhance the reconstruction quality, a cardiac phase fusion module is introduced to integrate cardiac phase priors as supplementary temporal information. Similarly, the decoder mirrors the encoder structure and includes a refinement block composed of two convolutional layers to generate the final reconstructed output. And a data consistency (DC) layer is subsequently applied to enforce fidelity to the original k-space measurements. After multiple iterations, we can obtain the final reconstructed images. Additionally, an ℓ_1 loss term is employed to optimize the network during training stage.

Local Enhanced Visual Mamba. The disturbance in k-space measurements could lead to the long-range distribution of artifacts in the image domain. Inspired by the recently proposed Mamba, which could mitigate the limitations of the inherent of CNN while decrease the complexity of the model, and achieved promising performance in sequence modeling. Moreover, achieving high-quality reconstruction performance requires not only capturing global contextual relationships but also preserving local contextual dependencies. Thereby, we design an adapted vision Mamba module for MRI reconstruction. As shown in Fig. 1, given the input x for our Local enhanced Visual Mamba (LeVM) module, it first through a Layer Normalization. And then, a multiple direction visual state space model (VSSM) module is used to capture the correlations hidden in the whole sequence. Subsequently, instead of the standard linear operation, we employ two convolutional layers to enhance the local context learning ability of the model. The process can be formulated as follows:

$$y = s_1 \cdot x + VSSM(LN(x)), \tag{8}$$
$$y = s_2 \cdot x + LFE(LN(x)), \tag{9}$$

where the LFE denotes the local feature enhancement module in the second stage. $s1 \in \mathbb{R}^C$ and $s2 \in \mathbb{R}^C$ are the learnable factors for skip connection.

Cardiac Phase Encoding and Fusion. The circulatory of the heart alternates between diastole and systole, while dynamic cardiac MRI are used to reflect heart structure at different moments in the cardiac cycle. To leverage this temporal information, as illustrated in Fig. 1 we design a cardiac phase fusion module to fuse two different modalities to enhance feature representation. First, to align the cardiac phase with the image sequence, we embed the cycle activity via the cosine function, where the end of diastole and systole mapping to maximum and minimum value, respectively. Inspired by [13], the phase encoding process is formulated as follows:

$$P^t = \begin{cases} \mathrm{Cos}(\pi \times \frac{t-ED}{ES-ED}), & \text{if } ED < t \leq ES \\ \mathrm{Cos}(\pi \times (1 + \frac{(t-ES)\%T}{T-(ES-ED)})), & \text{otherwise} \end{cases} \tag{10}$$

where P represent the encoded phase code, ED represents the end-diastole and ES represents the end-systole in a cardiac cycle. Subsequently, two convolution operations are used to achieve the encoded phase feature $F_p \in \mathbb{R}^{B,T,C}$, and use a activation function applied to it to modulate the learned image feature maps. This can be formulated as follows: $\hat{F}_{img} = Conv(F_{img} \cdot \sigma(F_p))$, where σ represents the Sigmoid function.

3   Experiments

3.1   Datasets and Baselines

In our experiments, we adopted two publicly available cardiac MRI dataset, Automated Cardiac Diagnosis Challenge dataset (ACDC) [1] and Kaggle second annual Data Science Bowl challenge dataset (KDSB)[1]. ACDC dataset was created from real clinical exams, where cine MR images were acquired in breath hold with a retrospective or prospective gating and with a SSFP sequence in short axis orientation. and spatial resolution goes from 1.37 to 1.68 mm^2/pixel. We random choose 50 cases for train, 20 cases for validation and 30 cases for test, and time phase varied from 12 to 30. KDSB dataset was acquired on a separate breath hold and the main view is the short axis stack, each slice contains approximately 30 images across the cardiac cycle. In addition, we compare the proposed method with five representative approaches, CRNN [20], CineLSTM [17], ReconFormer [7], L+S [8] and VRT [16]. All data were resized to 224 × 224, and different acceleration factors were employed in the experiments.

3.2   Implementation Details and Evaluation Metrics

The experiments were implemented by Pytorch deep learning framework on one NVIDIA H800 GPU card with 80G memory. The Adam optimizer with an initial learning rate 1.0×10^{-3}, $(\beta_1, \beta_2) = (0.9, 0.999)$ is used to optimize the parameters. We train the model with 100 epochs and the number of iteration is set to

---

[1] https://www.kaggle.com/c/second-annual-data-science-bowl.

Table 1. Quantitative comparision of different methods on ACDC dataset under random undersampling pattern with AF 6× and 8×. The best results are marked in **bold**.

Method	6×			8×		
	PSNR↑	SSIM↑	NMSE↓	PSNR↑	SSIM↑	NMSE↓
Zero Filled	23.32 ± 1.6	0.6124 ± 0.069	0.0653 ± 0.023	23.00 ± 1.6	0.5941 ± 0.070	0.0702 ± 0.024
CRNN [20]	34.05 ± 1.6	0.9306 ± 0.018	0.0058 ± 0.003	31.75 ± 1.4	0.8967 ± 0.023	0.0096 ± 0.003
CineLSTM [17]	29.22 ± 1.3	0.8576 ± 0.025	0.0152 ± 0.004	27.94 ± 1.2	0.8299 ± 0.030	0.0204 ± 0.005
ReconFormer [7]	29.47 ± 1.5	0.8491 ± 0.033	0.0166 ± 0.005	26.56 ± 1.6	0.7704 ± 0.047	0.0315 ± 0.009
L+S [8]	36.01 ± 1.7	0.9473 ± 0.016	0.0038 ± 0.002	33.47 ± 1.6	0.9176 ± 0.022	0.0066 ± 0.003
VRT [16]	28.10 ± 1.2	0.8260 ± 0.029	0.0213 ± 0.005	26.83 ± 1.3	0.7864 ± 0.036	0.0286 ± 0.008
CMambaR	**36.90 ± 1.7**	**0.9579 ± 0.015**	**0.0030 ± 0.001**	**36.27 ± 1.6**	**0.9524 ± 0.016**	**0.0034 ± 0.002**

Table 2. Quantitative comparision of different methods on KDSB dataset under random undersampling pattern with AF 6× and 8×. The best results are marked in **bold**.

Method	6×			8×		
	PSNR↑	SSIM↑	NMSE↓	PSNR↑	SSIM↑	NMSE↓
Zero Filled	26.61 ± 2.8	0.7336 ± 0.072	0.0467 ± 0.023	26.29 ± 2.8	0.7218 ± 0.074	0.0502 ± 0.025
CRNN [20]	35.41 ± 3.4	0.9261 ± 0.028	0.0063 ± 0.002	33.51 ± 3.2	0.9023 ± 0.034	0.0095 ± 0.004
CineLSTM [17]	31.49 ± 2.7	0.8751 ± 0.037	0.0137 ± 0.006	30.42 ± 2.7	0.8525 ± 0.041	0.0178 ± 0.009
ReconFormer [7]	32.91 ± 3.0	0.8879 ± 0.038	0.0118 ± 0.006	31.23 ± 3.0	0.8582 ± 0.047	0.0175 ± 0.010
L+S [8]	38.43 ± 4.1	0.9500 ± 0.023	0.0033 ± 0.001	36.44 ± 3.9	0.9321 ± 0.029	0.0051 ± 0.002
VRT [16]	30.57 ± 2.7	0.8521 ± 0.044	0.0185 ± 0.008	30.02 ± 2.7	0.8391 ± 0.047	0.0212 ± 0.010
CMambaR	39.32 ± 3.7	0.9590 ± 0.018	0.0026 ± 0.001	37.38 ± 3.3	0.9460 ± 0.021	0.0040 ± 0.002

$K = 3$. The number of hidden filters in first level is set to 48 and other layers are 64. In addition, three metrics are used for performance evaluation, including Peak Signal to Noise Ratio (PSNR), Structural Similarity Index Measurement (SSIM), and Normalization Mean Square Error (NMSE).

3.3 Experimental Results and Analysis

Quantitative Comparision. The quantitative comparison between the proposed method and other baselines on different datasets are presented in Table 1 and Table 2. We report three evaluation metrics in the form of mean value and standard deviation (mean ± std) under 1D cartesian random sampling pattern with different undersampling patterns. As shown from the results, the proposed method achieved consistent and superior performance across all undersampling rates regardless of the evaluation metrics compared other approaches. Compared to L+S method, our method achieved gains 2.8 dB and 0.94 dB on PSNR for the two datasets at AF 8×, respectively. Notice that, even ReconFormer achieves better performance on static MRI slice reconstruction, it hard to cope with the dynamic sequences. For a more intuitive comparison, we also report the evaluation results at AF 12× in Fig. 2.

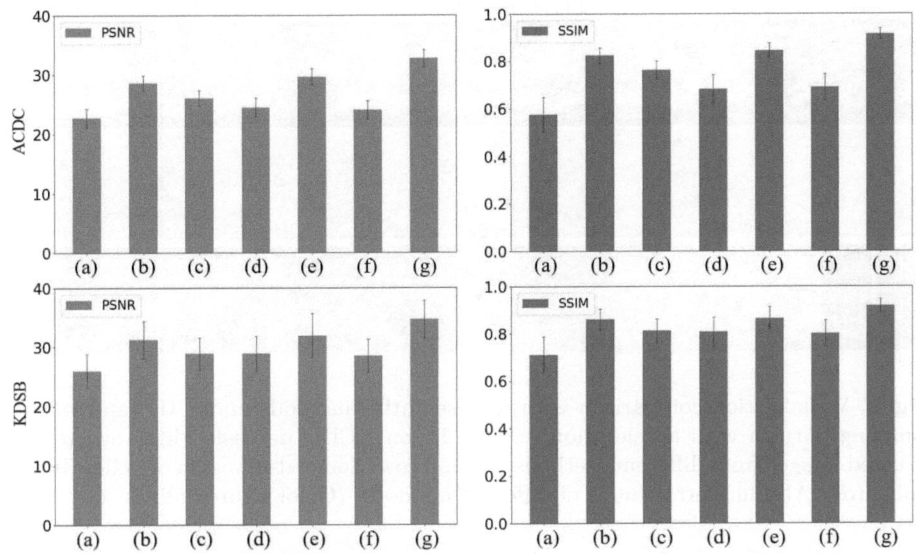

Fig. 2. Comparison with representative methods under 1D random subsampling pattern with acceleration factor 12×. (a) Zero Filled (b) CRNN (c) CineLSTM (d) Recon-Former (e) L+S (f) VRT (g) CMambaR.

Qualitative Comparision. Besides the quantitative comparision, we also provide the visualization results for qualitative comparison. Figure 3 showcases the reconstruction images from ACDC datasets under 1D random undersampling pattern. To facilitate comparison, we further presented the zoom-in detail and the error maps between ground truth with reconstructed results. CMambaR consistently outperforms all baseline methods with fewer reconstruction aliasing artifacts and less error value across different acceleration factors. Similar results can be found in Fig. 4, which demonstrate the effectiveness of the proposed method.

Table 3. Ablation studies on ACDC dataset under 8× acceleration factor.

PriorF	LeVM	PSNR↑	SSIM↑	NMSE↓
Zero Filled	Zero Filled	23.00 ± 1.6	0.5941 ± 0.0704	0.0702 ± 0.0239
✗	✗	34.27 ± 1.4	0.9361 ± 0.0170	0.0052 ± 0.0017
✓	✗	34.78 ± 1.5	0.9396 ± 0.0188	0.0047 ± 0.0018
✗	✓	35.72 ± 1.6	0.9490 ± 0.0166	0.0038 ± 0.0015
✓	✓	36.27 ± 1.6	0.9524 ± 0.0162	0.0034 ± 0.0015

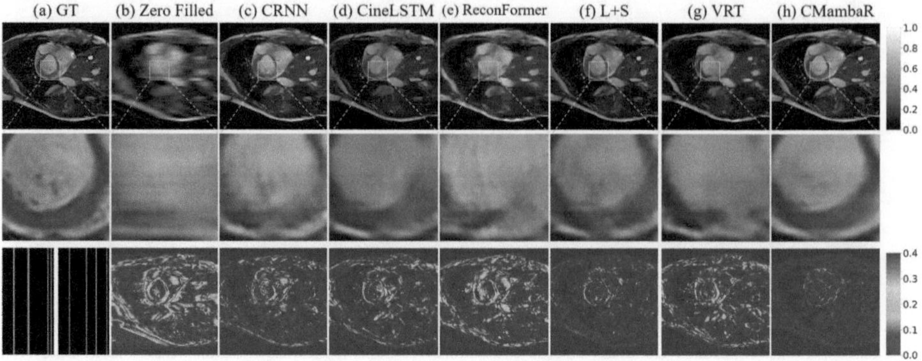

Fig. 3. Visualisation comparison with representative methods under 1D random subsampling pattern with acceleration factor 12× on ACDC dataset. First row: Reconstructed images from different methods; Second row: Zoomed-in region of yellow boxes; Third row: Absolute error maps of different methods. (Color figure online)

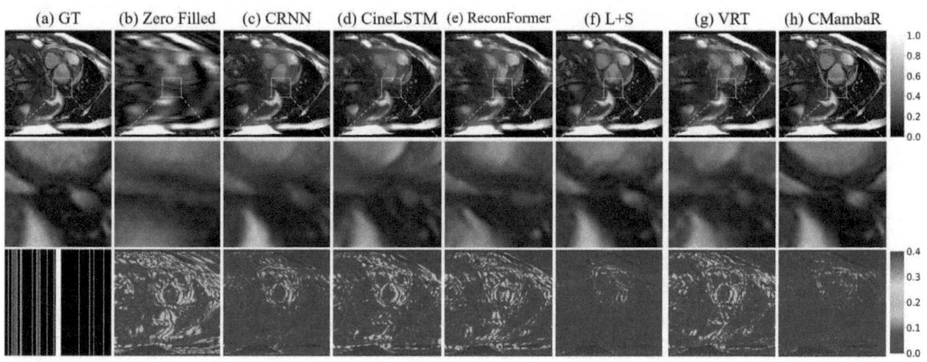

Fig. 4. Visualisation comparison with representative methods under 1D random subsampling pattern with acceleration factor 8× on KDSB dataset. First row: Reconstructed images from different methods; Second row: Zoomed-in region of yellow boxes; Third row: Absolute error maps of different methods. (Color figure online)

3.4 Ablation Study

In this section, we conduct ablation studies on ACDC dataset under AF 8× to evaluate the of the signification of each important components. We first assess the utility of the designed LeVM block, we replace it with the conventional structure, where linear operation is utilized for forward feature extraction instead of the convolution operation. Then, we further analyzed the effectiveness of the cardiac phase prior by removing the cardiac phase fusion procedure, denoted as PriorF. The results in Table 3 demonstrate that both the LeVM module and the cardiac phase fusion contribute to the accurate restoration of images. Moreover, we found that performing phase fusion at deeper layers of the model further improves reconstruction accuracy.

4   Conclusion

In this paper, we proposed CMambaR, a deep unrolling framework designed to accelerate cardiac MRI reconstruction. By unrolling a carefully designed learning-based reconstruction network into an iterative optimization structure, CMambaR effectively restores cardiac anatomy and enhances reconstruction quality. The proposed Local-enhanced Vision Mamba module could effectively capture the global and local dependencies to learn a better feature representation. Additionally, the integration of a cardiac phase prior fusion mechanism further improves reconstruction accuracy. In future work, we plan to conduct more extensive experiments to validate its generalizability.

Acknowledgements. This work was supported in part by the Qingdao Science and Technology Benefiting the People Demonstration Project (24-1-8-cspz-20-nsh); in part by the Key R&D Program of Shandong Province, China (Major Scientific and Technological Innovation Project) (2022CXGC010504), in part by the Fundamental Research Funds for the Central Universities (2022JC015), in part by "New Universities 20 items" Funding Project of Jinan under Grant (2021GXRC024), and in part by the Shandong Provincial Natural Science Foundation under Grant (ZR2021LZH009).

References

1. Bernard, O., Lalande, A., Zotti, C., et al.: Deep learning techniques for automatic mri cardiac multi-structures segmentation and diagnosis: is the problem solved? IEEE Trans. Med. Imaging **37**(11), 2514–2525 (2018)
2. Cao, C., et al.: High-frequency space diffusion model for accelerated mri. IEEE Trans. Med. Imaging **43**(5), 1853–1865 (2024)
3. Curtis, A.D., Cheng, H.L.M.: Primer and historical review on rapid cardiac cine mri. J. Magn. Reson. Imaging **55**(2), 373–388 (2022)
4. Duan, J., Liu, Y., Wang, J.: Accelerated spirit parallel mr image reconstruction based on joint sparsity and sparsifying transform learning. IEEE Trans. Comput. Imaging **9**, 276–288 (2023)
5. Fabian, Z., Tinaz, B., Soltanolkotabi, M.: Humus-net: hybrid unrolled multi-scale network architecture for accelerated mri reconstruction. Adv. Neural. Inf. Process. Syst. **35**, 25306–25319 (2022)
6. Gu, A., Dao, T.: Mamba: linear-time sequence modeling with selective state spaces. arXiv preprint arXiv:2312.00752 (2023)
7. Guo, P., Mei, Y., Zhou, J., Jiang, S., Patel, V.M.: Reconformer: accelerated mri reconstruction using recurrent transformer. IEEE Trans. Med. Imaging **43**(1), 582–593 (2024)
8. Huang, W., et al.: Deep low-rank plus sparse network for dynamic mr imaging. Med. Image Anal. **73**, 102190 (2021)

9. Kramer, C.M., Barkhausen, J., Bucciarelli-Ducci, C., Flamm, S.D., Kim, R.J., Nagel, E.: Standardized cardiovascular magnetic resonance imaging (cmr) protocols: 2020 update. J. Cardiovasc. Magn. Reson. **22**(1), 17 (2020)

10. Li, B., Hu, W., Feng, C.M., Li, Y., Liu, Z., Xu, Y.: Multi-contrast complementary learning for accelerated mr imaging. IEEE J. Biomed. Health Inf. **28**(3), 1436–1447 (2024)

11. Li, B., Wang, W., Tao, K., Cao, Y., Li, Y., Liu, Z.: Enhance cardiac mri reconstruction via unfolding network with hybrid mamba-lstm. In: 2025 IEEE 22nd International Symposium on Biomedical Imaging (ISBI), pp. 1–5 (2025)

12. Liang, D., Cheng, J., Ke, Z., Ying, L.: Deep mri reconstruction: unrolled optimization algorithms meet neural networks. arXiv preprint arXiv:1907.11711 (2019)

13. Lin, J.-Y., Chang, Y.-C., Hsu, W.H.: Efficient and phase-aware video super-resolution for cardiac MRI. In: Martel, A.L., et al. (eds.) MICCAI 2020. LNCS, vol. 12264, pp. 66–76. Springer, Cham (2020). https://doi.org/10.1007/978-3-030-59719-1_7

14. Liu, S., Thung, K.H., Qu, L., Lin, W., Shen, D., Yap, P.T.: Learning mri artefact removal with unpaired data. Nat. Mach. Intell. **3**(1), 60–67 (2021)

15. Liu, Y., et al.: kt self-consistency diffusion: a physics-informed model for dynamic mr imaging. In: International Conference on Medical Image Computing and Computer-Assisted Intervention, pp. 414–424. Springer, Heidelberg (2024). https://doi.org/10.1007/978-3-031-72104-5_40

16. Liu, Z., et al.: Video swin transformer. In: Proceedings of the IEEE/CVF Conference on Computer Vision and Pattern Recognition, pp. 3202–3211 (2022)

17. Lyu, Q., et al.: Cine cardiac mri motion artifact reduction using a recurrent neural network. IEEE Trans. Med. Imaging **40**(8), 2170–2181 (2021)

18. Oscanoa, J.A., et al.: Deep learning-based reconstruction for cardiac mri: a review. Bioengineering **10**(3), 334 (2023)

19. Pan, J., Hamdi, M., Huang, W., Hammernik, K., Kuestner, T., Rueckert, D.: Unrolled and rapid motion-compensated reconstruction for cardiac cine mri. Med. Image Anal. **91**, 103017 (2024)

20. Qin, C., Schlemper, J., Caballero, J., Price, A.N., Hajnal, J.V., Rueckert, D.: Convolutional recurrent neural networks for dynamic mr image reconstruction. IEEE Trans. Med. Imaging **38**(1), 280–290 (2019)

21. Schlemper, J., Caballero, J., Hajnal, J.V., Price, A.N., Rueckert, D.: A deep cascade of convolutional neural networks for dynamic mr image reconstruction. IEEE Trans. Med. Imaging **37**(2), 491–503 (2017)

22. Sun, H., et al.: Fourier convolution block with global receptive field for mri reconstruction. Med. Image Anal. **99**, 103349 (2025)

23. Wang, Z., et al.: A faithful deep sensitivity estimation for accelerated magnetic resonance imaging. IEEE J. Biomed. Health Inf. **28**(4), 2126–2137 (2024)

24. Yang, Y., Sun, J., Li, H., Xu, Z.: Admm-csnet: a deep learning approach for image compressive sensing. IEEE Trans. Pattern Anal. Mach. Intell. **42**(3), 521–538 (2018)

25. Zhu, L., Liao, B., Zhang, Q., Wang, X., Liu, W., Wang, X.: Vision mamba: efficient visual representation learning with bidirectional state space model. In: Forty-first International Conference on Machine Learning (2024)

SC-DSE-nnUNet: An Efficient Hippocampus MRI Segmentation Method

Bowen Xiao and Yu Ma[✉]

Ningxia University, Yinchuan 750021, China
`mayu95@163.com`

Abstract. To address the issues of poor accuracy caused by complex structures and noise interference in hippocampus MRI segmentation, an improved nnU-Net segmentation algorithm is proposed. First, the introduction of Self-Calibrated Convolutions enhances the ability to capture irregular targets and edge details. Second, an adaptive threshold-constrained dynamic channel attention mechanism is proposed to optimize the allocation of channel weights, strengthening the features of the target region while effectively suppressing noise interference. Experimental results show that the proposed algorithm significantly outperforms nnU-Net in terms of Dice coefficient, IoU, and sensitivity. On the MSD Hippocampus and LPBA40 datasets, the DSC improved by 1.72% and 4.52%, the IoU improved by 2.89% and 5.4%, and the recall rate improved by 1.55% and 4.21%, respectively. Further visualization analysis of the segmentation results confirms that the proposed algorithm demonstrates excellent performance in segmenting complex structures such as hippocampal boundaries, vascular bifurcations, and lung infection regions.

Keywords: nnU-Net · Self-Calibrated Convolutions · Attention Mechanism · Cross-validation

1 Introduction

The hippocampus, located between the thalamus and the medial temporal lobe, is a crucial part of the limbic system. It is closely involved in functions such as emotional regulation, memory formation, and spatial navigation. Research has shown that structural and functional abnormalities in the hippocampus are closely related to the pathogenesis of several neurological disorders, including Alzheimer's disease, epilepsy, and intellectual disabilities. Among these, hippocampal atrophy is the most common neuroimaging feature of Alzheimer's disease, and its degree of atrophy has been shown to correlate positively with the duration of the illness. Therefore, precise segmentation of the hippocampus holds significant clinical value in assisting doctors with the intervention and treatment of related psychiatric conditions [1].

With the continuous advancement of technology, magnetic resonance imaging (MRI) has become widely used in clinical examinations and research. Hippocampus segmentation aids doctors and researchers in better evaluating the structure and function of the hippocampus. Currently, segmentation methods for hippocampal MRI can be broadly categorized into manual segmentation, multi-atlas segmentation, and deep learning-based segmentation methods. Manual segmentation, which relies heavily on expert input, suffers from high subjectivity and low efficiency. Although multi-atlas segmentation improves accuracy by integrating multiple anatomical atlases, it still faces challenges in adapting to individual differences. As a result, deep learning-based methods for hippocampal MRI segmentation have gradually become a research hotspot.

Ronneberger et al. [2] proposed the U-Net network, which is an improvement based on fully convolutional networks. The design incorporates skip connections and builds a completely symmetric U-shaped encoder-decoder structure, which helps retain richer global context information in the image. Su et al. [3] introduced a multi-scale segmentation model, MSU-Net, which applies multi-scale blocks to extract and recover image features using convolutional kernels with different receptive fields [4], and enhances segmentation accuracy by applying interactive skip connections between features. Richard Joules et al. [5] proposed a deep learning-based method for automatic hippocampus segmentation using standard resolution T1-weighted MRI. This method improves model adaptability and application scope by simplifying the data processing pipeline. Sackl et al. [6] proposed a deep learning-based automated hippocampus segmentation method that improves the segmentation accuracy of standard T1-weighted MRI by first pre-localizing the hippocampus and then enhancing it using T2-weighted MRI images.

Despite significant progress in deep learning-based hippocampus MRI segmentation, there are still numerous technical challenges that remain to be addressed. First, the hippocampus exhibits irregular shapes, small volumes, and low contrast with surrounding tissues, which makes traditional convolutional operations prone to losing fine structural and edge information during feature extraction, thus affecting segmentation accuracy. Secondly, the common issues of low contrast, weak edge characteristics, and noise interference in hippocampus MRI datasets further complicate precise segmentation. Additionally, significant variations in scale, modality, and category distribution across hippocampus MRI datasets limit the generalization performance of existing models. To address these challenges, this paper proposes a hippocampus MRI segmentation algorithm based on an improved nnU-Net. It innovatively integrates Self-Calibrated Convolutions and dynamic channel attention mechanism, which enhances the model's multi-scale feature extraction and adaptive feature selection capabilities, effectively improving segmentation accuracy.

2   nnU-net Algorithm and Its Improvements

2.1   nnU-net Algorithm Architecture

nnU-Net is an adaptive framework [7]. After inputting the hippocampus MRI dataset, nnU-Net automatically analyzes the attributes of the target dataset to determine the most suitable inference parameters. These are then combined with pre-defined blueprint parameters such as the loss function and optimizer to generate a pipeline fingerprint. The pipeline fingerprint is subsequently used as the optimal parameter setting, allowing the adaptive generation of the corresponding network structure to complete the segmentation task, as shown in Fig. 1.

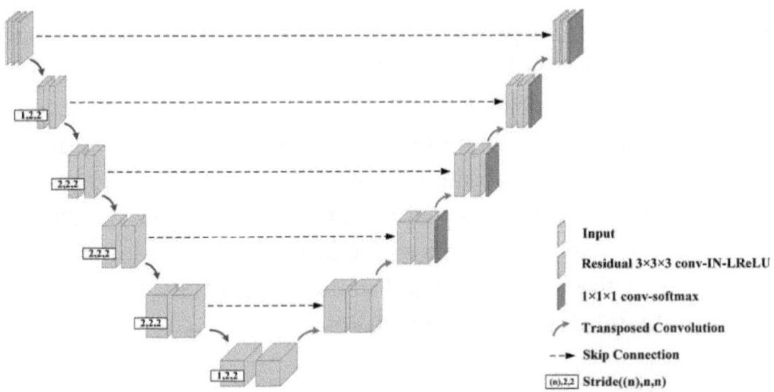

Fig. 1. Adaptive Network Architecture Generated by nnU-Net

Building upon the original U-Net architecture, nnU-Net replaces traditional batch normalization with instance normalization. By normalizing independently across each feature map, this modification effectively enhances the model's generalization ability across different medical image datasets. nnU-Net employs the Leaky ReLU (LReLU) activation function instead of the ReLU activation function to improve training stability and alleviate the vanishing gradient problem. Considering that directly using the cross-entropy loss function may lead to the loss of fine details in medical images, this paper chooses a hybrid loss function, combining the Dice loss function with the cross-entropy loss function for model training. The definition of this hybrid loss function is given in Eq. (1).

$$L_{Total} = L_{Dice} + L_{CE} \tag{1}$$

In the equation, L_{Dice} represents the Dice loss function, and its definition is given in Eq. (2).

$$L_{\text{Dice}} = -\frac{2}{|N|} \sum_{n \in N} \frac{\sum_{i \in I} r_i^n g_i^n}{\sum_{i \in I} r_i^n + \sum_{i \in I} g_i^n} \tag{2}$$

In the equation, N represents the total number of classes, I denotes the set of pixels, r_i represents the result of post-processing the neural network output with the Softmax function, g_i and represents the one-hot encoding of the ground truth labels.

2.2   nnu-Net-Based Improved Algorithm Architecture

Self-calibrated Convolutions

In neural networks, convolution operations serve as the core operation, primarily responsible for extracting local features from input images. However, traditional convolution operations have clear limitations. Exploring more efficient convolution methods to enhance the model's ability in global context awareness, detailed feature extraction, and adaptability to irregular targets is crucial for improving the accuracy of medical image segmentation.

Self-Calibrated Convolutions perform convolutional feature transformations by constructing a bi-scale feature space [8]. The self-calibration operation establishes spatial and channel dependencies, which not only significantly expands the receptive field of the convolutional layer but also strengthens the semantic representation of features. As shown in Fig. 2, the Self-Calibrated Convolution consists of two branches: the upper branch generates feature maps with adaptive correction weights through the self-calibration convolution operation, dynamically adjusting feature responses, while the lower branch retains the original spatial context information through convolution operations, ensuring the integrity of local features.

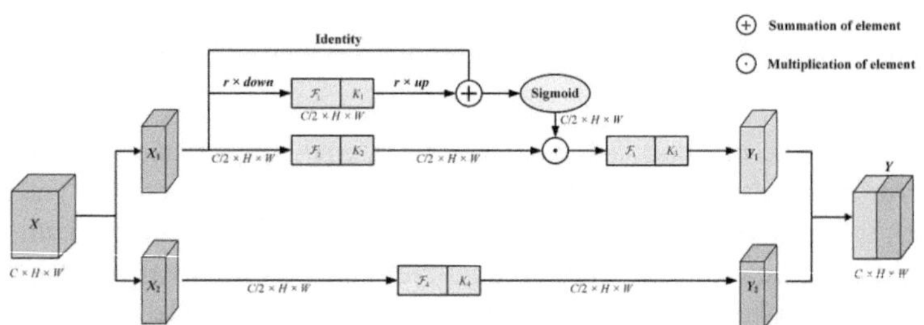

Fig. 2. Self-Calibrated Convolution Structure Diagram

Specifically, the input feature map X is divided along the channel dimension into two sub-feature maps, X_1 and X_2, which halves the number of channels while keeping the spatial dimensions unchanged. To effectively capture contextual information at each spatial location, the convolution kernels are divided into four parts: K_1, K_2, K_3 and K_4. In the upper branch, X_1 is first downsampled using an average pooling layer, then processed with the K_1 convolution kernel, followed by upsampling to restore the resolution. The result is added to the original features, and a Sigmoid activation function generates the self-calibration weights. These weights are then used to perform a weighted fusion with the feature map extracted by the K_2 convolution kernel, and finally, the feature map Y_1 is generated using the K_3 convolution kernel. The computation process is shown in Eq. (3). In the lower branch, directly extracts features using the X_2 directly extracts features using the K_4 convolution kernel, generating the feature map Y_2, as shown in Eq. (4). The feature maps Y_1 and Y_2 are then fused by concatenating along the channel dimension, resulting in the final output feature map Y.

$$Y_1 = f_3[\sigma(Up(f_1(Avgpool_r(X_1)))) * X_1) + f_2(X_1)] \tag{3}$$

$$Y_2 = f_4(X_2) \tag{4}$$

Dynamic Channel Attention Mechanism
The core principle of the attention mechanism lies in calculating the correlations between input features to adaptively adjust the allocation weights of different features in the input image. This allows the model to automatically focus on key regions of the image while

effectively suppressing the interference of irrelevant or redundant features. Among various attention mechanisms, channel attention mechanisms, as a key branch, enhance feature channel responses by assigning differentiated weights to different feature channels, thereby improving the model's ability to extract key features.

The SE (Squeeze-and-Excitation) attention mechanism is a typical application of the channel attention mechanism [9]. Through two key operations—squeezing and excitation—it learns the relationships between different channels while preserving the integrity of the original feature space. This mechanism assigns different weights to each channel to enhance the model's feature representation ability. In this paper, based on the SE attention mechanism, an innovative adaptive dynamic threshold mechanism is introduced, as shown in Fig. 3. By setting minimum and maximum thresholds to constrain the channel weights, the mechanism ensures that the weight values remain within a reasonable dynamic range. This effectively addresses the performance degradation problem caused by extreme channel weight values, while providing the model with the flexibility to dynamically adjust the weight range according to the distribution characteristics of the input features, significantly improving the model's ability to capture dependencies between channels.

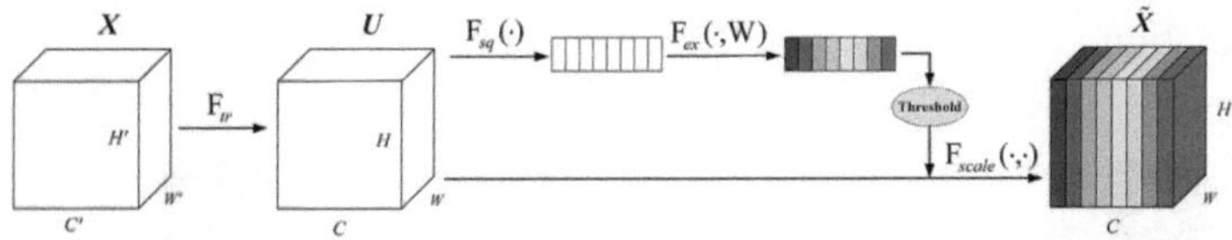

Fig. 3. Dynamic Channel Attention Mechanism Structure Diagram

First, the input feature map X is transformed into the feature map U through a transformation operation. In the Squeeze phase, global average pooling is applied to compress the spatial dimensions of the input high-dimensional feature map while keeping the channel dimension unchanged. Each channel is then represented by a single value. The computation process is shown in Eq. (5).

$$z_c = F_{sq}(u_c) = \frac{1}{H \times W} \sum_{i=1}^{H} \sum_{j=1}^{W} u_c(i, j) \tag{5}$$

In the Excitation phase, two fully connected layers with a bottleneck structure are used to model the nonlinear relationships between the channels. After the dimensionality reduction and subsequent dimensionality expansion through the fully connected layer transformation, the weights for different channels are generated. The Sigmoid activation function is then applied to map the channel weights to the range of (0, 1). The computation process is shown in Eq. (6).

$$s = F_{ex}(z, W) = \sigma(g(z, W)) = \sigma(W_2 \delta(W_1 z)) \tag{6}$$

In the equation, σ represents the Sigmoid activation function, δ represents the ReLU activation function, z is the output from the previous stage, W_1 is the input weight, and W_2 is the ReLU weight.

In the Scale phase, the adaptive dynamic threshold mechanism is used to assign weights to the feature map U based on the weight vector generated in the Excitation phase. Specifically, each channel is element-wise multiplied by the corresponding weight, resulting in an output feature map that has the same dimensions as U. The computation process is shown in Eq. (7).

$$\tilde{X}_c = F_{scale}(u_c, s_c) = s_c u_c \tag{7}$$

Improved Network Architecture

To address the limitations of nnU-Net in handling fine segmentation of complex structures and multi-scale feature adaptation, this paper optimizes and improves the network architecture based on the adaptively generated structure. As shown in Fig. 4, while retaining the original encoder-decoder structure and skip connections, the traditional convolutional layers are replaced with Self-Calibrated Convolutions, enhancing the model's ability to capture irregular targets and edge details. Additionally, by introducing a dynamic threshold-constrained channel attention mechanism, the feature channel weight distribution strategy is optimized. This not only strengthens the features of the target regions but also achieves a balance between noise suppression and the retention of key information.

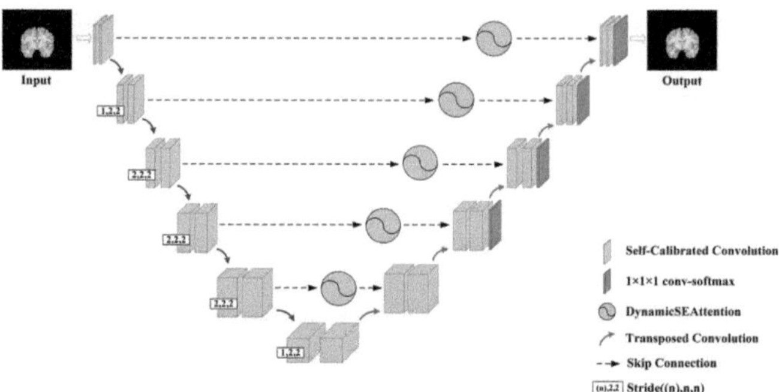

Fig. 4. Improved Network Architecture

3 Experiments

3.1 Experimental Environment and Configuration

To comprehensively evaluate the performance of the improved algorithm, two representative hippocampus MRI public datasets were selected for the experiments: the MSD Hippocampus dataset and the LPBA40 dataset. Both datasets were split into training and testing sets at a 3:1 ratio to ensure the validity of model training and the objectivity of the evaluation results.

Detailed information about the experimental environment is shown in Table 1.

Table 1. Experimental Environment

Component	Example
Operating System	Ubuntu22.04 LTS
Development Environment	Python3.8 PyTorch 2.5.1
CPU	Intel(R) Xeon(R) Platinum 8474C
Memory Capacity(GB)	80
GPU	RTX 4090D
VRAM Capacity(GB)	24
Acceleration Libraries	Cuda 12.1

The number of training iterations for the experiment was set to 1000, and the optimizer used was Stochastic Gradient Descent (SGD). The learning rate was dynamically adjusted using the Poly strategy, with the calculation formula provided in Eq. (8).

$$\mathrm{lr}(t) = \mathrm{initial\_lr} \times \left(1 - \frac{t}{T}\right)^{\alpha} \tag{8}$$

In the equation, initial_lr represents the initial learning rate, t and T represent the current training epoch and the total number of training epochs, respectively, and α is the hyperparameter that adjusts the decay rate.

The experiment used five-fold cross-validation, where the training set was randomly divided into five subsets. One subset was selected as the validation set in each iteration. Through five iterations, each subset was used once for validation and four times for training. The final model performance was evaluated by averaging the performance metrics from all five tests. The specific implementation process is shown in Fig. 5.

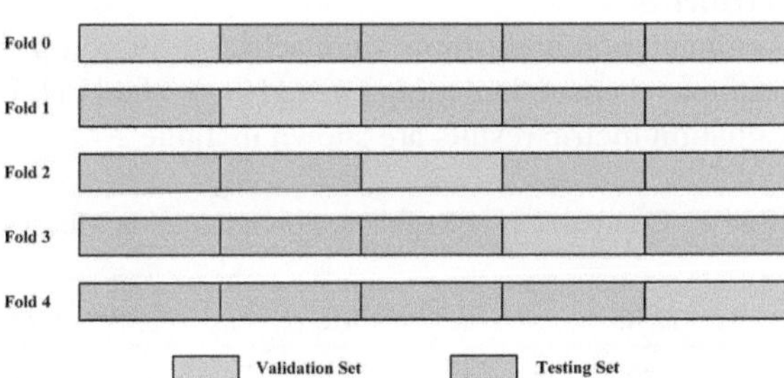

Fig. 5. Five-Fold Cross-Validation Example

3.2 Evaluation Metrics

The experiment used three evaluation metrics: Dice Similarity Coefficient (DSC), Intersection over Union (IoU), and Recall.

The Dice Similarity Coefficient (DSC) is used to measure the similarity between the segmentation result and the ground truth label. The closer the value is to 1, the better the segmentation performance. The calculation formula is shown in Eq. (9).

$$DSC(A, B) = \frac{2|A \cap B|}{|A| + |B|} \tag{9}$$

In the equation, A and B represent the segmentation result and the ground truth label, respectively. $|A \cap B|$ denotes the total number of overlapping pixels between the segmentation result and the ground truth label, while $|A|$ and $|B|$ represent the number of pixels in the segmentation result and the ground truth label, respectively.

Intersection over Union (IoU) is used to measure the overlap between the segmentation result and the ground truth label. The larger the value, the better the segmentation performance. The calculation formula is shown in Eq. (10).

$$IoU(A, B) = \frac{|A \cap B|}{|A \cup B|} \tag{10}$$

In the equation, $|A \cup B|$ denotes the total number of pixels marked as the target region in both the segmentation result and the ground truth label.

Recall is used to measure the algorithm's ability to recognize positive data, specifically the proportion of actual positive samples that are correctly predicted. The higher the recall, the smaller the likelihood that the algorithm misses the target region. The calculation formula is shown in Eq. (11).

$$Recall = \frac{TP}{TP + FN} \tag{11}$$

In the equation, TP represents the true positive samples that are predicted as positive, and FN represents the false negative samples that are predicted as negative.

3.3 Experimental Results and Analysis

Comparative Experiments

In this paper, four segmentation algorithms were selected for comparison experiments on the MSD Hippocampus dataset, including FCN [10], V-Net [11], U-Net [2], and 3D U-Net [12]. The evaluation metric results are shown in Table 2.

Table 2. Comparison of Segmentation Evaluation Metrics

Algorithm	DSC	IoU	Recall
FCN	0.6852	0.5212	0.6907
V-Net	0.8481	0.7363	—
U-Net	0.8487	0.7372	0.7392
3D U-Net	0.8752	0.7781	0.8874
SC-DSE-nnUNet	**0.9083**	**0.8344**	**0.9075**

As shown in Table 2, SC-DSE-nnUNet demonstrates significant advantages due to the integration of feature calibration and attention mechanisms, with all metrics significantly outperforming other algorithms. The DSE exceeds 90% and IoU exceeds 80%, confirming its outstanding performance in hippocampus segmentation tasks. Compared to other algorithms, SC-DSE-nnUNet also performs exceptionally well in Recall, reaching 90.75%, indicating its ability to effectively reduce the occurrence of false negatives.

Ablation Experiment

To further analyze the individual and synergistic effects of Self-Calibrated Convolutions and the Dynamic Channel Attention Mechanism, this paper uses the nnU-Net model as the baseline and integrates the Self-Calibrated Convolution structure (SC-nnUNet), the Dynamic Channel Attention Mechanism structure (DSE-nnUNet), and the combined structure of both (SC-DSE-nnUNet) for experimental validation on two datasets. The evaluation metric results are shown in Table 3, and the segmentation results are visualized in Fig. 5.

Table 3. Ablation Experiment Segmentation Evaluation Metric Results

Algorithm	Dataset	DSC	IoU	Recall
nnU-Net	MSD Hippocampus	0.8911	0.8055	0.8920
SC-nnUNet		0.8979	0.8161	0.9019
DSE-nnUNet		0.9073	0.8328	**0.9089**
SC-DSE-nnUNet		**0.9083**	**0.8344**	0.9075
nnU-Net	LPBA40	0.8911	0.8055	0.8920
SC-nnUNet		0.8979	0.8161	0.9019
DSE-nnUNet		0.9073	0.8328	0.9089
SC-DSE-nnUNet		**0.9083**	**0.8344**	**0.9075**

SC-nnUNet shows a 3.74% and 5% improvement in Dice coefficient and IoU, respectively, on the LPBA40 dataset compared to nnU-Net, confirming the effectiveness of Self-Calibrated Convolutions in extracting local features of small targets. DSE-nnUNet performs excellently on the MSD Hippocampus dataset, with improvements of 1.62%, 2.73%, and 1.69% in Dice coefficient, IoU, and Recall, respectively. On the LPBA40 dataset, DSE-nnUNet also shows improvements of 1.61%, 1.85%, and 0.88% in Dice coefficient, IoU, and Recall, respectively, confirming the Dynamic Channel Attention Mechanism's capability in recognizing target regions.

SC-DSE-nnUNet, by integrating Self-Calibrated Convolutions and the Dynamic Channel Attention Mechanism, achieves a complementary optimization in local feature capturing and global feature selection. In segmentation tasks, both Dice coefficient and IoU improve simultaneously, exceeding the individual contributions of Self-Calibrated Convolutions or Dynamic Channel Attention Mechanisms. On the MSD Hippocampus dataset, compared to nnU-Net, the Dice coefficient and IoU improve by 1.72% and 2.89%, significantly enhancing the segmentation accuracy of small targets.

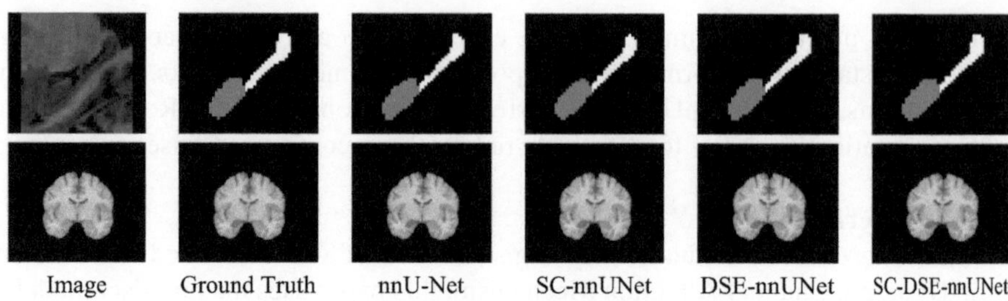

Image   Ground Truth   nnU-Net   SC-nnUNet   DSE-nnUNet   SC-DSE-nnUNet

Fig. 6. Hippocampus Segmentation Results

As shown in Fig. 6, the introduction of Self-Calibrated Convolutions effectively improves the continuity of segmentation boundaries for small targets. The Dynamic Channel Attention Mechanism enhances the signal-to-noise separation ability, achieving differentiated enhancement of the target region and background features. The synergistic effect of both methods yields significant results in segmentation tasks across both datasets, with clearer hippocampal boundaries and more complete structures.

Three-Dimensional Visualization of Segmentation Results
To visually assess model performance, the open-source software ITK-SNAP [13] was used for three-dimensional visualization of the hippocampus MRI segmentation results. As shown in Fig. 7, compared to the nnU-Net model, SC-DSE-nnUNet provides more accurate segmentation at the hippocampal anterior sulcus, with significant improvement in the continuity of the posterior surface topology. The overall segmentation results exhibit higher spatial consistency, validating the superior performance of the improved algorithm in segmenting complex structures.

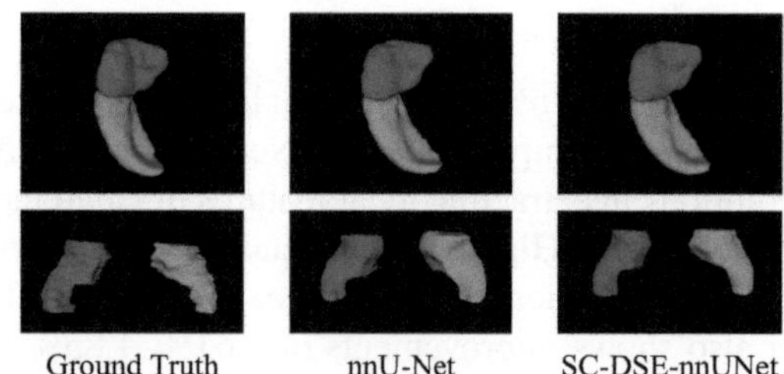

Ground Truth   nnU-Net   SC-DSE-nnUNet

Fig. 7. Three-Dimensional Visualization of Hippocampus Segmentation Results

4 Conclusion

Based on nnU-Net, this paper introduces the Self-Calibrated Convolution module to enhance the correction ability of multi-scale features, effectively improving feature extraction for irregular targets and edge details. Meanwhile, a dynamic channel attention mechanism with adaptive threshold constraints is designed to optimize the allocation of channel weights, effectively suppress noise interference while enhancing the feature representation of the target region. This method provides a new technical approach for hippocampus MRI segmentation and holds certain application value for related clinical diagnoses.

References

1. Morais-Ribeiro, R., Almeida, F.C., Coelho, A., et al.: Differential atrophy along the longitudinal hippocampal axis in Alzheimer's disease. Eur. J. Neurosci. **59**(12), 3376–3388 (2024)
2. Ronneberger, O., Fischer, P., Brox, T.: U-net: convolutional networks for biomedical image segmentation. In: Medical Image Computing and Computer-Assisted Intervention—MICCAI 2015: 18th International Conference, Munich, Germany, October 5–9, 2015, Proceedings, Part III, pp. 234–241. Springer, Heidelberg (2015)
3. Su, R., Zhang, D.Y., Liu, J.H., et al.: MSU-net: multi-scale U-net for 2D medical image segmentation. Front. Genet. **12**, 639930 (2021)
4. Li, Y. H., Chen, Y. T., Wang, N. Y., et al.: Scale-aware trident networks for object detection. In: 2019 IEEE/CVF International Conference on Computer Vision (ICCV), pp. 6053–6062. IEEE (2019)
5. Joules, R., Wolz, R.: Fully automatic deep-learning based segmentation of hippocampal subfields from standard resolution T1W MRI in Alzheimer's Disease. Alzheimer's Dementia **19**, e076575 (2023)
6. Sackl, M., Tinauer, C., Urschler, M., et al.: Fully automated hippocampus segmentation using T2-informed deep convolutional neural networks. Neuroimage **298**, 120767 (2024)
7. Isensee, F., Jaeger, P.F., Kohl, S.A., Petersen, J., Maier-Hein, K.H.: NnU-Net: a self-configuring method for deep learning-based biomedical image segmentation. Nat. Methods **18**(2), 203–211 (2021)
8. Liu, J.J., Hou, Q., Cheng, M.M., et al.: Improving convolutional networks with self-calibrated convolutions. In: Proceedings of the IEEE/CVF Conference on Computer Vision and Pattern Recognition, pp. 10096–10105. IEEE (2020)
9. Hu, J., Shen, L., Sun, G.: Squeeze-and-excitation networks. In: Proceedings of the IEEE Conference on Computer Vision and Pattern Recognition, pp. 7132–7141. IEEE (2018)
10. Long, J., Shelhamer, E., Darrell, T.: Fully convolutional networks for semantic segmentation. In: Proceedings of the IEEE Conference on Computer Vision and Pattern Recognition, pp. 3431–3440. IEEE (2015)
11. Milletari, F., Navab, N., Ahmadi, S.-A.: V-net: fully convolutional neural networks for volumetric medical image segmentation. In: Proceedings of the 4th International Conference on 3D Vision, pp. 565–571. IEEE, Piscataway (2016)
12. Wolny, A., Cerrone, L., Vijayan, A., et al.: Accurate and versatile 3D segmentation of plant tissues at cellular resolution. Elife **9**, e57613 (2020)
13. Yushkevich, P.A., et al.: User-guided 3D active contour segmentation of anatomical structures: Significantly improved efficiency and reliability. Neuroimage **31**(3), 1116–1128 (2006)

Spatiotemporal Feature Fusion for Glioblastoma Recurrence Prediction Using Mamba-Based Dual-Stream Framework

Chengwei Chen[1,2], Dong Huang[1,2,3], Yao Zheng[1,2], Jie Wei[1,2], Yuefei Feng[1,2], Tianci Liu[1,2], Junmei Feng[4], and Yang Liu[1,2,3(✉)]

[1] Department of Biomedical Engineering, Air Force Medical University, No. 169 Changle West Road, Xi'an 710032, Shaanxi, China
[2] Shaanxi Provincial Key Laboratory of Bioelectromagnetic Detection and Intelligent Perception, No. 169 Changle West Road, Xi'an 710032, Shaanxi, China
[3] Innovation Research Institute, Xijing Hospital, Air Force Medical University, No. 169 Changle West Road, Xi'an 710032, Shaanxi, China
yliu@fmmu.edu.cn
[4] Guangzhou Institute of Technology, Xidian University, Guangzhou 510555, China

Abstract. Glioblastoma (GBM) is the most aggressive glioma with a 5-year survival rate of only 6.8% and a median overall survival of 8 months. Accurate prediction of recurrence is essential for personalized treatment. Current imaging-based approaches face two major limitations: 1) reliance on single-time point images fails to capture tumor dynamics, and 2) the limited receptive fields of CNN and the quadratic complexity of Transformer hinder effective 3D MRI processing. To address these limitations, we leverage Mamba's linear computational complexity and global modeling capabilities, and our model employs the following techniques: 1) a dual-stream framework for prediction of recurrence; 2) the BiSMamba module for multi-scale feature extraction; 3) the multi-stage fusion module for capturing dynamic changes. Extensive experiments on two public datasets (RHUH-GBM and LUMEIERE) have shown that our approach achieves impressive results in prediction of glioblastoma recurrence.

Keywords: Glioblastoma · Recurrence prediction · 3D MRI · Deep learning · Mamba architecture

1 Introduction

Glioma, a common primary intracranial tumor derived from glial cells, has a malignant proportion of up to 80%. Its high recurrence rate and mortality rate pose a serious threat to human health [1]. According to the 2021 WHO Classification of Tumors of the Central Nervous System (2021 WHO CNS Classification), gliomas are graded I-IV by malignancy, with distinct differences in invasive patterns, treatment options, and prognosis across grades. The standard clinical

Z. Lin et al. (Eds.): ICIG 2025, LNCS 16161, pp. 352–363, 2026.
https://doi.org/10.1007/978-981-95-3398-5_29

treatment primarily involves surgical resection, but complete removal is challenging due to the tumor's aggressive growth and ill-defined boundaries. Data show that most patients, even with standard treatment, experience early progression or recurrence, accompanied by symptoms such as headaches, epilepsy, neurological deficits, and cognitive decline. After recurrence, tumors exhibit increased treatment resistance, while patient survival rates decrease. Glioblastoma (GBM), the most malignant type, has a median overall survival of only 8 months (after recurrence) and a 5-year survival rate of approximately 6.8%. Therefore, early and accurate prediction of GBM recurrence is crucial for formulating personalized treatment plans, slowing disease progression, and improving patient prognosis.

Non-invasive imaging such as MRI is now a research focus for predicting glioma recurrence. Traditional image analysis relies on morphological indicators (tumor size, enhancement features, and extent of edema) to determine recurrence, while machine learning and deep learning models, driven by big data, have significantly improved prediction accuracy by mining complex image features undetectable via traditional methods. For example, Mahootiha et al. [2] used preoperative MRI features with a UNet framework to predict postoperative recurrence risk in children with low-grade gliomas, and Ren et al. [3] distinguished true recurrence from treatment-related effects using image features of postoperative enhanced regions to aid clinical decisions. However, using only preoperative or postoperative images has limitations: preoperative MRI provides tumor biological characteristics (initial tumor volume, morphology, heterogeneity), but cannot provide postoperative treatment response; postoperative images reflect tumor changes after surgery or radiotherapy, but lack assessment of baseline biological behavior. Although Qin et al.'s model combines preoperative and postoperative clinical data to assess the risk of recurrence, it cannot determine the degree of tumor infiltration or minimal residue, as well as spatial information of tumor changes. Thus, combining preoperative and postoperative imaging for recurrence prediction more comprehensively reflects the dynamic evolution of tumors, offering a new strategy to improve the accuracy of glioblastoma recurrence prediction.

Based on the above problems, we propose a network framework for predicting tumor recurrence using preoperative and postoperative 3D MRI images, which not only preserves the spatial structural information of the tumor, but also focuses on temporal changes in the tumor region. Specifically, we construct a Mamba-based dual-stream framework and utilize the BiSMamba module to extract spatiotemporal features from preoperative and postoperative images. Additionally, a multi-stage fusion module is designed for effective fusion of preoperative and postoperative features to capture the dynamic evolution of the tumor.

Our main contributions are as follows:

- We design a Mamba-based dual-stream framework and proposed the BiSMamba module to model spatiotemporal features of preoperative and postoperative 3D MRI long sequence image data.

- We construct a multi-stage fusion module, which can effectively fuse pre-operative and postoperative features to capture the key processes of tumor development and change.
- Extensive experiments on the RHUH-GBM and LUMEIERE datasets show that the method achieved good results in predicting glioblastoma recurrence, which confirm the effectiveness of our proposed method.

2   Related Work

Recent years have seen notable progress in using medical images to predict tumor recurrence. For instance, Wang et al. [4] constructed a multi parameter radiomics model by extracting radiomics features from preoperative multi parameter MRI (T1WI, T2WI, T1CE sequences), which can effectively predict the risk of early postoperative recurrence in patients and provide reference for clinical treatment decision-making. However, preoperative imaging only represents the biological characteristics of the tumor and cannot reflect the impact of surgical and other treatment responses on recurrence. Meanwhile, Rykkje et al. [5] used early post-operative MRI to assess residual tumors for recurrence prediction but faced difficulties in distinguishing pseudo progression from actual recurrence. Thus, relying solely on preoperative or postoperative imaging has inherent limitations. Hence, building models that integrate both types of images is key to enhancing prediction accuracy.

Existing tumor recurrence prediction primarily focuses on medical image feature extraction, key feature fusion, and predictive model construction. Jia et al. [6] built a machine learning prediction model by combining preoperative MRI radiomic features with clinical factors, but this method required manual feature design with a complex selection process. Later, deep learning-based convolution neural network (CNN) enabled automatic feature learning from medical images and were widely adopted. Yang et al. [7] demonstrated the potential of a ResNet-34-based framework in predicting prognosis for hepatocellular carcinoma (HCC) patients. However, CNN architectures struggle to capture global information due to the local receptive field limitation of convolutional kernels. The Transformer architectures, with its self-attention mechanism, can improve prediction accuracy through its global receptive field when processing high-resolution, complex-structured medical images. Notably, Transformer architectures can effectively integrate multi-modal data to enhance prediction accuracy [8], but the quadratic complexity of their self-attention mechanism leads to significantly increased computational costs.

To overcome the challenges of modelling long sequences, the efficient Mamba architecture based on the State Space Model (SSM) [9] has emerged as an effective alternative. Its linear time complexity gives it an advantage over Trans-formers in handling long-sequence data. The Vision Mamba model [10], which performed well in multiple vision tasks, offered superior computational efficiency and memory usage. Thus, using Mamba to process preoperative and postoper-ative 3D MRI images can effectively achieve information complementarity and dynamic tracking of anatomical structure changes, thereby enhancing the performance of tumor recurrence prediction models to some extent.

3   Methodology

3.1   Detailed Description of the Framework

Our proposed tumor recurrence prediction network architecture (Fig. 1(a)) is a dual-stream model based on the Mamba framework, which combines computational efficiency with global dependency modeling. It employs a multi-stage strategy for multi-scale feature learning, comprising two 3D feature encoders constructed using the bidirectional spatial Mamba (BiSMamba) module, four multi-stage fusion modules, and a classification head.

The dual-stream network inputs preoperative and postoperative 3D MRI images and corresponding tumor masks to leverage information complementarity between time points. The encoder first extracts initial image features through convolution, normalization, and GELU activation. The BiSMamba module then extracts spatial features and constructs a multi-scale feature structure through down sampling. Preoperative and postoperative multi-scale features are fed into multi-stage fusion modules for spatiotemporal collaborative modeling, incorporating a learnable attention mechanism to adaptively weight their respective contributions. Feature maps from different stages undergo $1\times1\times1$ convolution to align dimensions, then are concatenated along the channel dimension and fed into the classification head. The classification head follows a three-step process: (1) performing global average pooling on fused 3D features to extract global context; (2) flattening and normalizing features to stabilize the input distribution; and (3) mapping high-dimensional features to classification probabilities via two fully connected layers for tumor recurrence prediction.

3.2   Bidirectional Spatial Mamba (BiSMamba) Module

To achieve effective medical image feature extraction, we design a hierarchical feature extraction module that leverages the complementary strengths of 3D convolution and State Space Model (SSM) to deeply mine spatial information from preoperative and postoperative multi-modal imaging data.

The bidirectional spatial Mamba (BiSMamba) module innovatively integrates 3D convolution and State Space Model (SSM) to build a unique hybrid architecture. As illustrated in Fig. 1(b), the input feature map F first passes through the Gated Spatial Convolution (GSC) component. This component employs a dual-path 3D convolution structure with a sigmoid-based gating mechanism to generate dynamic weights, enhancing the feature responses in lesion-relevant regions. Mathematically, this can be expressed as:

$$F_{GSC} = \mathcal{C}_{3\times3\times3}\left(\sigma(\mathcal{C}_{1\times1\times1}(F)) \odot \mathcal{C}_{3\times3\times3}(F)\right) \tag{1}$$

Among them, F_{GSC} is the final output feature, σ is the Sigmoid activation function, $\mathcal{C}_{3\times3\times3}$ represents a 3D convolution operation with a kernel size of

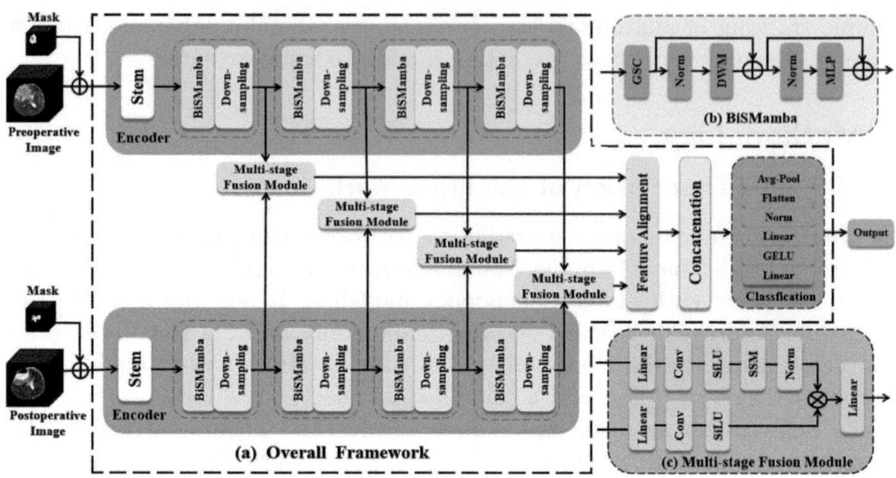

Fig. 1. The overall framework proposed in this study. (a) Overall framework: Preoperative and postoperative 3D images and Masks are input into the network. The encoder blocks extract features at four stages, which are then fed into the corresponding multi-stage fusion modules. After mapping the fused features of each stage to a unified number of channels and size, they are concatenated and transmitted to the classification head for prediction. (b) BiSMamba module (c) Multi-stage Fusion module.

$3 \times 3 \times 3$, and $\mathcal{C}_{1 \times 1 \times 1}$ represents a 3D convolution operation with a kernel size of $1 \times 1 \times 1$.

The output feature F_{GSC} of the GSC component passes through a residual block and, then undergoes normalization. Use Dual-Way Mamba (DWM) component for bidirectional sequence modeling. The DWM component employs a tensor rearrangement strategy: for 3D input features with dimensions (B, C, D, H, W), spatial dimensions are flattened in two orthogonal directions: firstly, flattened in the order of depth-height-width $(d - h - w)$ for forward Mamba computation; and secondly, flattened in the order of width-height-depth $(w - h - d)$ for backward Mamba computation. These two flattening methods enable the model to capture long-range feature dependencies from multiple dimensions and achieve in-depth interaction of global information. Ultimately, the results of bidirectional processing are dynamically fused via a learnable adaptive weighting mechanism to achieve efficient integration of local details with global contextual information. The process is expressed as:

$$F_{forward} = \text{Flatten}_{d-h-w}(F_{GSC}) = \text{Reshape}(F, (B, C, D \times H \times W)) \tag{2}$$

$$F_{backward} = \text{Flatten}_{w-h-d}(F_{GSC}) = \text{Reshape}(F, (B, C, W \times H \times D)) \tag{3}$$

$$M_{forward} = \text{Mamba}(F_{forward}) \tag{4}$$

$$M_{backward} = \text{Mamba}(F_{backward}) \tag{5}$$

$$M_{merged} = \alpha \cdot M_{forward} + (1 - \alpha) \cdot M_{backward} \tag{6}$$

$$\alpha = \sigma(\text{WeightNet}([M_{forward}; M_{backward}])) \tag{7}$$

Among them, $[M_{forward}; M_{backward}]$ represents the feature concatenation operation, and σ is the sigmoid function, ensuring that $\alpha \in [0, 1]$, WeightNet represents the adaptive weight calculation network.

After the primary hybrid features are obtained by summing the DWM component output with the residual path features, the channel interaction is enhanced by secondary residual concatenation, layer normalization, and introduction of a channel MLP with a channel expansion ratio of four. Finally, the residual path and MLP path outputs are fused to generate advanced features rich in semantic information to support tumor recurrence prediction.

3.3 Multi-stage Fusion Module

The dual-stream encoder directly feeds preoperative and postoperative features extracted at each level into the fusion module. Given that preoperative images contain intrinsic tumor biological features and postoperative images reflect treatment response information, these two types of features are highly complementary. To leverage this complementarity, we designed a multi-stage fusion module with a multi-path synergy mechanism (see Fig. 1(c)). The module is centered on parallel path construction to facilitate interaction between features at different scales and strengthen feature representation capability, containing two parallel processing paths:

Path 1: A $3{\times}3{\times}3$ convolutional kernel is employed for feature extraction. Through small receptive field convolutional operations, it captures local spatial details, effectively preserving anatomical continuity. It is particularly suitable for extracting high-frequency information such as organ edges and micro-lesions.

Path 2: First, a $1{\times}1{\times}1$ convolution is utilized for channel adjustment, then the SSM is introduced to establish long-range spatial dependence. This path can effectively capture global contextual information of the lesion area, enhancing the model's perception of overall tumor morphology.

The output features of the two paths are fused via element-wise multiplication. This non-linear interaction establishes deep cross-path feature associations. Finally, a $1{\times}1{\times}1$ convolution maps the fused features back to the original channel dimension to ensure compatibility with subsequent modules. Additionally, instance normalization is reapplied to further enhance the model's robustness across different samples. Through this multi-stage fusion module, the model fully integrates local details and global information, significantly improving the accuracy and reliability of tumor recurrence prediction.

4 Experiments

4.1 Data

This study used two datasets from different centers: RHUH-GBM (as an independent external validation cohort) and LUMEIERE (as the internal dataset).

The RHUH-GBM dataset [11], obtained from The Cancer Imaging Archive (TCIA), includes 120 records from 40 patients, with multi-parametric MRI sequences (T1WI, T2WI, FLAIR, T1CE, DWI) and expert-validated tumor sub-region segmentations from preoperative, postoperative, and follow-up scans.

The LUMEIERE dataset [12], sourced from Figshare, comprises longitudinal MRI data of 91 glioblastoma (GBM) patients (638 time points, 20082017), including the same MRI sequences and tumor sub-region segmentations via DeepBraTumIA and HD-GLIO-AUTO tools.

For this study, T2 modality and mask-guided feature extraction were used, with a 6-month time threshold as the label. Data with poor image quality, incomplete modalities, or unknown labels were excluded, resulting in 59 cases in the internal dataset (subjected to five-fold cross-validation) and 31 cases in the external dataset (used as an independent test set).

4.2 Implementation Details

This study preprocessed MRI data via intensity standardization and enhanced it through spatial transformation, intensity perturbation, and random occlusion. During training, dynamic Focal Loss (with adaptive gamma adjustment) and the AdamW optimizer (coupled with cosine annealing learning rate) were used, along with Dropout (p = 0.2–0.4) and gradient clipping (threshold 10.0) to boost model performance. All experiments ran on PyTorch 2.50 on a server, using Tesla-V100-PCIE-32GB.

4.3 Evaluation Indicators

In order to conduct a thorough and precise evaluation of the tumor recurrence prediction model, this study opted for five pivotal metrics: AUC, Accuracy, Precision, Recall, and F1. The calculation formulas for the indicators are as follows:

$$\text{Accuracy} = \frac{TP + TN}{TP + TN + FP + FN} \tag{8}$$

$$\text{F1} = 2 \times \frac{\text{Precision} \times \text{Recall}}{\text{Precision} + \text{Recall}} \tag{9}$$

$$\text{Precision} = \frac{TP}{TP + FP} \tag{10}$$

$$\text{Recall} = \frac{TP}{TP + FN} \tag{11}$$

Among them, AUC is the area under the receiver operating characteristic curve; TP, FP, TN, and FN represent true positive, false positive, true negative, and false negative, respectively.

4.4 Comparison with the Current Models

To evaluate the effectiveness and advantages of the model, we compared the proposed method with several mainstream models based on CNN and Transformer frameworks, including 3DResNet [13], TwinCNN [14], MVCNN [15],

EDCA-Net [16], nnFormer [17], and MedNeXt [18]. All existing models retained their core innovations and were reproduced as 3D MRI classification frameworks. The validation set results are shown in Table 1 and the test set results are presented in Table 2, where the optimal results are bolded. The ROC curves are shown in Fig. 2.

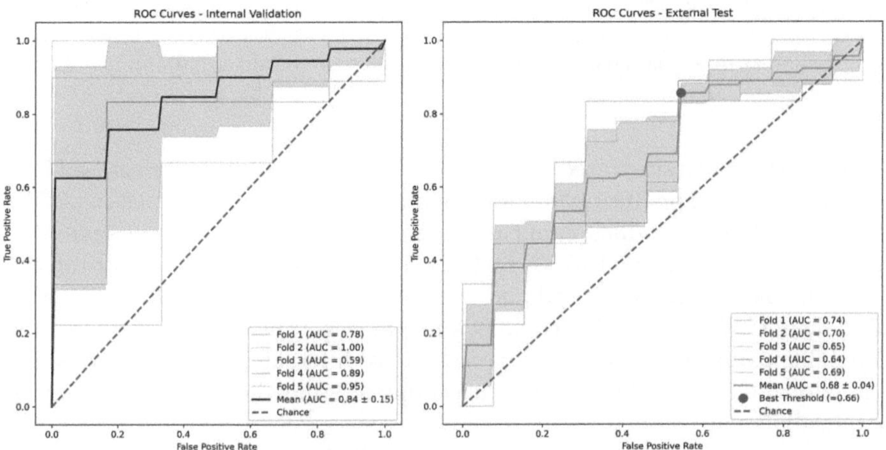

Fig. 2. ROC curves of the optimal model in Internal Validation and External Test.

Table 1. Comparison with the current model (Validation set)

Method	AUC	Accuracy	F1	Precision	Recall
3DResNet [13]	0.8245 ± 0.0890	0.7636 ± 0.0794	0.7861 ± 0.0992	0.9350 ± 0.0831	0.6921 ± 0.1393
TwinCNN [14]	0.7637 ± 0.1094	0.7288 ± 0.0323	0.7790 ± 0.0420	0.8611 ± 0.0824	**0.7243 ± 0.0930**
MVCNN [15]	0.8105 ± 0.0821	0.7470 ± 0.0713	0.7564 ± 0.1099	**0.9667 ± 0.0667**	0.6386 ± 0.1466
EDCA-Net [16]	0.8339 ± 0.0668	0.7121 ± 0.0380	0.7402 ± 0.0530	0.9267 ± 0.0904	0.6186 ± 0.0472
nnFormer [17]	0.6423 ± 0.0785	0.6439 ± 0.1331	0.6439 ± 0.1331	0.8562 ± 0.1410	0.6193 ± 0.2839
MedNeXt [18]	0.5522 ± 0.0860	0.6288 ± 0.0589	0.6833 ± 0.0896	0.7913 ± 0.1071	0.6286 ± 0.1579
Ours	**0.8419 ± 0.1450**	**0.7667 ± 0.1106**	**0.7915 ± 0.1073**	0.8867 ± 0.0933	0.7178 ± 0.1196

Our method demonstrated superior performance on the validation set, achieving the highest AUC (0.8419 ± 0.1450), indicating excellent generalization capability. With an accuracy of 0.7667 ± 0.1106 and the best F1 (0.7915 ± 0.1073), the model shows outstanding overall predictive performance and optimal balance between precision and recall. While precision (0.9667 ± 0.0667) was slightly lower than MVCNN, our approach maintained comparable recall (0.7178 ± 0.1196 vs TwinCNN's 0.7243±0.0930), effectively identifying positive samples without significant false negatives.

Table 2. Comparison with the current model (Test set)

Method	AUC	Accuracy	F1	Precision	Recall
3DResNet [13]	0.5833 ± 0.0230	0.5742 ± 0.0241	0.5633 ± 0.0749	0.7063 ± 0.0701	0.4889 ± 0.1077
TwinCNN [14]	0.5645 ± 0.0334	**0.6774 ± 0.0204**	**0.7504 ± 0.0291**	0.6831 ± 0.0346	0.8444 ± 0.0956
MVCNN [15]	0.4513 ± 0.0729	0.5419 ± 0.0826	0.5344 ± 0.2722	0.4872 ± 0.2469	0.6000 ± 0.3170
EDCA-Net [16]	0.4927 ± 0.0432	0.5613 ± 0.0724	0.5542 ± 0.1458	0.6551 ± 0.0637	0.5333 ± 0.2572
nnFormer [17]	0.5222 ± 0.0477	0.6194 ± 0.0428	0.6757 ± 0.0972	0.6613 ± 0.0283	0.7333 ± 0.2061
MedNeXt [18]	0.5872 ± 0.0937	0.6710 ± 0.0316	0.7190 ± 0.0491	0.7255 ± 0.0725	**0.7444 ± 0.1432**
Ours	**0.6829 ± 0.0387**	0.6774 ± 0.0408	0.7044 ± 0.0861	**0.7533 ± 0.0716**	0.7000 ± 0.1670

Our method demonstrated superior performance on the test set, achieving the highest AUC (0.6829±0.0387) among all models, notably surpassing 3DResNet (0.5833±0.0230), which confirms its enhanced discriminative capability. It attained the best precision (0.7533±0.0716) and matched TwinCNN for top accuracy, while maintaining balanced performance in F1 and recall. Although slightly behind TwinCNN's F1 and MedNeXt's recall, our approach shows more stable and reliable comprehensive performance across different clinical scenarios, making it particularly suitable for practical applications where both precision and generalizability are crucial.

In summary, the proposed method has reached or surpassed existing models across multiple key performance indicators. In particular, its strong performance in critical metrics such as AUC and precision fully validates the effectiveness and robustness of the method in practical applications, providing a more reliable solution for tasks in related fields.

4.5 Ablation Study

In order to comprehensively analyze the specific contributions of each component to the overall performance, ablation studies are conducted to systematically evaluate the key modules of the proposed model.

Effectiveness of Dual-Stream Framework. In order to verify the effect of the dual-stream framework, we compared models using only preoperative (Pre) or postoperative (Post) images against our dual-stream approach. As shown in Table 3, the dual-stream framework significantly outperformed single-input variants across all metrics, demonstrating that integrating both preoperative and postoperative imaging data substantially enhances predictive performance for tumor recurrence.

Effectiveness of BiSMamba Module. In order to verify the necessity of BiSMamba Module in feature extraction, we conducted comparative experiments replacing it with normal convolution (CNN) and residual convolution (ResNet). While performance differences on the validation set were marginal,

Table 3. Ablation experimental results of Dual-Stream framework

Dataset	Method	AUC	Accuracy	F1	Precision	Recall
Validation	Pre[1]	0.7660 ± 0.1311	0.6939 ± 0.1155	0.7248 ± 0.1310	0.8762 ± 0.1524	0.6693 ± 0.2029
	Post[2]	0.6440 ± 0.1643	0.5924 ± 0.0996	0.6257 ± 0.0860	0.8529 ± 0.1232	0.5121 ± 0.1232
	Ours	**0.8419 ± 0.1450**	**0.7667 ± 0.1106**	**0.7915 ± 0.1073**	**0.8867 ± 0.0933**	**0.7178 ± 0.1196**
Test	Pre[1]	0.5222 ± 0.0887	0.5871 ± 0.0851	0.5485 ± 0.1987	0.7299 ± 0.1433	0.5222 ± 0.2780
	Post[2]	0.5752 ± 0.1284	0.6129 ± 0.0456	0.6446 ± 0.0447	0.7303 ± 0.1350	0.6222 ± 0.1548
	Ours	**0.6829 ± 0.0387**	**0.6774 ± 0.0408**	**0.7044 ± 0.0861**	**0.7533 ± 0.0716**	**0.7000 ± 0.1670**

[1] Pre corresponds to the preoperative model in the ablation experiment of dual-stream framework

[2] Post corresponds to the postoperative model in the ablation experiment of dual-stream framework

BiSMamba demonstrated clear superiority on the test set (Table 4). These results confirm that BiSMamba's hybrid architecture - combining 3D convolution's local feature extraction with SSM's long-range modeling - is particularly effective for capturing the complex spatial patterns in tumor recurrence prediction.

Table 4. Ablation experimental results of BiSMamba Module

Dataset	Method	AUC	Accuracy	F1	Precision	Recall
Validation	CNN[1]	0.7941 ± 0.1365	**0.7803 ± 0.0834**	**0.8142 ± 0.0914**	0.8814 ± 0.1026	**0.7657 ± 0.1137**
	ResNet[2]	0.8275 ± 0.0620	0.7303 ± 0.0576	0.7625 ± 0.0606	**0.9333 ± 0.0816**	0.6557 ± 0.0928
	Ours	**0.8419 ± 0.1450**	0.7667 ± 0.1106	0.7915 ± 0.1073	0.8867 ± 0.0933	0.7178 ± 0.1196
Test	CNN[1]	0.5530 ± 0.1347	0.5871 ± 0.0689	0.5859 ± 0.1490	0.6872 ± 0.0581	0.5667 ± 0.2470
	ResNet[2]	0.5436 ± 0.0903	0.5226 ± 0.0376	0.4313 ± 0.1756	0.7334 ± 0.1405	0.3889 ± 0.2919
	Ours	**0.6829 ± 0.0387**	**0.6774 ± 0.0408**	**0.7044 ± 0.0861**	**0.7533 ± 0.0716**	**0.7000 ± 0.1670**

[1] CNN corresponds to the normal convolution module in the ablation experiment of BiSMamba Module

[2] ResNet corresponds to the residual convolution module in the ablation experiment of BiSMamba Module

Effectiveness of Multi-stage Fusion Module. In order to evaluate the effectiveness of the multi-stage fusion module, we compared our Mamba-based fusion against two alternatives: 1) linear projection with simple concatenation (Proj), and 2) early feature concatenation before fusion (Combined). As shown in Table 5, the multi-stage fusion module achieved superior performance across all metrics (AUC, F1), demonstrating optimal balance between sensitivity and specificity. The results confirm that our dual-path interaction mechanism effectively integrates global and local features, significantly outperforming conventional fusion approaches in tumor recurrence prediction.

Table 5. Ablation experimental results of Multi-stage Fusion Module

Dataset type	Method	AUC	Accuracy	F1	Precision	Recall
Validation	Combined[1]	$0{,}7352 \pm 0{,}0299$	$0{,}5924 \pm 0{,}0661$	$0{,}5613 \pm 0{,}1316$	$\mathbf{0{,}9267 \pm 0{,}0904}$	$0{,}5800 \pm 0{,}2097$
	Proj[2]	$0{,}7835 \pm 0{,}1779$	$0{,}7606 \pm 0{,}1279$	$0{,}7887 \pm 0{,}1138$	$0{,}9095 \pm 0{,}1170$	$\mathbf{0{,}7407 \pm 0{,}0897}$
	Ours	$\mathbf{0{,}8419 \pm 0{,}1450}$	$\mathbf{0{,}7667 \pm 0{,}1106}$	$\mathbf{0{,}7915 \pm 0{,}1073}$	$0{,}8867 \pm 0{,}0933$	$0{,}7178 \pm 0{,}1196$
Test	Combined[1]	$0{,}5333 \pm 0{,}0655$	$0{,}5935 \pm 0{,}0524$	$0{,}6332 \pm 0{,}1070$	$0{,}6567 \pm 0{,}0427$	$0{,}6556 \pm 0{,}2261$
	Proj[2]	$0{,}5256 \pm 0{,}0907$	$0{,}6000 \pm 0{,}0632$	$0{,}6399 \pm 0{,}0658$	$0{,}6834 \pm 0{,}0936$	$0{,}6222 \pm 0{,}1186$
	Ours	$\mathbf{0{,}6829 \pm 0{,}0387}$	$\mathbf{0{,}6774 \pm 0{,}0408}$	$\mathbf{0{,}7044 \pm 0{,}0861}$	$\mathbf{0{,}7533 \pm 0{,}0716}$	$\mathbf{0{,}7000 \pm 0{,}1670}$

[1] Combined corresponds to the concatenated input module in the ablation experiment of multi-stage fusion module.

[2] Proj corresponds to simple convolution module respectively in the ablation experiment of multi-stage fusion module

5   Conclusion

Aiming at the clinical challenges of high recurrence and high lethality of glioblastoma, as well as the problems of missing information, insufficient global modeling or high computational cost of existing methods, this study proposes a dual-stream neural network framework based on the Mamba framework for early recurrence prediction. The framework extracts preoperative and postoperative multi-scale spatiotemporal features through the dual-stream framework combined with the BiSMamba module, utilizes the multi-stage fusion module to achieve information interaction, and outputs the prediction results via the classification header. Experiments on the RHUH-GBM and LUMEIERE dual-center datasets show that the framework significantly improves the accuracy of glioblastoma recurrence prediction, which is better than traditional methods, and provides a new solution for clinical precision decision-making.

Acknowledgments. This work was supported by the National Natural Science Foundation of China under grant No. 82472053, No. 62403473, No. 62401570, No. 82572373; Key Research and Development Plan of Shaanxi Province No. 2025SF-YBXM-324; Joint Founding Project of Innovation Research Institute in Xijing Hospital No. LHJJ24YG01, No. LHJJ24YG07, No. LHJJ24YG13; and Natural Science Basic Research Program of Shaanxi Province No. 2024JC-YBQN-0675.

Disclosure of Interests. The authors have no competing interests to declare that are relevant to the content of this article.

References

1. Pan, Z., Zhao, R., et al.: EWSR1-induced circNEIL3 promotes glioma progression and exosome-mediated macrophage immunosuppressive polarization via stabilizing IGF2BP3. Molec. Canc. **21**(5), 16 (2022)
2. Mahootiha, M., Tak, D., Ye, Z., et al.: Multimodal deep learning improves recurrence risk prediction in pediatric low-grade gliomas. Neuro Oncol. **27**(1), 277–290 (2025)

3. Ren, J., Zhai, X., Yin, H., et al.: Multimodality MRI radiomics based on machine learning for identifying true tumor recurrence and treatment-related effects in patients with postoperative glioma. Neurol. Therapy **12**(5), 1729–1743 (2023)

4. Wang, Z.H., Xiao, X.L., Zhang, Z.T., et al.: A radiomics model for predicting early recurrence in grade II gliomas based on preoperative multiparametric magnetic resonance imaging. Front. Oncol. **11**, 684996 (2021)

5. Rykkje, A.M., Carlsen, J.F., Larsen, V.A., et al.: Prognostic relevance of radiological findings on early postoperative MRI for 187 consecutive glioblastoma patients receiving standard therapy. Sci. Rep. **14**(1), 10985 (2024)

6. Jia, X., Zhai, Y., Song, D., et al.: A multiparametric MRI-based radiomics nomogram for preoperative prediction of survival stratification in glioblastoma patients with standard treatment. Front. Oncol. **12**, 758622 (2022)

7. Yang, J., Dong, X., Wang, F., et al.: A deep learning model based on MRI for prediction of vessels encapsulating tumour clusters and prognosis in hepatocellular carcinoma. Abdominal Radiol. **49**(4), 1074–1083 (2024)

8. Sato, M., Moriyama, M., Fukumoto, T., et al.: Development of a transformer model for predicting the prognosis of patients with hepatocellular carcinoma after radiofrequency ablation. Hep. Intl. **18**(1), 131–137 (2024)

9. Gu, A., Dao, T.: Mamba: Linear-time sequence modeling with selective state spaces. arXiv preprint arXiv:2312.00752(2023)

10. Zhu, L., Liao, B., Zhang, Q., et al.: Vision mamba: Efficient visual representation learning with bidirectional state space model. arXiv preprint arXiv:2401.09417 (2024)

11. Cepeda, S., et al.: The Río Hortega University Hospital Glioblastoma dataset: a comprehensive collection of preoperative, early postoperative and recurrence MRI scans (RHUH-GBM). Data Brief **23**(50), 109617 (2023). https://doi.org/10.1016/j.dib.2023.109617. PMID: 37808543; PMCID: PMC10551826. https://www.cancerimagingarchive.net/

12. Lucraft, M., Allin, K., Baynes, G.: Challenges and Opportunities for Data Sharing in China. figshare. Journal contribution (2019). https://doi.org/10.6084/m9.figshare.7326605.v3

13. Ressa, G., Levi, R., Savini, G., et al.: AI differentiates radionecrosis from true progression in brain metastasis upon stereotactic radiosurgery: analysis of 124 histologically assessed lesions. Neuro-Oncology, noaf090(2025)

14. Oyelade, O.N., Irunokhai, E.A., Wang, H.A.: Twin convolutional neural network with hybrid binary optimizer for multimodal breast cancer digital image classification. Sci. Rep. **14**(1), 692 (2024)

15. Kang, G., Liu, K., Hou, B., Zhang, N.: 3D multi-view convolutional neural networks for lung nodule classification. PloS One **12**(11), e0188290 (2017)

16. Zhu, H., Wang, J., Wang, S.H., et al.: An evolutionary attention-based network for medical image classification. Int. J. Neural Syst. **33**(03), 2350010 (2023)

17. Zhou, H.Y., Guo, J., Zhang, Y., et al.: nnFormer: volumetric medical image segmentation via a 3D transformer. IEEE Trans. Image Process. **32**, 4036–4045 (2023)

18. Roy, S., Koehler, G., Ulrich, C., Baumgartner, M., et al.: Mednext: transformer-driven scaling of convnets for medical image segmentation. In International Conference on Medical Image Computing and Computer-Assisted Intervention, pp. 405–415. Springer, Cham (2023). https://doi.org/10.1007/978-3-031-43901-8_39

Automatic and Fast Segmentation of Cochlear Implant-Induced Artifacts in MR Images Using Deep Learning

Longtao Ma[1], Kaiyu Zhao[2], Siqi Gao[3], Lanyin Hu[4], Jintao Wei[1], Sui Huang[5], Yuan Li[3(✉)], Jiehua Ma[2(✉)], and Hongjian He[4(✉)]

[1] College of Biomedical Engineering and Instrument Science, Zhejiang University, Hangzhou, China

[2] Department of Radiology, Hangzhou Seventh People's Hospital, Hangzhou, China
`lengshimjh@163.com`

[3] Department of Otolaryngology, Affiliated Hospital of Hangzhou Normal University, Hangzhou, China
`liyuan81629@163.com`

[4] School of Physics, Zhejiang University, Hangzhou, China
`hhezju@zju.edu.cn`

[5] Zhejiang Nurotron Biotechnology Co., Ltd., Hangzhou, China

Abstract. Magnetic Resonance Imaging (MRI) plays a vital role in medical and biological applications. However, for patients with MRI-compatible implantable devices such as cochlear implants, the presence of integrated magnets often leads to large signal voids and severe artifacts, significantly compromising diagnostic accuracy. Although recent advances in deep learning have shown promise in artifact reduction and image enhancement, the quantitative assessment of artifact regions still heavily relies on manual annotation, which is labor-intensive and inconsistent. In particular, boundary distortions and tissue loss near cranial regions pose significant challenges for accurate artifact delineation, limiting the effectiveness of existing segmentation methods. To address these issues, we propose a novel 3D artifact segmentation framework that integrates reflective registration into a deep neural network combining U-Net and Transformer architectures. We conducted experiments on MRI data from 5 real-world patients with cochlear implants. Experimental results demonstrate that our method achieves state-of-the-art performance in implant-induced artifact segmentation, offering an efficient and reliable solution for automatic artifact evaluation in clinical settings.

Keywords: MRI Compatibility · Automated Artifact Segmentation · Deep Learning · Cochlear Implant

1 Introduction

Magnetic Resonance Imaging (MRI) has become an indispensable tool in modern medical diagnostics due to its high soft-tissue contrast, multi-planar and multi-parametric imaging capabilities, and the absence of ionizing radiation. It provides

Z. Lin et al. (Eds.): ICIG 2025, LNCS 16161, pp. 364–376, 2026.
https://doi.org/10.1007/978-981-95-3398-5_30

essential imaging support for the detection and evaluation of a wide range of diseases [1].

Cochlear implants (CIs), first introduced only about 60 years ago, have since become a routine part of clinical practice, offering renewed hope for patients with severe to profound hearing loss. To date, over 400,000 individuals worldwide have received CIs, and this number continues to grow as implantation criteria are progressively expanded [2,3]. Many cochlear implants (CIs) are not compatible with magnetic resonance imaging (MRI). Even MRI-compatible CIs may introduce severe artifacts in MRI scans, typically appearing as large regions of signal void surrounding the implant. The shape and extent of these artifacts vary depending on the imaging sequences used. Fundamentally, they are caused by local magnetic field disturbances induced by the magnetic components of the implant, resulting in abnormal signal accumulation or substantial signal attenuation— often seen as prominent black regions in the images [4]. According to the F2119 standard issued by ASTM International, any image region with pixel intensity differing by more than 30% from a reference region is defined as an artifact [5].

These artifacts not only disrupt the continuity of cranial boundaries and brain tissue structures but also severely affect image registration and anatomical reconstruction accuracy, thereby compromising the extraction of critical clinical metrics such as cortical thickness and regional brain volume. Existing neuroimaging tools, such as FreeSurfer [6] and FastSurfer [7], often fail or produce biased outputs when processing MRI images affected by such artifacts, primarily due to structural loss and registration failure caused by the artifacts.

To address this issue, Pollak et al. proposed FastSurfer-LIT [8], a lesion inpainting tool that restores structurally defective regions to resemble normal anatomy, thereby improving the accuracy of downstream segmentation and surface reconstruction. A key strength of FastSurfer-LIT lies in its localized inpainting mechanism, which restricts modifications strictly to user-defined lesion masks, thus preserving anatomical integrity in unaffected regions. However, this approach relies heavily on the availability of accurate artifact masks, which must currently be delineated manually by experienced clinicians. This process is time-consuming—often exceeding two hours per case—and subject to substantial inter-observer variability, limiting its scalability in clinical practice.

Against this backdrop, there is an urgent need for automated artifact segmentation. Although models such as 3D U-Net [9] have achieved remarkable success in general structural segmentation tasks, they often perform poorly in artifact regions. This is due to the low signal intensity of artifacts and the surrounding background, which leads to indistinct boundaries and over-segmentation, ultimately reducing accuracy and generalizability.

To tackle these challenges, we propose a novel method for automated MRI artifact segmentation. Our approach utilizes a dual-input neural network architecture that simultaneously processes the original image and its reflectively registered counterpart. By leveraging anatomical symmetry as an external supervisory signal, the model is guided to more precisely localize artifact boundaries. The proposed method integrates MRI preprocessing, deep learning-based segmentation, and symmetry-enhanced boundary refinement, offering a new technical framework and practical solution for accurate artifact quantification in clinical MRI applications.

The contributions of this work include the following two aspects:

We propose a novel method for quantitative MRI artifact assessment, specifically designed to accurately segment implant induced artifacts that result in skull structure loss. To the best of our knowledge, this is the first automatic 3D segmentation model explicitly developed for MRI artifact delineation.

We introduce reflective registration into the input data pipeline to supervise the segmentation boundaries. By aligning each image with its mirrored counterpart, the model leverages anatomical symmetry to improve the precision and robustness of boundary detection.

2   Method

2.1   Data Acquisition

All participants were scanned using two MRI systems affiliated with Hangzhou Normal University: a SIEMENS Area 1.5T scanner and a 3.0T GE Discovery MR750 scanner (GE Medical Systems, Waukesha, WI).

For the 1.5T scanner, the imaging protocol included three 2D axial sequences: (1) a T1-weighted Spin Echo (T1w SE) with repetition time (TR) = 500 ms, echo time (TE) = 14 ms, field of view (FOV) = $24 \times 24\,cm^2$, slice thickness (THK) = 6 mm, slice spacing (SP) = 1.5 mm, bandwidth (BW) = 31.2 Hz, flip angle (FA) = 75°, and matrix = 512×256; (2) a T2-weighted Fast Spin Echo (T2w FSE) with TR = 4000 ms, TE = 115.4 ms, FOV = $24 \times 18\,cm^2$, THK = 6 mm, SP = 1.5 mm, BW = 25 Hz, echo train length (ETL) = 15, FA = 90°, and matrix = 384×192; and (3) a T2-weighted Gradient Echo (T2w GRE) with TR = 420 ms, TE = 20 ms, FOV = $24 \times 18\,cm^2$, THK = 6 mm, SP = 1.5 mm, BW = 25.0 kHz, FA = 20°, and matrix = 256×192.

For the 3.0T scanner, the same imaging sequences were used, but with thinner slices. The parameters were: (1) T1w SE with TR = 500 ms, TE = 14 ms, FOV = $24 \times 24\,cm^2$, THK = 3 mm, SP = 1.5 mm, BW = 31.2 Hz, FA = 75°, and matrix = 512×256; (2) T2w FSE with TR = 4000 ms, TE = 115.4 ms, FOV = $24 \times 18\,cm^2$, THK = 3 mm, SP = 1.5 mm, BW = 25 Hz, ETL = 15, FA = 90°, and matrix = 384×192; and (3) T2w GRE with TR = 420 ms, TE = 20 ms, FOV = $24 \times 18\,cm^2$, THK = 3 mm, SP = 1.5 mm, BW = 25.0 kHz, FA = 20°, and matrix = 256×192.

The training dataset consisted of MRI scans from 12 healthy participants with external magnets affixed to the scalp to simulate artifact effects. The testing dataset included 5 real patients with clinically implanted cochlear devices. All experimental procedures complied with the Declaration of Helsinki and were approved by the Ethics Committee of the Affiliated Hospital of Hangzhou Normal University (Approval No. 2024(E2)-KS-153). All participants gave written informed consent and completed the study without any adverse events potentially related to the research or experimental conditions. The 12 healthy volunteers (6 males and 6 females) ranged in age from 23 to 27 years (mean age: 25.05 $\pm$ 1.19 years).

2.2   Data Preprocessing

In existing research, most symmetry modeling approaches typically adopt symmetric patch construction strategies [10, 11] or perform direct horizontal flipping of images [12]. However, these methods often overlook the inherent anatomical asymmetry of the brain and the potential rotational variations introduced during image acquisition. This issue becomes more pronounced in the presence of implants such as cochlear devices, where local magnetic field inhomogeneities further exacerbate structural deviations, making simple flipping and overlaying insufficient for constructing effective symmetry priors.

To address these challenges, inspired by the work of Xie et al. [13], we propose a reflection-based rigid registration strategy to generate more precisely aligned symmetric representations. For each original MRI volume (denoted as MRI_{gt}), we first generate a horizontally flipped version (denoted as MRI_f). The original image MRI_{gt} is used as the reference, and the flipped image MRI_f serves as the moving image. Rigid registration is performed using the FLIRT tool from the FMRIB Software Library (FSL) [14], resulting in a structurally aligned flipped image (denoted as MRI_{rf}). Finally, a weighted fusion of MRI_{gt} and MRI_{rf} is performed to produce the final symmetric representation, denoted as MRI_a. The entire procedure is illustrated in Fig. 1.

This strategy explicitly incorporates spatial alignment while accounting for anatomical asymmetries, improving hemispheric consistency and mitigating geometric distortions caused by implant induced artifacts and natural anatomical variations. It thus provides a more stable and reliable structural prior for downstream artifact segmentation tasks.

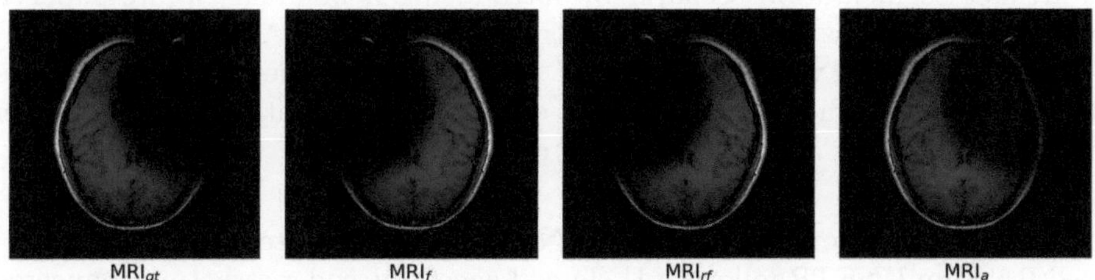

Fig. 1. Description of the reflective registration process. From left to right: the original image MRI_{gt}, the flipped image MRI_f, the reflectively registered image MRI_{rf}, and the final averaged image MRI_a.

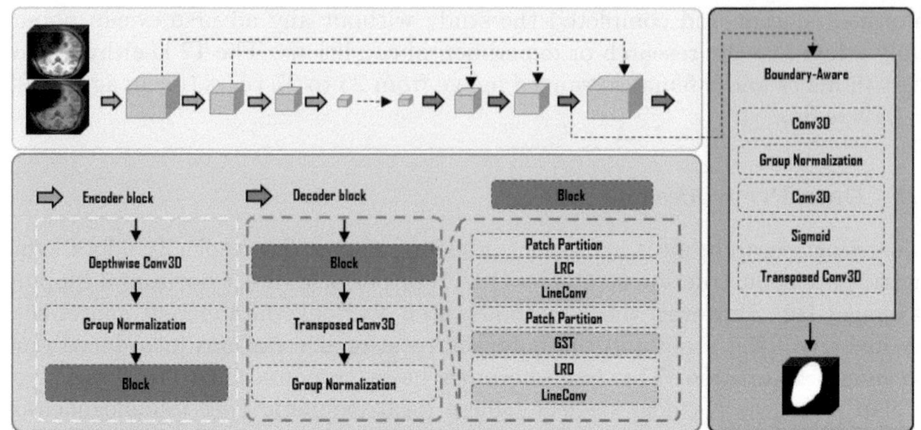

Fig. 2. Overall architecture of our proposed model. The network adopts a U-shaped encoderdecoder structure with skip connections. Each stage uses Slim UNETR blocks for efficient feature extraction and fusion. A boundary-aware supervision head is attached to mid-level decoder features to enhance edge localization through auxiliary ℓ_1 loss.

2.3   Network Architecture

Due to the large spatial size of both medical images and implant-induced artifacts, and the limitation of computational resources, we propose a lightweight 3D segmentation network inspired by Slim UNETR (Scale Hybrid Transformers to Efficient 3D Medical Image Segmentation Under Limited Computational Resources) [15]. The proposed model is tailored for segmenting brain MRI volumes suffering from severe structural distortion caused by implant-induced artifacts, particularly in cases where the skull boundary is partially or completely missing. While our architecture draws inspiration from the lightweight design of Slim UNETR—originally developed for tumor segmentation—we adapt it for the artifact segmentation scenario by introducing a boundary-aware supervision mechanism. This enhancement leads to the Boundary-Aware Slim UNETR (BA-Slim UNETR), which significantly improves the model's ability to delineate ambiguous artifact boundaries and enhances segmentation accuracy under structurally complex and artifact-heavy conditions.

Backbone: Overview of BA-Slim UNETR. As illustrated in Fig. 2, the proposed BA-Slim UNETR follows a U-shaped encoderdecoder structure connected via skip connections for multi-scale feature fusion. The encoder progressively downsamples a 3D input volume of size $H \times W \times D$ using convolutional layers, and the decoder restores the spatial resolution.

At each encoder level i ($i \in \{2, 3, 4\}$), the spatial resolution of the feature map is reduced to:

$$\frac{H}{2^{i+1}} \times \frac{W}{2^{i+1}} \times \frac{D}{2^{i+1}}.$$

Unlike prior works [9] that adopt standard convolutions for downsampling, we employ 3D *depthwise convolutions* in the encoder following the Slim UNETR design [15], which significantly reduces parameter count and memory cost.

Each encoder stage contains a contextual integration block, which efficiently extracts and aggregates representations using a hybrid of local convolutions and global attention. To further guide segmentation, an auxiliary boundary prediction branch is introduced at the decoder output.

Contextual Integration Block. The block, based on Slim UNETR [15], is composed of five submodules as shown in Fig. 2:

- **Patch Partition:** Employs 3D depthwise convolution to embed local features while introducing implicit spatial positional encoding without changing the spatial dimensions.
- **Local Representations Congregation (LRC):** Combines $1 \times 1 \times 1$ pointwise and $3 \times 3 \times 3$ depthwise convolutions to extract spatial neighborhood context. Residual connections and Group Normalization are included to enhance stability and representation capability.
- **LineConv:** Applies two sequential $1 \times 1 \times 1$ convolutions with GELU activation to perform channel-wise fusion, similar to feedforward networks in Transformer blocks.
- **Global Sparse Transformer (GST):** Leverages sparse token sampling and multi-head self-attention across selected tokens to model long-range dependencies with reduced computational cost.
- **Local Reverse Diffusion (LRD):** Uses transposed convolution followed by pointwise convolution to inject global contextual information back into the voxel space, enabling effective local-global feature fusion.

Together, these components form a closed-loop architecture of local encoding, global interaction, and local refinement, achieving efficient yet expressive feature learning for high-resolution 3D segmentation tasks.

Boundary-Aware Supervision Module. To improve edge localization, we add a parallel boundary-aware supervision head after the decoder. This module takes mid-level decoder features, passes them through two $3 \times 3 \times 3$ convolutions and a sigmoid activation, and outputs a boundary probability map of the same size as the segmentation output.

Ground-truth boundary maps are generated by applying a 3D Sobel operator to the artifact masks. During training, an ℓ_1 loss is applied between predicted and target boundaries, guiding the network to focus more on contour regions. This effectively reduces under-segmentation and helps recover artifact-contaminated boundaries.

2.4 Loss Function

To optimize segmentation performance and mitigate the impact of class imbalance, we adopt a combination of soft dice loss and focal loss as our primary segmentation objective. Additionally, to enhance boundary localization accuracy in implant induced artifact regions, we introduce a boundary-aware loss, forming a composite three-term total loss function.

The dice loss is defined as:

$$L_{\text{dice}}(G, Y) = 1 - \frac{2}{J} \sum_{j=1}^{J} \frac{\sum_{i=1}^{I} G_{i,j} Y_{i,j}}{\sum_{i=1}^{I} G_{i,j} + \sum_{i=1}^{I} Y_{i,j}} \tag{1}$$

The focal loss is defined as:

$$L_{\text{focal}}(G, Y) = - \sum_{j=1}^{J} \sum_{i=1}^{I} \big[Y_{i,j} G_{i,j}^2 \log(1 - G_{i,j}) \\ + (1 - Y_{i,j})(1 - G_{i,j})^2 \log(G_{i,j}) \big] \tag{2}$$

Here, I denotes the number of voxels, and J denotes the number of classes. $G_{i,j}$ and $Y_{i,j}$ represent the predicted probability and the ground truth (one-hot encoded) for class j at voxel i, respectively.

To explicitly supervise boundary learning, we define a boundary-aware loss as follows:

$$L_{\text{bnd}} = \| P_{\text{bnd}} - Y_{\text{bnd}} \|_1 \tag{3}$$

where P_{bnd} is the predicted boundary probability map from the auxiliary branch, and Y_{bnd} is the ground truth boundary map obtained by applying the Sobel edge detector to the segmentation mask. The L_1 loss penalizes discrepancies in predicted edge positions.

The final total loss function is formulated as:

$$L_{\text{total}} = \lambda_1 L_{\text{focal}} + \lambda_2 L_{\text{dice}} + \lambda_3 L_{\text{bnd}} \tag{4}$$

In our experiments, the loss weights are empirically set to $\lambda_1 = 1$, $\lambda_2 = 1$, and $\lambda_3 = 0.3$ by optimization of the grid search.

2.5   Implementation Details

The experiments were conducted on an NVIDIA RTX A4500 GPU equipped with 20 GB of memory. The training dataset comprised 12 subjects, each consisting of three co-registered 3D MRI modalities: T1-weighted spin echo (T1w SE), T2-weighted fast spin echo (T2w FSE), and T2-weighted gradient echo (T2w GRE). To augment data diversity and improve generalization, additional localizer sequences were incorporated. Furthermore, each sample was paired with its reflection registration counterpart, serving as a symmetric structural prior to facilitate robust modeling in regions affected by severe anatomical degradation.

Data preprocessing was performed using the MONAI framework [16], including orientation normalization, channel-first formatting, data type enforcement, multi-class label transformation, isotropic resampling ($1{\times}1{\times}1$ mm^3), spatial padding, center cropping, and random patch extraction (patch size:

160×160×160). Standard data augmentation techniques were applied, including random flipping along spatial axes, intensity normalization, and perturbation. Notably, skull stripping was omitted to preserve complete anatomical information during model training.

Model optimization was carried out using the AdamW optimizer with a weight decay coefficient of 0.4. The learning rate was initialized at 0.001 and scheduled using a linear warm-up strategy followed by cosine annealing to facilitate stable convergence.

3   Result

3.1   Segmentation Performance Evaluation

In this section, we conducted a study based on MRI data from 5 real clinical patients with cochlear implants. As illustrated in Fig. 3, we present a qualitative comparison of segmentation results on five representative T1-weighted MRI cases. Each column corresponds to one patient, with rows showing the original T1 image, the manually annotated ground truth (GT), and the predicted segmentation (Pred) from our proposed BA-Slim UNETR model. Despite variations in artifact intensity and distribution, the predicted masks align closely with the ground truth across all cases, confirming the robustness and accuracy of the model in delineating artifact regions.

To visually demonstrate the performance of different 3D segmentation models across anatomical planes, we utilized the AAHead_Scout sequence commonly available on SIEMENS MRI systems as the localizer image. This sequence rapidly acquires low-resolution images covering axial, sagittal, and coronal planes, making it suitable for assessing artifact boundary consistency across spatial dimensions. As shown in Fig. 4, we present representative segmentation results from 3D U-Net [9], nnU-Net [17], Slim UNETR [15], and the proposed BA-Slim UNETR. While other models show varying degrees of indentation or protrusion at the artifact boundaries, our BA-Slim UNETR generates continuous, smooth, and anatomically plausible contours, closely matching the manual annotations and offering the most visually accurate results.

To quantitatively evaluate segmentation performance, we adopted three widely used metrics: Dice Similarity Coefficient (DSC) [18], Intersection over Union (IoU) [19], and the 95th percentile Hausdorff Distance (HD95) [20]. These metrics comprehensively assess region overlap and boundary accuracy.

As shown in Table 1, BA-Slim UNETR demonstrates clear superiority across all evaluation criteria. Specifically, it achieves the highest Dice score (91.2%) and the best IoU (83.6%), indicating excellent performance in accurately covering the segmentation regions.

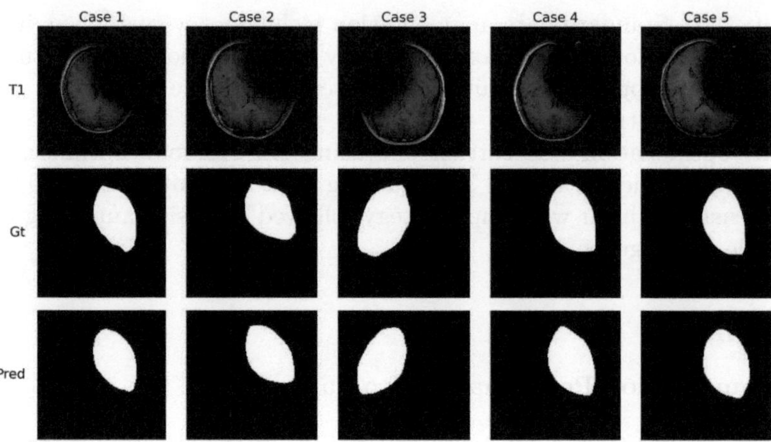

Fig. 3. Visual comparison of segmentation results on 5 representative clinical cases. From top to bottom: T1-weighted MRI images, ground truth (GT) segmentations, and predicted results (Pred) from the proposed model. The predictions demonstrate high agreement with manual annotations across varying artifact patterns.

Moreover, for boundary precision measured by HD95, BA-Slim UNETR achieves a strong average performance of 2.82 mm, further validating its robustness and accuracy in delineating anatomical boundaries under complex artifact conditions.

Table 1. Quantitative comparison of segmentation performance using Dice Similarity Coefficient (DSC), Intersection over Union (IoU), and 95th percentile Hausdorff Distance (HD95). Higher Dice and IoU and lower HD95 indicate better performance.

Method	Dice (%) ↑	IoU (%) ↑	HD95 (mm) ↓
3D U-Net [9]	85.3	75.2	7.56
nnU-Net [17]	88.7	80.3	6.15
Slim UNETR [15]	89.4	81.0	6.57
Ours (BA-Slim UNETR)	**91.2**	**83.6**	**2.82**

To further evaluate the cross-modality consistency of artifact segmentation, Fig. 5 presents the qualitative results on 5 representative clinical cases across both T1- and T2-weighted MRI images. Despite the lack of clear skull contours and the presence of signal inhomogeneities near the implant sites, the segmented artifact boundaries demonstrate strong visual alignment across modalities.

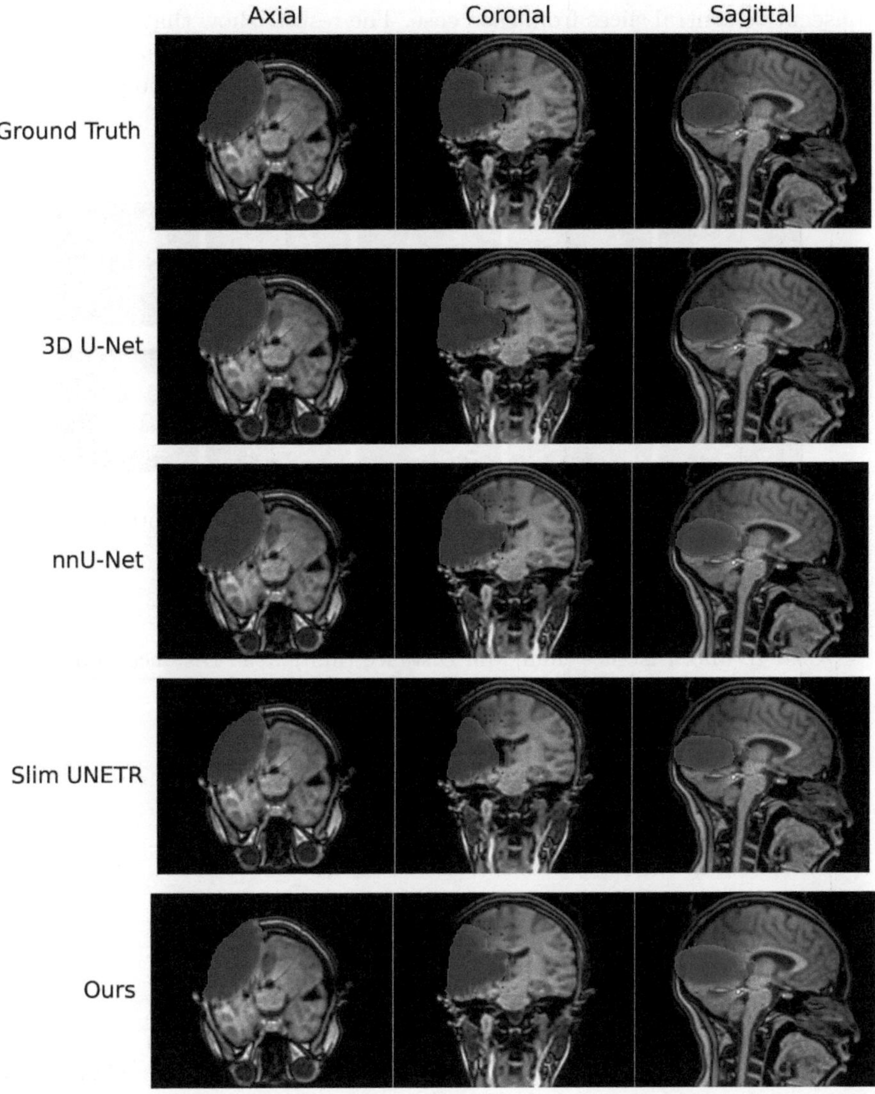

Fig. 4. Qualitative comparison of segmentation results across different models using multi-view MRI. Each row corresponds to a method (from top to bottom: Ground Truth, 3D U-Net, nnU-Net, Slim UNETR, and our BA-Slim UNETR), and each column displays the segmentation in one anatomical plane (Axial, Coronal, Sagittal). The results show that BA-Slim UNETR achieves better shape preservation and boundary consistency across all views.

In addition to the qualitative assessment, we performed a quantitative boundary discrepancy analysis as summarized in Table 2. To avoid bias from non-representative slices where artifacts do not reach the brain surface, we selected

10 consecutive central slices from each case. The results show that the maximum boundary deviations are all below 6.24 mm, and the average deviations are consistently below 3 mm. These findings confirm that the artifact boundaries have been accurately and robustly delineated across both modalities.

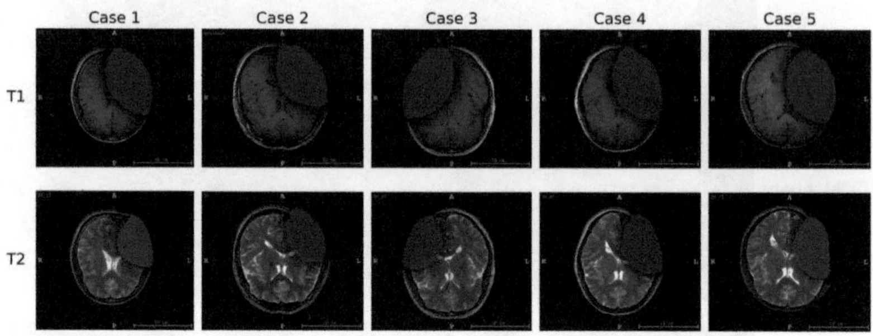

Fig. 5. Segmentation results of 5 representative clinical cases on both T1- and T2-weighted MRI images.

Table 2. Boundary distance statistics across 5 cases.

Case ID	Max Distance (mm)	Min Distance (mm)	Mean Distance (mm)
Case 1	5.82	0.0	2.53
Case 2	4.65	0.0	1.94
Case 3	6.24	0.0	2.75
Case 4	4.93	0.0	1.87
Case 5	5.33	0.0	2.40

3.2 Ablation Studies

To evaluate the individual contributions of key components in our proposed framework, we conducted an ablation study focusing on the effect of (1) reflection-registered input and (2) boundary-aware loss supervision. Four experimental groups were constructed as follows:

Group A (Baseline): The model was trained solely on raw MRI data without any auxiliary supervision. This serves as the baseline configuration.

Group B (Baseline + Reflection Input): The model was trained using both raw and reflection-registered inputs, allowing the network to leverage hemispheric symmetry as structural prior. This setting evaluates the effectiveness of reflective alignment in enhancing structural context.

Group C (Baseline + Boundary Loss): The model was trained on raw data with an additional boundary prediction head supervised by a boundary-aware loss. This setting examines the effect of explicitly modeling boundary information to improve segmentation precision.

Group D (Full Model): The model incorporates both reflection-registered inputs and boundary-aware supervision, representing the full configuration proposed in this study.

Experimental results demonstrate that incorporating either component individually leads to performance gains over the baseline. Notably, the full model achieves the best segmentation accuracy, especially in the delineation of implant induced artifact boundaries, confirming the complementary effectiveness of the proposed strategies.

4   Conclusion

In this study, we propose BA-Slim UNETR, a boundary-aware implant induced artifact segmentation network built upon the lightweight Slim UNETR framework. To address the challenges caused by severe anatomical distortions and boundary ambiguities introduced by implants in brain MRI, BA-Slim UNETR incorporates two key components: a reflection-registered dual-input encoder to leverage hemispheric symmetry priors, and a boundary-aware supervision module to enhance the localization of artifact edges.

The network adopts a U-shaped encoderdecoder architecture with lightweight contextual integration blocks, effectively capturing both local representations and global dependencies. Through this design, the model achieves accurate segmentation performance even in regions with missing or corrupted structures.

Extensive experiments and ablation studies demonstrate that each component of BA-Slim UNETR contributes significantly to its overall performance. The reflection-registered input improves structural inference in asymmetric regions, while the boundary-aware loss guides the model to better delineate artifact contours. Together, these enhancements enable BA-Slim UNETR to deliver robust segmentation results in artifact-degraded 3D medical imaging scenarios, providing a reliable basis for subsequent artifact reduction and neuroanatomical reconstruction.

Acknowledgments. This work has been supported by the "Leading Goose" R&D Program of Zhejiang (Grant No. 2023C03094) and the National Natural Science Foundation of China (Grant No. 82372036).

References

1. Srinivasan, R., So, C., Amin, N., Jaikaransingh, D., D'arco, F., Nash, R.: A review of the safety of MRI in cochlear implant patients with retained magnets. Clin. Radiol. **74**(12), 972-e9 (2019)
2. Canzi, P., et al.: MRI-induced artifact by a cochlear implant with a novel magnet system: an experimental cadaver study. Eur. Arch. Otorhinolaryngol. **278**(10), 3753–3762 (2021)
3. Carlson, M.L., et al.: Magnetic resonance imaging with cochlear implant magnet in place: safety and imaging quality. Otol. Neurotology **36**(6), 965–971 (2015)

4. Majdani, O., et al.: Artifacts caused by cochlear implants with non-removable magnets in 3t MRI: phantom and cadaveric studies. Eur. Arch. Otorhinolaryngol. **266**, 1885–1890 (2009)
5. ASTM International: Standard test method for evaluation of MR image artifacts from passive implants (2024). https://doi.org/10.1520/F2119-24, aSTM Standard F2119-24
6. Fischl, B.: Freesurfer. Neuroimage **62**(2), 774–781 (2012)
7. Henschel, L., Conjeti, S., Estrada, S.R., Diers, K., Fischl, B., Reuter, M.: Fastsurfer–a fast and accurate deep learning based neuroimaging pipeline. Neuroimage **219**, 117012 (2020)
8. Pollak, C., Kügler, D., Bauer, T., Rüber, T., Reuter, M.: Fastsurfer-lit: lesion inpainting tool for whole-brain mri segmentation with tumors, cavities, and abnormalities. Imaging Neuroscience **3**, imag_a_00446 (2025)
9. Çiçek, Ö., Abdulkadir, A., Lienkamp, S.S., Brox, T., Ronneberger, O.: 3D U-Net: learning dense volumetric segmentation from sparse annotation. In: Ourselin, S., Joskowicz, L., Sabuncu, M.R., Unal, G., Wells, W. (eds.) MICCAI 2016. LNCS, vol. 9901, pp. 424–432. Springer, Cham (2016). https://doi.org/10.1007/978-3-319-46723-8_49
10. Wang, Y., Katsaggelos, A.K., Wang, X., Parrish, T.B.: A deep symmetry convnet for stroke lesion segmentation. In: 2016 IEEE International Conference on Image Processing (ICIP), pp. 111–115. IEEE (2016)
11. Wu, X., Bi, L., Fulham, M., Feng, D.D., Zhou, L., Kim, J.: Unsupervised brain tumor segmentation using a symmetric-driven adversarial network. Neurocomputing **455**, 242–254 (2021)
12. Shen, H., Zhang, J., Zheng, W.: Efficient symmetry-driven fully convolutional network for multimodal brain tumor segmentation. In: 2017 IEEE International Conference on Image Processing (ICIP), pp. 3864–3868. IEEE (2017)
13. Xie, K., et al.: Gan-based metal artifacts region inpainting in brain MRI imaging with reflective registration. Med. Phys. **51**(3), 2066–2080 (2024)
14. Jenkinson, M., Beckmann, C.F., Behrens, T.E., Woolrich, M.W., Smith, S.M.: Fsl. Neuroimage **62**(2), 782–790 (2012)
15. Pang, Y., et al.: Slim unetr: scale hybrid transformers to efficient 3D medical image segmentation under limited computational resources. IEEE Trans. Med. Imaging **43**(3), 994–1005 (2023)
16. Cardoso, M.J., et al.: Monai: an open-source framework for deep learning in healthcare. arXiv preprint arXiv:2211.02701 (2022)
17. Isensee, F., Jaeger, P.F., Kohl, S.A.A., Petersen, J., Maier-Hein, K.H.: nnU-Net: a self-configuring method for deep learning-based biomedical image segmentation. Nat. Methods **18**(2), 203–211 (2021)
18. Dice, L.R.: Measures of the amount of ecologic association between species. Ecology **26**(3), 297–302 (1945)
19. Jaccard, P.: The distribution of the flora in the alpine zone. New Phytol. **11**(2), 37–50 (1912)
20. Huttenlocher, D.P., Klanderman, G.A., Rucklidge, W.J.: Comparing images using the hausdorff distance. IEEE Trans. Pattern Anal. Mach. Intell. **15**(9), 850–863 (1993)

Color and Multispectral Processing

End-to-End Diffusion Models with Physics Priors for Enhanced Spectral Super-Resolution

Xinxin Li and Jianjun Liu[✉]

School of Artificial Intelligence and Computer Science, Jiangnan University, Wuxi, China
liuofficial@163.com

Abstract. Spectral super-resolution aims to reconstruct high- dimensional hyperspectral images from low-dimensional multispectral or RGB inputs, enabling rich spectral information recovery for downstream vision tasks. In this paper, we propose EDSSR, a diffusion-based framework that reconstructs high-quality hyperspectral images by modeling complex spectral variations through an end-to-end trained sampling process. EDSSR incorporates a pretrained diffusion model as a prior to guide the reconstruction and improve spectral consistency. Additionally, a Physics-Guided Module is introduced to inject physical constraints into the U-Net backbone, enhancing high-frequency detail recovery in the reconstructed spectrum. Extensive experiments on two benchmark datasets demonstrate the effectiveness of our method in enhancing reconstruction accuracy and spectral fidelity.

Keywords: Spectral super-resolution · Diffusion models · Physics-Guided Module

1 Introduction

Hyperspectral images (HSIs) capture spectral information across a wide range of wavelengths, enabling detailed material identification and analysis. Unlike RGB images with only three color channels, HSIs contain hundreds of contiguous spectral bands, making them invaluable for applications such as environmental monitoring [1], agriculture [2], and mineral exploration [3].

However, acquiring images with both high spatial and spectral resolution remains a significant challenge due to hardware limitations and cost. This trade-off has led to growing interest in reconstructing hyperspectral images from more accessible multispectral images (MSIs). As a result, reconstructing HSI from MSI has become a major research focus. Spectral super-resolution (SSR) methods can be broadly classified into traditional approaches and deep learning-based techniques. Traditional methods often struggle to recover fine spectral details due to their limited capacity for nonlinear modeling. While convolutional neural networks (CNNs) are effective at capturing local features via convolutional kernels,

Z. Lin et al. (Eds.): ICIG 2025, LNCS 16161, pp. 379–390, 2026.
https://doi.org/10.1007/978-981-95-3398-5_31

they fall short in modeling the complex spectralspatial relationships and global dependencies inherent in hyperspectral data. Generative adversarial networks (GANs) [4] offer promise for producing high-quality images, but their training is frequently unstable and prone to convergence difficulties.

In recent years, diffusion models have emerged as a powerful framework for high-quality image generation [5], thanks to their ability to model complex data distributions through a gradual denoising process that reverses forward noise corruption. This iterative refinement allows for stable training and accurate data reconstruction, making diffusion models particularly suitable for capturing the intricate spectral characteristics of hyperspectral images. However, their application to hyperspectral image super-resolution remains limited, as training diffusion models typically requires large-scale datasets—resources that are often scarce and difficult to obtain in the hyperspectral domain.

To resolve the outlined issues, we propose the End-to-End Diffusion-Based Spectral Super-Resolution Network (EDSSR), which harnesses the powerful modeling capabilities of diffusion models for spectral super-resolution. Instead of explicitly designing regularization terms, we treat the reverse process of a pre-trained diffusion model as a prior constraint and fine-tune its sampling process in an end-to-end manner to directly learn the mapping from MSI to HSI. Additionally, we introduce a physics-guided module that incorporates known physical information into the U-Net's deep feature representations, effectively guiding the reconstruction process. Our main contributions are summarized as follows:

1) We propose EDSSR, a novel end-to-end framework that exploits the strengths of diffusion models to capture complex spectral variations, using a pretrained model as a prior to enable high-quality hyperspectral image reconstruction.
2) We introduce a Physics-Guided Module (PGM) that incorporates physical priors into the noise estimation network, effectively enhancing the recovery of high-frequency spectral details.
3) We validate our method on two benchmark datasets, demonstrating competitive performance compared to state-of-the-art approaches in both reconstruction accuracy and spectral fidelity.

2   Related Work

2.1   Spectral Super-Resolution

In recent years, spectral super-resolution has advanced considerably in reconstructing high-resolution HSIs from MSI or RGB inputs by exploiting the inherent spectralspatial correlations between the modalities. Traditional methods, which typically rely on handcrafted priors such as basis functions [6] or sparse representations [7], are fundamentally limited by the ill-posed nature of the task and their restricted ability to model nonlinear relationships. With the rise of deep learning, the focus has shifted toward data-driven approaches, which offer powerful nonlinear modeling capabilities and have achieved impressive performance improvements.

Recent studies have demonstrated diverse methodological advancements in this field. Galliani et al. [8] employed a DenseNet-based semantic segmentation architecture for RGB-to-HSI reconstruction, achieving improved performance compared to previous approaches. Dian et al. [9] developed a spectral super-resolution network combining imaging physics models with learning-based methods, showing enhanced robustness in experiments. Dai et al. [10] implemented an attention mechanism using second-order feature statistics, which improved the recovery of high-frequency details in reconstructed images. Liu et al. [11] explored the use of diffusion models for this task through their HyperLDM framework, processing hyperspectral data in a lower-dimensional latent space. However, these generative approaches currently face implementation challenges including substantial computational resources and large training datasets.

2.2   Diffusion Models

Diffusion models are deep generative frameworks that generate data through a gradual denoising process, beginning from samples of pure Gaussian noise. It comprises two main stages: a forward process that incrementally corrupts data by adding Gaussian noise until it resembles random noise, and a reverse process in which a neural network is trained to iteratively remove the noise, thereby recovering the data distribution. Ho et al. [12] introduced the Denoising Diffusion Probabilistic Model (DDPM), which laid the foundation for modern diffusion-based generative models by combining diffusion processes with probabilistic modeling. Building on this, Song et al. [13] proposed a score-based generative model that directly estimates the gradient of the log-density of the data distribution, offering a unified theoretical framework that bridges diffusion models and score-based approaches.

Owing to their remarkable modeling flexibility and stable training dynamics, diffusion models have been successfully applied to a wide range of challenging vision tasks, including image restoration [14], generation [5], and super-resolution [15]. Beyond generative applications, the rich feature representations learned by diffusion models have also proven highly effective in discriminative tasks such as image classification [16], object detection [17], and image segmentation [18].

However, the direct application of diffusion models to SSR poses significant challenges. In particular, hyperspectral images contain tens to hundreds of contiguous spectral bands, necessitating denoising in a high-dimensional spectral space. This imposes heavy computational demands and introduces considerable optimization complexity. Second, the strong spectralspatial coupling inherent in hyperspectral data necessitates that the model simultaneously preserve spectral continuity and spatial structural fidelity during the denoising process, which poses new architectural challenges for conventional diffusion models. To tackle these issues, we propose an end-to-end diffusion sampling framework that not only enhances reconstruction quality but also substantially reduces the number of required inference steps.

3   Method

3.1   Preliminaries of Denoising Diffusion Null Space Model

Denoising Diffusion Null Space Model (DDNM) [19] presents a zero-shot image restoration framework based on diffusion models, which effectively utilizes pre-trained diffusion models without requiring any fine-tuning to address multiple image inverse problems such as super-resolution, colorization, and deblurring. The key contribution is the optimization of the denoising procedure in DDPM via range-null space decomposition. The noise-free image restoration problem can be formally expressed as:

$$y = Ax \tag{1}$$

where x is the original image, y denotes the degraded observation, and A represents the degradation operator. DDNM reconstructs the image through the decomposition $\hat{x} = A^{\dagger}y + (I - A^{\dagger}A)x_r$, where $A^{\dagger}$ denotes the pseudo-inverse of A. The range-space term $A^{\dagger}y$ enforces exact data consistency $y = Ax$ while the null-space term $(I - A^{\dagger}A)x_r$ is optimized by the diffusion model to achieve perceptually realistic results.

To guide the reverse diffusion with degradation constraints, DDNM modifies the standard denoising step of DDPM. The reverse process at timestep t is defined as:

$$x_{0|t} = \frac{1}{\sqrt{\bar{\alpha}_t}}(x_t - \sqrt{1 - \bar{\alpha}_t}\epsilon_\Theta(x_t, t)), \tag{2}$$

$$x_{t-1} = \frac{\sqrt{\bar{\alpha}_{t-1}}\beta_t}{1 - \bar{\alpha}_t}\hat{x}_{0|t} + \frac{\sqrt{\alpha_t}(1 - \bar{\alpha}_{t-1})}{1 - \bar{\alpha}_t}x_t \tag{3}$$

where x_t is the noisy image at timestep t, x_{t-1} is the denoised estimate at timestep $t-1$, $x_{0|t}$ is the predicted clean image from the diffusion model, $\hat{x}_{0|t}$ is estimated by means of RND optimization, $\epsilon_\Theta(\hat{x}_t, t)$ is the noise predicted by the neural network at timestep t, α_t is the noise retention coefficient, $\beta_t = 1 - \alpha_t$ is the noise scheduling term, $\bar{\alpha}_t = \prod_{s=1}^{t} \alpha_s$ is the cumulative product. Throughout the reverse process, DDNM utilizes the intermediate prediction $x_{0|t}$ as the null-space component x_r, progressively refining it to simultaneously satisfy the degradation constraints while maintaining high perceptual quality.

3.2   End-to-End Training for Diffusion Sampling

Model Formulation. The objective of SSR is to reconstruct the target HSI from the observed MSI, formally modeled as:

$$Y = RX \tag{4}$$

where $X \in \mathbb{R}^{H \times W \times B}$ is the target HSI, with H, W as its height and width, respectively, and $Y \in \mathbb{R}^{H \times W \times b}$ is the observed MSI and $b < B$ is the number of spectral bands. $R \in \mathbb{R}^{b \times B}$ denotes the spectral response function (SRF) of the multispectral sensor. The reconstruction of high-dimensional data from low-dimensional observations constitutes an inherently ill-posed inverse problem,

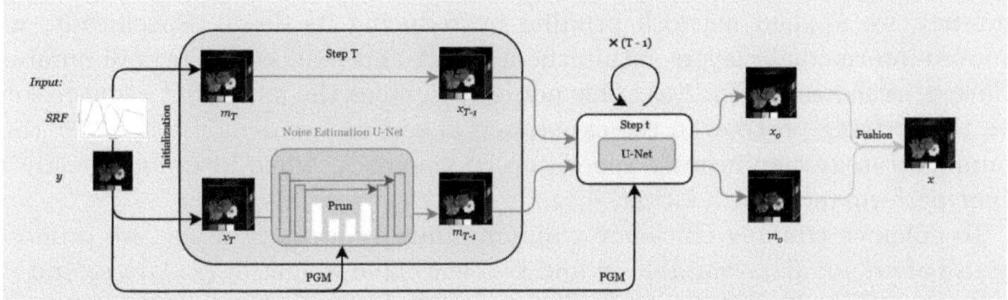

Fig. 1. Illustration of the proposed EDSSR framework. The model accepts the degraded image y and the SRF as inputs, incorporates the variable m_t, and conducts alternating updates between x and m via end-to-end diffusion sampling to achieve SSR.

where equation (4) admits infinite solutions. To regularize this underdetermined system, we formulate the optimization with explicit prior constraints:

$$\hat{X} = arg \min_{X} \|Y - RX\|^2 + \lambda\Psi(X) \tag{5}$$

where λ acts as a hyperparameter and $\Psi(\cdot)$ is a regularization function. Problem (5) can be efficiently solved through iterative optimization frameworks such as ADMM [20] and HQS [21], which employ variable splitting to decouple the operators and enable alternating minimization.

Network Framework. Inspired by [22], we employ the reverse denoising process of diffusion models to solve Problem (5), where the forward process gradually corrupts data into Gaussian noise while the reverse process reconstructs data through iterative denoising. In SSR, this can be viewed as an iterative optimization process where each denoising step acts as a regularization term enforcing image priors. To materialize this concept, we propose EDSSR. The network framework is shown in Fig. 1. By training the diffusion sampling process end-to-end, EDSSR directly learns the MSI-to-HSI mapping, effectively replacing traditional proximal operators with a neural network-learned nonlinear projection. This eliminates the need for explicit regularization design.

Hence, we recast DDNM's sampling procedure as a T-layer optimization network, with each layer representing a distinct sampling step:

$$x_{t-1} = \Phi_t(x_t; y, R) \tag{6}$$

The operator $\Phi_t(\cdot)$ represents the processes described in Eqs. (2) and (3). Unlike the classical diffusion models that sample from random noise, we propose an initialization strategy more suitable for SSR deterministic generation $x_T = \sqrt{\bar{\alpha}}R^{\dagger}y$. This strategy reduces the uncertainty in spectral reconstruction, effectively improving reconstruction quality and reducing computational costs.

The denoising network in the diffusion model adopts a U-Net architecture, which tends to be overly large and resource-intensive. To improve computational efficiency, we applied network pruning by reducing its depth. Specifically, we removed intermediate layers within the network and reduced the overall number of layers, as shown in Fig. 2(a). This not only lightens the model but also accelerates the training process. In the experimental section, we demonstrate that this pruning strategy significantly speeds up convergence, while introducing only a minor performance degradation.

To enhance training efficiency while minimizing memory usage, we propose the use of an auxiliary variable m and two learnable weighting scalars u_t and v_t ($u_t + v_t = 1$) in the diffusion sampling process. These scalars are used to scale the output and the transmitted data at each step. Mathematically, the forward and reverse operations of each connected layer are expressed as follows:

$$\text{Forward:} \begin{cases} x_t = u_t \Phi_t(x_t; \mathbf{y}, \mathbf{R}) + v_t m_{t-1} \\ m_t = x_{t-1} \end{cases} \tag{7}$$

$$\text{Inverse:} \begin{cases} x_{t-1} = m_t \\ m_{t-1} = [x_t - u_t \Phi_t(x_t; \mathbf{y}, \mathbf{R})] / v_t \end{cases} \tag{8}$$

Additionally, we introduce two learnable scalars, w_T and w_0, at the beginning and the end. Specifically, $m_T = w_T x_T$ is used to compute the input, while $\bar{x} = x_0 + w_0 m_0$ is used to compute the output. This ensures consistency between the input and output dimensions of the network.

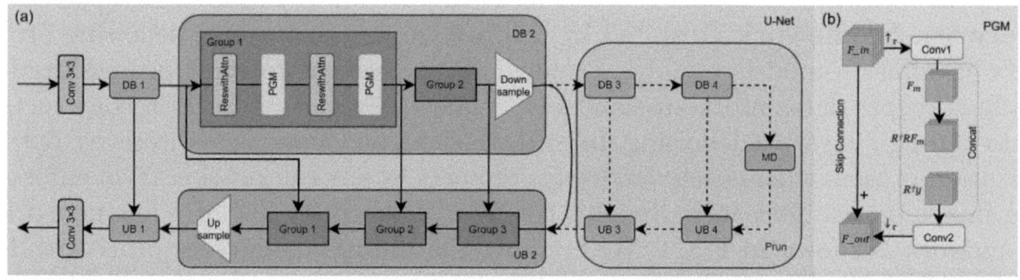

Fig. 2. Illustration of the modified denoising network U-Net in the diffusion model. (a) The PGM is added after each ReswithAttn module, and pruning is applied to the downsampling, upsampling, and middle blocks (marked as DB, UB, MD) within the network. (b) Detailed structure of the Physical Guidance Module (PGM).

3.3   Physical Guidance Module

As a high-dimensional data, HSI encounters various challenges during the reconstruction process, particularly when employing noise estimation networks for SSR. Noise estimation networks are typically focused on reducing image noise and enhancing image details. However, due to the complexity of hyperspectral images, relying solely on noise estimation networks may struggle to capture high-frequency information, particularly when there are subtle variations and details between different spectral bands of the hyperspectral data. To overcome this limitation, we propose the Physical Guidance Module (PGM), as illustrated in Fig. 2(b), which injects known physical information into the network to assist it in better understanding and reconstructing the high-frequency components of the image.

Here, $F_{in} \in \mathbb{R}^{(H/r)\times(W/r)\times(C\times r)}$ refers to the features of the intermediate network layer in U-Net, Our PGM injects physical information $\{y, R\}$ into the network as below:

$$F_m = Conv_1((F_{in})_{\uparrow r}), \tag{9}$$

$$F_{out} = F_{in} + Conv_2((concat[F_m, R^{\dagger}RF_m, R^{\dagger}y]))_{\downarrow r}. \tag{10}$$

where $Conv_1$ and $Conv_2$ refer to two 3×3 convolutional layers with a stride of 1 and padding of 1, while $(\cdot)_{\uparrow}/_{\downarrow r}$ denotes a Pixel-Shuffle/Unshuffle layer with a scaling ratio of r, used to align the feature space.

F_{in} is upsampled to restore the original image dimensions and serves as the initial feature input to the network. $R^{\dagger}R$ is the projection operator of the spectral response function, which projects F_m into the b-dimensional space of MSI and then maps it back into the B-dimensional HSI space via the inverse projection, ensuring spectral consistency and suppressing the formation of pseudo-bands. $R^{\dagger}y$ represents the least-squares inversion of the observed multispectral image y in the HSI space, further guiding the network's reconstruction. Finally, these three pieces of information (F_m, $R^{\dagger}RF_m$ and $R^{\dagger}y$) are concatenated and added to F_{in}, thereby enhancing high-frequency details without violating the physical observation constraints, ultimately improving the reconstruction quality.

The integration of physical information effectively introduces additional prior knowledge, significantly constraining the solution space, thereby greatly enhancing the final recovery quality. This allows the model to better preserve crucial spectral details, ultimately improving the overall accuracy of the recovery process and yielding more precise and realistic results.

4   Experiments

In this section, we validate the effectiveness of the proposed method through a series of experiments. In the experiments, we use a diffusion model pre-trained on remote sensing images, which was trained in an unsupervised manner using remote sensing data collected from Google Earth Engine, covering the RGB spectral range. The model's architecture is based on a five-layer U-Net, and in this paper, we simplify the model by reducing the number of layers to three for the experiments.

4.1   Datasets

The proposed method is evaluated on the CAVE [23] and Pavia University (PU) [24] datasets. The CAVE dataset contains 32 HSIs, each with a spatial resolution of 512×512 and 31 spectral bands. A random selection of 20 HSIs and their corresponding simulated RGB images are used for training, while the remaining 12 HSIs and simulated RGB images are used for testing. The PU dataset contains one HSI with 115 spectral bands. After removing water absorption and noisy bands, 103 bands remain. The original image has a resolution of 610×340 pixels, from which a 512×256 pixel region is cropped for the experiment. The top 256×256 pixel section is used as the training set, while the remaining portion is used as the test set. According to the Wald's protocol [25], the MSI images of the CAVE dataset are simulated using the SRF of a Nikon D700 camera, while the MSI images of the PU dataset are simulated using the SRF of the IKONOS satellite.

4.2   Implementation Details

To evaluate the similarity between the recovered images and the ground truth, we adopt three common evaluation metrics: peak signal-to-noise ratio (PSNR), root-mean squared error (RMSE), spectral angle mapper (SAM), structural similarity index (SSIM). These metrics are used to assess the quality of the reconstructed images from different perspectives, including pixel-wise accuracy, spectral fidelity, and structural similarity.

The proposed method is implemented based on the PyTorch framework, and the experiments were conducted on a desktop computer equipped with an Intel Core i9-14900K processor, an NVIDIA GeForce RTX 4090D graphics card, and 64 GB of memory. The model is trained for $T = 3$ iterations using the Adam optimizer with an initial learning rate of 2×10^{-4}, which is reduced by half every 30 iterations. The total number of training epochs is 200. The optimization objective for the model is defined using the basic L1 loss function. During training, all input image data are normalized to the range $[0, 1]$. Additionally, For the CAVE dataset, images are cropped into 32×32 patches with a stride of 16, while for the PU dataset, patches of size 16×16 are extracted with a stride of 8. The batch size is set to 32.

4.3   Ablation Study

In this section, we conduct ablation studies on the CAVE dataset to validate the effectiveness of the proposed components, including the reuse of pretrained model weights, the PGM module, and network pruning. The experimental results are presented in Table 1.

We evaluate the contribution of each component by removing them from the network individually. Specifically, under the condition of 200 training epochs, reusing the pretrained model within the network helps accelerate convergence. Although removing the PGM slightly reduces the training time per iteration, it leads to a performance drop across all evaluation metrics, indicating that the PGM effectively guides the image reconstruction process. When applying network pruning, the training time per iteration is reduced by approximately 33%, while the PSNR decreases marginally by 0.09 dB.

Table 1. Ablation study results on the CAVE dataset. Reu: reuse of pretrained model weights, PGM: physical guidance module, Pru: network pruning. PSNR: average PSNR (dB), SAM: average SAM (degrees), Tra: training time per epoch (s).

Reu	PGM	Pru	PSNR	SAM	Tra
✗	✗	✓	37.72	8.45	**137**
✗	✓	✓	37.89	7.79	154
✓	✓	✗	**38.34**	**7.38**	207
✓	✗	✓	<u>37.97</u>	7.81	**137**
✓	✓	✓	<u>38.25</u>	<u>7.41</u>	<u>154</u>

4.4 Effectiveness Evaluation

In this study, we conduct extensive comparative experiments between our method and several advanced spectral super-resolution approaches, including FMNet [26], MST++ [27], SSRAN [28], SSRNet [9] and LTRN [29]. To ensure fair and reliable comparisons, all methods are evaluated on the same datasets under consistent experimental settings.

Table 2. Quantitative results on the CAVE dataset.

	FMNet	MST++	SSRAN	SSRNet	LTRN	Ours
PSNR ↑	36.4962	38.0173	37.2391	37.5589	<u>38.1946</u>	**38.2513**
RMSE ↓	5.3531	**4.3727**	4.8023	4.8070	4.4864	<u>4.3809</u>
SAM ↓	12.8761	<u>7.4769</u>	8.3072	7.7742	7.6074	**7.4127**
SSIM ↑	0.9657	<u>0.9822</u>	0.9788	0.9797	0.9821	**0.9827**

Table 3. Quantitative results on the PU dataset.

	FMNet	MST++	SSRAN	SSRNet	LTRN	Ours
PSNR ↑	41.4531	<u>44.2583</u>	43.2564	44.5013	43.8463	**44.5856**
RMSE ↓	2.4361	<u>1.9511</u>	2.1623	1.9140	2.0026	**1.8681**
SAM ↓	2.7588	<u>2.3466</u>	2.4841	2.3457	2.3658	**2.2471**
SSIM ↑	0.9831	<u>0.9869</u>	0.9851	0.9866	0.9862	**0.9876**

Table 2 provides a detailed comparison of the experimental results of different methods on the CAVE dataset, where the best results are highlighted in bold and the second-best results are underlined. As shown in the table, the proposed method performs favorably across most metrics, achieving the best results in

PSNR, SAM, and SSIM, while closely following the best in RMSE, indicating strong error control. These results demonstrate that our method can not only accurately recover high-frequency details but also maintain good spectral fidelity and structural consistency.

Experimental results on the PU dataset are summarized in Table 3. Our proposed method achieves the best performance across all evaluation metrics, including PSNR, RMSE, SAM, and SSIM. It consistently outperforms all baseline methods, demonstrating superior reconstruction accuracy and spectral fidelity. These results confirm the effectiveness and robustness of our diffusion-based framework, enhanced with a physics-guided module, for hyperspectral image reconstruction across diverse datasets (Figs. 3 and 4).

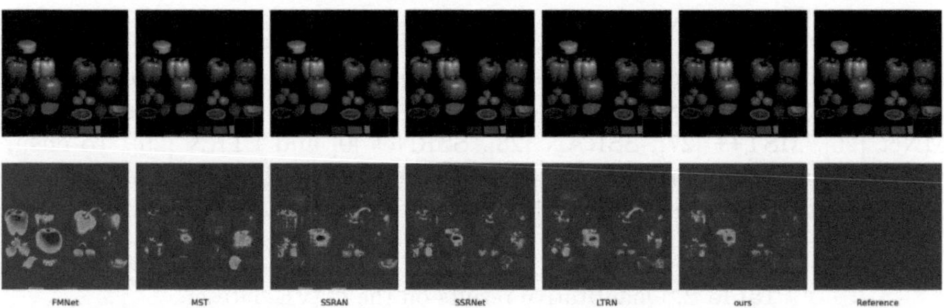

Fig. 3. Experimental results on the CAVE dataset: first row is the 25th-band reconstructions, and second row is the corresponding error maps.

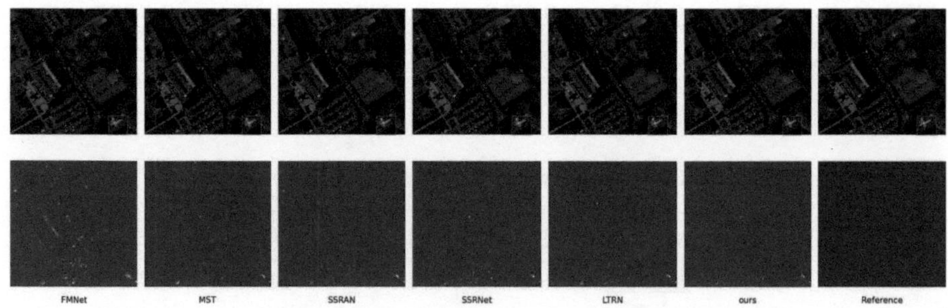

Fig. 4. Experimental results on the PU dataset: first row is the 79th-band reconstructions, and second row is the corresponding error maps.

5   Conclusion

In this work, we proposed a diffusion-based SSR framework that reconstructs high-quality HSI from MSI by modeling complex spectral correlations in an end-to-end manner. The framework leverages a pretrained diffusion model as a reconstruction prior and integrates a physics-guided module to enhance the recovery of high-frequency spectral details. Extensive experiments demonstrate that the proposed method achieves competitive performance across multiple benchmarks, highlighting the effectiveness of combining generative diffusion modeling with physics-informed network design. Future work will focus on extending the framework to real-world remote sensing applications and improving computational efficiency.

References

1. Wan, Y., et al.: UAV-ground hyperspectral monitoring of tailings reservoir disasters: a case study in Xinjiang. In: IGARSS, pp. 9713–9716 (2019)
2. Jia, J., et al.: Tradeoffs in spatial and spectral resolution of airborne hyperspectral systems: a crop identification case. IEEE Trans. Geosci. Remote Sens. **60**, 1–18 (2022)
3. Meyer, J.M., Kokaly, R.F., Holley, E.: Hyperspectral sensing of white mica: a review with spectrometer design insights. Remote Sens. Environ. **275**, 113000 (2022)
4. Goodfellow, I., et al.: Generative adversarial networks. Commun. ACM **63**(11), 139–144 (2020)
5. Dhariwal, P., Nichol, A.: Diffusion models beat GANs on image synthesis. In: NeurIPS, vol. 34, pp. 8780–8794 (2021)
6. Arad, B., Ben-Shahar, O.: Sparse recovery of hyperspectral signal from natural RGB images. In: Leibe, B., Matas, J., Sebe, N., Welling, M. (eds.) ECCV 2016. LNCS, vol. 9911, pp. 19–34. Springer, Cham (2016). https://doi.org/10.1007/978-3-319-46478-7_2
7. Fang, L., Zhuo, H., Li, S.: Super-resolution of hyperspectral image via superpixel-based sparse representation. Neurocomputing **273**, 171–177 (2018)
8. Galliani, S., Lanaras, C., Marmanis, D., Baltsavias, E., Schindler, K.: Learned spectral super-resolution. arXiv:1703.09470 (2017)
9. Dian, R., Shan, T., He, W., Liu, H.: Spectral super-resolution via model-guided cross-fusion network. IEEE Trans. Neural Netw. Learn Syst **35**, 10059–10070 (2023)
10. Dai, T., Cai, J., Zhang, Y.-B., Xia, S.-T., Zhang, L.: Second-order attention network for single image super-resolution. In: IEEE Conference Computer Vision and Pattern Recognition, pp. 11057–11066 (2019)
11. Liu, L., Chen, B., Chen, H., Zou, Z., Shi, Z.: Diverse hyperspectral remote sensing image synthesis with diffusion models. IEEE Trans. Geosci. Remote Sens. **61**, 5532616 (2023)
12. Ho, J., Jain, A., Abbeel, P.: Denoising diffusion probabilistic models. In: Advances in Neural Information Processing Systems, pp. 6840–6851 (2020)
13. Song, Y., Sohl-Dickstein, J., Kingma, D.P., Kumar, A., Ermon, S., Poole, B.: Score-based generative modeling through stochastic differential equations. In: International Conference on Learning Representations (2021)
14. Kawar, B., Elad, M., Ermon, S., Song, J.: Denoising diffusion restoration models. In: Advances in Neural Information Processing Systems (2022)
15. Saharia, C., Ho, J., Chan, W., Salimans, T., Fleet, D.J., Norouzi, M.: Image super-resolution via iterative refinement. IEEE Trans. Pattern Anal. Mach. Intell. **45**(4), 4713–4726 (2023)

16. Zhou, J., et al.: Exploring multi-timestep multi-stage diffusion features for hyperspectral image classification. IEEE Trans. Geosci. Remote Sens. **62**, 1–16 (2024). https://doi.org/10.1109/TGRS.2024.3407206
17. Bandara, W.G.C., Nair, N.G., Patel, V.M.: Remote sensing change detection using denoising diffusion probabilistic models. arXiv:2206.11892 (2022). https://doi.org/10.48550/ARXIV.2206.11892
18. Wolleb, J., Sandkühler, R., Bieder, F., Valmaggia, P., Cattin, P.C.: Diffusion models for implicit image segmentation ensembles. arXiv:2112.03145 (2021)
19. Wang, Y., Yu, J., Zhang, J.: Zero-shot image restoration using denoising diffusion null-space model. In: International Conference on Learning Representations (2023)
20. Boyd, S., Parikh, N., Chu, E., Peleato, B., Eckstein, J.: Distributed optimization and statistical learning via the alternating direction method of multipliers. Found. Trends Mach. Learn. **3**(1), 1–122 (2011)
21. He, R., Zheng, W.-S., Tan, T., Sun, Z.: Half-quadratic-based iterative minimization for robust sparse representation. IEEE Trans. Pattern Anal. Mach. Intell. **36**(2), 261–275 (2014)
22. Chen, B., et al.: Invertible diffusion models for compressed sensing. IEEE Trans. Pattern Anal. Mach. Intell. **47**, 3992–4006 (2025)
23. Yasuma, F., Mitsunaga, T., Iso, D., Nayar, S.K.: Generalized assorted pixel camera: postcapture control of resolution, dynamic range, and spectrum. IEEE Trans. Image Process. **19**(9), 2241–2253 (2010)
24. Dell'Acqua, F., Gamba, P., Ferrari, A., Palmason, J.A., Benediktsson, J.A., Árnason, K.: Exploiting spectral and spatial information in hyperspectral urban data with high resolution. IEEE Geosci. Remote Sens. Lett. **1**(4), 322–326 (2004)
25. Ranchin, T., Wald, L.: Fusion of high spatial and spectral resolution images: the arsis concept and its implementation. Photogramm. Eng. Remote. Sens. **66**(1), 49–61 (2000)
26. Zhang, L., et al.: Pixel-aware deep function-mixture network for spectral super-resolution. In: Proceedings of the AAAI Conference on Artificial Intelligence, vol. 34, no. 07, pp. 12821–12828 (2020)
27. Cai, Y., et al.: MST++: multi-stage spectral-wise transformer for efficient spectral reconstruction. In: Proceedings of the IEEE Conference on Computer Vision and Pattern Recognition (CVPR), pp. 744–754 (2022)
28. Zheng, X., Chen, W., Lu, X.: Spectral super-resolution of multispectral images using spatial-spectral residual attention network. IEEE Trans. Geosci. Remote Sens. **60**, 1–14 (2022)
29. Dian, R., Liu, Y., Li, S.: Spectral super-resolution via deep low-rank tensor representation. IEEE Trans. Neural Netw. Learn. Syst. **36**(3), 5140–5150 (2025)

Asymmetric Dual-Teacher Guided Knowledge Distillation for HSI-SR with Reconstructed Features

Ziqi Zhang and Jianjun Liu$^{(\boxtimes)}$

School of Artificial Intelligence and Computer Science, Jiangnan University, Wuxi, China
liuofficial@163.com

Abstract. Hyperspectral image super-resolution (HSI-SR) aims to reconstruct high-resolution (HR) images from their low-resolution (LR) counterparts while preserving spectral integrity. Existing knowledge distillation (KD) methods predominantly transfer knowledge from a single super-resolution network, which limits the student model's ability to learn multi-stage hierarchical features. To overcome this limitation, we propose an asymmetric dual-teacher KD framework where two specialized teachers guide the student network: The super-resolution teacher network provides the knowledge of feature extraction, and the reconstruction teacher network provides the knowledge of feature reconstruction. Furthermore, we designed a Dual Aggregation Transformer U-net (DATU-Net) that is applicable to this framework and to hyperspectral super-resolution. The loss function designed enables the student network to focus on the knowledge of the two teacher networks, we verified the proposed network on two datasets and proved that our knowledge distillation framework is superior to the latest methods. The effectiveness of this framework was proved through ablation experiments.

Keywords: Hyperspectral image super-resolution · Dual-teacher knowledge distillation · Transformer

1 Introduction

Hyperspectral imaging (HSI) captures three-dimensional data comprising hundreds of contiguous narrow spectral bands. This unparalleled spectral resolution has driven its adoption in critical applications [1, 2] ranging from precision agriculture and mineral exploration to medical diagnostics. However, inherent physical limitations, particularly the photon count trade-off between spectral and spatial resolutions, force HSIs to prioritize spectral fidelity at the expense of spatial detail [3]. Consequently, low spatial resolution HSIs hinder downstream tasks such as small object detection [4] and fine-grained classification [5], where localized spatial features are paramount. Although hardware advances (e.g. high-precision sensors) offer a direct solution, their prohibitive cost and engineering complexity [3] have shifted the research focus to computational HSI-SR. This paradigm aims to reconstruct high-resolution HSIs from low-resolution input while preserving spectral integrity, either through single-image enhancement [6] or multimodal fusion with high spatial resolution multispectral imagery (MSI) [7].

Z. Lin et al. (Eds.): ICIG 2025, LNCS 16161, pp. 391–402, 2026.
https://doi.org/10.1007/978-981-95-3398-5_32

Significant advances have been made in the development of hyperspectral imaging. In general, single-image HSI-SR methods are broadly categorized into two groups: traditional approaches and deep learning-based methods. Conventional techniques primarily rely on handcrafted priors and algorithmic models, such as bilinear interpolation, bicubic interpolation, and coupled nonnegative matrix factorization (CNMF) [8]. However, these traditional methods struggle to capture complex non-linear relationships in spectral-spatial feature mapping. The emergence of deep learning has brought a qualitative leap to HSI-SR. Deep learning approaches employ data-driven strategies to learn intricate mapping relationships between low-resolution and high-resolution images through end-to-end training paradigms [9]. This enables them to inherently model the nonlinear degradation process of hyperspectral data while preserving critical spectral signatures. Consequently, deep learning-based solutions demonstrate substantially superior performance compared to conventional methods. While convolutional neural networks (CNNs)achieve notable performance in HSI-SR, their local receptive fields constrain long-range dependency modeling—crucial for reconstructing spectral-spatial correlations. This stems from convolutional operations prioritizing local over global interactions. Transformers address this via self-attention mechanisms that dynamically link all spatial-spectral positions [10]. By processing the hyperspectral cube as token sequences, they explicitly preserve global relationships and high-dimensional structures.

However, the relentless pursuit of superior performance has driven modern models toward escalating architectural scale and computational complexity [11]. Compared to convolutional neural networks, transformer-based architectures incur significantly higher computational burdens due to their self-attention mechanisms, which exhibit quadratic complexity relative to input size. This inherent limitation renders them unsuitable for resource-constrained deployment scenarios like edge devices or real-time systems. To address this challenge, knowledge distillation emerges as a strategic solution, primarily through two strategies: (1) Model Compression, which transfers knowledge from heavyweight teachers to lightweight students, maintaining performance while slashing parameters and FLOPs; (2) Knowledge Fusion, which integrates complementary expertise from multiple teachers into a unified student model, achieving synergistic performance gains.

In this paper, we propose an asymmetric dual-teacher knowledge distillation framework. For the student network, it learns feature extraction knowledge from the encoder of Teacher Network A and feature reconstruction knowledge from the decoder of Teacher Network B. Both the teacher and student networks adopt a dual-aggregated U-Net architecture (DATU-Net) tailored for HSI-SR. To ensure that the student network's encoder and decoder focus on distinct knowledge from the two teachers, we design customized loss functions targeting multi-scale encoder and decoder outputs. These innovations enable the proposed network to achieve significant improvements over existing super-resolution networks.

In summary, the main contributions are as follows.

- An asymmetric dual-teacher knowledge distillation framework based on reconstruction information is proposed, enabling the student network to effectively learn distinct knowledge from each teacher network.
- Designed a dual-aggregation U-Net to effectively extract both spectral and spatial information from hyperspectral images.
- Designed a loss function to constrain the training process and ensure the student network focuses on the knowledge from both teacher networks.

2   Related Work

2.1   Single HSI-SR

Previous studies have primarily formulated HSI super-resolution as a constrained optimization problem. For instance, Zare M et al. [12] introduced a tensor factorization framework that decomposes HSIs into low-rank spatial-spectral components, explicitly preserving inter-band correlations through Tucker decomposition. Building on this, Dian et al. [13] combined non-local similarity constraints with a graph Laplacian prior to enhance spatial continuity while maintaining spectral consistency. Another notable approach by Yokoya et al. [14] employed coupled sparse and total variation (TV) regularization, where spatial TV minimized noise artifacts and sparse coding enforced spectral basis compactness.

Deep learning, particularly CNNs, has revolutionized HSI-SR by automating spatial-spectral feature learning. Yuan et al. [15] designed dual-branch CNNs for joint spatial-spectral optimization. However, CNNs' limited receptive fields hinder long-range spectral dependency modeling under data scarcity. Hybrid architectures like GDDRN [16] addressed this via band-grouped convolutions and hybrid SAM-MSE losses, reducing spectral distortion. Transformers have further advanced global spectral-spatial modeling: CLSCNet [17] employed LSTM to enhance spatial recovery performance, while SRDNet [18] enhanced spatial information and spectral coherence through 3d convolution.

Despite significant advancements, current HSI-SR methods still face critical challenges. Transformer-based approaches struggle to balance spatial-spectral interdependencies and effectively extract both spatial details and spectral features. Furthermore, existing methods often fail to achieve hierarchical feature fusion across network layers, lacking robust multi-scale feature integration capabilities. To address these limitations, we propose a novel dual-branch U-Net architecture specifically tailored for HSI-SR.

2.2   Knowledge Distillation

Knowledge distillation has emerged as a pivotal technique for transferring knowledge from computationally intensive teacher models to compact student networks while preserving performance. Knowledge distillation facilitates the transfer of learned knowledge from computationally intensive teacher models to compact student networks, allowing the latter to attain comparable or superior performance while maintaining significantly reduced complexity. As demonstrated in FitNets [19], enforcing similarity between the hidden layers of teacher and student networks can enhance the training of deeper and thinner student models. For HSI-SR, these methods face unique challenges due to the high-dimensional spectral-spatial correlations and the need for precise spectral fidelity preservation. Dual-teacher frameworks have also gained traction: Zhang et al. [20] employed a noisy reconstruction teacher network and a clean reconstruction network for image reconstruction. Building on these advances, particularly the success of intermediate-layer guidance and dual-teacher strategies, in this work we propose a knowledge distillation framework that augments the knowledge transfer from a teacher network by incorporating reconstruction-guided supervision, addressing the inherent limitations of single-teacher knowledge in modeling complex spectral-spatial interdependencies.

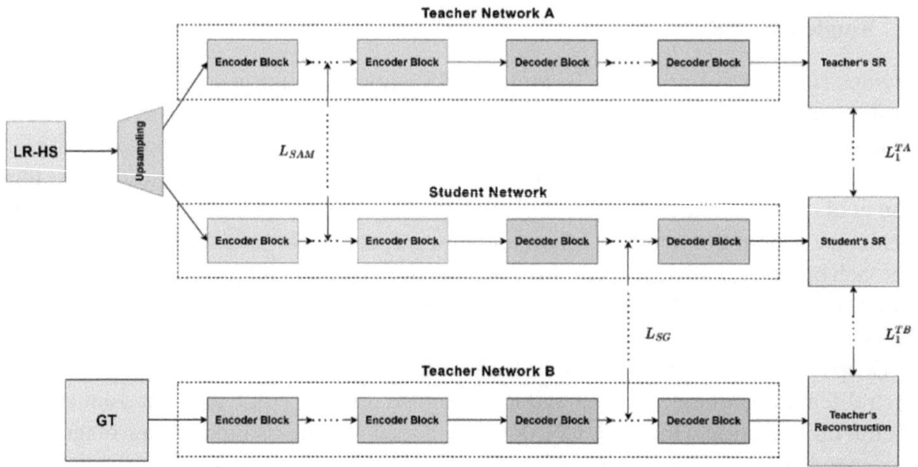

Fig. 1. The overall architecture of our proposed Asymmetric Dual-Teacher Guided Knowledge Distillation (ADTKD) strategy

3 Proposed Method

In this section, we will first present the overall framework of our proposed Asymmetric Dual-Teacher Guided Knowledge Distillation. Subsequent sections will provide a comprehensive description and analysis of the backbone architecture—the Dual-Aggregated Transformer U-Net—followed by an in-depth discussion of the proposed loss function.

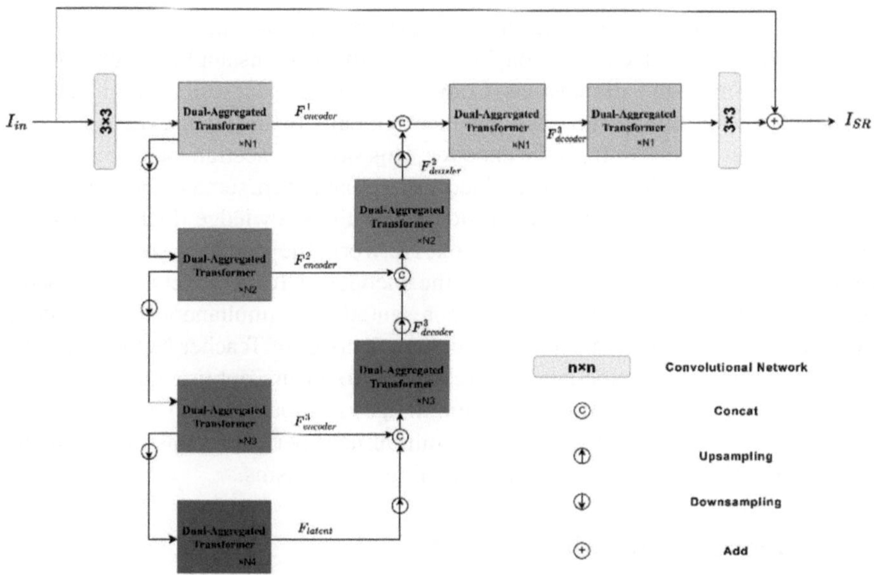

Fig. 2. The structure of our Dual-Aggregated Transformer U-Net.

3.1 Overall Architecture

As illustrated in Fig. 1. The overall architecture of our proposed Asymmetric Dual-Teacher Guided Knowledge Distillation strategy, our ADTKD strategy employs two pre-trained models: Teacher A (a super-resolution network) and Teacher B (an image restoration network). The student network is trained by distilling knowledge from both teachers. While the teacher and student architectures share structural similarities, the student network reduces computational complexity by using fewer intermediate features and fewer Transformer layers. Given $I_{LR} \in \mathbb{R}^{B \times H \times W}$ denote the input low-resolution hyperspectral image and $I_{GT} \in \mathbb{R}^{B \times rH \times rW}$ denote ground truth. $I^T_{SR} \in \mathbb{R}^{B \times rH \times rW}$, $I^S_{SR} \in \mathbb{R}^{B \times rH \times rW}$ and $I_{Recon} \in \mathbb{R}^{B \times rH \times rW}$ denote the super-resolved outputs from Teacher Network A, the Student Network and Teacher Network B, respectively, where W and H are the width and height of the low-resolution hyperspectral image(LR-HSI), B is the number of spectral bands, and r denotes the scaling factor for SR reconstruction. Our framework consists of three parallel branches: Teacher Network A, Teacher Network B, and the Student Network, as follows:

$$I^T_{SR} = Net_{TA}(I_{LR}) \tag{1}$$

$$I^S_{SR} = Net_{STU}(I_{LR}) \tag{2}$$

$$I_{Recon} = Net_{TB}(I_{GT}) \tag{3}$$

where $Net_{TA}(\cdot)$, $Net_{STU}(\cdot)$, $Net_{TB}(\cdot)$ denote the proposed Teacher Network A, Student Network, and Teacher Network B, respectively.

In the U-Net architecture, the encoder extracts multi-scale features from low-resolution images through convolutional layers and local downsampling operations, progressively reducing spatial dimensions. Conversely, the decoder restores high-resolution spatial details via upsampling layers, while hierarchically fusing features across scales by integrating skip connections from the encoder. This skip-connection mechanism enables the aggregation of both shallow, fine-grained textures and deep, semantic representations, thereby enhancing detail reconstruction fidelity. In the knowledge distillation strategy between Teacher Network A and the Student Network, the student's encoder is trained to learn feature extraction knowledge from the encoder of Teacher Network A, focusing on acquiring hierarchical spectral-spatial representations. Simultaneously, the student's decoder distills reconstruction expertise from the decoder of Teacher Network B, which specializes in high-fidelity spatial detail recovery. To ensure optimal knowledge transfer, we employ ground-truth high-resolution images as inputs to both teacher networks during distillation, enabling the student to mimic near-perfect reconstruction patterns through feature alignment and gradient matching mechanisms.

3.2 Dual-Aggregated Transformer U-Net

As illustrated in Fig. 2. The overall architecture of our proposed Dual-Aggregated Transformer U-Net. In this work, Teacher Network A and the Student Network share a nearly identical backbone architecture, both adopting the proposed Dual-Aggregated Transformer U-Net as their core framework. Teacher Network B employs Restormer [21], a state-of-the-art transformer-based reconstruction architecture, to provide complementary expertise in high-fidelity spatial detail recovery. To ensure dimensional alignment of intermediate features between the student and teacher networks, we apply bicubic upsampling to the low-resolution hyperspectral image prior to feeding it into both Teacher Network A and the student network within the DATU-Net framework. This preprocessing step guarantees consistent feature map dimensions across all network stages, enabling effective knowledge transfer through feature-level distillation.

Inspired by the design principles of Dual-Aggregation Transformer (DAT) modules [22], we propose the DATU-Net architecture as illustrated in Fig. 2. The network comprises eight cascaded DAT modules: The first three DAT modules progressively downsample spatial dimensions while extracting hierarchical spectral-spatial features. The fifth, sixth, and seventh DAT modules reconstruct high-resolution features through learned upsampling, with skip connections bridging complementary multi-scale representations from the encoder.

First, we extract shallow features through a 3×3 convolutional layer. These features are then sequentially passed through the encoder composed of DATBs (each containing a different number of DAT modules) and downsampling layers, facilitating multi-scale feature extraction, as follows:

$$F_{encoder}^{1} = DATB_1(Conv_{3\times3}(I_{in})) \tag{4}$$

$$F_{encoder}^{i+1} = DATB_{i+1}(Down(F_{encoder}^{i})) \tag{5}$$

where $Conv_{3\times3}(\cdot)$ denotes a 3×3 convolution. $Down(\cdot)$ denotes a downsampling layer. $F_{encoder}^{i}$ denote the feature output by the i-th encoder ($i = 1,2,3$) and $DATB_{i+1}(\cdot)$ denote the i-th DATB. I_{in} denotes the inputs of DATU-Net. The intermediate decoder features are obtained as follows:

$$F_{latent} = DATB_4\left(Down\left(F_{encoder}^3\right)\right) \tag{6}$$

$$F_{decoder}^3 = DATB_5\left(Cat\left(Up(F_{latent}), F_{encoder}^3\right)\right) \tag{7}$$

$$F_{decoder}^i = DATB_{8-i}\left(Cat\left(Up\left(F_{decoder}^{i+1}\right), F_{encoder}^i\right)\right) \tag{8}$$

where $Up(\cdot)$ denotes upsampling layer. $Cat(\cdot)$ denotes concat. $F_{decoder}^i$ denote the feature output by the i-th decoder ($i = 1,2,3$). Finally, the high-resolution result image is generated by processing $F_{decoder}^1$ through the final DATB.

$$I_{SR} = Conv_{3\times3}(DATB_8(F_{decoder}^1)) + I_{in} \tag{9}$$

In this work, we configure the number of DATBs (Dual-Aggregation Transformer Blocks) in each stage as $(N_1, N_2, N_3, N_4) = (2, 3, 3, 4)$ for the teacher network, and (1, 2, 2, 3) for the student network.

3.3 Loss Function

The L_1 loss is a standard choice in super-resolution tasks. In this work, we employ the L_1 loss to measure the discrepancy between the student network's output and the reconstructed results from both teacher networks, ensuring pixel-wise alignment while preserving spectral-spatial consistency.

$$L_1^{TA} = \|I_{SR}^S - I_{SR}^T\|_1 \tag{10}$$

$$L_1^{TB} = \|I_{SR}^S - I_{Recon}\|_1 \tag{11}$$

For the intermediate features between Teacher Network A and the student network's encoder, we introduce a Spectral Angle Mapper (SAM) loss to guide the student's spectral-aware feature extraction.

$$L_{SAM} = \frac{1}{N}\sum_{i=1}^{N} arccos\left(\frac{\langle x_i, y_i \rangle}{\|x_i\|_2 \cdot \|y_i\|_2 + \varepsilon}\right) \tag{12}$$

where N represents the total number of pixels in the image. x_i denotes the predicted spectrum and y_i denotes the ground truth spectrum. For the intermediate features between Teacher Network B and the student network's decoder, we select a Spectral Gradient Loss to enhance feature reconstruction fidelity.

$$L_{SG} = \frac{1}{c-1}\sum_{i=1}^{C-1}\left|(\hat{x}_{i+1} - \hat{x}_i) - (x_{i+1} - x_i)\right| \tag{13}$$

where C represents the number of spectral bands. $\hat{x}_i$ denotes the predicted spectrum and x_i denotes the ground truth spectrum.

Finally, the overall loss is formulated as:

$$L_{total} = L_1^{TB} + \alpha_1 L_1^{TA} + \alpha_2(L_{SAM} + L_{SG}) \tag{14}$$

In this work, we set the weighting coefficients α_1 and α_2 to 0.5 and 0.01, respectively.

4 Experiments

4.1 Datasets and Settings

Cave Dataset

The CAVE dataset [23] comprises 32 static high-resolution multispectral image scenes. Each scene is captured across 31 spectral bands, covering the visible light spectrum from 400 nm to 700 nm with a 10 nm wavelength interval. All band-specific images have a spatial resolution of 512×512 pixels and are stored as 16-bit grayscale images.

Pavia Centre Dataset

The Pavia Centre dataset [24] was acquired by the ROSIS sensor and covers the urban area of the city center of Pavia, Italy. The spatial resolution of this dataset is approximately 1.3 m per pixel, with image dimensions typically being 1096×715 pixels and it contains 102 spectral bands.

Implementation Details

Our framework is implemented in PyTorch with NVIDIA GeForce GTX 3080 GPU, using the Adam optimizer ($\beta_1 = 0.9$, $\beta_2 = 0.999$). Teacher Network A is trained for 150 epochs, Teacher Network B is trained for 60 epochs, and the Student Network is trained for 150 epochs. We set the batch size to 8, with a fixed patch size of 64. The initial learning rate is set to 0.0001 and gradually decreased to 1e-6.

Each dataset is partitioned into training and testing subsets. For the CAVE dataset, the first 20 scenes are allocated to the training set, while the remaining 12 scenes constitute the test set. During preprocessing, image patches of size 64×64 pixels are extracted with a stride of 16 and a downsampling ratio of $r = 4$ to generate low-resolution inputs. The teacher network employs 64 channels in its intermediate feature layers to preserve reconstruction fidelity, whereas the student network adopts a compressed configuration with 32 channels to reduce computational overhead.

For the PaviaC dataset, we first extract the top-left 1024×512-pixel region as the region of interest. Subsequently, 64×64-pixel patches are cropped with a stride of 16 and downsampled by a factor of $r = 4$ to generate low-resolution inputs. The dataset is partitioned by allocating 20% of the patches to the test set, while the remaining 80% are used for training.

Evaluation Metrics

To comprehensively evaluate the performance of our model in hyperspectral super-resolution knowledge distillation, we employ six widely-adopted quantitative metrics: cross correlation (CC) [25], spectral angle mapper (SAM) [26], peak signal-tonoise ratio (PSNR), root mean square error (RMSE), erreur relative globale adimensionnelle de synthese (ERGAS) [27], structure similarity (SSIM) [28].

4.2 Qualitative Results

We conduct comparative evaluations against six state-of-the-art hyperspectral super-resolution methods, including: GDRNN [16], SSPSR [29], ESSA [30], MCT [31], SRDNet [18], CLSCNet [17].

Table 1. Quantitative comparison of different methods on the CAVE dataset.

Method	CC	SAM	PSNR	RMSE	ERGAS	SSIM
Bicubic	0.9794	4.4308	33.6151	0.0228	7.6897	0.9678
GDRNN	0.9902	3.9122	37.3617	0.0159	4.6048	0.9786
SSPSR	0.9909	3.9429	37.4219	0.0156	4.5545	0.9801
MCT	0.9922	3.3735	38.8214	0.0139	4.0085	0.9827
ESSA	0.9915	3.8512	38.2935	0.0149	4.2541	0.9691
SRDNet	0.9923	3.5155	38.6033	0.0143	4.1291	0.9816
CLSCNet	0.9911	3.5776	38.1779	0.0150	4.3125	0.9806
OURS	**0.9931**	**3.4018**	**39.2933**	**0.0133**	**3.8128**	**0.9841**

Table 2. Quantitative comparison of different methods on the PaviaC dataset.

Method	CC	SAM	PSNR	RMSE	ERGAS	SSIM
Bicubic	0.7431	8.3681	26.8935	0.0503	9.4227	0.6586
GDRNN	0.8826	7.7234	29.5906	0.0348	6.9781	0.8332
SSPSR	0.9113	6.1915	30.7935	0.0304	6.0353	0.8811
MCT	0.9063	6.8465	30.4421	0.0324	6.4018	0.8536
ESSA	0.9411	5.6283	33.0093	0.0234	4.8054	0.9299
SRDNet	0.9503	5.8479	34.9242	0.0185	4.1976	0.9546
CLSCNet	0.9574	5.2417	35.1078	0.0183	3.9916	0.9589
OURS	**0.9723**	**4.4074**	**39.6698**	**0.0106**	**3.1649**	**0.9847**

Results on CAVE Dataset

As shown in Table 1. Quantitative comparison of different methods on the CAVE dataset. Traditional bicubic interpolation underperforms across all metrics compared to deep learning-based methods. Although GDRNN improves upon traditional approaches by learning the mapping from low-resolution to high-resolution images through recursive residual blocks, its reliance on convolutional operations limits its ability to handle complex spectral correlations and global dependencies in hyperspectral imagery, resulting in only marginal gains over conventional techniques. In contrast, SSPSR integrates spatial residual modules with spectral attention mechanisms, achieving superior performance to GDRNN. Nevertheless, conventional CNN architectures remain constrained by their local receptive fields, which hinder effective global feature extraction and reconstruction, ultimately rendering them less competitive than subsequent transformer-based or hybrid methods. The MCT method employs hybrid 2D/3D convolutions to jointly optimize spatial detail reconstruction and spectral fidelity. This comparison highlights a persistent performance gap between CNN-driven methods and Transformer-based architectures. Recent methods like ESSA, SRDNet, and CLSCNet leverage attention mechanisms to surpass CNN-based solutions, yet none match the efficacy of our proposed framework. Our approach uniquely integrates both spatial and spectral information while providing the student network with richer prior knowledge through a dual-teacher framework, where Teacher A specializes in spectral consistency and Teacher B focuses on high-frequency spatial refinement.

Results on PaviaC Dataset

As shown in Table 2. Quantitative comparison of different methods on the PaviaC dataset. The MCT method only marginally outperforms GDRNN on the PaviaC dataset, with negligible performance gaps among other competing methods. In contrast, our proposed approach consistently achieves superior results across all metrics, demonstrating its robustness in balancing spatial and spectral fidelity.

4.3 Ablation Study

As shown in Table 3, we conducted ablation experiments on the PaviaC dataset for ADTKD. The first row represents the removal of both teacher network B and the intermediate loss between the encoder and decoder. The second row removes only the intermediate loss, while the third row corresponds to the complete architecture. As shown in the table, the structure that incorporates Teacher Network B and the intermediate feature loss function achieves the best performance.

Table 3. Ablation study results on PaviaC

TB Network	$L_{SAM} + L_{SG}$	CC	SAM	PSNR	RMSE	ERGAS	SSIM
×	×	0.9700	4.8069	39.1436	0.0111	3.3441	0.9822
✓	×	0.9714	4.4644	39.5506	0.0109	3.1810	0.9818
✓	✓	**0.9723**	**4.4074**	**39.6698**	**0.0106**	**3.1649**	**0.9847**

5 Conclusion

This paper introduces a novel framework termed Asymmetric Dual-Teacher Guided Knowledge Distillation, which synergistically leverages expertise from a super-resolution teacher network and a reconstruction-oriented teacher network to guide the training of a compact student model. To tailor this framework for hyperspectral imaging, we propose the Dual-Aggregated U-Net as the backbone architecture. DATU-Net structurally decouples knowledge acquisition by dedicating its encoder to spectral-spatial feature extraction under the super-resolution teacher's guidance and its decoder to high-fidelity spectral reconstruction supervised by the reconstruction teacher. This asymmetric design explicitly aligns feature learning stages with teacher specializations, ensuring efficient knowledge transfer. Many experiments conducted on two benchmark hyperspectral datasets show that, compared with the traditional transformer-based methods, our framework achieves state-of-the-art performance while theoretically reducing complexity.

References

1. Wang, T., Zhu, Z., Blasch, E.: Bio-inspired adaptive hyperspectral imaging for real-time target tracking. IEEE Sens. J. **10**(3), 647–654 (2010)
2. Yuan, H., Tang, Y.Y.: Spectral–spatial shared linear regression for hyperspectral image classification. IEEE Trans. Cybern. **47**(4), 934–945 (2016)
3. Yokoya, N., Grohnfeldt, C., Chanussot, J.: Hyperspectral and multispectral data fusion: a comparative review of the recent literature. IEEE Geosci. Remote Sens. Mag. **5**(2), 29–56 (2017)
4. Niu, Y., Wang, B.: Hyperspectral anomaly detection based on low-rank representation and learned dictionary. Remote Sensing **8**(4), 289 (2016)
5. Jia, S., Deng, X., Zhu, J., et al.: Collaborative representation-based multiscale superpixel fusion for hyperspectral image classification. IEEE Trans. Geosci. Remote Sens. **57**(10), 7770–7784 (2019)
6. Pandey, G., Ghanekar, U.: Single image super-resolution using multi-scale feature enhancement attention residual network. Optik **231**, 166359 (2021)
7. Zhang, J., Liu, J., Yang, J., et al.: Crossed dual-branch U-Net for hyperspectral image super-resolution. IEEE J. Sel. Top. Appl. Earth Observations Remote Sens. **17**, 2296–2307 (2023)
8. Keys, R.: Cubic convolution interpolation for digital image processing. IEEE Trans. Acoust. Speech Signal Process. **29**(6), 1153–1160 (2003)
9. Li, Y., Hu, J., Zhao, X., et al.: Hyperspectral image super-resolution using deep convolutional neural network. Neurocomputing **266**, 29–41 (2017)
10. Hu, J.F., Huang, T.Z., Deng, L.J., et al.: Fusformer: a transformer-based fusion network for hyperspectral image super-resolution. IEEE Geosci. Remote Sens. Lett. **19**, 1–5 (2022)
11. Luo, X., Liu, D., Kong, H., et al.: Efficient deep learning infrastructures for embedded computing systems: a comprehensive survey and future envision. ACM Trans. Embed. Comput. Syst. **24**(1), 1–100 (2024)
12. Zare, M., Helfroush, M.S., Kazemi, K., et al.: Hyperspectral and multispectral image fusion using coupled non-negative tucker tensor decomposition. Remote Sensing **13**(15), 2930 (2021)
13. Dian, R., Fang, L., Li, S.: Hyperspectral image super-resolution via non-local sparse tensor factorization. In: Proceedings of the IEEE Conference on Computer Vision and Pattern Recognition, pp. 5344–5353 (2017)
14. Yokoya, N., Yairi, T., Iwasaki, A.: Coupled nonnegative matrix factorization unmixing for hyperspectral and multispectral data fusion. IEEE Trans. Geosci. Remote Sens. **50**(2), 528–537 (2011)
15. Yuan, Y., Zheng, X., Lu, X.: Hyperspectral image superresolution by transfer learning. IEEE J. Sel. Top. Appl. Earth Observations Remote Sens. **10**(5), 1963–1974 (2017)

16. Li, Y., Zhang, L., Dingl, C., et al.: Single hyperspectral image super-resolution with grouped deep recursive residual network. In: 2018 IEEE Fourth International Conference on Multimedia Big Data (BigMM), pp. 1–4. IEEE (2018)
17. Xu, Y., Hou, J., Zhu, X., et al.: Hyperspectral image super-resolution with ConvLSTM skip-connections. IEEE Trans. Geosci. Remote Sens. (2024)
18. Liu, T., Liu, Y., Zhang, C., et al.: Hyperspectral image super-resolution via dual-domain network based on hybrid convolution. IEEE Trans. Geosci. Remote Sens. (2024)
19. Romero, A., Ballas, N., Kahou, S.E., et al.: Fitnets: Hints for thin deep nets. arXiv preprint arXiv:1412.6550 (2014)
20. Zhang, Y., Yan, D.: Knowledge distillation for image restoration: simultaneous learning from degraded and clean images. arXiv preprint arXiv:2501.09268 (2025)
21. Zamir, S.W., Arora, A., Khan, S., et al.: Restormer: efficient transformer for high-resolution image restoration. In: Proceedings of the IEEE/CVF Conference on Computer Vision and Pattern Recognition, pp. 5728–5739 (2022)
22. Chen, Z., Zhang, Y., Gu, J., et al.: Dual aggregation transformer for image super-resolution. In: Proceedings of the IEEE/CVF International Conference on Computer Vision, pp. 12312–12321 (2023)
23. Yasuma, F., Mitsunaga, T., Iso, D., et al.: Generalized assorted pixel camera: postcapture control of resolution, dynamic range, and spectrum. IEEE Trans. Image Process. **19**(9), 2241–2253 (2010)
24. Gamba, P.: A collection of data for urban area characterization. In: IGARSS 2004. 2004 IEEE International Geoscience and Remote Sensing Symposium, p. 1. IEEE (2004)
25. Loncan, L., De Almeida, L.B., Bioucas-Dias, J.M., et al.: Hyperspectral pansharpening: a review. IEEE Geosci. Remote Sens. Mag. **3**(3), 27–46 (2015)
26. Yuhas, R.H., Goetz, A.F.H., Boardman, J.W.: Discrimination among semi-arid landscape endmembers using the spectral angle mapper (SAM) algorithm. In: JPL, Summaries of the Third Annual JPL Airborne Geoscience Workshop, vol. 1. AVIRIS Workshop (1992)
27. Wald, L.: Data Fusion: Definitions and Architectures: Fusion of Images of Different Spatial Resolutions. Presses des MINES (2002)
28. Wang, Z., Bovik, A.C., Sheikh, H.R., et al.: Image quality assessment: from error visibility to structural similarity. IEEE Trans. Image Process. **13**(4), 600–612 (2004)
29. Jiang, J., Sun, H., Liu, X., et al.: Learning spatial-spectral prior for super-resolution of hyperspectral imagery. IEEE Trans. Comput. Imaging **6**, 1082–1096 (2020)
30. Zhang, M., Zhang, C., Zhang, Q., et al.: Essaformer: efficient transformer for hyperspectral image super-resolution. Proceedings of the IEEE/CVF International Conference on Computer Vision, pp. 23073–23084 (2023)
31. Li, Q., Wang, Q., Li, X.: Mixed 2D/3D convolutional network for hyperspectral image super-resolution. Remote sensing **12**(10), 1660 (2020)

Gradient-Based Multi-focus Image Fusion with Focus-Aware Saliency Enhancement

Haoyu Li and Xiaosong Li[✉]

School of Physics and Optoelectronic Engineering, Foshan University, Foshan 528225, China
lixiaosong@buaa.edu.cn

Abstract. Multi-focus image fusion (MFIF) aims to yield an all-focused image from multiple partially focused inputs, which is crucial in applications cover surveillance, microscopy, and computational photography. However, existing methods struggle to preserve sharp focus-defocus boundaries, often resulting in blurred transitions and focused details loss. To solve this problem, we propose a MFIF method based on significant boundary enhancement, which generates high-quality fused boundaries while effectively detecting focus information. Particularly, we propose a gradient-domain-based model that can obtain initial fusion results with complete boundaries and effectively preserve the boundary details. Additionally, we introduce Tenengrad gradient detection to extract salient features from both the source images and the initial fused image, generating the corresponding saliency maps. For boundary refinement, we develop a focus metric based on gradient and complementary information, integrating the salient features with the complementary information across images to emphasize focused regions and produce a high-quality initial decision result. Extensive experiments on four public datasets demonstrate that our method consistently outperforms 12 state-of-the-art methods in both subjective and objective evaluations. The source code is available at https://github.com/Lihyua/GICI.

Keywords: Multi-focus image fusion · boundary preservation · focus detection · focus decision map

1 Introduction

Depth of field [1] significantly influences the range of clear imaging achievable by an optical system and reflects the overall imaging capability of that system. Due to the limited depth of field of a camera, only part of the scene is in focus while the rest of the scene appears blurred, which may hinder the complete presentation of useful information in the scene. The MFIF technology effectively solves this problem. This technique can synthesize images from different sources into one image of the same scene to produce a clear fused image. Currently, MFIF techniques can be broadly categorized into deep learning-based methods and traditional methods. Among them, deep learning-based methods mainly include classification and regression models, while traditional methods can be categorized into spatial domain methods, transform domain methods, and methods combining transform and spatial domains.

Z. Lin et al. (Eds.): ICIG 2025, LNCS 16161, pp. 403–416, 2026.
https://doi.org/10.1007/978-981-95-3398-5_33

Liu et al. [2] introduce deep learning into MFIF by learning a convolutional neural network model (CNN) to generate fusion rules and activity level measurements, strengthening their correlation and avoiding traditional manual design issues. Subsequently, deep learning models like CNN, Generative Adversarial Network model (GAN) and Self-Attention Mechanism model have been effectively applied in the domain of MFIF, yielding impressive results. In the classification model-based methods, Xiao et al. [3] used multi-scale features and attention mechanism to achieve accuracy for boundary segmentation, and proposed a global feature coding U-Net, which can obtain global semantic and boundary information more accurately. In contrast, among the based regression models, Zhu et al. [4] throwed in a generalized model built upon expert mixtures - task-customized adapter mixing, which can be utilized across a wide range of fusion tasks by adding only 2.8% of learnable parameters.

Traditional methods still hold considerable importance in the domain of MFIF. Among these, spatial domain-based methods directly process and fuse images in the spatial domain, obtaining features from the original images to assess activity levels, which are then used in fusion rules to combine the images based on the detected activity. For instance, You et al. [5] introduced a pixel-level fusion method called LSDGF1, which operates on the principle that clear pixels typically have a higher local variance, resulting in a higher local standard deviation. Unlike spatial domain methods, transform domain methods approaches involve three steps: image transformation, coefficient fusion and inverse transformation. Burt PJ et al. [6] applied the Laplacian pyramid in the MFIF field by using a Gaussian basis function as the pattern element, ensuring efficient and accurate transformations. Although transform domain methods better preserve image details, the conversion process is time-consuming and prone to errors, often resulting in artifacts and blurring.

Lately, significant advancements in MFIF have produce high-quality fused images, yet inherent issue cover blurred boundaries and loss of details remain. In response, we propose a MFIF method based on significant boundary enhancement. First, an initial fusion image is obtained, the saliency map is generated from both the initial fusion and the source image using Tenengrad [7] gradient saliency detection. Subsequently, we introduce a focus detection scheme based on gradient information and complementary information (GICI) to enhance the focus areas, and finally compares it with the saliency map of the initial fused image to obtain the initial decision map, and obtains the final fused image through post-processing methods. Comprehensive experimental results show that our method surpasses existing techniques, generating fused images with enhanced edge information and successfully mitigating problems like boundary detail loss and edge blurring. The key contributions of this work are as follows:

- We propose a MFIF method based on significant boundary enhancement to effectively solve blurring and detail loss at both focused and unfocused edges.
- We develop a novel focus detection scheme, which accurately distinguishes pixel focus attributes through gradient and complementary information, ensuring clear details retention in the fused image.
- We introduce a high-quality initial decision maps acquisition strategy via comparing the salient image of the enhanced source images, effectively preserves the details and edges of the source images.

The paper is organized as follows: Sect. 2 details the proposed method; Sect. 3 describes the experiments and discussion; Finally, Sect. 4 concludes the study.

2 Methodology

Figure 1 illustrates the proposed MFIF method, which is divided into two stages: (1) enhancement of the saliency map and acquisition of the initial decision map, and (2) optimization of the initial decision map and acquisition of the fused image. The following sections provide a detailed introduction and comprehensive analysis of each component of the model.

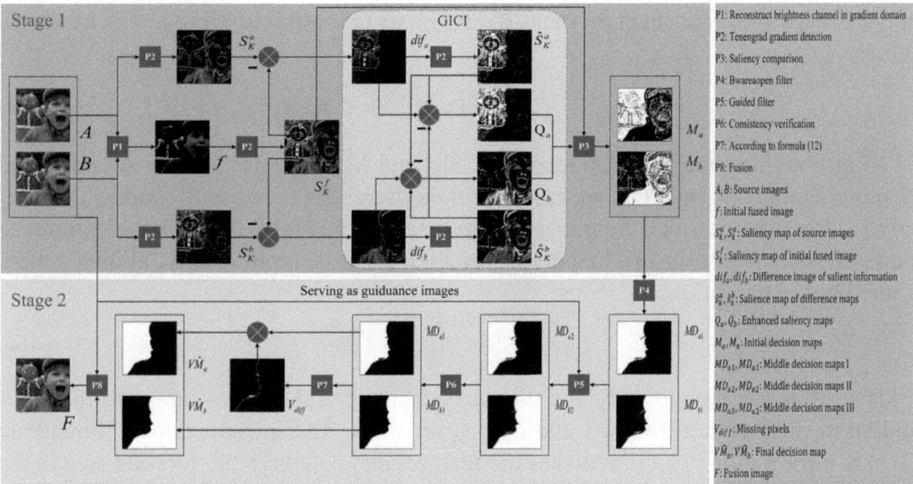

Fig. 1. Framework of the proposed MFIF algorithm

2.1 Acquisition of the Initial Decision Map

To address the issue of unclear edge detection in spatial domain methods, we propose an algorithm based on saliency information enhancement, which processes the saliency map of the input image to obtain a more accurate decision map. In transform domain methods, we find that gradient-based fusion methods are particularly effective in preserving the details of the source image. Therefore, we adopt the approach proposed by Paul S. et al. [8] to obtain the initial fused image f, which serves as a foundation for significant information enhancement. In this method, we focus exclusively on brightness fusion, as the brightness channel contains the primary structural details of the original image. This reduces the computational burden and improves efficiency.

Typically, the gradient of the source image brightness channel can be obtained as:

$$\Phi_\alpha^x(x, y) = \alpha(x + 1, y) - \alpha(x, y) \tag{1}$$

$$\Phi_{\alpha}^{y}(x, y) = \alpha(x, y+1) - \alpha(x, y) \tag{2}$$

For ease of discussion, we set the number of input images to 2. The extension to cases with multiple input images can be easily derived based on the two-image input formulation. Let $\alpha = A$ or B denote the input source images A and B, respectively. $\Phi_{n}^{x}(x, y)$ and $\Phi_{n}^{y}(x, y)$ are the gradient components of the image in the x and y directions, while (x, y) represents the pixel location in the image. Therefore, according to the method of Paul S. et al., we obtain the initial fusion image f.

According to the evaluation by Huang et al. [7], the Tenengrad detection method is highly sensitive to pixel variations, yielding clear and precise edge detection results. Therefore, we select the Tenengrad Gradient detection to perform significance measurements. This approach extracts gradient and edge details from the image, generating the saliency maps for input images A and B, as well as the initial fused image f, as shown below:

$$S_{K}^{\beta}(x, y) = \sum_{x=2}^{M-1} \sum_{y=2}^{N-1} |\nabla\theta(x, y)|^2 \ \theta \in A, B, f \ \beta \in a, b, f \tag{3}$$

After obtaining the saliency maps S_{K}^{a}, S_{K}^{b}, and S_{K}^{f} for input images A and B and the initial composite image f, we calculate the differences between S_{K}^{f} and S_{K}^{a}, and S_{K}^{f} and S_{K}^{b}, respectively. Since the initial composite image f is fully focused, this difference operation accentuates the original defocused regions in the input images, allowing them to stand out in the difference maps:

$$dif_{i} = S_{K}^{f} - S_{K}^{i} \ i \in a, b \tag{4}$$

The difference images dif_a and dif_b are generated and used as inputs to the GICI module to differentiate focused and defocused areas. The introduction of Tenengrad saliency information detection makes the features and details of the focused area in the saliency map richer, while reducing the features and details of the defocused area:

$$\hat{S}_{K}^{i} = \sum_{x=2}^{M-1} \sum_{y=2}^{N-1} |\nabla dif_{i}(x, y)|^2 \ i \in a, b \tag{5}$$

We obtain the saliency maps $\hat{S}_{K}^{a}$ and $\hat{S}_{K}^{b}$ from the difference images. Compared to directly extracting saliency maps from the source images, $\hat{S}_{K}^{a}$ and $\hat{S}_{K}^{b}$ provide a clearer distinction between defocused and focused areas, along with smoother boundaries. However, small alternating regions of focus and defocus near edges can result in unclear boundaries. To address this, we propose leveraging complementary information between images by combining saliency maps S_{K}^{a} and S_{K}^{b} with $\hat{S}_{K}^{a}$ and $\hat{S}_{K}^{b}$ from the difference images:

$$Q_{a} = S_{K}^{a} + \hat{S}_{K}^{a} - \hat{S}_{K}^{b} \times k \tag{6}$$

$$Q_{b} = S_{K}^{b} + \hat{S}_{K}^{b} - \hat{S}_{K}^{a} \times k \tag{7}$$

Among them, k serves to determine the extent of $\hat{S}_{K}^{b}$ or $\hat{S}_{K}^{a}$ to be subtracted, and k is set to 0.5 through parameter analysis. Through the above operation, the saliency map of the input image is enhanced in the focus area, and the initial fusion image obtained through the gradient domain can retain more details at the boundary and reduce the introduction of error information. Therefore, we choose f and the enhanced saliency maps Q_a and Q_b to obtain an initial decision map that has clearer edge details and retains richer edge details:

$$M_a(x, y) = \begin{cases} 1 & \text{if } Q_a(x, y) \geq S_K^f(x, y) \\ 0 & \text{otherwise} \end{cases} \tag{8}$$

2.2 Optimization and Acquisition of the Fused Image

To address potential errors that may occur during the initial decision map acquisition process, we employ the adaptive threshold "bwareaopen" filling filter to refine the initial decision map and rectify inaccurate pixels:

$$\widehat{M_a} = \text{bwareaopen}(M_a, t) \tag{9}$$

The filling filter eliminates all small areas smaller than t pixels in the initial decision map. However, if the size of t is set directly, the advantages of "bwareaopen" cannot be used due to the diversity of source image sizes. Therefore, to implement an adaptive threshold for t and maximize the advantages of "bwareaopen", we define the threshold t as $t = th \times S$, S is the size of the input image, and th is selected as 0.02 through multiple parameter experiments.

To preserve edge information, we introduce Guided Filtering:

$$FM_i = GF(\eta, \widehat{M_i}, r, \varepsilon) \; \eta \in A, B \tag{10}$$

where r and ε set to 5 and 0.3, respectively. To address the error information that may be introduced by Guided Filtering, we apply consistency verification to smooth and naturalize the decision map edges:

$$VM_i = \begin{cases} 1 & \text{if } \sum_{(x,y) \in \varphi} FM_i(x + a, y + b) \geq \frac{\varphi}{2} \\ 1 & \text{otherwise} \end{cases} \tag{11}$$

where $\varphi = q \times S, q = 5 \times 10^{-5}$. However, performing separate consistency verifications on the decision maps can lead to some pixels remaining unclassified in the focus-defocus boundary areas of the binary image. Therefore, we first find the pixels whose pixel value is 0 and whose focus attribute cannot be determined, and assign a value to this part:

$$V_{\text{diff}}(x, y) = \begin{cases} 1 & \text{if } VM_a(x, y) = VM_b(x, y) = 0 \\ 0 & \text{otherwise} \end{cases} \tag{12}$$

$$V\hat{M}_a(x, y) = \begin{cases} 0 & \text{if } V_{\text{diff}}(x, y) = 1 \\ VM_a(x, y) & \text{otherwise} \end{cases} \tag{13}$$

$$V\hat{M}_b(x, y) = \begin{cases} 1 & \text{if } V_{\text{diff}}(x, y) = 1 \\ VM_b(x, y) & \text{otherwise} \end{cases} \tag{14}$$

Then the final decision graphs $\widehat{VM}_a$ and $\widehat{VM}_b$ are obtained, ensuring that the addition of the two decision graphs is a binary graph with a value of all 1 and a size of S. This final decision map enhances the source image features, preserves edge details, and minimizes the introduction of error information.

The fused image is then generated from the final decision maps $\widehat{VM}_a$ and $\widehat{VM}_b$:

$$F(x, y) = \widehat{VM}_a(x, y) \times A(x, y) + \widehat{VM}_b(x, y) \times B(x, y) \tag{15}$$

3   Experiment

3.1   Experimental Settings

We validate our method on four publicly available MFIF datasets: the Lytro dataset [9], the MFFW dataset [10], the MFI-WHU dataset [11] and the GrayScale dataset [12]. For our experiments, we selected a representative image pair from Lytro dataset—"lytro-01"—for qualitative and quantitative analysis. Additionally, quantitative comparisons were conducted across all four public datasets.

To assess the usefulness of the proposed framework, we provide comparisons with 12 advanced methods. These methods encompass spatial domain methods: INS [13], IFD [14],MFIF-MMIF [15] and RDMF [16]; transform domain method: SAMF [17]; based on empty Methods that combine the inter-domain and transform domains: SIGPRO [18]; and deep learning methods: PMGI [19], MFIF-GAN [20], U2Fusion [21], MUFusion [22], SDNet [23] and MFEIF [24]. In this paper, VIF [25], $Q^{AB/F}$ [26], SF [26], NMI [27], Q_Y [28], and Q_{CB} [29] metrics are selected for comparative analysis to objectively evaluate the fusion results. In the experiments, red indicates first place, green indicates second, and blue indicates third.

3.2   Qualitative Comparisons

Due to the space limitations, we only present qualitative comparison using the Lytro dataset.

As shown in Fig. 2, it is evident that methods such as PMGI, INS, MUFusion, SDNet, MFEIF, and IFD retain significant residual information in the out-of-focus areas, suggesting their inability to accurately delineate focus regions and leading to detail loss along image edges. Furthermore, the difference maps reveal that MUFusion and MFEIF produce excessively bright outputs with lingering background textures, and IFD suffers from noise that blurs pseudo-color map details. These observations highlight that these methods struggle to precisely identify focus areas and maintain accurate edge representation.

In comparison, the fusion results of the SIGPRO, MFIF-GAN, U2Fusion, SAMF, RDMF and MFIF-MMIF methods show improved edge representation, but some issues persist. Due to improper processing of edge information, some artifacts and burrs appear on the edge of the club in the red frames of the SIGPRO and SAMF pseudo-color images. In the U2Fusion, RDMF and MFIF-MMIF pseudo-color images, misjudgment between the defocused area and the focus area results in the missing edges around the arm or the boundary is not obvious. Among all methods, the fused images produced by MFIF-GAN and the proposed method show superior visual quality, preserving smooth and clear boundaries. As depicted in Fig. 3, our method ranks in the top second across six metrics—achieving the highest score in four—demonstrating its advantage in accurately preserving focus-defocus boundaries and reliably identifying focus regions compared to 12 state-of-the-art techniques.

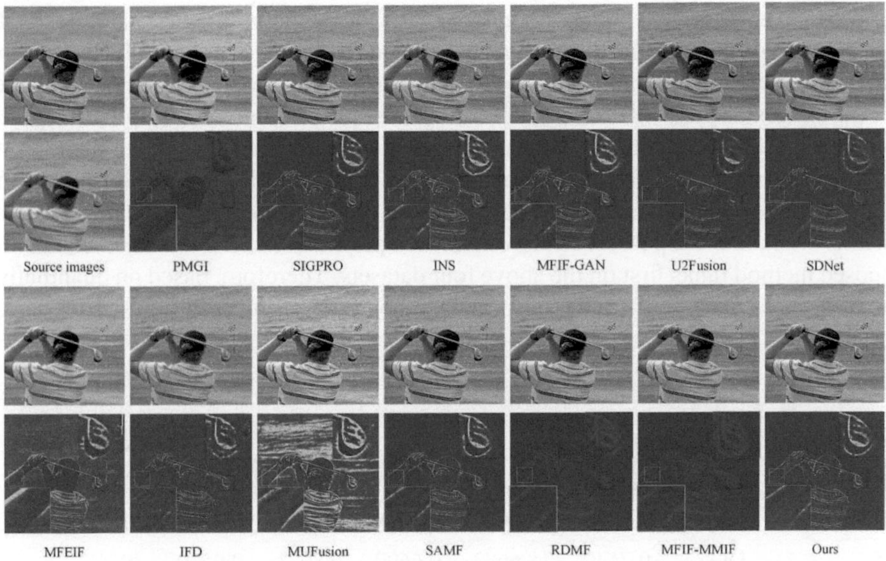

Fig. 2. The different fused images of the test image "lytro-01"

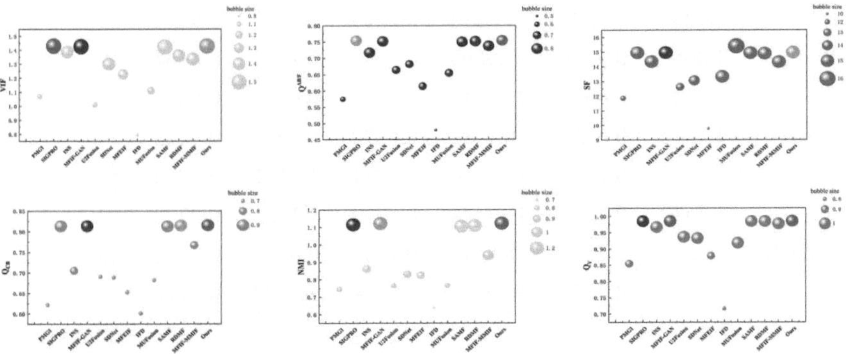

Fig. 3. Quantitative analysis of the fusion method for the source image "lytro-01" (where the bubble size q represents the range of the metric within range $(q - 0.1) \sim q$, and specifically for the SF, within range $(q - 1) \sim q$.)

3.3 Quantitative Comparisons

Tables 1, 2, 3 and 4 show quantitative comparisons of the methods presented in this paper with 12 other SOTA methods in the four datasets, respectively. In the Lytro dataset, all metrics of the proposed method ranked in the top two, with the highest scores in VIF and QCB metrics. Even if the source image of the MFFW dataset has a boundary DSE, our method can still handle the boundary problem better and obtain clear and accurate boundaries. All indicators of the proposed method are in the top three. The images in the MFI-WHU dataset have complex boundaries, and the proposed method can effectively extract boundary information, so it always ranks in the top two in the indicators. In the GrayScale dataset, even if affected by grayscale images, the proposed method can better express images in the MFI-WHU dataset have complex boundaries, and the proposed method can effectively extract boundary information, so it always ranks in the top two in the indicators. In the GrayScale dataset, even if affected by grayscale images, the proposed method can better express boundaries. Except for the NMI indicator, all other indicators rank in the top three. And from the comprehensive score of the indicators, the proposed method ranks first on the above four datasets. Therefore, based on quantitative evaluation, we concluded that the overview method outperforms other SOTA methods.

Table 1. Objective performance of different fusion methods on Lytro dataset

Method	VIF	$Q^{AB/F}$	SF	Q_{CB}	NMI	Q_Y	Score	Rank
PMGI	0.9634	0.5058	12.1405	0.5873	0.8001	0.8098	12	13
SIGPRO	**1.3633**	**0.7530**	19.4040	**0.8018**	**1.1261**	**0.9793**	67	3
INS	1.1477	0.7140	18.6682	0.6690	0.8931	0.9510	39	7
MFIF-GAN	1.3630	**0.7529**	**19.4271**	**0.8005**	**1.1313**	**0.9797**	68	2
U2Fusion	1.0248	0.6337	15.3529	0.6462	0.7891	0.8855	18	12
SDNet	1.1241	0.6803	17.8238	0.6519	0.8520	0.9076	31	9
MFEIF	1.0655	0.5779	11.9865	0.6096	0.8549	0.8304	19	11
IFD	1.0341	0.6356	**21.8814**	0.5767	0.6816	0.6871	23	10
MUFusion	1.1504	0.6624	18.9482	0.6770	0.7983	0.9068	34	8
SAMF	1.3575	0.7511	19.3820	0.7951	1.1191	0.9770	54	5
RDMF	**1.3679**	0.7518	19.3444	0.8010	1.1221	0.9790	62	4
MFIF-MMIF	1.2576	0.7318	18.5671	0.7338	0.9329	0.9632	45	6
Ours	**1.3644**	**0.7531**	**19.4306**	**0.8024**	**1.1292**	**0.9796**	74	1

Table 2. Objective performance of different fusion methods on MFFW dataset

Method	VIF	$Q^{AB/F}$	SF	Q_{CB}	NMI	Q_Y	Score	Rank
PMGI	0.8142	0.4698	13.8816	0.5262	0.7267	0.7097	10	13

(*continued*)

Table 2. (*continued*)

Method	VIF	$Q^{AB/F}$	SF	Q_{CB}	NMI	Q_Y	Score	Rank
SIGPRO	0.9732	**0.6360**	**22.6809**	0.6867	**0.7749**	**0.8540**	**68**	**2**
INS	0.85942	0.6069	21.6675	0.5993	0.7559	0.8340	43	6
MFIF-GAN	**0.9776**	**0.6306**	22.4090	**0.6884**	0.7735	**0.8512**	65	3
U2Fusion	0.7953	0.5461	16.5798	0.5786	0.7187	0.7577	19	11
SDNet	0.8578	0.5765	21.7309	0.5776	0.7478	0.7883	34	9
MFEIF	0.9285	0.5540	13.5768	0.5753	**0.8132**	0.8016	35	8
IFD	0.6902	0.4671	19.6419	0.5316	0.6104	0.6067	12	12
MUFusion	0.8537	0.5596	20.1091	0.6087	0.7199	0.7887	30	10
SAMF	0.9512	0.6292	**22.6846**	0.6693	0.7368	0.8125	51	5
RDMF	**0.9837**	0.6296	22.145	**0.6908**	0.7665	0.8499	64	4
MFIF-MMIF	0.9064	0.6219	21.3722	0.6375	0.7473	0.8327	43	6
Ours	**0.9752**	**0.6361**	**22.8127**	**0.6888**	**0.7742**	**0.8528**	**72**	**1**

Based on the scores and rankings in Tables 1, 2, 3 and 4, our method achieved the highest overall scores in all four public datasets, and performed particularly well in the Lytro and MFI-WHU datasets. To sum up, our method exhibits the highest fusion performance compared to the 12 state-of-the-art methods (Fig. 4).

Table 3. Objective performance of different fusion methods on MFI-WHU dataset

Method	VIF	$Q^{AB/F}$	SF	Q_{CB}	NMI	Q_Y	Score	Rank
PMGI	0.9733	0.5080	17.0356	0.6163	0.7552	0.7959	15	12
SIGPRO	**1.3808**	0.7280	**26.7604**	0.8222	**1.1845**	0.9835	**63**	**3**
INS	1.3274	0.7230	26.6967	0.7786	1.0381	0.9739	49	6
MFIF-GAN	1.3786	**0.7327**	**26.8503**	**0.8227**	1.1841	**0.9847**	67	2
U2Fusion	0.9622	0.5729	18.9410	0.6240	0.7079	0.8652	18	11
SDNet	1.2428	0.6856	26.2088	0.7196	0.8816	0.9448	37	8
MFEIF	1.1031	0.5662	15.6286	0.6846	0.8501	0.848	22	10
IFD	0.7830	0.4760	24.5354	0.6045	0.6179	0.6725	10	13
MUFusion	1.0656	0.5996	22.5857	0.6473	0.7287	0.8737	25	9
SAMF	1.3775	0.7263	26.6674	0.8203	**1.1883**	**0.9849**	62	4
RDMF	**1.3837**	**0.7289**	26.5912	**0..8236**	1.1743	0.9828	62	4
MFIF-MMIF	1.3174	0.7173	25.8464	0.7915	1.0381	0.9706	42	7
Ours	**1.3848**	**0.7330**	**26.7834**	**0.8253**	**1.1850**	**0.9848**	**74**	**1**

Table 4. Objective performance of different fusion methods on GrayScale dataset

Method	VIF	$Q^{AB/F}$	SF	Q_{CB}	NMI	Q_Y	Score	Rank
PMGI	0.9032	0.5334	16.6665	0.5774	0.7498	0.7535	12	12
SIGPRO	1.0657	0.5195	17.3427	0.6616	**0.9692**	**0.8879**	47	6
INS	1.0004	0.6306	22.2542	0.6521	0.8183	0.8679	40	8
MFIF-GAN	**1.0997**	**0.6424**	**22.5395**	**0.7077**	**0.8809**	0.8814	**68**	**2**
U2Fusion	0.8767	0.5559	16.6350	0.6130	0.7238	0.7810	12	12
SDNet	0.9535	0.5792	**23.3981**	0.6270	0.7657	0.8232	36	9
MFEIF	0.9673	0.5556	13.9899	0.6153	0.8215	0.8193	22	11
IFD	1.0341	0.6356	21.8814	0.6742	0.8237	0.8693	48	5
MUFusion	0.9965	0.5777	20.3517	0.6212	0.7289	0.8014	24	10
SAMF	1.077	0.6382	22.4320	0.7022	0.8649	0.8764	58	4
RDMF	**1.1011**	**0.6413**	22.4109	**0.7061**	**0.8816**	**0.8853**	67	3
MFIF-MMIF	1.0149	0.6301	21.4024	0.6675	0.7867	0.8706	41	7
Ours	**1.1010**	**0.6446**	**22.5101**	**0.7167**	<u>0.8804</u>	**0.8870**	71	1

3.4 Parameter Analysis

This section mainly assesses the influence of the parameter th in the adaptive threshold "bwareaopen" filling filter in Eq. (9) and the parameter k in Eq. (6) on the fusion results. To assess the influence of the parameter th on fusion performance, we fixed k at 0.5 and then examined the effect of varying th. The fusion outcomes were quantitatively evaluated using the Q_Y, VIF, and Q_{CB} metrics. The average scores of different th values in the data set Lytro are shown in Fig. 5. When $th = 0.02$, a significant improvement is observed in the overall fusion performance, so based on comprehensive analysis, we set the parameter $th = 0.02$. After setting parameter $th = 0.02$, we analyze the impact of parameter k on fusion performance. To more intuitively observe the impact of parameters on the fusion results, we use the input image pair "lytro-01" in the Lytro data set as the t experimental image to assess the impact of different parameters k on the final decision map, as shown in Fig. 6. In Fig. 6, it can be found that when k is greater than 0, the edge of the final decision is more accurate, so introducing parameter k is effective. When $k = 0.5$, some small structures on the edge almost completely disappear and edge information is retained. Comprehensive analysis of objective evaluation and subjective vision shows that when $k = 0.5$ it has good fusion performance, so the parameter k is set 0.5. Therefore, we set the two key parameters th and k to 0.02 and 0.5 respectively.

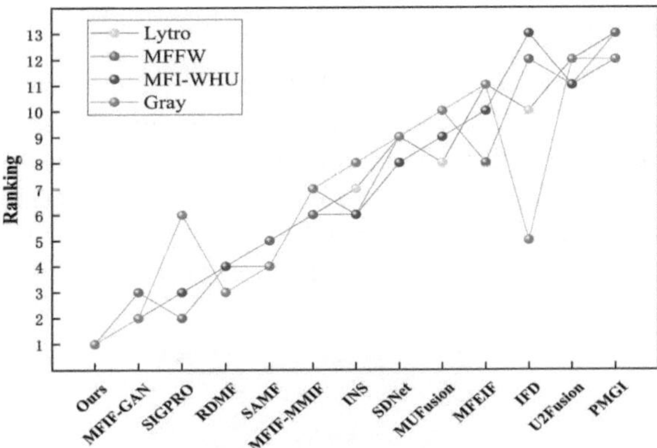

Fig. 4. Ranking of the 12 MFIF methods and the proposed method on the four datasets and the overall ranking (The proposed method ranking first.)

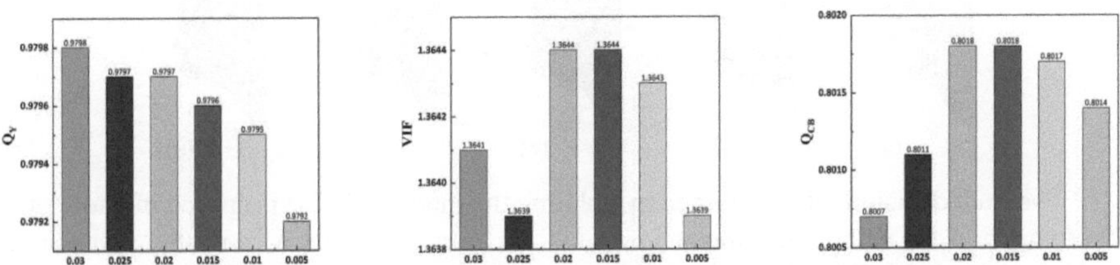

Fig. 5. Effect of parameter th on the fusion performance of the proposed method on the Lytro dataset. The index of the horizontal axis indicates the value of the parameter *th*.

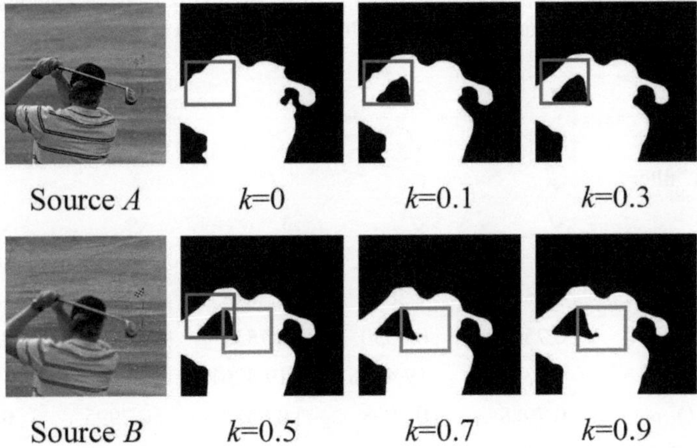

Fig. 6. Obtain the final decision maps with different parameters *k* in source images A, B.

3.5　Ablation Experiments

In the ablation studies, we conducted on the Lytro dataset to evaluate the impact of four key components: the edge enhancement strategy of the initial fused image, the adaptive threshold "bwareaopen" filling filter, guided filtering, and consistency verification. During testing, all settings were kept consistent across modules, except for the specific ablation module under evaluation. The experiments reveal the crucial importance of the proposed salient information enhancement and the employed post-processing strategies.

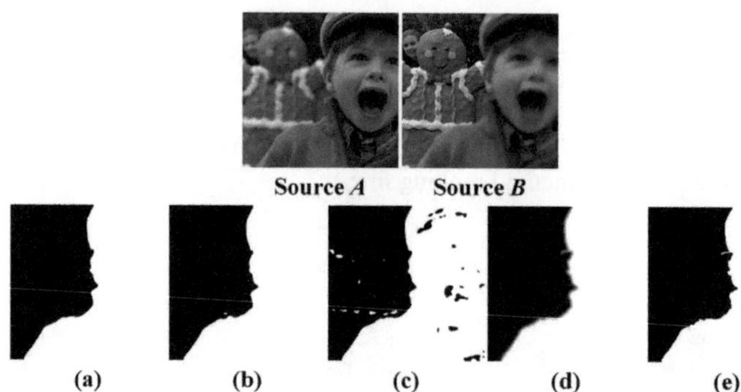

Fig. 7. The final decision maps obtained by ablating the modules in the proposed method. (a) the proposed method, (b) without significant information enhancement, (c) without the "bwareaopen" filter, (d) without guided filtering, (e) without consistency verification.

Table 5. Mean metric results of ablation experiments on the Lytro dataset. "\" indicates that the component was not used, and an "$\sqrt{}$" indicates that the component is used.

Index		1	2	3	4	5(Ours)
initial fusion image		\	$\sqrt{}$	$\sqrt{}$	$\sqrt{}$	$\sqrt{}$
"bwareaopen" filters		$\sqrt{}$	\	$\sqrt{}$	$\sqrt{}$	$\sqrt{}$
guided filters		$\sqrt{}$	$\sqrt{}$	\	$\sqrt{}$	$\sqrt{}$
consistency verification		$\sqrt{}$	$\sqrt{}$	$\sqrt{}$	\	$\sqrt{}$
metric	VIF	1.3541	1.3628	**1.3648**	1.3620	**1.3644**
	$Q^{AB/F}$	0.7509	0.7530	**0.7531**	0.7520	**0.7531**
	SF	19.3333	**19.4366**	19.4261	19.2639	**19.4306**
	Q_{CB}	0.7988	0.7998	**0.8012**	0.7995	**0.8018**
	NMI	**1.1299**	1.1290	**1.1299**	1.1125	**1.1303**
	Q_Y	**0.9800**	0.9785	0.9794	0.9789	**0.9797**

First, the saliency map of one input image is used in Eq. (5) instead of the initial fused image to enhance the saliency map of another input image. Second, we sequentially remove the adaptive thresholding "bwareaopen" filler filter, bootstrap filtering, and consistency validation, and verify its effectiveness. Table 5 presents the objective evaluation results of ablation experiments for each model on the Lytro dataset, demonstrating that the putted forward method outperforms all others across all metrics. To better illustrate the impact of each module on fusion performance, we use the input image pair "lytro-03" from the Lytro dataset to analyze the effect of different modules on the final decision map, as shown in Fig. 7. In Fig. 7, boundary issues are visible in decision maps (b)-(e). In contrast, decision map (a), generated by the proposed method, avoids these issues and achieves smooth, clear boundaries. In summary, any substitution or omission of parts results in block effects, blurring, and reduced overall fusion performance in the final decision map. These findings confirm that each component in the putted forward method is effective and significantly enhances fusion quality and performance.

4 Conclusions

This paper proposed in a MFIF method based on gradient detection and saliency enhancement. To obtain complete and clear focused edge information, we design a strategy based on salient edge enhancement. And we obtain an initial decision map with more accurate edges through the GICI module. We used six commonly used metrics to conduct qualitative and quantitative analysis in four datasets, and compared them with 12 SOTA methods. Experimental results shows that our method has obvious advantages in both subjective and objective evaluations, and the fusion result can better retain edge details and effectively solve the problem of boundary troubles.

Acknowledgement. This research was supported by the National Natural Science Foundation of China (No. 62201149), and the Natural Science Foundation of Guangdong Province (No. 2024A1515011880).

References

1. Wang, W., Chang, F.: A multi-focus image fusion method based on laplacian pyramid. J. Comput. **6**(12), 2559–2566 (2011)
2. Liu, Y., Chen, X., Peng, H., et al.: Multi-focus image fusion with a deep convolutional neural network. Inf. Fusion **36**, 191–207 (2017)
3. Xiao, B., Xu, B., Bi, X., et al.: Global-feature encoding U-Net (GEU-Net) for multi-focus image fusion. IEEE Trans. Image Process. **30**, 163–175 (2020)
4. Zhu, P., Sun, Y., Cao, B., et al.: Task-customized mixture of adapters for general image fusion. arXiv preprint arXiv:2403.12494 (2024)
5. You, C.S., Yang, S.Y.: A simple and effective multi-focus image fusion method based on local standard deviations enhanced by the guided filter. Displays **72**, 102146 (2022)
6. Burt, P.J., Adelson, E.H.: Merging images through pattern decomposition. In: Applications of Digital Image Processing VIII. SPIE, vol. 575, pp. 173–181 (1985)
7. Huang, W., Jing, Z.: Evaluation of focus measures in multi-focus image fusion. Pattern Recogn. Lett. **28**(4), 493–500 (2007)
8. Paul, S., Sevcenco, I.S., Agathoklis, P.: Multi-exposure and multi-focus image fusion in gradient domain. J. Circuits Syst. Comput. **25**(10), 1650123 (2016)

9. Nejati, M., Samavi, S., Shirani, S.: Multi-focus image fusion using dictionary-based sparse representation. Inf. Fusion **25**, 72–84 (2015)

10. Xu, S., Wei, X., Zhang, C., et al.: MFFW: a new dataset for multi-focus image fusion. arXiv: 2002.04780 (2020)

11. Zhang, H., Le, Z., Shao, Z., et al.: MFF-GAN: an unsupervised generative adversarial network with adaptive and gradient joint constraints for multi-focus image fusion. Inf. Fusion **66**, 40–53 (2021)

12. Guo, X., Nie, R., Cao, J., et al.: FuseGAN: learning to fuse multi-focus image via conditional generative adversarial network. IEEE Trans. Multimedia **21**(8), 1982–1996 (2019)

13. Li, X., Zhou, F., Tan, H., et al.: Multimodal medical image fusion based on joint bilateral filter and local gradient energy. Inf. Sci. **569**, 302–325 (2021)

14. Li, X., Zhou, F., Tan, H.: Joint image fusion and denoising via three-layer decomposition and sparse representation. Knowl.-Based Syst. **224**, 107087 (2021)

15. Li, X., Li, X., Ye, T., et al.: Bridging the gap between multi-focus and multi-modal: a focused integration framework for multi-modal image fusion. In: Proceedings of the IEEE/CVF Winter Conference on Applications of Computer Vision, pp. 1628–1637 (2024)

16. Yu, W., Nie, Y., Xiong, W.: An adaptive region division multi-focus image fusion algorithm with defocus diffusion mitigation mechanism. In: Proceedings of the 2024 2nd Asia Conference on Computer Vision, Image Processing and Pattern Recognition, pp. 1–6 (2024)

17. Li, X., Li, X., Tan, H., et al.: SAMF: small-area-aware multi-focus image fusion for object detection. In: ICASSP 2024–2024 IEEE International Conference on Acoustics, Speech and Signal Processing (ICASSP), pp. 3845–3849. IEEE (2024)

18. Li, X., Zhou, F., Tan, H., et al.: Multi-focus image fusion based on nonsubsampled contourlet transform and residual removal. Signal Process. **184**, 108062 (2021)

19. Zhang, H., Xu, H., Xiao, Y., et al.: Rethinking the image fusion: a fast unified image fusion network based on proportional maintenance of gradient and intensity. In: Proceedings of the AAAI Conference on Artificial Intelligence, vol. 34, no. 07, pp. 12797–12804 (2020)

20. Wang, Y., Xu, S., Liu, J., et al.: MFIF-GAN: a new generative adversarial network for multi-focus image fusion. Signal Process. Image Commun. **96**, 116295 (2021)

21. Xu, H., Ma, J., Jiang, J., et al.: U2Fusion: a unified unsupervised image fusion network. IEEE Trans. Pattern Anal. Mach. Intell. **44**(1), 502–518 (2020)

22. Cheng, C., Xu, T., Wu, X.J.: MUFusion: a general unsupervised image fusion network based on memory unit. Inf. Fusion **92**, 80–92 (2023)

23. Zhang, H., Ma, J.: SDNet: a versatile squeeze-and-decomposition network for real-time image fusion. Int. J. Comput. Vision **129**(10), 2761–2785 (2021)

24. Liu, J., Fan, X., Jiang, J., et al.: Learning a deep multi-scale feature ensemble and an edge-attention guidance for image fusion. IEEE Trans. Circuits Syst. Video Technol. **32**(1), 105–119 (2021)

25. Sheikh, H.R., Bovik, A.C.: Image information and visual quality. IEEE Trans. Image Process. **15**(2), 430–444 (2006)

26. Balasubramaniam, P., Ananthi, V.P.: Image fusion using intuitionistic fuzzy sets. Inf. Fusion **20**, 21–30 (2014)

27. Hossny, M., Nahavandi, S., Creighton, D.: Comments on Information measure for performance of image fusion' (2008)

28. Li, S., Hong, R., Wu, X.: A novel similarity based quality metric for image fusion. In: 2008 International Conference on Audio, Language and Image Processing, pp. 167–172. IEEE (2008)

29. Chen, Y., Blum, R.S.: A new automated quality assessment algorithm for image fusion. Image Vis. Comput. **27**(10), 1421–1432 (2009)

OME-Net: Optimization-Inspired Multi-domain Enhanced Network for Image Compressed Sensing Reconstruction

Ying Ma and Lijun Zhao[✉] [iD]

Taiyuan University of Science and Technology, Taiyuan 030024, China
`leejun@tyust.edu.cn`

Abstract. Traditional Compressive Sensing (CS) image reconstruction methods suffer from high computational costs and low reconstruction quality, so deep learning models are widely used to achieve non-linear projection for better reconstruction. Recently, CS unfolding networks can combine the advantages of deep learning and traditional optimization methods, but existing methods are still limited by single-domain information flow within unfolding networks, leading to information loss during image-to-image mapping. This paper proposes an Optimization-inspired Multi-domain Enhanced Network (OME-Net) based on multi-domain collaboration and frequency-domain enhancement. At each stage of OME-Net, there are two parts: the gradient descent module and proximal operator. Rather than only adopting pure gradient descent formula, the proposed OME-Net uses multi-domain gradient descent module to synchronously extract multi-domain information for feature complementarity. The proximal operator is approximated by frequency-domain guided multi-resolution reconstruction architecture that enhances features on Fourier domain and fuses features to retain high-frequency details. Experimental results show that the proposed OME-Net significantly outperforms several traditional methods and deep learning methods for image CS reconstruction task.

Keywords: Multi-domain gradient descent · Compressive sensing · Unfolding network · Image reconstruction

1 Introduction

With the rapid development of information technology, the scale of data generation and storage has been increasing exponentially, making efficient compression and high-quality signal recovery to be a critical research topic [1,2]. Compressive Sensing (CS) theory [3] demonstrates that when a signal x is sparse in an appropriate transform domain Ψ, it can be reconstructed using fewer measurements than the ones required by the Nyquist sampling theorem, which has garnered extensive attention in academia. As an inverse problem, CS reconstruction aims to restore x from its compressive sensing measurements $\mathbf{y} = \Phi x$, where Ψ is the measurement matrix. Due to the ill-posed nature of the inverse CS problem, the reconstruction can be formulated as the following optimization problem:

$$\min_{x} \|\Phi x - \mathbf{y}\|_2^2 + \lambda \|\Psi x\|_1 \tag{1}$$

Here, Ψ represents the prior knowledge, and λ is the regularization hyperparameter. Various iterative optimization algorithms often employ the proximal gradient descent method to solve the above problem, and the specific update step can be written as:

$$r^{(k)} = x^{(k-1)} - \rho \Phi^T \left(\Phi x^{(k-1)} - \mathbf{y} \right) \tag{2}$$

$$x^{(k)} = \arg \min_{z} \frac{1}{2} \|z - r^{(k)}\|_2^2 + \lambda \|\Psi z\|_1 \tag{3}$$

where k is the iteration index and ρ is the step size.

To effectively apply CS theory to practical scenarios, researchers have proposed various image reconstruction algorithms [4–10] for ill-posed CS problems. Traditional CS-based reconstruction approaches consist of iterative sparse reconstruction algorithms, matching pursuit methods, and convex optimization techniques. Among these, iterative sparse reconstruction algorithms are widely adopted. For instance, the Iterative Shrinkage Threshold Algorithm (ISTA) [5] achieves low computational complexity through iterative shrinkage threshold operations. Accelerated variants like Fast Iterative Shrinkage Threshold Algorithm (FISTA) with momentum term [5] and Two-step Iterative Shrinkage Thresholding (TwIST) algorithm via two-step iteration [6] can further improve convergence rates and reconstruction accuracy. While these methods effectively utilize image priors to preserve details and edges, they predominantly rely on fixed soft-threshold constraints, which leads to the lack of flexibility and adaptability.

Traditional CS image reconstruction methods face two key limitations: high computational costs from complex iterative algorithms, and the difficulty in meeting high-precision reconstruction requirements. Recent advancements in Deep Learning (DL) offer data-driven solutions. Notable examples include convolutional neural network [11–15], non-local neural networks [16], and denoising autoencoders [17], which leverage large datasets and advanced feature extraction to model real-world signals. Compared to traditional methods, DL-based approaches excel in signal reconstruction, especially in complex high-noise scenarios achieving more efficient and accurate recovery. To leverage DL and traditional CS's complementary strengths [18–20], deep unfolded CS networks [21–23] have been developed for high-quality reconstruction. For example, OPINE-Net [24] learns orthogonal yet binary constraint-based sampling matrices to improve CS reconstruction performance. MADUN [25] reduces information loss via memory modules, while FSOINet [26] enhances reconstruction in feature space. However, most of the existing models suffer from single-domain information flow constraints, limiting multi-domain feature exploitation and causing feature loss during image-to-image mapping.

To this end, we propose an Optimization-inspired Multi-domain Enhanced Network (OME-Net). At each stage of OME-Net, there are two key components: a gradient descent module and a proximal operator. Unlike traditional approaches that rely solely on pure gradient descent, the proposed OME-Net introduces a multi-domain gradient descent module. This module simultaneously extracts and integrates multi-domain information to achieve feature complementarity for CS reconstruction. For the proximal operator, OME-Net employs a frequency-domain guided multi-resolution reconstruction architecture. This architecture approximates the proximal operator by enhancing features in the Fourier domain and dynamically fusing them across resolutions. The rest of this paper is organized as follows. In Sect. 2, we will introduce the proposed method in detail. In Sect. 3, we will provide extensive experimental results. Finally, we will draw conclusions in Sect. 4.

2   The Proposed Method

2.1   Sampling Network

The input image $x \in \mathbb{R}^{H \times W}$ is divided into $\frac{H}{\sqrt{N}} \times \frac{W}{\sqrt{N}}$ non-overlapping image blocks, with each block having a size of $\sqrt{N} \times \sqrt{N}$. Each image block $x \in \mathbb{R}^{N}$ undergoes sparse sampling through spatial convolution with a stride of $\sqrt{N}$:

$$\mathbf{y} = \mathcal{F}_{\Phi}(x) = W_{\Phi} * x \tag{4}$$

Each row of $\Phi \in \mathbb{R}^{M \times N}$ is reshaped into a $1 \times \sqrt{N} \times \sqrt{N}$ convolution kernel W_{Φ}, which is optimized via a kind of end-to-end learning. This design adapts measurement to input content by replacing fixed Gaussian matrices, controlled by the measurement rate $r = \frac{M}{N}$ ($M = \lfloor rN \rfloor$).

2.2   Initial Reconstruction Network

The measurement value restores spatial domain information through pixel-shuffle upsampling f_{ps}, which can be written as:

$$x_{init} = \mathcal{F}_{\Phi^{T}}(\mathbf{y}) = f_{ps}(W_{\Phi^{T}} * \mathbf{y}) \tag{5}$$

This process obtains the initialized CS image served for latter image reconstruction. Based on the initialized CS image x_{init}, the initialized feature $x_f^{(0)}$ is obtained through a convolutional operation $\mathrm{Conv}(\cdot)$, which can be written as:

$$x_f^{(0)} = \mathrm{Conv}(x_{init}) \tag{6}$$

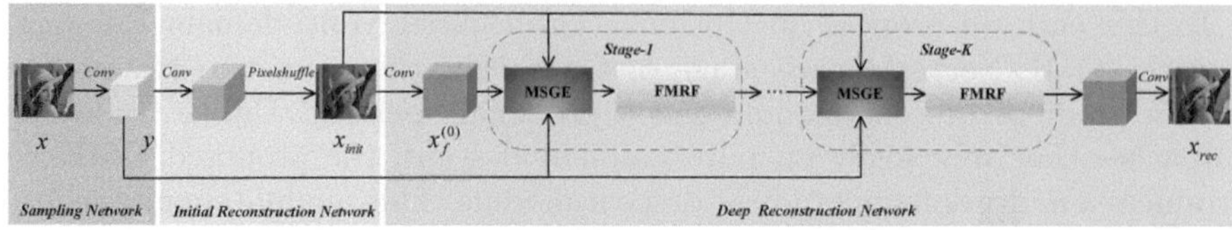

Fig. 1. The diagram of the proposed OME-Net.

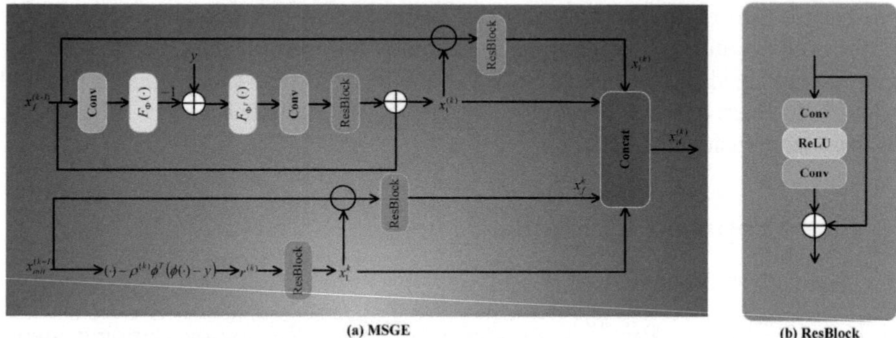

Fig. 2. The diagram of the proposed MSGE (a) and ResBlock (b).

2.3 Deep Reconstruction Network

As shown in Fig. 1, the deep reconstruction network of OME-Net consists of two parts: the Multi-domain Synergy Gradient Enhancement (MSGE) module and the Frequency-domain enhanced Multi-scale Residual Fusion (FMRF) module. Specifically, the MSGE module synchronously extracts the quadruple information from the feature domain, image domain, image residual domain, and feature residual domain. Through cross-domain concatenation, it fuses multi-scale features, compensating for the limitations of single domain information flow. Finally, the FMRF module constructs multi-resolution features through downsampling, and then it adopts a progressive multi-scale fusion strategy and residual connections. As a result, it significantly improves the quality of reconstructed images while maintaining computational efficiency.

MSGE Module. During the gradient update phase, OME-Net innovatively synchronizes feature extraction from the feature domain, image domain, image residual domain, and feature residual domain. As illustrated in Fig. 2, by concatenating features across these domains, the MSGE module achieves multi-domain feature complementarity, enriching the contextual information available for subsequent proximal mapping. This design enables the network to more precisely capture fine details and structural information in the image, thereby boosting CS reconstruction process. The feature domain gradient descent can be written as:

$$p^{(k)} = \Phi^T \left(\Phi x_f^{(k-1)} - \mathbf{y} \right)$$
$$z^{(k)} = \mathcal{F}_g \left(p^{(k)} \right)$$
$$x_t^{(k)} = \text{ResBlock} \left(z^{(k)} \right) + x_f^{(k-1)} \tag{7}$$

Here, $\mathcal{F}_g(\cdot)$ maps the gradient of the data fidelity term to the feature space through convolution. The image domain gradient descent can be written as:

$$r^{(k)} = x_{init}^{(k-1)} - \rho \Phi^T \left(\Phi x_{init}^{(k-1)} - \mathbf{y} \right)$$
$$x_1^{(k)} = \left(\mathcal{F}_i(r^{(k)}) \right) \tag{8}$$

Here, $\mathcal{F}_i$ denotes a functional mapping of ResBlock. The feature domain residual feature extraction can be written as:

$$x_i^{(k)} = x_t^{(k)} - x_f^{(k-1)}$$
$$x_i^{(k)} = \text{ResBlock}(x_i^{(k)}) \tag{9}$$

Here, $x_f^{(k-1)}$ denotes the initial features. The image domain residual feature extraction can be written as:

$$x_f^{(k)} = x_1^{(k)} - x_{init}^{(k-1)}$$
$$x_f^{(k)} = \text{ResBlock}(x_f^{(k)}) \tag{10}$$

Here, x_{init} denotes the initial image signal. Finally, $x_t^{(k)}$, $x_1^{(k)}$, $x_i^{(k)}$ and $x_f^{(k)}$ are concatenated together along the channel dimension, forming $x_A^{(k)}$ with rich cross-domain information, which can be written as:

$$x_A^{(k)} = \text{Concat}(x_t^{(k)}, x_1^{(k)}, x_i^{(k)}, x_f^{(k)}) \in \mathbb{R}^{B \times 2(C+1) \times H \times W} \tag{11}$$

This fusion enables the network to capture comprehensive image characteristics and differential information across domains, enhancing image reconstruction quality and network capacity.

FMRF Module. As shown in Fig. 3, the FMRF module is a core component of OME-Net, designed to achieve more efficient multi-resolution reconstruction guided by frequency-domain information. Firstly, the input features generate multi-resolution feature maps through three downsampling convolution and ResBlocks after one convolution operation to produce 1/2, 1/4, and 1/8 resolution branches. In the lowest resolution (1/8) branch, a Frequency-Domain Cross-Attention (FDCA) module is embedded into FMRF module, as shown in Fig. 4, which adaptively modulates frequency-domain information. Specifically, after the input features generate frequency-domain components via 1*1 convolutions and

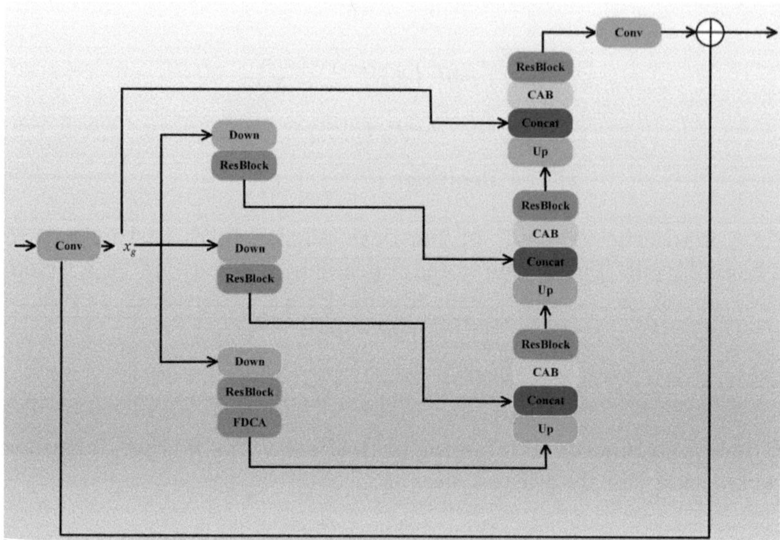

Fig. 3. The diagram of the proposed FMRF.

grouped convolutions, a frequency-domain cross-attention mechanism is used for fusion. Finally, spatial features are reconstructed via inverse Fourier transform and added to the initial low-resolution features as residuals, forming frequency-domain enhanced latent representations.

During the upsampling process, each level of feature maps is first restored to the previous level's resolution via bilinear interpolation, then concatenated with the corresponding branch's feature maps along the channel dimension. For example, at the 1/4 resolution level, the frequency-domain-enhanced 1/8 resolution features are upsampled and added in an element-wise manner to the original 1/4 resolution features to form the fused features containing multi-scale information. Then, the concatenated features are dynamically corrected by a channel attention block, which captures channel importance weights via global average pooling. Finally, the residual connection is used. After the reconstruction result is processed by one convolutional layer, it is fused with the coarse reconstruction result generated from the initial measurement values. This retains low-frequency background information while mitigating the deficiencies of traditional linear reconstruction through high-frequency details introduced by FMRF module.

2.4   Loss Function

For the original image x, the proposed method first obtains the CS measurement y through sampling, and then y is used to reconstruct x_{rec} via deep reconstruction network. The proposed network is optimized in an end-to-end way using the

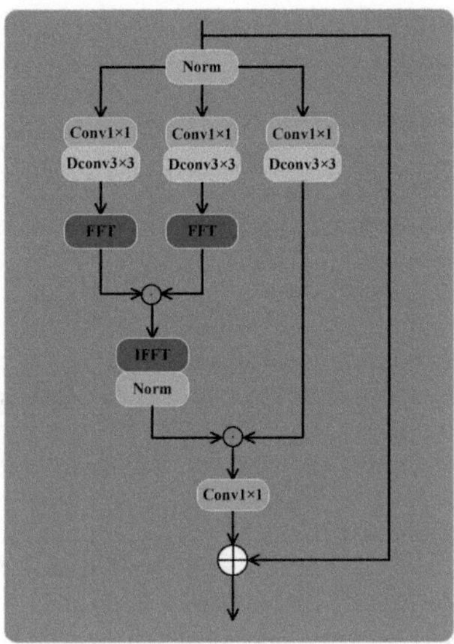

Fig. 4. The diagram of the used FDCA module.

following loss function:

$$\mathcal{L} = \mathcal{L}_{\mathrm{MSE}}(x_{\mathrm{rec}}, x) + \gamma \mathcal{L}_{\mathrm{orth}}(\Phi) \tag{12}$$

$\mathcal{L}_{\mathrm{mse}}$ denotes the Mean Squared Error (MSE) between the reconstructed image x_{rec} and the ground truth x, which can be written as: $\mathcal{L}_{\mathrm{MSE}}(x_{\mathrm{rec}}, x) = \frac{1}{N}\sum_{i=1}^{N}(x_{\mathrm{rec},i} - x_i)^2$. $\mathcal{L}_{\mathrm{orth}}$ enforces orthogonality constraints on the sampling matrix Φ, that is, $\mathcal{L}_{\mathrm{orth}}(\Phi) = \frac{1}{M^2}\|\Phi\Phi^T - I\|_F^2$. I is the identity matrix, and M is the length of measurement vector. In our experiments, the regularization parameter γ is set to 0.01 to balance reconstruction accuracy and measurement matrix quality.

3   Experimental Results

3.1   Implementation Details

Regarding training, in accordance with [16], we employ 400 images from BSDS-500's training and testing datasets [27]. Through data augmentation, the training images are cropped into 96×96 patches. As for the network setting, the sampling block size $\sqrt{N} * \sqrt{N}$ is set to 32*32, the number of channels C is 16, the number of stages is 16, and the batch size is 32. The size of the unspecified convolution kernel is 3×3. We utilize the Adam optimizer [28] to train the network. The initial learning rate is 2×10^{-4}, which is reduced to 5×10^{-5} over 100 epochs via the cosine annealing strategy [29], with three warm-up epochs. All experiments are carried out in PyTorch, with NVIDIA GeForce RTX 4090 GPU. For testing, we

Table 1. The average PSNR/SSIM comparison of interpretable CS methods on Set11, CBSD68 and Urban100 datasets.

Datasets	Methods	Sampling Ratio				
		0.1	0.25	0.3	0.4	0.5
Set11	ISTA-Net[+]	26.53/0.8066	32.44/0.9239	33.77/0.9388	35.99/0.9580	38.03/0.9704
	OPINE-Net[+]	29.81/0.8904	34.83/0.9514	36.04/0.9601	38.24/0.9721	40.20/0.9799
	MADUN	27.87/0.8470	33.28/0.9373	34.66/0.9494	36.85/0.9644	38.60/0.9739
	COAST	28.67/0.8608	–	35.07/0.9507	37.22/0.9655	39.03/0.9749
	DGU-Net[+]	28.86/0.8791	31.53/0.9266	34.26/0.9508	36.44/0.9662	39.13/0.9782
	FSOINet	29.80/0.8911	34.84/0.9526	36.18/0.9618	38.29/0.9727	40.17/0.9806
	OME-Net(Ours)	**30.89/0.9081**	**36.14/0.9613**	**37.31/0.9682**	**39.40/0.9774**	**41.27/0.9837**
CBSD68	ISTA-Net[+]	25.33/0.7011	29.29/0.8505	30.34/0.8777	32.18/0.9161	34.02/0.9423
	OPINE-Net[+]	27.81/0.8047	31.49/0.9064	32.51/0.9238	34.41/0.9487	36.32/0.9657
	MADUN	25.52/0.7191	29.35/0.8575	30.46/0.8837	32.22/0.9183	33.94/0.9424
	COAST	26.42/0.7434	–	31.15/0.8939	33.02/0.9273	34.82/0.9502
	DGU-Net[+]	26.89/0.7824	28.68/0.8639	30.97/0.9063	32.82/0.9351	35.09/0.9592
	FSOINet	27.64/0.8021	31.22/0.9025	32.32/0.9217	34.24/0.9474	36.03/0.9640
	OME-Net(Ours)	**28.37/0.8209**	**32.32/0.9194**	**33.39/0.9357**	**35.42/0.9584**	**37.45/0.9731**
Urban100	ISTA-Net[+]	23.52/0.7218	28.84/0.8830	30.17/0.9073	32.31/0.9371	34.41/0.9574
	OPINE-Net[+]	26.64/0.8375	31.44/0.9280	32.59/0.9417	34.69/0.9602	36.67/0.9728
	MADUN	25.08/0.7870	30.23/0.9079	31.53/0.9265	33.48/0.9483	35.28/0.9634
	COAST	25.80/0.8012	–	31.93/0.9305	34.11/0.9528	35.97/0.9670
	DGU-Net[+]	25.61/0.8152	28.99/0.9020	30.86/0.9278	32.96/0.9501	35.24/0.9674
	FSOINet	26.56/0.8412	31.49/0.9303	32.66/0.9438	34.77/0.9618	36.55/0.9728
	OME-Net(Ours)	**28.00/0.8706**	**33.17/0.9470**	**34.37/0.9573**	**36.33/0.9707**	**38.29/0.9800**

Table 2. The ablation study on proximal networks when testing on Set11 at the CS sampling ratio of 0.1.

Dataset	Proximal operator		
	VNet	**OINet**	**OME-Net**
PSNR/SSIM	29.33/0.895	29.90/0.8942	30.89/0.9081
Parameters	536257	536080	1248343

make use of three widely-used benchmark datasets, namely Set11 [30], BSDS68 [31], and Urban100 [32]. Color images are processed in the YCbCr space and evaluated on the Y channel. Two commonly-used image assessment metrics, Peak Signal to Noise Ratio (PSNR) and Structural Similarity (SSIM), are used to assess the reconstruction outcomes.

3.2   Performance Comparison

Extensive algorithmic validation demonstrates that learnable sampling matrices exhibit significant performance advantages over fixed Gaussian matrices. To objectively assess model capabilities, the proposed OME-Net in this paper is sub-

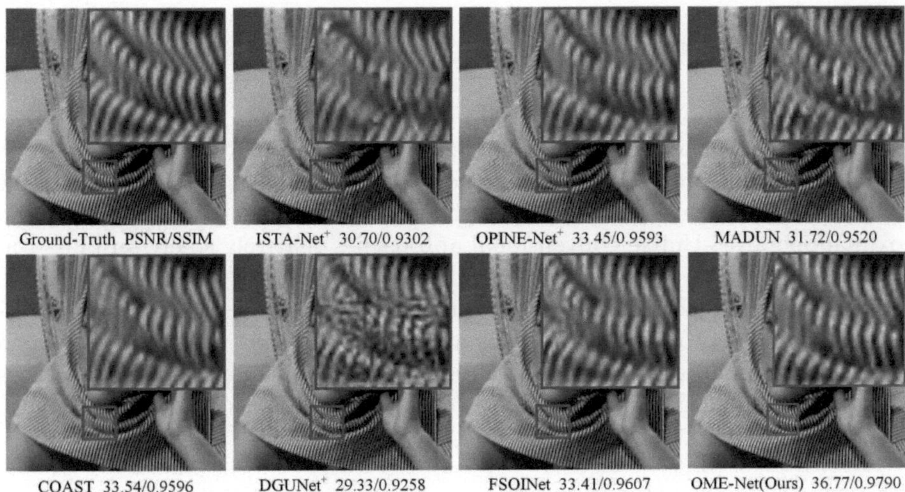

Fig. 5. Visual comparison of the recovery of the image named "Barbara" by our proposed method and several recent interpretable CS methods on the Set11 dataset under a CS ratio of 30%.

jected to a comprehensive comparative analysis with five state-of-the-art trainable sampling matrix-based compressed sensing methods, including ISTA-Net+ [5], OPINE-Net+ [24], MADUN [25], COASTNet [21], DGUNet [33]. As shown in Table 1 and Fig. 5, across compression sampling ratios ranging from 0.1 to 0.5, OME-Net (Ours) exhibits comprehensive superiority. Iterative optimization-based methods such as ISTA-Net+, OPINE-Net, and MADUN demonstrate better reconstruction quality compared to some traditional methods. Among them, the proposed method can improve CS reconstruction performance, particularly excelling in texture-rich areas, as clearly shown in Fig. 5, when tested on the Barbara image.

3.3   Ablation Study

This section explores the essential role of Feature-Space Gradient-descent Mapping (FSGM), which can be replaced by other modules. There are two comparative configurations: a baseline model (denoted as VNet) that removes FSGM to retain only measurement-based initial reconstruction for simulating conventional neural networks, and a hybrid model (denoted as OINet) that replaces FSGM with pixel-domain gradient-descent iteration to emulate traditional optimization-driven architectures. As shown in Table 2, at a low sampling ratio of 0.1, OINet exhibits a 0.99dB/0.0139 reduction in PSNR/SSIM compared to OME-Net, demonstrating that feature-space gradient operations effectively capture high-frequency information, while VNet shows an additional 0.57dB/0.0047 degradation relative to OINet.

4   Conclusion

To address high computational cost in traditional CS image reconstruction methods and the limitation of single-domain information flow in deep unfolding networks, this paper proposes an explicable network of OME-Net, which leverages multi-domain collaboration and frequency-domain enhancement. At each stage of OME-Net, there are two key components: a gradient descent module and a proximal operator. Unlike conventional approaches that rely solely on pure gradient descent, OME-Net employs a multi-domain gradient descent module to simultaneously extract and integrate complementary information across multiple domains. The proximal operator is approximated using a frequency-domain guided multi-resolution reconstruction architecture, which enhances features in the Fourier domain. The experimental results have demonstrated the effectiveness of the proposed method.

Acknowledgements. This work was supported by National Natural Science Foundation of China (62202323) and Shanxi Scholarship Council of China (2024-130).

References

1. Zhao, L., Zhang, Y., Wang, X., Zhang, J., Bai, H., Wang, A.: A survey on image compressive sensing: from classical theory to the latest explicable deep learning. Pattern Recogn. **170**, 112022 (2025)
2. Zhao, L., Wang, X., Zhang, J., Wang, A., Bai, H.: Boundary-constrained interpretable image reconstruction network for deep compressive sensing. Knowl.-Based Syst. **275**, 110681 (2023)
3. Donoho, D.L.: Compressed sensing. IEEE Trans. Inf. Theory **52**(4), 1289–1306 (2006)
4. Afonso, M.V., Bioucas-Dias, J.M., Figueiredo, M.A.T.: An augmented Lagrangian approach to the constrained optimization formulation of imaging inverse problems. IEEE Trans. Image Process. **20**(3), 681–695 (2011)
5. Beck, A., Teboulle, M.: A fast iterative shrinkage thresholding algorithm for linear inverse problems. SIAM J. Imag. Sci. **2**(1), 183–202 (2009)
6. Bioucas-Dias, J.M., Figueiredo, M.A.T.: A new twist: two-step iterative shrinkage thresholding algorithms for image restoration. IEEE Trans. Image Process. **16**(12), 2992–3004 (2007)
7. Chen, S.S., Donoho, D.L., Saunders, M.A.: Atomic decomposition by basis pursuit. SIAM Rev. **43**(1), 129–159 (2001)
8. Hale, E.T., Yin, W., Zhang, Y.: A fixed-point continuation method for L1-regularized minimization with applications to compressed sensing, CAAM TR07-07, Rice University 43 (44) (2007)
9. Hale, E.T., Yin, W., Zhang, Y.: Fixed-point continuation for L1-minimization: methodology and convergence. SIAM J. Optim. **19**(3), 1107–1130 (2008)
10. He, W., Yokoya, N., Yuan, X.: Fast hyperspectral image recovery of dual-camera compressive hyperspectral imaging via non-iterative subspace-based fusion. IEEE Trans. Image Process. **30**, 7170–7183 (2021)

11. Mousavi, A., Baraniuk, R.G.: Learning to invert: signal recovery via deep convolutional networks. In: Proceedings of IEEE International Conference Acoustics, Speech Signal Processing (ICASSP), pp. 2272–2276 (2017)
12. Zhang, K., Zuo, W., Gu, S., Zhang, L.; Learning deep CNN denoiser prior for image restoration. In: Proceedings IEEE Conference Computer Vision Pattern Recognition (CVPR), pp. 2808–2817 (2017)
13. Zhao, L., Wang, K., Zhang, J., Wang, A., Bai, H.: Learning deep texture-structure decomposition for low-light image restoration and enhancement. Neurocomputing **524**, 126–141 (2023)
14. Zhao, L., Zhang, J., Wang, X., Zhang, J., Wang, A.: Learning only two deep models of structure-texture decomposition neural networks for consecutive image smoothing. Neurocomputing **524**, 126–141 (2023)
15. Wang, K., Zhao, L., Zhang, J., Zhang, J., Wang, A., Bai, H.: Joint depth map super-resolution method via deep hybrid-cross guidance filter. Pattern Recogn. **136**, 109260 (2023)
16. Cui, W., Liu, S., Jiang, F., Zhao, D.: Image compressed sensing using non-local neural network. IEEE Trans. Multimedia **25**, 816–830 (2023)
17. Mousavi, A., Patel, A.B., Baraniuk, R.G.: A deep learning approach to structured signal recovery. In: Proceedings 53rd Annual Allerton Conference Communication, Control, Computing (Allerton), pp. 1336–1343 (2015)
18. Zhao, L., Zhang, J., Zhang, J., Bai, H., Wang, A.: Joint discontinuity-aware depth map super-resolution via dual-tasks driven unfolding network. IEEE Trans. Instrum. Meas. **73**, 1–14 (2024)
19. Zhang, J., Zhao, L., Zhang, J., Wang, A., Bai, H.: Joint deep-unfolding optimization learning for depth map arbitrary-scale super-resolution. IEEE Trans. Multimedia, 1–14 (2025)
20. Zhao, L., Chen, B., Zhang, J., Wang, A., Bai, H.: RIRO: From Retinex-inspired reconstruction optimization model to deep low-light image enhancement unfolding network. IEEE Trans. Comput. Imaging **10**, 969–983 (2024)
21. You, D., Zhang, J., Xie, J., Chen, B., Ma, S.: COAST: controllable arbitrary-sampling network for compressive sensing. IEEE Trans. Image Process. **30**, 6066–6080 (2021)
22. Xie, J., Zhang, J., Zhang, Y., Ji, X.: PUERT: probabilistic under-sampling and explicable reconstruction network for CS-MRI. IEEE J. Sel. Topics Signal Process. **16**(4), 737–749 (2022)
23. Wang, X., Zhao, L., Zhang, J., Wang, A., Bai, H.: A wavelet-domain consistency-constrained compressive sensing framework based on memory-boosted guidance filtering. IEEE Trans. Instrum. Meas. **73**, 1–16 (2024)
24. Zhang, J., Zhao, C., Gao, W.: Optimization-inspired compact deep compressive sensing. IEEE J. Sel. Top. Signal Process. **14**(4), 765–774 (2020)
25. Song, J.C., Chen, B., Zhang, J.: Memory-augmented deep unfolding network for compressive sensing. In: Proceedings 29th ACM International Conference Multimedia, pp. 4249–4258 (2021)
26. Chen, W.J., Yang, C.L., Yang, X.: FSOINet: feature-space optimization-inspired network for image compressive sensing. In: Proceedings 2022 IEEE International Conference Acoustics, Speech and Signal Processing (ICASSP), pp. 2460–2464 (2022)
27. Arbelaez, P., Maire, M., Fowlkes, C., Malik, J.: Contour detection and hierarchical image segmentation. IEEE Trans. Pattern Anal. Mach. Intell. **33**(5), 898–916 (2010)

28. Kingma, D.P., Ba, J.: Adam: a method for stochastic optimization. arXiv preprint arXiv:1412.6980
29. I. Loshchilov, F. Hutter, SGDR: Stochastic gradient descent with warm restarts, arXiv preprint arXiv:1608.03983
30. Kulkarni, K., Lohit, S., Turaga, P., Kerviche, R., Ashok, A.: ReconNet: non-iterative reconstruction of images from compressively sensed measurements. In: Proceedings of the IEEE Conference on Computer Vision and Pattern Recognition, pp. 449–458 (2016)
31. Martin, D., Fowlkes, C., Tal, D., Malik, J.: A database of human segmented natural images and its application to evaluating segmentation algorithms and measuring ecological statistics. In: Proceedings Eighth IEEE International Conference Computer Vision (ICCV), vol. 2, pp. 416–423 (2001)
32. Huang, J., Singh, A., Ahuja, N.: Single image super-resolution from transformed self-exemplars. In: Proceedings IEEE Conference Computer Vision Pattern Recognition, pp. 5197–5206 (2015)
33. Mou, C., Wang, Q., Zhang, J.: Deep generalized unfolding networks for image restoration. In: Proceedings of IEEE/CVF Conference Computer Vision Pattern Recognition, pp. 17399–17410 (2022)

Compression, Transmission, Retrieval

MARSNet: Scalable Deep Coding of LiDAR Point Clouds via Multimodal and Residual Learning

Yanji Huang[1], Runnan Huang[1], Jianlong Zhou[2]✉, Yingqi Zhuo[2], Yanshan Li[1], and Miaohui Wang[1]✉

[1] Guangdong Key Laboratory of Intelligent Information Processing, Shenzhen University, Shenzhen, China
huangyanji2021@email.szu.edu.cn, lys@szu.edu.cn, wang.miaohui@gmail.com
[2] China Overseas Property Management Co., Ltd., Shenzhen, China
{zhoujianlong,zhuoyingqi}@cohl.com

Abstract. The rapid adoption of LiDAR sensors in autonomous driving has led to an explosion of LiDAR point cloud (LPC) data, posing substantial challenges for storage and transmission. To address the complexity of large-scale and spatially non-uniform LiDAR point clouds, we introduce a new multimodal and residual-driven scalable framework (MARSNet) for LiDAR point cloud compression (LPCC). Our MARSNet integrates an end-to-end deep network with a residual-aware compression module that leverages multiple modalities. By aligning and jointly encoding point cloud, depth, segmentation, and residual information, the proposed approach generates ultra-low-bit latent representations while preserving fine-grained geometric details. Extensive experimental validations show that MARSNet consistently outperforms 16 advanced LPCC models, achieving superior reconstruction quality at ultra-low bitrates.

Keywords: LiDAR point cloud · multi-modality · scalable coding

1 Introduction

With the widespread adoption of LiDAR sensors in fields such as *autonomous driving, military security,* and *machine vision,* the volume of LiDAR point cloud (LPC) data has increased significantly [21]. This surge has placed substantial strain on existing storage and transmission systems. The escalating demand for high precision, quality, and efficiency in machine vision, coupled with the

This work was supported in part by the National Natural Science Foundation of China (No. 62472290), and in part by Natural Science Foundation of Guangdong Province (No. 2024A1515011972 and No. 2023A1515011197), and in part by the Research and Application of Key Technologies for Building a Livable, Friendly and Smart Community Service Platform (No. CSCEC-2024-Z-30-2).

Z. Lin et al. (Eds.): ICIG 2025, LNCS 16161, pp. 431–443, 2026.
https://doi.org/10.1007/978-981-95-3398-5_35

challenges posed by the large scale, spatial variability, and uneven distribution of LPC data, has been further exacerbated by the advancements in automation and artificial intelligence [23]. As a result, LiDAR point cloud compression (LPCC) [22] has become a critical technological focus, driving progress in 3D machine vision and autonomous driving domains.

LPC data is challenging due to the large scale, sparsity, and dynamic nature of outdoor LiDAR scans [11,19], which is quite different from the static point cloud (SPC) [34] and dynamic point cloud (DPC) [25,26]. It reflects the following distinct characteristics: 1) **Large-scale**. In a typical LPC acquisition device, the Velodyne HDL-64E LiDAR sensor generates nearly 120K points per frame [7]. 2) **Uneven spatial and categorical distribution**. LPCs are highly imbalanced as some classes, such as road or building, occur much more frequently than others, like bicycle or motorcycle [3]. 3) **Multi-modality**. LPCs may include various types of data, such as point clouds, depth, semantic segmentation, and color images [20]. 4) **Sparsity and unstructured**. LPCs are inherently sparse and exhibit an unstructured format, especially for distant and small objects [22].

In this paper, we present a new multimodal and residual-driven scalable framework (MARSNet) to address the challenges of LiDAR point cloud compression (LPCC). It enhances compression efficiency while maintaining high-fidelity reconstruction of LPCs under ultra-low distortion conditions. The performance of MARSNet outperforms 16 representative LPCC models on the SemanticKITTI dataset. The main contributions of MARSNet are as follows:

- To deal with large-scale inputs, we introduce a hierarchical strategy that decouples LPCs into a representative standard layer and multiple residual subsets on a per-frame basis. This enables a flexible, scalable compression paradigm by controlling the number of residual layers.
- To learn and obtain comprehensive coding representations, we propose a novel multimodal-driven LPCC framework that extracts and compresses features from point, depth, and semantic modalities in the standard layer. Through end-to-end alignment and fusion, the proposed framework achieves superior compression efficiency at ultra-low bitrates.
- To enhance reconstruction quality, we develop a dedicated residual data learning that learns compact representations from the multi-layered residual subsets, enabling high-fidelity recovery of fine-grained 3D structures.

2   Related Work

The mainstream representative methods of LPCC can be broadly classified into two general aspects : 1) transformation-based methods and 2) learning-based ones, each with its own distinct advantages and disadvantages. Most LPCC methods are generated from originated raw LPC data while the related residual data is usually overlooked which contains rich details.

Transformation-Based. Cutting-edge LPCCs convert raw sparse LiDAR point data into specific compact data structure through its inherent hierarchical structure, geometric spatial distribution and relevant feature, including tree-based structure and voxel-based structure. Octree-based methods [17] recursively divide an initialized bounding box into smaller cubes until each smaller cube contains a limited number of points composing an oct-tree structure while KD-Tree-based methods [13] implement LPCC through indexing. Although tree-based methods accomplish both swift retrieval and efficient compact data storage, it results in loss of details and huge computational complexity while facing large-scale and high-density dynamic LPC data with extremely complex details. Voxel-based methods [16] exploit fixed-size voxels to approximate and quantize the continuous 3D space, providing both lossless and lossy compression options.

Learning-Based. With the growing adoption of neural networks, end-to-end based LPCCs [16,18] have emerged as a dominant approach for LPC compression and reconstruction. Point cloud Transformer and variational autoencoder [2] leverage entropy models for efficient compression on modest-scale datasets, yielding higher ratios and more accurate latent representations. To further enhance reconstruction quality, Zhang *et al.* [32] introduced a multi-view framework using multimodal inputs, while Wang *et al.* [20] employed joint networks integrating texture and depth maps. However, these methods remain limited in scalability and struggle to preserve fine-grained details in large-scale datasets.

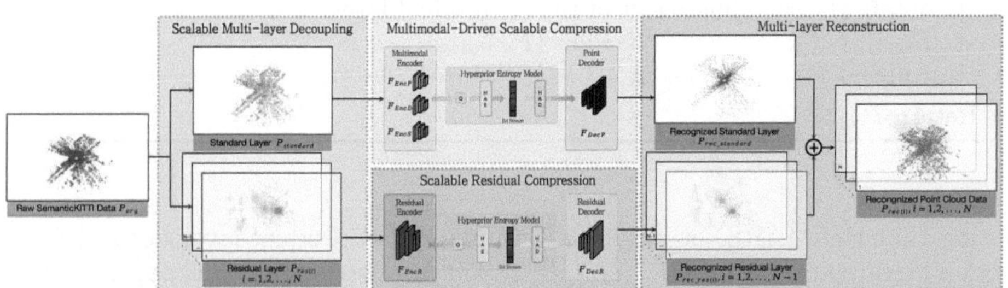

Fig. 1. Pipeline of the proposed multimodal residual-driven scalable LiDAR point cloud compression (MARSNet) framework. It consists of four key modules: scalable multi-layer decoupling, multimodal-driven compression, scalable residual compression, and multi-layer reconstruction.

3 Proposed MARSNet

The proposed MARSNet framework is mainly composed of four components: scalable multi-layer decoupling, multimodal-driven compression, scalable residual compression, and multi-layer reconstruction, as shown in Fig. 1. It is worth

---

Algorithm 1: Scalable Multi-layer Decoupling

Input: The standard layer of LiDAR point cloud data with M points, $P_{standard}$; The uniform LiDAR point cloud data with τ points, P_{org}; The point number of each residual layer $P_{res(i)}$, M; The total number of the decoupled layers, N

Output: The subset of residual layer,
$$P_{res} = \{P_{res(1)}, P_{res(2)}, ..., P_{res(j)}, ..., P_{res(N-1)}\}, \text{ where}$$
$$j = 1, 2, ..., N - 1$$

1 **if** $(N - 1) \times M > \tau$ **then**
2   Extend the size of P_{org} to τ points through random sampling without replacement;

3 Remove $P_{standard}$ from P_{org} to make P'_{org}: $P'_{org} = Remove(P_{org}, P_{standard})$;
4 Initialize residual-layer storage tensor and neighboring-layer storage tensor, each of size is $(N - 1) \times M \times 3$: P_{res}, P_{KNN};
5 **for** $i = 0$ *to* $M - 1$ **do**
6   Select a point p_i from $P_{standard}$ and use the KNN algorithm to find its $N - 1$ nearest neighboring points set $P_{KNN(i)}$ in P'_{org}:
    $P_{KNN(i)} = KNN(p_i, P'_{org}, N - 1)$ *s.t.*
    $P_{KNN(i)} = \{p_{KNN(0)}, p_{KNN(1)}, ..., p_{KNN(j)}, ..., p_{KNN(N-1)}\}$, where $p_{KNN(j)}$ stands for KNN points with x-y-z dimensions, $j = 1, 2, ..., N - 1$;
7   Remove $P_{KNN(i)}$ from P'_{org}: $P'_{org} = Remove(P_{org}, P_{KNN(i)})$;
8   Append $P_{KNN(i)}$ to P_{KNN} as a $1 \times (N - 1) \times 3$ row tensor;

9 **for** $i = 0$ *to* $N - 1$ **do**
10   Select points by column from P_{KNN} and subtract them from $P_{standard}$ to obtain the sampling result of the ith residual layer:
    $P_{res(i)} = P_{KNN}[:, i, :] - Reshape(P_{standard})_{1 \times M \times 3}$;
11   Append $P_{res(i)}$ to P_{res} as a $1 \times M \times 3$ row tensor;

12 Return P_{res};

---

noting that the MARSNet integrates standard and residual layer data, derived from a hierarchical decoupling module, to aid reconstruction. This approach preserves both global distribution and local structural details of LPCs. By leveraging residual layer data and the decoupling module, scalable layered compression is achieved, resulting in a more accurate and structurally complete reconstruction through dynamic adjustment of residual layers.

3.1   Scalable Multi-layer Decoupling

Concentrating on both global structural features and partial local details of LPCs, the proposed layered decoupling architecture combines a standard-layer module and a residual-layer module. This architecture utilizes farthest point sampling (FPS) [10], k-nearest neighbors (KNN) [10], and random sampling algorithm (RSA) [8] to effectively extract and decouple hierarchical features, enabling scalable structure. FPS is employed to capture global features, KNN is used to extract local structural details, and RSA ensures overall scale consistency. For example, the input LPC P_{org} is decoupled into two subsets: standard layers $P_{standard}$, which capture global information, and residual layers $\{P_{res(1)}, P_{res(2)}, P_{res(3)}, ..., P_{res(N-1)}\}$, which focus on local details.

$$P_{org} \rightarrow \{P_{standard}, P_{res(1)}, P_{res(2)}, P_{res(3)}, ..., P_{res(N-1)}\}. \tag{1}$$

Standard Hierarchical Decoupling. Considering the substantial data processing burden imposed by the large-scale LiDAR point clouds, we strategically extract the standard layer LPC data $P_{standard}$ from the consistent LPC data $P_{org\_consist}$ which is obtained directly through the unification of the original LPC frame P_{org}. This process involves a lossy mapping of approximately 120,000 large-scale LPC frames to τ points through FPS, resulting in the uniform LPC data $P_{org\_consist}$, which effectively preserves most of the structural characteristics of the original LiDAR point cloud. In addition, the standard layer $P_{standard}$ is then extracted from $P_{org\_consist}$ through FPS, containing M points.

Residual Hierarchical Decoupling. Based on the standard layer $P_{standard}$ with M points representing the global information through hierarchical decoupling, we use $P_{standard}$ as a reference layer to devide the remaining dataset within $P_{standard}$ for residual hierarchical decomposition through KNN. Additionally, each residual layer is formally required to maintain the same number of points as the standard layer to enable the hierarchical scalability of MARSNet. The residual hierarchical decoupling process is provided in Algorithm 1.

3.2   Multimodal and Scalable Compression

MARSNet combines a multimodal-driven scalable compression model and a scalable residual compression model, as illustrated in Fig. 2. The multimodal-driven model uses three modality encoders to collaboratively generate a comprehensive low-dimensional feature representation of the LPC layer data [20]. Minor adjustments were made to the convolutional layer sizes, and a novel compression encoding network was employed to extract the latent feature representation of the standard layer. Meanwhile, the scalable residual compression model captures latent features of local details and enhances the feature representation of the standard layer $P_{standard}$. The point cloud Transformer (PCT) network [8] is introduced, using residual layer data $P_{res\{1,2,...,N-1\}}$ as input for compression. The latent feature representation of the LPC frame can be expressed as:

$$f_{code} = \{F_{multimodal}(P_{standard}) \oplus F_{residual}(P_{res\{1,2,...,N-1\}})\}, \tag{2}$$

where $F_{multimodal}(\cdot)$ denotes our multimodal-driven scalable compression network, $F_{residual}(\cdot)$ represents the scalable residual compression network, $\oplus$ denotes the concatenation operation, and f_{code} is the concatenated latent feature representation of the entire LPC frame. $P_{standard}$ and $P_{res(i)}$ represent the LPC for the standard and residual layers, respectively.

Given that the reconstructed LPC data are represented as individual points, multilayer 1D deconvolution is employed in the reconstruction process, which precisely reconstructs LPC details from the multimodal latent feature representations. The reconstruction of the ith layer is expressed as:

$$P_{rec(i)} = F_{DecP}(f_{standard}) + F_{DecR}(f_{res(i)}), \tag{3}$$

where F_{DecP} and F_{DecR} are the reconstruction decoders for the multimodal-driven scalable compression network and the scalable residual compression network, respectively. $P_{rec(i)}$ represent the ith reconstructed LPC frame.

Multimodal-Driven Scalable Compression. The scalable compression method utilizes three modality encoders, as shown in Fig. 2: F_{EncP} for point modality with position information, F_{EncD} for depth modality with spatial data, and F_{EncS} for segmentation modality with category information. By aligning and fusing the latent features ($f_{standard\_point}$, $f_{standard\_depth}$, $f_{standard\_seg}$), a unified latent representation of the layer data, $f_{standard}$, is obtained. Specifically, scalable point cloud Transformer (PCT) is used for F_{EncP} and F_{EncS} [8], while point Transformer (PT) [33] serves as the depth encoder F_{EncD}. Modifications to the number of layers and the size of linear and self-attention layers improve the accuracy and suitability of the latent feature representations.

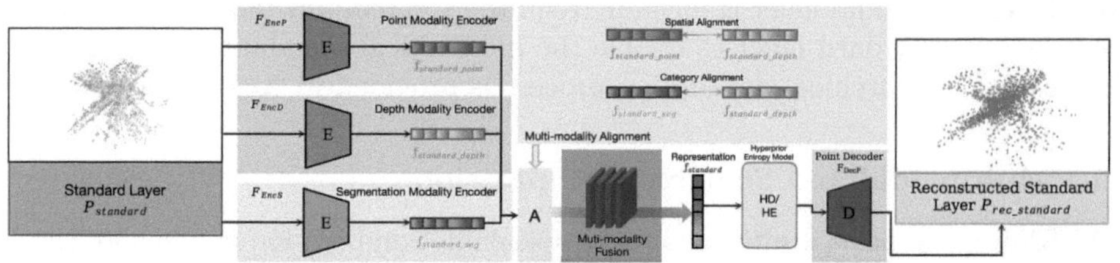

Fig. 2. Illustration of the proposed multimodal and scalable compression network.

The primary goal of multimodal-driven scalable compression is to reconstruct the global features of the original LPC via the standard layer, $P_{standard}$. The compression objective is to minimize the loss between $P_{rec\_standard}$ and $P_{standard}$, while also reducing the bitrate of the latent feature representation $f_{standard}$. This optimization process can be formulated as follows:

$$\min_{\omega_{mm},\omega_{DecP}} \quad \|F_{DecP}(f_{standard}, \omega_{DecP}) - P_{standard}\|_2^2 + BPP(f_{standard})$$
$$\text{s.t.} \quad f_{standard} = F_{Enc}(P_{standard}; \omega_{mm}) \tag{4}$$

where ω_{mm} represents the weights of the multimodal compression network, including those for the three modalities, alignment, and fusion. ω_{DecP} refers to the weights of the point modality decoding network, and $BPP(\cdot)$ calculates the bitrate of the latent feature representation based on the large-scale LiDAR point cloud data distribution using a hyperprior entropy model.

Scalable Residual Compression. Scalable residual compression leverages the end-to-end training of residual data for better adaptation to fine-grained geometry variations, as shown in Fig. 3. We use a scalable PCT model [8] as the residual encoder, replacing the original raw points P_{org} with residual data P_{res} derived from the raw and standard points $P_{standard}$. We use four self-attention layers to capture more local detail correlations among neighboring points.

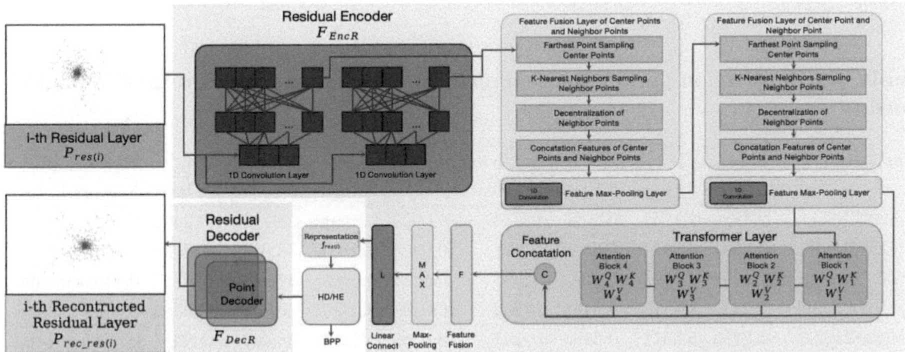

Fig. 3. Illustration of the proposed scalable residual compression network.

The main purpose of scalable residual compression is to reconstruct the refined LPC features. Therefore, we aim to minimize the loss between the reconstructed residual layer $P_{rec\_res(i)}$ and the original $P_{res(i)}$, as well as the bitrate of the latent feature representations $f_{res(i)}$ for the ith residual layer. The optimization process of scalable residual compression are formulated as:

$$\min_{\omega_{EncR}, \omega_{DecR}} \quad \|F_{DecP}(f_{res(i)}, \omega_{DecR}) - P_{res(i)}\|_2^2 + BPP(f_{res(i)})$$

$$\text{s.t.} \quad f_{res(i)} = F_{EncR}(P_{res(i)}; \omega_{EncR}) \tag{5}$$

where ω_{EncR}, ω_{DecR} denotes weights of residual encoder and decoder separately.

3.3 Multi-layer Reconstruction

The multi-layer reconstruction involves a point decoder F_{DecP} and a residual decoder F_{DecR}, each with three 1D deconvolutional layers. These decoders reconstruct the standard layer $F_{rec\_standard}$ and residual layer P_{rec_res}, respectively. The reconstruction process for the ith layer $P_{rec(i)}$ is given by:

$$P_{rec(i)} = F_{DecP}(f_{standard}; \omega_{DecP}) + F_{DecR}(f_{res(i)}; \omega_{DecR}) \tag{6}$$

where ω_{DecP} and ω_{DecR} denotes the weights of F_{DecP} and F_{DecR} respectively.

The reconstructed $P_{rec\_standard}$ and the ith layer $P_{rec\_res(i)}$ are combined to obtain the reconstructed point $P_{rec(i)}$ at the ith layer. By aggregating the reconstructed data from all layers $\{P_{rec\_standard}, P_{rec(1)}, \ldots, P_{rec(N-1)}\}$, the final reconstructed P_{rec} is obtained. As the number of layers increases, the reconstruction quality improves. The aggregation process is expressed as:

$$P_{rec} \to \{P_{rec\_standard}, P_{rec(1)}, \cdots, , P_{rec(N-1)}\}, \tag{7}$$

where P_{rec} aggregates N reconstructed layers, including the reconstructed standard layer $P_{rec\_standard}$ and all $N-1$ reconstructed layers $\{P_{rec(1)}, \ldots, P_{rec(N-1)}\}$.

Table 1. Compression performance comparison of 17 methods in terms of four LPCC metrics.

Methods	Loss$_{point}$ ↓		BPP ↓ (bits/point)		CD ↓ (m)		PSNR ↑ (dB)		RMSE ↓ (m)	
	5 layers	32 layers	5 layers	32 layers	5 layers	32 layers	5 layers	32 layers	5 layers	32 layers
Guo2021 [8]	2.4826	2.1744	0.2026	0.2644	0.0228	0.0191	38.1192	40.2492	0.2631	0.1948
BPG2018 [4]	4.6831	4.8114	0.8431	0.7514	0.0384	0.0406	38.9052	38.8023	0.1583	0.1394
JPEG XL2020 [1]	2.3793	3.5891	0.5393	0.7391	0.0184	0.0285	37.9424	37.9853	0.1493	0.1392
WebP2023 [29]	5.3435	4.4512	0.5135	0.4932	0.0483	0.0396	38.5318	39.0953	0.1653	0.1485
Wang2022 [24]	4.3793	3.5671	0.5193	0.5241	0.0386	0.0304	38.4031	41.9472	0.1934	0.1469
Yan2019 [27]	5.1731	4.8084	0.2431	0.2184	0.0493	0.0459	42.3946	43.8576	0.1348	0.1392
Huang2019 [12]	3.4664	4.2105	0.1864	0.2705	0.0328	0.0394	43.2914	43.9284	0.1540	0.1285
Gao2021 [6]	10.0493	7.7238	0.2193	0.2038	0.0983	0.0752	41.3587	44.8573	0.1583	0.1739
Zhao2021 [33]	3.9794	43.0239	0.1294	0.3839	0.0385	0.4264	44.7580	44.9758	0.1784	0.1876
Fu2022 [5]	5.7385	6.1547	0.2685	0.3247	0.0547	0.0583	42.9664	45.6791	0.1857	0.2050
Liang2022 [14]	3.3865	4.1174	0.2265	0.3074	0.0316	0.0381	41.2948	41.8392	0.1938	0.1724
Zhang2022 [31]	7.5783	4.5645	0.1983	0.2545	0.0738	0.0431	43.0314	45.0853	0.1772	0.1581
He2022 [9]	8.0944	3.5567	0.2544	0.3967	0.0784	0.0316	43.2985	43.5831	0.1593	0.0947
Liu2023 [15]	5.7698	4.9894	0.3798	0.4394	0.0539	0.0455	40.3895	42.7239	0.0984	0.1034
Yim2024 [28]	4.7623	4.2021	0.3823	0.4021	0.0438	0.0380	43.4864	45.5838	0.0849	0.0554
Zhang2024 [30]	7.1136	6.0873	0.1836	0.2073	0.0693	0.0588	41.0906	44.8993	0.0784	0.0622
Proposed	**2.4095**	**1.8872**	**0.0795**	**0.0872**	**0.0217**	**0.0164**	**48.8796**	**48.9047**	**0.1275**	**0.1174**

4   Experimental Results

In this section, we have conducted comprehensive experiments to verify the scalability and capability of our MARSNet. Moreover, some cutting-edge LPCC models are used to compare the compression performance with MARSNet.

4.1   Experiment Protocol

Datasets. SemanticKITTI [3] is a large-scale LPC dataset with over 22,000 frames captured from a vehicle equipped with a VelodyneHDL-64E LiDAR and cameras. It contains 22 sequences across 22 semantic classes (*e.g.*, road, sidewalk, and vehicle). For MARSNet evaluation, we follow the recommended partitioning: sequences 0007 and 0910 for training, 1121 for testing, and 08 for validation.

Evaluation Metrics. To evaluate MARSNet for lossy LPCC, we adopt four widely-used metrics [5,9,22]: Bits Per Point (BPP), Peak Signal-to-Noise Ratio (PSNR), Chamfer Distance (CD), and Root Mean Squared Error (RMSE). An enhanced scalable PCT [8] serves as the baseline model.

Implementation Details. We preprocess the original database using hierarchical decoupling, setting $M = 32$ decoupled layers, each with $N = 2048$ points, including the standard layer $P_{standard}$ and $N-1$ residual layers $P_{residual}$. MARSNet is implemented in *PyTorch* and trained on an *NVIDIA A100 80G*. For modality encoder training, we use a batch size of 32, and for multimodal alignment and fusion training, a batch size of 16. We apply the Adam optimizer with a learning rate of 0.001 for 200 epochs.

4.2   Performance Comparison

We compare the proposed MARSNet with 16 representative and state-of-the-art lossy LPCC methods, including cutting-edge learning-based approaches. Extensive experiments demonstrate that MARSNet significantly outperforms existing methods on large-scale LiDAR point cloud compression. Detailed comparisons are presented in Table 1.

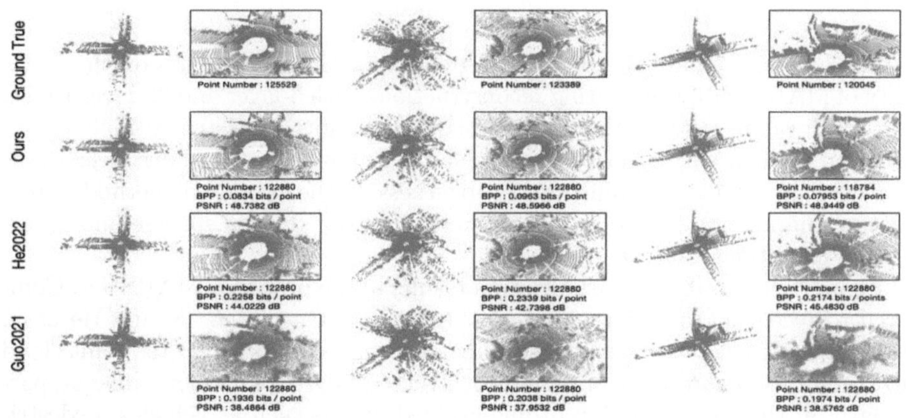

Fig. 4. Reconstruction results of the 08-000800, 08-000000, and 18-000300 (left to right) on the SemanticKITTI dataset. From top to down is the ground-truth LPC, our method, He *et al.* [9], and Guo *et al.* [8].

Table 1 provides a comprehensive comparison of our MARSNet model with other point-based LPCC models, based on the evaluation results obtained from the SemanticKITTI test dataset. As seen, our proposed MARSNet method achieves the highest PSNR and the lowest CD and BPP among all compared LPCCs, highlighting its superior LPC reconstruction capability under ultra-low bit rates. Notably, the majority of the bitrate in MARSNet is consumed by the compression of standard LiDAR point cloud layers using a multimodal-driven scalable compression module, while only approximately 0.02 bits/point are required for encoding the latent representations of the residual layer in scalable residual compression. This residual structure introduces a significant performance gain, yielding a PSNR improvement of nearly 10 dB compared to existing state-of-the-art models, while simultaneously reducing the bitrate by approximately 0.15 bits/point on average.

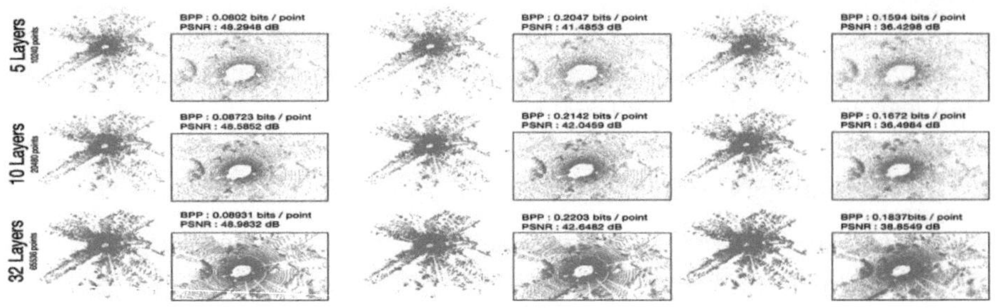

Fig. 5. Hierarchical reconstruction results of 08-000000 on the SemanticKITTI dataset, showing our method, He *et al.* [9], and Guo *et al.* [8] (left to right) with the 5th layer, 10th layer, and 32th layer reconstructions (top to bottom).

In addition, we have conducted a detailed quantitative analysis on the scalability of MARSNet by evaluating reconstructions with 5-layer and 32-layer LPCs. The results demonstrate that our method maintains consistently high reconstruction quality, with PSNR values remaining above 48 dB in both cases. This confirms the strong scalability and robustness of the proposed method across various compression levels, making it well-suited for diverse storage and transmission conditions.

Figure 4 illustrates the visualization results of the proposed MARSNet. Compared to recent learning-based approaches such as Guo *et al.*. [8] and He *et al.* [9], our framework demonstrates notable advantages in both LiDAR point cloud bitrate efficiency and the quality of reconstructed LiDARpoint cloud images, particularly in the reconstruction of fine-grained details such as vehicles, pedestrians, and trees. Under the condition of scalable layered reconstruction, the latent feature bitstream generated by the MARSNet network achieves approximately a 50 % reduction in storage. Moreover, the PSNR of the fully reconstructed LPCs is improved by up to 10 dB, corresponding to an approximate 25 % enhancement over the baseline method. In contrast, the compression performance of [9] noticeably degrades when extended to scalable layered reconstruction.

Furthermore, we perform scalable layered reconstruction based on the compressed latent feature bitstream. As illustrated in Fig. 5, we show the reconstructed LPCs at the 5th, 10th, and 32th layers, each consisting of 2,048 points. The proposed method enables progressive reconstruction, where the bitrate consistently remains below 0.1 BPP as the number of layers increases, while the

PSNR exhibits a steady improvement. Compared with other LPCC models, our MARSNet demonstrates superior performance in both reconstruction quality and bitrate efficiency under scalable layered settings.

5 Conclusion

LiDAR point cloud compression (LPCC) inherently involves a trade-off between compression efficiency and reconstruction fidelity. To address this, we present MARSNet, a novel LPCC framework that combines a residual-aware encoding network with a multimodal-driven scalable module. By leveraging a multilayer decoupling strategy and residual compression, MARSNet effectively preserves fine-grained geometric details while enabling flexible, scalable reconstruction. Extensive evaluations on the SemanticKITTI benchmark demonstrate that MARSNet achieves superior performance over 16 representative LPCC methods, offering high-quality reconstructions at significantly reduced bitrates.

References

1. Alakuijala, J., Boukortt, S., Ebrahimi, T., Kliuchnikov, E., Sneyers, J., Wassenberg, J.: Benchmarking jpeg xl image compression. In: Optics, Photonics and Digital Technologies for Imaging Applications VI, vol. 11353, pp. 187–206 (2020)
2. Ballé, J., Minnen, D., Singh, S., Hwang, S.J., Johnston, N.: Variational image compression with a scale hyperprior. arXiv preprint arXiv:1802.01436 (2018)
3. Behley, J., et al.: Semantickitti: a dataset for semantic scene understanding of lidar sequences. In: Proceedings of the IEEE/CVF International Conference on Computer Vision, pp. 9297–9307 (2019)
4. Bellard, F.: Bpg: Better portable graphics (2018). http://bellard.org/bpg. Accessed 12 Sept 2022
5. Fu, C., Li, G., Song, R., Gao, W., Liu, S.: Octattention: octree-based large-scale contexts model for point cloud compression. In: Proceedings of the AAAI Conference on Artificial Intelligence, vol. 36, pp. 625–633 (2022)
6. Gao, L., Fan, T., Wan, J., Xu, Y., Sun, J., Ma, Z.: Point cloud geometry compression via neural graph sampling. In: 2021 IEEE International Conference on Image Processing (ICIP), pp. 3373–3377. IEEE (2021)
7. Geiger, A., Lenz, P., Urtasun, R.: Are we ready for autonomous driving? The kitti vision benchmark suite. In: 2012 IEEE Conference on Computer Vision and Pattern Recognition, pp. 3354–3361. IEEE (2012)
8. Guo, M.H., Cai, J.X., Liu, Z.N., Mu, T.J., Martin, R.R., Hu, S.M.: Pct: point cloud transformer. Comput. Visual Media **7**, 187–199 (2021)
9. He, Y., Ren, X., Tang, D., Zhang, Y., Xue, X., Fu, Y.: Density-preserving deep point cloud compression. In: Proceedings of the IEEE/CVF Conference on Computer Vision and Pattern Recognition, pp. 2333–2342 (2022)
10. Hu, Y., Sun, H., Guo, C., Deng, Q., Ha, Y.: An energy-efficient and fast knn search accelerator for large scale point cloud map. In: 2023 30th IEEE International Conference on Electronics, Circuits and Systems (ICECS), pp. 1–4. IEEE (2023)
11. Huang, R., Wang, M.: Patch-wise lidar point cloud geometry compression based on autoencoder. In: Springer International Conference on Image and Graphics, pp. 299–310 (2023)

12. Huang, T., Liu, Y.: 3d point cloud geometry compression on deep learning. In: Proceedings of the 27th ACM International Conference on Multimedia, pp. 890–898 (2019)
13. Hubo, E., Mertens, T., Haber, T., Bekaert, P.: The quantized kd-tree: efficient ray tracing of compressed point clouds. In: 2006 IEEE Symposium on Interactive Ray Tracing, pp. 105–113. IEEE (2006)
14. Liang, Z., Liang, F.: Transpcc: towards deep point cloud compression via transformers. In: Proceedings of the 2022 International Conference on Multimedia Retrieval, pp. 1–5 (2022)
15. Liu, C.S., Yeh, J.F., Hsu, H., Su, H.T., Lee, M.S., Hsu, W.H.: Bird-pcc: bidirectional range image-based deep lidar point cloud compression. In: ICASSP 2023-2023 IEEE International Conference on Acoustics, Speech and Signal Processing (ICASSP), pp. 1–5. IEEE (2023)
16. Quach, M., Pang, J., Tian, D., Valenzise, G., Dufaux, F.: Survey on deep learning-based point cloud compression. Front. Signal Process. **2**, 846972 (2022)
17. Schnabel, R., Klein, R.: Octree-based point-cloud compression. PBG@ SIGGRAPH **3**(3) (2006)
18. Sun, X., Wang, M., Du, J., Sun, Y., Cheng, S.S., Xie, W.: A task-driven scene-aware LiDAR point cloud coding framework for autonomous vehicles. IEEE Trans. Ind. Inf. **19**(8), 8731–8742 (2022)
19. Sun, X., Wang, S., Wang, M., Wang, Z., Liu, M.: A novel coding architecture for LiDAR point cloud sequence. IEEE Rob. Autom. Lett. **5**(4), 5637–5644 (2020)
20. Wang, M., Huang, R., Dong, H., Lin, D., Song, Y., Xie, W.: msLPCC: a multimodal-driven scalable framework for deep LiDAR point cloud compression. In: Proceedings of the AAAI Conference on Artificial Intelligence, vol. 38, pp. 5526–5534 (2024)
21. Wang, M., Huang, R., Liu, Y., Li, Y., Xie, W.: suLPCC: a novel LiDAR point cloud compression framework for scene understanding tasks. IEEE Trans. Ind. Inf. **21**(5), 3816–3827 (2025)
22. Wang, M., Huang, R., Xie, W., Ma, Z., Ma, S.: Compression approaches for LiDAR point clouds and beyond: a survey. ACM Trans. Multimedia Comput. Commun. Appl. 1–30 (2025)
23. Wang, M., Yue, G., Xiong, J., Tian, S.: Intelligent point cloud processing, sensing, and understanding. Sensors **24**(283), 1–5 (2024)
24. Wang, S., Jiao, J., Cai, P., Wang, L.: R-pcc: a baseline for range image-based point cloud compression. In: 2022 International Conference on Robotics and Automation (ICRA), pp. 10055–10061. IEEE (2022)
25. Xiong, J., Gao, H., Wang, M., Li, H., Lin, W.: Occupancy map guided fast video-based dynamic point cloud coding. IEEE Trans. Circuits Syst. Video Technol. **32**(2), 813–825 (2021)
26. Xiong, J., Gao, H., Wang, M., Li, H., Ngan, K.N., Lin, W.: Efficient geometry surface coding in V-PCC. IEEE Trans. Multimedia **25**, 3329–3342 (2022)
27. Yan, W., Liu, S., Li, T.H., Li, Z., Li, G., et al.: Deep autoencoder-based lossy geometry compression for point clouds. arXiv preprint arXiv:1905.03691 (2019)
28. Yim, J.Y., Sim, J.Y.: Compression of large-scale 3d point clouds based on joint optimization of point sampling and feature extraction. arXiv preprint arXiv:2412.07302 (2024)
29. Zern, J., Massimino, P., Alakuijala, J.: Rfc 9649 webp image format. Animation **2**, 1–2 (2024)
30. Zhang, G., Zhao, W., Liu, J., Bai, Y., Jiang, J., Liu, X.: Pvcontext: hybrid context model for point cloud compression. arXiv preprint arXiv:2409.12724 (2024)

31. Zhang, J., Liu, G., Ding, D., Ma, Z.: Transformer and upsampling-based point cloud compression. In: Proceedings of the 1st International Workshop on Advances in Point Cloud Compression, Processing and Analysis, pp. 33–39 (2022)
32. Zhang, Z., et al.: Mm-pcqa+: advancing multi-modal learning for point cloud quality assessment. ACM Trans. Multimedia Comput. Commun. Appl. (2025)
33. Zhao, H., Jiang, L., Jia, J., Torr, P.H., Koltun, V.: Point transformer. In: Proceedings of the IEEE/CVF International Conference on Computer Vision, pp. 16259–16268 (2021)
34. Zhou, H., et al.: Cylinder3d: an effective 3d framework for driving-scene lidar semantic segmentation. arxiv 2020. arXiv preprint arXiv:2008.01550 (2020)

Accelerating Learned Video Compression via Low-Resolution Representation Learning

Zidian Qiu[1], Zongyao He[1], and Zhi Jin[1,2]([✉])

[1] School of Intelligent Systems Engineering, Shenzhen Campus of Sun Yat-sen University, Shenzhen 518107, Guangdong, People's Republic of China
{qiuzd,hezy28}@mail2.sysu.edu.cn, jinzh26@mail.sysu.edu.cn
[2] Guangdong Provincial Key Laboratory of Fire Science and Intelligent Emergency Technology, Shenzhen 518107, People's Republic of China

Abstract. Learned video compression achieves high compression ratios but often suffers from low speeds due to model complexity and high-resolution spatial operations. In this work, we propose an efficiency-optimized framework that emphasizes low-resolution representation learning to accelerate inference. Specifically, we reduce the resolution of reused inter-frame propagated features (including those from I-frames) and employ joint I/P-frame training to enhance feature interaction. Our method efficiently exploits multi-frame priors for parameter prediction with minimal additional decoding computation. Furthermore, we revisit the Online Encoder Update (OEU) strategy to boost compression performance without sacrificing decoding efficiency. Overall, our framework significantly improves the trade-off between compression efficiency and inference speed, achieving performance comparable to VTM-LDP. Compared to DCVC-HEM, it delivers a similar compression ratio while offering $3\times$ faster encoding and $7\times$ faster decoding, decoding 1080p frames in under 100ms on an RTX 2080Ti.

Keywords: Learned video compression · Efficiency · Online Update

1 Introduction

Video coding reduces video file size by compressing redundant intra- and inter-frame information. Traditional standards such as H.264/AVC [31], H.265/HEVC [27], AV1 [5], and H.266/VVC [4] employ complex algorithms to achieve high-quality compression, but lack end-to-end optimization. Recently, learned video compression has surpassed H.266 in compression ratio, though high complexity causes slow speeds, limiting practical applications. Optimizing learned compression thus demands framework redesign.

In end-to-end neural video codecs, components like motion estimation, compensation, and compression are implemented through neural networks for joint optimization. Existing methods mainly fall into residual coding and conditional

Z. Lin et al. (Eds.): ICIG 2025, LNCS 16161, pp. 444–456, 2026.
https://doi.org/10.1007/978-981-95-3398-5_36

coding. Residual coding encodes the difference between predicted and actual frames. DCVC [12] introduced conditional coding, using propagated features as context, with DCVC-DC [14] surpassing ECM [24] in compression ratio. However, high inference latency (e.g., ¿1 s/1080p frame) restricts practical use.

To address this, we propose an efficiency-optimized framework focusing on low-resolution representation learning to significantly improve encoding and decoding speeds (Fig. 1). We relocate high-resolution operations to low-resolution space and reuse decoded features, including I-frames, enabling joint I/P-frame optimization. Unlike previous works [8,15,17,22], we generate temporal priors at the decoding end with negligible overhead, improving entropy model prediction with multi-frame priors. Revisiting the Online Encoder Update (OEU) strategy [18] further boosts performance without slowing decoding. Our method achieves much faster decoding than other neural codecs, matches the low-decay P configuration of VTM [4], and outperforms it in MS-SSIM [30]. Our contributions are summarized as follows:

- We identify high-resolution spatial operations as the main source of decoding latency and mitigate this by relocating them to low-resolution spaces. We further introduce feature reuse across decoded frames (including I-frames) and jointly optimize I- and P-frame models to reduce computation costs.
- We enhance entropy model predictions by generating temporal priors in the low-resolution feature domain using multi-frame references, improving performance with negligible overhead. Additionally, we revisit the OEU strategy to boost compression without impacting decoding speed.
- Our method achieves comparable performance to VTM's low-delay P configuration [4], and compared to DCVC-HEM [13], achieves similar compression efficiency while delivering 3× faster encoding and 7× faster decoding.

2 Related Work

2.1 Traditional Video Compression

Traditional video codecs, such as H.264/AVC [31], H.265/HEVC [27], AV1 [5], and H.266/VVC [4], rely on complex, manually designed algorithms aiming for higher compression and quality, but lack end-to-end optimization.

2.2 Learned Video Compression

DVC [19] first introduced end-to-end learned video compression. FVC [10] improved compression by operating in the feature domain, while C2F [9] introduced coarse-to-fine motion estimation and adaptive compression. MMVC [16] adapted strategies based on motion patterns. DCVC [12] proposed an efficient conditional coding framework using temporal context features; DCVC-TCM [25] and DCVC-HEM [13] further improved performance with multi-scale contexts and advanced entropy models. DCVC-DC [14] enhanced optical flow-based coding with offset diversity and quadtree partitioning, surpassing ECM [24] in compression ratio. Despite their advances, neural codecs still lag behind traditional codecs in computational efficiency.

2.3 Efficient Learned Video Compression

Few works focus on computational efficiency. ELF-VC [22] optimized the network backbone, AlphaVC [26] reduced arithmetic coding cost via entropy skipping, and MobileCodec [11] enabled smartphone deployment through quantization and parallel entropy coding. Tian *et al.* [28] proposed a lightweight codec achieving real-time 720p decoding but exhibited performance comparable only to the medium preset of x265. In contrast, our framework achieves over 50% bitrate savings compared to Tian *et al.* while maintaining comparable decoding speed.

3 Method

3.1 Overall Framework

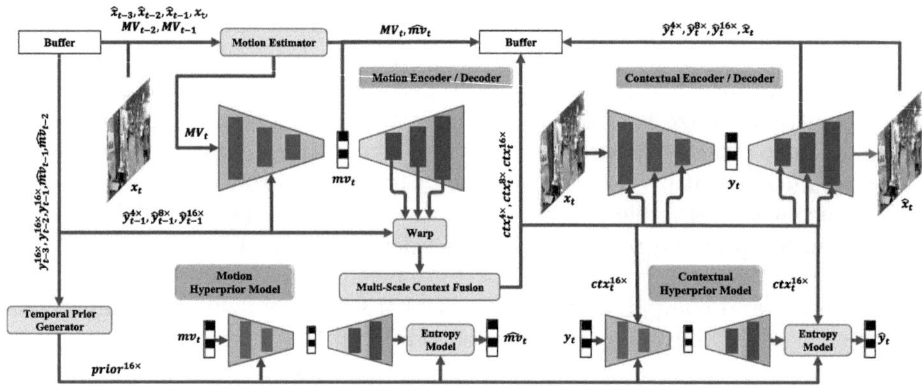

Fig. 1. Overview of our framework, where red lines represent data flows not included in the decoder side, while blue lines indicate data flows on the decoder side. x_t and $\hat{x}_t$ represent the input frame and reconstructed frame, respectively. MV_t, mv_t and $\hat{mv}_t$ denote the optical flow, motion vector and reconstructed motion vector, respectively. y_t and $\hat{y}_t$ represent the latent representation and reconstructed intermediate feature in the contextual decoder, and ctx_t is the learned temporal context, where the superscript $n\times$ denotes that the downsampling factor is n relative to the input resolution. (Color figure online)

To optimize network architecture for actual inference latency, we design the network using simple residual blocks and residual bottleneck blocks [7]. Since online video applications typically allow offline encoding, we emphasize decoding speed and adopt an imbalanced design, using lightweight decoders and higher-complexity encoders. For the I-frame model, the encoder stacks residual blocks, while the decoder stacks residual bottleneck blocks to reduce computational overhead. For P-frames, we adopt a conditional coding framework [13,14,25], as illustrated in Fig. 1. The main modules are as follows:

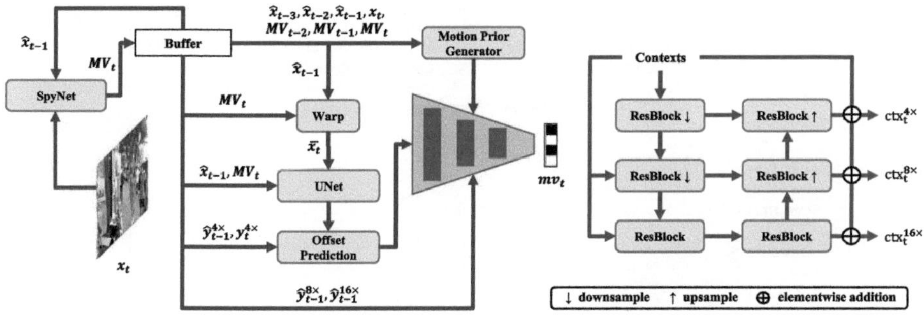

Fig. 2. Proposed motion encoder utilizing multi-frame priors (left) and multi-scale context fusion module (right).

Motion Estimation and Motion Encoding. We first estimate optical flow MV_t between the current frame x_t and the reference frame $\hat{x}_{t-1}$ using SpyNet [21]. Then, we refine motion features using a UNet [23] that takes the warped frame $\bar{x}t$ and optical flow as input. In parallel, we perform feature-level motion estimation to generate offsets, which are fused with the refined motion features. Additionally, temporal priors are extracted from previous frames and optical flows $(\hat{x}_{t-3}, \hat{x}_{t-2}, \hat{x}_{t-1}, MV_{t-2}, MV_{t-1})$ to assist motion encoding, as shown in Fig. 2.

Motion Decoding and Temporal Context Alignment. The compressed motion vector is decoded progressively. At each resolution, the decoded features serve as offsets for deformable alignment of the reference frame features. The aligned features are then fused by the multi-scale context fusion module to enhance temporal information.

Contextual Encoder-Decoder. During encoding, the current frame is conditionally encoded into latent representations using multi-scale contexts ($ctx_t^{4\times}$, $ctx_t^{8\times}$, $ctx_t^{16\times}$). During decoding, the latent representation $\hat{y}_t$ is reconstructed into the frame $\hat{x}_t$ using the same contexts. To reduce decoding cost, we employ a lightweight decoder without post-processing; to compensate for this, we scale up the encoder's depth and width following an imbalanced design.

Hyperprior Model and Entropy Model. We model the distributions of motion vectors and latent representations with Laplace distributions. Both our I-frame model and P-frame model utilize arithmetic coding skip entropy models [26] which are based on quadtree [14]. To exploit multi-frame priors efficiently at the decoding end, stacked residual bottleneck blocks generate temporal priors from latent representations in the decoding buffer, providing inputs to the hyperprior models for more accurate parameter prediction.

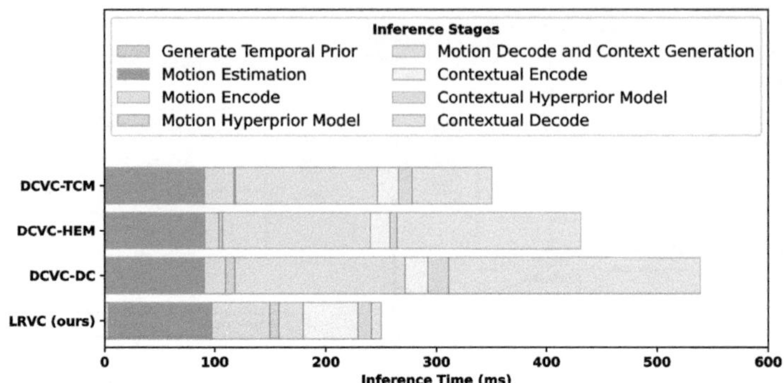

Fig. 3. Inference latency composition of different approaches. Tested on V100 using 1080p as the input.

3.2 Low-Resolution Representation Learning

Taking the DCVC series [13,14,25] as an example, Fig. 3 shows that decoding latency dominates overall inference latency. A significant portion of this latency stems from high-resolution spatial operations, such as context fusion for high-resolution contexts and post-processing in the contextual decoder. Simply reducing model depth or channels (Sect. 4.3) fails to address this and harms convergence. We tackle this by low-resolution representation learning.

Instead of using high-resolution multi-scale contexts as in DCVC-TCM [25], we reuse intermediate features ($4\times$, $8\times$, $16\times$ downsampled) from the previous timestep and dimensionally reduced to 64, 64, and 128 channels through lightweight adaptors. In contrast, prior works [13,14,25] extract context features by downsampling decoded frames, typically requiring costly high-resolution operations. Our method reuses decoded features directly, incurring no additional computational overhead.

Since optical flow alignment degrades at low resolutions, we redesign the motion decoder to use deformable convolution [6] for joint motion decoding and alignment in the feature domain, eliminating costly high-resolution operations. Context fusion is also performed entirely at low resolutions (Fig. 2).

3.3 Exploring Richer Prior Information

Prior information like optical flows and intermediate features has been widely exploited [8,15,17,22], but often at the cost of increased decoding complexity for limited gains. We enhance temporal priors by using more reference frames for better modeling. At the encoder, we leverage high-quality priors—reference frames and optical flows at original resolution—for improved motion estimation (Fig. 2). At the decoder, priors are generated from low-resolution features for the hyperprior models, introducing negligible overhead.

Furthermore, we directly reuse intermediate features from reference frame decoding, minimizing computation and information loss. Unlike prior works

[8,13,14,19,25] that treat I-frames separately, we strengthen I- and P-frame coupling by reusing I-frame features as temporal contexts for the first P-frame, enabling joint optimization and further improving performance.

Table 1. Comparison of model parameters (I model/P Encoder/P Decoder), MACs (Encoder/Decoder), encoding time (ET) and decoding time (DT) with 1080p resolution input.

Model	Params (M)	MACs (T)	ET (ms)	DT (ms)	Device
HM	–	–	42000	93	AMD EPYC 7352
VTM	–	–	189000	132	AMD EPYC 7352
DCVC-TCM [25]	23.7/**10.7/7.5**	2.960/1.908	632	341	V100
DCVC-HEM [13]	31.2/17.5/15.3	3.465/2.586	595	468	V100
DCVC-DC [14]	31.0/19.8/15.7	2.790/1.901	603	477	V100
LRVC (ours)	**12.5/35.1/10.6**	**1.824/0.277**	**257**	**86**	V100
DCVC-TCM [25]	23.7/**10.7/7.5**	2.960/1.908	892	479	RTX 2080Ti
DCVC-HEM [13]	31.2/17.5/15.3	3.465/2.586	974	679	RTX 2080Ti
DCVC-DC [14]	31.0/19.8/15.7	2.790/1.901	948	697	RTX 2080Ti
LRVC (ours)	**12.5/35.1/10.6**	**1.824/0.277**	**383**	**94**	RTX 2080Ti

3.4 Online Encoder Update Strategy

The online update strategy, known for its adaptability, has gained traction across various fields [2]. In video coding, applying this strategy enables improved rate-distortion performance without increasing decoding complexity. Prior work [18] proposed Online Encoder Update (OEU) for content-adaptive encoding but faced memory issues on high-resolution sequences like 1080p. Error propagation-aware training requires backpropagation through entire frames, resulting in prohibitive memory consumption.

Several schemes exist to address this issue, such as reducing the resolution of input sequences or conducting patch-wise training. Through extensive experiments, we find that simple overlapping patch-wise updates are effective. We update only the motion encoder, contextual encoder, and their associated hyperprior encoders in the P-frame model.

4 Experiments

4.1 Implementation Details

Dataset. We train on Vimeo-90k [32] with frames randomly cropped to 256 × 256. Evaluation is conducted on UVG [20], MCL-JCV [29], and HEVC B [3].

Training. We train four models targeting different rate-distortion points. The I-frame and P-frame models are first trained separately, then jointly fine-tuned, gradually increasing the number of training frames from 2 to 7.

Table 2. BD-Rate (%) comparison for PSNR and MS-SSIM on UVG, MCL-JCV (MCL), and HEVC B datasets. The anchor is VTM-LDB.

Method	PSNR			MS-SSIM		
	UVG	MCL	HEVC B	UVG	MCL	HEVC B
VTM-LDB	0	0	0	0	0	0
HM-LDB	36.26	41.78	39.06	27.26	35.59	38.27
DCVC	155.01	114.07	117.08	58.79	26.00	54.47
CANF-VC	64.54	65.34	60.49	39.86	22.43	42.80
DCVC-TCM	45.68	50.85	40.36	0.03	−10.58	−11.18
DCVC-HEM	2.79	8.74	5.08	−25.11	−36.12	−37.65
DCVC-DC	**−17.98**	**−10.53**	**−12.04**	**−32.50**	**−44.61**	**−47.57**
LRVC (ours)	21.55	30.56	32.07	−2.01	−8.58	−9.78
LRVC+OEU (ours)	14.76	18.99	22.93	−9.80	−15.61	−14.76

Table 3. BD-Rate (%) comparison for PSNR on UVG, MCL-JCV and HEVC B datasets. The anchor is VTM-LDP.

Dataset	VTM	HM	DCVC	ELF-VC	C2F	MMVC	LRVC	LRVC+OEU
UVG	0	33.24	95.87	65.03	16.79	2.53	4.91	**−1.06**
MCL-JCV	0	26.09	66.12	56.98	19.68	**−8.56**	5.29	−1.87
HEVC B	0	45.17	67.36	–	14.19	**−26.06**	29.18	20.26

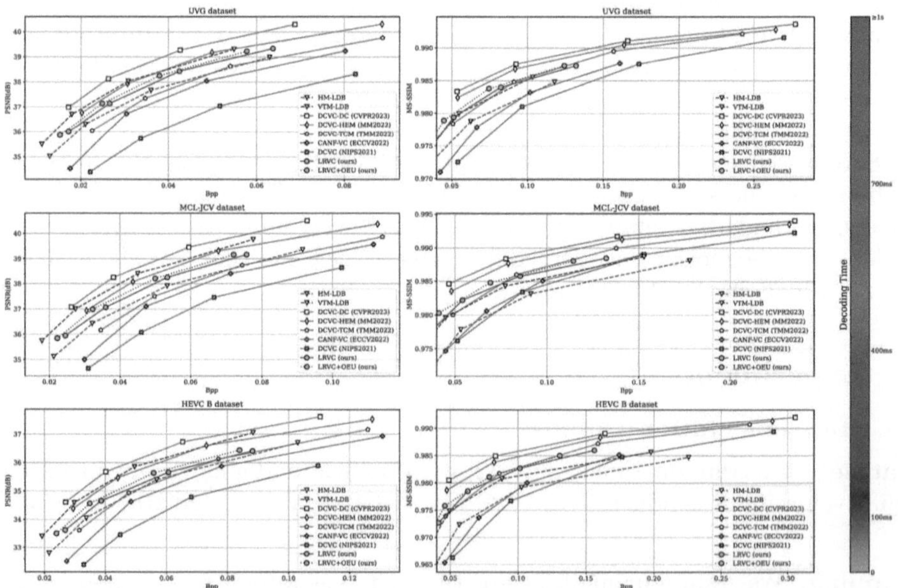

Fig. 4. Rate and distortion curves. The comparison is in RGB colorspace with BT.709 measured with PSNR and MS-SSIM. The line color represents the decoding time.

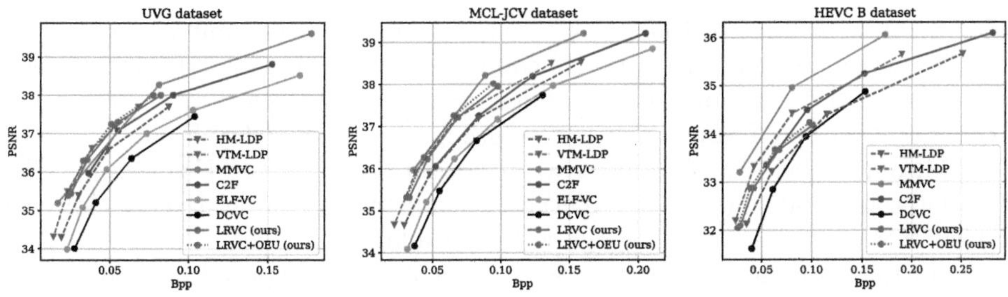

Fig. 5. Rate and distortion curves. The comparison is in RGB colorspace with BT.601 measured with PSNR.

Test Conditions. We evaluate using PSNR, MS-SSIM, and BD-Rate [1]. All comparisons are made in the RGB space; YUV420 inputs are converted following DCVC-DC settings (BT.709) or PyTorchVideoCompression standards (BT.601)[1]. We test with a GOP size of 32.

4.2   Comparison to Previous SOTA Methods

We compare against traditional codecs (HM [27], VTM [4]) and neural codecs (DCVC [12], ELF-VC [22], CANF-VC [8], DCVC-TCM [25], DCVC-HEM [13], DCVC-DC [14], C2F [9], MMVC [16]), as shown in Table 1-3, and Figs. 4, 5.

Efficiency. Table 1 summarizes model efficiency. Our method has 47.6M parameters in total, with the I-frame model at only 12.5M—much smaller than DCVC series. Although our P-frame model is relatively larger, the encoder-decoder imbalance design leads to a significantly lighter P-frame decoder. On 1080p inputs, our method requires 1.8T MACs, with decoding complexity of 277G—substantially lower than compared methods. For example, DCVC-HEM's encoding and decoding complexities are 1.9× and 9× higher, respectively, and DCVC-DC's decoding complexity is about 7× higher despite using efficient depth-wise convolutions.

We also evaluated actual encoding and decoding times (Table 1). Our method outperforms traditional codecs like HM (H.265 low-delay B) and achieves superior GPU encoding speeds, while decoding speeds are comparable. Against other neural codecs, our method approaches DCVC-HEM's rate-distortion performance but is 7× faster in decoding and 3× faster in encoding on RTX 2080Ti.

Quantitative Results. Table 2 show BD-Rate comparisons relative to VTM's low-delay B configuration. Our model exhibits only on average 18.9% PSNR performance gap compared to the optimal VTM configuration, but has competitive performance compared to DCVC-HEM. From the perspective of MS-SSIM, our

---

[1] https://github.com/ZhihaoHu/PyTorchVideoCompression.

codec saves an average of 13.39% bitrate across all datasets compared to VTM. Table 3 supplements the BD-Rate (%) comparison in terms of PSNR between our method and other methods under a different testing condition, using low-delay P configuration of VTM as anchor. Compared to the low-delay P configuration of VTM, our model exhibits better compression ratios on the UVG and MCL-JCV datasets. Additionally, our method demonstrates competitive or superior performance compared to other methods in Table 3.

To further compare with the efficient video codec proposed by Tian *et al.* [28], we tested our model under their settings at 720P resolution. As shown in Table 4, our method achieves 51.92% bitrate saving without OEU, with only minor decoding speed gaps despite not using model pruning.

Table 4. Comparison of complexity and decoding time for 720p resolution inputs. Note that MM 2023 [28] employs model pruning, reducing the complexity of the P-frame model from the original 1.1T to 162G MACs.

	BD-rate(%)	MACs (Enc/Dec)	Decoding time	Device
MM 2023 [28]	0	162G/76G	40 ms	RTX 2080
LRVC (ours)	−51.92	858G/130G	52 ms	RTX 2080Ti

4.3   Ablation Study

In this section, we present ablation experiments on various strategies mentioned in this paper.

Low-Resolution Representation Learning. We adjusted the depth and width of DCVC-DC [14] to evaluate the impact of high-resolution spatial operations. Post-processing in the context decoder was removed to maintain low latency, and modules/channels were reduced. However, decoding speed remained lower than ours, and the adjusted model failed to converge (Table 5), highlighting the necessity of low-resolution representation learning.

Table 5. BD-rate comparison for different strategies.

Strategy	BD-rate (%)	Decoding time
Ours	0	94 ms
Rescale DCVC-DC	5150.56	145 ms
Ours w/o deformable convolution	89.31	79 ms
Ours w/o joint training	18.95	94 ms
Ours w/o temporal prior	7.26	92 ms

Deformable Convolution vs. Optical Flow. We redesigned the motion decoder by decoding optical flow to original resolution, then downsampling for alignment. As shown in Table 5, replacing deformable alignment with optical flow alignment caused significant performance drops, demonstrating the superiority of our progressive deformable alignment at low resolutions.

Multi-frame Priors. Multi-frame priors are used for motion estimation at encoding and parameter prediction at decoding. Replacing them with single-frame priors led to noticeable bitrate increases (Table 5), demonstrating the advantage of leveraging longer temporal dependencies.

Joint Training. Jointly optimizing I- and P-frame models yields an additional 18.95% bitrate saving (Table 5) by enhancing feature reuse between I-frames and subsequent P-frames.

OEU Strategy. Table 6 shows the impact of our online encoder update. Simply downscaling high-resolution inputs yields limited gains, while cropping into overlapping patches (768×448 for 1080p) achieves better performance. We set training sequence length $T=8$ and steps $N=5$. Since frame positions within GOPs are fixed during testing, updating only the first T frames maintains performance while greatly reducing encoding time.

Table 6. BD-rate and Encoding time comparison for different OEU strategies on the V100 device. OEU strategies include: (a) Downsample and update all frames, (b) Crop and update all frames, and (c) Crop and update first T frames.

Strategy	BD-rate (%)	Encoding time
Ours	0	257 ms
Ours+OEU (a)	–2.43	257 ms + 154 ms × N Step
Ours+OEU (b)	–7.91	257 ms + 1719 ms × N Step
Ours+OEU (c)	–6.62	257 ms + 437 ms × N Step

5   Conclusion

We present an efficiency-optimized framework for learned video compression, centered around low-resolution representation learning. Through strategies such as feature reuse, joint training, multi-frame priors, and online encoder updates, our method achieves competitive compression ratios relative to VTM while substantially improving encoding and decoding speeds compared to existing neural codecs. Unlike traditional codecs, neural video compression eliminates the need for complex, handcrafted optimizations. Although challenges remain for deployment on power-constrained devices and compatibility issues must be addressed, our results demonstrate the significant potential of learned video compression for future video coding applications.

Acknowledgement. This work was supported by the National Natural Science Foundation of China under Grant U24A20251, 62071500, Shenzhen Science and Technology Program under Grant JCYJ20230807111107015.

References

1. Bjontegaard, G.: Calculation of average PSNR differences between RD-curves. VCEG-M33 (2001)
2. Bojanowski, P., Joulin, A., Lopez-Paz, D., Szlam, A.: Optimizing the latent space of generative networks. arXiv preprint arXiv:1707.05776 (2017)
3. Bossen, F., et al.: Common test conditions and software reference configurations. In: JCTVC-L1100 (2013)
4. Bross, B., et al.: Overview of the versatile video coding (vvc) standard and its applications. IEEE Trans. Circ. Syst. Video Technol. 3736–3764 (2021). https://doi.org/10.1109/tcsvt.2021.3101953
5. Chen, Y., et al.: An overview of core coding tools in the av1 video codec. In: 2018 Picture Coding Symposium (PCS) (2018). https://doi.org/10.1109/pcs.2018.8456249
6. Dai, J., et al.: Deformable convolutional networks. In: Proceedings of the IEEE International Conference on Computer Vision, pp. 764–773 (2017)
7. He, K., Zhang, X., Ren, S., Sun, J.: Deep residual learning for image recognition. In: Proceedings of the IEEE Conference on Computer Vision and Pattern Recognition, pp. 770–778 (2016)
8. Ho, Y.H., Chang, C.P., Chen, P., Gnutti, A., Peng, W.H.: Canf-vc: conditional augmented normalizing flows for video compression. ArXiv arxiv:2207.05315 (2022). https://api.semanticscholar.org/CorpusID:250451487
9. Hu, Z., Lu, G., Guo, J., Liu, S., Jiang, W., Xu, D.: Coarse-to-fine deep video coding with hyperprior-guided mode prediction. In: Proceedings of the IEEE/CVF Conference on Computer Vision and Pattern Recognition, pp. 5921–5930 (2022)
10. Hu, Z., Lu, G., Xu, D.: FVC: a new framework towards deep video compression in feature space. In: Proceedings of the IEEE/CVF Conference on Computer Vision and Pattern Recognition, pp. 1502–1511 (2021)
11. Le, H., et al.: Mobilecodec: neural inter-frame video compression on mobile devices. In: Proceedings of the 13th ACM Multimedia Systems Conference, pp. 324–330 (2022)
12. Li, J., Li, B., Lu, Y.: Deep contextual video compression. Adv. Neural. Inf. Process. Syst. **34**, 18114–18125 (2021)
13. Li, J., Li, B., Lu, Y.: Hybrid spatial-temporal entropy modelling for neural video compression. In: Proceedings of the 30th ACM International Conference on Multimedia, pp. 1503–1511 (2022)

14. Li, J., Li, B., Lu, Y.: Neural video compression with diverse contexts. In: Proceedings of the IEEE/CVF Conference on Computer Vision and Pattern Recognition, pp. 22616–22626 (2023)
15. Lin, J., Liu, D., Li, H., Wu, F.: M-lvc: multiple frames prediction for learned video compression. In: Proceedings of the IEEE/CVF Conference on Computer Vision and Pattern Recognition, pp. 3546–3554 (2020)
16. Liu, B., Chen, Y., Machineni, R.C., Liu, S., Kim, H.S.: Mmvc: learned multi-mode video compression with block-based prediction mode selection and density-adaptive entropy coding. In: Proceedings of the IEEE/CVF Conference on Computer Vision and Pattern Recognition, pp. 18487–18496 (2023)
17. Liu, C., Sun, H., Katto, J., Zeng, X., Fan, Y.: Learned video compression with residual prediction and loop filter. arXiv preprint arXiv:2108.08551 (2021)
18. Lu, G., Cai, C., Zhang, X., Chen, L., Ouyang, W., Xu, D., Gao, Z.: Content adaptive and error propagation aware deep video compression. In: Vedaldi, A., Bischof, H., Brox, T., Frahm, J.-M. (eds.) ECCV 2020. LNCS, vol. 12347, pp. 456–472. Springer, Cham (2020). https://doi.org/10.1007/978-3-030-58536-5_27
19. Lu, G., Ouyang, W., Xu, D., Zhang, X., Cai, C., Gao, Z.: Dvc: an end-to-end deep video compression framework. In: Proceedings of the IEEE/CVF Conference on Computer Vision and Pattern Recognition, pp. 11006–11015 (2019)
20. Mercat, A., Viitanen, M., Vanne, J.: Uvg dataset. In: Proceedings of the 11th ACM Multimedia Systems Conference (2020). https://doi.org/10.1145/3339825.3394937
21. Ranjan, A., Black, M.J.: Optical flow estimation using a spatial pyramid network. In: Proceedings of the IEEE Conference on Computer Vision and Pattern Recognition, pp. 4161–4170 (2017)
22. Rippel, O., Anderson, A.G., Tatwawadi, K., Nair, S., Lytle, C., Bourdev, L.: Elfvc: efficient learned flexible-rate video coding. In: Proceedings of the IEEE/CVF International Conference on Computer Vision, pp. 14479–14488 (2021)
23. Ronneberger, O., Fischer, P., Brox, T.: U-net: convolutional networks for biomedical image segmentation. In: Navab, N., Hornegger, J., Wells, W.M., Frangi, A.F. (eds.) MICCAI 2015. LNCS, vol. 9351, pp. 234–241. Springer, Cham (2015). https://doi.org/10.1007/978-3-319-24574-4_28
24. Seregin, V., Chen, J., Leannec, F., Zhang, K.: Jvet ahg report: Ecm software development (ahg6). JVET-AA0006 **1**, 8 (2022)
25. Sheng, X., Li, J., Li, B., Li, L., Liu, D., Lu, Y.: Temporal context mining for learned video compression. IEEE Trans. Multimedia (2022)
26. Shi, Y., Ge, Y., Wang, J., Mao, J.: Alphavc: high-performance and efficient learned video compression. In: European Conference on Computer Vision, pp. 616–631. Springer, Heidelberg (2022). https://doi.org/10.1007/978-3-031-19800-7_36
27. Sullivan, G.J., Ohm, J.R., Han, W.J., Wiegand, T.: Overview of the high efficiency video coding (hevc) standard. IEEE Trans. Circuits Syst. Video Technol. **22**(12), 1649–1668 (2012)
28. Tian, K., Guan, Y., Xiang, J., Zhang, J., Han, X., Yang, W.: Towards real-time neural video codec for cross-platform application using calibration information. In: Proceedings of the 31st ACM International Conference on Multimedia, pp. 7961–7970 (2023)
29. Wang, H., et al.: Mcl-jcv: a jnd-based h.264/avc video quality assessment dataset. In: 2016 IEEE International Conference on Image Processing (ICIP) (2016). https://doi.org/10.1109/icip.2016.7532610
30. Wang, Z., Simoncelli, E., Bovik, A.: Multiscale structural similarity for image quality assessment. In: The Thirty-Seventh Asilomar Conference on Signals, Systems & Computers, 2003 (2004). https://doi.org/10.1109/acssc.2003.1292216

31. Wiegand, T., Sullivan, G.J., Bjontegaard, G., Luthra, A.: Overview of the h. 264/avc video coding standard. IEEE Trans. Circ. Syst. Video Technol. **13**(7), 560–576 (2003)
32. Xue, T., Chen, B., Wu, J., Wei, D., Freeman, W.T.: Video enhancement with task-oriented flow. Int. J. Comput. Vision **127**(8), 1106–1125 (2019). https://doi.org/ 10.1007/s11263-018-01144-2

Optical Flow-Driven Fast CU Partition for Inter Prediction in Versatile Video Coding

Junhao Jiang[1], Shuangxing Tian[1], Dandan Ding[1(✉)], and Weiwei Xu[2]

[1] Hangzhou Normal University, Hangzhou 311121, Zhejiang, China
DandanDing@hznu.edu.cn
[2] Zhejiang University, Hangzhou 311121, Zhejiang, China

Abstract. The new generation video coding standard, H.266/VVC, introduces the quad-tree nested multi-type (QTMT) block partitioning structure and multiple inter coding modes, significantly improving coding efficiency but also increasing encoding time. To address this, we propose a coarse-to-fine fast partition decision (FPD) algorithm that collects both temporal and spatial information for inter CU partitioning. FPD first leverages co-located similarity between the current CU and its counterpart in the reference frame to capture global motion. High similarity indicates static regions, allowing early pruning of partition candidates. For CUs with low similarity, indicating complex local motions, we introduce a machine learning-based approach. Specifically, we extract temporal optical flow and spatial features (e.g., edges and gradients) to train a LightGBM classifier to predict the partition direction and skip the horizontal/vertical directions in advance. Experiments conducted under the common test condition of H.266/VVC demonstrate that our proposed FPD achieves a 37% runtime saving with only 0.99% coding performance loss, significantly surpassing state-of-the-art methods.

Keywords: Versatile Video Coding · CU partition · inter frame coding · optical flow

1 Introduction

With the increasing popularity of digital video, video compression has become a fundamental module in modern digital media communication. To this end, the international standardization committees sequentially concluded two video coding standards, High-Efficiency Video Coding (H.265/HEVC) [1] and its successor, Versatile Video Coding (H.266/VVC) [2], with H.266/VVC achieving about 40% higher coding efficiency over H.265/HEVC.

The high performance of H.266/VVC is obtained at the expense of increased computational resources and memory, posing challenges for practical applications and devices. In particular, apart from multiple newly added inter coding tools, H.266/VVC adopts a much more complex partition method than

H.265/HEVC by introducing the Multi-type Tree (MTT) structure for a Coding Tree Unit (CTU), forming the nested Quad-Tree plus Multi-type Tree (QTMT) partition structure [3]. QTMT consists of five partition modes for each Coding Unit (CU): QuadTree (QT), Binary Tree Horizontal (BTH), Binary Tree Vertical (BTV), Ternary Tree Horizontal (TTH), and Ternary Tree Vertical (TTV), to more efficiently adapt to the high-resolution images. However, the high performance of QTMT comes at the expense of intensive computational complexity and long encoding time, which challenges practical use. It has been observed in [4] that the reference software of H.266/VVC, VTM, dedicates 97% of its encoding time to searching for the optimal CTU partition. Therefore, accelerating the partition processing will greatly reduce the encoding time. This work thus focuses on the fast partition algorithm for H.266/VVC to balance the coding performance and computational complexity for real applications.

In the past years, researchers have proposed numerous fast CU partition techniques. These techniques mainly leverage texture features, such as image gradient [5], entropy [6], contrast [7], and residual information [8], for partition prediction. However, these features are all spatial information, only reflecting the texture characteristics, which are mostly used for intra CU partition. For inter CU partition, as temporal information is utilized in inter frame coding, the temporal motion also has a significant impact on the CU partition. To this end, many works incorporate temporal features, such as pixel difference and depth difference between current and matching blocks [9], for predicting the inter partition mode.

Based on these extracted spatial and temporal features, we can treat the CU partition as a classification problem and train machine learning (ML) models to decide the CU partition. Typical ML-based methods include the decision tree (DT) [10], the support vector machine (SVM) [11], and random forest (RF) [12]. On the other hand, some works proposed using neural networks (NNs) to automatically extract features and make decisions [13]. However, NN-based methods typically demand high-performance platforms, making them unfeasible for resource-constrained end devices. To facilitate the deployment of our method in existing devices, this work employs an ML-based model for the acceleration of inter CU partition.

As analyzed above, in inter partition, both spatial and temporal information should be considered for accurate prediction. The temporal features used in state-of-the-art methods, such as pixel difference across frames, generally reflect the global temporal motions, while ignoring the local motions in each CU. This may lead to low prediction accuracy in videos having complex motions because the local motion significantly affects the fine partition of each CU. To this end, this paper proposes a coarse-to-fine partition method, referred to as fast partition decision (FPD), jointly utilizing frame-level pixel difference and CU-level optical flow for temporal information representation. Moreover, we adopt texture edge and gradient for spatial representation. Using such temporal and spatial features, our FPD trains a LightGBM model to decide the partition direction, thereby skipping horizontal/vertical partition candidates.

The main contributions of this paper are as follows:

- We propose a coarse-to-fine algorithm, called FPD, to accelerate the inter partitioning process of H.266/VVC. FPD consists of two steps: it first uses temporal co-located similarity to assess the coarse motion of objects to determine whether to partition a CU or not; then it leverages the optical flow to capture the local motion of each CU to determine the fine partition.
- We treat the fine CU partition as a binary classification problem and train the LightGBM model for early prediction. In addition to temporal features, we incorporate spatial information related to the partition direction, including Canny edge, gradient, etc., to enhance the prediction accuracy.
- Experiments show the advanced performance of FPD. Under the common test condition of H.266/VVC, FPD archives 37% runtime saving with only 0.99% coding performance loss, surpassing state-of-the-art methods.

2   Related Work

2.1   Fast CU Partition

Currently, CU partition optimization in H.266/VVC falls into two main categories: machine learning-based and neural network-based methods.

Machine Learning-based Methods. The ML-based fast CU partition is to train ML models to learn the relationship between video features and CU partitions, thereby predicting partition probabilities or partition results for each CU. Two problems are deeply concerned with the partition accuracy: 1) the extracted video features, and 2) the ML model used. For inter frame coding, spatial and temporal features both contribute to the final results. For example, Grellert *et al.* [14] proposed an SVM-based approach, in which features like neighboring CU depth and rate-distortion cost were used to determine whether the next CU depth should be continued or not. Similarly, Zhang [15] used the improved directed acyclic graph support vector machine (DAG-SVM) model for determination. Tang *et al.* [16] calculated the three-frame difference to determine whether the current block represents a moving object and used the motion amplitude of the CU block content to decide whether or not the current block needed to be partitioned. Results showed that this algorithm achieved an encoding time reduction of 31.43% on VTM-4.0.1, with a BDBR increase of 1.34%.

Neural Network-Based Methods. Neural network-based methods have recently been incorporated into video encoders for encoding acceleration. Liu *et al.* [17] introduced a new representation for the QTMT partition and developed a U-Net model taking a multi-scale motion vector field as input, which accelerated the encoding time of H.266/VVC by about 16.5% to 60.2% under the random access configuration with an efficiency drop ranging from 0.44% to 4.59%. Li *et al.* [9] extracted spatial feature vectors based on the DenseNet model, and Merkle *et al.* [18] presented a convolutional neural network (CNN)-based method to improve the motion-compensated prediction. Tissier *et al.* [13] presented a method using the CNN model and the decision tree to accelerate the CU partition. Specifically, they used a CNN model to predict the partition probabilities of each 4×4 block, and then based on this probability information, a decision tree was applied to refine the partition results. On VTM-10.2, this method achieved a 31.8% reduction in time complexity with a 1.11% increase in coding efficiency.

While neural network-based methods effectively utilize data information to guide partitioning decisions, they require significant computational resources and training time, which is unfeasible for resource-constrained applications.

3   Proposed Method

3.1   Proposed Fast Partition Decision

In the encoding process of H.266/VVC, the encoder will traverse various QTMT partition candidates in each depth to find the one with the minimal rate-distortion (R-D) cost, which leads to intensive computational complexity. Thus, this paper proposes the FPD algorithm to speed up the above process.

Our FPD is motivated by the fact that the inter partition structure of a CU is highly associated with its spatial texture and temporal motion information. Most previous works are devoted to the fast intra partition, focusing on exploiting spatial correlation, such as entropy, contrast, and variance across pixels. However, for inter frame coding that leverages temporal reference frames for motion estimation and compensation, both spatial and temporal information will affect the partition result. Therefore, the central of FPD lies in the effective extraction and utilization of spatial and temporal information to strike a balance between accelerating speed and minimizing performance degradation.

As illustrated in Fig. 1, in the beginning, we extract the Canny edge information and the optical flow of the entire frame for later utilization in FPD. Then, for each CTU to be encoded, only CU blocks with sizes larger than 16×16 will go across the proposed FPD. Figure 2 further describes the flowchart of FPD, which adopts a coarse-to-fine mechanism. We first detect the coarse motion of objects at the frame level: if there is no horizontal/vertical motion, we can directly skip the horizontal/vertical partition. Otherwise, we further make decisions based on the fine motion of each CU via temporal optical flow and spatial texture, together with commonly used features, including CU area, quantization parameter, etc. More specifically, we first calculate the co-located similarity between the current CU and its co-located counterpart in the reference frame. Such co-located similarity reflects the global change degree of the current CU—a high similarity indicates that the current CU carries limited changes from its temporal prior and has no obvious horizontal and vertical motion. Then, we determine the partition direction based on the co-located similarity: If the similarity is greater than 95%, the horizontal and vertical partitions are directly skipped; otherwise, the current CU has a local motion, and an ML-based classifier, LightGBM, is further applied to predict its fine partition direction.

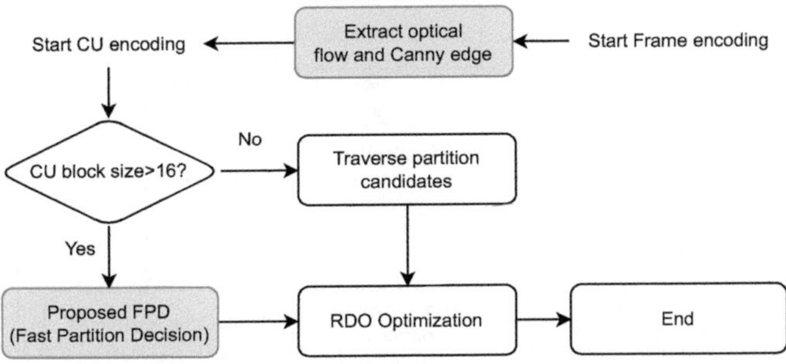

Fig. 1. Proposed fast partition decision algorithm. Canny edge information and optical flow are extracted and used in each CU for decision.

3.2 Classifier and Feature

In Fig. 2, we employ LightGBM as the classifier to further judge the fine partition direction of a CU. Note that the partition accuracy of LightGBM is closely related to its input features. Selecting appropriate features can not only enhance the classifier's discriminative ability but also improve its generalizability. Next, we will detail the features used in our FPD.

1) Temporal Co-located Similarity. In inter frame coding, the temporal correlation across adjacent frames is exploited to predict the pixels of the current frame. Consequently, if a CU in the current frame is highly similar to its co-located CU in the reference frame, the encoder can directly copy the co-located one for prediction without the complex partition process, thereby skipping the next horizontal/vertical partition steps. Inspired by this, we propose the co-located similarity feature for a coarse determination at the beginning, defined as the pixel difference $d(x, y)$ between CUs in the current frame I_i and its co-located counterpart in the first frame of the reference list I_{i-1}:

$$d(x, y) = |I_i(x, y) - I_{i-1}(x, y)|. \tag{1}$$

Then, a threshold $T = 2$ is defined to convert the obtained co-located similarity of a frame into a binary map:

$$D(x, y) = \begin{cases} 1 & d(x, y) \geq T \\ 0 & d(x, y) < T \end{cases}. \tag{2}$$

Finally, as described in Eq. (3), S_{split} is defined to represent the ratio of zero pixels in $D(x, y)$:

$$S_{split} = 1 - (\sum_{i=1}^{h} \sum_{j=1}^{w} D(i, j)/(h \times w)), \tag{3}$$

where h and w are the height and width of the current CU, respectively. In our FPD, when S_{split} exceeds 0.95, the current CU will skip horizontal and vertical

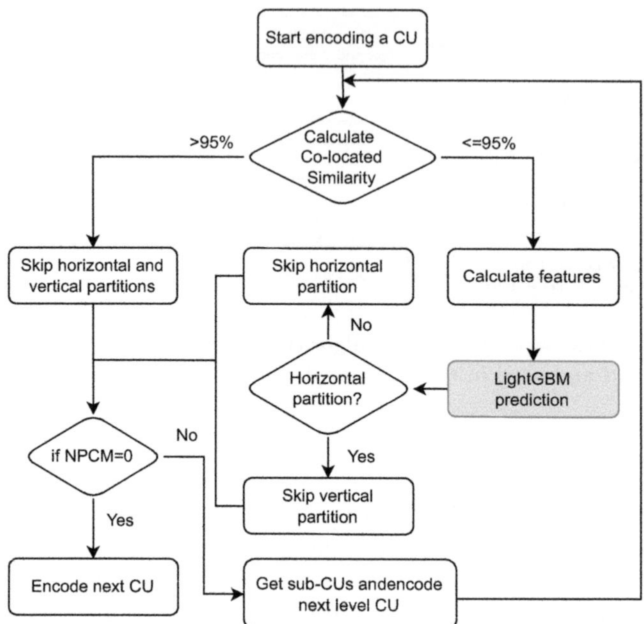

Fig. 2. The proposed FPD process where a coarse-to-fine decision is performed: the co-located similarity is first applied to directly skip horizontal/vertical partitions and then the LightGBM model is used to determine the fine partition direction for each CU. If the number of partition modes in the CU's mode candidate list (NPCM) is zero, it means the current CU has finished the encoding process. On the contrary, the CU will be partitioned into sub-CUs.

partitions. Otherwise, it is used as a feature input to the LightGBM model for further decision-making.

2) Temporal Optical Flow. The co-located similarity can be rapidly obtained to check the coarse motion of a CU. For the fine motion of each CU, we leverage the optical flow to calculate the motion vector for each pixel in a CU. Specifically, we use the *calcOpticalFlowFarneback* function in *OpenCV* to calculate the dense optical flow between the current frame and its nearest reference frame, as exemplified in Fig. 3.

Such optical flow features fully demonstrate the direction and speed of object motion across temporal frames. By calculating the mean and variance of the optical flow in the horizontal and vertical directions, we can determine the partition mode. We define the average horizontal optic flow as F_{Avgx} and the average vertical optic flow as F_{Avgy}, and set the mean feature $F_{avgSplit} = \frac{F_{Avgx}}{F_{Avgy}}$. Similarly, we derive the variance feature $F_{varSplit} = \frac{F_{Varx}}{F_{Vary}}$ using the variance of horizontal optic flow F_{Varx} and the variance of vertical optic flow F_{Vary}.

3) Spatial Edge Features. In general, the partition structure of a CTU is highly correlated to its texture complexity. For example, CTUs with complex

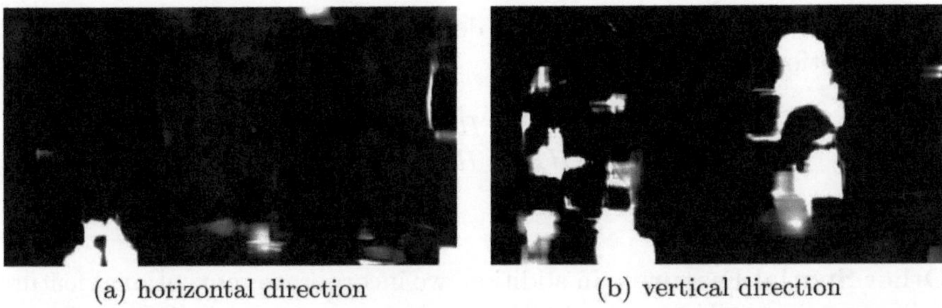

(a) horizontal direction   (b) vertical direction

Fig. 3. Dense optical flows between the current frame and its nearest reference frame in (a) horizontal direction and (b) vertical direction.

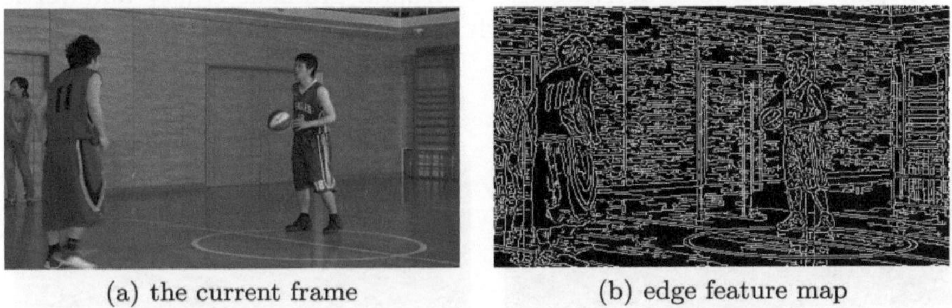

(a) the current frame   (b) edge feature map

Fig. 4. Edge feature map computed using the Canny operator: (a) the luminance component of the current frame and (b) its edge feature image.

textures are finely partitioned, and vice versa. Furthermore, the texture complexity of a CTU is related to the number and intensity of its edge features. For example, high-complexity CTUs typically have more edges, more complex object contours, and more details. Therefore, spatial edge features can be leveraged as texture characteristics for fast CU partition. In FPD, we use the Canny operator to calculate edge features in a frame, obtaining the edge feature map in Fig. 4.

In Eq. (4), we denote the edge value of the coordinate (x, y) as $Canny(x, y)$. In this way, we calculate the horizontal and vertical Canny features as he_i and ve_i and compute their respective differences HE and VE following:

$$\begin{cases} \begin{cases} ve_i = \sum_x Canny(x, y)|_{y=i} (x = 0, 1, ..., h - 1) \\ VE = \max(ve_j) - \min(ve_j)(j = 0, 1, ..., w - 1) \end{cases} \\ \begin{cases} he_i = \sum_y Canny(x, y)|_{x=i} (y = 0, 1, ..., w - 1) \\ HE = \max(he_j) - \min(he_j)(j = 0, 1, ..., h - 1) \end{cases} \end{cases} \quad (4)$$

As a result, the ratio of HE to VE, denoted as E_{split}, is used as the feature. The computation of E_{split} is as follows:

$$\begin{cases} E_{split} = 0 & HE = 0, VE = 0 \\ E_{split} = HE & HE \neq 0, VE = 0 \\ E_{split} = \frac{HE}{VE} & VE \neq 0 \end{cases} \tag{5}$$

4) Other Spatial Features. In addition, we incorporate conventional features, including gradient, CU area, and CU quantization parameter (QP) as features in FPD. Particularly, the frame complexity can also be reflected by its gradient to some extent. Here, we use the Sobel operator to calculate the gradient value of each pixel in a frame, deriving the horizontal gradient G_{Avgx} and vertical gradient G_{Avgy} shown in Fig. 5. Similarly, the gradient feature G_{split} is defined as $G_{split} = \frac{G_{Avgx}}{G_{Avgy}}$.

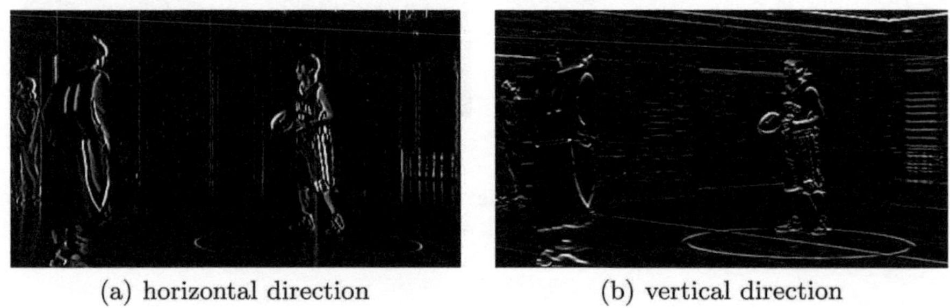

(a) horizontal direction   (b) vertical direction

Fig. 5. Gradient images in (a) horizontal and (b) vertical directions. We compute the gradient values using the Sobel operator.

3.3   Feature Evaluation

To validate the effectiveness of the selected features, the built-in tool of Light-GBM is used to evaluate the importance of each feature, as shown in Fig. 6.

It is observed that five features, including edge E_{split}, co-located similarity S_{split}, optical flow $F_{avgSplit}$, $F_{varSplit}$, and gradient G_{split}, lead the importance in FPD. This sufficiently demonstrates the effectiveness of our proposed edge, co-located similarity, and optical flow features. The other two features, CU area and CU QP, exhibit lower importance than the others, indicating their small impact on prediction outcomes. However, the inclusion of these features can adapt our LightGBM model to different QP values and CU sizes without training separate models, which significantly reduces the memory requirement. To this end, we incorporate these two features into our model.

4   Experiments and Results

Dataset. The proposed algorithm is implemented in C/C++ and integrated into the official H.266/VVC reference software VTM-15.0. We use VTM-15.0 to generate a dataset using four QP values, 22, 27, 32, and 37, under random access (RA) coding configuration. Our training dataset is built using seven sequences, namely *FoodMarket4* (3840×2160), *RitualDance* (1920×1080), *Cactus* (1920×1080), *BasketballDrive* (1920×1080), *RaceHorsesC* (832×480), *Blowing-Bubbles* (416×240), and *Johnny* (1280×720). The first two sequences are 10 bits while the others are 8 bits. Due to video resolution differences, these seven sequences have different numbers of CTUs per frame. To maintain the data balance in our training dataset, we adjust the number of frames used for training in each sequence:*FoodMarket4* uses 16 frames, *RitualDance* uses 32 frames, *Cactus* and *BasketballDrive* use 9 frames, *RaceHorsesC* uses 33 frames, *BlowingBubbles* uses 129 frames, and *Johnny* uses 17 frames.

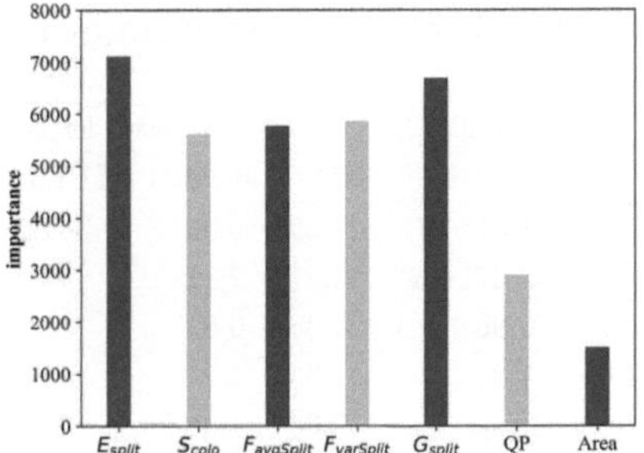

Fig. 6. Importance of selected features in the proposed FPD.

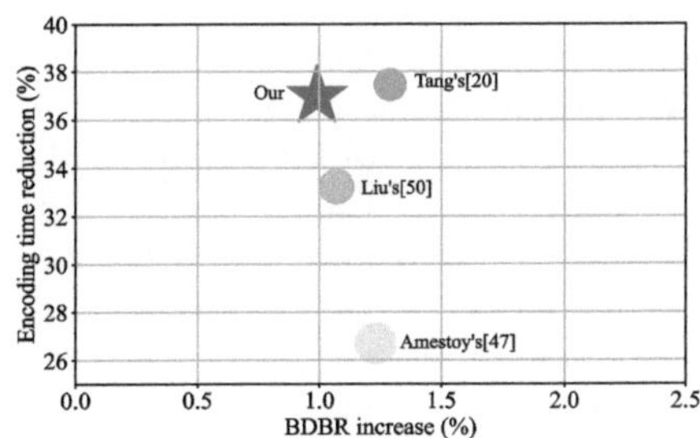

Fig. 7. Time reduction versus BDBR loss of compared methods on 8-bit sequences from JVET common test condition.

Table 1. Performance of the proposed FPD algorithm on 10-bit test sequences

Class	10-bit Sequence	BDBR (%)	TR (%)
A1	Tango2	2.77	49.63
	FoodMarket4	1.71	53.71
	CamNfire	1.21	45.97
A2	CatRobot1	1.29	41.06
	DaylightRoad2	2.13	45.45
	NarkRunning3	1.12	43.87
B	MarketNlace	2.16	39.79
	RitualDance	1.79	47.8
	Average	1.77	45.91

Setting. To test the coding performance of the proposed FPD algorithm, we use 22 video sequences officially used in the video coding standardization committee, Joint Video Experts Team (JVET), for performance evaluation. These test sequences include eight 10-bit sequences and fourteen 8-bit sequences, covering wide resolutions from 3840×2160 to 416×240. Our experimental settings follow the common test condition defined in H.266/VVC.

We use Bjøntegaard Delta Bit Rate (BDBR) [19] to evaluate the coding performance. For the coding complexity, we use the Time Reduction (TR) compared to the anchor VTM-15.0.

Overall Performance. Tables 1 and 2 present the performance improvement of the proposed FPD over the anchor H.266/VVC. For 10-bit sequences, our method saves 45.91% runtime and the BDBR loss is 1.77%. For 8-bit sequences from Class B to Class E, we achieve 37% encoding time reduction with only 0.99% BDBR loss.

Table 2. Performance comparison of the proposed FPD algorithm with state-of-the-arts on 8-bit test sequences

Class	8-bit Sequences	Amestoy's [12]		Liu's [17]		Tang's [16]		Proposed FPD	
		BDBR (%)	TR (%)	BDBR (%)	TR (%)	BDBR (%)	TR (%)	BDBR (%)	TR (%)
B	Cactus	1.26	28.24	1.32	44.03	1.51	42.59	0.95	41.78
	BasketballDrive	1.61	34.87	2.16	51.35	2.07	44.57	2.11	49.5
	BQTerrace	1.07	22.48	1.13	36.72	0.96	34.36	0.92	35.59
C	BasketballDrill	1.65	31.4	1.14	34.60	1.3	41.35	1.25	43.06
	BQMall	1.33	29.03	1.12	31.60	1.4	39.36	1.05	37.85
	PartyScene	1.31	29.03	0.93	41.15	0.61	34.01	0.57	34.57
	RaceHorses	1.39	35.52	1.13	49.10	1.12	40.4	1.07	42.26
D	BasketballPass	1.22	27.12	0.31	19.10	1.31	37.1	0.83	34.42
	BQSquare	0.71	23.97	0.79	18.95	0.88	28.87	0.09	29.35
	BlowingBubbles	1.91	26.83	0.27	24.46	1.22	35.41	0.85	34.28
	RaceHorses	1.98	35.52	0.77	26.70	0.96	37.1	1.2	38.59
E	FourPeoPle	0.69	17.53	0.81	31.69	1.26	37.07	0.84	32.48
	Johnny	0.5	15.38	1.27	25.62	1.38	34.81	0.9	30.59
	KristenAndSara	0.6	18.09	1.83	30.05	2.11	37.32	1.21	33.28
	Average	1.23	26.69	1.07	33.22	1.29	37.45	**0.99**	**36.97**

We further compare our coding performance with state-of-the-art fast inter CU partition methods in Table 2, including the ML-based method Amestoy *et al.* [12], the NN-based method Liu *et al.* [17], and the threshold-based method Tang *et al.* [16]. It is observed that FPD outperforms other methods with faster speed and/or less BDBR increase. Amestoy *et al.* is an ML-based method. It trained three RF-based binary classifiers, namely S-NS (Split or No Split), QT-BT (QT or BT), and BH-BV (BTV or BTH). On the one hand, the three classifiers are applied sequentially, costing significant time for determination. On the other hand, such sequential processing easily leads to error accumulation because errors in the first classifier will be propagated to the next, resulting in high BDBR loss. This is also revealed in our results: Amestoy *et al.* saved only 26.69% encoding time, while the BDBR loss is as high as 1.23%. Liu *et al.* is an NN-based method. It introduced the partition path as QTMT representation and used a U-Net-style network to predict the QTMT representation of the current CU from its original pixels. Experiments showed that in the case of threshold $Thm = 0.2$ and $QTskip = 0$, it achieved 33.22% runtime reduction, with BDBR increased by 1.07%. Tang *et al.* used a three-frame difference method with the pre-defined threshold to determine whether the current block is a moving object and whether the partition can be early terminated. While this method achieved a comparable runtime to ours, it resulted in a larger BDBR loss. This is because it solely relies on the global temporal motion information and ignores the impact of local motions in each CU, resulting in a rough partition decision.

By contrast, our FPD introduces a coarse-to-fine mechanism for fast partition determination. At the coarse level, it introduces co-located similarity to judge whether the partition is applied. At the fine level, it utilizes optical flow and Canny edges together for early termination. As a result, our FPD obtains a more balanced trade-off between the BDBR loss and runtime saving. For example, our runtime speedup is comparable to that of Tang *et al.* (36.97% versus 37.45%) while having less BDBR loss (0.99% versus 1.29%). Figure 7 demonstrates the BDBR loss versus runtime reduction of various methods.

5 Conclusion

This paper presents a fast inter partition algorithm for H.266/VVC. While previous works have focused on fast intra partition using various spatial features, inter-frame coding relies heavily on temporal correlations across neighboring frames, which significantly influence partition decisions. To address this, we propose a coarse-to-fine approach that integrates both spatial and temporal information. First, we use co-located similarity to capture global object motion and roughly determine the CU's motion direction, allowing early skipping of horizontal or vertical partitions. Then, for CUs with complex motion, we extract temporal optical flow and spatial features (e.g., edges and gradients) and train a LightGBM classifier for fine-grained partitioning. Experimental results demonstrate the effectiveness of the proposed method.

Acknowledgment. This work was supported by National Natural Science Foundation of China (62171174).

References

1. Sullivan, G.J., Ohm, J.R., Han, W.J., Wiegand, T.: Overview of the high efficiency video coding (HEVC) standard. IEEE Trans. Circuits Syst. Video Technol. **22**(12), 1649–1668 (2012)

2. Bross, B., Wang, Y.K., Ye, Y., Liu, S., Chen, J., Sullivan, G.J., Ohm, J.R.: Overview of the versatile video coding (VVC) standard and its applications. IEEE Trans. Circuits Syst. Video Technol. **31**(10), 3736–3764 (2021)
3. Huang, Y.-W., et al.: Block partitioning structure in the VVC standard. IEEE Trans. Circuits Syst. Video Technol. **31**(10), 3818–3833 (2021)
4. Tissier, A., Mercat, A., Amestoy, T., Hamidouche, W., Vanne, J., Menard, D.: Complexity reduction opportunities in the future VVC intra encoder. In: 2019 IEEE 21st International Workshop on Multimedia Signal Processing (MMSP), pp. 1–6. IEEE (2019)
5. Jiang, W., Ma, H., Chen, Y.: Gradient based fast mode decision algorithm for intra prediction in HEVC. In: 2012 2nd International Conference on Consumer Electronics, Communications and Networks (CECNet), pp. 1836–1840. IEEE (2012)
6. Ding, G., Lin, X., Wang, J., Ding, D.: Accelerating QTMT-based CU partition and intra mode decision for versatile video coding. J. Vis. Commun. Image Represent. **94**, 103832 (2023)
7. Song, Y., Zeng, B., Wang, M., Deng, Z.: An efficient low-complexity block partition scheme for VVC intra coding. J. Real-Time Image Process. **19**, 161–172 (2022)
8. Wang, Z., Wang, S., Zhang, J., Wang, S., Ma, S.: Probabilistic decision based block partitioning for future video coding. IEEE Trans. Image Process. **27**(3), 1475–1486 (2017)
9. Li, H., Zhang, P., Jin, B., Zhang, Q.: Fast CU decision algorithm based on CNN and decision trees for VVC. Electronics **12**(14), 3053 (2023)
10. Wen, S., Ding, G., Ding, D.: Paired decision trees for fast intra decision in H266/VVC. Displays **80**, 102545 (2023)
11. Yao, Y., Wang, J., Chenjie, D., Zhu, J., Xin, X.: A support vector machine based fast planar prediction mode decision algorithm for versatile video coding. Multimedia Tools Appl. **81**(12), 17205–17222 (2022)
12. Amestoy, T., Mercat, A., Hamidouche, W., Menard, D., Bergeron, C.: Tunable VVC frame partitioning based on lightweight machine learning. IEEE Trans. Image Process. **29**, 1313–1328 (2019)
13. Tissier, A., Hamidouche, W., Vanne, J., Menard, D.: Machine learning based efficient QT-MTT partitioning for VVC inter coding. In: 2022 IEEE International Conference on Image Processing (ICIP), pp. 1401–1405. IEEE (2022)
14. Grellert, M., Zatt, B., Bampi, S., da Silva Cruz, L.A.: Fast coding unit partition decision for HEVC using support vector machines. IEEE Trans. Circuits Syst. Video Technol. **29**(6), 1741–1753 (2018)
15. Zhang, Q., Wang, Y., Huang, L., Jiang, B., Wang, X.: Fast CU partition decision for H.266/VVC based on the improved dag-svm classifier model. Multimedia Syst. **27**, 1–14 (2021)
16. Tang, N., et al.: Fast CTU partition decision algorithm for VVC intra and inter coding. In: 2019 IEEE Asia Pacific Conference on Circuits and Systems (APCCAS), pp. 361–364. IEEE (2019)
17. Liu, Y., Riviere, M., Guionnet, T., Roumy, A., Guillemot, C.: CNN-based prediction of partition path for VVC fast inter partitioning using motion fields. arXiv preprint arXiv:2310.13838 (2023)
18. Merkle, P., Winken, M., Pfaff, J., Schwarz, H., Marpe, D., Wiegand, T.: Intra-inter prediction for versatile video coding using a residual convolutional neural network. In: 2022 IEEE International Conference on Image Processing (ICIP), pp. 1711–1715. IEEE (2022)
19. Bjøntegaard, G.: Calculation of average PSNR differences between rd-curves. In: ITU-T SG 16/Q6, 13th VCEG Meeting. Document VCEG-M33 (2001)

Semantic Maintained Video Compression by Background Blurring in Surveillance Scenarios

Wenpeng Cui[1], Xinwei Zheng[2(✉)], Hongming Zhang[2], and Wei Zeng[2]

[1] Beijing Smart-chip Microelectronics Technology Co., Ltd., Beijing, China
[2] School of Compute Science, Peking University, Beijing, China
{xwzheng,hmzhang76,weizeng}@pku.edu.cn

Abstract. This paper proposes a novel surveillance video compression framework that does not modify the encoder and decoder. By introducing background blurring before encoding, the method significantly enhances compression efficiency and semantic regions' signal. Background blurring is adopted to remove background texture and preserve signal of semantic regions(foreground) as a preprocessing step. This preprocessing yields higher compression gains and improves foreground signal simultaneously. This paper also presents the first quantitative model relating compression gain to ROI area ratio and blurring degree. It provides a theoretical basis for our approach's compression capability. Additionally, a video caching scheme is proposed to temporarily store original videos at the camera end. This enables lossless video retrieval in emergencies as a supply. Extensive experimental results are given and demonstrate our method's effectiveness and efficiency. At equivalent bitrates, the average PSNR of semantic regions increases about 1.22 dB. Our approach presents a simple but highly efficient solution for surveillance video compression without changing the encoder and decoder.

Keywords: Surveillance Video Compression · ROI Compression · Background Blurring

1 Introduction

Video compression is a long term evolving technology. Researchers persistently pursue high compression performance, and leading to series of compression technologies and standards such as MPEG-4, H.265, AVS-3 [1]. Video compression technologies and standards are applied in various scenarios, e.g. video conferencing, movie, surveillance, mobile phones, etc. Among these scenarios, video surveillance has among the highest demands due to the large number of cameras deployed worldwide. Most surveillance videos must be transmitted to supervision centers for monitoring and storage.

Unlike other video compression scenarios, surveillance video contains a large portion of background that is typically unimportant to observers. Viewers primarily focus on events and objects related to security-relevant activities. These security-critical elements represent the core semantics of surveillance. For example, electronic police cameras focus on vehicles; security cameras focus on individuals; traffic cameras focus on

Z. Lin et al. (Eds.): ICIG 2025, LNCS 16161, pp. 469–478, 2026.
https://doi.org/10.1007/978-981-95-3398-5_38

vehicle trajectories. In such cases, background regions or irrelevant objects can be disregarded. Based on this premise, region of interest (ROI) compression and background compression techniques have been developed specifically for surveillance video. Foreground/ROI regions receive greater bit allocation during encoding, while the background receives fewer bits. The separation between foreground/ROIs and background enables additional compression gains. However, these surveillance video compression methods require encoder and decoder modifications to embed the separation scheme. Such systems necessitate redesign of both components, presenting challenges for hardware implementation.

This paper proposes a novel surveillance video compression approach that introduces a non-ROI region blurring process prior to encoding. The method comprises three key steps: semantic object detection, background blurring, and encoding. Semantic objects are first detected or selected after objection. The objects are then treated as ROIs in total. Subsequently, non-ROI regions (background) undergo blurring via standard image processing techniques. Finally, ROIs are combined with the blurred background and fed into a traditional encoder for compression. The core principle underlying our method is that background blurring will remove texture and yields obvious compression gains. The contributions of this paper are listed as follows:

(1) We propose a novel compression approach that achieves high compression of surveillance video without modifying the encoder or decoder.
(2) For the first time, we present a model that reveals relationship between compression gain, blurring degree, and foreground area. This provides a theoretical analysis of our method's compression capability.
(3) A video caching scheme is introduced to systematically compensate the loss of ROI information in emergencies.

2 Related Work

Surveillance video compression aims to compress background as much as possible while preserving foreground or ROIs. Most surveillance video compression technologies follow the traditional block encoding schema [3–7]. Due to emergence of deep learning, end-to-end surveillance video encoding algorithms occur recently [8–13]. Li et al. summarized various surveillance video compression algorithms as an overview [2].

Traditional surveillance video compression algorithms incorporate background modeling into the compression pipeline. Fewer bits and accurate motion estimation are employed for efficient background compression [3–7]. Wu et al. proposed a foreground-background parallel compression method with residual encoding, which adopts an adaptive Gaussian mixture model to separate foreground and background regions before compressing them separately [3]. Zhao et al. introduced an adaptive surveillance video compression framework (ASVC) based on background hyper-priors, extracting background information from GOPs as hyper-priors to assist I-frame and P-frame compression [4]. Addressing spatiotemporal background properties, the Time Domain Adaptive Learning Compression (TALC) method was developed [5]. This approach incorporates a Forward Time Domain Adaptation (FTA) module and a Backward Time Domain Adaptation (BTA) module that dynamically select appropriate enhancement strategies by analyzing optical flow error accumulation and residual errors. Sengar et al. presented an adaptive particle swarm optimization (PSO) technique utilizing motion segmentation [6], combining both elements to overcome block encoding limitations while maintaining object encoding flexibility. Beyond improving compression efficiency, fine-grained compression can be achieved. Zhao et al. developed a method that enhances compression performance through dual reference frames (background and foreground reference frames) to separately address background and foreground redundancy [7].

Similar approaches of background compression have been adopted in end-to-end compression techniques [8–13]. Wang et al. proposed an end-to-end video compression method that combines optical flow residual encoding and decoding-end optical flow optimization [8]. Zhao et al. proposed an end-to-end unsupervised foreground-background separation network, UVCNet [9]. UVCNet uses its Mask Net module to perform unsupervised separation of foreground and background in real time, while fully utilizing the relatively static nature of the background. Lu et al. proposed a deep compression technique for apron surveillance videos that separates moving objects from stationary objects using object detection techniques [10]. Wu et al. proposed a generative framework that decomposes video signals into global spatiotemporal features (termed memory) and the structural skeleton of each frame (termed cue) [11]. At the decoding end, a generative adversarial network reconstructs video frames. Beye et al. proposed a recognition-aware deep video compression method, which trains a convolutional encoder-decoder neural network combined with novel random quantization techniques for video compression optimized toward object detection [12]. Meng et al. proposed an image-feature parallel compression framework that divides a video into two parts: a background image and foreground features for separate compression [13].

Another type of surveillance video compression is Region of Interest (ROI) compression [14–19]. These methods treat the ROI as foreground, and non-ROI areas as background. Hapsari et al. proposed a video compression method that separates foreground (ROI) and background using a background subtraction algorithm [14]. Only the foreground regions are encoded, thereby significantly improving the compression ratio. Fadel et al. proposed an efficient compression method that encodes and transmits only ROI regions containing motion [15]. Liao et al. proposed an ROI encoding method that determines ROIs based on prior knowledge and employs a weighted rate control strategy to allocate more bits to these regions to preserve their quality [16]. Liu et al. proposed an ROI-aware dynamic quantization method [17], which allocates high bit widths to ROI regions and low bit widths to non-ROI areas. Zhao et al. proposed a video compression algorithm that divides frames into background, foreground, and foreground ROI regions [18]. These distinct regions are allocated different bit allocations during compression.

Beyond background and ROI compression, regions exhibiting semantic relevance can be separated and encoded more efficiently [19, 20]. Shanmugam et al. proposed a semantic-aware compression strategy based on the H.264 video compression format, which combines block-based encoding with deep-learning semantic segmentation to achieve region-specific quantization for regions of interest versus non-ROI areas [19]. Htike et al. proposed a two-stage intelligent compression system for surveillance videos [20], where only temporally encoded semantic event video segments are processed.

To the best of our knowledge, most existing surveillance video compression methods require modifications to both encoder and decoder. Limited research offers solutions that preserve standard encoding/decoding frameworks. In this paper, we present a novel approach for surveillance video compression that operates without modifying the encoder or decoder.

3 Proposed Method

Our method introduces a background blurring pre-processing step prior to frame compression. Semantic regions – typically foreground objects or manually labeled regions – are designated as preserved areas, which are treated as ROIs. ROIs are obtained by object detection algorithms [21]. Subsequently, pixel-level blurring is applied to non-ROI regions, and yielding blurred background. The modified frames are synthesized by combining original ROIs with blurred background. These processed frames are fed into an encoder for compression. The overall workflow is shown in Fig. 1.

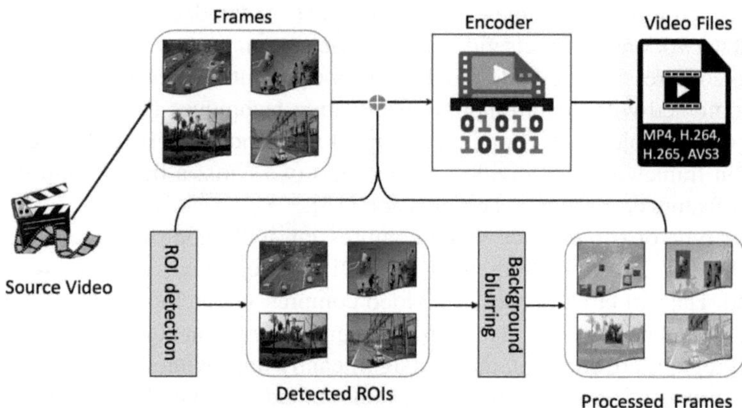

Fig. 1. The overall process of the proposed algorithm.

3.1 Basic Paradigm

Give an input video V that consists of a series of frames: $V = \{I_1, I_2, ..., I_t, , .., I_n\}$. The first step of our algorithm is to extract or set ROIs in each frame. All ROIs compose the ROI set $R = \{ROI_1, ROI_2, ..., ROI_t, , .., ROI_n\}$. A blurring process is performed on non-ROI regions, obtaining blurred background frames $B = \{B_1, B_2, ..., B_t, , .., B_n\}$. The ROI and background are merged at the pixel level. The synthesized video is $V\prime = \{I\prime_1, I\prime_2, ..., I\prime_t, , .., I\prime_n\}$. At last, V' is fed to an encoder for traditional compression. The steps are formulated as:

$$B_t = blur(I_t),$$
$$I_t' = merge(ROIs_t, B_t) \tag{1}$$
$$V'' = encode(V'),$$

V" is the final encoded video.

The compression gain in our algorithm depends on the degree of background blurring and the total area of ROIs. In general, higher degree of background blurring yields greater compression gain. Conversely, a smaller ROI area also results in higher compression gain. This occurs because the gain is achieved by smoothing background texture, which leads to fewer bits allocated during encoding. Let the blurring degree be parameterized as δ, and let r represent the percentage of ROIs within a frame. The compression gain Δg is then given by:

$$\Delta g = 0.23 * \ln(1 + \delta) - 0.4 * r^{1/2} - 0.006 * crf + 0.34, \tag{2}$$

where *crf* denotes the constant rate factor used by the FFmpeg encoder [22], ranging from 0 to 51. Equation 2 indicates that the compression gain exhibits a linear relationship with $\ln(1 + \delta)$, and an linear relationship with both *sqrt* (the square root of the ROI area ratio) and *crf*. We derived this model through curve fitting based on empirical compression gain data. Figure 2 illustrates the relationship between compression gain and blurring degree for varying ROI percentages.

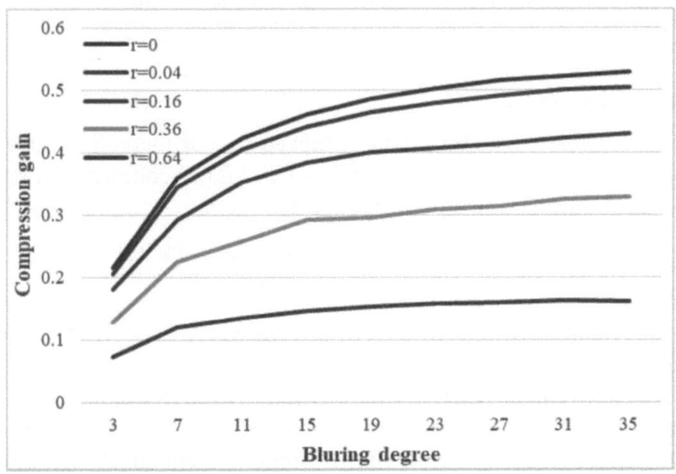

Fig. 2. The curves of compression gain and blurring degree under different percentage of ROIs

3.2 Advanced Paradigm

Although our method efficiently compresses surveillance video, background texture is blurred and consequently lost. To address the potential requirement for viewing background details in emergencies, we propose a video caching mechanism. This mechanism involves a temporary buffer at the camera side to store the original video stream directly. When users need to retrieve the original, lossless video, they can request the camera to transmit the cached video on demand. Given the infrequency of critical surveillance events, such requests are expected to occur occasionally. The workflow of the video caching mechanism is illustrated in Fig. 3.

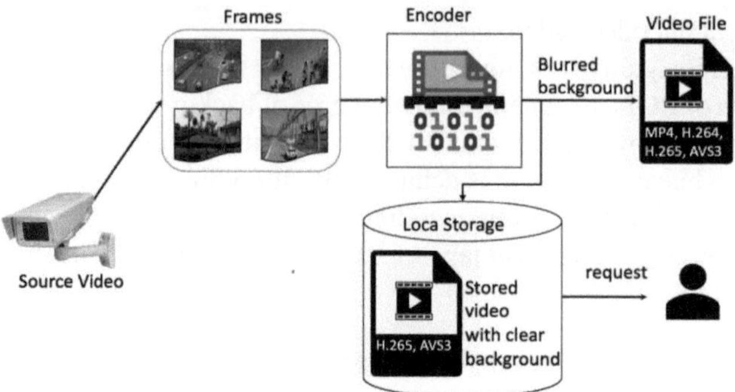

Fig. 3. The flow of the video caching scheme.

4 Experiments

To evaluate the proposed approach, we selected 10 videos as a test dataset. The videos were primarily collected from various surveillance devices capturing real-world scenes. The scenes encompassed traffic, shopping malls, and campuses. We employed two evaluation metrics: compression gain and the peak signal-to-noise ratio (PSNR) improvement within the ROI.

4.1 Evaluation Metrics

Compression gain refers to the bit saving achieved by our method relative to the conventional method (without background blurring). A higher compression gain indicates greater bit saving. Compression gain is defined as:

$$\Delta g = \frac{bits\big(encode(V) - bits\big(encode(V')\big)\big)}{bits(encode(V))}, \tag{3}$$

while *bits(V)* is the number of bits of the compressed video V; V' is the blurred video as in Eq. 1. *Encode()* is the adopted encoder for compression.

The PSNR improvement refers to the increase in PSNR achieved by our method within the semantic ROIs, relative to traditional compression. A higher PSNR improvement indicates better preserved fidelity of the foreground signal. PSNR improvement is defined as:

$$\Delta P = \frac{PSNR\big(ROI \in V'\big)}{PSNR(ROI \in V)}, \tag{4}$$

while V and V' is the original video and blurred video of our approach.

4.2 Compression Gain Experiments

To evaluate the impact of blurring degree and ROI percentage on compression gain, we systematically varied blurring values and ROI proportions, and applied multiple quality control factors during video compression. The average compression gains across all videos were calculated for each parameter combination. The results are presented in Table 1.

Table 1. Compression gain under different blurring degree and percentage of ROIs

Blurring degree	Percentage of ROIs								
	0	0.01	0.04	0.09	0.16	0.25	0.36	0.49	0.64
3	0.215	0.213	0.205	0.196	0.180	0.159	0.129	0.101	0.072
7	0.359	0.355	0.344	0.323	0.292	0.261	0.225	0.169	0.120
11	0.423	0.418	0.405	0.380	0.353	0.308	0.258	0.205	0.135
15	0.461	0.455	0.441	0.418	0.383	0.342	0.292	0.215	0.147
19	0.485	0.479	0.463	0.440	0.400	0.349	0.295	0.224	0.153
23	0.502	0.496	0.479	0.451	0.407	0.358	0.308	0.236	0.158
27	0.514	0.508	0.490	0.462	0.413	0.377	0.313	0.248	0.159
31	0.522	0.515	0.500	0.464	0.423	0.381	0.325	0.239	0.163
35	0.528	0.521	0.503	0.476	0.430	0.381	0.327	0.248	0.160

The results reveal a clear trend in compression gain. It increases with higher blurring degree, validating the effectiveness of our method. Additionally, as the proportion of ROIs increases, the blurrable background area decreases, leading to a reduction in compression gain.

Table 2. Compression gain under different blurring degree and CRFs

Blurring degree	Constant Rate Factor(CRF)				
	18	23	28	33	38
3	0.194	0.183	0.162	0.106	0.056
7	0.314	0.294	0.255	0.184	0.114
11	0.363	0.341	0.296	0.218	0.143
15	0.393	0.369	0.321	0.239	0.162
19	0.405	0.380	0.333	0.251	0.174
23	0.417	0.392	0.344	0.258	0.180
27	0.426	0.400	0.352	0.268	0.190
31	0.432	0.405	0.356	0.271	0.193
35	0.435	0.408	0.359	0.275	0.197

Table 2 and Fig. 4 summarize the compression gains achieved by our method under different CRF settings, reflecting variations in blurring degree. The results demonstrate that compression gain consistently increases with higher blurring degree across all CRF configurations. However, when the CRF is set to higher values, the additional compression gain attributable to blur processing diminishes. This occurs because larger CRF values cause the encoder to apply more aggressive compression, which inherently involves filtering operations that discard texture. This effect parallels blurring before encoding to some extent. Consequently, the benefits of our approach partially overlap with the encoder's inherent compression mechanisms (including filtering) at high CRF settings.

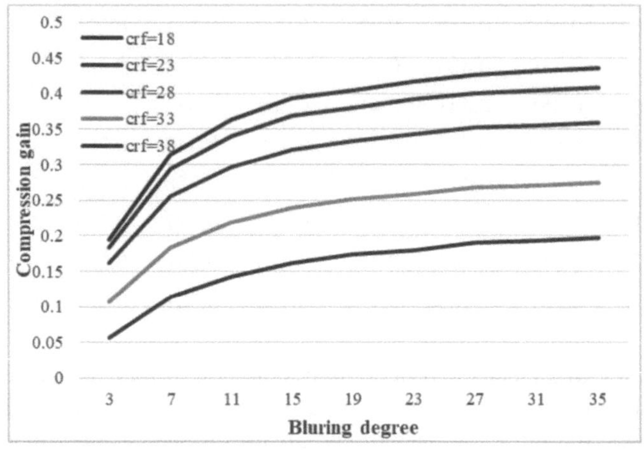

Fig. 4. The relationship between compression gain and blurring degree under different CRF settings

4.3   PSNR Improvement Experiments

For surveillance video, bandwidth is an expensive resource. Our method facilitates superior preservation of ROI signals. Using the same experimental dataset as in Sect. 4.2, we encoded videos at target bitrates of 200–500 kbps and compared the PSNR within ROI regions between traditional compression and our method. The results are presented in Table 3.

Table 3. PSNR(dB) comparison between our method and conventional methods in ROIs under different bitrates

Percentage of ROIs	bitrate = 200kbps		bitrate = 300kbps		bitrate = 400kbps		bitrate = 500kbps	
	w/o our method	w/ our method	w/o our method	w/ our method	w/o our method	w/ our method	w/o our method	w/ our method
0.04	37.81	38.83	40.11	41.58	40.92	42.67	41.57	43.51
0.16	37.05	37.89	38.44	39.61	39.22	40.70	39.87	41.56
0.36	36.26	36.73	37.89	38.60	38.68	39.62	39.34	40.48
Avg.	37.04	37.82	38.81	39.93	39.60	41.00	40.26	41.85
Improve	0.78		1.12		1.39		1.59	

The results demonstrate that our method provides significant improvement in preserving ROI signals, achieving an average PSNR improvement of 1.22 dB. This enhancement offers high flexibility in bandwidth allocation. For instance, when targeting a PSNR of 40 dB for ROI regions, conventional methods require approximately 460 kbps, while our proposed method achieves the same PSNR with only 301 kbps. This represents an approximately 35% reduction in bitrate compared to conventional approaches.

5 Conclusions

This paper proposes a novel semantic-preserving video compression framework for surveillance scenarios. The core contribution lies in decoupling semantic-aware processing from standard encoding, thereby eliminating the need to modify existing encoders and decoders. The framework establishes a new video compression paradigm that integrates object detection, background blurring, and traditional encoders. By controlling the blurring degree applied to background/non-ROI regions, the method significantly reduces background texture complexity, and leads to substantial compression gains. We also present a quantitative model and give theoretical analysis of the proposed method. Experimental results on real surveillance videos demonstrate effectiveness and efficiency of our method.

Our work paves the way for novel surveillance systems featuring highly efficient, flexible compression and transmission in a simple framework. Future work will explore dynamic adaptation of blurring on ROIs and background, as well as more precise blurring control for refined bitrate setting.

Acknowledgments. This study is supported by the Joint R&D Fund of Beijing Smart-chip Microelectronics Technology Co., Ltd (Grant no. SGSC0000NXJS2401305).

References

1. Ma, S., et al.: Evolution of AVS video coding standards: twenty years of innovation and development. Sci. China Inf. Sci. **65**(9), 1–24 (2022)
2. Li, L., Hu, X., Zhou, W., Zhang, P., Cai, L.: Overview of surveillance video compression for power system. In: International Conference on Artificial Intelligence and Computer Engineering, pp. 707–711, IEEE, Wuhu (2024)
3. Wu, L., Huang, K., Shen, H., Gao, L.: Foreground-background parallel compression with residual encoding for surveillance video. IEEE Trans. Circuits Syst. Video Technol. **31**(7), 2711–2724 (2021)
4. Zhao, Y., Tang, S., Ye, M.: Adaptive surveillance video compression with back-ground hyperprior. IEEE Signal Process. Lett. **32**, 456–460 (2025)
5. Zhao, Y., Ye, M., Ji, L., Guo, H., Zhu, C.: Temporal adaptive learned surveillance video compression. IEEE Trans. Broadcast. **71**(1), 142–153 (2025)
6. Sengar, S., Mukhopadhyay, S.: Motion segmentation-based surveillance video compression using adaptive particle swarm optimization. Neural Comput. Appl. **32**(15), 11443–11457 (2020)

7. Zhao, L., Wang, S., Ye, Y., Ma, S., Gao, W.: Enhanced surveillance video compression with dual reference frames generation. IEEE Trans. Circuits Syst. Video Technol. **32**(3), 1592–1606 (2022)
8. Wang, S., Zhao, Y., Gao, H., et al.: End-to-end video compression for surveillance and conference videos. Multimedia Tools Appl **81**, 42713–42730 (2022)
9. Zhao, Y., Luo, D., Wang, F., Gao, H., Ye, M., Zhu, C.: End-to-end compression for surveillance video with unsupervised foreground-background separation. IEEE Trans. Broadcast. **69**(4), 966–978 (2023)
10. Lu, Z., Xu, X.: Deep compression: a compression technology for apron surveillance video. IEEE Access **7**, 129966–129974 (2019)
11. Wu, Y., He, T., Chen, Z.: Memorize, then recall: a generative framework for low bit-rate surveillance video compression. In: IEEE International Symposium on Circuits and Systems, pp.1–5. IEEE, Seville (2020)
12. Beye, F., Itsumi, H., Vitthal C., Nihei, K.: Recognition-aware deep video compression for remote surveillance. In: IEEE International Conference on Image Processing, pp. 1986–1990, IEEE, Bordeaux (2022)
13. Meng, Y., Wang, H., Yin, H., Yu, L., Lai, C., Wang, G., Li, T.: Image-feature parallel compression for indoor surveillance video. In: 25th International Workshop on Multimedia Signal Processing, pp. 1–5. IEEE, Poitiers (2023)
14. Hapsari, D., Madenda, S., Subali, M., Talita, A.: A novel approach to video compression using region of interest (ROI) method on video surveillance systems". Int. J. Adv. Comput. Sci. Appl. **13**(6), 125–130 (2022)
15. Fadel, M., et al.: Reducing bandwidth and storage requirements for surveillance videos using ROI extraction and compression. In: 17th International Conference on Development in eSystem Engineering, pp. 281–286. IEEE, Khorfakkan (2024)
16. Liao, L., Hu, R., Xiao, J., Zhan, G., Chen, Y., Xiao, J.: An analysis-oriented ROI based coding approach on surveillance video data. In: Chen, E., Gong, Y., Tie, Y. (eds) Advances in Multimedia Information Processing - PCM 2016. PCM 2016. Lecture Notes in Computer Science, vol. 9917, pp. 428–437. Springer, Cham (2016)
17. Liu, J., Zhang, B., Cao, X.: ROI-aware dynamic network quantization for neural video compression. In: Antonacopoulos, A., Chaudhuri, S., Chellappa, R., Liu, CL., Bhattacharya, S., Pal, U. (eds.) PATTEN RECOGNITION 2024, Lecture Notes in Computer Science, vol. 15305. Springer, Cham (2025)
18. Ramadoss, M., Mahendran, S.: Design of lossy and lossless algorithms for roi-based video compression. Int. J. Sci. Technol. Res. **8**(9), 1439–1443 (2019)
19. Shanmugam, V., Maheswari, B.: A semantic-aware compression strategy for intelligent vehicles. Procedia Comput. Sci. **2025**, 2544–2553 (2025)
20. Htike, K.: A two-stage intelligent compression system for surveillance videos. J. Theor. Appl. Inf. Technol. **93**(1), 1–9 (2016)
21. Pagire, V., Chavali, M., Kale, A.: A comprehensive review of object detection with traditional and deep learning methods. Signal Process. **237**, 1–28 (2025)
22. FFmpeg Documentation. http://ffmpeg.org/documentation.html. Accessed 20 May 2025

Learning Based Fast Coding Unit Decision for Video-Based Point Cloud Compression

Lewen Fan and Yun Zhang[✉]

School of Electronics and Communication Engineering, Sun Yat-Sen University,
Shenzhen Campus, Shenzhen, China
`fanlw3@mail2.sysu.edu.cn`, `zhangyun2@mail.sysu.edu.cn`

Abstract. The Moving Picture Experts Group (MPEG) standardized Video-based Point Cloud Compression (V-PCC) is an emerging coding standard for 3D dynamic point clouds. V-PCC projects point clouds into geometry and attribute videos and uses Versatile Video Coding (VVC) as a video encoder to improve compression efficiency, but it also results in a huge coding complexity. To reduce the coding complexity, we propose a fast Coding Unit (CU) decision algorithm based on a Support Vector Machine (SVM) for VVC coding of geometric and attribute videos in V-PCC. First, we extract different features based on CU types, including texture feature, coding feature, inter feature, and geometric feature. Second, we trained discriminators for various sizes of CUs and selected different weight factor for each discriminator to achieve a trade-off between coding complexity and Rate-Distortion (RD) performance. The experimental results show that the proposed fast decision method reduces the complexity by 27.49% with Bjónteggard Delta Bit Rate (BDBR) of 1.23% and 1.36% compared to the anchor VVC-based V-PCC.

Keywords: Video-based Point Cloud Compression · Versatile Video Coding · SVM · Low Complexity · CU partition

1 Introduction

Virtual Reality (VR) and Augmented Reality (AR) have emerged as transformative technologies for immersive experiences with the rapid development of 3D sensing technologies. Point Cloud has become an important imaging modality with great value for 3D representation. However, the massive data volume of dynamic point clouds (DPCs) poses critical challenges for real-time transmission and rendering, particularly in resource-constrained scenarios. To address this challenge, the Moving Picture Experts Group (MPEG) standardized Video-based Point Cloud Compression (V-PCC) [1], which projects 3D point clouds into 2D video videos (occupancy, geometry, and attribute) and compresses them using existing coders such as High-Efficiency Video Coding (HEVC) [2] and

Z. Lin et al. (Eds.): ICIG 2025, LNCS 16161, pp. 479–490, 2026.
https://doi.org/10.1007/978-981-95-3398-5_39

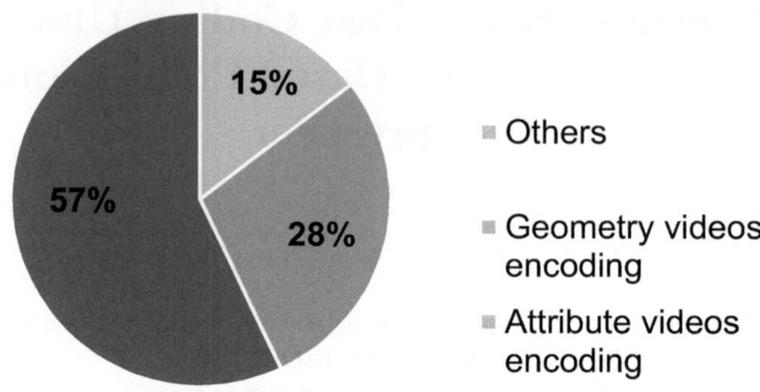

Fig. 1. Proportion of encoding time in VVC-based V-PCC.

Versatile Video Coding (VVC) [3]. While V-PCC achieves high compression efficiency, its computational complexity remains prohibitive, especially in geometry and attribute video encoding. As shown in Fig. 1, the statistics showed that 28% and 57% of the time was spent coding geometric and attribute videos. This is because V-PCC projects a point cloud from one frame to two frames of near and far images, and the generated geometry/attribute video has more empty pixels and higher complexity. In addition, VVC-based V-PCC has higher computational complexity due to VVC achieving superior compression performance but significantly higher coding complexity through enhanced coding tools such as flexible block splitting and advanced internal prediction modes.

Although there has been a great deal of research in the area of fast video coding [4–12]. This fast coding methods for 2D video may not achieve optimal performance when applied to V-PCC, because the videos generated by V-PCC are different from traditional 2D videos. Currently, there are many optimization algorithms for point cloud encoding [13–19], but fast compression algorithms are still relatively scarce. Xiong *et al.* [20] proposed fast Coding Unit (CU) size and mode decision strategies for CUs with different occupancy types. Yuan *et al.* [21] fully exploited the VPCC alternating projection property and designed a new RD cost-guided learning method by using the correlation between geometry and attribute videos. Wang *et al.* [22] proposed an early termination method for static blocks, an adaptive motion search area method for complex blocks, and an early prediction mode decision algorithm for affine motion areas in ordinary blocks. Liu *et al.* [23] proposed a LightGBM-based fast CU decision algorithm for geometric video coding, which explores the relationship between multidirectional edge distributions, segment-smoothed block attributes in CUs, and CU segmentation. Gao *et al.* [24] introduced a fast algorithm leveraging cross-projection data to enhance CU partitioning prediction accuracy, coupled with a rate-distortion optimized learning method to refine CU decision precision. Wang *et al.* [25] was the first to propose a fast VVC-based V-PCC algorithm, which proposes an early termination method for low-complexity blocks and devises an optimal CU splitting based on the transformer model for predicting attribute-occupied blocks.

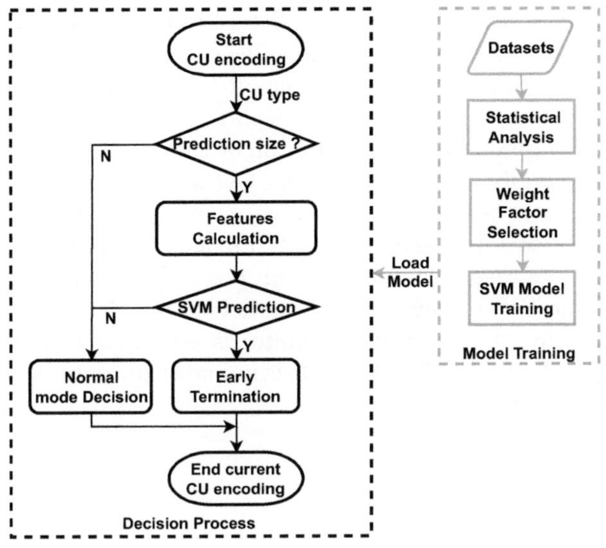

Fig. 2. Over workflow of the proposed method.

However, the above work does not exploit CU correlations further. The effect of different sizes of CUs on computational complexity and reconstruction quality has not been considered.

With the development of machine learning, Support Vector Machine (SVM) methods have been widely used to accelerate the coding process. In this paper, we propose an SVM-based fast CU decision algorithm for geometric/attribute video coding of VVC-based VPCC. We selected several features for different CU types and trained discriminators with different CU sizes. Then, the impact of different CU sizes on coding complexity and quality loss is measured by precoding, and the weight factor of each discriminator is selected to achieve the trade-off between coding complexity and RD performance. When the discriminator believes that the CU does not need to be split further, it performs an early termination operation.

The rest of this paper is organized as follows. Section 2 describes the proposed SVM-based fast CU decision method. Experiments and analyses are performed in Sect. 3. Section 4 draws conclusions.

2   Proposed Method

2.1   Overview

In this paper, we use SVM as a discriminator to determine whether the current CU is splitting or not. The overall workflow of the algorithm is shown in Fig. 2. At first, we need to determine whether the size of the current CU is the predicted size, and we consider CUs of sizes M × N and N × M as the same type of CUs.

Experimental results show that directly determining whether a large-size CU (e.g., 64 × 64) is splitting or not and performing early termination leads to a huge loss in coding performance. In addition, small CUs (e.g. 8 × 4, 8 × 8) do not require much coding time, so there is no need to implement fast algorithms for these CU sizes. The prediction sizes of our algorithm are 32 × 32, 32 × 16, 16 × 16, and 32 × 8. Secondly, the corresponding features are calculated according to the CU type. The gray box represents offline training of the model. Considering that different sizes of CUs have different impacts on coding complexity and quality loss, we select weight factors through pre-coding and statistical analysis. Then, we train the SVM discriminator model with different sizes for various CU types. Eventually, the SVM discriminator is used to determine whether the current CU can be further split. If the discriminator outputs non-split (Y), the current CU is terminated early.

2.2 Feature Selection

(1) Texture Feature

Texture complexity: In VVC encoding, the Quadtree with nested Multi-type Tree (QTMT) partition structure is highly correlated with the texture complexity of the encoded frame. In general, texture complex regions tend to be further partitioned. The variance of a CU is chosen to calculate the texture complexity TC , which is

$$TC = \frac{1}{w \times h} \sum_{0}^{w-1}\sum_{0}^{h-1}(x_{i,j} - \bar{x})^2 \tag{1}$$

where w and h represent the width and height of the current CU. $x_{i,j}$ and $\bar{x}$ respectively denote the Luma value of each pixel in the current CU and the average pixel Luma value.

Texture variance of Quadtree (QT) mode: Considering the multiple segmentation modes of VVC, the average texture complexity of subregions divided by QT mode QT_{diff} is added as a supplementary feature, which is:

$$\begin{aligned}
QT_{\text{diff}} = \frac{1}{w \times h} \Bigg[&\sum_{0}^{\frac{w}{2}}\sum_{0}^{\frac{h}{2}}(x_{i,j} - \bar{x}_1)^2 + \sum_{\frac{w}{2}}^{w-1}\sum_{0}^{\frac{h}{2}}(x_{i,j} - \bar{x}_2)^2 \\
&+ \sum_{0}^{\frac{w}{2}}\sum_{\frac{h}{2}}^{h-1}(x_{i,j} - \bar{x}_3)^2 + \sum_{\frac{w}{2}}^{w-1}\sum_{\frac{h}{2}}^{h-1}(x_{i,j} - \bar{x}_4)^2 \Bigg]
\end{aligned} \tag{2}$$

where $\bar{x}_1$, $\bar{x}_2$, $\bar{x}_3$, and $\bar{x}_4$ respectively denote the average pixel Luma value in each subregion.

(2) Coding Feature

RD cost of the next level: Each step of a partitioning decision of CU is based on the RD cost generated by different partitioning modes. The RD cost of the next level has already been calculated before the decision-making of the current CU and can be used as a reference for the current partitioning decision.

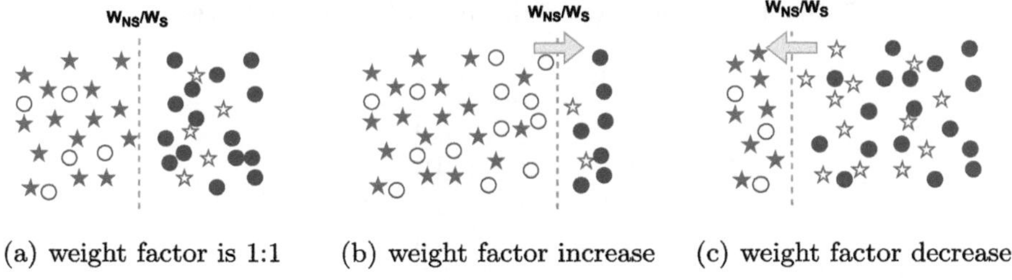

(a) weight factor is 1:1   (b) weight factor increase   (c) weight factor decrease

Fig. 3. Schematic classification of weight factor.

(3) Inter Feature

RD cost and depth of the intra-frame CU in the same position: In all-intra configuration, the V-PCC alternately encodes IP frames that refer to the information of the intra-frame of the CUs in the same position when coding inter-frame. Therefore, when deciding on the inter-frame CU, the RD cost and the depth of its corresponding intra-frame CU are used as the feature.

(4) Geometric Feature

RD cost of the corresponding geometric CU: Since the geometry video is encoded before the attribute video, the RD cost information associated with each CU in the geometry video can be effectively utilized as a reference when determining the optimal partitioning and coding modes for the corresponding CUs in the attribute video.

Texture complexity of the corresponding geometric CU: The region of complex geometric video texture identifies the surface primitive point cloud where there are a large number of geometric deformations and uneven regions, and such regions are often prone to large texture fluctuations as well, e.g., the human face; Therefore, the texture complexity of the corresponding geometric CU can also be used as a guideline for the attribute video coding.

2.3   Weight Factor Selection

Different sizes of CUs affect the quality of the reconstructed point cloud and the coding complexity reduction to different degrees. To achieve a good trade-off between coding quality and computational complexity reduction, optimization strategies should be different for CUs with various sizes. When training the SVM discrimination model, it is necessary to set the weight for each category separately. The weight indicates the penalty when the prediction of the category is wrong. The larger the weights are set, the larger the penalty is, and the classifiers will be more cautious in discriminating the category. Therefore, we introduce the concept of weight factor, which is expressed as the ratio of the non-split weight to the split weight W_{NS}/W_S. The schematic classification of the weight factor is shown in Fig. 3.

In Fig. 3, the star-shaped represents the samples that will not be further partitioned, and the circle-shaped represents the samples that will eventually be

Table 1. Weight factor of different CU types and sizes.

CU Type	32×32	32×16	32×8	16×16
Geo-intra	1:4	1:2	1:1	1:2
Geo-inter	1:1	1:1	1:1	1:1
Att-intra	1:4	1:1	1:1	2:1
Att-intre	1:2	1:1	1:1	1:1

further partitioned. The solid graph means that the sample is correctly predicted, and the opposite is true for hollows. The weight factor can be visualised as the boundary lines between the two categories. When the weight factor is 1:1, most of the samples in both categories are predicted correctly, and a small number of samples are misclassified. When the weight factor increases, the boundary line shifts to the right when more star-shaped samples are correctly predicted, as opposed to more incorrectly predicted circle-shaped samples. Represented in the coding as more early terminations will be performed, which will lead to better performance for complexity savings, but will also lead to a greater loss of reconstructed point cloud quality due to more incorrect terminations of CUs that continue to split. When the weighting factor reduces, the classifier will be biased towards predicting splits, which ensures more CUs perform further partitioning at the cost of reduced complexity savings.

Based on the above analysis, CUs with a significant impact on quality need to be set with a smaller weight factor, while CUs with significant time complexity savings and a small impact on quality can be set with larger weight factors. We perform pre-coding and statistical analysis to select the weight factors based on the time complexity savings and quality loss for each size CU. We set weight factor of 4:1, 2:1, 1:1, 1:2 and 1:4 to train the SVM model. We then calculated the average complexity savings and quality loss. The final weight factors were selected based on excellent complexity savings and smaller quality loss. Table 1 shows the weight factors of different CU types and sizes, CU types including geometry, attribute, intra-frame, and inter-frame. The weight factors for 32×32 are significantly smaller than the other sizes, and the weight factors for intra-frame are usually smaller than for inter-frame. Since these types and sizes have a huge effect on quality, the larger weight factor will result in significant quality loss.

3   Experimental Results and Analysis

3.1   Experimental Settings

To demonstrate the effectiveness of the proposed method, we applied it to the V-PCC standard software TMC2 V15.0 [26]. In terms of encoding configurations, we used All-intra as the main setting and conducted experiments under five standard bit rates (r1–r5), and the rest of the configurations referenced the CTC

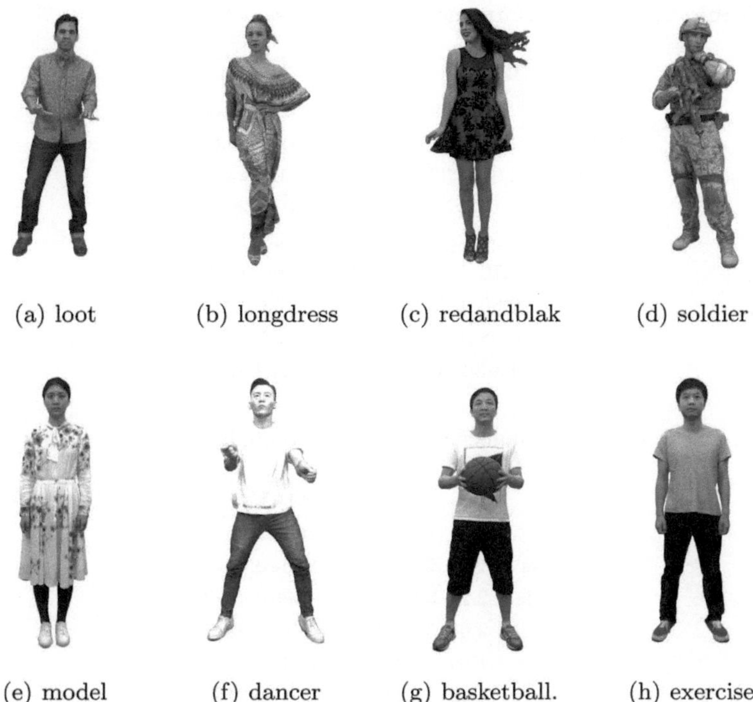

(a) loot   (b) longdress   (c) redandblak   (d) soldier

(e) model   (f) dancer   (g) basketball.   (h) exercise

Fig. 4. Visualization of Experimental Point Cloud Sequences.

[27]. We selected eight standard DPCs (loot, longdress, redandblack, soldier, model, dancer, basketball-player, exxercise) as the experimental sequences shown in Fig. 4. All experiments were performed on a workstation equipped with an Intel(R) Core(TM) i9-10900X CPU @ 3.70GHz and an NVIDIA GeForce RTX 3090 GPU.

The training datasets consist of features and split/non-split labels of different size CUs in the longdress, redanblack, soldier, model sequence. To eliminate the dimensionality effect between features, the data is normalised before training. The ratio of split to non-split samples was selected as 1:1, the penalty factor was set to 100, as well as the weights were set according to the weight factor selected in Table 1. SVM models with CUs in different sizes and types were trained.

3.2   Performance Evaluation

The coding performance is measured by the Bjóntegaard Delta Bit Rate (BDBR) and the complexity reduction. The lower values of BDBR and higher values of complexity reduction signify better performance. Specifically, the BDBR for the geometry part of the point cloud is measured jointly using point-to-point (D1) and point-to-plane (D2) PSNR. The BDBR for the colour part of the point cloud is measured using PSNR for luminance and chrominance (Luma, Cb, Cr)

Table 2. Coding performance of the reconstructed video [Unit: %].

Sequence	D1	D2	Luma	Cb	Cr	ΔTG	ΔTA
loot	0.32	1.29	1.14	4.06	5.54	11.05	38.37
longdress	2.77	3.89	1.34	0.44	0.42	25.86	40.51
redandblack	2.97	4.30	1.03	-2.17	0.02	23.16	30.40
soldier	2.13	3.28	1.89	2.56	-0.18	22.28	43.44
model	1.36	2.70	1.65	4.08	1.55	13.41	39.32
dancer	1.70	1.99	1.23	0.43	2.66	10.36	29.78
exercise	0.80	1.07	1.79	2.39	5.63	10.65	29.68
basketball.	0.98	1.36	1.26	0.78	1.28	10.36	30.94
Avg.	**1.63**	**2.48**	**1.42**	**1.57**	**2.12**	**15.88**	**35.30**

Table 3. Coding performance of the reconstructed point cloud [Unit: %].

	D1	D2	Luma	Cb	Cr	ΔTV
loot	0.54	1.97	0.90	2.86	3.92	26.86
longdress	1.21	2.97	1.43	0.70	0.64	37.37
redandblack	2.24	3.85	1.29	−1.06	0.49	27.11
soldier	2.00	3.64	1.75	2.37	0.23	35.33
model	1.09	2.98	1.53	3.43	1.46	29.31
dancer	1.32	1.76	1.27	0.83	2.21	21.02
exercise	0.57	0.66	1.59	2.04	4.32	21.15
basketball.	0.87	1.37	1.11	0.68	1.12	21.79
Avg.	**1.23**	**2.40**	**1.36**	**1.48**	**1.80**	**27.49**

in YUV format. In terms of complexity reduction, we give the complexity reduction for geometric coding, attribute coding, and video coding, respectively. We calculated the average complexity reduction at the five-bit rates as

$$\Delta T = \frac{1}{5} \sum_{i=1}^{5} \frac{T_O(i) - T_F(i)}{T_O(i)} \times 100\% \tag{3}$$

where $T_O(i)$ and $T_F(i)$ are the encoding time of the original V-PCC and the proposed mode decision at the bit-rate r_i.

Table 2 and Table 3 show the coding performance of the proposed algorithm compared to V-PCC TMC2 V15.0. when compared with the original V-PCC, the proposed method greatly reduces the complexity for all sequences, and gets an average complexity reduction of 15.88%, 35.30%, and 27.49% for geometric coding, attribute coding, and video coding. It can be observed that our method performs better on 10-bit sequences, which may be related to the characteristics of the sequences. Experiment results show that the BDBRs of the proposed methods are 1.63%, 2.48% and 1.42%, 1.57%, 2.12% when the video bit rate is counted and the quality of the reconstructed geometry and attribute videos are

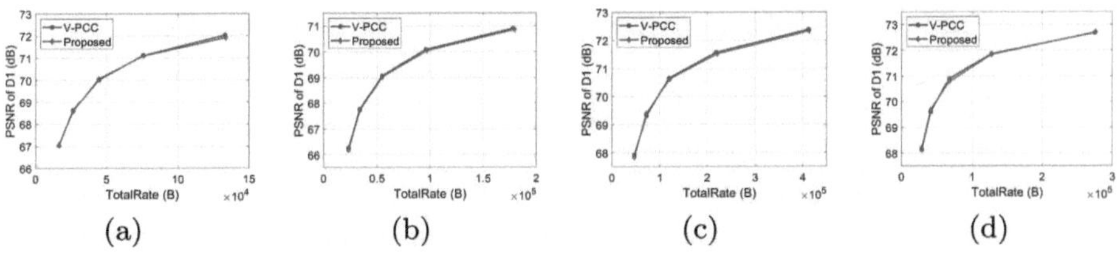

Fig. 5. Geometry RD performance of the anchor V-PCC and the proposed method, where the quality of reconstructed point cloud is measured with the PSNR of D1. (a)loot, (b)redandblack, (c)model, (d)exercise.

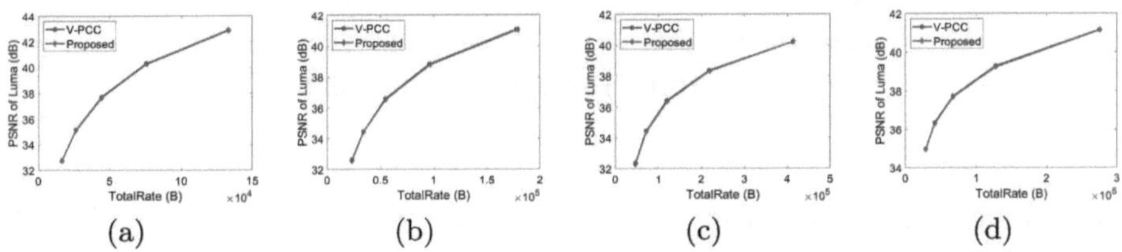

Fig. 6. Attribute RD performance of the anchor V-PCC and the proposed method, where the quality of reconstructed point cloud is measured with the PSNR of Luma. (a)loot, (b)redandblack, (c)model, (d)exercise.

measured with D1, D2, Luma, Cr, and Cr. At the same time, the BDBRs of reconstructed point clouds are 1.23%, 2.40% and 1.36%, 1.48%, 1.80% when the total bit rate is counted. The proposed methods perform better when the quality is measured with D1 and Luma because we select weight factors based on these two metrics. Meanwhile, the proposed method performs better on the attribute channel and achieves greater complexity savings with a smaller BDBR. This is because more features are selected for the attribute channel and attribute coding takes much longer than geometric coding. Fig. 5 and Fig. 6 show the geometry and attribute RD performance of four sequences for the anchor V-PCC and the proposed method, where the quality is measured with the PSNR of D1 and Luma. The proposed method exhibits similar RD performance to the anchor V-PCC. This means that the method can guarantee the quality of the reconstructed point cloud while reducing computational complexity. The proposed method only considers four CU sizes and the weights are all integers, it has already achieved good performance. In addition, considering the remaining CU sizes and optimizing the selection of weight factors further enhance performance.

Furthermore, Table 4 indicates the complexity reduction from low bit-rate to high bit-rate. Compared with the original V-PCC, the average complexity savings of the proposed method are about 10.66%, 19.94%, 28.48%, 35.54%, and 43.04% under r1 to r5. Complexity savings increase with increasing bit-rate, suggesting that our method is more suitable for high bit rates with higher complexity. The complexity savings of exercise sequence is -1.63% at the $r1$ bit-rate, which shows that the time taken for feature calculation and SVM model prediction exceeded the time saved by early termination. However, in most cases, the

Table 4. Complexity reduction under each bit-rate [Unit: %].

Sequence	r1	r2	r3	r4	r5
loot	8.44	22.41	30.37	35.89	37.18
longdress	29.85	30.36	33.98	38.18	54.47
redandblack	12.67	20.40	28.76	33.29	40.43
soldier	21.01	35.85	36.41	38.50	44.91
model	13.36	24.84	27.04	35.96	45.36
dancer	0.89	9.24	22.54	33.17	39.27
exercise	-1.63	5.70	25.81	34.31	41.54
basketball.	0.66	10.76	22.90	33.42	41.19
Avg.	**10.66**	**19.94**	**28.48**	**35.34**	**43.04**

proposed method can effectively reduce computational complexity, even if SVM inference time is required.

4 Conclusion

In this paper, we proposed a Support Vector Machine (SVM) based fast Coding Unit (CU) decision algorithm for VVC coding of geometric and attribute videos in Video-based Point Cloud Compression (V-PCC). Firstly, several features are selected according to the CU types, including texture feature, coding feature, inter feature, and geometric feature. Based on this, an efficient SVM algorithm for predicting whether a CU is split or not is carefully designed. We train SVM discriminators for CUs of different sizes and types to improve the accuracy and reduce the complexity of training. In addition, we adjusted the weighting factors according to the specifics of each CU type and size with the aim of achieving a trade-off between coding complexity and Rate-Distortion (RD) performance. Experimental results show that the proposed algorithm can reduce the computational complexity by 27.49% with Bjónteggard Delta Bit Rate (BDBR) of 1.23% and 1.36% compared to the anchor V-PCC.

Acknowledgment. This work was supported in part by the National Natural Science Foundation of China under Grant 62172400, in part by Shenzhen Key Science and Technology Program under Grant JCYJ20241202124415021 and Shenzhen Natural Science Foundation under Grant JCYJ20240813180503005

References

1. Jang, E.S., et al.: Video-Based point-cloud-compression standard in MPEG: from evidence collection to committee draft. IEEE Sign. Process. Mag. **36**(3), 118–123 (2019)

2. Sullivan, G.J., Ohm, J.R., Han, W.J., Wiegand, T.: Overview of the high efficiency video coding (HEVC) standard. IEEE Trans. Circuit Syst. Video Technol. **22**(12), 1649–1668 (2012)
3. Bross, B., et al.: Overview of the versatile video coding (VVC) standard and its applications. IEEE Trans. Circuit Syst. Video Technol. **31**(10), 3736–3764 (2021)
4. Wang, L.L., Siu, W.C.: Novel adaptive algorithm for intra prediction with compromised modes skipping and signaling processes in HEVC. IEEE Trans. Circuit Syst. Video Technol. **23**(10), 1686–1694 (2013)
5. Zhang, T., Sun, M.T., Zhao, D., Gao, W.: Fast intra-mode and cu size decision for HEVC. IEEE Trans. Circuit Syst. Video Technol. **27**(8), 1714–1726 (2016)
6. Xu, M., Li, T., Wang, Z., Deng, X., Yang, R., Guan, Z.: Reducing complexity of HEVC: a deep learning approach. IEEE Trans. Image Process. **27**(10), 5044–5059 (2018)
7. Wang, T., Li, F., Qiao, X., Cosman, P.C.: Low-complexity error resilient HEVC video coding: a deep learning approach. IEEE Trans. Image Process. **30**, 1245–1260 (2020)
8. Li, Y., Yang, G., Song, Y., Zhang, H., Ding, X., Zhang, D.: Early intra CU size decision for versatile video coding based on a tunable decision model. IEEE Trans. Broadcast. **67**(3), 710–720 (2021)
9. Wu, S., Shi, J., Chen, Z.: HG-FCN: hierarchical grid fully convolutional network for fast VVC intra coding. IEEE Trans. Circuit Syst. Video Technol. **32**(8), 5638–5649 (2022)
10. Zhao, T., Huang, Y., Feng, W., Xu, Y., Kwong, S.: Efficient VVC intra prediction based on deep feature fusion and probability estimation. IEEE Trans. Multimedia **25**, 6411–6421 (2023)
11. Zhang, S., Feng, S., Chen, J., Zhou, C., Yang, F.: A GCN-based fast CU partition method of intra-mode VVC. J. Vis. Commun. Image Represent. **88**, 103621 (2022)
12. Feng, A., Liu, K., Liu, D., Li, L., Wu, F.: Partition map prediction for fast block partitioning in VVC intra-frame coding. IEEE Trans. Image Process. **32**, 2237–2251 (2023)
13. Zhang, Y., Ding, K., Li, N., Wang, H., Huang, X., Kuo, C.-C.J.: Perceptually weighted rate distortion optimization for video-based point cloud compression. IEEE Trans. Image Process. **32**, 5933–5947 (2023)
14. Wang, S., Zhu, M., Li, N., Xiao, M., Liu, Y.: VQBA: visual-quality-driven bit allocation for low-latency point cloud streaming. In: Proceedings of ACM International Conference on Multimedia, pp. 9143–9151. ACM, New York (2023)
15. Wang, J., Ding, D., Li, Z., Feng, X., Cao, C., Ma, Z.: Sparse tensor-based multiscale representation for point cloud geometry compression. IEEE Trans. Pattern Anal. Mach. Intell. **45**(7), 9055–9071 (2023)
16. Yang, H., Zhang, Y., Yang, Q., Shan, Z., Xu, Y., Guan, Y.: Cross-modal distortion approximation for fast bit allocation of video-based point cloud compression. In: IEEE 26th International Workshop Multimedia Signal Processing, pp. 1–6. IEEE, West Lafayette (2024)
17. Chiang, J.-C., Wu, Y.-T., Hsieh, H.-Y., Tsai, Y.-C.: Enhanced temporal consistency for global patch allocation in video-based point cloud compression. IEEE Trans. Multimedia **26**, 6917–6930 (2024)
18. Chen, P., Wang, S., Li, Z.: Occupancy map guided attributes artifacts removal for video-based point cloud compression. ACM Trans. Multimedia Comput. Commun. Appl. **20**(12), 1551–6857 (2024)

19. Guo, Z., Zhang, Y., Zhu, L., Wang, H., Jiang, G.: TSC-PCAC: voxel transformer and sparse convolution-based point cloud attribute compression for 3D broadcasting. IEEE Trans. Broadcast. **71**(1), 154–166 (2025)
20. Xiong, J., Gao, H., Wang, M., Li, H., Lin, W.: Occupancy map guided fast video-based dynamic point cloud coding. IEEE Trans. Circuit Syst. Video Technol. **32**(2), 813–825 (2021)
21. Yuan, H., Gao, W., Li, G., Li, Z.: Rate-distortion-guided learning approach with cross-projection information for V-PCC fast cu decision. In: Proceedings of ACM International Conference on Multimedia, pp. 3085–3093. ACM, New York (2022)
22. Wang, Y., Wang, Y., Cui, T., Fang, Z.: Occupancy map-based low complexity motion prediction for video-based point cloud compression. J. Vis. Commun. Image Represent. **100**, 104110 (2024)
23. Liu, Z., Liu, J., He, B., Huang, C., Li, Q., Zhang, M.: Fast cu decision algorithm based on LightGBM for geometry video in V-PCC. In: Proceedings of International Conference on Electronics Information Technology and Computer Engineering, pp.362–367. ACM, New York (2024)
24. Gao, W., Yuan, H., Li, G., Li, Z., Yuan, H.: Low complexity coding unit decision for video-based point cloud compression. IEEE Trans. Image Process. **33**, 149–162 (2024)
25. Wang, Y., Wang, Y., Cui, T., Fang, Z.: Fast video-based point cloud compression based on early termination and transformer model. IEEE Trans. Emerg. Top. Comput. Intell. **8**(3), 2336–2348 (2024)
26. MPEG: Point cloud compression category 2 reference software, TMC2 15.0 (2021). http://mpegx.int-evry.fr/software/MPEG/PCC/TM/mpeg-pcc-tmc2.git
27. Schwarz, S., Martin-Cocher, G., Flynn, D., Budagavi, M.: Common test conditions for point cloud compression. Document ISO/IECJTC1/SC29/WG11 w17766, Ljubljana, Slovenia (2018)

Computational Imaging

Leveraging a Dual-Learning Methodology Based on Degradation Modeling and Fractional Fourier Image Transformer for Light Field Image Super-Resolution

Haiyang Liu[1], Jian Ma[1,2]([✉]) [ID], Sheng Chen[3], Dong Liang[1], Linsheng Huang[1], and Rui Xu[1]

[1] School of Internet, Anhui University, Hefei 230039, China
[2] College of Computing, City University of Hong Kong, Hong Kong 999077, China
`jian.ma@cityu.edu.hk`
[3] Jianghuai Advance Technology Center, Hefei 230039, China

Abstract. Light Field Super-Resolution (LFSR) endeavors to reconstruct high-resolution (HR) light field images from their low-resolution (LR) counterparts by capitalizing on multi-view image information. This process not only enables a more efficient restoration of high-frequency details but also preserves the geometric structure of the scene. Nevertheless, prevailing methods encounter difficulties in capturing the long-range spatial and angular dependencies inherent in light field data, as well as their high-frequency spectral characteristics. Moreover, the availability of high-quality paired training data for real-world scenarios remains limited. To address these challenges, this paper presents DFFIT (Dual learning and Fractional Fourier Image Transformer), a novel LFSR framework that seamlessly integrates frequency-domain analysis with a dual-learning strategy grounded in degradation modeling. We introduce the Fractional Fourier Image Transformer (FrIT), which ingeniously combines the fractional Fourier transform (FrFT) with Transformer-based long-range dependency modeling. This integration effectively captures frequency-specific features while guaranteeing cross-view consistency. Additionally, our dual-learning framework generates a variety of LR training samples by emulating real-world degradation processes, thereby narrowing the domain gap between synthetic and real-world data. Experimental results verify that the proposed method exhibits remarkable performance in enhancing the resolution of light field images.

Keywords: Light field Super-Resolution · Dual Learning · Fractional Fourier Image Transformer · Degradation Model

This work was supported in part by the National Natural Science Foundation of China under Grants 61906118, 62273001, Jianghuai Advance Technology Center Dream-Chasing Fund under Grants 2023-ZM01D009, AnHui Natural Science Foundation under Grants 2108085MF230 and Anhui Province Outstanding Scientific Research and Innovation team Grants 2022AH010005.
H. Liu and J. Ma—Co-first authors.

1   Introduction

Light Field Super-Resolution (LFSR) leverages the unique capabilities of light field imaging to enhance image resolution beyond that of traditional two-dimensional (2D) methods. Unlike conventional 2D imaging, which captures only spatial intensity, light field cameras record both spatial and angular information of light rays [1]. This rich four-dimensional (4D) representation enables a more comprehensive understanding of the three-dimensional (3D) scene geometry, offering inherent advantages for super-resolution (SR) tasks through the fusion of multiview information [2]. As a result, LFSR has found widespread applications in fields such as 3D reconstruction, immersive virtual reality—including foreground de-occlusion [3], depth estimation [4].

While traditional single image super-resolution (SISR) techniques have achieved remarkable progress, they often suffer from limitations imposed by simplified degradation assumptions and susceptibility to noise, which hinder their ability to restore realistic high-frequency details and preserve structural fidelity. In contrast, LFSR offers the ability to utilize angular redundancy and complementary views to reconstruct fine textures and restore accurate spatial structures. Early deep learning-based LFSR models such as LFCNN [5] pioneered the joint optimization of spatial and angular features, while LF-DFNet [6] introduced deformable convolutions to mitigate parallax-related distortions across views. Zhang et al. [7] proposed an end-to-end network for full-view reconstruction, and Wang et al. [8] developed a directional disentanglement approach to exploit orthogonal spatial correlations. More recently, Liang et al. [9] incorporated Transformer-based spatial-angular attention to model long-range dependencies. Despite these advances, several challenges remain unresolved.

Firstly, most existing approaches struggle to effectively model long-range dependencies across spatial and angular domains. Light fields inherently contain structured patterns—such as epipolar plane images (EPIs)—that are more naturally expressed and analyzed in the frequency domain. However, prior methods rarely exploit frequency domain representations, thereby limiting their ability to fully leverage the structured geometry embedded in light fields. Secondly, current supervised learning paradigms rely heavily on large-scale, high-quality, paired datasets, which are difficult to acquire in real-world settings due to the high cost and complexity of capturing pixel-aligned, diverse light field images. Moreover, synthetic degradation via bicubic downsampling, commonly used to generate training data, fails to emulate realistic distortions such as dynamic blur and sensor noise, leading to performance degradation when models are applied to real-world light field data [10].

To overcome these challenges, we propose a novel dual-branch framework named DFFIT (Dual learning and Fractional Fourier Image Transformer), which introduces two key innovations. Firstly, inspired by the successful application of the fractional Fourier image transformer in multimodal remote sensing image classification [11], we design a plug-and-play Fractional Fourier Image Transformer (FrIT) module tailored for LFSR. This module synergistically integrates the parameterized time-frequency representation capability of the Fractional Fourier Transform (FrFT) with the global modeling power of the Transformer architecture. FrIT enables adaptive focus on frequency-specific structural information—such as the slope variations in EPIs correlated with disparity—and facilitates coherent feature aggregation across views, thereby enhancing spatial detail reconstruction and maintaining angular consistency. Secondly, to address the scarcity and limitations of real-world paired data, we introduce a degradation-model-based dual learning framework. Drawing inspiration from recent advances in realistic degradation modeling for natural image SR [12] and the dual learning paradigm in image-to-image translation [13], we develop a degradation simulation pipeline that mimics real-world light field degradation processes. This includes random combinations of blur kernels, additive noise, and downsampling operations to synthesize low-resolution (LR) images from high-resolution (HR) light field data. These synthetic HRLR pairs are then used to jointly train the DFFIT network, allowing it to generalize more effectively to practical LF images captured under uncontrolled conditions. By narrowing the domain gap between synthetic and real-world data, this dual learning strategy significantly boosts the robustness and generalization ability of the proposed LFSR model.

In summary, our contributions are two-fold: (1) the development of a FrFT-based Transformer module (FrIT) that bridges spatial and frequency domains for enhanced light field representation learning; and (2) a realistic degradation-aware dual learning framework that facilitates effective training under limited real-world supervision. Together, these innovations enable DFFIT to achieve state-of-the-art performance in reconstructing high-quality light field images across both synthetic and real-world scenarios.

2   Related Works

2.1   Traditional LFSR Methods

Before the advent of deep learning, research on LFSR primarily relied on traditional algorithms grounded in physical modeling and mathematical optimization. These approaches aimed to reconstruct HR light field images from their LR counterparts by leveraging prior knowledge and hand-crafted assumptions. For instance, Wanner et al. [2] introduced a variational framework based on depth map estimation derived from EPIs analysis. Mitra et al. [14] employed Gaussian mixture models to encode the intrinsic structure of light fields for applications including depth estimation, view synthesis, and SR. Farrugia et al. [15] proposed a subspace-based method that linearly projected LR patches into HR subspaces by exploiting local coherence across views. Egiazarian et al. extended BM3D denoising to the light field domain, resulting in the LFBM5D method [16,17], which proved effective for both denoising and SR tasks. Rossi et al. [18] developed a graph-based optimization method to recover HR views by modeling the geometric structure of the light field. Although these traditional methods demonstrated the potential to model light field structure, they were fundamentally limited by their reliance on fixed priors and handcrafted features, rendering them less effective in recovering complex textures and high-frequency details. Moreover, their generalization to diverse real-world scenarios remained inadequate due to the inflexible nature of their underlying assumptions.

2.2   Deep Learning-Based LFSR Methods

Recent advances in deep learning have brought transformative progress to LFSR, enabling substantial improvements in reconstruction fidelity through data-driven learning of spatial-angular correlations. Yoon et al. [5] were the first to introduce convolutional neural networks (CNNs) to the LFSR task with their LFCNN model, which jointly optimized spatial and angular information. Yuan et al. [19] extended this idea by applying enhanced deep residual networks (EDSR) to each view independently. Zhang et al. [20] proposed a residual learning framework that aggregated features from neighboring views to enhance the central view reconstruction. To better address geometric disparities across views, Wang et al. [6] introduced LF-DFnet, incorporating deformable convolutions to dynamically align features with varying parallax. Jin et al. [21] designed LF-ATO to preserve the parallax-consistent structure of light fields during upsampling. In pursuit of full-view SR, Zhang et al. [7] developed an end-to-end network that simultaneously reconstructed all angular views. Wang et al. [8] proposed a directional disentanglement strategy to separate spatial features along orthogonal directions, thereby exploiting the intrinsic structure of light fields. More recently, Liang et al. [9] employed Transformer architectures for LFSR, introducing spatial and angular attention mechanisms to better model long-range dependencies.

While these CNN- and Transformer-based methods have significantly enhanced LFSR performance, several challenges remain. First, most existing approaches primarily concentrate on spatial and angular feature fusion, with limited attention to frequency domain representations—despite the fact that light fields inherently contain structured frequency components (e.g., EPI line slopes) that are critical for high-frequency detail reconstruction. Second, the effectiveness of supervised learning methods depends heavily on the availability of large-scale, high-quality LR-HR training pairs. However, acquiring such datasets for real-world light fields is extremely labor-intensive and often impractical. As a result, models trained on synthetically downsampled data frequently exhibit degraded generalization performance when applied to complex, noisy, and variably degraded light field inputs encountered in real-world scenarios.

3   Method

The DFFIT framework comprises two core components: a generative model G and a degradation model D. The generative model reconstructs HR light field images by integrating spatial-angular decoupling, multi-scale fusion, and frequency-domain attention to enhance detail and preserve angular consistency. The degradation model simulates realistic LR inputs using residual blocks, adaptive Gaussian blur, and stochastic noise, thereby improving training realism and model generalization.

3.1   Network Architecture

The overall architecture of the proposed model is illustrated in Fig. 1. The input LR sub-aperture image (SAI) array, denoted as $I_{LR}^{SAIs} \in \mathbb{R}^{AH \times AW}$ is first transformed into a LR Macro-Pixel Image (MacPI), represented as $I_{MacPI}^{LR} \in \mathbb{R}^{AH \times AW}$, where U and V correspond to the angular dimensions, and H and W denote the spatial dimensions. We set U = V = A, where A represents the angular resolution. Subsequently, a 3×3 convolutional kernel is employed to perform preliminary feature extraction on the MacPI. Inspired by prior works [22,23], we propose a DFFIT model comprising multiple hierarchical residual structures. Specifically, the model includes four residual groups, each consisting of four Disentangled Fractional Fourier Image Transformer (DFrIT) blocks. These blocks are designed to effectively extract spatial, angular, EPI, and frequency-enhanced features from the MacPI representation.

As depicted in Fig. 1(c), we adopt the decoupling strategy introduced in [8], where features are extracted separately through different branches: spatial (F_{spa}), angular (F_{ang}), horizontal EPI (F_{epih}), vertical EPI (F_{epiv}). The F_{spa} operation performs convolution over pixels that share the same angular coordinates, thereby isolating spatial features while minimizing interference from angular variations. Conversely, F_{ang} focuses on pixels with identical spatial coordinates, effectively suppressing aliasing effects caused by spatial inconsistencies and emphasizing the extraction of angular features. Furthermore, to capture the intrinsic correlation between spatial and angular domains, we exploit the line structural properties in EPIs. Specifically, F_{epih} and F_{epiv} are employed to model spatial-angular interactions by extracting features along the horizontal and vertical epipolar directions, respectively. The outputs of these branches are subsequently concatenated into a unified feature representation, denoted as $\mathcal{F}_{cat}$, which is then processed by the Fractional Fourier Image Transformer (FrIT) module. This module further enhances high-frequency components in both the angular and frequency domains. The combination of these operations constitutes a complete DFrIT block.

Following feature extraction, the resulting feature maps are converted from the MacPI domain back to the SAI domain. First, a 1×1 convolution is employed to expand the channel depth to $a^2 C$, where a represents the spatial upscaling factor. This step facilitates the subsequent spatial upsampling. Next, a 2D pixel shuffle operation rearranges the feature maps such that each input channel is decomposed into a^2 sub-channels, which are then spatially reorganized to construct the super-resolved output of dimensions $aAH \times aAW$. Finally, a 1×1 convolutional layer reduces the number of output channels to one, yielding the HR SAIs. Note that, consistent with conventional practices in LFSR [6,21,24], the input images are first converted to the YCbCr color space. SR is performed only on the luminance (Y) channel, while the chrominance channels (Cb and Cr) are upsampled using bicubic interpolation.

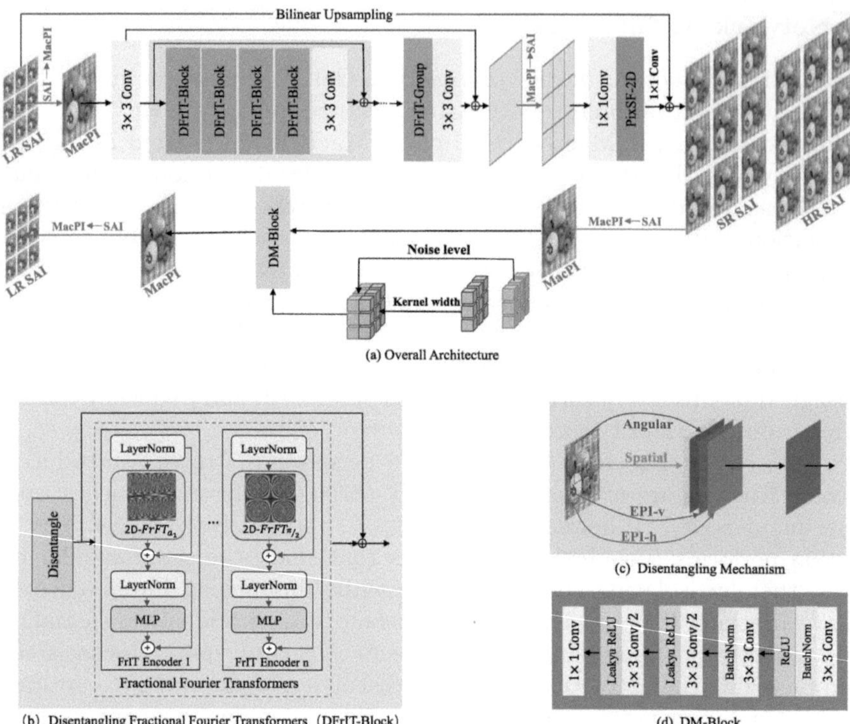

Fig. 1. An overview of our proposed DFFIT.

3.2 Fractional Fourier Image Transformer

In traditional Vision Transformer (ViT) architectures, the self-attention mechanism—though powerful—is inherently complex and computationally intensive when compared to conventional CNNs. To mitigate these challenges, we propose a novel Fractional Fourier Image Transformer (FrIT) module, wherein the standard Multi-Head Attention (MHA) mechanism in ViT is replaced with the Fractional Fourier Transform (FrFT). This substitution allows the FrIT to dynamically balance spatial and frequency domain representations by modulating the transform order parameter (α), thereby enabling more effective and efficient feature fusion and reconstruction for LFSR across both multiview and frequency domains. By explicitly embedding frequency-domain representations into the attention mechanism, the proposed module enhances the model's capacity to capture subtle scene characteristics, including disparities, occlusions, and high-frequency textures inherent to light field data. This frequency-aware design not only improves detail preservation and artifact suppression but also reduces computational redundancy typically associated with self-attention. As illustrated in Figure (b), the FrIT module consists of a 2D Discrete Fractional Fourier Transform (2D-DFrFT) layer, as introduced in [25], followed by a multi-layer perceptron (MLP). These components are integrated with layer normalization and residual connections to ensure stable training and effective information flow. The mathematical formulation of the FrIT module is detailed as follows:

$$\text{FrIT}(\mathcal{F}_{\text{cat}}) = \mathcal{F}_{\text{cat}} + \text{Conv}(\text{ETP}(FNet(\mathcal{P}(\text{PTE}(\mathcal{F}_{\text{cat}})))))\tag{1}$$

$$FNet_{out}(x^{(0)}) = LN(x^{(L)} + x^{(0)})\tag{2}$$

$$x^{(l)} = x^{(l-1)} + DFrFT(LN(x^{(l-1)})) + MLP(LN((x^{(l-1)}))\tag{3}$$

In FRiT, the input tensor F_{cat} first undergoes patch embedding, followed by processing with the FNet block. The resulting features are then restored to their original dimensions via an inverse transform, after which convolution and residual concatenation are applied to produce the final output. Here, $ETP(\cdot)$ denotes the patch embedding operation, $PTE(\cdot)$ represents the corresponding inverse transform, $\mathcal{P}(\cdot)$ represents positional encoding, and $LN(\cdot)$ indicates layer normalization. The DFrFT is mathematically defined as follows:

$$X^a(m) = F^a[x(n)] = \sqrt{\frac{\sin a - j\cos a}{N}} \cdot \exp\left(\frac{j}{2}\cot a\, m^2\right)$$
$$\cdot \sum_{n=0}^{N-1} \exp\left(-j\frac{2\pi nm}{N}\right) \cdot \exp\left(\frac{j}{2}\cot a\, n^2\right) x(n)\tag{4}$$

In each FrIT block, the features $\widehat{\mathbf{Z}}_l$ extracted by DFrFT are fed into the MLP block:

$$\mathbf{Z}_l = \text{MLP}\left(\text{LN}(\hat{\mathbf{Z}}_l) + \hat{\mathbf{Z}}_l\right)\tag{5}$$

$$\hat{\mathbf{Z}}_l = \mathcal{F}^a(LN(\hat{\mathbf{Z}}_{l-1})) + \hat{\mathbf{Z}}_{l-1}\tag{6}$$

Here, $\hat{\mathbf{Z}}_l$ denotes the output of the l-th FrIT block, where $\mathcal{F}^a$ represents the Fractional Fourier Transform (FrFT) with transform angle α, and $l = 1,\dots,L$ indexes the FrIT blocks. The MLP block comprises two linear layers separated by a GELU activation function. The normalized features $\mathbf{Z}_l$ are then used as the input to the subsequent FrIT block. To improve computational efficiency, following [11], we adopt the 2-D Simplified Fractional Fourier Transform (SFrFT) [26]. Owing to the composite properties of FrFT, concatenating multi-domain information enhances the robustness of the encoder. By adjusting the transform angle α, each FrIT encoder can dynamically balance and integrate information from both the spatial and angular domains of light field images, thus enabling the extraction of features at specific scales and angular-frequency ranges.

3.3   Degradation-Aware Dual Learning

Inspired by the dual learning frameworks proposed in [12,13], we propose a dual learning strategy grounded in a degradation model to address the scarcity of paired datasets in real-world scenarios. As illustrated in Fig. 1(a), the proposed Degradation-Aware Dual Learning model is designed to simultaneously learn the forward mapping from LR images to HR images and the inverse mapping from super-resolved images back to LR images. The process begins by transforming the super-resolved SAI into the MacPI format. A generated blur kernel is then applied to the HR image, followed by downsampling via random convolution. Gaussian noise is subsequently added to the degraded image. Finally, the degraded MacPI is converted back into the SAI format, yielding a synthesized LR dual light field image. Consequently, if the super-resolved image closely approximates the HR image, the resulting degraded light field image should be highly consistent with the original LR image. The mathematical formulation of the degradation model is as follows:

$$I_{u,v}^{lr} = (I_{u,v}^{hr})\!\downarrow_a + N_{u,v} \tag{7}$$

Here, $I_{u,v}^{hr} \in \mathbb{R}^{H \times W \times 3}$ represents the input HR SAI of view (u,v), $I_{u,v}^{lr} \in \mathbb{R}^{aH \times aW \times 3}$ denotes the corresponding LR SAI, and $\otimes$ signifies the convolution process. $k_{u,v} \in \mathbb{R}^{21 \times 21}$ and $N_{u,v} \in \mathbb{R}^{H \times W \times 3}$ represent the blur kernel and the generated random noise for view (u,v) respectively. $\downarrow_a$ indicates the bicubic downsampling process. In the following, we detail the three key components of the proposed light field degradation model: blur kernel, noise, and downsampling.

1) Blur Kernel: To emulate realistic degradation caused by camera shake, lens aberrations, or motion blur, we adopt an isotropic Gaussian blur kernel following [27,28]. The kernel is parameterized by its width and standard deviation (σ), simulating typical optical blurring effects.

2) Noise: To reflect real-world interference such as sensor and quantization noise, we add channel-independent additive white Gaussian noise during degradation. Each element in the noise tensor $N \in \mathbb{R}^{H \times W \times 3}$ is sampled from a zero-mean Gaussian distribution with a controllable standard deviation.

3) Downsampling: Bicubic interpolation is employed for downsampling, implemented iteratively using a loop-based approach.

By incorporating realistic blur and noise into the degradation pipeline, the model better captures the HR-to-LR transformation, improving robustness and generalization to real-world data.

3.4   Loss Function

The proposed loss function comprises three components:

Pixel Loss: Measures the pixel-wise difference between the SR and HR light field images.

Structural Similarity Loss (SSIM): To preserve structural and edge details, especially in the Y channel, we incorporate SSIM loss. Unlike pixel loss, SSIM emphasizes perceptual quality by capturing structural information, thereby mitigating over-smoothing and enhancing texture reconstruction.

Degradation Consistency Loss: Leveraging dual learning, this term computes the pixel-wise loss between the degraded SR image and the original LR input, ensuring consistency under the degradation model.

Table 1. Datasets used in our experiments.

	EPFL	HCInew	HCIold	INRIA	STFgantry
Training	70	20	10	35	9
Test	10	4	2	5	2

The overall loss function is formulated as follows:

$$loss = \sum_{i=1}^{M} L_{SR} + \lambda L_{Dual} + \gamma L_{SSIM} \tag{8}$$

$$L_{SR} = L_1(S(I_{lr}^i, I_{hr}^i)) \tag{9}$$

$$L_{Dual} = L_1(D(S(I_{lr}^i)), I_{lr}^i) \tag{10}$$

$$L_{SSIM} = 1 - SSIM(S(I_{lr}^i), I_{hr}^i) \tag{11}$$

Here, $S(\cdot)$ represents the SR network, and $D(\cdot)$ denotes the dual learning network based on the degradation model, and $SSIM(\cdot)$ denotes the structural similarity loss. The parameters λ and γ are weighting factors. Specifically, for images with a scaling factor of $\times 2$, λ is set to 0.01 and γ to 0.02; for $\times 4$ SR images, λ is set to 0.1 and γ to 0.2.

4   Experiments

4.1   Datasets and Implementation Details

We conduct experiments on five publicly available datasets: EPFL [29], HCInew [30], HCIold [31], INRIA [32], and STFgantry [33]. The training and testing splits are detailed in Table 1. All light field images have an angular resolution of 5×5. During training, light field images are cropped into 160×160 SR patches, with corresponding LR patches of 32×32 generated via bicubic downsampling.

We use peak signal-to-noise ratio (PSNR) and structural similarity index measure (SSIM) [34] for quantitative evaluation. Data augmentation is applied through random horizontal/vertical flips and $90°$ rotations, increasing the training set eightfold. To maintain light field structure, spatial and angular dimensions are jointly transformed.

The model is trained using a composite loss function that combines pixel-wise (L_1 and L_2) loss, structural similarity (SSIM) loss, and degradation consistency loss. Optimization is performed using the AdamW optimizer [35]. For $2\times$ SR and $4\times$ SR, the batch sizes are set to 2 and 4, respectively. The initial learning rate is 2×10^{-4} and decays by half every 15 epochs. Training concludes after 50 epochs. All experiments are implemented in PyTorch and run on a workstation with dual NVIDIA RTX 4090 GPUs.

Table 2. PSNR/SSIM Values Achieved by Different Methods for 2× and 4× SR.

Method	Scale	EPFL	HCInew	HCIold	INRIA	STFgantry
Bicubic	2x	29.50/0.935	31.69/0.933	37.46/0.977	31.10/0.956	30.82/0.947
VDSR [36]	2x	32.50/0.959	34.37/0.956	40.61/0.986	34.43/0.974	35.54/0.979
EDSR [37]	2x	33.09/0.963	34.83/0.959	41.01/0.987	34.97/0.976	36.29/0.981
RCAN [22]	2x	33.16/0.963	34.98/0.960	41.05/0.987	35.01/0.976	36.33/0.982
resLF [20]	2x	32.75/0.967	36.07/0.971	42.61/0.992	34.57/0.978	36.89/0.987
LFSSR [38]	2x	33.69/0.974	36.86/0.975	43.75/0.993	35.27/0.983	38.07/0.990
LF-ATO [21]	2x	34.27/0.976	37.24/0.977	44.20/0.994	36.15/0.984	39.64/0.993
LF-InterNet [39]	2x	34.14/0.972	37.28/0.977	44.45/0.995	35.80/0.985	38.72/0.992
LF-DFnet [6]	2x	34.44/0.977	37.44/0.979	44.23/0.994	36.36/0.984	39.61/0.993
LF-TGUnet [40]	2x	34.67/0.978	37.80/0.979	44.78/0.995	36.46/0.986	39.95/0.994
LFT [9]	2x	34.80/0.978	37.84/0.979	44.52/**0.995**	36.59/**0.986**	40.51/0.994
DistgSSR [8]	2x	34.80/**0.979**	37.95/**0.980**	**44.92/0.995**	36.58/**0.986**	40.37/0.994
LF-CFUnet [41]	2x	34.78/0.978	**38.04/0.980**	44.77/0.995	36.72/**0.986**	40.59/0.994
DFFIT (Ours)	2x	**35.03/0.979**	37.98/**0.980**	44.85/**0.995**	**36.94/0.986**	**40.65/0.995**
Bicubic	4x	25.14/0.831	27.61/0.851	34.42/0.934	26.82/0.886	25.93/0.843
VDSR [36]	4x	26.82/0.869	29.12/0.876	34.01/0.943	28.87/0.914	28.31/0.893
EDSR [37]	4x	27.82/0.892	29.94/0.893	35.53/0.957	29.86/0.931	29.43/0.921
RCAN [22]	4x	28.31/0.899	30.25/0.896	35.89/0.959	30.36/0.936	30.25/0.934
resLF [20]	4x	27.86/0.899	30.37/0.907	36.12/0.966	29.72/0.936	29.64/0.927
LFSSR [38]	4x	29.16/0.915	30.88/0.913	36.90/0.970	31.03/0.944	30.14/0.937
LF-ATO [21]	4x	28.52/0.912	30.88/0.914	37.00/0.970	30.71/0.949	30.61/0.943
LF-InterNet [39]	4x	28.67/0.914	30.98/0.917	37.11/0.972	30.64/0.949	30.53/0.943
LF-DFnet [6]	4x	28.77/0.917	31.23/0.920	37.32/0.972	30.83/0.950	31.15/0.949
LF-TGUnet [40]	4x	28.96/0.919	31.42/0.922	37.63/0.973	31.28/**0.953**	31.36/0.951
LFT [9]	4x	29.25/**0.921**	31.46/0.922	37.63/**0.974**	31.20/0.952	31.86/**0.955**
DistgSSR [8]	4x	28.98/0.919	31.38/0.922	37.55/0.973	30.99/0.952	31.63/0.953
LF-CFUnet [41]	4x	29.24/**0.921**	**31.54/0.923**	**37.75/0.974**	31.32/**0.953**	31.68/0.954
DFFIT (Ours)	4x	**29.27/0.921**	31.43/0.922	37.67/**0.974**	**32.26/0.953**	**31.89/0.955**

4.2   Comparison to State-of-the-Art Methods

We compare DFFIT against several state-of-the-art methods, including three
SISR approaches [22,36,37], and nine LFSR methods [6,8,9,20,21,38–41].

Quantitative Results: Table 2 compares DFFIT with state-of-the-art SR
methods on both 2× and 4× SR tasks. DFFIT consistently achieves competitive PSNR and SSIM scores across all five datasets. Leveraging the proposed
DFrIT module, our method effectively handles complex scenarios and delivers
superior performance across the board.

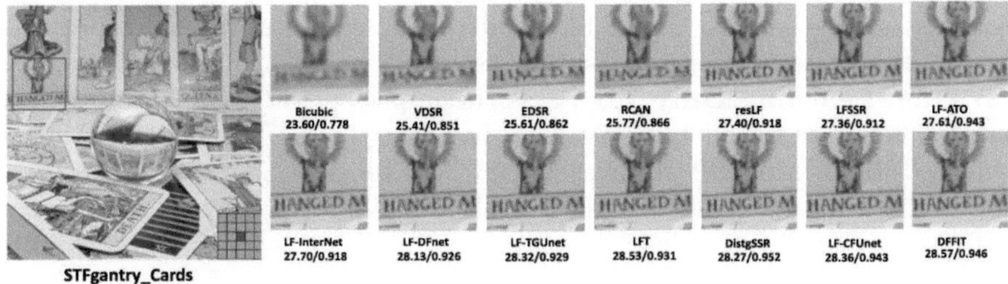

Fig. 2. Visual comparisons for 4×SR on STFgantry.

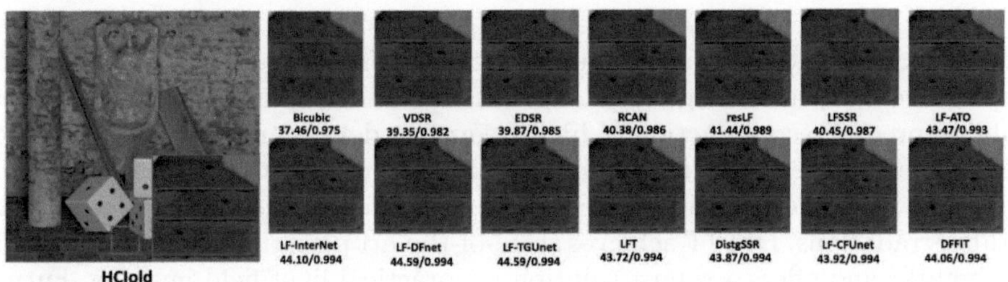

Fig. 3. Visual comparisons for 2×SR on HCIold.

Table 3. Ablation Study on Network Design for DFFIT.

	DM-Dual learning	Distg	DFrIT-block	EPFL	HCInew	HCIold	INRIA	STFgt	Average
0		✓		34.80	37.95	44.92	35.58	40.37	38.92
1		✓	✓	35.00	37.80	44.88	36.84	40.43	38.99
2	✓	✓		34.69	37.92	**44.91**	36.64	40.59	38.95
3	✓	✓	✓	**35.03**	**37.97**	44.85	**36.94**	**40.65**	**39.09**

Qualitative Results: Figures 2 and 3 illustrate the visual performance of various methods on 2× and 4× super-resolution tasks. Compared to existing state-of-the-art approaches, DFFIT demonstrates clear advantages in detail reconstruction, yielding richer textures and sharper structural features, which highlights its superior visual quality and fidelity.

Ablation Study: To assess the contribution of each component within the DFFIT architecture, we conducted ablation studies by progressively removing key modules. Specifically, Model 1 excludes the dual learning mechanism, and Model 2 omits the DFrIT-block. Table 3 summarizes the PSNR results of these variants. For fair comparison, all Distg-based methods [8] were retrained using the same training dataset as our approach.

1) DFrIT-block Only: To evaluate the impact of the DFrIT-block, we compared Model 1 (with DFrIT) and Model 0 (without DFrIT). As shown in Table 3, Model 1 achieves an average PSNR improvement of 0.07 dB over Model

0, demonstrating that the DFrIT-block effectively enhances feature representation and contributes to improved super-resolution performance.

2) Dual-Learning Only: To assess the impact of the dual-learning mechanism, we compared Model 2 (with dual learning) to Model 0 (without it). As shown in Table 3, Model 2 achieves a 0.03 dB average PSNR gain over Model 0, confirming that the dual-learning module contributes positively to SR reconstruction.

5   Conclusion

This paper proposes DFFIT, a novel LFSR framework that integrates frequency-domain analysis with a degradation-aware dual learning strategy. The FrIT module effectively captures long-range dependencies and frequency-specific features, enabling precise reconstruction of high-frequency details and consistent angular views. The dual learning mechanism, grounded in realistic degradation modeling, alleviates the need for paired data and enhances generalization to real-world degradations. DFFIT achieves state-of-the-art performance across multiple benchmarks and offers a robust solution for practical light field imaging. Future work will focus on improving the utilization of light field data and addressing the challenges of model lightweighting and few-shot learning in LFSR.

References

1. Ng, R., Levoy, M., Brédif, M., Duval, G., Horowitz, M., Hanrahan, P.: Light field photography with a hand-held plenoptic camera. Ph.D. thesis, Stanford university (2005)
2. Wanner, S., Goldluecke, B.: Variational light field analysis for disparity estimation and super-resolution. IEEE Trans. Pattern Anal. Mach. Intell. **36**(3), 606–619 (2013)
3. Wang, Y., Wu, T., Yang, J., Wang, L., An, W., Guo, Y.: DeOccNet: learning to see through foreground occlusions in light fields. In: Proceedings of the IEEE/CVF Winter Conference on Applications of Computer Vision, pp. 118–127 (2020)
4. Wang, T.-C., Efros, A.A., Ramamoorthi, R.: Depth estimation with occlusion modeling using light-field cameras. IEEE Trans. Pattern Anal. Mach. Intell. **38**(11), 2170–2181 (2016)
5. Yoon, Y., Jeon, H.-G., Yoo, D., Lee, J.-Y., Kweon, I.S.: Learning a deep convolutional network for light-field image super-resolution. In: Proceedings of the IEEE International Conference on Computer Vision Workshops, pp. 24–32 (2015)
6. Wang, Y., et al.: Light field image super-resolution using deformable convolution. IEEE Trans. Image Process. **30**, 1057–1071 (2020)
7. Zhang, S., Chang, S., Lin, Y.: End-to-end light field spatial super-resolution network using multiple epipolar geometry. IEEE Trans. Image Process. **30**, 5956–5968 (2021)
8. Wang, Y., et al.: Disentangling light fields for super-resolution and disparity estimation. IEEE Trans. Pattern Anal. Mach. Intell. **45**(1), 425–443 (2022)
9. Liang, Z., Wang, Y., Wang, L., Yang, J., Zhou, S.: Light field image super-resolution with transformers. IEEE Signal Process. Lett. **29**, 563–567 (2022)

10. Ma, J., Li, Z., Cheng, J., An, P., Liang, D., Huang, L.: Light field image super-resolution based on dual learning and deep Fourier channel attention. Opt. Lett. **49**(11), 2886–2889 (2024)
11. Zhao, X.: Fractional Fourier image transformer for multimodal remote sensing data classification. IEEE Trans. Neural Netw. Learn. Syst. **35**(2), 2314–2326 (2024)
12. Wang, Y., Liang, Z., Wang, L., Yang, J., An, W., Guo, Y.: Real-world light field image super-resolution via degradation modulation. IEEE Trans. Neural Netw. Learn. Syst. (2024)
13. Yi, Z., Zhang, H., Tan, P., Gong, M.: DualGAN: unsupervised dual learning for image-to-image translation. In: Proceedings of the IEEE International Conference on Computer Vision, pp. 2849–2857 (2017)
14. Mitra, K., Veeraraghavan, A.: Light field denoising, light field superresolution and stereo camera based refocussing using a GMM light field patch prior. In: 2012 IEEE Computer Society Conference on Computer Vision and Pattern Recognition Workshops, pp. 22–28. IEEE (2012)
15. Farrugia, R.A., Galea, C., Guillemot, C.: Super resolution of light field images using linear subspace projection of patch-volumes. IEEE J. Sel. Top. Sig. Process. **11**(7), 1058–1071 (2017)
16. Egiazarian, K., Katkovnik, V.: Single image super-resolution via BM3D sparse coding. In: 2015 23rd European Signal Processing Conference (EUSIPCO), pp. 2849–2853. IEEE (2015)
17. Alain, M., Smolic, A.: Light field denoising by sparse 5D transform domain collaborative filtering. In: 2017 IEEE 19th International Workshop on Multimedia Signal Processing (MMSP), pp. 1–6. IEEE (2017)
18. Rossi, M., Frossard, P.: Geometry-consistent light field super-resolution via graph-based regularization. IEEE Trans. Image Process. **27**(9), 4207–4218 (2018)
19. Yuan, Y., Cao, Z., Lijuan, S.: Light-field image superresolution using a combined deep CNN based on EPI. IEEE Signal Process. Lett. **25**(9), 1359–1363 (2018)
20. Zhang, S., Lin, Y., Sheng, H.: Residual networks for light field image super-resolution. In: Proceedings of the IEEE/CVF Conference on Computer Vision and Pattern Recognition, pp. 11046–11055 (2019)
21. Jin, J., Hou, J., Chen, J., Kwong, S.: Light field spatial super-resolution via deep combinatorial geometry embedding and structural consistency regularization. In: Proceedings of the IEEE/CVF Conference on Computer Vision and Pattern Recognition, pp. 2260–2269 (2020)
22. Zhang, Y., Li, K., Li, K., Wang, L., Zhong, B., Fu, Y.: Image super-resolution using very deep residual channel attention networks. In: Ferrari, V., Hebert, M., Sminchisescu, C., Weiss, Y. (eds.) ECCV 2018. LNCS, vol. 11211, pp. 294–310. Springer, Cham (2018). https://doi.org/10.1007/978-3-030-01234-2_18
23. HeK, M., RenS, Q., et al.: Deep residual learning for image recognition. In: 2016 IEEE Conference on Computer Vision and Pattern Recognition, pp. 770–778 (2016)
24. Wu, G., Zhao, M., Wang, L., Dai, Q., Chai, T., Liu, Y.: Light field reconstruction using deep convolutional network on EPI. In: Proceedings of the IEEE Conference on Computer Vision and Pattern Recognition, pp. 6319–6327 (2017)
25. Pei, S.-C., Ding, J.-J.: Closed-form discrete fractional and affine Fourier transforms. IEEE Trans. Signal Process. **48**(5), 1338–1353 (2000)
26. Pei, S.-C., Ding, J.-J.: Simplified fractional Fourier transforms. JOSA A **17**(12), 2355–2367 (2000)
27. Zhang, K., Zuo, W., Zhang, L.: Learning a single convolutional super-resolution network for multiple degradations. In: Proceedings of the IEEE Conference on Computer Vision and Pattern Recognition, pp. 3262–3271 (2018)

28. Gu, J., Lu, H., Zuo, W., Dong, C.: Blind super-resolution with iterative kernel correction. In: Proceedings of the IEEE/CVF Conference on Computer Vision and Pattern Recognition, pp. 1604–1613 (2019)
29. Rerabek, M., Ebrahimi, T.: New light field image dataset. In: 8th International Conference on Quality of Multimedia Experience (QoMEX) (2016)
30. Honauer, K., Johannsen, O., Kondermann, D., Goldluecke, B.: A dataset and evaluation methodology for depth estimation on 4D light fields. In: Lai, S.-H., Lepetit, V., Nishino, K., Sato, Y. (eds.) ACCV 2016, Part III. LNCS, vol. 10113, pp. 19–34. Springer, Cham (2017). https://doi.org/10.1007/978-3-319-54187-7_2
31. Wanner, S., Meister, S., Goldluecke, B.: Datasets and benchmarks for densely sampled 4D light fields. In: VMV, vol. 13, pp. 225–226 (2013)
32. Le Pendu, M., Jiang, X., Guillemot, C.: Light field inpainting propagation via low rank matrix completion. IEEE Trans. Image Process. **27**(4), 1981–1993 (2018)
33. Vaish, V., Adams, A.: The (new) Stanford light field archive, computer graphics laboratory (2008)
34. Wang, Z., Bovik, A.C., Sheikh, H.R., Simoncelli, E.P.: Image quality assessment: from error visibility to structural similarity. IEEE Trans. Image Process. **13**(4), 600–612 (2004)
35. Loshchilov, I., Hutter, F.: Decoupled weight decay regularization. arXiv preprint arXiv:1711.05101 (2017)
36. Kim, J., Lee, J.K., Lee, K.M.: Accurate image super-resolution using very deep convolutional networks. In: Proceedings of the IEEE Conference on Computer Vision and Pattern Recognition, pp. 1646–1654 (2016)
37. Lim, B., Son, S., Kim, H., Nah, S., Lee, K.M.: Enhanced deep residual networks for single image super-resolution. In: Proceedings of the IEEE Conference on Computer Vision and Pattern Recognition Workshops, pp. 136–144 (2017)
38. Yeung, H.W.F., Hou, J., Chen, X., Chen, J., Chen, Z., Chung, Y.Y.: Light field spatial super-resolution using deep efficient spatial-angular separable convolution. IEEE Trans. Image Process. **28**(5), 2319–2330 (2019)
39. Wang, Y., Wang, L., Yang, J., An, W., Yu, J., Guo, Y.: Spatial-angular interaction for light field image super-resolution. In: Vedaldi, A., Bischof, H., Brox, T., Frahm, J.-M. (eds.) ECCV 2020, Part XXIII. LNCS, vol. 12368, pp. 290–308. Springer, Cham (2020). https://doi.org/10.1007/978-3-030-58592-1_18
40. Li, H., Lv, T., Yingchun, W., Chen, J.: A light field image super-resolution network based on dual-path guided update. Opto-Electron. Eng. **51**(12), 63–75 (2024)
41. Chen, J., Yingchun, W., Lyu, T., Liu, L., Zhao, X.: Light field image super-resolution network based on interleaved feature update. Acta Electron. Sin. **52**(12), 4113–4124 (2024)

Video Stabilization Based on MeshFlow Motion Model in Dynamic and Complex Scenes

Jun Liu[1,2], Hao Ning[1,2], Jing Huang[1,2], Yingjie Xia[1,2], Qun Xie[3], Jun Zhou[4], and Jinping Li[1,2(✉)]

[1] School of Information Science and Engineering, University of Jinan, Jinan 250022, Shandong, China
ise_lijp@ujn.edu
[2] Shandong Provincial Key Laboratory of Ubiquitous Intelligent Computing, Jinan 250022, Shandong, China
[3] School of Civil Engineering and Architecture, University of Jinan, Jinan 250022, Shandong, China
[4] School of Mechanical Engineering, Shandong University, Jinan 250061, Shandong, China

Abstract. Due to the influence of both internal and external factors, fixed installed surveillance cameras often suffer from shakiness. In dynamic and complex scenes, frequent discontinuous depth variations and large foreground moving objects lead to multi-plane motion. This can lead video stabilization algorithms to misjudge local plane motion as global camera shakiness, resulting in stabilization failure or degraded performance. To address this problem, we propose a video stabilization algorithm based on the MeshFlow motion model. First, we propose a shakiness detection method and rules, which enables the stabilization algorithm to process only shaky frames, thus improving computational efficiency. Then, during motion estimation, we divide each frame into multiple mesh and construct a sparse motion field using motion vectors from mesh vertices to extract the camera's shakiness trajectory. Finally, we apply Kalman filtering for trajectory smoothing, and use motion compensation to generate stabilized video. Experimental results show that the stabilized video achieves a PSNR improvement of 30% over the original video, only 0.23 dB lower than the SOFT algorithm. Additionally, the processing speed reaches 32 frames per second, which is 78% faster than SOFT algorithm, thereby meeting the requirements of practical applications.

Keywords: Video Stabilization · Motion Estimation · Motion Compensation · MeshFlow Motion Model

1 Introduction

Although surveillance cameras are typically fixed, their captured videos can still suffer from shakiness due to internal factors like the rolling shutter effect and external disturbances such as wind or vibrations from passing vehicles. This shakiness degrades visual quality and hinders subsequent video analysis, making stabilization essential for improving processing accuracy.

Early camera stabilization, dating back to the 1960s–70s, relied on mechanical devices and gyroscopes [1]. Modern methods fall into three categories: mechanical, optical, and electronic [2–5]. Mechanical and optical approaches depend heavily on hardware precision, which degrades over time and compromises performance, while also increasing device size and reducing portability. In contrast, electronic methods use image processing algorithms, require no extra hardware, and are more cost-effective.

Despite their advantages, electronic stabilization methods face two main challenges: (1) low real-time performance due to slow processing speed, and (2) interference from multi-plane motion. In dynamic scenes, frames often contain both global camera shake and local motion-such as large moving objects (Fig. 1a) or depth discontinuities from perspective effects (Fig. 1b). Misinterpreting these local motions as camera shake can lead to motion estimation errors and reduced stabilization quality.

(a)

(b)

Fig. 1. Multi-plane motion scene

Video stabilization typically involves three stages: motion estimation, trajectory smoothing, and motion compensation. Motion estimation uses techniques like feature matching or optical flow to capture camera shake [6, 7]; smoothing applies filtering or interpolation to suppress jitter [8–10]; and compensation adjusts frames to produce a stable video [11–13].

A key task in motion estimation is distinguishing between different motion patterns, i.e., identifying multi-plane motion. Based on the estimation method, stabilization algorithms are categorized as 2D, 2.5D, or 3D.

2D stabilization is the most basic approach. Early methods, like Liu et al.'s grid-based technique [14], estimated transformation matrices per grid to handle multi-plane motion, but struggled with large moving foregrounds. To address this, Wu [15] used superpixels and K-means clustering to separate foreground and background motion, improving accuracy but at high computational cost, limiting real-time use. In 2023, Hao et al. [16] distinguished camera shake from intentional motion using variational modal decomposition, further enhancing motion separation. Overall, 2D methods are low in complexity, scalable, and widely used as preprocessing in video tasks.

2.5D stabilization assumes small camera rotations around a central point and uses pseudo-3D modeling to address multi-plane motion. Liu et al. [17] introduced subspace constraints and view re-mapping to estimate foreground trajectories but relied on stable viewpoints and dominant background motion. To handle unstable views, Shang et al. [18] applied low-rank regularization and path prediction to smooth trajectories and suppress foreground interference, though their method assumes scenes can be approximated by planes.

3D stabilization reconstructs camera motion in 3D space using point clouds or motion trajectories, allowing better separation of multi-plane motion and actual shake. Structure from Motion (SfM) is commonly used to recover camera pose [19]. Liu et al. [20] applied SfM and least-squares optimization to generate stabilized frames but ignored depth distinctions. To improve this, Mehala et al. [21] used a Gaussian Mixture Model to estimate both absolute and relative depth, combining feature extraction, Bezier curves, and Kalman filtering to handle complex motion. While 3D methods offer high accuracy, they are computationally intensive, sensitive to scene changes, and depend heavily on video quality.

Fixed surveillance cameras typically lack complex motions like zoom or large rotations and require real-time, low-power processing. While 2.5D and 3D methods offer better stabilization, their high computational cost makes them impractical. In contrast, 2D methods are more suitable for such scenarios.

However, 2D stabilization still faces two main issues: (1) local planar motion, such as depth changes or large moving foregrounds, is often mistaken for global camera shake; (2) limited processing speed restricts real-time application.

To address this, we propose:

(1) A mesh-based motion estimation method that builds a sparse motion field from vertex motion vectors to better capture true camera shake. Kalman filtering is then applied for smoothing, followed by motion compensation to stabilize the video.
(2) A shakiness detection strategy that enables the algorithm to process only shaky frames, reducing unnecessary computation and improving efficiency.

2 Proposed Method

2.1 Algorithm Flow

The overall flow of the algorithm is shown in Fig. 2. In practical applications, video shakiness does not always occur. Therefore, the first step is to determine whether shakiness exists in the current video frame by calculating the similarity of projection curves within fixed-position windows between different frames. Then, applied shakiness rules to update the stable frames. For frames identified as exhibiting shakiness, SIFT feature points are detected and matched between different frames. The motion vectors of the matched feature points are propagated to the mesh vertices to construct the sparse motion field and obtain the motion trajectory. Finally, apply the Kalman filter to smooth the motion trajectory and use affine transformation to process the video frames, generating stabilized video.

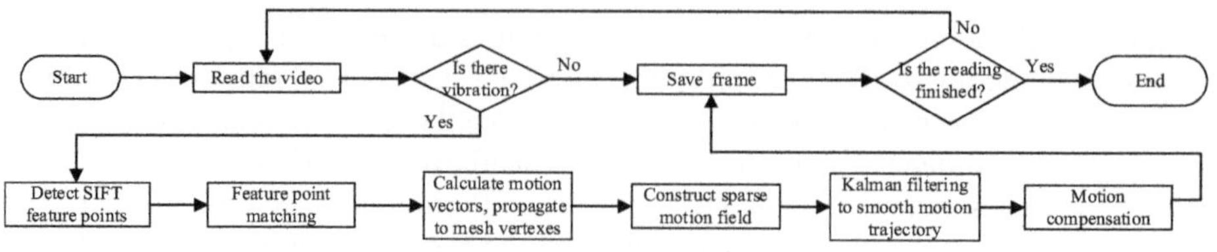

Fig. 2. Algorithm flow chart

2.2 Shakiness Detection

Shakiness Detection Method. In fixed-camera scenarios, shakiness appears as displacement in overlapping regions between frames. To detect it, we use image matching: a fixed window is selected, and horizontal and vertical projection curves are computed (Fig. 3). Based on the principle that shaky frames yield differing curves, we calculate the Pearson Correlation Coefficient between frames to determine if shakiness is present, as shown in Eq. (1).

$$r = \frac{\sum\limits_{i=1}^{n} (S_i - \bar{S})(U_i - \bar{U})}{\sqrt{\sum\limits_{i=1}^{n} (S_i - \bar{S})^2} \sqrt{\sum\limits_{i=1}^{n} (U_i - \bar{U})^2}} \tag{1}$$

where S_i and U_i are data points of horizontal and vertical projection curves, $\bar{S}$ and $\bar{U}$ denote their mean values, and n is the number of points. A Pearson Correlation Coefficient near 1 indicates similar images, while a value near -1 signals shakiness.

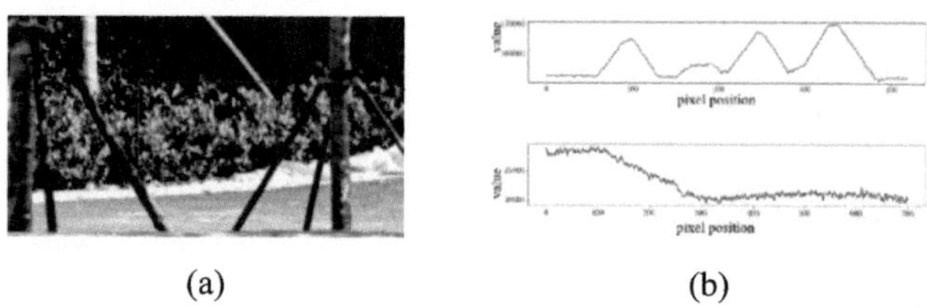

(a)   (b)

Fig. 3. Shakiness detection method. (a) Fixed-position window. (b) Horizontal and vertical projection curves

Shakiness Detection Rules. Frames without shakiness are defined as stable frames and serve as references for aligning subsequent shaky frames. The first frame is used as the initial stable frame and is updated over time to adapt to scene changes. The update rules are as follows (Table 1):

Table 1. Shakiness Detection Rules

Shakiness Detection Rules
1. Read the video
2. Set stabilized frame Z as the first frame
3. Initialize counter = 0
4. For each current frame Y:
If no shakiness detected between Y and previous frame X:
Increment counter
If counter $\geqslant$ 25, update stabilized frame Z=$Y$and reset counter to 0
Else:
Stabilize Y by aligning it with stabilized frame Z

Vibrating frames are aligned to the stable frame rather than consecutively to avoid two issues: (1) poor-quality initial frames (e.g., blurry or black) can degrade the entire video; (2) consecutive alignment causes cumulative errors (Fig. 4a), leading to residual shakiness. Aligning with a stable frame offers greater consistency (Fig. 4b).

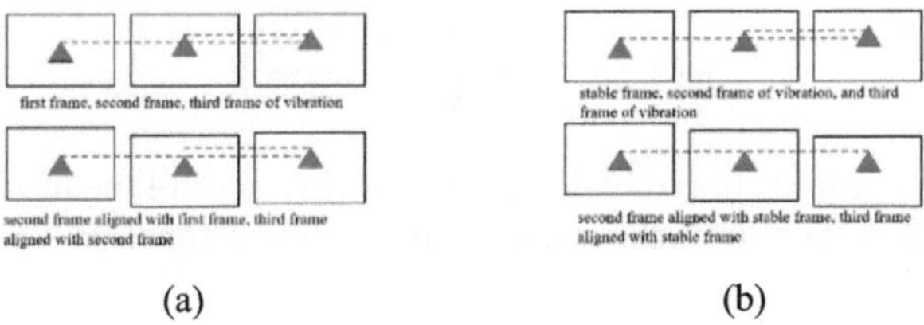

Fig. 4. Video frame alignment schematic diagram. (a) Cumulative error. (b) Aligned with stable frame

2.3 MeshFlow Motion Model

Shakiness results from camera shake during capture, making accurate motion estimation crucial. The MeshFlow model, composed of motion vectors at mesh vertices, effectively handles spatial motion caused by depth changes [22]. Compared to optical flow [23], it is more efficient, avoiding costly feature matching.

Feature Matching. SIFT features are extracted from the stable and current frames for matching. To remove mismatches, RANSAC [24] is applied, which randomly samples data to fit a model and identifies inliers by checking consistency. This filters out outliers and improves matching accuracy. Final results are shown in Fig. 5.

Motion Vector Propagation. Each matched feature point pair generates a motion vector $v_p = p_n - p_t$, where the direction indicates movement direction and magnitude represents displacement, as shown in Fig. 6.

Fig. 5. SIFT feature point matching

Fig. 6. Motion vector

The video frame is divided into regular $M \times N$ grids, as shown in Fig. 7. The motion vectors in the video frame are propagated to the nearby mesh vertices. On one hand, this can improve the accuracy of motion estimation in multi-plane motion. On the other hand, high-quality feature points are usually evenly distributed across various regions of the image, ensuring that each region contains a sufficient number of feature points and thereby guaranteeing the comprehensiveness of the motion estimation.

To maximize motion vector propagation, a rectangular region around feature point p (matching the eight-neighborhood grid) is used (Fig. 7a). The vector v_p is propagated to all mesh vertices in this region, weighted by a Gaussian function to reduce instability from distance effects (Eq. 2). The propagation result is shown in Fig. 7b.

$$w(h, u) = \exp\left(-\frac{h^2 + u^2}{2\sigma^2}\right) \tag{2}$$

where h and u represent the horizontal and vertical distances of the mesh vertex relative to the feature point p, σ controls the range of the Gaussian function's spread.

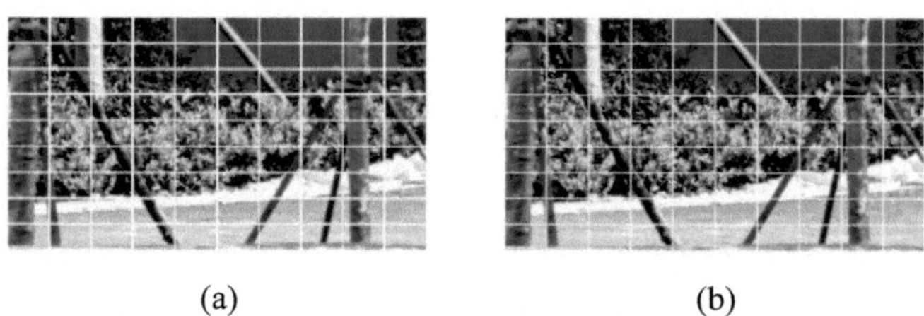

(a)   (b)

Fig. 7. Motion vector propagation. (a) Propagation range. (b) Propagation result.

As shown in Fig. 8, after propagating motion vectors, each mesh vertex may receive multiple vectors from different feature points. To ensure each vertex has a unique motion vector, filtering is required.

Motion Vector Filtering. Median filtering is a nonlinear denoising method that replaces each pixel with the median value of its neighborhood using a sliding window, effectively removing noise. Since each mesh vertex may receive motion vectors with varying directions, median filtering is used to remove irregular motion and assign a unique vector. As shown in Fig. 9, vertex v receives 7 vectors; after sorting by direction and magnitude, the median is selected as the final motion vector.

Once each mesh vertex has a unique motion vector, a sparse motion field is formed, representing camera motion between frames. As shown in Fig. 10, it effectively captures regional motion under multi-plane conditions.

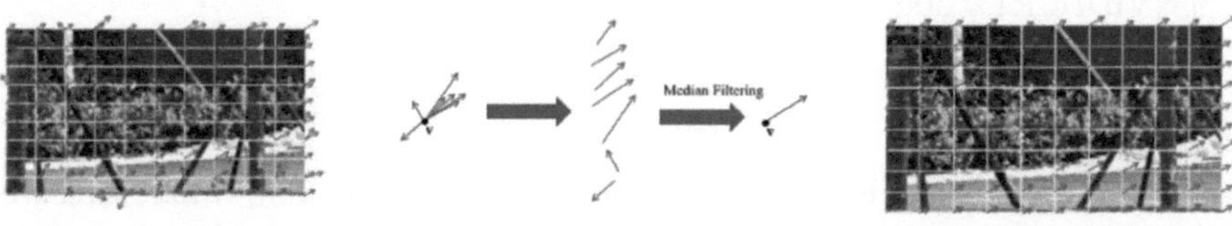

Fig. 8. Vector propagation   **Fig. 9.** Vector selection   **Fig. 10.** Sparse motion field

2.4 Motion Trajectory Smoothing and Motion Compensation

Motion Trajectory Smoothing. At each mesh vertex, motion vectors v_i from nnn shaky frames form a motion trajectory set $V = \{v_i | i = 1, 2, ..., n-1\}$. Kalman filtering smooths V into a stable trajectory $V' = \{v_i | i = 1, 2, ..., n-1\}$. as shown in Fig. 11, this removes fluctuations and stabilizes the motion path.

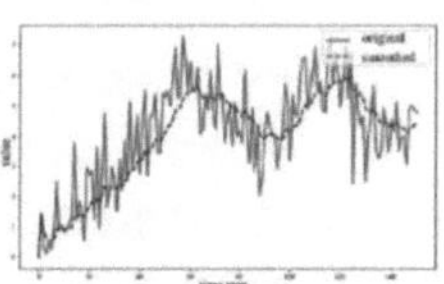

Fig. 11. Motion trajectory smoothing

Motion Compensation. Motion compensation eliminates camera-induced displacement by applying image registration based on the smoothed motion trajectory. Using affine transformation, it aligns the current frame to the stable frame through rotation, translation, and scaling. The steps are as follows:

1. The motion vectors at all mesh vertices form the motion trajectory of the video along the time sequence, $C = \{V_j | j = 1, 2, ..., N\}$ where N is the number of mesh vertices, and V_j represents the set of motion vectors collected over time for vertex j.
2. Apply Kalman filtering to the motion trajectory V_j of each vertex j, obtaining the smoothed camera motion trajectory $C' = \{V'_j | j = 1, 2, ..., N\}$.
3. Compute the transformation matrix based on C and C', then apply affine transformation to the current frame to align it with the stabilized frame.
4. Black borders introduced by alignment are cropped to improve visual quality, and the stabilized frame is output.

3   Experiments

To evaluate the algorithm, we conducted video stabilization and comparison experiments on a Windows system using Python 3.8. The hardware included an Intel i5-12490F CPU and an NVIDIA RTX 3060 GPU (12 GB).

3.1   Datasets

Currently, most video stabilization datasets focus on camera motion, with few recorded by fixed cameras. To address this, we collect videos of outdoor natural scenes captured by a fixed camera under varying conditions, including: (1) Scenes: airport runways, open water, and natural environments; (2) Time: early morning to evening; (3) Weather: sunny, cloudy, and rainy; (4) Stability: stable, continuous jitter, and intermittent jitter; (5) Content: large moving objects, parallax, and depth discontinuities.

The DS-2CD3T86FWDV3 camera (Fig. 12) was used to capture 115 video clips with both continuous and intermittent shakiness. Sample videos are shown in Fig. 13. Resolutions were 1920 × 1080 or 2560 × 1440 at 25 fps, with durations of 10–20 s.

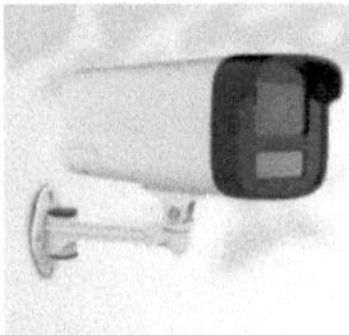

Fig. 12.   Camera

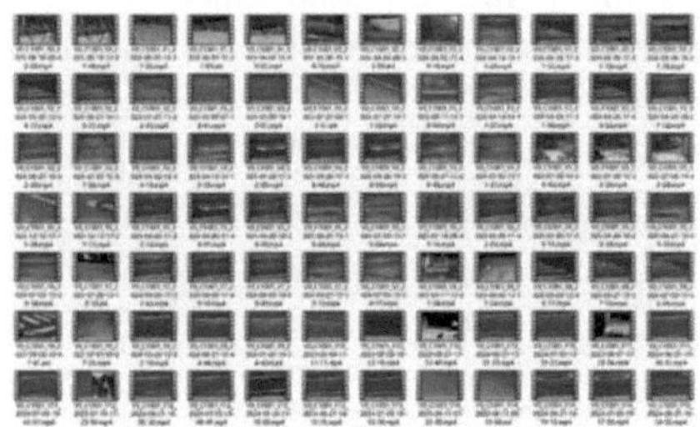

Fig. 13.   Experimental video

3.2   Video Stabilization Experiment

The effectiveness of video stabilization was evaluated based on grayscale difference images and Peak Signal-to-Noise Ratio (PSNR).

Grayscale Difference Images.   Grayscale difference images, computed by pixel-wise grayscale value subtraction, intuitively reflect image similarity—smaller differences indicate greater similarity.

Analyzing grayscale difference images helps evaluate video stabilization: the more stable the video, the closer pixel differences are to zero. As shown in Fig. 14, the difference image before stabilization contains many non-black pixels, which are significantly reduced after stabilization, indicating improved frame alignment.

(a)   (b)   (c)

Fig. 14. Grayscale difference comparison diagram. (a) Original Adjacent two frames. (b) Difference image before stabilization. (c) Difference image after stabilization

PSNR. In video stabilization research, Peak Signal-to-Noise Ratio (PSNR) [25] is widely used to measure frame similarity. It is calculated between adjacent frames using the following equation:

$$PSNR = 10 \times \log_{10}\left(\frac{L_{\max}^2}{MSE}\right) \tag{3}$$

$$MSE = \frac{1}{W \times H} \sum_{x=1}^{W} \sum_{y=1}^{H} \left[K_1(x, y) - K_2(x, y)\right]^2 \tag{4}$$

where W and H are the image width and height. $K_1(x, y)$ and $K_2(x, y)$ are pixel values at (x, y) in the current and next frames. L_{max} is the max pixel value (e.g., 255 for 8-bit). MSE is the average squared pixel difference between frames. Smaller MSE means higher PSNR, indicating better alignment and stability.

To evaluate overall stabilization, the average PSNR ($PSNR_\mu$) across all N_f frames is calculated as shown in Eq. (5). Table 2 presents results from six sample clips, showing that $PSNR_\mu$ improves by about 30% after stabilization, validating the effectiveness of the proposed algorithm.

$$PSNR_\mu = \frac{1}{N_f - 1} \sum_{k=1}^{N_f - 1} PSNR_k \tag{5}$$

1where $PSNR_k$ is calculated in the same way as in Eq. (3).

Table 2. Video stabilization results

Video ID	1	2	3	4	5	6
Before $PSNR_\mu$/dB	21.96	23.86	28.20	18.86	18.35	30.40
After $PSNR_\mu$/dB	29.66	31.11	36.94	25.70	24.70	37.69

3.3 Comparative Experiment

As our algorithm targets fixed-camera scenes, and public datasets mainly involve moving cameras, comparisons were conducted on our collected videos. We compared it with traditional methods (MeshFlow [22], Ref. [26]) and unsupervised deep learning methods (DUT [27], SOFT [28]), as no ground-truth stable videos were available.

Figure 15 shows visual results of three consecutive shaky frames and their processed versions. The scene includes large moving objects (e.g., swaying trees), parallax, depth discontinuities, and camera shake.

Figure 16 presents grayscale difference images after stabilization by various methods. More black pixels indicate better results, with pixel values enhanced threefold for clarity. Reference [26] performs poorly, failing to align swaying leaves. MeshFlow improves but still shows many white pixels. SOFT's result has white bands caused by high cropping, which removes black borders to enhance visual quality.

We processed 115 shaky videos with different algorithms and calculated the average PSNR ($PSNR_w$) and processing speed (Table 3). SOFT achieved the highest $PSNR_w$ of 31.74 due to its strong deep learning features. Our method performed comparably, with a $PSNR_w$ just 0.23 dB lower, while running at 32 fps-78% faster than SOFT and 33% faster than MeshFlow (24 fps). This speedup owes to our shakiness detection reducing computation.

Considering both stabilization performance and processing speed, our proposed method exhibits greater potential in certain application scenarios.

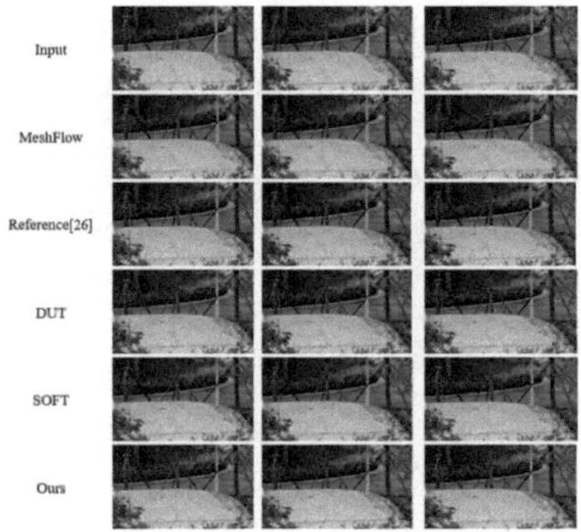

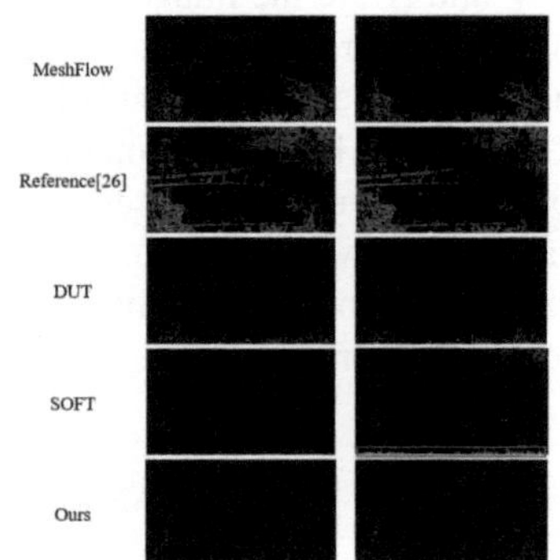

Fig. 15. Comparison of stabilization algorithms

Fig. 16. Difference image of two frames after stabilization

Table 3. Results of comparative experiment

Method	$PSNR_w$	Speed
MeshFlow [22]	24.33	20 fps
Reference [26]	26.89	24 fps
DUT [27]	30.16	15 fps
SOFT [28]	**31.74**	18 fps
Ours	31.51	**32 fps**

3.4 Ablation Study

An ablation study tested the proposed shakiness detection method's impact on runtime and stabilization. Table 4 shows that adding shakiness detection reduces runtime by up to 60%, while $PSNR_\mu$ drops by less than 5% compared to processing all frames.

The impact of shakiness detection varies by video. For intermittent shakiness (e.g., Video 4), runtime dropped by 60% since fewer frames needed processing. For continuous shakiness (e.g., Video 1), runtime savings were minimal, and overhead caused a slight 0.5-s increase. Overall, for intermittent shakiness, the proposed detection method effectively reduces computation and improves efficiency.

Table 4. Ablation experiment results of shakiness detection

Video ID		1	2	3	4
Video Duration(s)		15	12	20	15
Algorithm Runtime (s)	Without	12.0	9.8	17.3	13.5
	With	12.5	5.0	13.1	5.8
$PSNR_\mu$ (dB)	Original	18.85	28.05	26.64	31.06
	Without	23.63	34.41	34.06	37.15
	With	23.37	34.89	33.90	38.02

4 Conclusion

In dynamic scenes with depth variations and large foreground motion, multi-plane motion occurs. To handle this, we use the MeshFlow model for stabilization, improving PSNR by 30%. SIFT features are matched between current and stable frames to compute motion vectors, which form a sparse motion field. Kalman filtering smooths the trajectory, and affine transformation stabilizes the video.

To reduce computation, we introduce shakiness detection so only shaky frames are processed, greatly improving efficiency. Experiments show the method balances speed and stabilization well for practical use.

Future research can focus on the following two aspects:

1. Optimizing for intense motion, where blur reduces feature quality and hinders matching.
2. Adapting and improving real-time performance on low-power platforms while maintaining stabilization quality.

Acknowledgments. This study is funded by Shandong Provincial Project of Innovation Ability Enhancement Engineering for Technology Oriented Small and medium-sized enterprises (2022TSGC1047); Central Guidance Funding Projects for Local Scientific and Technological Development of Shandong Province (YDZX2024078); University of Jinan Disciplinary Cross-Convergence Construction Project 2023 (XKJC-202310).

Disclosure of Interests. The authors have no competing interests to declare that are relevant to the content of this article.

References

1. Li, Q.: Research on Full-Frame Video Stabilization Method Based on Optical Flow and Grid Trajectory. Wuhan University of Technology, Wuhan (2022)
2. Gao, T., Li, R., Sun, L.: Research on video stabilization methods for mobile robots. J. Harbin Inst. Technol. **09**, 1379–1382 (2007)
3. Zhao, F., Lu, H.: Digital image stabilization algorithm based on the combination of gray-level information and feature information. Comput. Appl. **S2**, 66–68 (2007)
4. Wei, X.: Research and Implementation of Real-Time Image Stabilization Algorithm for Mobile HD Video. North China University of Technology, Beijing (2018)
5. Wei, S., Xie, W., He, Z.: A review of digital video stabilization technology. J. Comput. Res. Dev. **54**(09), 2044–2058 (2017)
6. Puglisi, G., Battiato, S.: A robust image alignment algorithm for video stabilization purposes. IEEE Trans. Circuits Syst. Video Technol. **21**(10), 1390–1400 (2011)
7. Yu, J., Ramamoorthi, R.: Selfie video stabilization. In: Proceedings of the European Conference on Computer Vision (ECCV). Springer (2018)
8. Chen, B.Y., Lee, K.Y., Huang, W.T., et al.: Capturing intention-based full-frame video stabilization. In: Computer Graphics Forum, vol. 27, no. 7, pp. 1805–1814. Blackwell Publishing Ltd, Oxford (2008)
9. Jia, C., Evans, B.L.: Online motion smoothing for video stabilization via constrained multiple-model estimation. EURASIP J. Image Video Process. **2017**, 1–13 (2017)
10. Souza, M.R., Pedrini, H.: Digital video stabilization based on adaptive camera trajectory smoothing. EURASIP J. Image Video Process. **2018**, 1–11 (2018)
11. Zhang, L., Chen, X.Q., Kong, X.Y., et al.: Geodesic video stabilization in transformation space. IEEE Trans. Image Process. **26**(5), 2219–2229 (2017)
12. Zhao, M., Ling, Q.: Adaptively meshed video stabilization. IEEE Trans. Circuits Syst. Video Technol. **31**(9), 3504–3517 (2020)
13. Huang, Q., Liu, J., Jiang, C., et al.: DMCVS: decomposed motion compensation-based video stabilization. IET Image Proc. **18**(6), 1422–1433 (2024)
14. Liu, S., Yuan, L., Tan, P., et al.: Bundled camera paths for video stabilization. ACM Trans. Graph. (TOG) **32**(4), 1–10 (2013)
15. Wu, R.: Research on Video Stabilization Algorithm Based on Complex Motion. University of Chinese Academy of Sciences (Institute of Optoelectronics, Chinese Academy of Sciences), Chengdu (2022)
16. Hao, D., Shi, W., Li, C., et al.: Digital image stabilization method based on variational mode decomposition and sampling fluctuation analysis. Acad. J. Comput. Inf. Sci. (AJCIS) **6**(8), 8–21 (2023)
17. Liu, F., Gleicher, M., Wang, J., et al.: Subspace video stabilization. ACM Trans. Graph. (TOG) **30**(1), 1–10 (2011)
18. Shang, Z., Chu, Z.: Video stabilization based on low-rank constraint and trajectory optimization. IET Image Proc. **18**(7), 1768–1779 (2024)
19. Özyeşil, O., Voroninski, V., Basri, R., et al.: A survey of structure from motion. Acta Numer **26**, 305–364 (2017)
20. Liu, F., Gleicher, M., Jin, H., et al.: Content-preserving warps for 3D video stabilization. In: Seminal Graphics Papers: Pushing the Boundaries, vol. 2, pp. 631–639 (2023)
21. Mehala, R., Mahesh, K.: An effective absolute and relative depths estimation-based 3D video stabilization framework using GSLSTM and BCKF. SIViP **19**(5), 1–16 (2025)

22. Liu, S., Tan, P., Yuan, L., et al.: MeshFlow: minimum latency online video stabilization. In: Computer Vision–ECCV 2016: 14th European Conference, Amsterdam, The Netherlands, 11–14 October 2016, Proceedings, Part VI 14, pp. 800–815. Springer (2016)
23. Lucas, B.D., Kanade, T.: An iterative image registration technique with an application to stereo vision. In: IJCAI 1981: 7th International Joint Conference on Artificial Intelligence, vol. 2, pp. 674–679 (1981)
24. Fischler, M.A., Bolles, R.C.: Random sample consensus: a paradigm for model fitting with applications to image analysis and automated cartography. Commun. ACM **24**(6), 381–395 (1981)
25. Roberto e Souza, M., Maia, H.A., Pedrini, H.: Survey on digital video stabilization: concepts, methods, and challenges. ACM Comput. Surv. (CSUR) **55**(3), 1–37 (2022)
26. Grundmann, M., Kwatra, V., Essa, I.: Auto-directed video stabilization with robust l1 optimal camera paths. In: Conference on Computer Vision and Pattern Recognition, pp. 225–232. IEEE (2011)
27. Xu, Y., Zhang, J., Maybank, S.J., et al.: Dut: learning video stabilization by simply watching unstable videos. IEEE Trans. Image Process. **31**, 4306–4320 (2022)
28. Wang, N., Zhou, C., Zhu, R., et al.: SOFT: self-supervised sparse Optical Flow Transformer for video stabilization via quaternion. Eng. Appl. Artif. Intell. **130**, 107725 (2024)

Dual-Edge Consistency Constrained Unfolding Network for Depth Map Super-Resolution

Hao Ren[1], Lijun Zhao[1(✉)] , Jinjing Zhang[2] , Huihui Bai[3],
and Anhong Wang[1]

[1] Taiyuan University of Science and Technology, Taiyuan 030024, China
`leejun@tyust.edu.cn`, `s202315110476@stu.tyust.edu.cn`
[2] North University of China, Jiancaoping District, Taiyuan 030051, China
[3] Institute of Information Science, Beijing Jiaotong University, Beijing 100044, China

Abstract. Recently, several newest Depth Map Super-Resolution (DMSR) methods have incorporated depth edge prediction as auxiliary guidance into the optimization model, creating a dual-task driven unfolding network for enhancing depth edge refinement. Nevertheless, these approaches either overlook explicit dual-edge consistency constraint or merely fuse color edges with depth edges once. This oversight results in diminished generalization ability and subpar performance. To this end, we transform the DMSR problem as a triple-task optimization model explicitly constrained by dual-edge consistency. According to the Alternating Direction Method of Multipliers (ADMM) theory, the proposed model can be cast as iterative sub-optimizations for color-edge update, depth-edge update, depth map update, and augmented Lagrange multiplier update. These sub-optimizations can be further unfolded into an interpretable ADMM network. Within this network, we integrate learnable modules into the initial pure formula expansion, enabling high-throughput information transmission and thereby enhancing the network's representational power. A large number of experiments have demonstrated that the proposed method achieves better reconstruction results as compared with several DMSR methods.

Keywords: Depth map super-resolution · Edge consistency constraint · Deep unfolding network · Image reconstruction

1 Introduction

Depth maps serve as fundamental cues for 3D scene perception, playing a pivotal role in diverse computer vision tasks. However, acquiring High-Resolution (HR) depth maps remains challenging due to hardware constraints of consumer-grade depth cameras. Notably, most depth sensing devices are co-integrated with color image sensors, enabling simultaneous acquisition of color images and Low-Resolution (LR) depth maps. For color-guided Depth Map Super-Resolution

Z. Lin et al. (Eds.): ICIG 2025, LNCS 16161, pp. 520–532, 2026.
https://doi.org/10.1007/978-981-95-3398-5_42

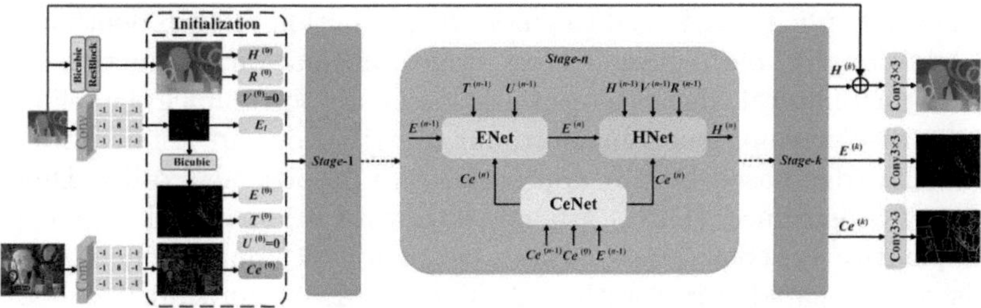

Fig. 1. The diagram of the proposed DEC-Net.

(DMSR), a core assumption underpinning its effectiveness is the structural consistency between color images and depth maps in the same scene [1]. This inherent similarity allows color information to guide the recovery of fine-grained details in LR depth maps, addressing the resolution gap imposed by hardware limitations.

Recent advancements in DMSR focus on mitigating color-induced artifacts through various strategies. Notable approaches include designing sophisticated adaptive weighting schemes for optimization model-based DMSR [2,3], and learning complementary information from RGB-D pairs [4], achieving joint filtering via non-convex optimization and weighted least squares frameworks [5], and integrating explicit inconsistency measurements between color images and depth maps [6]. Accurate edge reconstruction remains a critical challenge in DMSR, prompting several studies [7,8] to use edge refinement networks for progressive depth map reconstruction. However, conventional edge detection often yields fragmented or inaccurate edges, while LR depth maps alone lack sufficient details for precise edge extraction. Existing methods typically concatenate color/depth edge maps with the upsampled inputs, leading to unidirectional information flow that propagates artifacts and blurriness around object boundaries. Furthermore, CNN-based approaches often suffer from interpretability issues due to their black-box architectures [9–11], which rely heavily on implicit expert knowledge rather than principled modeling. These limitations underscore the need for bidirectional information exchange and physically-motivated network designs to enhance edge fidelity and reconstruction transparency.

Building on the above analysis, the core theoretical contribution of this work lies in rethinking the utilization of structural consistency between depth maps and their corresponding color images. Addressing the inherent inconsistency between color and depth domains, we propose an explicit dual-boundary consistency-constrained triple-task optimization model, as illustrated in Fig. 1, inspired by traditional optimization frameworks [6]. Leveraging the Alternating Direction Method of Multipliers (ADMM), our model is decomposed into iterative sub-optimization processes: color edge update, depth edge update, depth map update, and augmented Lagrange multiplier update, yielding an interpretable DMSR framework. This formulation is further expanded as an interpretable ADMM network. In each sub-optimization stage, the bilateral edge consistency is explicitly enforced to guide the prediction of both depth and color edges. Additionally, bidirectional cross-stage information interaction is introduced into the bilateral edge sub-optimization model to enhance the reliability of depth edge discontinuity cues. In short, our contributions are listed as follows: 1) Motivated by edge-based DMSR approaches, we propose an explicit Dual-Edge Consistency-constrained (DEC) triple-task optimization model that explicitly embeds quantitative consistency metrics between depth and color edges to facilitate discontinuous edge restoration. 2) The ADMM algorithm is employed to unfold the DEC model into an interpretable ADMM network. Within this architecture, the bilateral edge sub-optimization module utilizes bidirectional cross-stage information flow to provide robust depth edge discontinuity information for high-fidelity depth reconstruction. 3) The ADMM network progressively extracts structural features from the color edge sub-network (named CeNet) and depth edge sub-network (named E-Net), which are then fused and refined through the high-fidelity sub-network (named HF-Net) to enhance depth boundary accuracy.

The rest of this paper is organized as follows. In Sect. 2, we will present the proposed method. In Sect. 3, experimental results are provided and analyzed. Finally, conclusions are given in Sect. 4.

2   The Proposed Method

2.1   Problem Formulation

Existing edge-guided DMSR methods exploit edge information from LR depth maps or color images to aid depth reconstruction. However, the inaccuracy of LR depth edges limits high-quality depth edge recovery, while color image textural edges may be misidentified as depth edges, inevitably causing texture-copying artifacts. Motivated by these issues, we reformulate the DMSR problem as a triple-task joint optimization with dual-edge consistency constraints, which can be written as follows:

$$\arg\min_{H,E_h,Ce} \frac{1}{2}\|L - D_d K_d H\|_2^2 + \frac{\alpha}{2}\varphi(H \mid E_h, Ce) + \frac{1}{2}\|E_l - D_e K_e E_h\|_2^2$$
$$+ \frac{\gamma}{2}\|E_h - Ce\|_2^2 + \frac{\beta}{2}\varphi_1(E_h \mid Ce) + \frac{1}{2}\|Ce - Ce^{(0)}\|_2^2, \tag{1}$$

where $\varphi(\cdot)$ and $\varphi_1(\cdot)$ denote two regularization terms. Ce represents HR color-edge map. α, γ and β are three hyper-parameters. $\|\cdot\|_2$ is the L_2-norm. Additionally, $E_l \in \mathcal{R}^{1\times\, h\times w}$ and $E_h \in \mathcal{R}^{1\times H_t\times W_h}$ denote the spatially down-sampled LR and target HR depth edge maps, respectively.

Updating Ce. When updating Ce at the n-th stage in Eq. (1), the terms independent of Ce are treated as constants, and then the color-edge feature update rule is derived as:

$$Ce^{(n)} = \underset{Ce}{argmin}\, \frac{1}{2}\|Ce - Ce^{(0)}\|_2^2 + \frac{\gamma}{2}\|E_h - Ce\|_2^2. \tag{2}$$

While a closed-form solution for Ce exists via Eq. (2), it necessitates inverting a large matrix, leading to low computational efficiency. To address this, we employ gradient descent to update the Ce, which can be written as:

$$Ce^{(n)} = Ce^{(n-1)} - \delta_1 \nabla g_1(Ce^{(n-1)}), \nabla g_1(Ce^{(n-1)}) = Ce^{(n-1)} - Ce^{(0)} + \gamma(E_h^{(n-1)} - Ce^{(n-1)}), \tag{3}$$

where ∇ and δ_1 represent the gradient operator and learnable step size.

Updating E_h. In Eq. (1), treating the terms independent of E_h as constants, we introduce an auxiliary variable T for decoupling, reformulating the Eq. (1) as:

$$\arg\min_{E_h} \frac{1}{2} \|E_l - D_e K_e E_h\|_2^2 + \frac{\gamma}{2} \|E_h - Ce\|_2^2 + \frac{\beta}{2} \varphi_1 (E_h \mid Ce), \quad \text{s.t. } T = E_h. \tag{4}$$

Then, the ADMM algorithm is employed to optimize Eq. (4). The corresponding augmented Lagrangian function can be written as:

$$\mathcal{L}(E_h, T, P) = \arg\min_{E_h} \frac{1}{2} \|E_l - D_e K_e E_h\|_2^2 + \frac{\gamma}{2} \|E_h - Ce\|_2^2$$
$$+ \frac{\beta}{2} \varphi_1 (E_h \mid Ce) + \langle P, T - E_h \rangle + \frac{\rho}{2} \|T - E_h\|_2^2, \tag{5}$$

Here, P represents the Lagrangian multiplier. ρ is the penalty factor. $\langle A, B \rangle$ denotes the inner product of matrices A and B. For simplify, the scaled Lagrangian multiplier is defined as $U = \frac{P}{\rho}$. Then Eq. (5) is decomposed into three sub-problems optimized separately for E_h, T, and U:

$$E_h^{(n)} = \arg\min_{E_h} \frac{1}{2} \|E_l - D_e K_e E_h\|_2^2 + \frac{\gamma}{2} \|E_h - Ce\|_2^2 + \frac{\rho}{2} \|T - E_h + U\|_2^2, \tag{6}$$

$$T^{(n)} = \arg\min_T \frac{\rho}{2} \|T - E_h + U\|_2^2 + \frac{\beta}{2} \varphi_1(T \mid Ce), \tag{7}$$

$$U^{(n)} = U + \rho (T - E_h). \tag{8}$$

Here, three variables can be updated in an alternating manner while keeping the others fixed at each iteration step.

Step 1. When Ce and H are provided, we hold T and U constant to update E_h. The gradient descent method is applied to solve Eq. (6), yielding:

$$\begin{cases} E_h^{(n)} = E_h^{(n-1)} - \delta_2 \nabla g_2 \left(E_h^{(n-1)} \right), \\ \nabla g_2 \left(E_h^{(n-1)} \right) = (D_e K_e)^T \left(E_l - D_e K_e E_h^{(n-1)} \right), \\ + \gamma \left(E_h^{(n-1)} - Ce^{(n)} \right) + \rho \left(T^{(n-1)} - E_h^{(n-1)} + U^{(n-1)} \right), \end{cases} \tag{9}$$

where δ_2 and $(\cdot)^T$ represent the learnable step size and transpose operation.

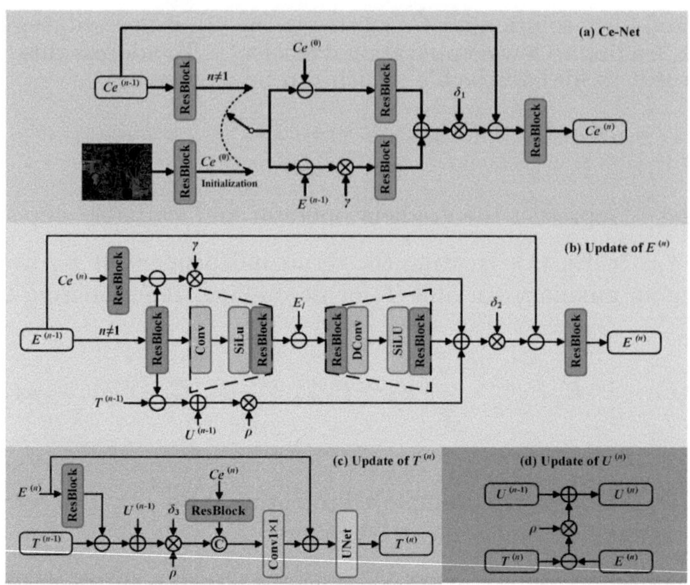

Fig. 2. The structures of the Ce-Net (a) and basic components of E-Net (b–d).

Step 2. With E_h and U keeping constant and using the proximal gradient descent algorithm, Eq. (7) is reformulated as:

$$\begin{cases} T^{(n)} = prox_{\varphi_1}(T^{(n-1)} - \delta_3 \nabla g_3(T^{(n-1)})), \\ \nabla g_3(T^{(n-1)}) = \rho(T^{(n-1)} - E_h^{(n)} + U^{(n-1)}), \end{cases} \tag{10}$$

where $prox_{\varphi_1}$ denotes a nonlinear proximal operator associated with the regularization term $\varphi_1(\cdot)$, and δ_3 represents the learnable step size.

Step 3. Finally, the update rule for the Lagrangian multiplier is given by:

$$U^{(n)} = U^{(n-1)} + \rho(T^{(n)} - E_h^{(n)}) \tag{11}$$

Updating H. Following the updates to Ce and E_h, Eq. (1) is reformulated as:

$$\arg\min_{H} \frac{1}{2} \|L - D_h K_h H\|_2^2 + \frac{\alpha}{2} \varphi(H \mid E_h, Ce) \quad \text{s.t. } R = H. \tag{12}$$

Further, the augmented Lagrangian function can be written as:

$$\mathcal{L}(H, R, Q) = \underset{H}{\arg\min} \frac{1}{2} \|L - D_h K_h H\|_2^2 + \frac{\alpha}{2} \varphi(R \mid E_h, Ce) + \langle Q, R - H \rangle + \frac{\lambda}{2} \|R - H\|_2^2. \tag{13}$$

where Q denotes the Lagrangian multiplier and λ represents the penalty parameter. The scaled Lagrangian multiplier is defined as $V = \frac{Q}{\lambda}$. Consequently, Eq. (13) is decomposed into three sub-problems optimized over H, R, and V:

$$H^{(n)} = \arg\min_{H} \frac{1}{2} \|L - D_h K_h H\|_2^2 + \frac{\lambda}{2} \|R - H + V\|_2^2, \tag{14}$$

$$R^{(n)} = \arg\min_R \frac{\lambda}{2}\|R - H + V\|_2^2 + \frac{\alpha}{2}\varphi(R|E_h, Ce), \tag{15}$$

$$V^{(n)} = V + \lambda(R - H). \tag{16}$$

Step 1. When Ce and E_h are provided, we hold R and V constant to update H. Solving Eq. (14) via gradient descent yields:

$$\begin{cases} H^{(n)} = H^{(n-1)} - \delta_4 \nabla g_4\left(H^{(n-1)}\right), \\ \nabla g_4\left(H^{(n-1)}\right) = (D_h K_h)^T \left(L - D_h K_h H^{(n-1)}\right) + \lambda\left(R^{(n-1)} - H^{(n-1)} + V^{(n-1)}\right). \end{cases} \tag{17}$$

Step 2. With H and V keeping constant and using the proximal gradient descent algorithm, Eq. (15) is reformulated as:

$$R^{(n)} = prox_\varphi(R^{(n-1)} - \delta_5 \nabla g_5(R^{(n-1)})), \nabla g_5(R^{(n-1)}) = \lambda(R^{(n-1)} - H^{(n)} + V^{(n-1)}), \tag{18}$$

where $prox_\varphi(\cdot)$ denotes a nonlinear proximal operator about φ, and δ_5 is the learnable step size.

Step 3. Finally, the update of Lagrangian multipliers can be written as:

$$V^{(n)} = V^{(n-1)} + \lambda(R^{(n)} - H^{(n)}). \tag{19}$$

2.2   The Unfolding of The Proposed Model (DEC-Net)

DEC-Net is primarily composed of k iterative stages. At the n-th stage, the optimization model is decomposed into three model-driven sub-networks: Ce-Net, E-Net and HF-Net. Specifically, Eq. (3) is unfolded as Ce-Net, while Eq. (9), Eq. (10), and Eq. (11) are jointly unrolled to form E-Net. HF-Net is derived by expanding Eq. (17), (18), and (19). The update order follows Ce-Net $\Rightarrow$ E-Net $\Rightarrow$ HF-Net. In detail, learnable convolutional edge operators are utilized to extract edges from color and depth maps. The LR depth map is first up-sampled via Bicubic interpolation to generate an initial HR depth map. Both the input image and the extracted edge maps are passed through initialization module, e.g., the *ResBlock*, to transform them into high-dimensional feature representations. Following these steps, $H^{(0)}$, $Ce^{(0)}$, $E^{(0)}$, and E_l are fed into the network. These feature representations undergo iterative updates and reconstructions through three sequential sub-networks.

Color-Edge Features Reconstruction Sub-network (Ce-Net): To illustrate the unfolding process of Ce-Net, as depicted in Fig. 2(a), the optimization model in Eq. (3) can be reformulated as:

$$\begin{cases} Ce_a^{(n)} = Res([Res(Ce^{(n-1)}) - Ce^{(0)}]), Ce_b^{(n)} = Res(\gamma[Res(Ce^{(n-1)}) - E^{(n-1)}]), \\ Ce^{(n)} = Res(Ce^{(n-1)} - \delta_1[Ce_a^{(n)} + Ce_b^{(n)}]). \end{cases} \tag{20}$$

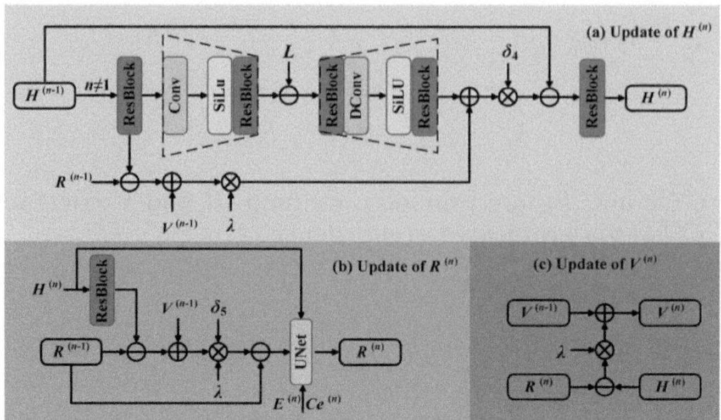

Fig. 3. The structures of basic components of HF-Net.

Here, $Ce_a^{(n)}$ ensures that the updated color edges $Ce^{(n)}$ align with the initially extracted color edges $Ce^{(0)}$. Meanwhile, $Ce_b^{(n)}$ preserves consistency between color and depth edges, generating edge features that are coherent with depth edges. This dual mechanism enables the network to precisely align edge information across modalities, ensuring that essential structural details are effectively transferred from color to depth. The *ResBlock* is employed to ensure robust feature propagation across iterations, maintaining both high-quality representations and efficient information flow.

Depth Edge Features Reconstruction Sub-network (E-Net). As depicted in Fig. 2(b), (c), (d), the alternately-updated Eq. (9), Eq. (10), and Eq. (11) are unfolded through three sequential steps to construct the E-Net for deriving depth edge features E_h.

Step 1. As shown in Fig. 2(b), the Eq. (9) can be rewritten as:

$$\begin{cases} E_a^n = Up[E_l - Down(E^{(n-1)})], E_b^n = \gamma[Res(Ce^{(n)}) - Res(E^{(n-1)})], \\ E_c^n = \rho[T^{(n-1)} - E^{(n-1)} + U^{(n-1)}], E_d^n = E^{(n-1)} - \delta_2(E_a^n + E_b^n + E_c^n), E^n = Res(E_d^n). \end{cases} \tag{21}$$

Here, E_a^n establishes the mapping between prior-stage depth edge features and LR depth edge features E_l. This mapping is represented by the blur kernel and downsampling operator $D_e K_e$ (denoted as $Down$), approximated via $Res(SiLU(Conv(\cdot)))$. The inverse operator $(D_e K_e)^T$ (denoted as Up) is learned through $Res(SiLU(DConv(Res(\cdot))))$, enabling efficient cross-resolution transmission and recovery of depth edge features. Next, E_b^n quantifies the disparity between color and depth edge features, ensuring consistency across dual-modal boundaries. To refine the depth edge reconstruction, a constraint error compensation term E_c^n is introduced within the ADMM framework to rectify reconstruction errors. Concurrently, E_d^n implements gradient descent updates on $E^{(n-1)}$. Finally, one residual block (ResBlock) is applied to enhance feature propagation and optimize information flow in E_d^n.

Step 2. As shown in Fig. 2(c), we rewrite Eq. (10) as:

$$\begin{cases} T_a^n = T^{(n-1)} - \delta_3 \rho(T^{(n-1)} - Res(E^{(n)}) + U^{(n-1)}), \\ T^n = UNet((Conv1[T_a^n, Res(Ce^{(n)})]) + E^{(n)}). \end{cases} \qquad (22)$$

Here, $[,]$ denotes the concatenation operation, and $Conv1$ represents the 1×1 convolution. ρ and δ_3 are learnable parameters, while T_a^n corresponds to the gradient descent update of the auxiliary variable. Finally, T_a^n is fed into the proximal operator (denoted by $prox$), where it is guided by the color edge Ce to reconstruct depth edge features. By leveraging Ce as the color-edge prior, the network efficiently exploits color edge information in each iteration to optimize depth map edge reconstruction. Given the superior performance of the U-Net architecture in the depth map super-resolution (DMSR) domain, we substitute the traditional $prox$ operator with the U-Net.

Step 3. The augmented Lagrangian multiplier equation corresponding to Eq. (11) is expanded as follows:

$$U^{(n)} = U^{(n-1)} + \rho(T^{(n)} - E^{(n)}). \qquad (23)$$

High-Fidelity Sub-network (HF-Net). As illustrated in Fig. 3, following the processing by Ce-Net and E-Net, HF-Net acquires the color edge prior $Ce^{(n)}$ and depth edge prior $E_h^{(n)}$, which serve as critical prerequisites for high-quality DMSR. By adopting a strategy analogous to that of E-Net, Eq. (17), Eq. (18), and Eq. (19) are collectively unfolded to form HF-Net.

Step 1. As shown in Fig. 3(a), the Eq. (17) can be rewritten as:

$$\begin{cases} H_a^n = f_{Up}[L - f_{Down}(H^{(n-1)})], \ H_b^n = \lambda(R^{(n-1)} - H^{(n-1)} + V^{(n-1)}), \\ H_c^n = H^{(n-1)} - \delta_5(H_a^n + H_b^n), H^n = Res(H_c^n). \end{cases} \qquad (24)$$

Here, H_a^n denotes the mapping relationship between HR and LR depth map features, enabling effective propagation and reconstruction of depth information across scales. H_b^n functions as a constraint regularization term within the ADMM framework, ensuring alignment between feature representations and optimization objectives. H_c^n implements gradient-based updates to iteratively refine feature representations. Finally, one residual block (ResBlock) is incorporated to stabilize feature propagation, minimize information loss, and enhance the fidelity of reconstructed depth maps.

Step 2. As shown in Fig. 3(b), the Eq. (18) is rewritten as:

$$\begin{cases} R_a^n = R^{(n-1)} - \delta_5 \lambda(R^{(n-1)} - Res(H^{(n)}) + V^{(n-1)}), \\ R^n = UNet(R_a^n, Ce^n, E^n, H^n). \end{cases} \qquad (25)$$

Here, λ and δ_5 are learnable parameters. R_a^n denotes the optimization of depth map features via a gradient descent process. We leverage the U-Net to approximate the proximal operator.

Step 3. As shown in Fig. 3(c), the augmented Lagrange multiplier is updated via $V^{(n)} = V^{(n-1)} + \lambda(R^{(n)} - H^{(n)})$.

Table 1. Objective performance comparison of different DMSR approaches Middlebury RGB-D dataset in term of MAD (The lower, the better).

Methods	Art			Books			Dolls			Laundry			Moebius			Reindeer		
	4×	8×	16×	4×	8×	16×	4×	8×	16×	4×	8×	16×	4×	8×	16×	4×	8×	16×
Bicubic	1.10	2.10	4.02	0.35	0.67	1.29	0.36	0.68	1.25	0.60	1.12	2.13	0.36	0.70	1.32	0.58	1.09	2.18
PAC [12]	0.34	1.12	2.13	0.19	0.62	1.13	0.23	0.70	1.18	0.22	0.74	1.25	0.19	0.51	0.92	0.24	0.74	1.20
DMSG [13]	0.46	0.76	1.53	0.15	0.41	0.76	0.25	0.51	0.87	0.30	0.46	1.12	0.21	0.43	0.76	0.31	0.52	0.99
DJFR [14]	0.35	0.76	1.68	0.17	0.34	0.74	0.22	0.41	0.79	0.21	0.48	1.10	0.19	0.37	0.75	0.23	0.44	0.99
DSRNet [15]	0.25	0.53	1.44	<u>0.11</u>	0.26	0.67	<u>0.16</u>	0.35	0.65	0.16	0.36	0.76	**0.13**	0.27	0.69	0.17	0.35	0.77
PMBANet [16]	0.26	0.51	<u>1.22</u>	0.15	0.26	0.59	0.19	0.32	0.59	0.17	0.34	<u>0.71</u>	0.16	0.26	0.67	0.17	0.34	0.74
BridgeNet [17]	0.30	0.58	1.49	0.14	0.24	0.51	0.19	0.34	0.64	0.19	0.34	<u>0.71</u>	0.15	0.26	0.52	0.19	0.31	0.70
AHMF [18]	0.22	0.51	1.26	0.13	0.25	0.48	0.17	0.32	0.62	0.15	0.32	0.74	0.14	0.26	0.52	<u>0.15</u>	0.31	<u>0.62</u>
EC-DSRNet [8]	0.31	0.44	1.35	0.16	<u>0.23</u>	0.55	0.22	0.33	0.66	0.21	0.34	0.89	0.18	0.26	0.67	0.24	0.31	0.70
HER-Net [7]	<u>0.20</u>	0.46	1.37	0.13	0.24	0.54	0.18	0.32	0.61	0.15	0.33	0.84	0.14	0.25	0.50	<u>0.15</u>	0.28	0.68
HCGNet [19]	0.21	<u>0.41</u>	1.38	0.13	<u>0.23</u>	<u>0.44</u>	0.17	<u>0.31</u>	**0.57**	<u>0.14</u>	<u>0.28</u>	0.78	0.14	<u>0.24</u>	**0.45**	<u>0.15</u>	<u>0.26</u>	0.64
DEC-Net (Ours)	**0.14**	**0.34**	**0.78**	**0.10**	**0.19**	**0.40**	**0.15**	**0.29**	<u>0.58</u>	**0.13**	**0.27**	**0.64**	**0.13**	**0.23**	<u>0.48</u>	**0.14**	**0.24**	**0.53**

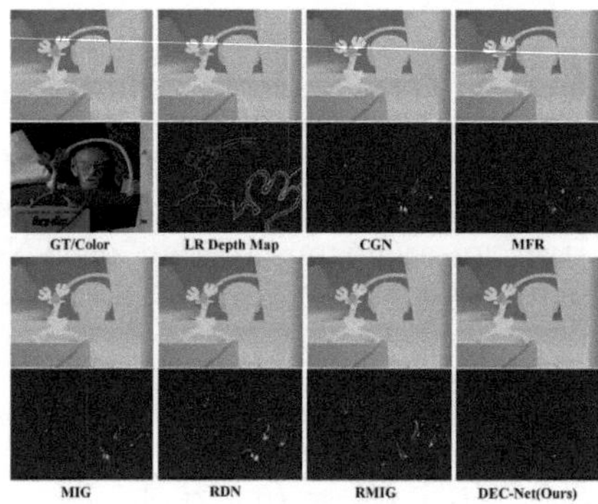

Fig. 4. Visual comparison of 8× up-sampling results and error maps of the "Reindeer" depth map from the Middlebury RGB-D dataset.

2.3   Loss Function

In DMSR, the $L1$ norm is used to measure the distance between SR target image H_{SR} and the Ground Truth (GT) depth map H_{GT}, which can be written as: $Loss_1 = \frac{1}{N} \sum_{i=1}^{N} \|H_{SR,i} - H_{GT,i}\|_1$ For the depth edge map SR model, the $L2$ norm is used to measure the distance between SR depth edge map E_{SR} and GT edge map E_{GT}, that can be written as: $Loss_2 = \frac{1}{N} \sum_{i=1}^{N} \|E_{SR,i} - E_{GT,i}\|_2$ The total loss is defined as $L_{sum} = Loss_1 + \mu Loss_2$. μ is used to make trade-off between two loss functions, i represents the i-th pixel of the image, and N is the total pixel number of the entire image.

3   Experimental Results

3.1   Implementation Details

We implement our network using the PyTorch framework. Training is performed on an NVIDIA GeForce RTX 3090 GPU with the Adam optimizer. The initial learning rate is 10^{-4}. A total of 200 epochs are used for training with a batch size of 4. The weighting parameter μ is set as 0.5. The number of stages n is 4. For training, we use thirty-six 1312×1072 RGB-D images from Middlebury RGB-D dataset (6, 9 and 21, and six 640×480 RGB-D images (Art, Books, Dolls, Laundry, Moebius and Reindeer) are collected from Middlebury RGB-D dataset for testing. To facilitate training, the HR depth map is randomly cropped to 256×256 as GT depth map. The LR depth maps are down-sampled via Bicubic interpolation from the GT depth maps at $4\times$, $8\times$ and $16\times$.

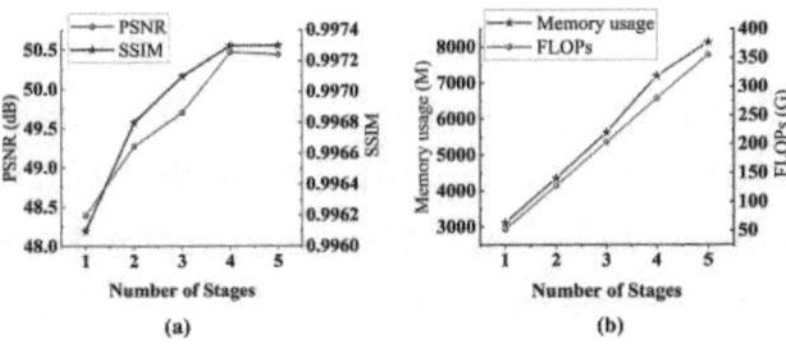

Fig. 5. Curve of DEC-Net's PSNR, SSIM, FLOPS and Memory usage with the number of stages.

3.2   Comparison with the Latest DMSR Methods

As shown in Table 1, the proposed DEC-Net is compared with a large number of DMSR methods, such as Bicubic, PAC [12], DMSG [13], DJFR [14], DSRNet [15], PMBANet [16], BridgeNet [17], AHMF [18], EC-DSRNet [8], HERNet [7] and HCGNet [19]. Here, the bold font and underline font denote the best and second-best performance respectively. From this table, among 18 times evaluation, DEC-Net achieves the optimal performance in 16 cases and the second-best performance in the remaining 2 metrics. Figure 4 presents a visual comparison of the $8\times$ up-sampling results and error maps of the "Reindeer" depth map from the Middlebury RGB-D dataset. Our method is compared with CGN [20], MFR [21], MIG [22], RDN [23], and RMIG [24]. For visual comparison, our method depicts the depth details of the "Reindeer" model and its surrounding objects more exquisitely, such as the antlers of the "Reindeer". In the error maps, the areas highlighted by red boxes show that the error of our method is significantly smaller than that of the other compared methods. This indicates that our method has a higher accuracy in depth reconstruction, enabling a more precise restoration of depth information.

3.3 Ablation Study

The impact of the stage number on the model's performance is analyzed by setting the stage number n as a scaler integer value ranging form one to five. As shown in Fig. 5, we quantitatively compare the performance of the model using four metrics: PSNR, SSIM, FLOPs, and Memory usage. Taking $n = 1$ as the baseline, there is a continuous performance improvement of the proposed method on the Middlebury dataset as n is increased to 4. However, when the stage number exceeded 4, the quantitative results exhibit a slight decline. As illustrated in Fig. 5(b), the complexity increase linearly with the stage number. Therefore, we set $n = 4$ as the default stage number for comparison.

4 Conclusion

In this paper, an explicit dual-boundary consistency constrained triple-task optimization model is proposed to address the limitations of existing DMSR methods either treating color image as static priors or lacking dual-boundary consistency constraints, leading to compromised performance and interpretability. This model is solved by the ADMM algorithm and its iterative sub-optimizations are jointly expanded into an explicable DEC-Net for color-edge refinement, depth-edge enhancement, and depth map reconstruction, ensuring dynamic alignment between modalities. This network explicitly enforces dual-boundary consistency through bidirectional cross-stage interactions, rectifying the texture-copying artifacts and boundary blurring issues inherent in prior approaches. To enhance feature fusion and network expressivity, we integrate learnable modules into the ADMM unfolding process, enabling high-throughput information propagation.

Acknowledgements. This work was supported by National Natural Science Foundation of China (62202323, 62331003), Shanxi Scholarship Council of China (2024-130), Shanxi Province Science Foundation for Youth (202203021222047), The Shanxi Province Third Batch of Outstanding Doctoral Research Initial Funding in 2022 (98001836), and The First Batch of Doctoral Research Initial Funding in 2023 (110136051).

References

1. Zhang, J., Zhao, L., Zhang, J., Wang, A., Bai, H.: Joint deep-unfolding optimization learning for depth map arbitrary-scale super-resolution. IEEE Trans. Multimedia
2. Dong, W., Shi, G., Li, X., Peng, K., Wu, J., Guo, Z.: Color-guided depth recovery via joint local structural and nonlocal low-rank regularization. IEEE Trans. Multimedia **19**(2), 293–301 (2017)
3. Huang, M., Xiang, X., Chen, Y., Fan, D.: Weighted large margin nearest center distance-based human depth recovery with limited bandwidth consumption. IEEE Trans. Image Process. **27**(12), 5728–5743 (2018)

4. Kim, Y., Jung, H., Min, D., Sohn, K.: Deeply aggregated alternating minimization for image restoration. In: IEEE Conference on Computer Vision and Pattern Recognition, pp. 284–292 (2017)

5. Li, Yu., Min, D., Do, M.N., Lu, J.: Fast guided global interpolation for depth and motion. In: Leibe, B., Matas, J., Sebe, N., Welling, M. (eds.) ECCV 2016. LNCS, vol. 9907, pp. 717–733. Springer, Cham (2016). https://doi.org/10.1007/978-3-319-46487-9_44

6. Zuo, Y., Wu, Q., Zhang, J., An, P.: Minimum spanning forest with embedded edge inconsistency measurement model for guided depth map enhancement. IEEE Trans. Image Process. **27**(8), 4145–4159 (2018)

7. Zhang, S., Pan, Z., Lv, Y., Lin, Y.: Hierarchical edge refinement network for guided depth map super-resolution. IEEE Trans. Comput. Imaging **10**, 469–478 (2024)

8. Zhao, L., Zhang, J., Zhang, J., Bai, H., Wang, A.: Joint discontinuity-aware depth map super-resolution via dual-tasks driven unfolding network. IEEE Trans. Instrum. Meas. **73**, 1–14 (2024)

9. Zhao, L., Chen, B., Zhang, J., Wang, A., Bai, H.: RIRO: from Retinex-inspired reconstruction optimization model to deep low-light image enhancement unfolding network. IEEE Trans. Comput. Imaging **10**, 969–983 (2024)

10. Wang, X., Zhao, L., Zhang, J., Wang, A., Bai, H.: A wavelet-domain consistency-constrained compressive sensing framework based on memory-boosted guidance filtering. IEEE Trans. Instrum. Meas. **73**, 1–16 (2024)

11. Zhao, L., Zhang, Y., Wang, X., Zhang, J., Bai, H., Wang, A.: A survey on image compressive sensing: from classical theory to the latest explicable deep learning. Pattern Recognit., 112022 (2025)

12. Su, H., Jampani, V., Sun, D., Gallo, O., Learned-Miller, E., Kautz, J.: Pixel-adaptive convolutional neural networks. In: IEEE/CVF Conference on Computer Vision and Pattern Recognition, pp. 11158–11167 (2019)

13. Hui, T.-W., Loy, C.C., Tang, X.: Depth map super-resolution by deep multi-scale guidance. In: Leibe, B., Matas, J., Sebe, N., Welling, M. (eds.) ECCV 2016. LNCS, vol. 9907, pp. 353–369. Springer, Cham (2016). https://doi.org/10.1007/978-3-319-46487-9_22

14. Li, Y., Huang, J., Ahuja, N., Yang, M.-H.: Joint image filtering with deep convolutional networks. IEEE Trans. Pattern Anal. Mach. Intell. **41**(8), 1909–1923 (2019)

15. Sun, B., Ye, X., Li, B., Li, H., Wang, Z., Xu, R.: Learning scene structure guidance via cross-task knowledge transfer for single depth super-resolution. In: IEEE Conference on Computer Vision and Pattern Recognition, pp. 7788–7797 (2021)

16. Ye, X., et al.: PMBANet: progressive multi-branch aggregation network for scene depth super-resolution. IEEE Trans. Image Process. **29**, 7427–7442 (2020)

17. Tang, Q., et al.: BridgeNet: a joint learning network of depth map super-resolution and monocular depth estimation. In: ACM International Conference on Multimedia, pp. 2148–2157 (2021)

18. Zhong, Z., Liu, X., Jiang, J., Zhao, D., Chen, Z., Ji, X.: High-resolution depth maps imaging via attention-based hierarchical multi-modal fusion. IEEE Trans. Image Process. **31**, 648–663 (2022)

19. Cong, R., et al.: Learning hierarchical color guidance for depth map super-resolution. IEEE Trans. Instrum. Meas. **73**, 1–13 (2024)

20. Zuo, Y., Fang, Y., An, P., Shang, X., Yang, J.: Frequency-dependent depth map enhancement via iterative depth-guided affine transformation and intensity-guided refinement. IEEE Trans. Multimedia **23**, 772–783 (2021)

21. Zuo, Y., Wu, Q., Fang, Y., An, P., Huang, L., Chen, Z.: Multi-scale frequency reconstruction for guided depth map super-resolution via deep residual network. IEEE Trans. Circuits Syst. Video Technol. **30**(2), 297–306 (2020)
22. Zuo, Y., Wang, H., Fang, Y., Huang, X., Shang, X., Wu, Q.: MIG-Net: multi-scale network alternatively guided by intensity and gradient features for depth map super-resolution. IEEE Trans. Multimedia **24**, 3506–3519 (2022)
23. Zuo, Y., Fang, Y., Yang, Y., Shang, X., Wang, B.: Residual dense network for intensity-guided depth map enhancement. Inf. Sci. **495**, 52–64 (2019)
24. Zuo, Y., Fang, Y., Yang, Y., Shang, X., Wu, Q.: Depth map enhancement by revisiting multi-scale intensity guidance within coarse-to-fine stages. IEEE Trans. Circuits Syst. Video Technol. **30**(12), 4676–4687 (2020)

Computer Graphics and Visualization

Isotropic Remeshing with Inter-angle Optimization

Hanbing Zheng and Chenlei Lv$^{(\boxtimes)}$

College of Computer Science and Software Engineering, Shenzhen University, Shenzhen, China
chenleilv@mail.bnu.edu.cn

Abstract. As an important metric for mesh quality evaluation, the isotropy property holds significant value for applications such as texture UV-mapping, physical simulation, and discrete geometric analysis. Classical isotropy remeshing methods adjust vertices and edge lengths, which exhibit certain limitations in terms of input data sensitivity, geometric consistency control, and convergence speed. In this paper, we propose an improved isotropy remeshing solution with inter-angle optimization during mesh editing to enhance shape control capability and accelerate convergence. The advantage of the solution lies in its ability to predict the impact of edge length adjustments on subsequent optimization by monitoring angle transformations. It avoids inefficient editing that may cause performance fluctuations, thereby improving efficiency. Experiments demonstrate that the proposed method effectively improves the overall efficiency of mesh optimization. (The code has been released at Isotropic-Remeshing-InterAngle.

Keywords: Triangular Mesh · Isotropic Remeshing · Inter-Angle Optimization

1 Introduction

As a classical 3D data representation, triangular mesh models have been widely employed in various applications, including facial recognition [22,23], digital infrastructure [11,30], gaming&film production, and geographic information systems. Due to the excellent computability, adaptability to physical properties, and clear data structure, mainstream 3D geometry engines universally adopt triangular meshes as the standard data format for storage and computation. The initial triangular mesh is constructed either through shape reconstruction methods [15,19] or manual editing in CAD software. From the perspective of discrete differential geometry, shapes of triangular facets within the mesh exhibit randomness and often fail to satisfy the Delaunay condition [29], which is unfavorable for subsequent numerical computations. Therefore, isotropic remeshing methods are proposed for raw mesh optimization.

Supported by the National Key R&D Program of China (2024YFB3908500, 2024YFB3908503), Guangdong Basic and Applied Basic Research Foundation (2023A1515110292), Scientific Foundation for Youth Scholars of Shenzhen University.

Z. Lin et al. (Eds.): ICIG 2025, LNCS 16161, pp. 535–546, 2026.
https://doi.org/10.1007/978-981-95-3398-5_43

The concept of isotropic remeshing was proposed as early as the 1990s [3]. The primary objective is to transform an unconstrained triangular mesh (anisotropic) into a new one composed of approximately equilateral triangles (isotropic) while preserving geometric consistency. There are two technical solutions for the target, including Centroidal Voronoi Tessellation (CVT) [16] and four-steps strategy [4]. CVT iteratively adjusts vertex positions to uniform vertex-based Voronoi cells by employing Lloyd's relaxation. Limitations include sensitivity to initial mesh, slow convergence rates, and high computational coupling. Four-steps strategy is to reconnect edges between vertexes with position adjustment. It contains four basic operations (split, collapse, flip, and tangent smoothing) to efficiently adjust vertex-based distances. Intuitively, edge reconnection appears more efficient, but the original scheme still exhibits deficiencies in result stability and convergence efficiency due to insufficient consideration of shape affection.

In this paper, we propose a new isotropic remeshing method based on four-steps strategy. We redesign shape constraints with inter-angle optimization, which ensures better shape controlling in edge reconnection and prevents inefficient editing operations. The inter-angle optimization enhances the efficiency of edge-based operations during each iteration while mitigating cross-interference between different edge operations. To better preserve geometric consistency, we additionally employ point cloud up-sampling with Moving Least Squares (MLS) [1] remapping, ensuring adjusted vertices remain constrained to the original mesh-defined surface. Contributions can be summarized as:

- We present an inter-angle optimization scheme to control basic operations in the isotropic remeshing. It is useful to enhance convergence efficiency while mitigating aggressive shape deformation, thereby maintaining superior geometric consistency.
- We propose a MLS-based solution for geometric consistency keeping. The proposed solution eliminates the need for tangent smoothing, preventing vertex optimization from deviating from the MLS surface. Particularly for sparse meshes, it guarantees the stability for the vertex adjustment.

2   Related Works

As mentioned before, there are two technical solutions for isotropic remeshing, including CVT-based and four-steps remeshing.

CVT-Based Remeshing. Such solutions employ the Voronoi Diagram or Delaunay triangulation to implement remeshing. Representative methods include Restricted Voronoi Diagram (RVD) [27], improved RVD [26], weighted diagram optimization [10], intrinsic Delaunay remeshing [18], geodesic-based CVT [28], parallel CVT [31], and RVD with signed distance field (SDF) [12]. Such methods enhance the original CVT scheme by incorporating intrinsic metrics to suppress geometric artifacts induced by tangent-space displacements, thereby improving the stability of vertex neighborhood structures. However, such improvements inevitably introduce computational overhead, which compromises overall efficiency. Parallel optimization presents a potential solution, yet the inherently high coupling within CVT inevitably compromises isotropic quality.

Four-Steps Remeshing. Edge reconnection-based or four-steps remeshing implement mesh optimization based on four basic operations, including split, collapse, flip, and tangent smoothing. Such operations directly modify edge lengths and vertex degrees, which are more efficient than CVT-based remeshing. Representative methods include principal direction field-based remeshing [2], dynamic surface remeshing [14], adaptively isotropic remeshing [9,21], implicit domain-based remeshing [7], manifold-constrained remeshing [13], and intrinsic&isotropic remeshing [20]. In practice, some researchers have found that introducing shape control mechanisms into the four-steps strategy is essential for performance improvement. Wang *et al.* [24] proposed an isotropic remeshing method by removing large and small angles. Xu *et al.* [25] designed a new edge reconnection strategy to reduce the occurrence of obtuse angles. It does not pursue the strictly isotropic property. Lv *et al.* [21] employs angle-based constraints to judge the implementation of some edge editing operations. Such studies have established preliminary strategies for inter-angle optimization, which inspire our more comprehensive solution.

3   Background

As mentioned in early four-steps scheme [4], basic operations for isotropic remeshing include split, collapse, flip, and tangent smoothing, which uniform edge length. Defining a regular edge length l, the split inserts a new vertex for a long edge ($>4/3l$) and the collapse merges a short edge ($<4/5l$). The flip remove a edge for two vertexes and add a new edge between their common neighbors, which optimizes the vertex-based degree. The tangent smoothing is to adjust vertex positions to achieve accurate isotropic property.

Iteratively processing the four operations can implement the isotropic remeshing for a raw mesh. However, in the original implementation, coupling effects between the four operations are not taken into consideration. For instance, when performing collapse operations, the change in vertex degrees may increase the computational load for flips. Therefore, we aim to achieve more efficient control through inter-angle optimization at each step, thereby reducing mutual interference and enhancing the algorithm's convergence performance.

4   Methodology

We re-design basic operations (split, collapse, and flip) with more reasonable inter-angle optimization for triangular faces. The primary objective is to introduce more precise shape controlling to constrain remeshing operations and prevent "fixing one issue while creating another". In addition, we employ a MLS-based up-sampling to control vertex positions in the tangent smoothing for geometric consistency keeping. It is useful for some regions with few vertexes or sharp curvature changing.

4.1   Inter-angle Optimization

The proposed inter-angle optimization provides shape constraints during the isotropic remeshing. According to different edge editing operations, we develop related inter-angle checking to predict potential shape degradation, thereby preventing the execution of detrimental mesh editing operations. Basically, the optimization includes three parts: split, collapse, and flip schemes.

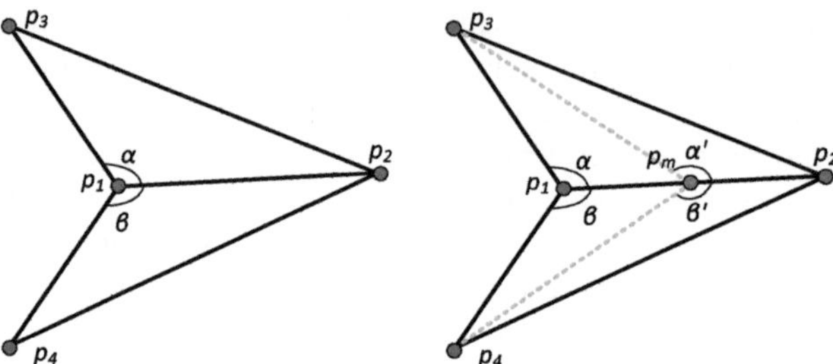

Fig. 1. Inter-angle optimization for split scheme. Angles $\angle\alpha$ and $\angle\beta$ control the split operation for $\overline{p_1p_2}$, which prevent the formation of $\angle\alpha'$ and $\angle\beta'$.

Split Scheme. Controlling split operation is simpler because adding edges to existing faces for splitting does not change the original geometry. Nevertheless, the implementation of angular surveillance remains imperative. The reason is that performing a split operation may introduce lower-quality obtuse triangles, thereby degrading isotropic property. An instance is shown in Fig. 1. If determined solely by edge length criteria, the edge $\overline{p_1p_2}$ should be split. However, since angles $\angle\alpha$ and $\angle\beta$ in the original face are obtuse, performing the split would generate new triangles with even larger obtuse angles $\angle\alpha'$, $\angle\beta'$. These highly distorted triangular elements would adversely affect the convergence of isotropic remeshing. Therefore, it is necessary to evaluate whether any of its four adjacent angles ($\angle\alpha, \angle\beta, \angle p_3p_2p_1$, and $\angle p_4p_2p_3$) are obtuse before splitting.

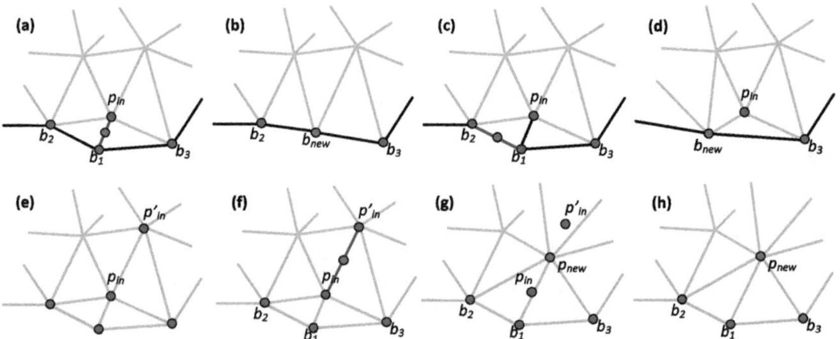

Fig. 2. Inter-angle optimization for collapse scheme. (a)∼(d) show the boundary condition; (e)∼(h) show the degree judgment.

Collapse Scheme. In practice, the collapse operation induces the most significant geometric alterations, not only reducing the vertex count but also directly modifying vertex-based degrees, while causing substantial angular distortions. For collapse scheme, we employ two additional constraints: boundary condition and degree judgment. The boundary condition means that if one point of an edge belong to a boundary edge, then the collapse operation should be blocked, as shown in Fig. 2. Edge points b_1, b_2, and b_3 connect a boundary line labeled by black color. Once we collapse either $\overline{p_{in}b_1}$ (Fig. 2a) or $\overline{b_1b_2}$ (Fig. 2c), the geometry of the boundary line is changed, which breaks the geometric consistency and becomes severe with more iterations.

Another constraint is the degree judgment, which estimates the impact of the collapse operation on vertex degrees to determine whether to proceed. Without vertex-based degree analysis may lead to abnormal degree assignments for the new vertex, consequently increasing the difficulty of subsequent flip operations. From the perspective of inter-angle view, an excessively high vertex degree implies that the average inter-angle associated with that vertex will fall below the ideal threshold ($60°$). It means the collapse operation may disrupt the isotropic property of the local region. An instance is also shown in Fig. 2. The degree values of p_{in} and p'_{in} are $deg(p_{in}) = 5$ and $deg(p'_{in}) = 6$ (average inter-angle is $65°$, see in Fig. 2e). Once the collapse operation is implemented, the degree of new point p_{new} change to $deg(p_{new}) = 7$ (average inter-angle is $50°$, see in Fig. 2h). Evidently, performing collapse on $\overline{p_{in}p'_{in}}$ reduces the isotropic quality. Combined mentioned constraints, collapse scheme is completed.

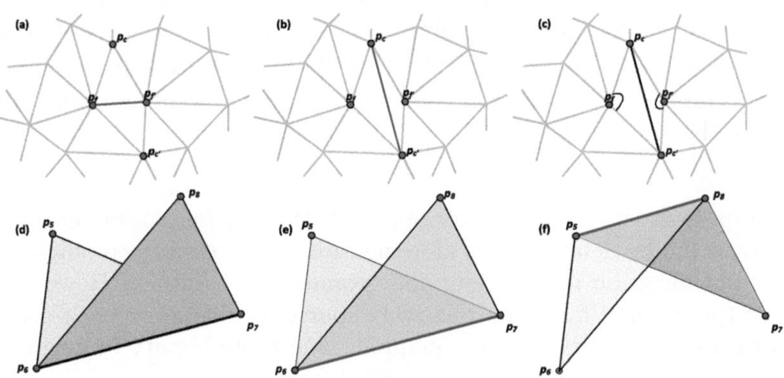

Fig. 3. Inter-angle optimization for flip scheme. (a)∼(c) show the inter-angle constraint; (e)∼(f) show the shape control.

Flip Scheme. Beyond the primary objective of degree optimization, flip operation must account the inter-angle constraint, which is similar to the split scheme. An instance is shown in Fig. 3. When determining whether to flip a given edge $\overline{p_f p'_f}$, we first compute the post-flip degree for each affected vertex. It is clear that the flip can optimize most vertexes, $deg(p_c) = 6, deg(p_f) = 6, deg(p'_f) = 6$, as shown in Fig. 3b. However, generated new obtuse angles ($\angle p_c p_f p'_c$ and $\angle p_c p'_f p'_c$ in

Fig. 3) violate shape control requirements in the isotropic remeshing. Therefore, the flip operation should be blocked for such condition.

An additional consideration is the geometric alteration induced by the flip operation. In fact, unless all four vertices involved in the flip operation are coplanar, it inevitably modifies the local geometry, as shown in Fig. 3e and Fig. 3f. If edge $\overline{p_6 p_7}$ lies precisely on a sharp feature boundary, performing the flip operation would introduce geometric artifacts along the boundary, thereby breaking the sharp feature. To mitigate the issue, we implement a face-based dihedral angle checking. Based on the instance in Fig. 3d, we compute the normal vectors of $\triangle p_5 p_6 p_7$ and $\triangle p_8 p_7 p_6$, and judge the vector-based intersection angle θ. Once $\theta > \varepsilon (\varepsilon = 20°$ by default), the flip operation is blocked for shape controlling. Combined split, collapse, and flip Schemes, the complete inter-angle optimization is established.

4.2   Geometric Consistency Keeping

The last operation of the four-steps remeshing is the tangent smoothing or vertex relocation, which adjusts vertex positions toward to their 1-ring neighborhood centers (gravity-weighted centroid [4]). The center can be formulated as

$$p_i' = \sum_{p_j \in N(p_i)} w_j p_j, \tag{1}$$

where p_i' is the center for the region of point p_i, p_j is 1-ring neighbor of p_i, w_j is the weight of p_j, which is typically represented by the area or cotangent weights corresponding to p_j to describe its influence on p_i. According to the vector $\overrightarrow{p_i p_i'}$ (mapped on the tangent plane of p_i) with a "pulling back" function, p_i can be updated

$$p_i' = p_i + \lambda (I - n_i n_i^T) \overrightarrow{p_i p_i'}, \tag{2}$$

where n_i represent the normal vector of p_i, λ is the control parameter for update step size ($\lambda = 0.5$ by default). The aforementioned process is a common practice for vertex optimization while preserving geometric consistency. However, if the vertices of the original mesh are relatively sparse, the "pulling back" operation may fail to produce correct surface mapping due to ambiguity in neighborhood determination, resulting in local geometric distortion.

To address the issue, we propose a mesh up-sampling step to insert new points into different faces. Firstly, inserting the centroid of a triangular face. Then, based on the centroid, inserting the midpoints of the line segments between each vertex of the triangle and the centroid. Subsequently, inserting new centers between these newly created midpoints. Then, seven new points can be inserted for a single triangle. We adjust these new points' positions by MLS remapping [1]. Finally, we achieve an up-sampled point set that takes more accurate geometric representation. Once we implement the tangent smoothing, the "pulling back" function is based on the neighborhood defined on the up-sampled point set. The local geometric distortion can be significantly suppressed.

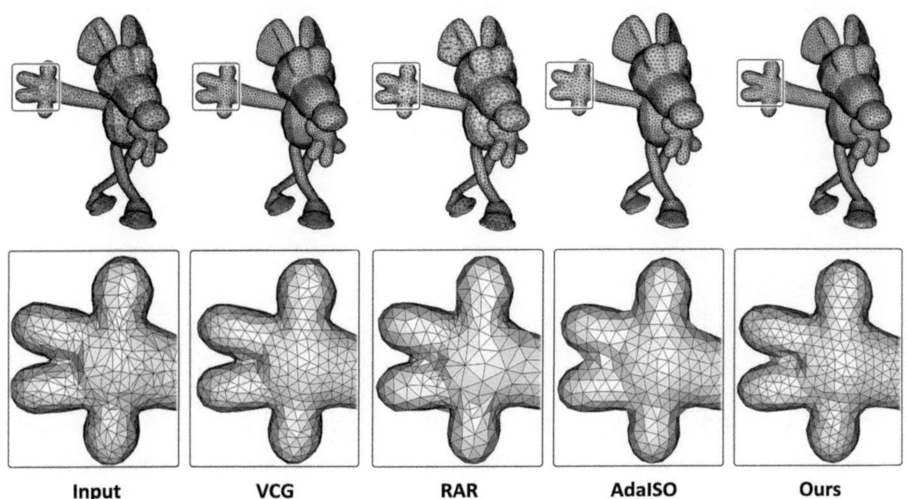

Fig. 4. Some remeshing results by different methods.

Table 1. Quantitative analysis of different remeshing methods. Hd: Hausdorff distance; Md: mean distance; θ_{max}: maximum degree of inter-angel; θ_{avg}: mean degree of inter-angel ($\pi/3 - \sum |\theta_i - \pi/3|$, θ_i is an inter-angel).

Model	VCG [4]				RAR [9]				AdaISO [21]				Ours			
	Hd	Md	θ_{max}	θ_{avg}	Hd	Md	θ_{max}	θ_{avg}	Hd	Md	θ_{max}	θ_{avg}	Hd	Md	θ_{max}	θ_{avg}
T0	0.0159	0.0016	151.5°	50.9°	**0.0130**	0.0016	179.1°	46.5°	0.0157	0.0017	179.9°	52.7°	0.0179	**0.0015**	**118.7°**	**52.8°**
T1008	0.0127	0.0017	167.2°	50.5°	**0.0115**	0.0018	166.8°	48.7°	0.0116	0.0017	179.9°	**53.7°**	0.0129	**0.0016**	111.1°	52.9°
T1022	0.0076	0.0010	164.8°	50.3°	–	–	–	–	**0.0070**	0.0011	179.9°	**52.6°**	0.0072	**0.0009**	**146.2°**	52.5°
T1036	0.0121	0.0016	145.8°	53.2°	0.0117	0.0016	159.1°	46.3°	**0.0111**	0.0017	179.9°	**53.5°**	0.0137	**0.0016**	**110.7°**	53.1°
T1050	0.0097	0.0011	172.5°	51.7°	**0.0089**	0.0013	154.4°	49.3°	0.0090	0.0012	179.9°	**53.4°**	0.0101	**0.0011**	**172.8°**	53.1°
T1064	0.0231	0.0026	177.4°	49.7°	0.0201	0.0028	176.8°	44.1°	**0.0176**	0.0028	180.0°	**53.1°**	0.0202	**0.0026**	**151.6°**	52.7°
T1078	0.0146	0.0020	176.9°	47.7°	0.0156	0.0020	174.8°	48.1°	–	–	–	–	0.0159	**0.0020**	**167.7°**	**52.6°**
T1092	0.0165	0.0017	169.9°	52.9°	**0.0162**	0.0018	177.1°	46.5°	0.0163	0.0019	180.0°	53.2°	0.0180	**0.0017**	**106.0°**	**53.3°**
T1106	0.0105	0.0014	178.2°	50.7°	0.0110	0.0016	175.8°	47.6°	0.0107	0.0015	179.9°	**53.4°**	**0.0096**	0.0014	119.6°	53.1°
T112	0.0244	**0.0031**	177.1°	46.9°	–	–	–	–	–	–	–	–	**0.0227**	0.0034	145.1°	**52.4°**
T1120	0.0155	0.0023	175.7°	49.3°	0.0177	0.0023	174.4°	46.3°	**0.0138**	0.0024	180.0°	53.1°	0.0157	**0.0023**	137.1°	**53.2°**
T1134	0.0086	0.0012	175.3°	49.6°	**0.0076**	0.0013	173.7°	48.5°	–	–	–	–	0.0080	**0.0011**	138.6°	**53.0°**
T1155	0.0165	0.0020	173.1°	51.7°	**0.0109**	0.0021	176.0°	48.4°	0.0147	0.0021	79.9°	**53.4°**	0.0177	**0.0020**	114.9°	53.0°
Avg	0.0120	0.0017	175.6°	50.4°	0.0107	0.0017	169.6°	48.6°	**0.0105**	0.0017	179.7°	52.9°	0.0116	**0.0016**	113.8°	**53.0°**

5   Experiments

In this part, We evaluate the performance of our remeshing scheme. The experimental machine equipped with Intel(R) i9-13900K 3.00 GHz, 128G RAM, GeForce RTX4090. The running system is Windows 11 with Visual Studio 2022 (64 bit). Firstly, we introduce the employed dataset and metrics. Then, we compare the performance between different methods. Finally, we show some applications based on our remeshing scheme and provide a discussion.

Dataset and Metrics. The experimental raw meshes are selected from SHREC [5], including non-rigid transformations. For quantitative analysis, we

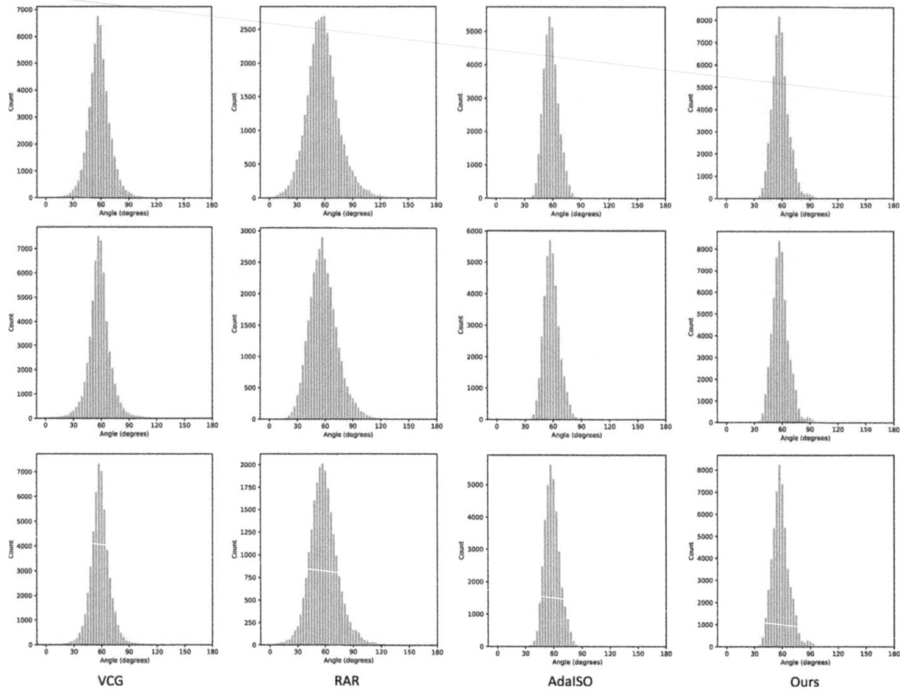

VCG   RAR   AdaISO   Ours

Fig. 5. Inter-angle distribution histograms of re-meshed models (T0, T14, T28).

Table 2. Time cost report for different methods.

	VCG [4]	RAR [9]	FCVT [8]	AdaISO [21]	Ours
T0	19.86 s	9.08 s	400.25 s	31.64 s	**8.93 s**
T14	21.26 s	**2.95 s**	381.85 s	39.72 s	11.26 s
T28	23.56 s	**1.58 s**	387.19 s	43.03 s	13.26 s
Avg	20.63 s	–	391.21 s	38.93 s	**10.89 s**

report Hausdorff distance, mean distance, average and maximum inter-angle values to measure the geometric consistency and isotropic property.

Comparisons. We compare different methods to show the performance of our remeshing scheme, including VCG-based isotropic remeshing (same to Mesh-Lab version [4,6]), RAR remeshing [9], and adaptive isotropic remeshing [21]. Figure 4 shows some remeshing results by different methods. Our solution takes better balance between geometric consistency and isotropic property. Table 1 reports quantitative results based on SHREC models. Our method demonstrates superior shape control for large obtuse triangles (θ_{max} is smaller).

Benefiting from the implementation of geometric consistency keeping, our approach achieves better geometric consistency (Md value is lower). Figure 5 shows some histograms of inter-angle distribution. AdaISO and our solution

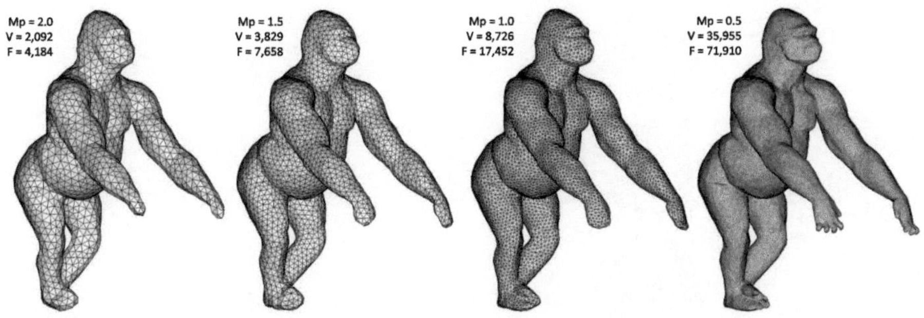

Fig. 6. Remeshing results by our method with different multi-parameters. Mp: multi-parameter value; V: vertex number; F: face number.

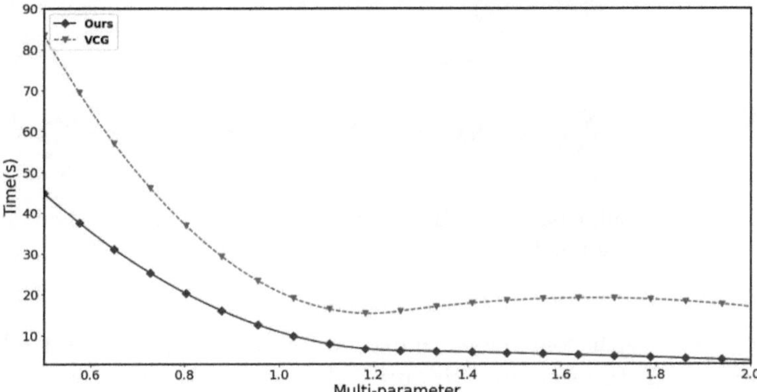

Fig. 7. Time cost curves for different methods with related multi-parameters.

take better distributions (concentrated around 60°). Table 2 reports computational efficiency for different methods. Our solution is faster than VCG-based isotropic remeshing and AdaISO solution, even they share similar four-steps strategy. RAR solution achieves faster runtime speeds for certain models, but fails to converge for some ones based on a larger test dataset. In addition, we employ a CVT-based solution (FCVT) [8] to be a reference in Table 2. According to statistical data, FCVT requires 30 times longer to achieve results comparable to our method. Significantly, our method holds advantages in terms of efficiency and stability.

Applications. A classical application of remeshing is the multi-resolution editing. By modifying the target edge length, we can either simplify or refine the input mesh. We assign different multi-parameters and multiply them by the average edge length to obtain new target edge lengths, thereby generating remeshing results with varying resolutions. Figure 6 shows some remeshing results by our method with different multi-parameters. The mesh resolution can be adjusted while preserving the isotropic property. We also report the time

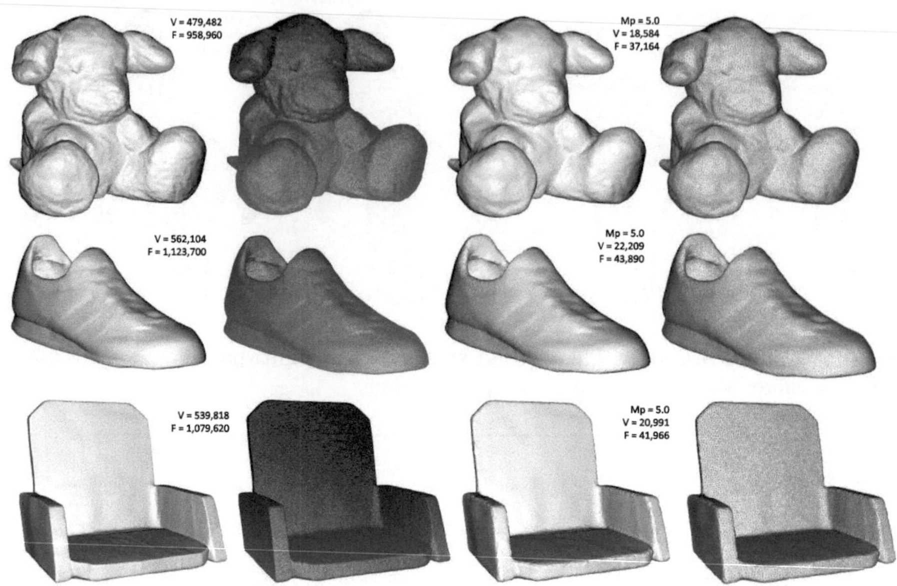

Fig. 8. Remeshing results based on 3D mesh generation framework. Left: generated meshes; right: remeshing results.

cost of remeshing with continuous multi-parameter variations, and add VCG-based remeshing as the reference. Figure 7 shows related time cost curves. Our method demonstrates superior time efficiency in both mesh simplification and refinement.

Another important application is assisting 3D-AIGC tasks. Currently, mainstream 3D mesh generation methods primarily rely on implicit reconstruction, driven by semantic and image features to produce accurate mesh outputs. However, they suffer from poor isotropic quality and excessive mesh volume. Our method can effectively enhance the isotropic quality of meshes while simultaneously simplifying them. Based on the generated results by MeshFormer [17], our remeshing is used to improve the mesh quality. Figure 8 shows some instances. It can be clearly observed that both the mesh volume and isotropic quality are optimized.

Discussion. Compared to the VCG-based remeshing solution, our method utilizes inter-angle control to avoid cross-interference between each basic operation, thereby improving convergence efficiency. Tables 1 and 2 demonstrate that our approach outperforms VCG-based version in both mesh optimization quality and computational efficiency. Compared to the CVT-based approach, our method inherits the advantages of isotropic remeshing while demonstrating significant superiority in convergence speed. The core reason is that our basic operations enable more direct updates to triangle shapes. In contrast, the CVT-based method relies on Voronoi cell computation and centroidal optimization for mesh editing, which inherently suffers from efficiency limitation.

6   Conclusions

In this paper, we propose a new isotropic remeshing method with inter-angle optimization. Angle-based constraints are incorporated into the basic operations (split, collapse, and flip) to suppress the generation of obtuse triangles. Compared to the original four-steps isotropic remeshing, our method effectively reduces repetitive edge editing and improves convergence efficiency. Benefited from a mesh-based up-sampling scheme, the quality of isotropic remeshing can be significantly improved. Experimental reports demonstrate that our solution exhibits comprehensive advantages in isotropic property optimization, geometric consistency keeping, and computational efficiency.

References

1. Alexa, M., Behr, J., Cohen-Or, D., Fleishman, S., Levin, D., Silva, C.T.: Point set surfaces. In: Proceedings of the Visualization, pp. 21–29. IEEE (2001)
2. Alliez, P., Cohen-Steiner, D., Devillers, O., Lévy, B., Desbrun, M.: Anisotropic polygonal remeshing. In: Proceedings of the SIGGRAPH, pp. 485–493 (2003)
3. Bern, M., Eppstein, D., Gilbert, J.: Provably good mesh generation. J. Comput. Syst. Sci. **48**(3), 384–409 (1994)
4. Botsch, M., Kobbelt, L.: A remeshing approach to multiresolution modeling. In: Proceedings of the Eurographics Symposium on Geometry Processing, pp. 185–192 (2004)
5. Bronstein, A., et al.: Shrec 2010: robust large-scale shape retrieval benchmark. Proc. 3DOR **5**(4), 1–8 (2010)
6. Cignoni, P., Callieri, M., Corsini, M., Dellepiane, M., Ganovelli, F., Ranzuglia, G.: MeshLab: an open-source mesh processing tool. In: Scarano, V., Chiara, R.D., Erra, U. (eds.) Eurographics Italian Chapter Conference, pp. 129–136. The Eurographics Association (2008)
7. Dapogny, C., Dobrzynski, C., Frey, P.: Three-dimensional adaptive domain remeshing, implicit domain meshing, and applications to free and moving boundary problems. J. Comput. Phys. **262**, 358–378 (2014)
8. Du, X., Liu, X., Yan, D.M., Jiang, C., Ye, J., Zhang, H.: Field-aligned isotropic surface remeshing. In: Computer Graphics Forum, vol. 37, pp. 343–357. Wiley Online Library (2018)
9. Dunyach, M., Vanderhaeghe, D., Barthe, L., Botsch, M.: Adaptive remeshing for real-time mesh deformation. In: Proceedings of the Eurographics, pp. 29–32. The Eurographics Association (2013)
10. Goes, F., Memari, P., Mullen, P., Desbrun, M.: Weighted triangulations for geometry processing. ACM Trans. Graph. **33**(3), 28:1–28:13 (2014)
11. He, X., Lv, C., Huang, P., Huang, H.: Windpoly: polygonal mesh reconstruction via winding numbers. In: Proceedings of the European Conference on Computer Vision, pp. 294–311. Springer, Cham (2024)
12. Hou, W., et al.: SDF-RVD: restricted Voronoi diagram on signed distance field. Comput.-Aided Des. **144**, 103166.1–103166.12 (2022)
13. Hu, B.Y., Ye, C., Su, J.P., Liu, L.: Manifold-constrained geometric optimization via local parameterizations. IEEE Trans. Visualization Comput. Graph. **29**(2), 1318–1329 (2021)

14. Jiao, X., Colombi, A., Ni, X., Hart, J.: Anisotropic mesh adaptation for evolving triangulated surfaces. Eng. Comput. **26**(4), 363–376 (2010)
15. Kazhdan, M., Hoppe, H.: Screened Poisson surface reconstruction. ACM Trans. Graph. **32**(3), 29:1–29:13 (2013)
16. Lévy, B., Liu, Y.: Lp centroidal Voronoi tessellation and its applications. ACM Trans. Graph. **29**(4), 119:1–119:11 (2010)
17. Liu, M., et al.: Meshformer: high-quality mesh generation with 3D-guided reconstruction model. arXiv preprint arXiv:2408.10198 (2024)
18. Liu, Y.J., Xu, C.X., Fan, D., He, Y.: Efficient construction and simplification of delaunay meshes. ACM Trans. Graph. **34**(6), 174:1–174:13 (2015)
19. Lv, C., Lin, W., Zhao, B.: Voxel structure-based mesh reconstruction from a 3D point cloud. IEEE Trans. Multimed. **24**, 1815–1829 (2021)
20. Lv, C., Lin, W., Zhao, B.: Intrinsic and isotropic resampling for 3D point clouds. IEEE Trans. Pattern Anal. Mach. Intell. **45**(3), 3274–3291 (2022)
21. Lv, C., Lin, W., Zheng, J.: Adaptively isotropic remeshing based on curvature smoothed field. IEEE Trans. Visualization Comput. Graph. **30**(7), 3196–3209 (2024)
22. Lv, C., Wu, Z., Wang, X., Zhou, M.: 3D facial similarity measurement and its application in facial organization. ACM Trans. Multimed. Comput. Commun. Appl. **16**(3), 82:1–82:20 (2020)
23. Lv, C., Wu, Z., Wang, X., Zhou, M., Toh, K.A.: Nasal similarity measure of 3D faces based on curve shape space. Pattern Recogn. **88**, 458–469 (2019)
24. Wang, Y., et al.: Isotropic surface remeshing without large and small angles. IEEE Trans. Visualization Comput. Graph. **25**(7), 2430–2442 (2018)
25. Xu, Q.C., Yan, D.M., Li, W., Yang, Y.L.: Anisotropic surface remeshing without obtuse angles. In: Computer Graphics Forum, vol. 38, pp. 755–763. Wiley Online Library (2019)
26. Yan, D.M., Guo, J., Jia, X., Zhang, X., Wonka, P.: Blue-noise remeshing with farthest point optimization. In: Computer Graphics Forum, vol. 33, pp. 167–176. Wiley Online Library (2014)
27. Yan, D.M., Lévy, B., Liu, Y., Sun, F., Wang, W.: Isotropic remeshing with fast and exact computation of restricted Voronoi diagram. In: Computer Graphics Forum, vol. 28, pp. 1445–1454. Wiley Online Library (2009)
28. Ye, Z., Yi, R., Yu, M., Liu, Y.J., He, Y.: Geodesic centroidal Voronoi tessellations: theories, algorithms and applications. arXiv preprint arXiv:1907.00523 (2019)
29. Yi, R., Liu, Y.J., He, Y.: Delaunay mesh simplification with differential evolution. ACM Trans. Graph. **37**(6), 263:1–263:12 (2018)
30. Zhang, R., Pan, S., Lv, C., Gong, M., Huang, H.: Architectural co-lod generation. ACM Trans. Graph. (Proc. SIGGRAPH Asia) **43**(6), 193:1–193:16 (2024)
31. Zheng, J., Tan, T.S.: Computing centroidal Voronoi tessellation using the GPU. In: Symposium on Interactive 3D Graphics and Games, pp. 1–9 (2020)

AlignMR: Design of a Home Yoga Self Learning System Based on MR Technology

Huangyiming Wu, Tuotuo Yang, and Xiaona Ma[✉]

School of New Media Art and Design, Beihang University, Beijing 100191, China
373547114@qq.com

Abstract. Yoga practice doesn't require costly equipment, and learners can teach themselves by watching online video tutorials. However, to keep the screen in view during practice, learners often disrupt their movement balance, which affects execution and hinders learning. Moreover, improper yoga postures may cause negative effects. This paper introduces a home-based self-practice yoga system using Mixed Reality (MR) technology and the OpenPose framework to address disrupted movement postures during yoga learning. By providing an instructor video interface that tracks the user's head movements, the system helps users focus on both the screen and their physical movements without distraction. It overlays real-time captured full-body user postures with instructional videos, allowing users to visually compare their movements with standard postures and correct errors, thus addressing the lack of feedback during self-practice. Research shows that this design enables learners to perform technical movements more smoothly and accurately, demonstrating its wide applicability and high practicality.

Keywords: Mixed Reality · Yoga · OpenPose · User Experience Design

1 Introduction

In the post-pandemic era, enhancing national health literacy has emerged as a critical agenda, sparking a surge in home-based fitness trends. Yoga fosters balance through seamless transitions between postures and regulated breathing, aiding in physical and mental relaxation, muscle strengthening, and blood pressure reduction [1]. During practice, beginners frequently find it challenging to enhance their skills without guidance and correction from an experienced instructor. Yet, professional instructors are costly and limited by time and location constraints. Many beginners opt for self-study via recorded yoga videos or live-streamed online courses. In yoga, sustaining a steady movement pace is crucial for promoting blood circulation, preventing injuries, and supporting meditation [2]. Research shows that interruptions in movement postures lead to reduced focus and lower exercise quality [3]. For example, in Tai Chi, head direction is considered a crucial criterion for movements, but learners cannot freely move their heads while maintaining screen viewing [4]. Similarly, in golf, when learners turn their heads to watch the screen, proper posture collapses [5]. Unlike personal training where instructors can provide immediate feedback or adjust the pace, learning yoga from videos at home makes it challenging to maintain a consistent movement pace, as learners frequently interrupt their actions to refer to the screen for movement cues.

Z. Lin et al. (Eds.): ICIG 2025, LNCS 16161, pp. 547–558, 2026.
https://doi.org/10.1007/978-981-95-3398-5_44

All physical activities carry inherent risks. If beginners practice with incorrect postures for extended periods, it may lead to issues such as spinal injuries or muscle strains. Online yoga learners cannot ascertain whether their movements are standard, preventing them from objectively evaluating their learning progress. Existing literature suggests that observing successful performances can enhance exercise success, and integrating successful and unsuccessful performances (i.e., expert models vs. novice models) has proven effective for motor learning [6]. In the real world, learners can compare their performances with the instructor's optimal performance in a mirror. However, this requires learners to map their own performance to that of the target while attempting to infer potential problems in their execution, which increases cognitive demands.

To address these issues, this paper explores the applicability of Mixed Reality (MR) in home-based fitness and presents an MR yoga learning system developed based on OpenPose. By wearing HoloLens 2, the system allows users to interact with virtual interfaces in real-world environments, enabling learners to maintain head freedom while watching the instructor's movements on the interface, thus avoiding movement interruptions and preserving normal vision to navigate obstacles. Leveraging OpenPose for keypoint data extraction, the system achieves low-cost real-time posture estimation using a smartphone. During autonomous practice, it captures users' movement data in real-time, abstractly visualizes both the instructor's and user's performances, and overlays them on the interface. When deviations exceed a preset threshold, the user's movement trajectory is highlighted to assist in correcting actions, thereby enhancing learning effectiveness and exercise motivation.

2 Related Work

In recent years, due to the growing demand for home fitness, extensive research has been conducted to analyze factors influencing exercise experiences using artificial intelligence, as well as to evaluate user satisfaction. This section will mainly discuss two key areas: advancements in human pose estimation research and the applications of virtual reality (VR) and augmented reality (AR) in exercise and fitness.

2.1 Human Posture Estimation

The assessment of human movement in both spatial and temporal dimensions holds significant applications across various research fields. Currently, AI-based pose analysis methods in the literature primarily include wearable devices and video-based motion tracking approaches.

The current gold standard for precise motion capture involves combining infrared cameras with reflective markers attached to the target object. In the realm of yoga, some immersive commercial applications [7, 8] employ layouts with head-mounted displays (HMDs) and 3D virtual coaches positioned in front of and around the user. However, this approach necessitates the deployment of a large number of sensors on the user's body, making it cumbersome, expensive, and requiring maintenance. Moreover, it may affect the user's motion performance, rendering such solutions difficult to popularize in home settings.

Computer vision-based pose estimation can address the limitations of marker-based motion capture systems. By recording videos of users' movements and applying pose estimators, researchers can obtain human joint positions for kinematic analysis. Given the high quality of modern smartphone cameras, motion capture using smartphones is often adequate, enhancing portability and accessibility. Moreover, without the need to attach reflective markers, users can move naturally during capture, making this approach better suited for amateur training and home fitness scenarios. Currently, most methods employ image-based techniques to extract static features from each frame and feed them into a temporal encoder to model frame-to-frame continuity. This allows for the regression of human parameters into the SMPL model for human pose modeling. Among these methods, OpenPose [9] is a deep learning-based framework for real-time human pose estimation. It relies on convolutional neural networks (CNNs) to detect human keypoints through deep learning image processing. Since the process is automated and requires no manual labeling or model retraining by users, OpenPose is increasingly adopted for human pose detection. S.-W. Shen [10] et al. created a learning assistant system using OpenPose and fuzzy technology. The system analyzes initial and key frames to identify posture differences between the instructor and user, then calculates scores with a fuzzy theory-based scoring system. It effectively detects and scores corresponding video frames, facilitating dynamic yoga self-practice at home.

Researchers have used wearable sensors, Kinect, and 3D reconstruction to advance intelligent fitness, creating lightweight, intuitive systems for tai chi [4, 11], sports assistance [12], and physical rehabilitation [13]. However, wearable sensors can interfere with natural motion, reducing the enjoyment and immersion of fitness activities, and they require specialized facilities, limiting the system's versatility. Given that the target users are the general public who cannot afford personal trainers, this paper proposes a video-based approach to estimate the movements and positions of both learners and trainers.

2.2   Virtual Reality (VR)/Augmented Reality (AR) for Exercising

With the continuous development of emerging technologies such as virtual reality (VR) and augmented reality (AR), the "intelligent + scientific fitness" model has become a prevailing trend. For instance, Kosmala [14] et al. introduced a video recording and playback system that provides an enhanced third-person perspective of experienced climbers, which can be displayed on Google Glass or projected onto climbing walls. Hoang [11] et al. proposed using a head-mounted display (HMD) to obtain a first-person perspective of a tai chi instructor's avatar in virtual reality. Meanwhile, Plante et al.'s [15] research found that participants experienced higher heart rates, greater enjoyment, and lower fatigue levels in VR compared to traditional exercise.

The instant feedback mechanisms and intuitive visual simulations provided by VR/AR technologies are crucial for understanding one's own movement deficiencies and making timely corrections. However, there are still some drawbacks to using VR for home exercise, particularly because users are unable to see their physical surroundings and obstacles. This raises safety concerns such as falls, trips, and collisions with objects [16]. Mixed reality (MR) can alleviate these safety concerns by allowing users to interact with virtual objects in a real environment, enabling them to clearly see their surroundings while keeping their hands free from device handling.

3   The AlignMR System

To better illustrate our proposed system, we have summarized its key features and positioning. The system mainly addresses issues in home fitness, such as disrupted movement continuity, the absence of corrective feedback, and safety concerns. Table 1 provides a comparison between AlignMR and previously developed motion learning systems.

Table 1. Comparison of VoLearn system with previous motion-learning systems

System	Device	Application	Corrective feedback	Movement continuity
AlignMR (This paper)	HoloLens2 Smartphone	Yoga	Real-time visual feedback (Pose overlay + Color coding)	Yes (Free head movement)
YogaVR [7]	VR HMD	Yoga	None	No (Fully virtualized environment)
Rhythm Yoga [8]	VR HMD	Yoga	None	No (Fully virtualized environment)
Shen et al. [10]	Camera OpenPose	Yoga	Post hoc fuzzy scoring	No (Need to see screen)
Hoang et al. [11]	HMD (VR)	Tai Chi	None	No (Immersive sheltered environment)

This chapter introduces a MR training system that leverages the OpenPose framework to support the practice of full-body yoga postures. By processing human skeletal information, the system determines the similarity between the user's and the instructor's poses to provide assessment and feedback. To ensure that users can safely move and practice at home, the authors have opted for the HoloLens 2. This device combines virtual content overlay with a live external camera feed, enabling users to see their own limbs and potential obstacles in their surroundings while engaging with virtual content.

3.1   Overall System Architecture Design

The system architecture is divided into three layers based on requirements: the Perception Layer, the Processing Layer, and the Interaction Layer, forming a complete closed-loop from user motion capture to MR feedback (see Fig. 1).

Perception Layer. The hardware components include the HoloLens 2 for rendering the MR environment and spatial anchoring, as well as a smartphone for recording videos to provide real-time joint information for OpenPose.

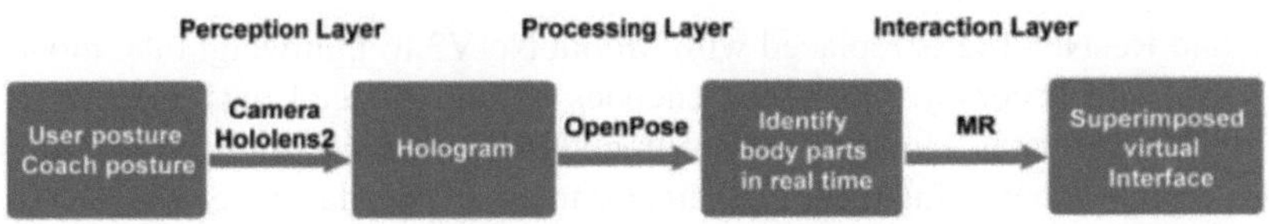

Fig. 1. System framework

Processing Layer. The core modules include the pose fusion module, which employs a Kalman filter to integrate 2D (OpenPose) and 3D (HoloLens spatial mapping) data to address self-occlusion issues (such as limb occlusion when the user is in a side profile) with monocular cameras. Additionally, there is the motion assessment module, which utilizes the Dynamic Time Warping (DTW) algorithm to calculate the differences between the user's motions and standard motions, enabling key error detection.

Interaction Layer. The scoring system determines whether the user's yoga poses are performed correctly through an overall coarse assessment module. MR provides feedback through visual cues. When the user's deviation exceeds a preset threshold, the incorrect posture is superimposed onto the virtual instructor's projection and highlighted.

3.2 Mixed Reality Scene and Posture Evaluation and Feedback Function

The system utilizes the mixed reality features of the HoloLens 2 to create a virtual screen overlay effect. Using C# and Unity 3D, it calculates the spatial positioning of these screens. The code and videos are preloaded onto the head-mounted device, allowing for unrestricted use and movement. In this mixed reality setup, the real world and virtual space operate with separate spatial coordinate systems. The user-anchored interface implemented in this study positions the virtual screen independently from the real-world environment. As the user moves or changes posture, the screen follows the user's head in a local coordinate system. Following ergonomic guidelines [17], the screen is set at a fixed distance of 1.3 m in front of the user's head, angled backward by 6 degrees. This ensures users can observe reference motions comfortably, regardless of their posture, without disrupting their own movements.

The system employs two video capture methods: (1) standard videos enabling access to instructional content from platforms like YouTube, featuring expert demonstrations of movement techniques for system input; and (2) real-time videos recording user motions using tripod-mounted smartphones. For fixed-perspective capture, key challenges include occlusions, user orientation, and body proportion variations, requiring standardized instructor video angles and user camera placement for accurate pose evaluation. This study established specifications based on high-view yoga videos: instructor videos must have $\geq 1920 \times 1080$ resolution with instructors wearing form-fitting clothing, horizontal perspective centered on the direct side ($\pm 20°$), and vertical perspective capturing full motion ranges from standing to lying. User cameras must be positioned horizontally 2–3 m away, with lying poses placing the user in the screen's lower quarter while maintaining ≥ 0.5 body width clearance on both sides.

OpenPose provides pose recognition for faces, hands, and the body. To achieve low-latency pose estimation optimization, the COCO joint model (with 18 key points) is retained, and ResNet-152 is replaced with MobileNetV3 to lightweight the model, balancing speed and accuracy. OpenPose encodes human skeletal data as a set of two-dimensional coordinates. However, environmental factors and variations in body shapes mean that directly comparing these coordinates to assess similarity between the instructor and user would lead to inaccurate results. Therefore, the virtual joints of the 3D trainer character must first be adjusted to align with the user's actual joints. Ari Shapiro [18] provided a method for automatic calibration.

The yoga learning system initiates by gathering standard motion data. Uploaded instructor video clips that meet the system's recognition criteria are divided into meaningful segments, with individual yoga motion sequences identified. Keyframes (video frames capturing the instructor in a static pose held for a duration) are extracted to evaluate the similarity between the user's and instructor's poses. To help users more easily and intuitively assess whether their fitness motions are correct and to provide targeted guidance, this study introduces a fitness assessment and guidance model based on 3D human pose estimation. This model includes an overall coarse assessment as well as detailed evaluations of key body parts (see Fig. 2). The coarse assessment evaluates only 14 joint poses, while the detailed assessment evaluates all 18 joint poses.

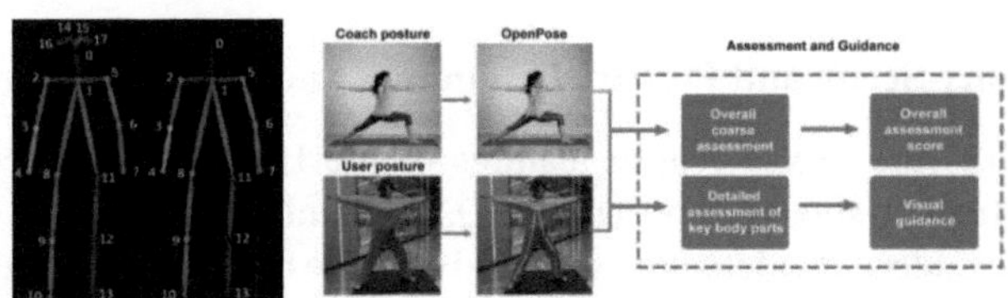

Fig. 2. The simplification of human body joint points and the overall structure of the fitness assessment and guidance model

In the pose assessment phase, the uploaded instructor's yoga poses and the real-time videos recorded by the smartphone are input separately to obtain the human pose parameters for all video frames.

Overall Coarse Assessment. Similarity calculations are conducted on the 14 joint pose parameters across all frames for both the instructor and the learner. This evaluates whether the learner's movements during the fitness routine are accurate and checks for unnecessary twists, reversals, or shakes, resulting in an overall score for the learner's performance. Since the overall coarse assessment must consider the entire sequence of video frames, and given that individuals vary in reaction times, start times, speeds, and accelerations during movement execution, leading to differences in frame counts and timing of identical movements between the instructor and learner, the system employs a sequence alignment algorithm, Dynamic Time Warping (DTW), to develop an overall coarse assessment method based on DTW. This approach calculates the overall similarity between the two sets of movements. DTW applies dynamic programming principles to compute the optimal matching between two sequences (see Fig. 3). First, the distances between each frame of the learner's fitness video sequence and the instructor's sequence are calculated. Next, local paths are constrained to identify the shortest path within the distance matrix, representing the optimal path for local alignment. Finally, the cumulative distance along this optimal path is computed to determine the globally optimal path. After averaging these distances, the similarity of the overall fitness movement sequences is derived, enabling the overall coarse assessment. Based on the average globally optimal distance, a final overall evaluation is provided.

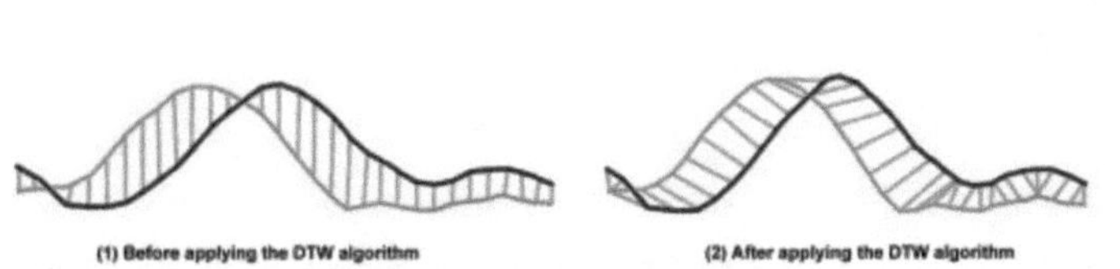

Fig. 3. Use DTW to achieve optimal matching between two sequences

Detailed Assessment of Key Body Parts. The process of detailed assessment for key body parts involves calculating the similarity of the complete 18 pose parameters from key frames to evaluate the standardization of specific body parts in the learner's fitness movements. The matching degree between the user's posture and the correct posture is determined by calculating the percentage of cosine similarity:

Cosine similarity is used to calculate the similarity between two vectors (e.g., vector A representing the user's posture and vector B representing the standard posture).

$$\text{Similarity}(A,\ B) = \frac{A \cdot B}{\|A\| \times \|B\|} = \frac{\sum_{i=1}^{n}(A_i \times B_i)}{\sqrt{\sum_{i=1}^{n} A_i^2} \times \sqrt{\sum_{i=1}^{n} B_i^2}} \tag{1}$$

Here, A·B represents the dot product of vectors A and B, and $\|A\|$ denotes the magnitude (Euclidean length) of vector A. The value of cosine similarity ranges from $[-1, 1]$, where -1 indicates complete dissimilarity and 1 indicates complete similarity. Based on this, thresholds for acceptable posture deviations can be established (e.g., >0.95 as "correct" and <0.8 as "needing correction"). By calculating the similarity of the 18 joint pose parameters, with a focus on joints with poor similarity and key joint areas, a detailed assessment of the critical body parts in the learner's yoga pose key frames is provided, along with guidance suggestions to enable targeted improvements by the learner.

In yoga pose training, the system utilizes an intuitive, easy-to-understand visually augmented feedback mechanism to guide users in performing precise and synchronized yoga movements. An instructor is displayed on the MR interface as a visual guide, demonstrating the correct position and speed of standard movements (see Fig. 4). When the user's posture perfectly matches the target posture and follows the intended trajectory, only the instructor's image is shown, indicating full synchronization. If the deviation value of any body part is below 0.95, the user's deviated posture is overlaid on the instructor's posture on the screen. The user's posture is represented by individual 3D markers that fade linearly over 5 s until they disappear. As deviation increases, these markers gradually shift from pink to red, turning completely red when the deviation value drops below 0.8. This combination of the instructor and the user's deviated posture provides clear, real-time feedback, helping users quickly identify and correct deviations from the target movements. The color-coding of the user's posture further enhances their ability to instantly gauge the extent of the deviation, enabling swift adjustments.

Fig. 4. Visual poses corresponding to different degrees of deviation values

4   User Study and Analysis

This section introduces the evaluation of the AlignMR system, which is divided into two parts. First, the performance of the MR virtual interface and visual feedback design was tested through user studies. Finally, the proposed system was evaluated with individuals engaged in sports-related professions to better position the overall system design.

4.1   User Study on Mixed Reality Interface and Visual Feedback Design

As described in Sect. 3, the visually augmented feedback module is implemented through pose analysis and evaluation based on video input provided by a smartphone or camera (see Fig. 5). Six classic yoga poses were selected for the participants to learn in the study (Upward-Facing Dog, Goddess, Downward-Facing Dog, Side Plank, Tree, and Warrior II). Therefore, two sets of experiments were designed: Group (a) received feedback consisting of the instructor's image along with the user's deviated posture, while Group (b) only received the instructor's image. This approach facilitated the validation of the effectiveness of the visually augmented feedback.A total of 36 participants were recruited, including 22 females and 14 males, aged between 18 and 56 years, with an average age of 31.0 years (standard deviation = 8.5). Among them, 10 individuals had a regular exercise habit, with 8 of them exercising more than twice a week. Among these exercisers, 8 practiced yoga at varying frequencies. All participants had normal or corrected-to-normal vision. The entire experiment lasted approximately 60 min.

Fig. 5. Setup, Six key poses from YouTube video and UI interface

Range of Motion and Temporal Error. The overall coarse assessment proposed in Sect. 3 was used to evaluate how closely the participants' movements matched the given poses in both time and space. To collect these data, participants were divided into Groups (a) and (b). Each participant randomly selected 3 out of 6 sets of yoga poses, repeating each set 3 times. Each experimental session lasted 5 min. If the augmented visual feedback facilitated the learning of movements, then Group A, which utilized visual feedback, should exhibit a smaller average global optimal distance as calculated by the algorithm compared to Group B, which did not use visual feedback.

Cognitive Load. The cognitive load was measured to assess whether the additional visual feedback increased the participants' attention and mental burden during the training phase. The NASA-TLX questionnaire [19] was used to measure the cognitive load, and comparisons were made between participants who used and did not use the visually augmented feedback.

User Comments. To evaluate visual feedback usability, participants provided system feedback after completing consent forms and demographic surveys. Following an introduction to MR interface operations for pose selection and video control, participants performed 5-min warm-ups before commencing the experiment. Participants were asked to stand at a designated position in front of a fixed camera, wear the Hololens 2, and perform coordinate calibration. Group A then learned yoga poses from the virtual instructor with visual feedback, while Group B only learned poses from the virtual instructor. During operation, a virtual UI interface displayed selectable yoga poses via gesture control. Through the footage captured by the mobile phone camera, participants followed the virtual instructor to complete the yoga poses. Finally, the participants' completed fitness videos were input into the previously established fitness assessment and guidance model, enabling a simulated MR fitness experiment. All participants completed NASA-TLX questionnaires and interviews addressing satisfaction with AlignMR, appealing aspects, and interface performance in movement motivation/guidance/standardization, with the entire process camera-documented. The DTW algorithm computed distances between instructor and participant fitness video sequences to compare pose similarity. The charts displayed the average global optimal distances calculated using the overall coarse analysis method proposed in this paper for the six yoga poses. Table 2 revealed a significant reduction in the average global optimal distance for Group (a) compared to Group (b), demonstrating visual feedback learners achieved higher pose similarity and superior outcomes.

Table 2. Average global optimal distance and overall score

Type	Upward-Facing Dog	Goddess	Downward-Facing Dog	Side Plank	Tree	Warrior II
(a)	0.29	0.43	0.61	0.57	1.19	0.22
(b)	0.47	0.74	1.32	1.06	1.81	0.41

The experimental results showed that participants using visual feedback took more time during the learning process, as they needed to adjust their postures based on the feedback. Our objective was to correct users' movements and enhance the accuracy of their poses during practice. Thus, it is reasonable to conclude that the introduction of the feedback mechanism led participants to spend more time in order to achieve better learning results. Notably, there was no significant difference in cognitive load, suggesting that while users spent more time using visual feedback, AlignMR did not impose an additional burden. Additionally, although the system boasts high feedback visibility, it still has defects like joint posture recognition errors and screen flickering. Subsequent work should prioritize research on hardware optimization and system architecture improvement plans.

Most participants expressed satisfaction with the system, noting that visual feedback reduced learning errors and helped them perform poses better. Some user feedback emphasized the overall value of the system, such as: "The MR environment let me move my head and limbs freely while watching the video, making yoga learning smoother," "The system gave me clear training goals, reducing boredom," and "Visual feedback on incorrect movements helped me understand differences and make timely adjustments." We also compared their experiences of using our system with virtual avatars and visual feedback compared to learning yoga independently by watching traditional tutorial videos. Most participants believed that the system offered a good interactive experience, enhancing the interactivity, engagement, effectiveness, and fun of fitness training. However, one participant held a neutral view: "Voice feedback on movement techniques would make the system more useful." while another recommended using different evaluation criteria for users with varying yoga experience levels.

4.2 Evaluation by Professional Users

Finally, we invited two experts from the yoga-related field to demonstrate all the functions of our system and conducted semi-structured interviews with them to gather opinions on the system's feedback mechanisms.

A professional yoga instructor noted that the video input feature could enable her to offer personalized guidance to remote students. She emphasized that practicing yoga alone without supervision is difficult, and this system could help students ensure proper movements through effective feedback after classes.

The other interviewee, a therapist from a rehabilitation hospital, believed the system could serve as a effective auxiliary tools for rehabilitation therapy. Patients typically receive corrective training three to four times a week under a therapist's supervision, but often call for guidance when practicing at home. If patients could use this system, it would help reduce the therapist's workload.

5 Conclusion

This study aimed to tackle challenges in home fitness—such as disrupted movement postures caused by static video sources, insufficient feedback during independent practice, and safety risks—by developing a Mixed Reality (MR)-based home yoga learning system. Built on the Unity 3D platform, the system incorporates the OpenPose framework for human pose recognition and uses the HoloLens 2 as its main hardware. The system supports gesture-based interaction and provides visually enhanced feedback, making the yoga learning more convenient and efficient. It offers guidance on standard yoga poses through a virtual interface that follows the user's head movements. Practical results show that it provides accurate, real-time movement feedback by visually comparing the coach's professional demonstration with the user's performance, helping users learn yoga poses smoothly and correctly, thus achieving its intended goals. Additionally, the system is also applicable to other models with similar movement characteristics and processes.

The system still has several shortcomings. The human body recognition algorithm requires further improvement, and the superimposed user models may still suffer from issues such as lagging and incorrect feedback. To address these problems, in-depth research can be conducted in the following directions: at the algorithmic level, parameter settings can be optimized; additionally, more measurements can be employed to verify movement accuracy, and system functions can be refined by evaluating learning outcomes.

References

1. Ashraf, F.B., Islam, M.U., Kabir, M.R., Uddin, J.: YoNet: a neural network for yoga pose classification. SN Comput. Sci. **4**(2), 198 (2023). https://doi.org/10.1007/s42979-022-016 18-8
2. Iyengar, B.K.S.: Light on yoga: the definitive guide to yoga practice. Schocken Books (1979)
3. Jackson, S.A., Csikszentmihalyi, M.: Flow in sports. Human Kinetics (1999)
4. Han, P.-H., Chen, Y.-S., Zhong, Y., Wang, H.-L., Hung, Y.-P.: My Tai-Chi coaches: an augmented-learning tool for practicing TaiChi Chuan. In: Proceedings of the 8th Augmented Human International Conference, pp. 1–4 (2017)
5. Ikeda, A., Hwang, D.-H., Koike, H.: A real-time projection system for golf training using virtual shadow. In: 2019 IEEE Conference on Virtual Reality and 3D User Interfaces (VR), pp. 1527–1528. IEEE (2019)
6. Andrieux, M., Proteau, L.: Mixed observation favors motor learning through better estimation of the model's performance. Exp. Brain Res. **232**, 3121–3132 (2014). https://doi.org/10.1007/ s00221-014-4000-3
7. Jijia: Home YogaVR. virtual reality application (2021). https://www.oculus.com/experiences/ quest/4828252637184827/. Accessed 15 Sept 2022
8. Soaring Roc Studio: Rhythm Yoga. Virtual reality application (2021). https://www.viveport. com/apps/70755b3a-4397-46a8-a33b-5abb9f832f32/. Accessed 15 Sept 2022
9. Cao, Z., Hidalgo, G., Simon, T., Wei, S.-E., Sheikh, Y.: OpenPose: realtime multi-person 2D pose estimation using part affinity fields. IEEE Trans. Pattern Anal. Mach. Intell. **43**(1), 172–186 (2021)
10. Shen, S.-W., Huang, W.-C., Anggraini, I.T., Funabiki, N., Fan, C.-P.: Exercise and performance learning assistant system for self-practice dynamic yoga by OpenPose and fuzzy based design. In: 2022 10th International Conference on Information and Education Technology (ICIET), pp. 16–21. IEEE (2022). https://doi.org/10.1109/ICIET55102.2022.9778954
11. Hoang, T.N., Reinoso, M., Vetere, F., Tanin, E.: Onebody: remote posture guidance system using first person view in virtual environment. In: Proceedings of the 9th Nordic Conference on Human-Computer Interaction, pp. 1–10 (2016)
12. Dayrit, F.L., Nakashima, Y., Sato, T., Yokoya, N.: Free-viewpoint AR human-motion reenactment based on a single RGB-D video stream. In: 2014 IEEE International Conference on Multimedia and Expo (ICME), pp. 1–6. IEEE (2014)

13. Stütz, T., et al.: An interactive 3D health app with multimodal information representation for frozen shoulder. In: Proceedings of the 19th International Conference on Human-Computer Interaction with Mobile Devices and Services, pp. 1–11. ACM (2017)
14. Kosmalla, F., Daiber, F., Wiehr, F., Krüger, A.: Climbvis: investigating in-situ visualizations for understanding climbing movements by demonstration. In: Proceedings of the 2017 ACM International Conference on Interactive Surfaces and Spaces, pp. 270–279 (2017)
15. Plante, T.G., Aldridge, A., Bogden, R., Hanelin, C.: Might virtual reality promote the mood benefits of exercise? Comput. Hum. Behav. **19**(4), 495–509 (2003). https://doi.org/10.1016/S0747-5632(02)00074-2
16. Mostajeran, F., Steinicke, F., Nunez, O.J.A., Gatsios, D., Fotiadis, D.: Augmented reality for older adults: exploring acceptability of virtual coaches for home-based balance training in an aging population. In: Proceedings of the 2020 CHI Conference on Human Factors in Computing Systems (CHI 2020), pp. 1–12. Association for Computing Machinery (2020). https://doi.org/10.1145/3313831.3376565
17. Shin, J.G., Kim, D., So, C., Saakes, D.: Body follows eye: unobtrusive posture manipulation through a dynamic content position in virtual reality. In: Proceedings of the 2020 CHI Conference on Human Factors in Computing Systems, pp. 1–14 (2020)
18. Shapiro, A., et al.: Rapid avatar capture and simulation using commodity depth sensors. Comput. Anim. Virtual Worlds **25**(3–4), 201–211 (2014)
19. Hart, S.G., Staveland, L.E.: Development of NASA-TLX (Task Load Index): results of empirical and theoretical research. In: Advances in Psychology, vol. 52, pp. 139–183. Elsevier (1988)

Bi-IRNet: A Transformer-Based Binaural Impulse Response Generation Guidance Model

Yisheng Zhang and Shiguang Liu[✉]

College of Intelligence and Computing, Tianjin University, Tianjin 300350, China
lsg@tju.edu.cn

Abstract. In the field of acoustic simulation, widely applied methods rely on the impulse response (IR) and its convolution relationships. However, most deep learning-based approaches for generating IRs are limited to monaural IRs. Some methods for generating binaural IRs require specialized binaural IR datasets, which are costly to collect and difficult to obtain under extreme conditions, such as underwater environments. Therefore, this paper introduces a low-cost and practical technique, Bi-IRNet, which guides various IR generation models to produce corresponding binaural IRs using positional information as input. Our method leverages transformer networks and the Head-Related Transfer Function (HRTF) database to train a binaural IR generation guidance module. This module can be easily embedded into other IR generation models, enabling end-to-end generation of spatially aware binaural IRs. With this module, IR generation models can produce spatial binaural IRs without the need for a binaural IR dataset, significantly reducing the cost of deep learning-based binaural IR generation.

Keywords: impulse response · deep learning · acoustic · transformer

1 Introduction

Acoustic simulation plays a crucial role in various applications, such as virtual reality, underwater acoustics, and spatial audio systems [9]. One of the key components of acoustic simulation is the accurate representation of the impulse response (IR), which describes how sound propagates through a given environment. Traditional methods for obtaining IRs rely on physical measurements or simulations, where convolution of the IR with sound signals helps to recreate the acoustic characteristics of a space. Although these methods are effective, they often require significant computational resources or expensive measurement equipment, especially in complex environments.

Recent advances in deep learning have opened new possibilities for generating IRs, particularly through data-driven models. However, most existing deep

This work was partly supported by the Natural Science Foundation of China under grant no. 62072328.

Z. Lin et al. (Eds.): ICIG 2025, LNCS 16161, pp. 559–571, 2026.
https://doi.org/10.1007/978-981-95-3398-5_45

learning-based IR generation methods focus on generating mono-channel IRs, which only capture sound propagation in a single channel. Although there are some methods designed to generate binaural IRs, they often require large and expensive datasets. These binaural IR datasets, which capture sound from two channels (left and right), are particularly difficult and costly to collect, especially in challenging environments such as underwater settings, where the physical and technical challenges of data acquisition are amplified.

To overcome these challenges, this paper introduces a novel, cost-effective, and practical technique, Bi-IRNet, to generate binaural IRs. Unlike existing approaches, which rely on the availability of large binaural datasets, Bi-IRNet utilizes positional information as input to guide various IR generation models in creating corresponding binaural IRs. Our method combines the power of Transformer [7] networks with the Head-Related Transfer Function [6] (HRTF) database to train a guidance module that can be embedded in other IR generation models. This module enables end-to-end generation of spatially aware binaural IRs, which are critical for applications that require immersive audio experiences.

2   Related Work

Traditional sound propagation methods Until now, many wave-based, geometric, and hybrid interactive sound propagation algorithms have been proposed to simulate sound propagation in complex scenes [2–4,11,12,16,18].

Among them, wave-based algorithms precompute the IR for static scenes and calculate the IR for arbitrary listener positions through efficient interpolation techniques at runtime. However, these methods are computationally expensive. Recent approaches indirectly generate RIR (Room IR) by first estimating acoustic parameters, such as reverberation time (RT60), the time RIR needs to decay 60dB, direct-toreverberant ratio (DRR), the energy ratio of direct sound to reflected sound, or match the distribution of such acoustic parameters in real-world RIR. Additionally, several machine learning algorithms have been proposed to estimate RIRs for specific environments [5,8,10,13–15,19]. One innovative learning-based approach is the generation of RIRs from a single RGB image of a physical environment, including pioneering work such as Image2Reverb [17], which utilizes a conditional Generative Adversarial Network (GAN) architecture. In the field of acoustic simulation, Convolutional Neural Networks (CNNs) have been applied to estimate the late reverberation statistics from images. These studies build on the premise that experienced acoustic engineers can estimate a space's IR or reverberation characteristics from visual scenes.

Most existing deep learning methods focus solely on generating monaural IR, which only captures sound propagation in a single channel. Although some methods aim to generate binaural IR, they typically rely on large and expensive datasets. To address this, we propose Bi-IRNet. A key advantage of Bi-IRNet is that IR generation models embedded with this module can generate spatial binaural IRs without the need for specialized binaural datasets. By leveraging the HRTF database and a transformer-based architecture, our method significantly reduces the cost and complexity of generating high-quality binaural IRs. This opens up new possibilities for acoustic simulation in environments where collecting binaural data is impractical, such as underwater or other extreme conditions.

3   Method

3.1   Overview

To enable UnderwaterImage2IR to generate binaural IRs with spatial awareness, this paper introduces an HRTF- and Transformer-based IR generation guidance module. This module is designed to predict HRIRs for arbitrary source and receiver position relationships. The model presented in this paper consists of two main components: (1) the spectral position context encoder, and (2) the conditional HRIR predictor. The spectral position context encoder builds an implicit model of environmental acoustic characteristics by extracting multimodal cues from the input spectrum and position relationship context. The conditional HRIR predictor uses this implicit representation to predict the corresponding HRIR based on queries for the positions of any given source and receiver. The model is trained end-to-end, with additional training objectives aimed at reducing the error between the predicted HRIR and the actual HRIR. The training objectives not only encourage the model to match the target HRIR at the spectral level but also ensure that the predicted HRIR and the target HRIR are similar in key high-level acoustic parameters, thereby improving the prediction quality. The following sections provide a detailed description of these two model components and the proposed training objectives.

3.2   Training Dataset

This study uses the CIPIC dataset [1], which includes head-related transfer function data with azimuth and elevation angles, to train the guidance module. The module is designed to guide the generation of binaural IRs with spatial awareness when generating IRs in the UnderwaterImage2IR network. Each sample in the dataset includes the azimuth and elevation angles of the sound source, along with the corresponding Head-Related Impulse Response (HRIR) spectrogram. The specific representation of azimuth and elevation is shown in Fig. 1, where azimuth is denoted as (θ, ϕ). Point P represents the sound source, and point O represents the receiver. The six example directions are as follows: directly in front $(0°, 0°)$; directly above $(0°, 90°)$; directly behind $(0°, 180°)$; directly below $(0°, 270°)$; directly to the left $(-90°, 0°)$; and directly to the right $(90°, 0°)$.

3.3   Guidance Model Architecture

The network architecture of the guidance module is shown in Fig. 2, and it is divided into two main parts: (1) the spectral position context encoder, and (2)

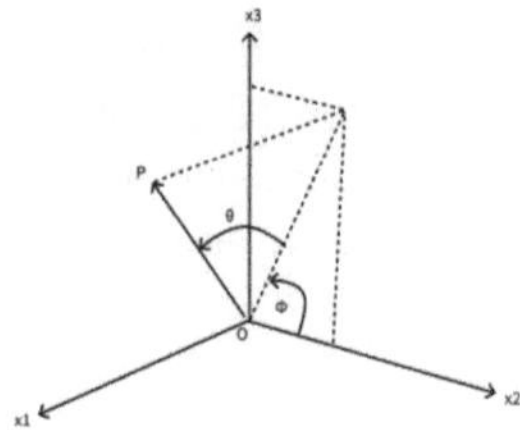

Fig. 1. HRTF azimuth representation.

the conditional HRIR predictor. The spectral position context encoder builds a latent vector of position information and HRIR from the input spectrogram and position information, while the HRIR predictor receives the latent vector and predicts the corresponding HRIR based on the input position information. The specific components of the context encoder are as follows:

- **Spectral Encoder:** The HRIRs are first processed with the Short-Time Fourier Transform (STFT) to obtain their log-frequency spectrograms. The spectrogram is then encoded using a convolutional neural network, which includes two convolutional layers, each followed by a ReLU activation function and a max-pooling layer. The first convolutional layer converts the single-channel spectrogram input to 16 channels, and the second layer converts the 16 channels to 32 channels. The output is then flattened and passed through a fully connected layer to produce a 512-dimensional feature vector.
- **Position Encoder:** For the position information, this paper does not directly encode the azimuth and elevation angles into the latent vector. Instead, the azimuth θ and elevation ϕ are transformed into a four-dimensional vector $[cos\theta, sin\theta, cos\phi, sin\phi]$ using sine and cosine functions, which is then further processed through a fully connected layer to produce a feature vector. The use of sine and cosine functions helps the model effectively understand the periodic nature of angle data, as angles repeat after a full cycle (for example, $360°$ is equivalent to $0°$). This encoding ensures smooth transitions between angles, mitigating the discontinuities that would arise from directly using angle values in degrees or radians.
- **Transformer Encoder:** The outputs of the spectral encoder and the position encoder are fused and passed into a Transformer encoder based on the self-attention mechanism. The encoder uses a multi-head attention mechanism to learn the complex relationships between the input features. The Transformer encoder consists of six layers, each with 8 attention heads and a 2048-dimensional feedforward network.

For the overall workflow of the context encoder, we concatenate the feature vectors from the spectral encoder and the position encoder, and project them through another linear layer to obtain the acoustic input S_i^A. This creates a multimodal memory of size N, denoted as $S = S_0^A, S_1^A, ...S_N^A$. Next, the context encoder utilizes the self-attention mechanism to focus on the embeddings in S, capturing both intra-modal and cross-modal short-range and long-range dependencies, and learns the implicit representation of the corresponding acoustic properties of the position relationships, denoted as $I = I_0, I_1, ... I_N$. This representation can model the acoustic characteristics of the relationship between the sound source and the listener. This representation is then passed to the next module, the conditional HRIR predictor, which generates the corresponding HRIR for any given position query.

For the conditional HRIR predictor, our approach first normalizes the position information and encodes each posture using sine-based position encoding, as done in the position encoder. Then, a single linear layer is used to connect and project the encoding to obtain the query code q. The HRIR predictor uses q as a condition and applies the Transformer decoder [20] to perform cross-attention on the learned implicit representation and generate the target HRIR encoding d^Q for the query Q (i.e., $HRIR^Q$). A multi-layer transposed convolution network U is used to upsample d^Q via transposed convolutions to predict the magnitude spectrogram of the HRIR in log-space. This log-magnitude spectrogram is then converted back to linear space to obtain the predicted HRIR for the query Q, denoted as $(HRIR^Q)^*$. Finally, a loss function is computed to optimize the various components.

3.4 Loss Function and Training Process

This guidance module is optimized in a supervised manner to predict the target HRIR for a given query Q, denoted as $(H^Q)^*$. The loss function L combines two aspects: the accuracy of the predicted spectrum and the high-level acoustic properties of the prediction $(H^Q)^*$ compared to the ground truth H^Q. The loss function consists of two parts: a reconstruction-based loss L_1 for the HRIR's spectrogram, and an energy decay matching loss L_E.

For the target binaural spectrogram H^Q, the L_1 loss aims to reduce the average prediction error in the time-frequency domain, defined as follows:

$$L_1 = \frac{1}{2 \times F \times T} \sum_{i=1}^{2F \times T} \left\| (H_i^Q)^* - H_i^Q \right\|_1, \tag{1}$$

where F represents the frequency bins, T represents the time window, and $|.|_1$ denotes the L_1 norm, which is the sum of the absolute values of the elements in the vector.

For the L_E loss component, the L_E loss attempts to capture the reverberation characteristics of the room impulse response (RIR) by matching the energy time decay of the predicted RIR with the target values. This approach allows the model to reduce errors in key reverberation parameters, such as T_{60} error and the direct-to-reverberant energy ratio. Although previous studies attempted to directly minimize such errors, it is infeasible to incorporate the loss into the training objective due to the non-differentiable nature of the function. In contrast, the proposed L_E loss in this paper is fully differentiable and can be combined with any other IR training objective. To compute L_E, we first sum

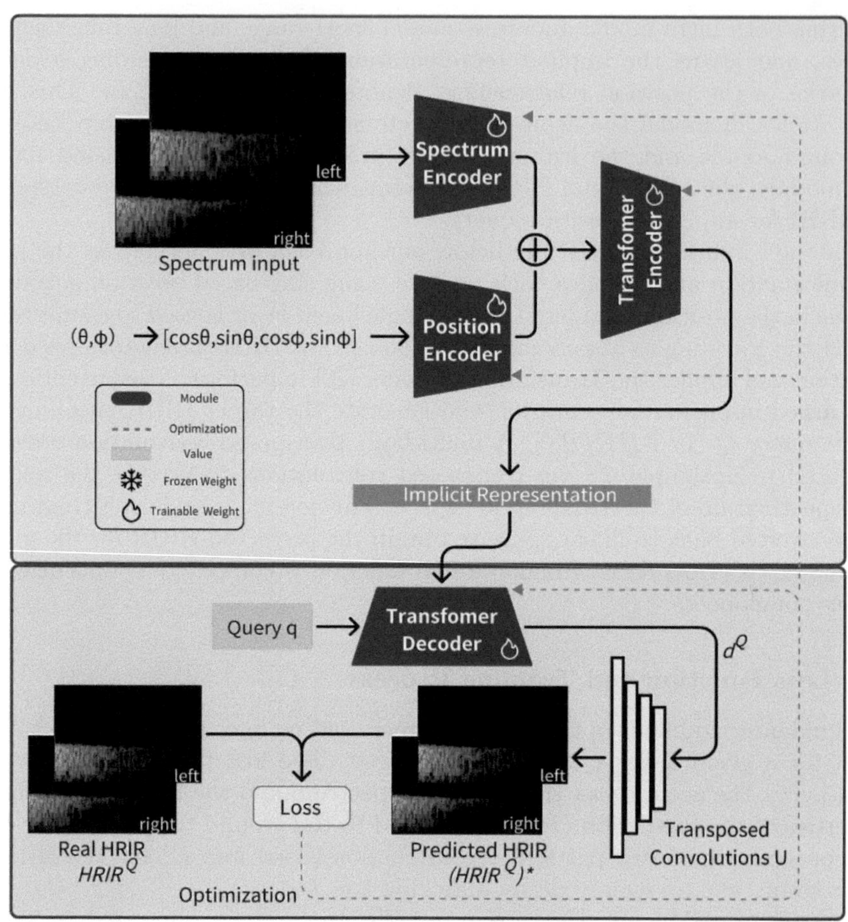

Fig. 2. Network architecture.

the spectrogram of the HRIR along the frequency axis (similar to the method described in [17]) to obtain the full-band amplitude envelope, from which the energy decay curve is derived. The decay curve D_e is then calculated using Schroeder's backward integration algorithm. However, unlike the method in [17], which calculates values from the decay curve using a series of non-differentiable operations, the L_E loss in this paper directly measures the error between the predicted and target energy decay curves, ensuring the complete differentiability of the loss and enabling the capture of other energy-based acoustic characteristics, such as the direct-to-reverberant energy ratio and early decay time. Additionally, by calculating the absolute error of D_e between the predicted $(H^Q)^*$ and the target H^Q at the non-zero time positions of the target energy decay D_e, the model can ignore the all-zero tail of shorter RIRs, further improving the model's applicability and accuracy. The definition of the L_E loss is as follows:

$$L_E = \frac{1}{2T} \sum_{i=1}^{2T} \left| D_e((H_i^Q)^*) - D_e(H_i^Q) \right|, \tag{2}$$

Here, $D_e((H_i^Q)^*)$ and H_i^Q represent the energy decay values of the predicted and true RIR at time point i, respectively. $2T$ denotes the total duration considered, typically twice the duration of the RIR, to ensure that all relevant decay information is captured. The design of this loss function aims to directly optimize the energy decay characteristics of the predicted HRIR, enabling the model to better learn and simulate the energy decay differences generated by binaural receptors when receiving sound from different directions.

Finally, the overall training loss function is $L = L_1 + \lambda L_E$, where λ is the weight of the L_E loss, with $\lambda = 10^{-2}$.

3.5 Model Architecture

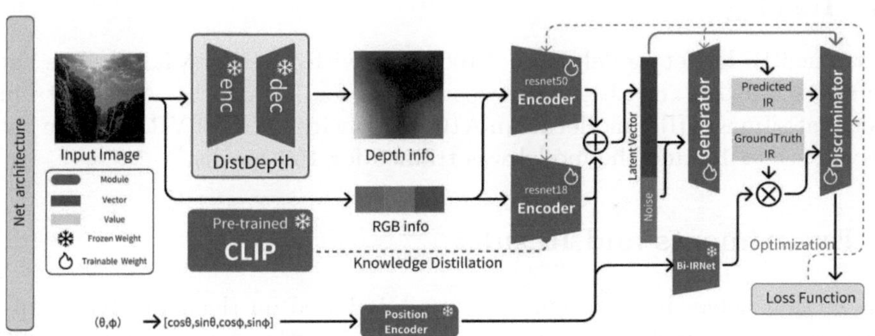

Fig. 3. UnderwaterImage2IR+

In our work, we introduce an IR generator based on deep neural network learning, UnderwaterImage2IR [21], capable of generating IRs at interactive rates for given underwater scene images. We embedded Bi-IRNet into Underwater-Image2IR and named it UnderwaterImage2IR+. The network can be formally described as follows:

$$IR_{x,p} = N(E_{\theta 1}(x \oplus N_{depth}(x)) \oplus E_{\theta 2}(x) \oplus E_P(P)), \tag{3}$$

Here, $IR_{x,p}$ represents the binaural predicted IR with spatial awareness generated from the given image x and position p, and E_P denotes the position encoder. N refers to the overall CGAN network, while $E_{\theta 1}$ and $E_{\theta 2}$ are two pre-trained ResNet encoders used for extracting spatial features and underwater environmental features from the images, respectively. N_{depth} is the pre-trained monocular depth estimation network. The symbol $\oplus$ denotes the concatenation operator. The overall network architecture is illustrated in Fig. 3, with further details provided in the following section.

After adding the HRTF- and Transformer-based guidance module, the overall network architecture of UnderwaterImage2IR is shown in Fig. 3, which mainly consists of the encoder part and the GAN network part. The input image first passes through the DistDepth network to generate the depth map, which is then fed along with its RGB image into two pre-trained encoders. The position information is processed using a sine function and sent to the position encoder and the HRTF- and Transformer-based guidance module. The outputs of the encoders are concatenated with noise to form the latent vector, which is then passed to the generator. The HRTF- and Transformer-based guidance module receives the real IR and position information, and after processing, outputs the binaural IR with spatial awareness as the real IR information. The discriminator obtains information from the latent vector and the real IR processed by the guidance module to distinguish the authenticity of the predicted binaural IR, compute the loss, and optimize the other components.

3.6   Training

We trained Bi-IRNet model on an A100 GPU with 24GB of VRAM. The batch size was set to 20, and the model was trained for 150 epochs. And we trained UnderwaterImage2IR+ model on an A100 GPU with 24GB of VRAM. The batch size was set to 16, and the model was trained for 150 epochs.

4   Experiments and Results

This section delves into the guidance module based on Head-Related Transfer Function (HRTF) technology and its application in the "UnderwaterImage2IR" system. The system can accept arbitrary underwater images and positional information as input and directly synthesize underwater acoustic impulse responses with stereo spatial perception.

4.1   Examples

The tests in this study cover underwater environments, non-underwater environments, real-world environments, and fully virtual environments to ensure the broad applicability and robustness of the system. Figure 4 presents some test examples, where binaural IRs with spatial awareness were generated from various scene images and compared with real IRs obtained through direct convolution with HRTF data. In each example, the frequency spectrogram of the binaural IR was generated from two random directions and compared with the real IR spectrogram obtained by directly convolving with HRTF data. Since the sampling angles of HRTF data are fixed, for angles not directly included in the test data, the nearest sampling points were selected for convolution.

From these spectrograms, it is clearly observed that, whether in underwater or non-underwater scenes, the reverberation time and intensity are closely related to the direction of the sound source. Specifically, the IR intensity and reverberation time are stronger from the direction of the sound source. In Fig. 4, the reverberation time and intensity in the spectrogram match the direction of the sound source, with higher energy intensity and longer reverberation time corresponding to the sound source direction. If the source is directly behind, there is almost no difference. In underwater scenes, due to the acoustic properties of water, the frequencies are generally lower and the reverberation time is longer. In non-underwater scenes, higher frequencies and relatively shorter reverberation times are observed. Additionally, in semi-enclosed spaces, the reverberation time increases as the space size grows, whereas in open areas, the reverberation time is relatively shorter, demonstrating the significant impact of spatial dimensions on sound propagation characteristics.

4.2   Comparisons

Due to the lack of existing work that can directly generate binaural IRs for various environments based on images, this study chose to conduct comparative experiments by directly convolving with HRTF data based on the model UnderwaterImage2IR. The T_{60} error is used as the evaluation criterion. Since the IR is binaural, the average error is taken as the result. Both methods are capable of generating underwater binaural IRs. The specific details can be found in Table 1.

Table 1. T_{60} Error(%) in the Custom Dataset Tests.

T_{60} Error (%)	μ	σ
UnderwaterImage2IR	-6.33	77.4
UnderwaterImage2IR+	-6.58	78.6

In the table, UnderwaterImage2IR refers to the results of the UnderwaterImage2IR model directly convolving with HRTF data, while UnderwaterImage2IR+ is the model with the added guidance module. It can be seen that the model with the guidance module (UnderwaterImage2IR+) has a larger error compared to the UnderwaterImage2IR model that directly convolves with HRTF data. The reason for this is that the real IR data used for comparison is also obtained by directly convolving real IR with HRTF data, so the accuracy of the UnderwaterImage2IR+ model is naturally lower than that of the UnderwaterImage2IR model.

However, UnderwaterImage2IR+ is an end-to-end model that directly generates binaural IR, which is much more efficient than the UnderwaterImage2IR model, which first generates an IR and then convolves it with HRTF data (see Table 2). Additionally, UnderwaterImage2IR+ is not limited by the finite sampling points of the HRTF dataset and can take any angle as input to generate the

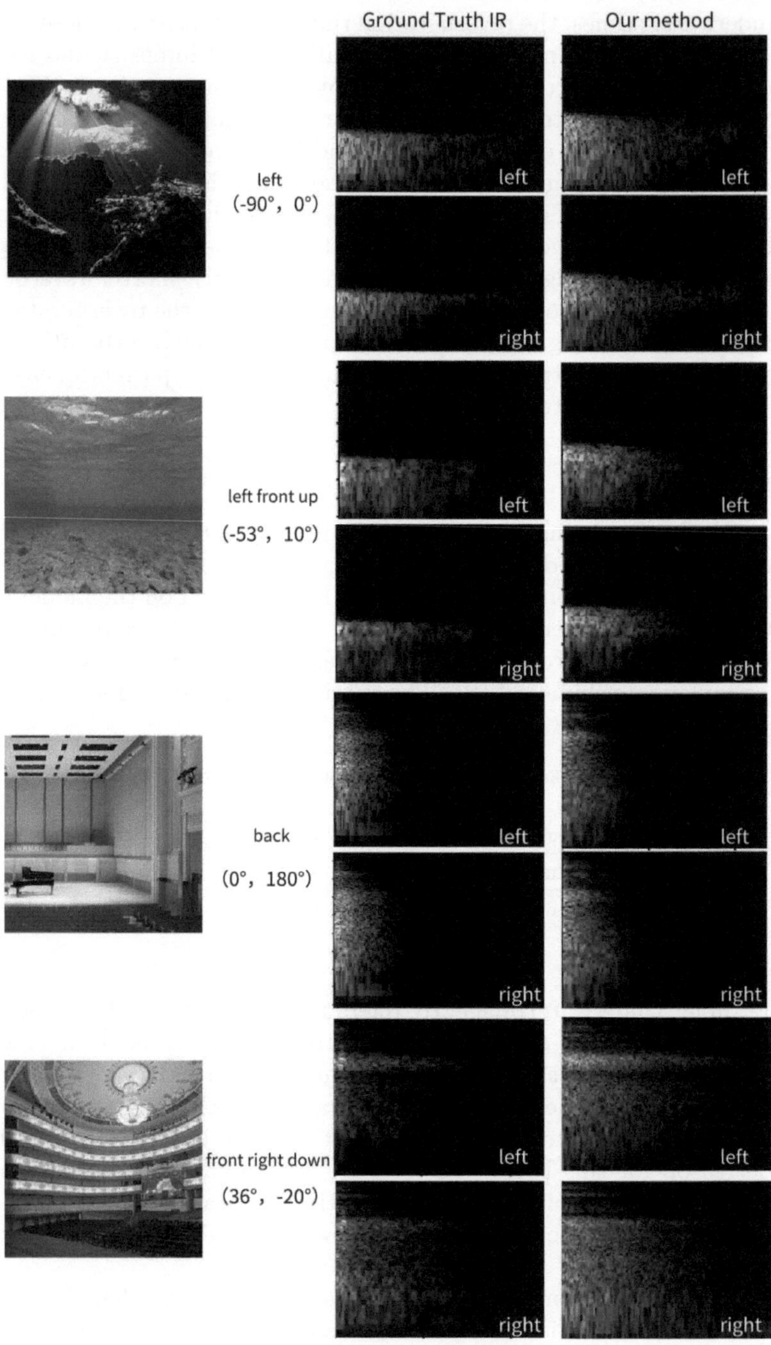

Fig. 4. Examples.

corresponding binaural IR. Compared to the process of first generating the IR and then performing the convolution, the end-to-end direct generation of binaural IR in UnderwaterImage2IR+ improves efficiency by 63%.

Table 2. The average time it takes to process an image to generate a binaural IR.

module	$time(s)$
UnderwaterImage2IR	0.108
UnderwaterImage2IR+	0.066

4.3 Ablation Experiments

To validate the effectiveness of each component in the proposed model, a series of ablation experiments were conducted. The experimental strategy involved removing certain key components from the model and then comparing the performance of the simplified model with that of the full model. The specific key components include the spectral encoder, the sine processing of positional information, and the energy decay matching loss L_E in the loss function.

Table 3. ablation

T_{60} Error (%)	μ	σ
UnderwaterImage2IR+	−6.58	78.6
-spcenc	−7.82	78.9
-posenc	8.11	82.7
-L_E	13.26	96.4

The T60 error results are shown in Table 3. "-Spectrum Encoder" refers to the removal of the spectrum encoder module, "-Sine Processing" refers to the cancellation of the sine processing operation for positional information, and "-L_E" indicates the removal of the energy decay matching loss L_E. Compared to models with key components removed, the complete model in this paper demonstrates lower mean error and standard deviation, proving that our model performs more stably and consistently across various scenarios. In particular, when the energy decay matching loss L_E is removed, the performance degradation of the model is particularly noticeable.

5 Conclusion

This study introduces Bi-IRNet, a transformative approach in the field of acoustic simulation, particularly in generating binaural IR from positional data without the need for extensive binaural datasets. By leveraging a transformer-based architecture and the Head-Related Transfer Function database, our method facilitates the integration of a guidance module into existing IR generation frameworks, promoting efficient end-to-end synthesis of spatially aware binaural IRs. This innovation significantly reduces the complexity and cost associated with binaural IR generation, especially in challenging environments like underwater settings where data acquisition is substantially difficult.

References

1. Algazi, V.R., Duda, R.O., Thompson, D.M., Avendano, C.: The CIPIC HRTF database. In: Proceedings of IEEE Workshop on the Applications of Signal Processing to Audio and Acoustics, pp. 99–102 (2001)
2. Bao, X., Zhu, J., Huang, Z.: Blind speech dereverberation based on a statistical model. In: IEEE International Conference on Multimedia and Expo, pp. 467–472 (2012)
3. Cao, C., Ren, Z., Schissler, C., et al.: Interactive sound propagation with bidirectional path tracing. ACM Trans. Graph. **35**(6), 1–11 (2016)
4. Ding, R., Liu, S.: Underwater sound propagation for virtual environment. Vis. Comput. **37**(9–11), 2797–2807 (2021)
5. Donahue, C., McAuley, J., Puckette, M.: Adversarial audio synthesis. arXiv preprint arXiv:1802.04208 (2018)
6. Evans, M.J., Angus, J.A., Tew, A.I.: Analyzing head-related transfer function measurements using surface spherical harmonics. J. Acoust. Soc. Am. **104**(4), 2400–2411 (1998)
7. He, Y., Xu, X., Liu, X., Ou, W., Lu, H.: Multimodal transformer networks with latent interaction for audio-visual event localization. In: 2021 IEEE International Conference on Multimedia and Expo (ICME), pp. 1–6. IEEE (2021)
8. Jiang, Y., Wang, Q., Du, J., et al.: Exploring audio-visual information fusion for sound event localization and detection in low-resource realistic scenarios. In: IEEE International Conference on Multimedia and Expo (ICME), pp. 1–6 (2024)
9. Liu, S., Dinesh, M.: Sound Synthesis, Propagation, and Rendering. Springer, Cham (2022)
10. Majumder, S., Chen, C., Al-Halah, Z., Grauman, K.: Few-shot audio-visual learning of environment acoustics. In: Proceedings of the Advances in Neural Information Processing Systems, vol. 35, pp. 2522–2536 (2022)
11. Mechel, F.P.: Improved mirror source method in room acoustics. J. Sound Vib. **256**(5), 873–940 (2002)
12. Mehra, R., Raghuvanshi, N., Antani, L., Chandak, A., Curtis, S., Manocha, D.: Wave-based sound propagation in large open scenes using an equivalent source formulation. ACM Trans. Graph. **32**(2), 19:1–19:13 (2013)
13. Ratnarajah, A., Zhang, S.X., Yu, M., Tang, Z., Manocha, D., Yu, D.: Fast-rir: fast neural diffuse room impulse response generator. In: Proceedings of the IEEE International Conference on Acoustics, Speech and Signal Processing, pp. 571–575 (2022)
14. Ratnarajah, A., Ghosh, S., Kumar, S., Chiniya, P., Manocha, D.: Av-rir: audio-visual room impulse response estimation. In: Proceedings of the IEEE/CVF Conference on Computer Vision and Pattern Recognition, pp. 27164–27175 (2024)
15. Ratnarajah, A., Tang, Z., Aralikatti, R., Manocha, D.: Mesh2ir: neural acoustic impulse response generator for complex 3D scenes. In: Proceedings of the 30th ACM International Conference on Multimedia, pp. 924–933 (2022)

16. Sakamoto, S., Ushiyama, A., Nagatomo, H.: Numerical analysis of sound propagation in rooms using the finite difference time domain method. J. Acoust. Soc. Am. **120**(5), 3008 (2006)
17. Singh, N., Mentch, J., Ng, J., Beveridge, M., Drori, I.: Image2reverb: cross-modal reverb impulse response synthesis. In: Proceedings of the International Conference on Computer Vision, pp. 286–295 (2021)
18. Thompson, L.L.: A review of finite-element methods for time-harmonic acoustics. J. Acoust. Soc. Am. **20**(3), 1315–1330 (2006)
19. Van Den Oord, A., Dieleman, S., Zen, H., et al.: Wavenet: a generative model for raw audio. arXiv preprint arXiv:1609.03499 (2016)
20. Vaswani, A., Shazeer, N., Parmar, N., et al.: Attention is all you need. In: Proceedings of the Advances in Neural Information Processing Systems, pp. 6000–6010 (2017)
21. Zhang, Y., Liu, S.: Underwaterimage2ir: underwater impulse response generation via dual-path pre-trained networks and conditional generative adversarial networks. Comput. Anim. Virtual Worlds **35**(3), e2243 (2024)

16. Sakamoto, S., Takenouchi, A.: Registration of 3D normalized atlas of [illegible] brain by shape [illegible] comparing the finite differences of [illegible] method of [illegible] Atlas [illegible] (2008)

17. Shen, D., Davatzikos, C.: Hammer: [illegible] transformation. In: Proceeding of the [illegible] International Conference on Computer Vision, pp. [illegible] (2002)

18. Simpson, [illegible]: A survey of [illegible] classification of [illegible] registration [illegible] Trans. Med. Imaging [illegible] (19[illegible])

19. Woods, R.P., [illegible], Mazziotta, J.C., [illegible]: [illegible] Registration [illegible] MRI [illegible] the [illegible]

20. Zhang, Z., [illegible]: [illegible] Finite [illegible] method [illegible] registration [illegible] of the Asymmetric [illegible] normalization [illegible] In: Proceeding [illegible] pp. [illegible] (1999)

21. [illegible]: [illegible]

Author Index

Han, Shicong   III-313
Han, Songde   I-212
Hao, Wanming   II-168
He, Fei   I-187
He, Hongjian   I-364
He, Huiguang   I-102
He, Qingwen   II-340
He, Wei   II-267
He, Zhenyu   II-116, II-267, II-328
He, Zongyao   I-444
Hong, Hanyu   III-410
Hong, Jiheng   III-102
Hong, Wei   III-3
Hou, Jiani   II-316
Hou, Zhiqiang   II-194
Hu, Huan   I-89
Hu, Junlin   III-40
Hu, Lanyin   I-364
Hu, Tengjie   III-102, III-212
Hu, Tianyu   I-212
Hu, Xiangrui   II-231
Hu, Yuanda   II-316
Hu, Yue   II-365
Huang, Chaoyi   III-102, III-212
Huang, Dong   I-352
Huang, HouHong   III-564
Huang, Jiale   II-567
Huang, Jing   I-507, II-143
Huang, Jinghao   II-541
Huang, Junjie   II-578
Huang, Likun   III-52
Huang, Linsheng   I-493
Huang, Mengcheng   I-187
Huang, Runnan   I-431
Huang, Shanshan   I-224
Huang, Shuangping   II-505
Huang, Sui   I-364
Huang, Tuhao   III-528
Huang, Xiaohua   II-479, II-567
Huang, Xinjian   III-3
Huang, Yan   II-243, III-187
Huang, Yanji   I-431
Huang, Yuli   II-517
Huiting, Gao   III-497
Huo, Junyuan   III-323
Huo, Lina   I-249, III-260

I

Ibrayim, Mayire   III-150, III-162

J

Ji, Lifan   II-206
Jia, Xiuyi   II-255
Jian, Meng   I-236
Jiang, Han   I-65
Jiang, Junhao   I-457
Jiang, Ruixuan   III-323
Jiang, Wenqian   II-479, II-567
Jiang, Zetao   I-15
Jiang, Zhengang   I-187
Jiang, Zhiqiang   II-578
Jiao, Yujie   III-513
Jin, Kekun   I-199
Jin, Yi   III-348
Jin, Zhi   I-444
Jiu, Mingyuan   III-138

K

Kamara, Alhassan   III-90
Kang, Ao   III-440
Kang, Jianjun   III-162

L

Lai, Jianhuang   II-181, II-517, II-554
Lan, Rushi   III-102, III-212, III-336
Lang, Langchen   I-236
Lei, Bingrui   II-567
Lei, Gaoyu   III-410
Lei, Xiaochun   I-15
Li, Bangjun   I-330
Li, Bin   II-54, II-390, II-541
Li, Biying   II-492
Li, Boqian   II-168
Li, Boyang   III-126
Li, Boyuan   I-306
Li, Changliang   III-375
Li, Cheng   III-64
Li, Chenglong   II-42
Li, Fangqi   III-313
Li, Guoli   III-440
Li, Guoping   I-199
Li, Haoyu   I-403, III-485
Li, He   III-485
Li, Jiahao   III-102, III-212, III-336
Li, Jing   III-425
Li, Jinping   I-507, II-54, II-143, II-390
Li, Kaihua   II-168
Li, Qiang   III-52
Li, Senmao   II-168

If you have any questions about our books,
please contact us or
ProductSafety@springernature.com

In case of product complaints, please contact the importer located in the EU:
Springer Nature Customer Service Center GmbH
Europaplatz 3, 69115 Heidelberg, Germany

Printed by Books on Demand Book Service
in Hamburg, Germany